HANDBOOK OF MIDDLE AMERICAN INDIANS

EDITED AT MIDDLE AMERICAN RESEARCH INSTITUTE, TULANE UNIVERSITY, BY

ROBERT WAUCHOPE, *General Editor*
MARGARET A. L. HARRISON, *Associate Editor*
INIS PICKETT, *Administrative Assistant*
FRANK T. SCHNELL, JR., DAVID S. PHELPS,
THOMAS S. SCHORR, *Art Staff*
JAMES C. GIFFORD, *Indexer*

ASSEMBLED WITH THE AID OF A GRANT FROM THE NATIONAL SCIENCE FOUNDATION, AND UNDER THE SPONSORSHIP OF THE NATIONAL RESEARCH COUNCIL COMMITTEE ON LATIN AMERICAN ANTHROPOLOGY

Editorial Advisory Board

HANDBOOK OF MIDDLE AMERICAN INDIANS

ROBERT WAUCHOPE, General Editor

VOLUME SIX

Social
Anthropology

MANNING NASH, Volume Editor

UNIVERSITY OF TEXAS PRESS · AUSTIN

Published in Great Britain by the
University of Texas Press, Ltd., London

Library of Congress Catalog Card No. 64-10316
Copyright © 1967 by the University of Texas Press
All rights reserved.

The preparation and publication of
The Handbook of Middle American Indians
has been assisted by grants from
the National Science Foundation.

Typesetting by G&S Typesetters, Austin, Texas
Printing by the Meriden Gravure Company, Meriden, Connecticut
Binding by Universal Bookbindery, Inc., San Antonio, Texas

CONTENTS

HANDBOOK OF MIDDLE AMERICAN INDIANS, VOLUME 6

Social Anthropology

GENERAL EDITOR'S NOTE

The manuscripts for the following articles were submitted at various dates over a period of several years. Because of revisions and minor updatings made from time to time, it is difficult to assign a date to each article. In some cases, an indication of when an article was completed can be had by noting the latest dates in the list of references at the end of each contribution.

1. Introduction

MANNING NASH

IN PREPARING the following articles on the social anthropology of the Indians of Middle America, the authors have relied on the accumulated ethnography of the region, but instead of giving broad historical treatment or ethnological emphasis, they were urged to be synthetic, comparative, and topical. These three directives govern the organization of the individual contributions and the volume as a whole. A synthetic view of the ethnography of Middle America aims to establish empirical generalizations of two sorts. The first set seeks to make more or less definitive assertions about the uniformities and varieties of culture, society, and personality, then proceeds to characterize the nature of indigenous social life, and to shape the general pattern of Middle American culture and its variations. The second set aims to account for the observed regularities and varieties in Middle American culture and society. Although resting on ethnographic fact and faithful to it, this set derives from a body of more or less articulated concepts, what in bolder moments is sometimes called a theory. The success of any synthesis depends on the facts and concepts it utilizes. Further field work in the active area of Middle America will certainly add new information as well as change the significance of material now at hand. The value of any synthesis lies almost as much in the act of superseding it as in the work of constructing it.

The regularities and varieties in Middle America are established in these articles by comparisons, mostly within the culture areas of Middle America but sometimes directly or indirectly with other regions of the world. The techniques of comparison run the gamut of the comparative logic of anthropology: in terms of statistical indices, along axes of social structural variation, by themes or patterns, by the erection of types, and by the device of levels of complexity and development. The use of a logic of comparison and contrast to arrive at tentative generalizations means that data are presented selectively and used chiefly to buttress assertions. Volume 7 of the *Handbook of Middle American Indians,* on the ethnology of Middle America, gives full factual coverage and cultural-historical ori-

3

entation, which allows contributors to Volume 6 to concentrate on a synthesis by comparative methods.

The substantive material is ordered by topic. Some topics reflect the ordinary categories of social anthropology (e.g., economy, religion, polity, kinship, personality); others are the special aspects of culture (e.g., crafts, music, dance). These topics focus on some of the current social and cultural dynamics, such as urbanization, acculturation, industrialization, and national incorporation.

Within the inevitable growth of Middle American anthropological studies from exploratory fact gathering to descriptive generalization and then on to conscious manipulation of data in terms of social and cultural regularity and processes there has been a minor cycle, a movement from culture history to social anthropology as the dominant way of work. Almost all of the earlier field studies were concerned with seeing how the living Indians of Middle America might shed light on the ethnology of the vanished high civilization of the Maya, Nahuatl, Zapotec, or other cultures. Survivals, parallels, clues to esoteric monuments and documents were what the early students sought and, of course, found. There was, however, a movement growing out of the nascent theory of community studies to see the Indians as members of living social systems. This focus demanded rounded descriptions and analyses of a given community or group in terms of some problem in general social science, irrespective of the light such an inquiry might shed on problems of cultural history. For a time these separate research frames—historical with an interest in the high civilizations, structural and functional with a concern toward contributing to a science of man—drew farther and farther apart. The social anthropologists and the cultural historians had little overlap in problem selection, in concepts, and in evaluation of results. Between Redfield's study of Tepoztlan (1930)

and Kirchhoff's attempts to delimit the historical core of Mesoamerica (1943) falls the shadow of an intellectual great divide.

Latterly, however, there is some trend, as there is in American anthropology in general, to seek a fusion of the historical and the generalizing modes of work. The tendency of modern students to view history and science, or the ideographic and nomothétic approaches, as complimentary rather than antithetical has not yet led to a viable fusion of method, concept, or agreement on research strategies. Several major research projects in Middle America, however, have done enough to indicate that archaeologists, linguists, social anthropologists, and ethnohistorians can fruitfully cooperate on the same body of data and mutually enrich each others' understanding. Vogt (1964c) and his students have explicitly used contemporary studies to portray the society and culture of the vanished Maya civilization. The rapprochement between the historical and functional studies appears to follow one major orientation: cultural historical problems, set by archaeological excavation or documentary testament, not by trait distribution or age-area speculation, are viewed through the lens of functional and dynamic theory. This line of attack is giving rise to a "genetic" interpretation of the historical development of the major groups of Indians, and is contributing to a social anthropology with temporal depth and historical control over its generalizations.

The nature of Middle American peoples has been an abiding concern in the social anthropology of the region. Kroeber (1940, pp. 460–87) made the following observations:

It [Indian population] is usually Christian, often fitted into the political institutions of the country and always into the economic one. Even where the Indians are bilingual or still mainly speak their native idiom, they no longer possess a native culture but instead live in a hybrid one. The active process of acculturation is so far behind them that they do not remember it, let alone the pure indigenous culture which preceded it. . . . The Indian cultures are neither native nor dying; they are almost invariably well hybridized and usually healthy. To understand these Indian cultures of Latin America it is obviously necessary to know as thoroughly as possible the two streams of ingredients of which they are composed. Inasmuch as these have generally been intermingling for centuries, the approach cannot but be historical if the results are to have any real significance.

Ignoring the biological analogy of hybrids and the dicta of a single necessary approach to problems of Middle America, this is an astute recognition of the dominant fact about the social life of the people of Middle America. These Indians are *part societies* and *part cultures,* enmeshed everywhere in wider networks of political and economic bonds, and their cultures are the results of the interactions of different civilizations. LaFarge's brilliant and widely cited sequences for Maya culture (1940) are the first major attempt to implement Kroeber's plea for historical understanding of the nature of Middle American culture. LaFarge's essay has served as a building block and model for Beals' (1951a) extension of the sequences of cultural change for Middle America as a whole.

In 1937, Tax laid the foundation for understanding the peoples of Guatemala, and he and Redfield (1952) later essayed the delineation of the major contours of Middle American culture. With the older cultural historical interests the unit of ethnological investigation in Middle America was taken to be either a "tribe" or a language group. Investigators like Schultze Jena wrote about the beliefs and social organization of the "Quiche" (1945); other students wrote of social or cultural "entities" like the Zapotec or the Nahuatl. With a posited, but undemonstrated, entity like the Quiche or the Nahuatl, Schultze Jena could indiscriminately use informants and information from Momostenango or Quezaltenango or Zunil and

blend all the differences, all the contradictions, all the anomalies into a single description. But such a description bears little or no relation to any organized society. It is not the culture of any living group, and was not the culture of any vanished group. Such a misconstruction of the basic unit of ethnological investigation results in monographs that are only artifacts of the investigators' methods and hence raise hosts of pseudohistorical and functional problems which no amount of further field work can possibly resolve. Tax conclusively demonstrated that the social locus of Middle American culture in Guatemala was a municipio, a locally organized society with a particular variant of the regional culture, and that further progress in Middle American studies must be inductive. Local communities must be studied, and when enough are known, the problem of whether or not there is such an entity as "Quiche" culture can then be meaningfully approached. The cultural varieties of Middle America must be the outcome of research, not the product of a naive identification of language, culture, and a social entity which bears them. In the wake of the demonstration that the unit of ethnological research was a local society bearing a particular version of regional culture, coupled with the application of the emerging community study method, came a wave of community studies in Middle America. Most of these monographs (the articles in this volume and their bibliographies rely chiefly on that literature) developed a single problem or else aimed at descriptive completeness for a single community. The building blocks of Middle American social anthropology and ethnology came as community studies, with only passing attention to comparison and slight interest in relating the contemporary scene to the preconquest civilizations or the four centuries of interaction between indigenous and nonindigenous cultural streams. This is not to ignore efforts like Parsons' (1936) to categorize the culture of Mitla into three streams, or to overlook Redfield's attempt to give historical depth to the Yucatan material he and co-workers gathered (1941), and similar attempts in the Tarascan region or the Totonac, and Beals' work with the Cahita peoples, but only to remark that most of the field work from the 1920's to the 1960's focused on a problem derived from general social science and on a single or a couple of closely related communities. Consequently, although information on ethnic relations, or the economy of a community, or the kinship system of a society, or the psychology of a municipio continued to swell in volume, the apparently simple questions of what are the general lineaments of Middle American culture and society or whether one (say) Quiche community is more like a remote Quiche-speaking community or more like its next door Tzutuhil-speaking community went either unanswered or met conflicting and idiosyncratic views.

In the *Heritage of Conquest* (1952a) Tax attempted to bring together not only the various strands of research on the contemporary peoples of Middle America but also many of the investigators who have woven the tapestry of Middle American ethnology and social anthropology. Starting with the earlier work of Kirchhoff (1943) and Redfield and Tax (1952), the volume set out to find the commonalities and range of Middle American culture and society. This was to be done against a background of "degrees" of acculturation, or assessing where in the culture area what aspects of "Indian" culture were most retained or most eroded. The general features of Middle American culture, as described in the above synthesis, are fairly familiar to students of the region:

There is a located community with a center housing a patron saint.

Maize agriculture is the subsistence core.

Families live in separate structures.

Male and female costume is differentiated.

The division of labor is along sexual and age lines with men doing heavy work, women domestic tasks; men are in charge of indigenous cults, women are more prominent in European-derived religion.

The market and market mentality is dominant in economic life; there is little taboo or other restriction on economic activity, but modern economic organization is absent.

Families tend to articulate directly with larger community without the intermediacy of clans, but in larger communities there are territorial divisions between the family and the larger community.

Families are hierarchial, with male dominance; both lines of descent are recognized, but there is a patrilineal tendency in transmitting names and some real property.

Marriage tends to be negotiated by elders for sons and daughters with fixed visits and gift exchange, and there is not infrequently wife service, or temporary uxorlocality; marriage is brittle, with serial monogamy until children arrive, and then it is typically stable.

Political organization is a central building, and the personnel form a hierarchy of officials, the top members being recognized by the formal government of the national state; the political offices are closely interwoven with a similar hierarchy serving the interest of the local church and related festal activities; there are annual ritual changes of offices in both hierarchies.

Social classes are absent, but there are considerable differences in prestige, due to wealth, power, and personal achievement.

The age hierarchy, especially among males, is notable and tied to performance in the civil-religious hierarchy.

Life-cycle events of importance are baptism and marriage; there are no puberty rites; death is accepted as a matter of course and followed by a Catholic wake.

Concepts of disease are unsystematic and include air and wind invasions of the body, identification of illness with disturbed emotional states, and period of delicacy when illness most likely strikes; the notions of hot and cold and strong and weak are used in curing and in diagnosis; curers are specialists or semispecialists, who are often bearers of noxious magic as well.

The *sacra* include a large number of supernatural beings and places; theirs is a vague hierarchy of deities sometimes with God at the apex, various saints combine Christian and pagan attributes and powers, and some truly pagan forces are identified or associated with natural forces like wind, rain, and lightning; theirs is a strongly marked saint cult centering around the housing of effigies in house altars or special temples; liquor is part of the sacred ceremonies and a *sacra* itself.

The annual cycle is regulated by the European calendar and is punctuated by various festivals, the chief of which is the patron saint ritual; All Saints' Day, All Souls' Day, Easter Week, and the Day of the Cross are major rituals; there is a pagan calendar, chiefly involved in divination and in some agricultural ritual.

The world view is animistic in the sense that the world is peopled by spirits, souls, ghosts, witches, and forces that affect the daily life of persons; omens, dreams, and talismans are important.

Physical contacts, except when intoxicated, are disfavored, great ambition is discouraged, but industry and application are lauded.

Ritual conformity is more important than inner piety; slander and gossip and envy are greatly condemned, but these are chief means of social control.

There is great respect for writing and books (though most Indians are illiterate).

There is great dependence on law, and formal organization is more important to leadership than is personal attribute.

These features of Middle American society and culture are here summarized so that the reader may compare the validity and adequacy of their substantive content against the contributions in this volume. Certainly the nearly two decades of field work since these assertions were assembled have extended, modified, refined, and negated some of them. In the main, however, they stand as a good approximation of the particular cluster of features which gives Middle America its distinct cast. What such a characterization does not do, and did not attempt to do, is link the features in any functional or causal series. The articles in this volume reflect the growing concern in anthropology to make statement of functional or causal interdependence, to attempt to distinguish between fortuitous coexistence of social facts in time and space and necessary or functional concomitance of social features.

From the efforts to see patterns and structures in Middle America as a whole, along with regional differences or subcultural variations, investigators have moved to making other sorts of typologies or categorizations of Middle American societies. One of the most fruitful and provocative typologies was erected by Wolf (1955b). In this attempt to sort out the types of peasantry in Middle America, the basic social and cultural facts about the region are already absorbed. Wolf, like other students of the region, can, because of the volume of ethnography in Middle America, take for granted that: (1) these people are peasants (part societies and part cultures); (2) their internal, local societies interact in complex ways with environing external national and world society; (3) ecological and historical factors have governed cultural retention and social persistence; and (4) political and economic processes are probably dominant in accounting for where a particular community fits in any typology.

With these established coordinates, Wolf describes two basic types of Middle American peasantry: the corporate peasantry and the open peasantry. Already, in the language and in the opposition of types, is seen the clear imprint of theoretical concerns general to anthropology and not specific to Middle American studies alone. The corporate peasantry are chiefly those Indian communities with spatial and structural boundaries, with temporal continuity, in which localized cultural heritages are transmitted, and the community and its members are in a defensive stance against the larger, encroaching society and economy. From this selection of features flows a set of consequences which Wolf spells out. In short, this is an admirable example of

7

the tendency alluded to earlier to find functional or causal and not merely fortuitous coexistence of parts of social life.

Another attempt to put the Indians of Middle America into a theoretically meaningful category is that of Wagley and Harris (1955), who use a different set of dimensions from Wolf's. They aim to view the Indians of Middle America (and indeed all "Indians" of Latin America) as a subcultural variant of Latin American culture. They hold that the Indians of Middle America are a subculture stabilized a century or more ago. The content of this cultural type is a fusion of cultural elements from the aboriginal background and the Spanish colonial heritage, overlaid with features from the modern national cultures. Wagley and Harris also are part of the stream of effort to assimilate the social anthropology of Middle America into wider and wider comparative frames and to more and more systematic apprehension.

Enough has been said now to see the major contours of Middle American Indian culture and society and to see where the chief descriptive and conceptual lacunae are. The trends I have adduced in Middle American studies are but a localized expression of American anthropology in general. A look at the list of research and problem leads spelled out by Beals, Redfield, and Tax (1943) shows how far most of the informational problems have been overcome and have been replaced by questions stemming from method and from theory.

Later pleas for pursuing research in a given direction frequently move completely away from specific data gaps and call directly for selection of a research site in terms of a particular problem for which the Middle American locale seems likely to provide telling exemplars or critical instances. There are four classes of problems which apparently engage most of the effort of social anthropology in Middle America in this decade. These are (and it would be

instructive, though not germane to this introduction, to compare Middle America to other regions of the world where a comparatively high volume of field research is under way): (1) the part-whole question of complex societies; (2) social and cultural change stemming from urbanization, industrialization, acculturation, and directed change; (3) the perennial problem of validity, replicability, and reliability of ethnographic data; and (4) the detail or depth portrayal of individuals, families, or a single aspect of a society or culture. Explicating these clusters of problems will place into proper perspective the contribution and aims of this volume.

The very nature of the segments that anthropologists study in Middle America brings them into confrontation with the mooted question of parts and wholes, of the *pars pro toto* aspect as well as the manner in which a highly differentiated social system can be conceptualized, or even studied from observations made merely upon some of the parts. Wolf (1956) has argued the position that complex societies like Mexico can be understood not through building a mosaic of community studies and capping that with a study of national institutions, but rather through the investigation of the ties that bind social groups throughout all levels of society. This focus on group relations in a complex society is a partial answer to how a highly differentiated social system may be thought about. It leads to an interest in the processes of conflict and of accommodation between groups with different orientations, and to a particular emphasis on the economic and political brokers who mediate the conflicts. Such study, of course, needs historical controls, but the history it requires is not the reconstruction of an aboriginal culture and its modifications through time. The history needed is shifting power relations among groups aiming at the widest levels of social and political integration. Perhaps anthropologists following Wolf's clues will have to make their own social histories of Middle America.

Elsewhere (1957a) I have offered the notion of a multiple society with plural cultures as a means of approximating the kind and level of social integration in these national societies. This model strives to locate the sources of stability and lability in a national society through assessing the scale of command of persons and resources of different social segments and the nature of their stake or discontent in a going order. The notion of a multiple society with plural cultures I derived in part from reading about social fragmentation and attempts at modernization in southeast Asia, and I find it of interest that Wolf also turned to Java when he sought a comparative frame for Middle America. These attempts to conceptualize a complex, differentiated society in order to understand its historical trajectory and perhaps triangulate its future states, were paralleled by Mexican anthropologists concerned with smaller-scale hypotheses and more practical questions of immediate policy about Indian populations. The reports of the Instituto Nacional Indigenista (Caso, 1954) show this concern.

At the same time efforts were made to see how representational, or sampling, accuracy could be furthered in anthropological field work. Three studies will, I believe, encompass the major efforts to see the part-whole problem in terms of what part is how representative of the larger whole. R. N. Adams (1957a) developed a meticulous and painstaking inventory of cultural items and complexes throughout the southern part of Middle America. Through survey field work and by mapping the actual distributions of cultural features, knowledge of the regional distinctiveness, as well as the cultural uniformities, has been greatly extended and deepened. A different view of the question of representational adequacy is found in studies by Edmonson and others (1957). Edmonson's concluding paper is a provocative if not wholly convincing effort to triangulate the major features of Mexican culture. The more purely survey approach to the part-whole question is the last method of finding some employment in Middle America, but it is less used by the anthropologist than by the sociologist or the social historian. It ranges from the use of national census figures coupled with anthropological monographs (Whetten, 1948, 1961) to questionnaire surveys (Young, 1960a,b) on to combinations of historical and census samples (Cline, 1962). It is clear, however, that Middle American social anthropology, like anthropology as a whole, is probably concerned with the double aspects of the part-whole problem for some time yet, and that the complexity and heterogeneity of Middle America is an ideal laboratory in which to fashion and test formulations of this order.

To contemporary field workers in Middle America the overriding problems of economic and political modernization of the nations seem to set the background against which all other studies must be placed. Such publications as the series put out in Guatemala under the title Integración Social (1956) indicate the level of attainment of social anthropology in handling the complex problems of urbanization, industrialization, and Ladinoization, all substrands of the tensions involved in the movement (or lack of it) toward a generically modern society. Generally, of course, anthropologists have viewed the Indian or peasant components as they react to the multifarious winds of change. I have studied (1958a) the impact of a factory on Indians in Guatemala, Lewis (1952) has been concerned with urbanization as has Beals (1951b), and there is a plethora of good work by both North and Middle American anthropologists on the various aspects of national incorporation, acculturation, and induced or directed cultural change. The Memorias

9

of the Instituto Nacional Indigenista of Mexico report a wide range of experience in the process of induced or directed change, and the continuing publications of the Seminario de Integración Social in Guatemala provide a similar but less extensive corpus of findings. Foster's handbook for technical assistance workers and project planners on the role of culture and society and personality in economic and social change (1961b) could not have been written without the body of work done in Middle America. In brief, not only is the tendency to devise models to account for the cultural and social complexity and integration in Middle America, but to use these models as tools for understanding the major cultural dynamics involved in the problems of modernization. Also, in the study of change, the work in Middle America shows its share of one of the most potent means of understanding dynamics—the "dual synchronic" study. This cross-sectional, two-time-period study of the same community provides one of the best controls in the analysis of change. Redfield's restudy of Chan Kom (1950), Lewis' of Tepoztlan (1951), and Tax's on-going work in Panajachel are among the most salient of these dual synchronic efforts.

Vogt's (1960) "anthropologist in continual residence" for a generation still needs time to be worked out, but likewise promises control over the frame of inference in studying change.

Anthropologists, like the fellow human beings they study, live in a world of changing ideas and technology. The recent developments converging in a cluster of related studies under the tent of "ethnoscience," the growing attempts to use the discovery and eliciting procedures from formal linguistics in other domains of culture, and the technology of the computer, tape recorder, and motion picture camera have had their repercussions on the social anthropology of Middle America. The chief effect of these notions and devices has been

to encourage a more rigorous collection of data, and to make these data reflect the informant's view of his world. The range of such studies is approximated by Guiteras Holmes' *Perils of the Soul* (1961) on one side, and the methodological essay by Metzger and Williams (1963a). These studies, of course, raise the problems of how far field work methods can be formalized, of whether or not formal eliciting procedures are useful for areas of culture that are not highly "terminologized" or structured like language. It will be a long time yet before enough work is done to place in proper perspective the work now going on in Middle America, but it is in this region that it is being prosecuted as vigorously as anywhere in the world. Parallel to the stress on gathering reliable and valid field data congruent with the informant's psychological realities is the need to cope with the volume of data already gathered. Problems of information retrieval, quantitative manipulation, coding and categorizing large bodies of fact seem ideally suited for the new information technology of the digital computer. Students in Middle America have made some efforts, particularly at Stanford University, to employ the computer for ethnographic data. Of course, the large-scale testing of hypotheses will inevitably require some use of the computers, and eventually, I suppose, simulation of ethnographic reality will be programmed, too. These are exciting vistas and are still hidden behind the clouds of promise, but they have been glimpsed in the social anthropology of Middle America.

As data accumulate and generalizations become compendent, the social anthropology of a region begins to see real actors, real lives, real personalities, and specific microaspects of culture and social structure as worthy and amenable to investigation. In Middle America, an outstanding example of depth study of people and aspects of society and culture is found in the work of Oscar Lewis (1959b), who followed a

10

family's fortunes from Tepoztlan to Mexico City. His detailed natural history of this and four other families is an important document on a microaspect of society using real, as against typical, people. His later study (1961a), the detailed description of the children of one of the families, is probably the most comprehensive life-history document in Middle American studies. This concentration on a single life, or a small segment of society, has dual consequences. It leads the anthropologist back to closer touch with the literary, interpretative skills of the humanist, reminding him that after all it is man and human nature, not a set of formal categories, which is the subject of his discipline, and at the same time it conduces to the placing in of content, of the humanization, of the more general concepts with which the social anthropologist, in his guise as scientist, must employ. Lewis' development of the notion of a "culture of poverty" on the basis of his Balzac-like reporting of life in Mexico City is the outstanding example of this interplay.

The full-scale attempt at biography is exhibited in the work of Pozas with the Chamula. So successful among the literati of Mexico has his *Juan Jolote* (1952b) been that Chamula has become a generic designation for all the Indians of Chiapas. Attempts to focus on particular microsegments of society and culture flourish in the regions with the highest level of monographic density, and examples are now becoming plentiful, in the Tarascan area, in the midwestern highlands of Guatemala, and among the Tzeltal and Tzotzil.

The following articles point clearly to the established islands of knowledge, the tentative generalizations formulated, and the directions and locations for further research which may consolidate the islands into a land mass. Placing these contributions into the perspective of general developments in American anthropology (of both hemispheres) is a tribute to the many scholars throughout the world who have constructed the factual and conceptual edifice on which a volume like this rests.

REFERENCES

Adams, R. N., 1957a
Beals, 1951a, 1951b
——, Redfield, and Tax, 1943
Caso, 1954
Cline, 1962
Edmonson, 1957
Foster, 1961b
Guiteras Holmes, 1961
Integración Social, 1956
Kirchhoff, 1943
Kroeber, 1940
LaFarge, 1940
Lewis, 1951, 1952, 1959b, 1961a

Metzger and Williams, 1963a
Nash, M., 1957a, 1958a
Parsons, 1936
Pozas, 1952b
Redfield, 1930, 1941, 1950
—— and Tax, 1952
Schultze Jena, 1945
Tax, 1937, 1952a
Vogt, 1957, 1960, 1964c
Wagley and Harris, 1955
Whetten, 1948, 1961
Wolf, 1955b, 1956
Young and Young, 1960a, 1960b

2. Indian Population and its Identification

ANSELMO MARINO FLORES

FROM THE ARRIVAL of the Spanish conquerors toward the end of the 15th century in what they—getting off to a bad start—called the Indies, there begin the processes of acculturation and racial mixture of the autochthonous population with the white which, despite the passage of almost half a millennium, has not yet ended. Now in the Americas, one can locate with some precision Mestizo zones and native zones which vary by country in number and proportion of Indian and Mestizo. It is therefore relevant to ask who and how numerous are the inhabitants of America who should be considered Indian.

In some cases it is easy to identify them. In nations with a small number of Indians living in geographically and administratively delimited areas who do not mix with other groups, no real difficulty is involved. But in those countries where the indigenous population is proportionately numerous a strong demographic pressure develops, and it is very difficult to specify who are Indians and who are not. In these places, for some people it is the physical characteristics which are decisive; for others, such features have a transitory value and are subordinate to culture and language indicators. These and divergent opinions are not only expressed but frequently passionately discussed.

The coexistence of the two situations—a biological versus a social definition—indicates that the colonization and the sociojuridical relations between conquerors and conquered, varied from place to place and time to time. The geographical and ecological differences in the American continent, the differing developmental levels of the native societies, the demographic composition, and the cultures of these societies were decisive factors which underlay differences in colonial regimes. Against this background the present American states became structured socially, politically, and administratively. Examination of the historical antecedents of each of these countries is indispensable to an understanding of the role of the indigenous population in the making of the nation and to an understanding of the present situation of Indian populations.

CRITERIA FOR THE DEFINITION OF THE NATIVE POPULATION

Physical or Somatic Criterion and Legal Criterion

Attempts to justify the cruelty characteristic of most of the conquerors alleged at the outset that the Indians belonged neither to the human species nor to the kingdom of God. The more benevolent Spaniards accepted Indians as persons, but distinguished Indians from themselves by using *gentes de razón* for Europeans and "Indian" as a pejorative term for the native population. It was doubted, and even denied publicly, that the Indians might be rational beings. This idea was the subject of polemics by colonizers, statesmen, and religious leaders that ended on the papal pronouncement that all men were equal before God.

As time went on, despite attempts to differentiate the two racial stocks, a new type began to appear—the Mestizo—eventually threatening to predominate numerically. At first the Mestizo, product of white and Indian, enjoyed almost the same rights as his European father; but soon, when many Mestizos were the product of more than three generations, legal restrictions were instituted. The colonial ruling class was dismayed by the Mestizo, in whom it saw a threat to its position. How could the process of race mixture be controlled to the social and political advantage of the ruling class?

The conquerors remained obstinate in their fallacy that the indigenous peoples were mentally backward, incapable of adapting themselves to new forms of life. They sought for full justification of slavery and exploitation; subjugation of the natives was their duty by law. Juan Comas (1955, p. 139) makes this clear:

The immigrant Europeans, the colonizers of that period, considered it their right to trade and to gain a good profit in their new dominions, even though in order to do so they might have to exploit and even eliminate the aborigines who were opposed to their designs. The abuses and unrestricted greed of the conquerors went to such an extreme as to subject the Indians to captivity on the pretext of a "just war"; so that Emperor Charles V ordered "no one in time of war, though it be just and ordered by Us and by representatives of Our power, may dare to capture the aforesaid Indians." But the economic interests were so strong that this order was disregarded four years later (1534).

In the *Leyes Nuevas de Indias (New Laws of the Indies)*, 1542, the prohibition on placing the Indians in captivity was again ordered. Actually, legal slavery lasted in America only until the first half of the 16th century, but there are those—the *encomienda*, personal servitude, and a number of other similar forms—which covered over a single fact: the economic exploitation of the American Indian by the European.

The colony needed the Indians, at whatever cost, and so justified the racial discrimination which became an integral part of the regime and was seemingly the formula for salvation which guaranteed its existence for 300 years. Rosenblat (1954, p. 133) explains:

To the degree that the colonial society became structured and acquired more precise contours, it gave ever more importance to purity of blood and adopted on the basis of this purity a hierarchial and aristocratic mode which was not completely achieved seemingly until the 18th century. The colonial regime of the Spanish then designated the results of the mixture of races with the name of *castas* and the Indian legislation specified clearly the rights and duties of each of them. The legislation assigned to persons a distinct position according to ethnic composition. And even more stringently than the legislation and the authorities, society or certain sectors of society which sprang forward as jealous guardians of racial distinction did so. The colonial regime came to be a caste regime.

In this period, the Indian was the principal target of exploitation and it was thus necessary to differentiate him from the non-

Indian. Consequently society was divided into three caste groups—European, Indigenous, and Negro—which ramified into ridiculous classifications, including all possible combinations of racial mixture.

The apex of the social pyramid was formed of Spaniards and Creoles; under them were Mestizos but only the Euro-Indians (product of Indian and Spaniard); the Indo-Negroes (product of Indian and Negro) occupied inferior levels. Farther down the scale were *cuarterones, zambos, lobos, saltapatras,* hybrids with little or no Spanish inheritance. In the proportion of his Negro or European ancestry was the Indian's socio-economic situation determined. Obviously this classification had to be based on uniquely and exclusively biological characteristics. The Chilean investigator Lipschütz (1944, p. 70) has created a word—pigmentocracy—for this state of affairs. He writes: "To any scaling of social functions from top to bottom, there corresponds a scale or spectrum of racial colors intermediate between white and Indian." Skin color was the criterion for locating an individual in social strata. Such importance was given to purity of blood that at times only a rumor was sufficient to cause the destruction of a family.

To the biological criterion for identification of populations corresponded a legal one. The law specified the human quality of each kind of individual and the rights and obligations inherent in his rank. For this arrangement to work individuals were assigned to category on the parochial birth, death, and marriage registers. This assignment theoretically governed all administrative, legal, and even religious relationships. Rosenblat (1954, p. 180) says of this legal aspect:

In the 18th century there was frequent recourse to the *Audiencia* in all Spanish colonies for certification of purity of blood. Purity of blood did not, however, signify absolute purity of white blood. At the beginning of this century, a Bull of Clemente XI established that quadroons and octoroons who were baptized should be considered white. By the Royal Cédula of Aranjuez of February 10, 1795, one could attain the dispensation of the rank of quadroon for 800 *reales de vellón*. This consideration was called the *gracias al sacar,* removal thanks. For the same thanks, illegitimate children could buy the right to be scribes and even *hidalgos.*

It is clear that when an individual was classified as Indian, it was done from both the somatic and the legal indicators. This racial discrimination took into account physical characteristics and was legally sanctioned. It was a powerful instrument of the colonial government and enormously facilitated exploitation and enslavement of the Indian.

After three centuries had passed, national independence movements sprang up. Constitutional acts were now promulgated for governing the young, recently emancipated peoples. Slavery was abolished; men were declared equal, legally and socially, despite color and ethnic origin. The system of castes was legally destroyed. With independence of the Americas it would seem that the spectre of racism had disappeared from the continent, but this was not altogether so. Comas writes (1955, p. 139): "From the 16th century until the present date, some sectors of the white group have continued to be persuaded that civilization is synonymous with their civilization and consequently consider men of other regions and other cultures and colors as 'savages' or 'barbarians' whom it is legitimate to exploit in every sense."

Now after some 400 years of living together, the Indians, Negroes, and whites have produced a racial mixture that makes it virtually impossible to identify pure Indians. Consequently, attempts to establish differences based on somatic or physiological characteristics such as skin color, eye color, color and texture of the hair, form of the cranium, and blood group yield no consistent classifications. The somatic criterion has for some years been totally set aside, since it has been amply demonstrated that morphological features of individuals have no significance in the social, economic, or psychological world and raise no significant or interesting biological problems.

The biological meaning of "race" (and the only one which can be given to it) has often been misunderstood even among anthropological specialists. With considerable frequency there is mention of the Aztec race, the Maya race, or the Tarascan race to designate native groups. The error of associating the biological term "race" with the ethnohistorical terms such as "Aztec" or ethnolinguistic terms like "Maya" or "Tarasca" is patent. Linguistic and cultural classifications of the American Indians are precise and generally accepted. Morphological variation is minimal, and there is no reason for subclasses based on linguistic, ethnic, or historical criteria. For these reasons, then, the biological criterion for defining the Indian is not very useful. It is cited only as a historical antecedent for understanding the evolution and present state of the Indian in America.

Cultural Criterion and Linguistic Criterion

In 1940 the first Interamerican Indigenist Congress met in Patzcuaro, Michoacan, Mexico. Delegates from most of the American countries came to discover practical means for improvement of life for the American Indians. To assess the magnitude of the problem, the first question was: Who is to be considered an Indian? An answer is essential to knowing who is to be aided or benefited. Despite the breadth of discussion no agreement was reached; the delegates left with a feeling of the urgency of defining clearly who the Indians are so that they could formulate programs of economic and social rehabilitation for their benefit.

The Patzcuaro meeting marks an important point in the Interamerican Indigenist movement. From that date began systematic studies on the history, theory, practice, and administration of the native populations. Nevertheless, apart from the promises undertaken personally by the congress members and the solid Interamerican cooperation required to attack the problem, certain countries had already taken steps to include in their population censuses in 1940 questions designed to quantify the Indian nuclei and their linguistic characteristics. Mexico, Guatemala, and Panama, for example, knew by that date the number of inhabitants speaking Indian languages and used this figure as a total for the Indian population. But anthropologists were not satisfied that the linguistic criterion was sufficient.

Gamio (1942a, p. 17) made the first detailed analysis of the Indian problem on the basis of linguistic and cultural criteria. He held that the linguistic facts in the census by themselves do not clearly indicate who the Indians are or which groups should be categorized as Indian. Gamio maintained that cultural criteria were needed. Indian should mean anyone who possessed Indian cultural features, without regard to somatic characteristics and even if he did not speak a pre-Hispanic language or dialect.

Use of the cultural criterion raises difficulties in practical application. The works published on Indian questions (mostly inspired by sentiments of good will) provided limited materials. These data make it impossible to handle the questions they asked. It was necessary to undertake new and more rigorous investigations.

For Gamio, these later investigations were not new. After his work at Teotihuacan (1922) he went on to make further studies (1937a, 1939) oriented to a cultural definition of the Indian. The basis of cultural classifications he explains (1942b, p. 16): "Our system, which was limited to classifying characteristics of material culture, applied in various regions of Mexico, consisted in making an inventory of all the objects possessed by a series of families of the particular region." The classificatory system was a function of three groups of cultural characteristics: Indian characteristics proper, those of foreign culture, and mixed. The presence or absence of elements such as the *metate,* phonograph, machete, *huaraches,* riding saddle, determined the value of the index for the classification of material culture. Gamio noted (1942b, p. 16):

When the sum of these three columns is added up, it can happen that the number of objects of Indian culture constitutes a high percentage with respect to the total number of objects of the three types cited, in which case the families classified can be considered as Indian, even though the individuals composing them do not present the racial characteristics of pure Indians, but rather those of Mestizos or whites.

To the degree that proportion of characteristics of pre-Spanish origin becomes reduced and that of characteristics of European origin increases, the group study can be considered as culturally mixed and less and less Indian. When this proportion is very small and the European characteristics very frequent, the groups and individuals are no longer culturally Indian even though from the racial point of view they may be so. . . . This procedure [he warned, p. 19] can help us to make a census representative of the characteristics of material culture, and by doing so we shall have achieved something. But there are important questions which remain to be resolved with respect to intellectual culture, aesthetic ideas, ethical ideas and religious ones, concepts governing the family and social organization, knowledge of a scientific character, and concepts of a conventional nature, and so forth. The topic is difficult, and although we have given special attention to it, we can still say nothing with respect to it.

The works of Gamio, path-breaking as they were, achieved nothing definitive. In 1946 on the Day of the Indian, Gamio, then director of the Interamerican Indigenist Institute, said (1946, p. 101): "Those [classifications] based on assessment of a cultural type and on the determination of needs and deficiencies appear to be the most convenient, but the elaboration of them requires a long time and numerous technical and economic elements on which not all countries can count. Furthermore, given that the problem presents some peculiar aspects of each country, there is a lack of adequate methods; and one cannot make an international generalization, even though that might bring, among other advantages, an economy in time and money."

Goubaud Carrera (1945, p. 378), at that time director of the National Indigenist Institute of Guatemala, makes the same point: "The third basis has been the cultural one; that is, the one which by means of inventories of traits both material and spiritual attempts to determine the person as Indian. In the cultural complex of countries with a high Indian population, this basis and such indices have proved inadequate for classifying the Indian because there are culturally subsequent features of problematic efficacy."

At the First Indigenist Congress the discussion of what should be understood as Indian put special emphasis on the cultural aspect. Conclusions of the Final Act read: "XXXI. On the Inclusion in Censuses of Cultural Characteristics of the Indian and Mestizo Groups. Conclusions: I. It is recommended to the countries of America who may have Indian groups that in the census and other ordinary statistics, there be included the cultural characteristics of the population and a basis of interamerican comparability. II. That in utilizing cultural characteristics for classifying groups of the population, a weighting procedure should be applied according to importance." The idea proposed was correct in principle, but unfortunately it could not be carried into practice. However, the insertion of these recommendations into the Final Document of the Congress demonstrates first, the existing interest in elucidating the problem, and, second, the recognition of the lack of data and the request that these be collected according to a single formula throughout America.

To show the changing definitions since the First Interamerican Indigenist Congress, the important contributions of indigenist studies from 1940 to date are outlined. In presenting the events in chronological sequence, we include the needed dimension of time.

In the list of topics for the First International Demographic Congress in Mexico City in 1943, the point referring to Indian problems in America was included. Efforts of the demographers towards a better knowledge of a quantitatively and qualitatively important sector of the American population were obvious in the following resolutions:

III. Cultural Characteristics in Population Censuses. Let the governments of the American countries with Indian economy and culture follow in the formulation of their respective censuses processes similar to those employed by Mexico in taking the Census of 1940, for which purpose one would have to determine sufficiently in advance and with appropriate coordination the cultural characteristics which each country should investigate in its Census of Population beginning in 1950. . . .

XII. Racial Prejudices. 1. To recommend to the American governments that they reject absolutely any policy or discriminatory action of a racial character. 2. That, to this end, the word "race" not be used in the sense implied beyond common inheritance; physical characteristics; psychological characteristics; or cultural, religious, or linguistic, taking into consideration that valid criteria of racial classification connote only somatic heredity characters without implication of any other psychological or cultural character.

For Mexico this first declaration was a matter of pride. In the Sixth Population Census of 1943 of the United States of Mexico (1943, p. 34), for the first time cultural data were collected in addition to the linguistic data already considered in previous censuses, such as: the population which eats wheat bread, which sleeps on the floor, which sleeps in *tapexco,* which sleeps in a hammock, which sleeps on a cot or bed. Similarly, it was indicated how many people went barefoot, how many wore sandals, and how many wore shoes. The General Directorate of Statistics, officially charged with collecting, classifying, and publishing census data, provided first-hand information for studying the degree of correlation, dependence, or dissociation of quantified cultural characteristics. In the matter of racial prejudices, the resolution was brusque; every form of racial discrimination was absolutely rejected.

Lewis and Maes, fundamentally interested in the improvement of Indian groups, consider practical action the main work of locating distinctive characteristics of Indians. They argue (1945, p. 113):

We are of the opinion that from the point of view of the person practically interested in indigenist work, the important thing is first to determine the data needed in relation to the administration of specific programs in various fields of social action (agriculture, health, education, etc.). For this purpose it seems to us that rather than to begin with an analysis of culture, it would be better to begin with an analysis of existing social services. . . . [The data needed by an administrator to carry out a program of improvement are:] 1. Data indicating the most acute economic and social deficiences of the groups in question. 2. Data showing differences among the needs and deficiencies of the various groups included in the compilation. 3. Data indicating the groups within which special techniques should be employed in programs designed to resolve the various aspects of the problem. 4. Data which serve as a basis for determining special adaptations must be produced in the existing national programs in each country so that these can reach the groups with the greatest need.

The classification they propose can be applied only through designing inventories of needs and social services of each group.

"Indeed, in our opinion, when a group has a maximum number of needs and quantitative deficiencies found in a people together with the maximum frequency of qualitative needs and deficiencies, we are in the presence of a group which we can call Indian. On the other hand, if it is a matter of a case in which the numerical frequency is minimal, we are in the presence of a Mestizo or non-Indian group."

This new emphasis on investigation is very valuable for indigenist action. Nothing could be more correct than the declaration that there is no Indian problem but Indian problems, and that their solution depends less on historical and theoretical analysis than on precise action programs based on the specific conditions of life of each of them. We therefore completely agree with their assertion: "We believe that it is necessary and practical to define the Indian on the basis of an internationally acceptable concept. Nevertheless, we recognize that the specific factors which will be employed in each country must necessarily differ. Our criterion for the definition of the Indian will serve not only to establish the differences between one country and another, but also to permit determination of differences among the Indian groups of the various regions of a single country."

For Julio de la Fuente, the important thing is the process of change taking place from day to day and through which the Indian ceases to be only such but moves into the Mestizo or non-Indian group. The progress of the Indian is realized despite barriers, among which racial discrimination still figures. De la Fuente remarks (1947a, p. 63):

As for *racial attitudes,* it is obvious that they exist. Dark color (as of an Indian or Negro) is linked to low status and consequently extended to biological extraction. Notions of innate inferiority of the Indian are common, and the employment of terms like *indio, indiote, naco,* and others in a pejorative sense is more or less general. The non-Indian usually looks down on the Indian, and both groups tend to rationalize the undesirable conditions in which they live by casting responsibility for these upon Indian extraction. To resolve the Indian problem by liquidating the Indians is considered the most reliable means by not a few people. It can be said, all in all, that as a result of the prolonged contact and the relatively scant attention it has received, the race has awakened.

Undoubtedly there is much truth here, but racial discrimination does remain, more in some places than in others. In Mexico extreme attitudes are among the Maya of Quintana Roo, the Tzeltal of Chiapas, and the Yaqui of Sonora.

Rorty has this to say (1960, p. 217): "It is generally asserted that there is no racial discrimination in Mexico. This is altogether true with respect to the juridical aspect and to national policy. Nevertheless, Mexico is not lacking in ethnic problems, one symptom of which is a certain discrimination, more of a cultural than a racial character. This affirmation is particularly appropriate to regions located south of the Isthmus of Tehuantepec."

De la Fuente is in agreement with the practical program of Lewis and Maes for the definition of what is an Indian, but for him this focus is incomplete unless we also consider the facts of constant change. The complexity of the topic is manifest in this warning (1947b, p. 215): "From what has been said, it should not be concluded that the process described in such broad strokes is the same throughout the country nor that either the passage or the disappearance of it is a phenomenon which in either a natural way or through the operation of directed action can be produced with the speed implied when one refers pointblank to the effect of the present disappearance of the Indian. In fact, there are groups which by reason of their marginality or for other special causes resist the modifications described."

Fernando Cámara (1947) also stresses the idea of the changing Indian. As a social anthropologist he accepts the cultural criterion for the distinction, but observes that cultures are not static but are continually undergoing transformation; in these conditions Gamio's classification of cultural elements into *eficientes*, *deficientes*, and *perjudiciales* has only transitory value. "It would be necessary to make, from time to time, changes and modifications in the elements classified since the transformation and advancement of science would give greater value to some elements which we are not now considering while perhaps there would remain some importance to others which we now consider as *eficientes*."

Cámara's more telling objections are in reply to the practical approach Lewis and Maes assigned to their system:

Although the authors mentioned assert that it is not necessary in principle to make an analysis of the culture, I believe that the means to be employed must always be based upon such an analysis. . . . [He disagrees with the value attributed to necessities:] The investigators cited reached the conclusion that a group can be called indigenous or Indian when it has a maximum of quantitative and qualitative necessities and deficiencies and that it should be Mestizo when these necessities and deficiencies are minimal. To this conclusion it may be added that a *blanco* is a person who has no necessities and deficiencies, but reality shows us quite the opposite. The groups which live in the suburbs of a city—even a great city like Mexico, New York, Buenos Aires, or Rio de Janeiro—may be, and actually in many cases are, in a more deficient and precarious socioeconomic situation than the very groups considered Indian and established in rural zones. That is to say, in any community we can encounter a whole spectrum of differences with respect to necessities and deficiencies.

Alfonso Caso published in 1948 a definition of the Indian even more complete. To the founder and present director of the Instituto Nacional Indigenista of Mexico it is of little importance to classify an individual as indigenous or not. Rather, the task is to define the community so as to apply appropriate formulas for its national incorporation. Caso proceeds: "I would say, 'He is an Indian who feels himself to belong to an Indian community; and an Indian community is one in which non-European somatic elements predominate, which speaks by preference an Indian language, which has in its material and spiritual culture a high proportion of Indian elements, and which finally has a social sense of community isolated among the other communities surrounding it which causes it to distinguish itself from the towns of blancos and Mestizos.'"

In 1949 the Second Interamerican Indigenist Congress, in Cuzco, Peru, made the following resolutions:

Section I: Biology. 1. The Second Interamerican Indigenist Congress condemns any concept of physical or intellectual degeneration of the indigenes, recognizing that they possess all normal potentiality and faculties for adaptation to modern life. . . . Section II: Anthropology. 10. The Second Interamerican Indigenist Congress resolves: That from the anthropological point of view, Indian and what is Indian can be defined in the following form: The Indian is the descendant of the pre-Columbian peoples and natives who have a common social consciousness of their human condition, correspondingly considered by themselves and foreigners in their system of work, in their language, and in their tradition even though these may have suffered modifications through foreign contacts.

What is Indian is the expression of a social consciousness tied to the systems of work and the economy, with its own language and respective national tradition of the aboriginal peoples or nations.

Such definitions have absolutely no effect on the condition of the Indian in those countries whose special legislation establishes some other legal characterization.

As these resolutions have been little disseminated, the definition is not widely known and is cited infrequently.

In the Third Interamerican Indigenist Congress, at La Paz, Bolivia, in 1954, the Indian population was again discussed. The Final Act (1954a) declared simply: "The Third Interamerican Indigenist Congress resolves: To recommend to the governments of the American countries that for purposes of census and interamerican statistical information, the linguistic, cultural, and social criteria be taken into account in the identification of the Indian." A special number of the *Boletín Indigenista* gave further explanations (1954b, p. 193): "Vote No. 15. All of us have had some experience with the fact that there are still great imperfections in regard to the demography of the Indian populations of the Americas, for we begin with the difficulty of defining what, strictly speaking, should be understood to be Indian or indigenous. This recommendation is dedicated to getting around these deficiencies by counseling improvement of statistics on indigenous populations, taking into account linguistic, cultural, and social criteria and not only unilaterally physical-anthropological criteria which frequently lead to mistakes or prejudices of a racist character."

The Fourth and last Interamerican Indigenist Congress, in Guatemala City in 1959, declared in its Final Agreements:

X. On the Improvement of Population Censuses. The Fourth Interamerican Indigenist Congress, considering that up to the present time the size of the indigenist population of America is not exactly known, that it is indispensable that we have complete statistical data to be able to help the American countries to make effective the social policy of Indian integration, therefore be it resolved: To recommend to the American countries that the Census of the Americas to be undertaken in 1960 take into account an appropriate interest in including data relative to the Indian population, taking into consideration the dispositions on the matter which the Interamerican Indigenistic Congresses have promulgated and in consultation with the National Indigenist Institutes or the Interamerican Indigenist Institute in those countries where national institutes do not exist.

Even with the results of indigenist investigations from 1940 to 1960 the problem of who and how many are the Indians of the Americas is still before us. Because the numerous points of view expressed are partial and of little practical value, they have not advanced us in this difficult topic. What solution, then, can there be, even on some provisional basis?

Since the only aspect which can be quantified is the linguistic one, the majority of American countries have taken the Indian language as a basis for their censuses, tabulating it as the maternal language, the language habitually spoken, the language spoken in the home, and so forth in order to determine the total native population. The data are cited in Table 1.

Figures on Indian Population

The Committee on Latin American Studies of the University of California in Los Angeles has published the second edition of the *Statistical Abstract of Latin America*, which covers the year 1956 and from which we select the data for Table 1 (for greater detail see *Boletín Indigenista*, 1958, p. 6).

TABLE 1—CENSUS DATA

Country	Estimated Population for 1956	Indian Population
Costa Rica	998,000	2,700
El Salvador	2,269,000	. . .
Guatemala	3,303,000	1,479,200
Honduras	1,711,000	80,700
Mexico	30,538,000	795,000
Nicaragua	1,261,000	20,000
Panama	934,000	. . .

The final column refers to the speakers of Indian languages (monolingual or bilingual), except for Mexico and Nicaragua, where it is limited to monolinguals.

MEXICO. According to the Census of 1950, the total population was 25,791,017, of whom 2,490,909 spoke Indian languages. After calculating the population over five

TABLE 2—REPUBLIC OF MEXICO, DISTRIBUTION OF INDIAN-SPEAKERS BY STATES

States	Speaking Indian Languages	Percentage*	Number of Monolinguals	Percentage of Monolinguals
Aguascalientes	42	...	1	...
Baja California Norte	354	...	9	...
Baja California Territorio Sur	74	...	...	...
Campeche	32,816	31.9	5,351	5.1
Coahuila	500	...	141	...
Colima	165	...	1	...
Chiapas	198,087	26.2	104,244	13.7
Chihuahua	22,448	3.1	9,707	1.3
Federal District	18,812	...	170	...
Durango	2,592	...	422	...
Guanajuato	4,650	...	336	...
Guerrero	124,693	16.0	59,241	7.6
Hidalgo	179,629	25.2	60,401	8.4
Jalisco	5,303	...	956	...
Mexico	183,051	15.6	39,207	3.3
Michoacan	51,273	4.3	12,106	1.0
Morelos	11,764	5.1	816	...
Nayarit	3,866	1.6	332	...
Nuevo Leon	198	...	6	...
Oaxaca	586,853	48.4	212,520	17.5
Puebla	297,490	21.6	118,971	8.6
Queretaro	13,257	5.5	4,824	2.0
Quintana Roo	9,599	43.7	1,335	6.0
San Luis Potosi	89,096	12.4	28,972	4.0
Sinaloa	8,940	1.7	954	...
Sonora	25,058	5.8	1,892	...
Tabasco	24,486	8.1	873	...
Tamaulipas	696	...	1	...
Tlaxcala	22,213	9.2	435	...
Veracruz	252,739	14.7	87,318	5.0
Yucatan	279,380	63.8	43,523	9.9
Zacatecas	284	...	2	...
TOTALS	2,490,909	11.2	795,069	3.6

*Percentages refer to the population over five years of age.

years of age (the group able to communicate orally) we get a proportion of 11.2 per cent. Expressed in other terms, for each 10 speaking Castilian, there is one who still speaks an Indian tongue.

These two and a half million Indian-speakers are scattered throughout almost all the federal states. There are strongly Indian states like Oaxaca or Yucatan and others like Aguascalientes, Tamaulipas, or Nuevo Leon with no native population (see Tables 2–4).

The distribution of Indian-speakers is counted as follows:

Oaxaca: more than 500,000 speakers.

Puebla, Veracruz, Yucatan: 200,000–300,000 speakers.

Chiapas, Guerrero, Hidalgo, Mexico: 100,000–200,000 speakers.

Michoacan, San Luis Potosi: 50,000–100,000 speakers.

Campeche, Chihuahua, Federal District, Morelos, Queretaro, Sonora, Tlaxcala: 10,000–50,000 speakers.

Durango, Guanajuato, Jalisco, Nayarit, Quintana Roo, Sinaloa: 1,000–10,000 speakers.

Aguascalientes, Baja California Norte, Baja California Territorio Sur: less than 1,000 speakers.

TABLE 3—REPUBLIC OF MEXICO, DISTRIBUTION OF INDIAN-SPEAKERS BY LANGUAGE

Language	Total Speakers	Monolinguals	Percentage of Monolinguals
Amuzgo	12,826	5,839	45.5
Cora	3,125	228	7.3
Chatino	13,446	8,259	61.4
Chinantec	35,654	15,702	44.0
Chol	31,139	18,898	60.7
Chontal	24,703	1,539	6.2
Huastec	66,646	17,276	25.9
Huichol	3,449	1,035	30.0
Kikapu	500	132	26.4
Maya	328,255	50,912	15.5
Mayo	31,053	2,509	8.1
Mazahua	84,125	16,254	19.3
Mazatec	77,530	47,167	60.8
Mixe	46,101	21,005	45.6
Mixtec	185,470	76,946	41.5
Nahuatl	641,334	212,813	30.1
Otomi	185,656	57,559	31.0
Popoloca	17,163	1,564	9.1
Tarahumara	18,421	9,796	22.2
Tarasco	44,102	8,166	44.3
Tepehuano	4,677	1,583	33.8
Tlapaneco	18,139	12,234	67.4
Totonac	106,696	54,333	50.9
Tzeltal	48,279	31,856	66.0
Tzotzil	74,827	44,103	58.9
Yaqui	2,640	199	7.5
Zapotec	226,995	60,680	26.7
Zoque	18,023	4,804	26.7
Others	139,935	11,678	
TOTAL	2,490,909	795,069	32.0

TABLE 4—REPUBLIC OF GUATEMALA, INDIAN DISTRIBUTION BY DEPARTMENTS

Department	Census of 1950
Guatemala: Cakchiqueles predominate; also Pocomanes, Quiches, Mames	79,514
El Progreso: Quiches predominate; also Cakchiqueles, Pocomanes, Kekchis	4,482
Sacatepequez: principally Cakchiqueles, some Quiches, Kekchis	30,994
Chimaltenango: mainly Cakchiqueles, a few Quiches, Pocomanes, Mames	94,243
Escuintla: principally Cakchiqueles, then central Pocomanes and Quiches, some Kekchis	19,660
Santa Rosa: Quiches, Cakchiqueles, some Kekchis	10,294
Solola: mostly Indian, principally Quiches, Cakchiqueles, and Tzutujiles; also some Pocomanes, Kekchis	77,817
Totonicapan: 96.8 per cent Indian, almost all Quiches; also some Cakchiqueles	96,138
Quezaltenango: principally Mames and Quiches; also Cakchiqueles, some Pocomanes, Kekchis	124,473
Suchitepequez: Quiches predominate; also Cakchiqueles, Tzutujiles, Mames, some Kekchis	84,252
Retalhuleu: Quiches predominate; also Mames, Cakchiqueles, some Kekchis	34,696
San Marcos: Mames predominate; also Quiches and Cakchiqueles and a few Kekchis	168,540
Huehuetenango: principally Mames and Kanjobales; also Jacaltecos, Chuj, Cakchiqueles	146,628
El Quiche: almost all Quiches, but also Ixiles, Mames, Cakchiqueles, Kekchis, Uspantecos	147,094
Baja Verapaz: Quiches predominate; also Pocomchis, Kekchis, Cakchiqueles	38,776
Alta Verapaz: principally Kekchis and Pocomchis; also Cakchiqueles, Quiches	177,308
El Peten: all are Kekchis except 215 Lacandones	4,431
Izabal: principally Kekchis; also Caribe Araguacs	9,466
Zacapa: Chortis predominate; also Quiches, Cakchiqueles	13,359
Chiquimula: solely Chortis	69,843
Jalapa: Pocomanes predominate; also Cakchiqueles	38,004
Jutiapa: Pocomanes	27,249

The Census of 1950 showed 795,069 Mexicans who knew no Spanish and spoke only Indian languages. In other words, for each 100 individuals who knew Spanish four did not.

The languages with the largest number of monolinguals are:

	Speakers
Chinantec	15,702
Chol	18,898
Huastec	17,276
Maya	50,912
Mazahua	16,254
Mazatec	47,167
Mixe	21,005
Mixtec	76,946
Nahua	212,813
Otomi	57,559
Tlapanec	12,234
Totonac	54,333
Tzeltal	31,856
Tzotzil	44,103
Zapotec	60,680

The geographic distribution of the Indian languages by states is:

Campeche: Maya.
Chiapas: Chol, Mame, Maya, Tojolabal, Tzeltal, Tzotzil, Zoque.
Chihuahua: Tarahumara, Tepehuano.
Guerrero: Amuzgo, Nahua, Mixtec. Tlapanec.
Hidalgo: Nahua, Otomi.
Mexico: Mazahua, Nahua, Otomi.
Michoacan: Tarasco.
Morelos: Nahua.
Nayarit: Cora.
Oaxaca: Chatino, Chinantec, Chontal, Mazatec. Nahua, Mixe, Mixtec, Zapotec, Zoque.
Puebla: Mazatec, Nahua, Mixtec, Otomi, Popoluca, Totonac, Zoque.
Queretaro: Otomi.
Quintana Roo: Maya.
San Luis Potosi: Huastec, Nahua, Pame.
Sinaloa: Mayo.
Sonora: Mayo, Papago, Yaqui.
Tabasco: Chontal.
Tlaxcala: Nahua.
Veracruz: Huastec, Nahua, Otomi, Popoluca, Totonac, Zapotec.
Yucatan: Maya.

The Indian demography of Mexico has been studied fairly broadly. For more information see Alaniz Patiño (1946), Parra (1950), Marino Flores (1956), and León-Portilla (1956).

GUATEMALA. According to Juan de Dios Rosales, the population of Guatemala in 1950 was 2,790,868; speakers of Indian languages numbered 1,497,261. Of these, 78 per cent are monolingual and 22 per cent bilingual.

The speakers from each group are (Rosales, 1959, p. 117):

	Speakers
Quiche	339,232
Cakchiquel	167,363
Tzutuhil	18,761
Uspantec	12,089
Mam	178,308
Aguacatec	8,401
Jalaltec	13,941
Kanjobal	41,622
Chuj	10,771
Ixil	25,025
Kekchi	153,971
Pocomchi	37,546
Eastern Pocoman	5,226
Central Pocoman	6,208
Chorti	12,048
Chol Lacandon	......
North Lacandon	......
Carib Araguac	1,116

The Indian population is concentrated in the western highlands, which at some points reach 4000 m. elevation. This zone represents nearly a fourth of the area of the country, where approximately 1,000,000 Indians live, belonging to the linguistic groups Quiche-Cakchiquel (west-central) and Mam (extreme west). The remainder of the aboriginal population is distributed in the central and north regions of the republic (see Table 4).

EL SALVADOR. This nation has an Indian population, culturally speaking, but there are no figures on the speakers of Indian languages.

HONDURAS. The principal Indian groups of Honduras are Jicaques, Payas, Sumos, Zambos, and Miskitos. The statistics are deficient. Núñez Chinchilla states (1959, p. 230):

The data we find in the most recent censuses are the following: 1935—89,665 Indians; in the year 1940, an Indian population of 105,752 was counted; in the year 1945, it was 80,660. And in the most recent census—in which the Honduran population reached almost 2,000,000 inhabitants—there is no box for the Indian population; that is to say that the authorities charged with the statistics of the country believed, reasonably or not, that the Indian race has been extinguished or should not appear as such in relation to the remainder of Honduras.

NICARAGUA. The population of Nicaragua, according to the Census of 1950, is 1,057,023; those over six years of age number 854,413, of whom 21,496 speak Indian languages (747 Sumo; 20,723 Miskito; and 26 other dialects). The Indian population of Nicaragua is 2.4 per cent. Monolinguals number 15,931, bilinguals 5,565.

The distribution of populations speaking Indian languages or dialects in the home, whether or not they speak Spanish, is listed in Table 5.

TABLE 5

Language	Department of Jinotega	Department of Zelaya	Comarca of Cabo Gracias a Dios
Sumo	238	509	. . .
Miskito	519	7,685	12,339
Other	. . .	26	. . .

The greatest concentration, in Cabo Gracias a Dios, takes up 57.4 per cent of the total Indian population; 39.1 per cent are in Zelaya; 3:5 per cent in Jinotega.

COSTA RICA. Figures on the Indian population of Costa Rica are very scarce, most of them being personal estimates. Rosenblat (1954) indicates that in 1942 the population was calculated at 687,354 inhabitants, among them 3500 Indians and 18,000 Negroes. Some people calculated that 90 per cent of the population is white, and the remainder is distributed among Mestizos,

Indians, and Negroes. Rosenblat states: "The census of the 22nd of May of 1950 reached 800,875 inhabitants distributed as follows: white, 782,041 (97.65 per cent); Negro, 15,118 (1.89 per cent); yellow, 933 (0.12 per cent); Indian, 2,692 (0.33 per cent); and other, 91 (0.01 per cent)."

PANAMA. The important Indian groups in Panama are the Guaymíes, the Kunas, and the Chocoes.

The Guaymíes are in the mountains, valleys, and plains of the interior of Chiriqui, Veraguas, Bocas del Toro. Those of Chiriqui are numerous in the districts of Remedios, Tole, San Felix, and San Lorenzo and total 19,135 individuals (1940), of whom 11,115 live in Tole. Those of Veraguas constitute the plains and Move-Valiente subgroups which live especially in the districts of Cañazas, Las Palmas, Santa Fe and total scarcely 1500 individuals. Those of Bocas del Toro total 6100 and live mostly in the district of Chiriqui Grande.

The Cunas live in the extreme east of the Isthmus, together with the Chocoes, occupying the region known by the name of the Comarca de San Blas.

The Indian population of Panama is geographically distributed as follows (1940):

TABLE 6

Province	Indian Population
Bocas del Toro	6,574
Cocle	. . .
Colon	20,822
Chiriqui	19,135
Darien	6,651
Herrera	. . .
Los Santos	. . .
Panama	1,329
Veraguas	1,476
TOTAL	55,987

REFERENCES

Alaniz Patiño, 1946
Cámara Barbachano, 1947
Caso, 1948
Comas, 1955, 1961
Congreso Indigenista, 1949, 1954a, 1954b, 1959
De la Fuente, 1947a, 1947b
Gamio, 1922, 1937a, 1939, 1942a, 1942b, 1946
Goubaud, 1945
Inst. Indigenista Interamericano, 1958
Klineberg, 1952
León-Portilla, 1956

Lewis and Maes, 1945
Lipschütz, 1944
Marino Flores, 1956
Mexico, 1943, 1953
Nicaragua, 1954
Núñez Chinchilla, 1959
Parra, 1950
Rorty, 1960
Rosales, 1959
Rosenblat, 1945, 1954
Vivó, 1943

3. Agricultural Systems and Food Patterns

ANGEL PALERM

AGRICULTURE CONTINUES TO BE the principal economic activity and the primary means of subsistence for the Indian groups of Mesoamerica. This is perhaps the only generalization possible in a comparison between the pre-Hispanic, colonial, and independence periods. The position and function of Indian agriculture within the framework of national society, however, have undergone profound and irreversible modifications, especially in the last 50 years. Less important yet highly significant changes have also occurred in agricultural technology and in the implements utilized; in methods of cultivation and kinds of plants grown; in the social forms of agricultural activity; and in other closely related cultural aspects (markets and marketing, land tenure, religious and magical beliefs and practices).

PLACE OF INDIAN AGRICULTURE IN THE NATIONAL SOCIETY

From the standpoint of the national societies of Mesoamerica as a whole, the main change consists in the increasingly marginal position assigned to Indian groups as such and to their economic activities, especially agriculture. Another change is the equally rapid integration and absorption of Indians as individuals or communities into the national society. The integration of the individual is brought about particularly through new economic activities, secondarily agricultural; that of communities is effected chiefly through the commercialization of traditional agricultural activities. Thus Indian agriculture presents a picture not only of deculturation and acculturation accompanied by geographic and socioeconomic marginalization, but also of the transformation of a dual society (dating from the Spanish conquest) and a multicultural society (dating from the pre-Hispanic era) into a modern society, national in character and uniform in culture.

In finding out how these changes occurred, we shall consider Mesoamerican Indian agriculture in terms of its present situation and its role in Indian communities within modern national society. We are concerned with both theoretical and practical aspects. For example, the decline of the *chinampas* ("floating gardens") in

26

the Valley of Mexico is related to flood prevention, to the acquisition of land for urban expansion, and to the appropriation of water sources to supply Mexico City. Conservation of the remaining chinampas is not so much for agricultural purposes as for their value as a tourist attraction. Restoration of the archaeological terrace system of the Texcoco piedmont was brought about by the appearance of a permanent and readily accessible market for flowers and fruits, by the return of water for irrigation to the Indian communities, and by the destruction of the hacienda system by the Mexican Revolution. The raising of cochineal was abandoned after the development of synthetic dyes in Germany, which caused many parts of Oaxaca to revert to the cultivation of subsistence crops. Since Western markets were not able to secure vanilla from Oriental producers during World War II, vanilla cultivation was intensified in Veracruz to the detriment of corn crops.

These phenomena, resulting from the increasing impact on Indian agriculture of the fluctuations and crises affecting national society, are accompanied by an accentuation of the marginal geographic position assigned to Indian agricultural activities. Areas characterized by a predominance of Indian agricultural systems are those least favored by natural conditions and least suited to the essential crops cultivated by the national society. This occurs, for example, in the tropical rain forest, in extremely arid or humid zones, in the mountains, and, in general, in regions isolated from urban centers and lacking means of communication and transportation. In some cases, however, specific needs for seasonal labor, as in the coffee-, banana-, and sugar-cane-raising areas, have helped keep nearby Indian groups engaged in traditional agricultural practices.

This marginalization is socio-economic as well as geographic. Indian agriculture has declined quantitatively and qualitatively, especially with respect to its strategic position within national society. From being the principal support of urban centers and the major economic activity during the pre-Hispanic era, it became simply an auxiliary source of supply during the colonial era, in which haciendas and plantations acquired a predominant role. Today Indian agriculture is losing even this function, frequently through the abandonment of certain crops that cannot withstand the competition of modern agriculture. This has happened with the growing and refining of sugar cane, and with cotton cultivation and home weaving. Both activities have been displaced by the highly technical farming practices and industrial manufacturing systems characteristic of a national society.

On the other hand, the role of transforming economic function into economic power does not belong to the Indian groups but, as a rule, to middlemen who stand between them and the national society. A case in point is the opportunity to accumulate wealth and to exert economic and social pressures afforded by gaining control of the vanilla grown by the Totonacs. It is not the Indian but the traders and other middlemen, members of the national society, who utilize this opportunity. The same can be said of the control of the Indian labor force in the coffee, banana, henequen, and sugar-cane areas. Logically, the marginal situation as regards economic, social, and political power helps to accentuate the marginalization of Indian agriculture in its geographic, technological, crops, marketing, and price aspects. Such factors as these require that we consider Indian agriculture in the context of the national society.

INDIAN AGRICULTURE AND ITS GEOGRAPHIC ENVIRONMENT

We look first at the influence of the national society, its demands, rewards, and pressures at all levels, and then at the specific geographic environment within which the Indian groups produce their crops.

Mesoamerica has repeatedly been described as a geographic mosaic of incredible fragmentation, variety, and contrast. It is not solely or even principally a question of latitude, extending from 10° to 20° N., but essentially of altitude, ranging from sea level to elevations of more than 5000 m. It is also a matter of prevailing winds and rains and complicated topography.

In describing features pertinent to agriculture, we shall follow the traditional classification of *tierra fría, tierra templada,* and *tierra caliente* (cold country, temperate country, and hot country).

Tierra Fría, Tierra Templada, Tierra Caliente

The tierra fría lies above 1600 m. It has two main seasons, dry and rainy, and a single annual growing period for corn, the principal native plant. The agricultural cycle unfolds between the beginning of the rainy season and the first night frosts.

The tierra fría has humid pockets in which the start of the rains does not affect farming overmuch. Arid zones are more abundant, however, where the start of the rains is critical, where auxiliary or emergency irrigation may be required especially when the corn is germinating. Without irrigation, such plants as maguey, nopal, and mesquite can be cultivated.

The tierra templada lies between 800 and 1600 m. It also has rainy and dry seasons, but is generally more humid than the tierra fría. A more moderate mean temperature and the almost total absence of frosts frequently permit two plantings of corn a year. Pockets in which humidity is above or below average either relieve the farmers of their dependence on rainfall, or oblige them to resort to irrigation or to the cultivation of plants adapted to arid conditions.

Plants such as coffee, citrus fruits, and sugar cane, of Old World origin and of great economic importance, have been better adapted to the tierra templada than to any other region of Mesoamerica.

The tierra caliente is located between sea level and 800 m.; it has a short dry season and a period of regular and abundant rainfall. The mean annual temperature and rainfall are sufficient to assure two corn-growing seasons a year. In some dry areas of the tierra caliente, however, irrigation must be utilized, or desert plants such as henequen must be cultivated.

Highlands and Coastal Regions

The main part of Mesoamerica consists of a mass of highlands or plateaus, bounded by mountain ranges parallel to the Pacific, Caribbean, and Gulf coasts. We can distinguish three zones of highlands: (1) the central zone, bounded on the east and west by the Sierra Madre Oriental and the Sierra Madre Occidental, on the north by the cultural frontier of Mesoamerica, and on the south by the Neovolcanic range which runs from east to west through the center of Mexico; (2) the southern zone, bounded by the Sierra Madre of Oaxaca and the Sierra Madre del Sur, with the Neovolcanic range to the north and the depression of the Isthmus of Tehuantepec to the southeast; (3) the southeastern zone, extending from the Isthmus of Tehuantepec to the southern border of Mesoamerica.

The coastal regions are generally small compared with the highlands. The principal exceptions are the Yucatan Peninsula and, to a certain degree, the coastal plains at the base of the Sierra Madre Oriental north of the state of Veracruz, Mexico, and the Caribbean coastal plains in Central America.

The Pacific coast is generally narrow and dry, with desert and semidesert characteristics. The Gulf-Caribbean coast is wider and more humid, mostly covered by tropical rain forest that extends without interruption from Veracruz to the southern border of Mesoamerica. The division of the Pacific and Gulf-Caribbean coastal areas into sections corresponding to the central, southern, and southeastern highlands is especially important for the cultural history of Mesoamerica. It is significant even for the analysis of modern conditions, particularly in zones of diversified agriculture where the Indians seek to supplement their resources by active barter.

Almost all the central highlands are tierra fría; the southern highlands are tierra templada with important areas of tierra caliente; the southeastern highlands are a mixture of tierra templada and tierra fría; the Pacific and Gulf-Caribbean coastal areas are tierra caliente. The mountain ranges bordering the highlands are made up of belts of the three climates, according to altitude.

In an area of this terrain we observe that (1) the largest concentrations of Indians are in the tierra caliente of the Gulf-Caribbean coastal area, and on the corresponding mountain slopes; (2) even today, Indian communities are scattered throughout Mesoamerica, in all geographic regions and on all types of terrain. This can be explained by the marginalization of Indian groups, by the geographic fragmentation and diversity; and by certain specific needs of national society, especially for labor.

Indian Cultivation Systems

Every system of cultivation may be viewed as an adaptation of agriculture to the conditions either of the geographic environment or of the socio-economic environment. These two environments have different intensities, according to the isolation of a group from national society. Wherever demands of national society are felt most strongly, agriculture tends to respond more rapidly and intensely to socio-economic adaptation; wherever these pressures decline, agriculture tends to respond to geographic adaptation.

Although we can thus expect to find a great variety of cultivation systems, we can group them into four types: (1) the *roza* (slash and burn); (2) the *barbecho* (fallowing); (3) the *secano intensivo* (dry farming); and (4) the *humedad y riego*

FIG. 1—FUTURE CORNFIELD CUT, DRIED, AND READY FOR BURNING, YUCATAN. (From Steggerda, 1941, pl. 17,c.)

(moisture and irrigation). Our typology is based on the ways land and water are used, omitting, for the moment, both the variety of tools and the repertory of plants in order to concentrate our attention on corn, the most important crop for Indian agriculture.

The distribution in Mesoamerica of these four systems is significant. The roza system is typical of tierra caliente; it predominates on the coasts, particularly those of the Gulf and Caribbean. The barbecho system is more typical of tierra fría than of tierra templada, although it is often found there; this system prevails in the highlands and particularly in the central highlands. Although the secano-intensivo system has a distribution similar to that of the barbecho, it is more restricted. This is true also of the humedad-y-riego system, whose distribution is determined both by dry conditions and by the availability of water.

From the standpoint of geographic conditions, each system represents a different level of adaptation to, or control of, the mean environment; from the standpoint of national society, each system represents a different state of socio-economic dependence.

Roza System

The roza system consists primarily in fell-

29

FIG. 2—BURNING THE FUTURE CORNFIELD, YUCATAN. Many small fires are started to insure a good burning. The milpero whistles a plaintive tune while starting the fires. (From Steggerda, 1941, pl. 17,*d.*)

FIG. 3—BURNED MILPA READY FOR PLANTING, NEAR CHICHEN ITZA, YUCATAN. (From Steggerda, 1941, pl. 18,*a.*)

30

ing a portion of woods at a suitable time of year so that the cut vegetation will dry and be ready for burning. The plot is planted after the burning, and later is weeded periodically. When the yields decline, after a generally brief time, the land is abandoned, permitting regeneration of woods and soil. A new section of woods is felled to continue the agricultural cycle.

The following description of the process may be applied to most tierra caliente, with some variations to be pointed out later.

Clearing (fig. 1) consists of three phases: first, the undergrowth, vines, and low branches are cut; second, all large trees are felled except those of special value, whose preservation may be desirable; third, tree trunks and thick branches are split for easier burning. Clearing is generally performed without interruption during April, May, or June, depending on weather and approach of the rainy season. During this phase, trees of good wood are selected for constructing houses and making home and work tools (spade and hoe handles, benches). Firewood to be carted home is also set aside.

The cleared land is burned (fig. 2) when the vegetation is sufficiently dry, and before the rains begin, on a day without wind. In addition, a firebreak is made; a strip around the area to be burned is cleared of all vegetation in order to keep the fire from spreading to the rest of the forest. This also protects valuable trees not felled during clearing. Once burned, the cleared land (fig. 3) constitutes a source of charred firewood to be used in the home.

When the cleared area is ready for planting, it is covered with ashes, thick branches, charred and split tree trunks, and roots, which are not removed from the ground. Planting starts with the arrival of the rains, generally between the latter part of June and the beginning of August.

Seed, selected from the best ears of corn of the preceding harvest, is put in water for 24 hours, and later wrapped in green plantain leaves or other pulpy leaves and set in the sun. Planting may be started as soon as the seed germinates. The soil is not prepared for planting in any special way. The seeds (from three to five) are placed by hand in rows of holes about 20 cm. deep, leaving approximately a meter or a meter and a half between rows and holes. As soon as the sprouts reach the surface, seed is put into the holes from which no plants have grown.

Constant effort is required to prevent weeds from growing in the cultivated area (maize field) and to keep birds and other animals away. It is usually necessary to weed at least once a month.

Corn planted between the end of June and the beginning of August starts to ripen in early November. In many places the ears are then bent (fig. 4). The farmer starts to use part of the crop and picks the tender ears from the field; the rest is harvested later and taken home. As soon as the first crop is harvested, a second crop is planted in the same field. Omitting clearing or burning, the process is the same. The new seed is planted between the rows of the first crop. The second crop ripens by the middle of April and is harvested in the same manner.

The roza system has a great many local variations. Rainfall, for example, will affect the farming schedule. Many farmers do not bother to preserve valuable trees. Others do not fell large trees, but kill them by making deep circular cuts in the trunks. The custom of soaking the seed to germinate is not general, nor is that of bending the ears when ripe. There are marked differences in the frequency of weeding that are not always determined by natural conditions. In some areas weeds are pulled up by the roots; in others they are merely cut off at ground level. In some places, all the corn is harvested at once and placed in special granaries. Sometimes the second crop is planted on separate fields.

PERMANENCE OF CROPS AND REGENERA-

FIG. 4—CORNFIELD WITH BENT STALKS, YUCATAN. (From Steggerda, 1941, pl. 20,*a*.)

FIG. 5—INDIANS HARVESTING CORN, YUCATAN. Baskets carried by tumpline. One milpero is throwing corn into his basket. (From Steggerda, 1941, pl. 20,*b*.)

31

TION OF THE SOIL. The main problem of the roza system, however, is not related to these local variations, but centers around the permanence of cultivation on the same soil, and the ability of the forest and soil to regenerate.

In the greater part of humid tierra caliente, covered by the tropical rain forest, a cultivation period of three years seems to be the norm; that is, there are three summer harvests and three winter harvests. After three years, the land is abandoned to the growth of natural vegetation and is not ready to be cleared again until the forest has developed sufficiently.

The fallow period, between the end of cultivation and the new clearing, varies substantially, not only with natural conditions (especially the quality of the soil), but also with demographic conditions, the system of land tenure, crop rotation, and principally agricultural techniques. For example, if demographic pressure exists, the fallow period is shorter and land is cleared not only in well-developed forest areas but in young forest areas as well, and even in areas having an undergrowth. If the regeneration cycle is too short, productivity declines, until it sometimes becomes impossible to raise two crops on the same soil in a single year. The system of land tenure frequently has the same result, through relative overpopulation, poor distribution of land ownership, or the inadequate size of individual plots.

On the other hand, in certain regions of Mesoamerica the cultivation of corn is frequently followed by the cultivation of certain plants (vanilla and cacao, for example) that permit partial regeneration of selected forests. At the same time, this system involves a rotation of crops that helps the soil to regain its fertility.

The techniques used in clearing and weeding are also very significant to the agricultural cycle. If clearing completely destroys all vegetation and the ground is weeded by uprooting plants, erosion and leaching are more intense, and the possibility of rapid forest regeneration is thus more remote. The opposite effect is produced when the most valuable trees in the cleared area are preserved and when weeding does not destroy the roots of wild plants.

Converting the tropical rain forest into savanna has been the subject of much discussion and is just as important to Mesoamerican culture history as it is to modern agriculture. Since this ecological phenomenon does not occur under normal roza conditions, it would seem to be produced by a combination of too long a cultivation period, excessive clearing, and the uprooting of weeds. The conversion of forest into savanna practically eliminates agricultural possibilities under the technological practices characteristic of Indian groups in humid tierra caliente.

Indian agriculturists have a special terminology to describe the variegated development of wild vegetation. A few frequently used terms are *monte alto* (large tree forests); *monte bajo* (young tree forests and shrub forests); *acahual* (undergrowth); and *zacatal* (savanna).

In spite of the variation implied by the factors mentioned, it is possible to establish an average ratio between the amount of land under cultivation and that which must be held in reserve. This ratio has been estimated at 1:8; thus, for each hectare presently under cultivation, eight cultivable hectares should lie fallow or remain unused.

SUBTYPES. Roza-system subtypes are fundamentally related to characteristics determined by the national society and, in a very special way, to the regulations imposed by the system of land ownership. Wherever areas of national ownership exist (generally very isolated, with a sparse Indian population having little contact with national society), there is still found a roza-system subtype that can truly be called itinerant. The farmer selects the land he wishes to clear, without any practical restriction other than

Fɪɢ. 6—PREPARING VEGETABLE GARDEN, PANAJACHEL, GUATEMALA. (From McBryde, 1947, pl. 20,*a.*)

the mutual desires of his neighbors and the recognition of certain limits fixed by the proximity of other groups and of well-established communities. Even in such cases, he follows a fairly well set pattern within a fixed area. The practice does not really constitute a nomadic or migratory form of agriculture, as it has sometimes been called. This subtype is infrequent in Mesoamerica today, and it is rapidly disappearing. A second subtype appears when the roza system operates within the territorial boundaries of an established community that owns the land communally, either by historical tradition or by modern legislation *(ejidos)*. In these cases, there is always a formal or informal land-use code, and it strictly limits the size and location of the clearings. A third subtype occurs when the community land is parceled out, and title to it is distributed among members of the community. The range of agricultural activity for

each family is thus reduced and limited to the area occupied by its plot.

Some results of these subtypes of the roza system will be discussed later. For the moment it is clear that each reflects a different degree of the national society's influence and authority over Indian communities and that each may at the same time express a different form of adaptation to specific natural conditions.

A fourth subtype of the roza system exhibits quite specific differences. The roza of *siembra cubierta* might be justified as a special category, but we shall here regard it as a major subtype. The siembra cubierta is characteristic of tropical forest areas where rain falls throughout the year and where the soil is constantly flooded by the overflow from rivers and swamps. It is therefore a highly specialized technique adapted to the particular natural environment.

Operations begin with planting, with no

33

previous preparation of the soil. Corn seed is sown, and helpers, who follow the planters, cut low vegetation (shrubs, branches, vines, grass). Next, big trees are felled. The cut vegetation is burned, but left as it falls, in a layer on the ground. The soil then remains virtually untouched; it is neither weeded nor tilled. Only when the corn has grown is it protected from animals until harvest.

The siembra cubierta requires the *chocosito* (named after its probable place of origin, Choco, Colombia), which has been genetically described as a very primitive type of corn. The distribution of the chocosito as well as that of the siembra cubierta was long thought to be entirely South American, with extensions in Panama, but recent data indicate the existence of both on the southern border of Mesoamerica and their probable presence in the Peten region.

Barbecho System

From a brief description of the operations involved in the barbecho system, we might easily come to the erroneous conclusion that they are identical to those of the roza system. Both systems have been too frequently confused in a manner that obscures important aspects and consequences of each one. The differentiating characteristics, however, are sufficiently numerous and marked to justify their separation. The following description of cultivation methods is applicable in general to tierra fría and tierra templada, with variations that will be indicated further on.

Theoretically, the barbecho system also begins with clearing, but in fact usually little cultivable land remains to be cleared. The permanence and regularity of cultivation does not give the forest sufficient time to regenerate. Moreover, forest regeneration is much slower in tierra fría and templada than in tierra caliente. In practice, therefore, clearing operations under this system are very rare.

When clearing is done, however, there are important differences from the way in which it is practiced under the roza system. Trees are not only felled at ground level, but frequently uprooted as well. Tree trunks and large branches are carted from the field to the home to be used in construction, for firewood, or for sale. The future cornfield is almost completely cleared, except for small branches, undergrowth and common bushes. Only the undergrowth and small branches remain to be burned. If the soil has previously been cultivated, cornstalks and stubble are burned during the dry season. After burning, the relatively clean and cleared earth is tilled once or twice before summer planting begins. Seeds are sown by hand in parallel rows of holes. The distance between rows and holes is frequently a meter or less (closer together than in tierra caliente). Dried seeds (from three to five) are generally used, and the ground is reseeded more intensively than in tierra caliente. The soil is weeded and prepared for cultivation at the same time. It is turned frequently, and the growth of weeds is not quite the menace that it is in tierra caliente. When the corn has grown sufficiently, earth is heaped around the stalks to form small mounds.

Corn planted in summer ripens at the beginning of winter. As in tierra caliente, there is the custom of bending the ears and of starting to consume tender corn gathered from the field, but usually the crop is harvested at one time and stored in sheltered, well-built granaries.

Under barbecho-system conditions, no second or winter crop is planted in tierra fría. A second harvest is frequently found in warmer and more humid parts of tierra templada.

Most of the variations in the barbecho system are related to the tools used in cultivation, and for that reason we shall discuss them later. Other variations are related to the cultivation cycle and soil regeneration and, in general, to methods of crop rotation, and are discussed below.

PERMANENCE OF CROPS AND REGENERATION OF THE SOIL. The essential difference between the roza and barbecho systems consists in the ability of the soil to regenerate and in the permanence of crops. In most of tierra fría and tierra templada, it is sufficient, for the soil to regain its fertility, to let it lie fallow for roughly the same period of time that it was under cultivation. Within these limits, the cultivation-fallow cycle varies greatly, even within the same area. These variations are almost always related to the quality of the soil. For example: rich soil may be cultivated two or three consecutive years and then left fallow one year; other less fertile soils, which are more abundant, are cultivated one year and left fallow the next; poor soils are cultivated once and left fallow two or three years.

Consequently, the forest seldom has time to regenerate. Naturally, geographic conditions, the uprooting of trees, and constant tillage of the soil contribute greatly to the destruction of the forest. However, there is a great temptation to open up new cultivation areas wherever forest reserves exist because of the economic stimulus provided by marketable trees; the need for fuel, which is frequently a salable product; and the higher yields from first crops planted in a newly cleared forest area. In this way, the progressive eradication of the forest in tierra fría and tierra templada continues, frequently without any real need for more farm land.

In spite of the variations indicated in crop permanence and regeneration cycles, it is possible to estimate that for each hectare presently under cultivation, two or three cultivable hectares should either lie fallow or remain unused.

CROP AND LAND ROTATION. Although the barbecho system may at first glance be mistakenly defined as a roza system carried over from tierra caliente and adapted to geographic conditions in tierra fría and tierra templada, the obvious implications of both systems, together with their technological characteristics, forbid this interpretation.

The barbecho system is correctly defined as a cultivation system in which, in the absence of fertilizers and irrigation, a method of land and work rotation has been established to prevent soil exhaustion and to favor soil regeneration. When the method of land rotation is further complemented by a method of crop rotation and constant tillage, we begin to enter into a category that we call the secano-intensivo system. On the other hand, the barbecho system is generally associated with other, more complex cultivation techniques, such as fertilizers, *calmil* (land cultivated next to the farmer's house), terraces, irrigation, and chinampas. Agriculturists in tierra fría and tierra caliente frequently cultivate several fields at the same time, utilizing not one but two or more agricultural techniques, which will be described here and further on.

Secano-Intensivo System

Under the secano-intensivo system practiced in tierra fría and tierra templada, the stability of the cultivation area is practically complete. The same soil is cultivated year after year without leaving its regeneration to natural factors or to simple fallow methods and the elementary rotation of crops. Clearing does not occur, except when new cultivation areas are needed. Consequently, there is no burning except occasionally for the removal of stubble.

On the other hand, tillage is intense and constant, even during the periods between harvest and planting. More concentration and care go into planting, reseeding, and weeding. There is always a deliberate rotation of crops. The soil is fertilized with manure, green manure, and chemical products, and the harvest is put into silos or special granaries.

Climatic conditions in tierra fría do not permit a second crop, but it is not unusual in warmer and more humid areas of tierra templada.

The secano-intensivo system presents a great variety of techniques and types that until now have not been sufficiently studied. We list some of those that are better known and most frequently found in Mesoamerica and that are usually associated with the barbecho system.

The Nahuatl name for the "calmil" sub-type (*calmil*, 'home maize field') adequately describes its nature. It consists of a small tract of land (generally half a hectare) adjacent or near to the farmhouse. The soil is constantly tilled and fertilized with garbage from the house, with dung collected from the farmyard where domestic animals are kept, and with leaves and branches. From the standpoint of cultivation, the stability of the calmil is complete. Because of the "pantry" nature of the calmil, crop rotation and mixed crops are normal techniques. The calmil is frequently used as a fruit-tree nursery or seed plot for transplanting at the proper time of year.

Dry-farming terraces and bancales might be strictly considered as erosion-control techniques and, in other cases, as cultivation methods typical of the irrigation system. However, they are also found under dry conditions, where they produce the secondary effect of maintaining soil fertility without much need of fertilizers.

Bancales and terraces are found throughout most of the tierria fría and tierra templada, especially on steep slopes and on the edges of ravines. We use the term "terrace" to describe constructions with stone or adobe retaining walls; the term "bancal" is used when the soil is retained by hedges. In general, the terraces are narrow and found on steep slopes; the bancales are wider and are used on more gradual slopes. Both techniques protect the soil against erosion, which seems to be their principal object. Both, however, have the secondary effect of retaining rainwater more effectively and permitting the accumulation, on each level, of certain amounts of alluvium, which is later distributed over the ground to increase its fertility.

Dry-farming terraces and bancales are normally associated with tillage; with the use of manure, green manure, and chemical fertilizers; and with mixed crops and crop rotation.

The stability of this type of cultivation is normally complete. However, the small area of land that it occupies allows it to function as a complement of the barbecho system.

Humedad-y-Riego System

We have grouped into this category a great variety of techniques that are typical of arid and semiarid climates in tierra caliente, tierra templada, and tierra fría, though they are found most frequently in the two last climates. These techniques cover various situations that may go from one extreme to another: from the need of crops for more moisture than that provided by insufficient and irregular rainfall, to the impossibility of cultivation without irrigation; from the need to hasten the crops to maturity before winter frosts set in, to intensification of the crop yield to its maximum.

The marginalization of Indian agriculture, sometimes confused with technological primitivism, has frequently distracted attention from these complex methods of cultivation. Most of them, however, are very old and possibly were the techniques most used by the Indian population at the time when its agriculture and society formed the basis and mainstay of national life. They are still very important today and can be found throughout Mesoamerica.

SOIL MOISTURE. This is the least complicated technique. It merely consists in cultivating moist river and lake banks, as well as areas inundated during the rainy and flood seasons. In the latter case, sediment deposits help keep the soil fertile. This technique is frequently associated with drainage systems.

ARTIFICIAL FLOODING. Small structures

are built in the streams to cut off all or part of its water, raise its level, and flood the adjacent land. After this has been done, the water is released and the wet earth is cultivated. This process may be repeated in dry periods if any water is available. Drainage is also frequent.

WELL IRRIGATION. Wells of different shapes and circumferences are dug wherever there is underground water at not too great a depth. Water is drawn in buckets or containers, and poured either on the ground or into small tanks from which it runs through channels to the farmland.

CANAL IRRIGATION. This technique varies substantially, especially in the way water is supplied. (1) A trench or canal is dug from a partially dammed-up stream to allow the water to flow to the fields. (2) A dam is built in the stream in order to raise the water level and direct it through a canal. This system assures a more regular water supply and permits cultivation on higher levels. (3) In either of the foregoing, but especially in the latter, work is sometimes complemented by the construction of one or more tanks for storing water. (4) A special technique of canal irrigation is that of opening a canal from the bank of a fresh-water lake or pond. The canal gradually deepens, allowing the water to flow easily to the fields. Water is drawn from the canal manually, and irrigation is carried on in the same manner as under the system of well irrigation. (5) Spring water is directed through canals to the fields; water-storage tanks are frequently built. (6) Circular stone and earth walls are built on relatively flat hilltops to collect rainwater and channel it down to the fields. Sometimes the reservoir is excavated to increase its capacity. At other times, dikes are constructed across the watercourses in barrancas, and the water collected. When the water deposit dries up, the farmer frequently uses the bottom and banks for moisture of flood cultivation.

All types of canal irrigation are frequent-ly associated with bancales and terraces, fertilizers, mixed-crop rotation, nurseries, and seed plots.

CHINAMPAS. The chinampas, erroneously termed "floating gardens," represent the most specialized and complex cultivation technique of Mesoamerica. At the same time, it is today the most geographically localized technique, being limited to the Valley of Mexico and to the sources of the Lerma River. Its previous distribution was probably wider.

The chinampa is a small artificial island built in the shallow waters of a fresh-water lake. First a suitable construction site is found, where the waters are shallow and there are no strong currents. Next, the perimeter is marked off with willow stakes and sticks; usually a long rectangular shape is preferred, 6–10 m. wide and 100–200 m. long. Layers of aquatic vegetation, dirt, and mud are deposited within the rectangle until the chinampa surface rises 20–30 cm. above the water level. Willow stakes are then driven in every 4 or 5 m. to prevent erosion. When the soil settles and decomposition of the organic matter is advanced, the ground is ready for cultivation.

The chinampa does not need irrigation. Since it is narrow and surrounded by water, filtration provides sufficient moisture. If more is necessary, lake water is poured from buckets or other receptacles. Neither does it require fertilizing; the organic composition of the soil, constantly replaced by more mud and aquatic vegetation, makes fertilizing practically unnecessary. In the chinampas we find the most advanced systems of crop rotation and mixing, as well as the most intense use of nurseries and seed plots. The chinampa produces all year, year after year. It is possibly one of the world's most stable, intensive, and productive cultivation systems.

37

PERMANENCE AND PRODUCTIVITY OF CULTIVATION SYSTEMS

The four cultivation systems described represent different degrees of crop permanence, with complete stability being reached in the chinampas and well-organized irrigation systems. The ratio of cultivable land that should be held in reserve to the area under cultivation varies from 8:1 under the roza system to 3:1 or 2:1 under the barbecho system. Theoretically, under the secano-intensivo and humedad-y-riego systems, no reserve land is required. The productivity per area cultivated, as distinct from that of the total area, does not have such clear characteristics. Productivity per cultivated area is substantially greater under roza-system conditions (with two annual crops) than under barbecho-system conditions (one crop a year). Thus an Indian family that requires a minimum of 1.5 hectares under the roza system will require 2.5 hectares under the barbecho system in order to obtain a similar yield of corn. These requirements decrease to 0.86 hectares under the irrigation system, and to approximately 0.4 hectares under the chinampa system.

The productivity per cultivated area and that of the total area are naturally very different questions from per capita and family-unit productivity. Under the present conditions of the roza system, it is difficult to say whether or not the average that must be cultivated for family subsistence equals the possible maximum, but seemingly it is not. Access to national markets has suddenly increased the amount of land cultivated by each family. In other words, the roza-system farmer can increase family productivity considerably merely by extending the area under cultivation, but this carries with it the risk of hastening soil-restoration cycles to the point of forest depletion and disappearance. On the other hand, production increase based on extending cultivation will necessarily reduce the tolerable density of agricultural population.

Once the inital investment of work is made in hydraulic, terrace, and chinampa constructions, family production, as well as production per cultivated area and per total area, increases enormously under the secano-intensivo and humedad-y-riego systems. The differences, in these cases, are sufficiently great to make it clear that the roza farmer is in the worst position to participate actively in the national economy and society, from the viewpoint of his ability to produce marketable surpluses. Barbecho farmers would be in an intermediate position were it not for such technological innovations as the plow and draft animals. Using these methods, the barbecho farmer tends to increase family production by extending cultivation, but he is in a better position to do so than is the roza farmer, for technological and environmental reasons. However, some specialized crops of the roza farmer that are adequate to natural conditions of tierra caliente (vanilla and cacao, for example) may produce noticeable local variations. These changes become rarer and less likely as the national society's modern agriculture is extended.

In summary, the problems raised by the nature, stability, and productivity of the various cultivation systems in Mesoamerica can be, and should be, analyzed in terms of the relationship of the Indian groups with the national society, and in terms of their predisposition to create and develop processes of acculturation, integration, and absorption by the national society. Population density and the concentration and type of settlement—so closely related to the nature of cultivation systems—may also be studied from this viewpoint.

SOME SPECIAL CROPS AND CULTIVATION TECHNIQUES

As noted earlier, our typology of Indian cultivation systems omitted all cultivated plants except corn, the basic crop. Other crops, however, require a number of special agricultural techniques of great economic and cultural importance.

Mesoamerican Indian agriculture has frequently been described as a system of intensive cultivation within a small area, involving a great deal of individual attention to the plants, the use of hand tools, and a considerable amount of work. Although this statement is especially applicable to pre-Columbian agriculture, the same conditions obtain today except for the important extensive systems developed with the introduction of the plow. The permanent installations such as terraces, irrigation canals, and chinampas sometimes represent an enormous amount of work, but individual care of plants and certain specialized techniques continue to be distinguishing features of Indian agriculture. Cultivation of certain economic and nutritive plants illustrates this point.

Maguey

Maguey cultivation typifies adaptation of Indian agriculture in tierra fría to marginal situations characterized by extreme aridity. The maguey not only withstands drought, poor soils, and frosts, but prevents erosion, forms bancales on the slopes, and contains eroded soil later used to reconstruct cultivation areas.

The maguey is an important item in the Indian diet in the highlands, especially in the form of pulque, the fermented *aguamiel,* or sap. Unfermented aguamiel is also drunk, and shoots of the plant are eaten. It is still economically important, though less than in pre-Columbian times, even though maguey cultivation on the haciendas and large-scale pulque production have substantially displaced Indian production from the national market.

When the maguey reaches a certain point of growth, shoots appear alongside the base of the plant; they are uprooted and allowed to dry for several months before replanting. Around September, holes approximately 50 cm. deep are dug for planting the shoots.

The earth around the holes is carefully weeded, but no fertilizers or irrigation is used. It takes about seven years for the plants to reach maturity; that is, to begin producing aguamiel. During this period and afterward, the plants are individually cared for, weeding and piling up earth around them. For a period of four months, the aguamiel is extracted from the plant twice a day by a kind of suction pump. The daily aguamiel yield is approximately 6 liters, reduced after fermentation to 4 liters of pulque. At the existing rates of consumption and the growth and production periods of the maguey, a family requires approximately 60 plants in different stages of growth.

Nopal

This is another plant adapted to cold and dry highland regions and to poor and shallow soils. Although its fruit *(tunas)* and shoots are eaten and it is also used for hedges, it is of little economic importance. The leaves *(pencas)* that fall on the ground strike roots that frequently give rise to new plants. These shoots are transplanted in the rainy season. If there is a period of drought, the new plants are watered by hand. They must be pruned frequently. The plant begins to bear fruit in its third year, but the tender leaves may be eaten earlier. The nopal yields for some 25 years, and the fruit is picked from early spring until late fall.

Cacao

This plant is typical of humid tierra caliente, but is successfully grown in dry tierra caliente with the aid of frequent irrigation. In the absence of irrigation there must be heavy rainfall and a very short dry season. Besides being of great importance on the national market, cacao is used to make chocolate, which, like the maguey pulque, was one of the pre-Columbian beverages of Mesoamerica.

The cacao cultivation process begins with the felling and burning of a section of

39

woods; frequently a milpa abandoned after two years of corn cultivation may be used. In order to grow properly, the cacao tree requires a vegetative cover—that is, shade-tree protection—but only certain kinds of trees are suitable and they must be planted before the cacao field is established.

Cacao seeds are first germinated in a seed bed, in soil carefully tilled and manually irrigated at frequent intervals. The seed bed is covered with plantain leaves for 15 days and when the leaves are removed the shoots are protected by a covering of branches. Six to eight months later they are transplanted, together with the block of earth in which they grew, into holes about 60 cm. deep, in rows between the trees that are to shield them from the sun and wind. The soil is weeded carefully and frequently, and the plants are pruned with great caution. In dry tierra caliente there must also be frequent canal irrigation.

The cacao tree begins to bear fruit in its third year, reaches maximum production between the tenth and fifteenth, and enters a period of decline in its twentieth year. The seed pod is cut with a knife, and the beans are cleansed in a basket of water and left out in the sun to dry.

Coffee

The techniques of coffee cultivation, introduced from the Old World, are an extension of those used in cacao cultivation. In fact, the mixed planting of coffee and cacao is common. Production begins in the second year and usually ends between the twelfth and fifteenth. Sometimes the seed-plot technique is not used for coffee, but instead slips from the mature plants are transplanted.

Vanilla

The cultivation of this economically valuable vine is typical of humid tierra caliente. Its peculiar requirement is manual pollination.

The process begins with the selection of a milpa where corn has been grown for several years, and where a number of special vine-supporting trees and shrubs have been permitted to develop. Vanilla is planted before the rainy season. Long cuttings from old plants are placed in holes about 15 cm. deep at the base of the supporting tree. The soil is not weeded, but the top and branches of the trees are pruned to prevent them from growing too rapidly and to lessen the thickness of foliage that would deprive the vine of sun. The vanilla plant begins to produce flowers in profusion in its third year. The flowering period lasts approximately three weeks, and each blossom opens only once a day, in the morning. Thus, pollination of the entire vanilla field must be accomplished during this brief period. This is done by cutting off the proper portion of each flower with a sharply pointed stick, which is also used to gather the pollen and place it in the corresponding organ. This long and arduous task requires care and precision. A few weeks after pollination, the pods begin to appear.

After the pods are gathered they are dried first in the shade and later, for an hour a day, in the sun. The drying process may take several months, depending on climatic conditions.

Other Special Techniques

Such techniques as artificial germination, seed plots, transplanting, and the use of cuttings and shoots for plant reproduction are remarkably widespread and important in Indian agriculture. It is strange to note the low incidence of plant grafting and hybridization, especially in view of the importance of fruit trees in Indian agriculture and certain indications that grafting was known in pre-Columbian times.

A LIST OF CULTIVATED PLANTS

The list of plants cultivated in Mesoamerica includes practically all those known at the time of the Spanish conquest (nearly a hundred species), plus those subsequently introduced from the Old World and South America. The length of the list is impressive, but only a few plants are of economic importance, and basic nutrition is provided by a small number, generally those of pre-Columbian origin.

Pre-Columbian Nutritive Plants

Of all the plants cultivated, corn (Zea mays) is foremost and basic in the Indian economy and diet. Indian cultivation systems may thus be classified and analyzed according to their corn crops without thereby being too arbitrary. As a matter of fact, plants of secondary importance generally have the same geographic distribution as corn and are cultivated together with it. Exceptions to this mixed cultivation are found in very specialized agricultural areas, generally irrigation and chinampa areas. Of the few geographic limitations to corn cultivation, altitude is the most restrictive, confining the crop to elevations under 3000 m.

The bean (Phaseolus), next in importance, is found all over Mesoamerica and is cultivated together with corn. The various species have different and little-known geographic distributions. The tepari (P. acutifolius) grows in northwest Mexico and the part of Mesoamerica that extends southeast from the Tehuantepec isthmian region. The ayécotl or címatl (P. coccineus) is found in Mexico and Guatemala, as is the haba (P. lunatus). The common bean (P. vulgaris) is distributed throughout Mesoamerica.

As are corn and beans, the squash or pumpkin (Cucurbita) is distributed amply throughout Mesoamerica and is usually cultivated with them. Few plants are used so completely in the diet. Only the seeds of corn and bean are eaten, either green and tender or ripe and dry, but squash and pumpkin provide edible seeds, flowers, tender leaves, and pulp.

The chile (Capsicum annuum, C. frutescens, C. pubescens), used primarily as a seasoning, constitutes the fourth universal element of Indian agriculture and diet. Its cultivation is usually associated with that of the other three plants.

Small green cooking tomatoes, called "tomates," and common tomatoes, called "jitomates" (Physalis ixocarpa, Lycopersicum esculentum) are regarded as a fifth staple and are cultivated together with the four plants already mentioned. The geographic distribution of the Lycopersicum is largely in tierra caliente of the Gulf-Caribbean coastal area, the Physalis principally in tierra fría and tierra templada (that is, in the central, southern, and southeastern highlands).

Huauhtli or alegría (Amaranthus leucocarpus, A. cruentus) may be added to this list of cultivated plants. In pre-Hispanic times it ranked with corn and beans, but its cultivation has been declining ever since colonial times, although huauhtli seeds are important to Indian ceremonies and rituals. The Amaranthus are cultivated on a small scale, mainly in the highlands.

There are other, but secondary, pre-Columbian nutritive plants still cultivated. The pineapple (Ananas comosus) is grown for its fruit in tierra caliente. Its pre-Columbian cultivation was at one time doubted, but now seems to be firmly established. The white haba (Canavalis ensiformis) has been substituted by other more productive or popular beans (Phaseolus). The epazote or huauhzontli (Chenopodium nuttaliae) is related to the South American quinoa (C. quinoa) family. In Mesoamerica, however, the tender bunches are eaten, and not the seed. The sunflower (Helianthus annuus) is grown only in northwest Mexico, for its seeds. The large lime-leaved sage (Hyptis suaveolens) is grown for its seeds in western and central Mexico. The camote (Ipomoea batatas), important because of its tubers, is distributed throughout Mesoamerica. The yucca or manioc (Manihot esculenta, M. dulcis), valued for its roots, is limited principally to tierra caliente. The jícama (Pachyrrhizus erosus), cultivated for its roots, is of special importance in the highlands. The true lime-leaved sage (*Salvia hispanica*) is grown for its seeds, probably throughout Mesoamerica. The chayote (*Sechium edule*), a vine of general distribution, provides edible fruit, tender leaves, shoots, and roots. Vanilla (*Vanilla planifolia*), which has great commercial value, is used in making beverages (particularly chocolate); its distribution is limited to Gulf-coast areas.

Another important group of pre-Columbian nutritive plants comprises those typical of deserts or dry regions. The maguey (*Agave*), limited to central Mexico, is used chiefly in making aguamiel and pulque, but the shoots are also eaten. The pitahaya (*Hylocerus undatus*), a vine of similar distribution, is grown for its fruit. The nopal (*Opuntia ficus-indica*) is more widely distributed; it is usually cultivated for its fruit, but the shoots are also eaten. The pitayo (*Pachycereus emarginatus*) is a cactus grown for its fruit; its distribution is similar to that of the nopal. The mezquite (*Prosopis*) is cultivated for its fruit, whose seeds are eaten.

Pre-Columbian Fruit Trees

The number of tree species that are of pre-Columbian origin and still cultivated today is surprisingly large. A third of the total cultivated plants known at the time of the Spanish conquest were trees. The role of fruit in the Indian diet is very important today, but with the exception of a few commercialized species, trees are not cultivated in large numbers; instead there is a great variety of species, with only a few of each cultivated.

Anonas, especially chirimoya (*Annona cherimolia*), are among the most popular fruit trees. The ilama (*A. diversifolia*) is limited mainly to the Pacific coast.

The achiote (*Bixa orellana*) has principally a tropical distribution. The pulp around the seeds is used for seasoning and coloring foods, and also as a dye and cosmetic.

The ox or ramón (*Brosimum alicastrum*) is especially abundant in Yucatan. The fruit and seeds are eaten, and sometimes the seeds are pounded into flour.

The nanche or nance (*Byrsonima crassifolia*) is very important in the area extending from southern Veracruz to Central America.

The sweet sapota (*Calacarpum mammosum*) is widely cultivated in Mesoamerica, as is the related green sapota (*C. viride*), which has smaller fruit and a more predominantly Central American distribution. Two other important varieties are the white sapota (*Casimiroa edulis*), of general distribution in Mesoamerica, and the matasano (*C. sapota*), which is chiefly Central American. The brown sapota (*Dyospiros ebenaster*) is among the most popular in Mexico, as is the chicozapote (*Manilkara zapotilla*), which is cultivated in tierra caliente for its fruit; in its wild state it is used as a source of chicle.

The papaya (*Carica papaya*) is really a grass that grows to about the size of a tree; it is distributed throughout Mesoamerica, though not in tierra fría.

The tepejilote (*Chamaedorea tepejilote*) is cultivated for the most part in Mexico and Central America. The clusters of flowers are eaten.

The tejocote (*Crataegus pubescens*) is widely cultivated, especially in tierra fría and tierra templada.

The alligator pear (*Persea americana*) is probably the most important tree in the Mesoamerican diet, from the standpoint of being used almost as frequently as squash or pumpkin, chiles, the small green tomato, and the common tomato.

The capulín (*Prunus serotina*), similar to the cherry, is principally and widely cultivated in the highlands, as are the guava (*Psidium guajava*), which has more general distribution, and the jocote (*Spondias purpurea*), sometimes called yellow plum.

The cacao (*Theobroma cacao, T. angustifolium, T. bicolor*), aside from its great commercial importance, is used to prepare beverages (chocolate); it is limited to the Pacific and Gulf-Caribbean coastal areas.

The izote *(Yucca elephantipes)* is often used as a hedge, and its flowers are eaten, as are those of the pichoco *(Erythrina americana)*, which is an ornamental tree.

The chalahuite *(Inga paterno)* and the leleke *(Leucaena glauca)*, whose fruits are eaten, have very limited distribution.

Important Pre-Columbian Commercial Plants

All the nutritive plants mentioned are of commercial importance, but their value depends on their role in the national diet and the capacity to produce considerable surpluses. Since the national diet has adopted almost all the Indian foods, there is a constant open market for them. The only restricting factors are market accessibility and unbalanced competition between traditional Indian agriculture and modern national agriculture.

Main commercial corn-growing areas have been displaced from predominantly Indian regions to those more suitable for mechanization and large-scale cultivation. This is true also in the growing of beans, tomatoes, and jitomates and, to a lesser extent, chiles and cucurbits.

On the other hand, Indian agriculture still controls the production of vanilla, probably because its cultivation requires specialized and careful techniques with which modern agriculture has not yet been able to compete. In contrast, from the beginning of the colonial period, Indian cacao cultivation met with strong competition from the Spaniards. Large-scale maguey cultivation and pulque production on the huge haciendas of the colonial and independence periods almost completely barred Indian farmers from this market. Nopal is still cultivated for the most part by Indians, perhaps because of its limited commercial profitableness.

Alligator pears and papaya, very popular on the national market, are now produced on a large scale by modern agriculture, less and less by Indian agriculture. This same trend is noticed also in some non-nutritional pre-Columbian plants. Henequen *(Agave sisalana, A. fourcroydes)* is grown for its fiber in Yucatan and northeastern Mexico, by Indian labor, but production is concentrated into large units of agricultural exploitation. The same happens with the agaves *(A. tequilana)*, used in central Mexico for making distilled beverages. The coconut *(Cocos nucifera)*, cultivated for industrial purposes (oils and soap), is almost monopolized by modern agriculture.

Cotton *(Gossypium hirsutum)* cultivated by Indians has been displaced from the national market by modern mechanized and large-scale agriculture, and Indians are even giving up the domestic production of textiles in favor of the fabrics manufactured by national society. So too is tobacco *(Nicotiana tabacum, N. rustica)*, the process here reinforced by change in preference from cigars and pipes to industrially manufactured cigarettes.

We have already described what happened to the raising of the cochineal and the nopal *(Nopalea cochenillifera)* on which it feeds, when synthetic anilines were developed. Indigo *(Indigofera suffruticosa)*, once used for dyeing fabrics, is a similar case. Another is the piñoncillo *(Jatropha curcas)*, the plant host for the axi or axin insect, which produces a wax used in making varnish.

The exclusion or marginalization of Indian agriculture from the national market, and its limitation to strictly local markets, is not always the result of competition influenced by purely economic, technological, and market-access factors. Although geographic marginalization is important, political factors are perhaps the most significant. On the other hand, preferential rules favoring national agriculture have existed since the colonial era, and frequently produce monopolies, particularly among maguey

43

and tobacco cultivation, pulque and textile production.

Post-Columbian Nutritive Plants

The centrifugal effects of a socio-economic and cultural nature produced by unbalanced competition between Indian and national agriculture have been largely counterbalanced by the Indians' adoption, as crops and articles of diet, of a considerable number of plants of Old World origin that are characteristic of national society and culture. The adoption of these foodstuffs is unbalanced and discontinuous, but is highest under the irrigation and chinampa systems and lowest under the roza system. Accessibility to the national market and proximity to urban centers are primary, but perhaps most significant is the absence of strong cultural resistance to the introduction and use of foreign plants, though preferences, sometimes quite marked, may exist for the native ones. In the same manner, national society has not excluded cultivation and use of Indian plants.

Old World cereals, though widely accepted by Mesoamerican Indian farmers, have never replaced corn, either as a crop or in the diet. Perhaps the most extreme exceptions are in western Mexico and in southern Puebla, where wheat is intensively cultivated today and frequently used in the diet. Rice has proved a valuable food in humid tierra caliente and tierra templada, not only where it is grown but also in distant areas where it must be bought.

Wheat, barley, and oats are most widely grown in high areas where frosts are especially critical. These cereals have extended the cultivation area to many altitudes prohibitive for corn and have also been accepted on Indian farms as alternates to corn, in a crop rotation typical under barbecho and secano-intensivo conditions.

Easy salability of the Old World cereals on the national market provides one of the greatest inducements for their cultivation. This in turn has promoted the introduction and distribution of Old World tools and agricultural techniques. Today, corn is grown in many places by the same methods as wheat and barley—plowing, broadcasting, weeding and tillage with plowing, elimination of beans and cucurbits from the field.

Potatoes are less widespread than cereals, but their nutritional role has increased. So have a group of legumes (chickpea, European haba, pea, chickling-vetch, lentils) probably grown more for commercial purposes than for foodstuff.

Of all the introduced plants, coffee has probably had the greatest success. It is cultivated both for market and for individual consumption wherever natural conditions permit. Most Mesoamerican Indian communities consume large quantities; when it becomes very expensive, it is mixed with small quantities of, or even substituted by, roasted corn or other seeds.

Sugar cane closely parallels coffee. Many Indian farmers begin small enterprises on their own to make molasses and a type of sugar commonly called "piloncillo" or "panela." This is one of the few examples in Mesoamerica of industries set up by the Indians for the processing of introduced plants.

The ajonjolí or sesame is another introduced plant whose use in the Indian diet generally equals indigenous produce. The cacahuate or peanut, probably brought from the Caribbean, has not been similarly accepted; its cultivation is important in some areas, but mainly for commercial use.

However important to Indian agriculture these plants have been, undoubtedly they now suffer from unequal competition with national agriculture, the most obvious being coffee and sugar cane, which have become products of large-scale modern agriculture. It is evident, however, that this will not cause introduced plants to drop out of the Indian diet.

The acceptance of Old World vegetables, greens, and fruits has been conspicuous, especially in the humedad-y-riego and chinampa cultivation systems. The traditional techniques of these systems and the accessibility of urban centers have brought about the extraordinary growth of prosperous and efficient horticulture. The competition of national agriculture is here less harmful, which is perhaps attributable both to the horticultural production scale and to the traditional ability of Indian irrigation and chinampa farmers. All this offers immediate advantages over modern cultivation on a large scale by machinery instead of manual labor.

These horticultural plants include onions, turnips, beets, garlic, eggplant, cabbage, carrots, lettuce, cucumbers, cauliflower, spinach, celery, parsley, mint, melons, watermelons, and strawberries. Although cultivated primarily for the national market, many have become very much a part of the Indian diet.

Fruit trees, introduced in large numbers, generally are cultivated in much the same way as are Indian species; that is, none are grown on a large scale, but in small numbers of each species.

Most important to Indian agriculture are oranges, lemons, limes, apples, peaches, figs, "perón," quince, pears, mangoes, pomegranates, and apricots, together with grapes, bananas, and various nut trees. Many are now essential to the Indian diet, particularly citrus fruits and bananas. Their commercial importance is mainly local, especially since the large-scale development of banana plantations and citrus orchards.

Floral, Medicinal, and Other Plants

Floriculture is a special aspect of Indian agriculture. Although Mesoamerican flower cultivation has a long history, only recently has it acquired great commercial importance. Many terraces and irrigated lands, as well as chinampas, which once were devoted to subsistence crops and commercial horticulture, are now given over to floriculture, especially near urban centers or in places that have adequate transportation and communication facilities. Decorative plants from the Old and New Worlds are cultivated indiscriminately: cempoaxúchitl or flower of the dead, gardenia, carnation, alcatraz or calla lily, rose, camelia, gladiolus, orchid, nochebuena, cornflower, dahlia, and tuberose.

Some, such as the cempoaxúchitl, are mostly local and are linked to religious ceremonies and rituals, but most are cultivated for the national market.

It is difficult to separate the plants cultivated for subsistence or commerce from those grown for medicinal purposes only. Some medicinal value is attributed to almost all cultivated plants, including corn, and they are used medicinally. Moreover, no strictly medicinal plants (the cathartic jalap root, sarsaparilla) are seriously cultivated any longer.

Among cultivated native plants not yet mentioned is the tecomate or gourd (*Crescentia cujete, Lagenaria sicenaria*) whose fruit is much used as a container, a plate or bowl. A number of grasses, generally called zacates (*Imperata contracta, Panicum purpurascens, Panicum maximum, Cynodon dactilon*), are also cultivated for cattle and bird feed, and for thatching roofs. They are never used for human consumption, although references from northwest Mexico, outside of Mesoamerica proper, mention a zacate (*Panicum sonorum*) cultivated for cereal. The bamboo (*Guadua aculeata*) is sometimes grown for use in house construction.

Besides plants under cultivation are a large number either semicultivated or whose spontaneous growth is encouraged and protected that further serve the Mesoamerican Indian.

AGRICULTURAL IMPLEMENTS

The list of implements used in Indian agriculture is small, though it includes as many aboriginal as Old World tools. They range from the very simple (the *espeque* or planting stick) to the fairly complex (the plow).

Fig. 7—CHORTI FARMERS, GUATEMALA, WITH DIGGING STICKS, MACHETES, AND GOURDS. (From Wisdom, 1940, p. 45.)

The extent of each one's use seems to be inversely related to its complexity: the simpler the tool, the wider its distribution. However, the geographic distribution of some implements is associated mainly with certain cultivation systems: the plow with the barbecho and secano-intensivo systems; the *azada* (hoe) with the chinampa and humedad-y-riego systems; and the *coa* (aboriginal hoe) and machete with the roza system.

The adoption of some Old World tools (the plow, for example) and steel implements (the machete and axe) has modified certain Indian agricultural techniques and, in others, helped to speed up the performance of such traditional tasks as the felling of trees and the breaking up of ground. From this viewpoint, the impact of their introduction has been greater than from the introduction of cultivated plants.

Espeque

This simplest and possibly oldest farming implement in Mesoamerica is a stick of hard wood with a sharp tip (fig. 7). Often, as in pre-Columbian times, the pointed end is hardened by fire or fitted with a metal tip; or it is selected from the burned roza area and is thus already hardened by fire. The espeque's thickness varies but is never so great as to prevent comfortable gripping or so little as to break easily. Its length also varies from nearly 3 m. to the average height of a person. It is mainly used to make holes in the ground into which the seed is placed but serves for removing roots of weeds and for digging up tubers.

The espeque is the implement most commonly used in Indian agriculture, but it is associated more closely with the roza system than with any other. With the coa and the machete, it forms a trio of indispensable tools. Not even the plow has completely replaced the espeque, which is still often used for sowing the seeds of aboriginal plants in furrows. Its use diminishes under riego-system conditions, particularly in the chinampas, and in cultivation of Old World plants, especially cereals.

Coa

This is the implement most often used for preparing the soil before planting, and for weeding, uprooting underbrush, and tilling. The aboriginal azada, it comes in many different shapes, usually adapted to soil conditions and cultivation systems. The simplest kind of coa is an espeque that, in place of a sharp tip, has a wide, flat, thin blade with sharp edges. The edges are sometimes bordered with metal, for greater effectiveness and durability. This is most likely a pre-Columbian practice; today, a one-piece coa, with or without metal edges, is a rarity in Mesoamerica, even in zones of soft and loose soil. The coa usually consists of two pieces: a wooden handle and a wide, flat, thin metal blade with sharp edges and a shaft in which the handle is set. Very rarely is the blade made of hard wood, with or without metal edges. In every case blade and handle are mounted on the same axis.

The coa is almost always associated with the espeque and the roza system. As a rule, barbecho, secano-intensivo, and humedad-y-riego farmers prefer the Old World azada as a manual tool. The coa, azada, and espeque are generally used with different movements and in different bodily positions. The espeque is gripped with one or both hands, the body and the espeque upright, striking downward at almost right angles to the ground. The azada is gripped with both hands held relatively close together, the body bent at the waist and knees; to strike the ground, the azada describes a wide arc downward, toward the worker. The coa is gripped with both hands held apart and the body bent, usually at the waist; the blade strikes downward at acute angles to the ground, away from the worker. These differences seem to depend on the shape of the implements and on the techniques peculiar to the cultivation.

Machete

This third farming implement, like the espeque and the coa, is closely associated with the roza system, but is almost universal in Mesoamerica. The machete is principally used for cutting and weeding but has many other uses, such as chopping of firewood, construction of houses and furniture, personal protection.

The modern steel machete, usually manufactured in foreign countries, seems to be the successor of a similar implement, the wooden *macana* incrusted with flint (sometimes metal) blades, which was used as a

FIG. 8—DIGGING CORNFIELD FURROWS WITH HOES, GUATEMALA HIGHLANDS. Between San Pedro Jocopilas and Sacapulas. (From McBryde, 1947, pl. 30,*c.*)

weapon and as a farming implement in pre-Columbian times. The modern machete, a large knife, has many different shapes and sizes (long and narrow, short and wide, straight and curved) designed according to needs and preferences. Since Indian farmers make very effective use of the machete, the axe is not needed for felling tropical forests, except when tree trunks are exceedingly thick or the wood is very hard.

It is doubtful, however, that the steel machete has substantially modified roza agriculture in the tropical forest, especially in large areas, for under this system, keeping the fields free of underbrush takes more time than any other operation, including that of felling trees. Thus the machete's principal impact is on the organization of tree-felling work, since steel tools (machete and axe) have made the group labor of neighbors and relatives practically unnecessary.

Axe

This is another, not exclusively agricultural, steel implement manufactured either in foreign countries or in workshops of the national society. Although not as common as the machete, it is general throughout

47

Mesoamerica. In agriculture it is used to fell forests in tierra fría and hardwood trees.

Azada

Under the barbecho, secano-intensivo, and humedad-y-riego systems, the Old World azada has almost entirely replaced the aboriginal coa, especially in tilling (fig. 8) and weeding. It is also invading roza-system areas as well as accompanying the widespreading use of the plow outside these areas.

The azada's steady replacement of the coa seems to be largely attributable to greater effectiveness, especially on hard ground and savannas, and to furrowing deeper than strict roza-system conditions require. Moreover, the azada lasts longer and is more obtainable on the national market.

Plow

The tool that has really revolutionized Indian agriculture is the plow.

First, the plow permits the extension of agriculture to areas that are fertile but practically impossible to cultivate with manual implements, such as savanna soil with herbaceous vegetation too dense and root-snarled to be worked with a coa or even an azada. Likewise, areas of insufficient rainfall yield to plow cultivation using the traditional secano (dry-farming) techniques of the arid Mediterranean area.

Second, the relatively deep furrows that can be made with the plow—even a wooden one, with or without metal tip—retain moisture more effectively and make it possible to prolong the soil's fertility. This signifies not only greater stability of the cultivation fields but also denser planting and better yields per unit of area.

Third, the use of the plow considerably increases the area that can be worked by each family; per capita production rises significantly. The plow thus turns Indian agriculture from intensive cultivation—characteristic of coa and azada techniques—to

extensive cultivation of large areas, producing less per unit of area than certain intensive systems but more per capita. From this standpoint, the difference between azada and plow cultivation is perhaps more significant than the difference between the animal-drawn and the mechanized plow.

Fourth, the use of the plow makes it necessary to bring in cattle wherever there are none as yet. It is rare to find a place where there are horses, mules, or oxen that does not also use plow cultivation. The exception is mainly in roza-farming areas.

Fifth, the plow modifies not only tilling but planting and weeding techniques as well. Broadcasting the seeds of native plants, such as corn and beans, has in many instances replaced the traditional technique of sowing with the espeque. Weeding with a plow has frequently superseded weeding with a machete, coa, or azada.

Finally, although this is not a complete list of significant changes, the use of the plow stimulates introduction of Old World plants, especially cereals and legumes. It is possible that, in the beginning, European plants were introduced before the plow, but, as with cattle, both phenomena develop almost simultaneously.

As a general result of the changes brought about by the plow, Indian farmers participate in the national market more intensively and extensively, thereby entering into a more interdependent relationship with national society. They have both more produce to take to the market and products that are more salable.

In Mesoamerica the plow is used predominantly in tierra fría and tierra templada and is associated with the barbecho, secano-intensivo, and humedad-y-riego systems. The roza system is not at all suitable to the plow, chiefly because of the practice of not uprooting trees and of leaving the charred trunks on the ground. Another obstacle is shallowness of the topsoil in a large part of the tropical forest or steepness of the mountain slopes. The chinampas are also not adapted to the plow nor are other techniques of terrace cultivation and horticulture. The system of land tenure, either small holdings or exploitation units (a phenomenon quite frequent in Mesoamerican Indian agriculture), is also a big hindrance to the introduction of the plow. Under these specific conditions, plowing is not the most effective or favorable form of cultivation, but its continuous expansion is still one of the most powerful forces for change in Mesoamerican Indian agriculture.

The plows used by Indian farmers are essentially the same as those introduced from Spain, especially from the southern part of the peninsula, since the 16th century. Nevertheless, their lack of variety, in comparison with those in Spain, is remarkable, as is their archaic nature. Today, the old wooden Roman plow, sometimes having metal parts, is being replaced by steel plows and others that have metal plowshares. Horses, oxen, mules, asses, and even cows are used as draft animals. The technique of cutting crosswise furrows is also of Old World origin; but some complementary implements, like the harrow and the threshing machine, and some techniques, like cutting contour furrows into hillsides, are uncommon.

Other Farming Implements

Among the most generally utilized implements in Indian agriculture discussed here are the Old World sickle, used principally for reaping cereals and forage crops, indicating absence of the scythe; the shovel and pickaxe, for constructing terraces and digging and maintaining irrigation ditches and canals; the *azadón,* a different kind of azada. Other implements, probably pre-Columbian, are the woven bags for carrying the seeds to be planted; armadillo shells for the same purpose; weeding hoes or large wooden hooks to hold back the underbrush and facilitate weeding with a machete; and the woven baskets and nets for hauling the harvest.

Another group of agricultural implements relates to irrigation. The most common and simple, probably of pre-Hispanic origin and principally associated with the chinampas, consists of a bucket at the end of a long pole. Water from the chinampa channels is poured from the bucket onto the cultivated area. This form of manual irrigation is very expensive and is used under drought conditions and to water transplants in the seed beds.

In irrigation zones where water is located in excavations or deep irrigation ditches, farmers employ the *tahona,* or scoop-bucket, a balancing pole placed on an axle, with a bucket on one end and a counterweight on the other. The water caught in the bucket is raised by manual traction, the effort being modified by the counterweight. This mechanism seems to be of Spanish origin and is rarely found in Mesoamerica.

The water wheel, whether turned manually or by the flow of water (Persian water wheel) is very rare in Mesoamerica, especially among the Indians. This is also true of the *noria* (chain bucket), whether made to revolve by animal traction or wind pressure.

ORGANIZATION AND CHARACTERISTICS OF AGRICULTURAL LABOR

The organization of agricultural labor presents variations that are principally related to family and community organization, technology and land tenure, and specific influences of national society.

Family Unit, Age, and Sex

The family, sometimes simple and frequently complex, constitutes the basic unit of work. Within the family, work is divided according to age and sex. Children and elderly people do the light work. In areas where national society's influence is greater and established schools exist, children start to work later or only part time. Work specialization according to sex starts at the same time as the children's apprenticeship. Age does not affect the division of work ac-

49

cording to sex, with the exception of the assignment of lighter work to children and elderly people.

The pattern of dividing agricultural work according to sex is variable. In most of Mesoamerica, the participation of women is either very rare, at least as an ideal norm, or limited to gathering and harvesting of semicultivated and wild crops. In other places, especially along the Gulf coast, women participate in weeding, tilling, and harvesting, but not in slash-and-burn operations. There are no known cases of women using the plow or machete. Breaking the ground and clearing is specifically men's work. In very rare instances, it is preferred that the women do the planting. Women do the same work as men in some special operations, such as manual vanilla pollination, vanilla and cacao harvesting, and fruit gathering.

It does not appear to be possible to establish a relationship between the participation of women in agriculture and the cultivation systems. Under the roza system, for example, there are cases of full participation by women as well as of their utter exclusion. Nevertheless, the participation of women in agriculture is more important wherever polygyny and complex families exist. This would seem to indicate a relationship between the amount of exclusively domestic work, the number of women in the family unit, and their participation in agriculture. However, in monogamous- and simple-family areas having intensive cultivation systems, women play a predominant or almost exclusive role in certain agricultural tasks. At other times, women are limited to housework and the care of domestic animals.

Our general impression is that there does not exist in Mesoamerica a uniform cultural tradition as regards the division of agricultural work according to sex, but there does exist an ideal norm in most of Mesoamerica, especially in the highlands, excluding women from agricultural work. This practice approaches the ideal norm as national socie-

ty's influence increases and as the use of tools, plants, and domestic animals from the Old World (plow, azada, some cereals, hens) becomes more widespread. Another ideal norm excludes women from work that is considered harder and more dangerous (plowing, clearing, burning); in this situation, the practice is very close to meeting the norm.

Mutual Aid and Remunerated Work

When a job, because of its size or its urgency, is beyond the capability of a family unit, outside help, usually from the same community, is utilized. This additional help is obtained through mutual aid (without cash payment but somehow recompensed) or through salaried workers (paid in cash, in kind, or both).

The importance and frequency of the mutual aid system rapidly declines, and the tendency to use salaried workers increases, with the incorporation of new techniques and implements and the increasing commercialization of Indian agriculture. However, some circumstances of a noneconomic nature help perpetuate forms of mutual aid.

For example, under roza-system conditions in the tropical forest, clearing must be completed within a certain time in order to accomplish the burning process before the rainy season. The introduction of steel implements (axe and machete) enables the family unit to carry out the work by itself. Today, there is no technical reason to resort to mutual aid, except in extraordinary cases. However, clearing is a task still executed by asking help from outside the family unit; it is recompensed by food, drink, or services whenever the participants ask for it. In this way, laboring jointly is turned into a festive affair that strengthens important social bonds.

Much more common than this system of mutual aid, in some places called *mano vuelta* (recompensing work by work, plus food and drink), is the system of paid workers (*mozos* or peons). Generally the peons are persons who either do not own land or have only small holdings; they may belong to the same or neighboring communities or to distant ones. The difference between highland and coastal cultivation periods permits seasonal migrations of salaried workers. Wages are paid in cash or in both cash and kind (food, drink, shelter); rarely is payment made entirely in cash. Salaried labor is used more intensively as cultivation systems become more modern, as agriculture becomes more commercial, and as national society's general influence increases.

Just as farm workers are hired, so too are implements, draft animals, and beasts of burden. Plows with draft teams, harrows and threshing machines, horses, mules, and asses to pull loads are frequently rented. Less often, some farmers rent axes and even azadas.

Communal Labor

Certain agricultural operations require communal labor, which is not recompensed directly. In many areas inhabited by Indians, especially in Mexico, the community is committed to contribute to the support of the rural school with proceeds from a milpa. In other places, the community supports a church or finances a project of general interest (construction of a bridge or public building) in the same manner. In all these cases, the participation of one member of each family is obligatory subject to fine, but they may discharge their obligation by hiring a mozo or peon to do the work. Local authorities organize the work, regulate shifts, and impose sanctions.

Another typical situation is that of communal labor organized for irrigation work and construction of irrigation facilities. There are cases in which the community as a whole owns the irrigation system; i.e. all the families have irrigation land and the right to use the water. This situation is generally found in places where traditional irrigation systems exist, frequently of pre-Columbian origin. Keeping the hydraulic

system (dams, canals, channels) in good repair is a communal operation strictly regulated by local authorities. Sanctions include not only fines, but also deprivation of water for irrigation for a certain length of time.

There are cases in which the irrigation system benefits only part of the community, generally in places where the irrigation systems are recent. Consequently, there are regulations for organizing work and irrigation that affect only the beneficiaries; there are also special authorities and sanctions of the type mentioned above.

Calendar

The annual agricultural work cycle follows the seasons and varies according to local conditions and the requirements of certain special crops. The modern calendar is the general guide for planning work. Religious festivals, sometimes superimposed on pre-Columbian festivals, are major points of reference. Rarely do Indian farmers use the position of the stars or that of the sun to determine the end of the seasons or as a guide to begin certain agricultural tasks. Pre-Columbian calendars, wherever they still exist, are used for ritual and magical purposes exclusively, though in some places they are still employed to regulate the assignment of turns to use water for irrigation.

Conclusions

Perhaps the most relevant conclusion is that of the complexity of Mesoamerican Indian agriculture. This complexity is manifested chiefly in the adaptation to widely varied environmental conditions, in the different general and special cultivation systems, and in the variety of plants, implements, and techniques utilized.

We note also that increasing marginalization within the national territory, economy, and society is characteristic of Indian agriculture. Here the marginalization does not signify isolation and self-sufficiency, but rather more dependence on, and vulnerability to, society and the national and international economy.

Indian agriculture is in a continuous state of change, both in its position in the nation (relative change) and its own structure and character (absolute change). At the same time that Indian agriculture is being marginalized as a whole, it is being integrated part by part, and modified in its entirety, by national society.

Indian agriculture does not essentially constitute a separate economy of subsistence and prestige; rather it is part of national market economy. As such, it is subject to price fluctuations and profit incentives; and, because of its marginal position, it is very much affected by market trends and compe-

tition from the agricultural sectors of the national and international economy.

Our impression is that the relatively slow rate of change (progress) in Indian agriculture is not chiefly attributable to cultural factors (conservatism, traditionalism). Considering the existence of economic motivations and participation in national and international markets, the slow rate of change is better explained by the geographic, socioeconomic, and political marginalization of its position. At the same time, the marginalization of Indian agriculture is basically an aspect and a result—not a cause—of the defects in, and general slowness of, national development.

4. Settlement Patterns

WILLIAM T. SANDERS

THIS SUBJECT is presented here from a strictly ecological approach. The ecology of the large urban centers in Mesoamerica is not attempted. Generally, the discussion is developed from the viewpoint of an archaeologist whose interest in contemporary settlement patterns stems from the need for comparative modern community data to interpret site patterns.

As the settlement pattern of any given area is the result of multiple factors, we will briefly discuss such nonecological factors as political and religious institutions and their effects. It is maintained here, however, that the primary determinant of rural settlement patterns in a peasant society is the agricultural system practiced. It is further postulated that the agricultural system in such a society is primarily the product of interaction of technology and environment. This does not mean that secondary factors do not operate throughout the cause and effect relationship. We shall here attempt to isolate the primary factor and only incidentally discuss other determinants of settlement patterns in our test areas.

By *settlement patterns* we refer to the distribution of human population in a given geographical region and the analyses of factors responsible for such distributions. By *ecology* we mean cultural ecology, which we define as the study of interrelationships between environment and culture. I previously stated (1956) that settlement pattern studies fall into two types, zonal and community:

In our discussion of settlement patterns the data naturally fall into two separate categories. First, we have "community settlement patterns," which are the individual units of population, including such data as types of communities, organization of public buildings, street and population distribution and form, density of community population, and character of the resident population. It would also include house types and solar organization. Second, we have "zonal settlement patterns," which are concerned with the distribution of community sizes, distances between communities, density of population, and the symbiotic interrelationship between communities—societal, economic, or religious.

Here we discuss zonal and community patterns in four test areas, using the following definitions in our community typology.

I. Nucleated community—any community in which the population density of the residential area is markedly higher than the total area used for subsistence.

    A. Village—a nucleated community with a minimum of 100 inhabitants and in which at least 75 per cent derive at least 75 per cent of their income from agriculture.

        1. Compact village—a village with a population density exceeding 1000 per square kilometer and in which only a small fraction of the subsistence crop is produced within the residential area.

        2. Scattered village—a village with population density below 1000 per square kilometer and in which a substantial part of the subsistence crop is grown within the residential area.

        3. Hamlet—a village with less than 100 inhabitants.

    B. Town—a rural community in which most of the population are subsistence farmers but where trade and craft specialization are added as secondary activities, reducing the percentage of the population dedicated to agriculture to below 75 per cent. In Mexico most communities classed as towns are usually municipal centers and in general are larger in population than villages. All towns measured have population densities exceeding 1000 per square kilometer.

    C. City—no population density measurements were made of this type of community but most Mexican cities have population densities at the upper end of the range given in this study for villages. Most Mexican cities have populations exceeding 10,000 people. Our primary basis of separating towns and cities is again occupational. All communities in which over 75 per cent of the population are nonagricultural are classified as cities. All Mexican cities are political centers of at least municipal rank.

II. Ranchería—defined as any agricultural community in which the population density of the residential area is the same as the area used for subsistence.

III. Concourse center—this is a term used by Borhegyi (1956a) for a community type apparently found only in the Guatemala highlands. "Still another type of settlement is that of the concourse center with a highly important plaza which serves to unite villagers from a large region on important secular or religious occasions. . . . The third type of present day settlement pattern, the concourse village or 'vacant town,' may reflect the concept of the pre-Columbian ceremonial center. Santo Tomas Chichicastenango is an example. In the municipio there are 27,718 people, according to the 1950 census, although only 1,622 people live in the actual town. The greatest part of the population lives in houses widely scattered over the neighboring cornfields, although many families maintain 'town houses' in which they live while holding public office and during feast days and use as headquarters for the Thursday and Sunday markets. Only 697 Indians live in the town continuously. The fact that the people habitually congregate in Chichicastenango and even bother to maintain special houses for use during ceremonial and market occasions suggests that it was perhaps the locale of a pre-Columbian ceremonial center."

Because our approach is ecological we have selected our four test zones from areas with striking differences in altitude, climate, vegetation, soil, topography, and hydrography.

Mesa Central. This includes two subareas, both in the Valley of Mexico: the Teotihuacan subvalley and the Chinampan. This area is semiarid elevated tableland situated about 2200–2400 m. above sea level.

The annual rainfall varies from 20 to 40 inches, with progressively drier conditions from south to north. In the Valley of Mexico the area of heavy agricultural utilization is flat plain or gentle slope, vegetation is sparse, and winter frosts constitute the primary agricultural hazard. Agriculture is primarily subsistence maize in type and a variety of systems is practiced. In all systems land use is intensive and in some parts of the valley irrigation and terracing are practiced. The two test areas selected provide a good range of ecological variation within the valley as a whole since the Teotihuacan subvalley is in the drier north and the Chinampan is in the more humid southern part. As a check on these two field studies, which I conducted in 1953–54, comparative data from highland Michoacan are also summarized (West, 1948).

Gulf Coast. The primary test area here is part of the region known as the Chontalpa in the municipio of Huimanguillo, state of Tabasco. It is an area of flat coastal plain, crossed by a major river (Grijalva) with an extensive flood plain. It is tierra caliente, average rainfall is 80 inches, and natural plant cover is tropical forest. Several agricultural systems are practiced: (a) large plantations in permanent cultivation—banana, sugar cane, and cacao, (b) slash-and-burn subsistence maize cultivation, (c) an intermediate system practiced by small farmers who have a few hectares in plantation crops and cultivate the balance of holdings in maize with the slash-and-burn technique. To fill out the picture for the Gulf Coast we have added comparative data for hillier, more rolling tropical forest plain from Kelly and Palerm's study of the Tajin Totonac (1952).

Northern Yucatan. This is a huge broken limestone plain with little real relief but considerable microtopography. The area of heavy occupation lies below 100 m. above sea level, soil cover is very scanty, surface drainage is nearly absent, and rainfall varies considerably from 20 inches in the northwest to 60 inches in the southeast. Rainfall gradually increases to the east and south from Progreso in northwest Yucatan. With the shift in rainfall we find a corresponding increased lushness of vegetation, from thorny bush around Progreso to high zapote forests in the southeast. It is hot country, as is the Gulf Coast, but here rainfall is more sharply seasonal and annual precipitation is generally lower. Streams flow underground and natural wells or cenotes are one of the main direct environmental determinants of settlement distribution. Agricultural systems vary with the amount of annual rainfall. In the drier northwestern center of the state of Yucatan there is emphasis on permanent henequen cultivation whereas in the more humid east and south slash-and-burn subsistence maize cultivation is practiced. The data for this area are based on my field studies and on publications of Carnegie Institution of Washington's Department of Archaeology.

Highland Guatemala. The Guatemala highlands are an area of rugged topography, small mountain valleys and more humid climate than in the Mexican Plateau, the average rainfall being almost double that of the latter area. Agriculture, in general, except for lakeshore plains, seems to be less intensive than in the Valley of Mexico but much more so than the slash-and-burn system practiced in the tropical lowlands. Irrigation plays only a minor role (for winter garden crops in limited areas). To judge from Stadelman's data, the most common system is Palerm's calmil-barbecho. The two most important points in connection with the ecological system are the lack of irrigation and requirements for centralized control of water rights but the presence of a semi-intensive agricultural system permitting dense population. The data summarized here are entirely based on published sources: McBryde, 1947; Borhegyi, 1956a; and Stadelman, 1940.

55

VALLEY OF MEXICO

Teotihuacan Valley Subarea

Ecologically, the Teotihuacan Valley may be divided into three subunits. (1) The Lower Valley and Delta includes the flat, level, deep soil plain from San Juan Teotihuacan to Tepexpan. At San Juan are numerous springs that provide a constant supply of water, which is used for irrigation of nearly 4000 hectares of rich grain land. The land is cropped continuously all year round, the population is very dense, holdings are tiny, and all the communities belong to an organization called the Junta de los Manantiales de Teotihuacan for regulating water distribution and irrigation system maintenance. (2) The Middle Valley is the area between San Juan and Otumba. Part of it is gentle slope, which is dry-farmed; erosion is controlled by maguey hedges. The rest is deep soil, flat plain. There are no permanent water sources but the surrounding ranges are high and trap a considerable volume of rainwater, which flows through arroyos to the main stream. Dams are constructed across these arroyos, stopping the runoff, which is then conducted to the fields. The fields are prepared by throwing up low embankments around them to retain the water and they are flooded completely. In spite of the lack of regularity of the water source, the combination of heavy irrigation and excellent dry-farming techniques results in a system of agriculture almost as productive as the perennial system noted for the Lower Valley. (3) The Upper Valley includes that area above Otumba. This is an area of stony thin soil on sloping terrain. It is bordered by low hills that receive very little more rain than the valley floor itself and therefore irrigation is lacking. Cultivation is by dry farming, is notably precarious, and as a result is a maguey- rather than maize-producing area.

Today most of the population of the Teotihuacan Valley live in nucleated settlements. The majority of the settlements fall in our category of "village," being inhabited entirely by farmers. Two of the communities, San Juan and Otumba, should rather be classed as true towns, as both possess numerous stores and workshops and many nonagricultural specialists and both are weekly market centers for the surrounding villages. Other municipio centers such as Calvario Acolman and San Martin de las Pyramides are transitional town-villages. For most of the population of the valley San Juan Teotihuacan is the main shopping center and has the largest market and the greatest volume of trade. (Principal market days are Sunday and Monday.) Agricultural activities are paramount in all communities although a few villages such as San Sebastian have secondary specializations (pottery and roof-tile manufacture).

The general plan of the nucleated community is quite uniform. In most cases in the center of the community is a central plaza with church, municipal buildings, and a few shops; houses are scattered about in all directions from this center. Except for a few principal streets the Spanish grid street pattern is not characteristic in the smaller communities. In the larger, more urban community we often find a more consistent use of the grid, as at San Martin, but San Juan, the most urban of all the communities, lacks a consistent grid pattern. A number of communities are compound, i.e., they are a single physical entity but are made up socio-politically of two or more joined villages. Often the component parts are called *barrios* instead of villages. San Juan Teotihuacan is a notable example. First we have the community of San Juan itself officially classed as a *villa* or town, and the urban elements are found only in this part of the community. Joined to it on the east is the barrio of La Purificacion and on the western edge the two barrios of Puxtla (south of the highway) and San Juan Evangelista (north of the highway). The latter barrios lack urban features and the inhabitants are peasant farmers. These four units form a single physical community. Aside from this we find another detached barrio, Maquixco, 2.5 km. to the west. In 1940 the Villa de San Juan alone possessed 1353 inhabitants, but the physical community San Juan–Puxtla–Purificacion–San Juan Evangelista possessed 2600 and together with Maquixco makes a total of 3059 inhabitants.

San Juan is not alone as a compound community. We find at least two others: San Juanico and San Bartolo Acolman, and Santa Catarina Acolman–Tenango. The origin of these compound communities in part goes back before the conquest. In some cases the ancient community was divided up into anywhere from two to six or even more subdivisions called *calpulli*, translated by the Spaniards as barrios. In other cases a large central community would have a number of physically separate dependent communities made up of just one calpul each and thus translated by the Spaniards as barrios also, although in reality they would be better called *aldeas*. Following the conquest, in many cases, the Spanish priests moved the population of these little aldeas to the central town to facilitate conversion, thus creating artificial compound communities as each moved community tended to preserve its social separativeness. In some cases (but rarely in the Teotihuacan Valley) in the Valley of Mexico the old calpul or barrio escaped Spanish settlement policies, and so we find in the census lists communities still listed as barrios rather than as pueblos.

In the case of some communities, such as the compound community of San Juan, the basic radial settlement pattern has been altered by the building of the highway. The houses are today stretched out linearly along the highway instead of being distributed equally around the central plaza. The effect of this change is quite dramatic, leaving the principal church of the community stranded solitary in the midst of chinampas well south of the edge of town.

The bulk of the population, ranging between 400–700 inhabitants, live in villages. Only one-third of the population of the valley live in communities with over 1000 inhabitants (Otumba, Tolman, San Martin, San Juan, Tepexpan, Cuanalan, Atlatongo, Nesquipayac, and Ixtapan).

Fig. 1—COMPACT VILLAGE, STREET IN ATLATONGO

The internal population densities of the nucleated communities divide sharply into two classes. All the villages with economies based on irrigation (permanent) have similar densities.

TABLE 1

Community	Area (hectares)	Density (per sq. km.)
Calvario Acolman . . .	15	5000
Cuanalan	30	3600
Chipiltepec	25	3300
Santa Catarina Acolman .	17	4000
Xometla	18	4000
Santa Maria Acolman . .	3	4000
San Juanico–Bartolo . . .	11	5000

The densities run 3300–5000 with five of the seven communities falling in the 4000–5000 bracket.

One of the interesting aspects of community growth is the relationship between the growth of its population and its physical expansion. We find that Gamio's estimate

FIG. 2—COMPACT VILLAGE, HOUSE LOT IN ATLATONGO

(1922) of the surface area of Xometla and Calvario Acolman in 1917 is exactly the same as our estimates. In other words, these communities have not expanded in area; what has happened is that the population density has increased. Evidently in an expanding community this is the first step. Later, when fractioning of house lots is no longer possible, new colonies tend to appear on the outskirts. Atlatongo is a good example of the latter stage.

The nucleated communities of the Middle Valley have much lower densities.

TABLE 2

Community	Area (hectares)	Density (per sq. km.)
San Francisco Mazapan . .	60	1250
San Sebastian	40	1250
Santa Maria Coatlan . .	25	1150
San Martin	100	2500

The higher figure for San Martin is probably due to the urbanization taking place in the blocks just off the plaza. The main reason that these communities show lesser densities than those in the Lower Valley undoubtedly lies in nopal orchard cultivation. One of the important sources of rural income is the tuna (the fruit of the nopal),

and each house is surrounded by a sizable orchard. The average house lot—buildings and orchards—measures 0.4 hectares. Farther up the valley outside of the nopal cultivation zone in the flood water, irrigated, deep soil plain is San Pablo Isquitlan with a density of 5000 sq. km., thus equaling our Lower Valley communities.

Aside from the compact nucleated community there are three other settlement types in the Teotihuacan Valley. One of these, here called a scattered village, includes such centers as Cuauhtlancingo, Oztotipac, Santiago Tolman, and Axapusco. The first three lie sprawled over long low ridges and lack any street organization of the grid type. Tolman lies on the lower flanks of Cerro Gordo. They all have plazas, however, and are classified as *pueblos* in the census lists. The major difference between communities of this type and the true nucleated center is in the internal population density. Tolman with 1000 inhabitants is spread over 100 hectares of slope; Cuauhtlancingo with 718 inhabitants is scattered even more diffusely over 160 hectares. This type of settlement is found all over the Valley of Mexico but is not common and generally occurs in marginal slope and hilly areas rather than on the flat plain. It is often associated with "Indian" conservatism

FIG. 3—SCATTERED VILLAGE, HOUSE LOT IN OXTOTIPAC

Fig. 4—SCATTERED VILLAGE, GENERAL VIEW OF TILANTONGO (MIXTEC), OAXACA, MEXICO. (From F. Starr, 1899, pl. 55.)

culturally (i.e., many villagers speak Nahuatl, use regional dress). In one case, Oztotipac, each house is near a small cave which is used as a corral and kitchen. Therefore, we have a direct geographical factor promoting a scattered settlement pattern.

A second type of settlement is called *ranchería* in the census lists. It is a subsistence farmer community but lacks the plaza, and each house is even more widely spaced than in the scattered village. Palapa, for example, has 400 inhabitants scattered over 200 hectares of slope or 200 per sq. km. This type of settlement is very rare in the Valley of Teotihuacan; all three (Palapa, Ixtlahuaca, and Tlachinolpa) are situated on the slopes of Cerro Gordo and Cerro Malinalco and in the dry marginal valley between them. The population are farmers practicing maguey and rainy-season cultivation on poor soils with some nopal orchard cultivation.

The final settlement type includes the *hacienda* and *rancho*. Today this type of settlement is of very slight demographic importance, and even in Gamio's time the actual resident population was small since most of the labor was part-time from the nearby villages. Today we find usually only a single resident family and a few full-time hands.

Within modern Mesoamerica there are only two large areas with population densities exceeding 40 per sq. km. One of these is highland Guatemala, the other the Mexican Plateau or Mesa Central. With the more intensive system of agriculture practiced in the latter we then have a denser population. This is especially true in small subareas where irrigation plays a key role and zonal densities often exceed 100 per sq. km.

59

This concentration of population is nowhere more evident than in the Valley of Mexico. Within the Valley local variations in climate and agricultural technology result in variant zonal settlement patterns. One of our test zones, Teotihuacan Valley, is part of a larger area of similar ecological features and agricultural technology, which in pre-Hispanic times formed a single political unit called Acolhuacan. Acolhuacan was the rural hinterland that supported the huge urban complex of Texcoco so there is some historical value in treating it as a unit for settlement pattern purposes. The area included the early 20th-century distritos of Texcoco and Otumba. The demographic history of this area by municipio since 1900 is summarized in Table 3.

The municipio in the Valley of Mexico is not a settlement unit as in parts of highland Guatemala. It is principally an administrative unit which includes several to a score or more separate, permanent physical communities, each nucleated and clearly defined. One of these is usually larger and serves as the administrative center.

Table 3 shows an interesting total picture. Between 1900 and 1930 the situation is a static one; following this is a striking total increase to about 40 per cent of the 1900 figure. The main reasons for this undoubtedly relate to the agrarian reforms and breakdown of the big haciendas during the 1920's and to the urban growth of Mexico providing a labor market easily available to villagers by bus. Looking at those municipios from the Teotihuacan Valley, we find a close correlation between agricultural system and population density. Acolman with a density of about 100 persons per square kilometer in 1950 is an area of permanent irrigation, San Martin with 80 is an area of deep soils and flood water irrigation, whereas Axapusco, a municipio con-

TABLE 3

	1900	1910	1930	1940	1950	Density (1940)	Area
District of Texcoco:							
Texcoco	20,161	19,171	21,517	24,812	32,265	53.92	460.17
Teotihuacan	5,175	5,570	5,418	6,667	8,348	88.41	75.41
Acolman	5,822	5,522	5,827	7,234	9,422	83.83	86.29
Tepetlaoxtoc	5,772	5,365	5,032	5,379	5,373	42.00	128.06
Chimalhuacan	4,603	4,746	6,213	7,399	13,004	141.61	52.25
Atenco	3,848	3,275	4,463	5,023	5,424	69.53	72.24
La Paz	2,714	2,803	2,503	3,052	4,194	77.88	39.19
Chiautla	3,119	2,730	3,205	3,479	3,867	151.52	22.96
Chicaloapan	2,618	2,420	2,278	2,417	3,229	43.93	55.02
Chiconcoac	2,311	2,383	3,086	3,587	4,520	312.46	11.48
Tezoyuca	1,837	1,709	1,960	2,161	2,531	83.34	25.93
Papalotla	941	853	859	815	705	62.40	13.06
San Martin (with Otumba)			3,717	4,171	4,718	72.18	57.79
District of Otumba:							
Otumba		11,264	7,167	7,584	8,407	43.94	172.59
Axapusco		7,944	7,049	7,662	7,598	29.87	256.51
Tamascalapa	36,218	7,074	7,304	8,136	8,191	55.03	147.85
Tecamac		6,293	6,863	7,718	9,094	52.48	147.06
Nopaltepec		2,580	2,333	2,709	2,931	35.55	76.20
TOTAL	95,139	91,702	96,794	112,005	133,817	60.0 (70 in 1950)	1,900.06

TABLE 4—POPULATION CLASSES

Municipio	Under 100	100–500	500–1000	1000–2000	2000–5000	Over 5000
Texcoco	4	19	11	3	. . .	1
Teotihuacan	0	8	3	1	. . .	. . .
Acolman	0	9	4	2	. . .	. . .
Tepetlaoxtoc	2	5	1	2	. . .	. . .
Chimalhuacan	. . .	3	2	3	. . .	. . .
Atenco	. . .	1	2	2	. . .	. . .
La Paz	. . .	1	2	1	. . .	. . .
Chiautla	1	7	3	. . .	. . .	. . .
Chicaloapan	. . .	. . .	. . .	. . .	1	. . .
Chiconcoac	. . .	. . .	1	1	. . .	. . .
Tezoyuca	. . .	. . .	1	1	. . .	. . .
Papalotla	. . .	. . .	1	. . .	. . .	. . .
San Martin	2	5	. . .	. . .	1	. . .
Otumba	. . .	8	4	2	. . .	. . .
Axapusco	. . .	10	4	2	. . .	. . .
Tamascalapa	0	4	3	3	0	0
Tecamac	0	5	6	1	0	0
Nopaltepec	0	2	2	. . .	. . .	. . .
TOTAL	9	87	50	24	2	1

taining mainly thin soil and slope topography with maguey and precarious rainy-season cultivation, had but 30. A rough calculation indicates that the Valley floor of Teotihuacan had an over-all population density in 1950 of nearly 150 per sq. km. in the flood water and permanent irrigation area—a striking testimony to the efficiency of irrigation agriculture.

The size of communities is detailed in Table 4, which does not include haciendas and ranchos.

Official names of settlements in the census lists are distributed as in Table 5.

The high number of ranchos and haciendas is misleading as they include but a very small fraction of the population and most of them are in the single municipio of Texcoco (47, of which 42 are small cattle ranches). The lack of importance of this type of settlement is clearly indicated by the fact that even in the municipio of Texcoco only one-twelfth of the population live in them. At least 90 per cent of the population live in pueblos, villas, and barrios.

On the basis of Table 5, the breakdown by community size in terms of actual population residing in each size category calculates as in Table 6.

In the Teotihuacan Valley today a highway connects Tepexpan with Otumba, a distance of 28 km. On or within a kilometer

TABLE 5

	District of Texcoco	Otumba	Total
Pueblos and villas .	68	42	110
Rancherías . . .	5	4	9
Barrios . . .	44	4	48
Haciendas, ranchos .	72	11	83
Ejidos, colonias, estaciones . . .	9	4	13

TABLE 6

Reside in Communities with	Number of Communities	Percentage of Population Residing in Size Classes
More than 2000 population	3	9.5
Between 1000–2000 . .	24	34.0
Between 500–1000 . .	50	36.0
Between 100–500 . . .	87	21.0
Below 100	9	0.5
TOTAL	173	101.0

61

Fig. 5—CHINAMPA AREA, LAKESIDE EDGE OF TOWN OF XOCHIMILCO, D.F., MEXICO

of it are no less than 14 separate physical communities with an average distance of but 2.0 km. The total population of these communities is 13,478 or approximately 481 per linear kilometer. The range of community size is 269–2600 with the average of 962 per community. This traverse plus the tables indicate an area of dense rural population with the standard settlement unit classifiable as a nucleated village of medium to large size (i.e., 70 per cent of the population live in communities of 500–2000 inhabitants).

Chinampan Subarea

The Chinampan is the ancient name for the southwestern part of the Valley of Mexico, or the ancient province of Xochimilco. In my study of demographic and zonal settlement patterns I have included also the old province of Chalco, so the total area includes the entire southern Valley of Mexico. Here the elevation is the same as the Teotihuacan Valley but the rainfall is approximately double, some 30 inches on the lake-shore increasing to 50 farther up the slopes. Soils are fertile and rainy-season crops abundant and secure; it is probably the most favorable part of the Mesa Central for agriculture without irrigation. However, the southwestern part, or old province of Xochimilco, is characterized by a very reduced lakeshore plain and is an area of steep slopes. In response to this geographical setting intensive agriculture of two basic types occurs. First are the chinampas, artificial islands built in the lake itself, which in terms of labor and production represent the most intensive form of agriculture in modern or ancient Mesoamerica. The technological aspects of the system have been summarized by West and Armillas (1950); I have completed a study of its economic aspects. The second system consists of completely terracing the steep slopes with stone terraces and the gentle slopes with maguey hedges.

Throughout the southern Valley of Mexico the bulk of the population live in nucleated settlements of either town or village

62

type. Although isolated ranchos and haciendas along with a few rancherías do exist, they certainly do not account for more than 2 or 3 per cent of the total population.

Of the 111 communities of the nucleated type listed in the census for the southern valley (delegaciones of Tlalpan, Milpa Alta, Tlahuac, Xochimilco plus the old distrito of Chalco) six may be classified as towns: Chalco, Xochimilco, Tlalpan, Amecameca, Tlahuac, and Milpa Alta. The rest are villages.

The congestion of population within these nucleated centers is almost, if not quite, as heavy as in an urban center. A glance at the aerial photos gives one the impression that the basic pattern is aboriginal, with a later veneer of the Spanish grid pattern added to group the basically irregular house lots into true squares and rectangles. Each of these measured rectangles is divided and subdivided by scores of winding alleys.

In some cases there is no observable grid at all, as at Mixquic. In this community we find a very compact densely concentrated village in which over 3000 people are compressed into an area of 30 hectares; the average individual has about 100 sq. m. of living room. In the center of the village is the plaza; streets and canals spread out in thin wavy or winding lines radially in all directions, often becoming lost in the maze of massed dwellings. Mixquic, entirely a Chinampa community in economy, lies on a small piece of high ground or island in the center of what was once an ancient bay of Lake Chalco. Today this bay is covered by 400–500 hectares of chinampas. The farthest field is only 1.0 km. from the village.

Tecomitl, on the other hand, a lakeshore-plain community without chinampas, has a completely regular grid of streets.

TABLE 7

Community	Area (hectares)	Density (per sq. km.)
Mixquic	30	8,500
Tecomitl	25	7,500
Ixtayopan	25	7,700
Tulyahualco	40	7,000
Tlahuac	50	6,600
Tlaltenco	40	6,700
Zapotitlan	25	8,900
Tlaxialtemaco	10	7,800
Atlapulco	40	10,200
Acalpixca	25	7,900

The observations listed in Table 7 refer only to the Chinampa and other lakeshore communities in the delegaciones of Tlahuac and Xochimilco. In all these communities the internal population density is extremely high, far surpassing even communities in the irrigated Lower Teotihuacan Valley.

TABLE 8

Delegación	1900	1910	1930	1940	1950	Area	Density
Chinampa-Terrace Area:							
Xochimilco	42,610	30,093	27,712	33,313	47,082	131	360
Tlahuac, including Xochimilco			11,780	13,843	19,511	82	238
	42,610	30,093	39,492	47,156	66,593	213	313
Barbecho Area:							
Milpa Alta	9,415	16,268	12,608	14,786	18,212	269	68
Chalco	69,478	71,930	64,566	79,656	96,767	1,606	60
Tlalpan	12,522	15,448	15,009	19,299	. . .	309	. . .
	91,415	103,646	92,183	113,741		2,184	
Total Area . . .	134,025	133,739	131,675	160,897		2,397	

The sample shows a range of population density running from 6600 to 10,200 per sq. km., and all the communities except Tlahuac are villages.

The southwestern or Xochimilco portion of the test area is occupied by a rural population practicing the most intensive system of agriculture found anywhere in Mesoamerica. The southeastern or Chalco portion is the scene of a simple rainy-season cultivation system, called "barbecho" by Palerm (1955), under highly favorable conditions (i.e., deep fertile soils and abundant dependable rainfall). The area includes the modern delegaciones of Xochimilco, Tlahuac, Milpa Alta, and Tlalpan and the old distrito of Chalco.

I doubt that any other rural area in modern Mexico has as dense a population as this area. The demographic history is summarized in Table 8.

A comparison of the data from Teotihuacan reveals some significant facts. First, the history of population growth shows an almost identical pattern, probably because the same factors are operative. Second, they clearly show the demographic results of chinampa agriculture with double the density of the irrigated valley floor at Teotihuacan. On the other hand, rainy-season agriculture even in this highly favorable area supports only half the population density of the irrigated Teotihuacan Valley, but double the population of nonirrigated lands in the latter area.

For community size the data sort out as in Table 9.

TABLE 9

Delegación and Distrito	Under 100	100– 500	500– 1000	1000– 2000	2000– 5000	Over 5000
Xochimilco	1	4	5	3	3	1
Tlahuac	0	1	1	1	4	...
Milpa Alta	0	5	2	4	1	0
Chalco	1	28	11	17	7	1
Tlalpan	...	2	3	3	1	1
TOTAL	2	40	22	28	16	3

64

Here, as in Acolhuacan, most of the population live in nucleated villages and towns. There is no other settlement type in the delegaciones of Xochimilco, Tlahuac, or Milpa Alta. In Tlalpan there are three ranchos, two haciendas, and two rancherías. In the rainy-season agricultural district of Chalco there are more nonvillage settlements with 15 hâciendas, 32 ranchos, 2 rancherías, and 11 miscellaneous community types. For all practical purposes these odd types may be ignored in our discussion.

In actual percentage of population living in settlements of the various size categories our data break down as in Table 10.

TABLE 10

Reside in Communities with	Number of Communities	Percentage of Population Residing in Size Classes
Over 5000 population . .	3	25
Between 2000–5000 . .	16	32
Between 1000–2000 . .	28	25
Between 500–1000 . .	22	10
Between 100–500 . . .	40	7
Under 100	2	2
TOTAL	111	101

Of the 19 communities containing more than 2000 inhabitants, six are towns and the rest are just big villages. Over half the population live in villages with more than 2000 inhabitants, and 83 per cent live in villages larger than 1000. Most of the smaller communities are up on the slopes, almost all lakeshore communities are of large size.

From the town of Xochimilco to the town of Chalco is almost exactly the distance from Tepexpan to Otumba; a highway runs along the old lakeshore between the two points. Along this stretch of 28 km. are 14 communities, 2 towns, and 12 villages. The average distance between communities is 2.0 km. The major difference between the zonal pattern of this area and the Teotihuacan Valley lies in the size of the settlements. They vary from 200 to 20,000, most of them

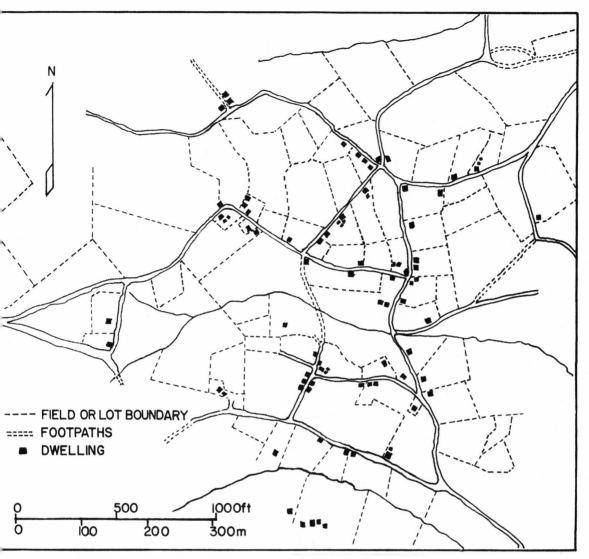

N

--- FIELD OR LOT BOUNDARY
===== FOOTPATHS
▪ DWELLING

| 0 | 500 | 1000ft |
| 0 | 100 | 200 | 300m |

FIG. 6—SCATTERED VILLAGE, URINGUITIRO, MICHOACAN. (From West, 1948, Map 15.)

falling between 1000–6000 (9 of the 14). The total population of the communities linked by this highway is over 50,000 people or 1800 per linear kilometer.

COMPARATIVE DATA. In highland Michoacan West (1948) defines two settlement types which he calls rancho and pueblo. Ordinarily the term "rancho" in Mexico refers to an isolated livestock ranch, but here it is often applied to hamlets or villages of farmers.

Rancho settlements occur mainly in the slope and mountain areas, and consist of scattered dwellings which lack orderly street patterns and are quite widely spaced. It is not clear in West's text whether or not these settlements possess plazas. His plan of Uringuitiro indicates that they did not, but he only gives one rancho plan. Approximately 287 people lived there at the time of his study and were scattered over an area of about 50 hectares or about 577 per sq. km. The density and pattern of settlement is typical of our scattered-village type of the Teotihuacan Valley, although in this case the plaza is lacking as in the Teotihuacan ranchería. The size and pattern resemble closely those of Santiago Tolman or

65

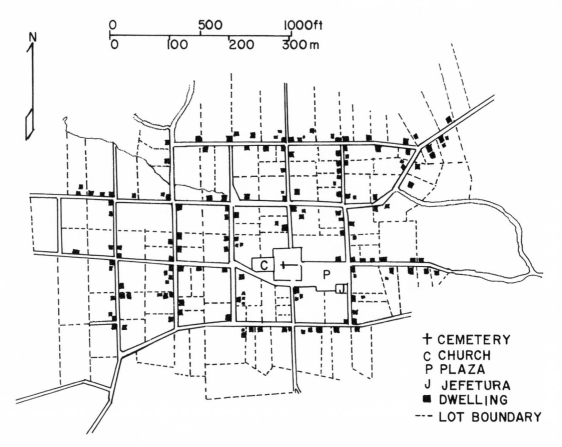

Fig. 7—COMPACT LOW DENSITY VILLAGE, AHUIRAN, MICHOACAN. (From West, 1948, Map 16)

+ CEMETERY
C CHURCH
P PLAZA
J JEFETURA
■ DWELLING
--- LOT BOUNDARY

Cuauhtlancingo in the Teotihuacan Valley.

The other type of community is the pueblo or village, differing from the rancho in its generally larger size (population varying from 200 to 34,000, whereas the rancho ranges from 9 to 900), in its regular grid street pattern, and in the presence of the typical plaza. In the broken areas the village is of compact but lower density, in the lakeshore plains and valleys it runs to higher density, compact type. Ahuiran is a good example of the first; although the streets are regularly laid out in a checkerboard pattern, the houses are widely spaced. In 1940 Ahuiran had 593 inhabitants living in an area of 25 hectares with a density of 2400 per sq. km. Tirindaro is representative of the high density subtype; here 1252 people live on 22 hectares of land or in a density of 5600 per sq. km.

Our settlements in highland Michoacan,

then, duplicate the types we defined for the Teotihuacan Valley. In terms of frequency of the two basic types, rancho and pueblo, by ecological area, we analyze West's data in Table 11.

TABLE 11

Ecological Area	Pueblos	Ranchos	Villas or Ciudades (Towns)
Sierra . . .	44	61	3
Lake area . . .	20	32	3
Northern plateau .	8	6	3
La Cañada . . .	11	2	1
Tierra templada .	4	2	1
TOTAL . . .	87	103	11

Aside from these units there are few communities of the hacienda or rancho type. Highland Michoacan is an area of villages. Most of the population live in the pueblo

66

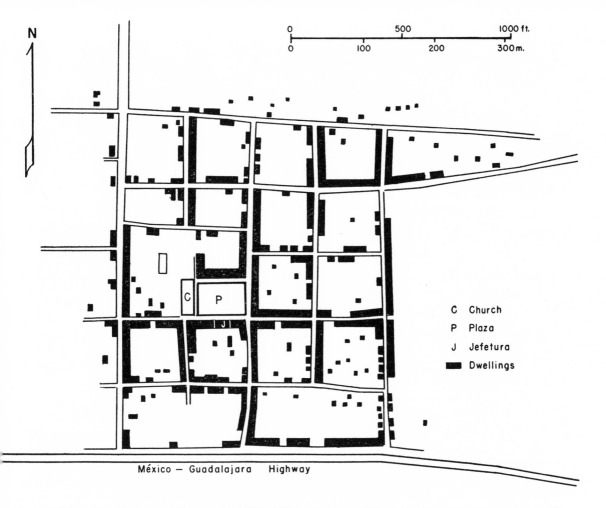

Fig. 8—COMPACT HIGH DENSITY VILLAGE, TIRINDARO, MICHOACAN. (From West, 1948, Map 17.)

type of settlement, and many of the settlements are of large size (over 1000 inhabitants). Table 12 summarizes the range of settlement sizes by number of settlements and also by percentage of the population represented in the size categories.

To sum up, nearly 69 per cent of the population live in big villages and towns, 89 per cent live in communities exceeding 500 in-

TABLE 12

Settlement Size	Number	Per cent
Under 100 inhabitants . .	57	2
100–500 inhabitants . . .	61	9
500–1000 inhabitants . . .	41	20
1000–2000 inhabitants . .	25	23
2000–3000 inhabitants . .	8	12
3000–4000 inhabitants . .	4	9
Over 4000 inhabitants . .	5	25

habitants, and only 2 per cent live in what we are calling hamlets.

THE GULF COAST PLAIN–THE CHONTALPA

Tabasco, along with most of the Gulf Coast Plain, was almost depopulated during the century following the Spanish conquest and even until the end of the 19th century was still thinly populated. The population has grown steadily since 1900 and is still climbing. The demographic limit under the present economic system has nearly been achieved in certain areas, but there are still vast areas of unoccupied tropical forest, especially in the Tonala river basin to the west. The population of the state in 1900 was only 159,834, in 1910 it rose to 187,834, and by 1940 it reached 285,659. The last census (1950) recorded 363,501 inhabitants

67

TABLE 13

Population Unit	Classification	Population in 1950
Huimanguillo	town	3,084
Caobanal	ranchería	1,186
Chicoacan	ranchería	356
Desecho	ranchería	452
Guiral y Gonzales	ranchería	512
La Libertad	ranchería	426
Monte de Oro	ranchería	636
Los Naranjos	ranchería	803
Ostitan	ranchería	595
El Puente	ranchería	485
Rio Seco y Montaña	ranchería	855
Tierra Nueva	ranchería	788
Villa Flores	ranchería	657
Ocuapan	nucleated village	625
		11,462

with a density of 16 per sq. km. Of this to-tal 10 per cent live in the one true city, the capital Villa Hermosa. In 1950 the munici-pio of Huimanguillo had a population of 24,575 inhabitants in an area of 3520 sq. km. or an over-all density of 7.0.

The figure for Huimanguillo is somewhat misleading as most of the population lives in a fertile riverside strip, and the bulk of the municipio is unpopulated. Huimangui-llo is part of a larger region called the Chontalpa, which is the center of Tabasco's cacao and banana production. Within the municipio I have selected a small test zone 10 km. wide and 30 km. running along the riverbank, which includes most of the muni-cipio's population and is heavily exploited for plantation and slash-and-burn maize cultivation. It is one of the most favorable small areas in Tabasco for agriculture and thus provides us with a test zone of optimal ecological conditions for the Gulf Coast Plain.

Within our test area of 300 sq. km. there are 12 rancherías, one town, and one nucle-ated village (Table 13). It would be help-ful to be able to divide the surface area by rancherías but such data were not available to me.

The total population for this area is 11,-

462, density 37 per sq. km. This excessive density for a Gulf Coast region offers a startling contrast to the average population density of but 7 for the municipio as a whole. The higher density is a striking dem-onstration of the more effective use of land, in which a semicommercial system partly based on permanent crops such as cacao is compared to simple slash-and-burn agricul-ture. The strictly rural population of our test zone is approximately 8000, the average areal size of a ranchería is 2300 hectares, and the average ranchería has 650 people. Each family has theoretically at its disposal 18 hectares of land. Actually the situation for the small farmer is not so favorable as there are large holdings, and many towns-men in the community of Huimanguillo own large plantations.

Within our test area of 300 sq. km. we find three types of individual community patterns: (a) the urban town, (b) the nu-cleated village, and (c) the ranchería. This situation is characteristic of most of Tabas-co except that in the east a fourth type, the isolated cattle ranch or rancho, must be added.

In the state as a whole we find one large city, Villa Hermosa, which is the capital. Within the state are 16 municipios other than that of the capital itself (El Centro). Each of these municipios has a center, a small urban town of 1500–4000 inhabitants. They are true towns with a mainly non-farming population and are religious, com-mercial, and administrative centers for the municipio. Approximately 10–15 per cent of the municipio population live at these cen-ters, of which Huimanguillo is one. If we were to make a trip from Estación Ferro-carril Chontalpa to the coast, we would find the following communities of this type along the highway: from the station, Hui-manguillo is situated at Km. 22, Cardenas Km. 42, Comalcalco Km. 82, Paraiso Km. 100; the last lies a few kilometers from the beach. These four communities in 1950 pos-sessed 3000–4000 inhabitants.

The ranchería is the most important settlement type in the Chontalpa and throughout most of Tabasco. It can not truly be called a community since it lacks the cohesion and function of a true community. The ranchería is an administrative unit and nothing more. There is generally no center; when it does exist, it consists of a pole-and-thatch church, a schoolhouse, and a small general store. We may find a slight clustering of houses around these structures, a dozen or so, but as each individual lives on his own agricultural holding these can not be numerous. We see a similarity in general pattern to the ranchería of Palapa in the Teotihuacan Valley, with the difference that, as the holdings are much larger here, the population is less dense. Each man has his house on his land, and as most farmers hold from 6 to 30 hectares the pattern is very scattered. The population of a ranchería forms a diffuse, extremely unstable social unit. The only symbol of social unity is the office of Comisario, whose main function is to act as the mouthpiece of the Presidente Municipal at Huimanguillo. He may, on occasion, following orders from the town authorities, organize the adult males of the ranchería for construction of a trail or bridge, but such communal activities are rare. He is also the representative of "law and order," principally reporting the frequent homicides which take place in these exceedingly diffuse, individualistic "communities." There is a near-lack of community spirit either for ingroup activities or against outsiders. The ejido system is in vogue as elsewhere in Mexico. Most farmers are ejiditarios and hold ejido lands; in this case the ejido is parceled out in family lots. Most farmers who have private land are those whose ancestors were big landowners of pre-agrarian revolution days or who have purchased land from such people. The ejido may or may not correspond to the ranchería.

In the type of community we are calling rancherías the community population density is the same as the areal population density. The exact concentration depends directly on the agricultural resources of the particular area.

The second, and a very minor, community type is the true village, of which Ocuapan is the only one in our test area. Within the municipio of Huimanguillo there are three altogether, with populations of 744, 250, and 625 inhabitants (Tecominuacan, Mecatepec, and Ocuapan). There was a fourth, San Miguel, but this has dispersed into a typical ranchería. Actually Mecatepec also can no longer be classified as a true village. It used to be a pilgrimage center because of its sacred arroyo, but with the over-all decline of the Church following the agrarian revolution it has lost its importance, and the population has scattered into the forest. All these centers are in the poorer agricultural region inland from the flood plain; some are even on the edge of savannas. A generation ago Nahuat was commonly spoken in all of them. They evidently are ancient Indian villages, the product of the Spanish colonial centralization policy of the 16th century. All hold ejidos which are operated as in northern Yucatan—the so-called open ejido system in which land is not parceled out but anyone can clear forest anywhere within the ejido. To a certain extent this explains the survival of these colonial communities in an area where rancherías are the typical form of rural settlement. On the other hand, it is of interest to note that the decline of the Church has been responsible for the disbanding of one and possibly two of them, the original Spanish centralization being due to religious factors (to facilitate conversion). Evidently without strong centralized control these communities do not hold together, and tend to scatter into a dispersed settlement pattern, which is more suited to slash-and-burn agriculture.

Each of the villages has an open plaza, a small church, and a few shops, together forming a complex which is the center of village social life. Houses are widely spaced but probably no more than the scattered villages of the Teotihuacan Valley. No aerial photos were available for exact classification.

The final community type is the urban town, of which there is one in every Tabascan municipio. Huimanguillo, the only such community in our test area, possessed in 1950 slightly over 3000 inhabitants. It is not a village but a true town and is the administrative, religious, and commercial center of the municipio. It has a very regular street grid and covers a rectangle 1500 m. north-south by 700 m. east-west (about 105 hectares). Its main street, the only paved one, is that which is part of the Chontalpa highway. The settlement pattern is not typically Mexican as the church does not face the main plaza, which is on the north edge rather than in the center of the community. Furthermore, social life is as much centered on the main street as it is on the plaza.

It has highway connections to Villa Hermosa, the state capital, and is further linked to that center by daily mail-passenger plane service. A paved highway runs from it to the Estación Chontalpa, and from that point a railroad service to Mexico City. On leaving Huimanguillo, the Chontalpa highway connects the town with Cardenas, Comalcalco, and the coast, but it is not paved through this section. A number of dirt roads run west from the community, connecting it to nearby rancherías, but these are only passable during the winter and spring.

Most of the houses in the center of the community are large, well-furnished, brick-and-masonry structures joined wall-to-wall with shops interspersed between the houses. The community has a movie, several hotels, cantinas, a telegraph office, mail service, and numerous shops of the general-store type.

A very low percentage of the population of the community are farmers, that is, people who work their own lands. Land ownership and agricultural production, however, are the bases of its existence, and most people live directly or indirectly from them. It is a small urban center collecting the products of the neighboring rancherías and fincas for foreign exportation. It is full of specialists: merchants, carpenters, bakers, tailors, seamstresses, masons, mechanics, bar and restaurant operators, stevedores, barbers, beauticians. An extraordinary percentage of the population, if not to be classed as millionaires by Mexican standards, certainly would be put in the middle class or lower upper-class in Mexican society. The basis of this wealth lies in land, cattle, and wholesaling of rural products plus retailing of consumer goods to the townsmen and farmers of the rancherías. Most of the wholesaling of products is in the hands of three cooperatives: one of cattle owners, and the other two banana and cacao growers. The wealthiest people have achieved their status mainly by a combination of several or all of the mentioned activities, and the technique of monopoly provides one of the main mechanisms for social advancement. A very sharp class system on three levels exists, the basis being a combination of family origin and capital wealth. The area offers an extraordinary opportunity for such an economic and social system owing to the high value of its products for the international market. In short, in spite of its small size, this community is fully urban, much more so than San Juan Teotihuacan, and is the most urban in our four test areas. There is some justification, then, for the community's official title of "ciudad" since urbanization is more marked than in most Mexican towns.

Of the population in our test area, 27 per cent live in the one urban town, 67 per cent live in rancherías, and 6 per cent live in the one village.

COMPARATIVE DATA FROM PAPANTLA. Kelly and Palerm (1952) have analyzed the economic and ecological setting of this area in detail. It is an area of rolling tropical lowlands with hilly topography, tropical forest cover, and humid climate. Their report deals with a single community, Tajin, inhabited by Totonac-speaking farmers practicing slash-and-burn maize agriculture.

The community of Tajin is in the municipio of Papantla in the state of Veracruz. Papantla municipio in 1940 covered an area of 1184 sq. km. and possessed a total population of 34,257 people, with a density of just under 29 persons per sq. km. Of this total 6644 lived in Papantla, which is a town of the type described for Huimanguillo. The rest of the population, or 82 per cent, lived in two types of settlements: the typical Tabascan ranchería and the congregación. Ranchos and haciendas are rare; only nine were counted in the 1940 census, when 1 ciudad (Papantla), 63 congregaciones, and 35 rancherías were listed in the municipio.

The life of the modern congregación of Tajin may be said to have really begun in 1875; before that date there were few inhabitants in the area. In 1876 as part of a general federal policy of coastal colonization the government opened up to settlement an area of over 6000 hectares, divided into parcels of some 31 hectares each, and offered the parcels for sale. Most of the buyers were native Totonac culled from a larger number of neighboring communities. The sale provided for two large areas to be set aside for villages, where the buyers were supposed to reside. The actual results are fascinating. One of the areas has never been occupied as a community; the other is the modern Fondo Legal of Tajin. The latter community was divided into regular blocks and streets, has a plaza, school, jail, municipal office, and two small shops. Although this center was set up originally as a future village, only 20 per cent of the population of the congregación actually live there; the rest of the population live scattered, each house surrounded by its fields. The congregación in all includes some 186 families, of which but 35 live in the Fondo Legal or

nucleated center. The Fondo Legal itself is spread over an area of some 50 hectares; the density of population is but 400 per sq. km., approximately that of our Teotihuacan Valley rancherías and scattered villages.

The settlement pattern described for Papantla is characteristic of the slash-and-burn areas of the Gulf Coast Plain. At Santiago Tuxtla, for example, in the San Martin area in southern Veracruz we find a municipio population of 16,064, of which 5392 live in the small city or center of the municipio and the remainder, the rural population, roughly two-thirds of the total population, live scattered in 17 congregaciones of the Tajin type, 28 rancherías, and 6 ranchos. The census of 1940 listed for the state of Veracruz as a whole 28 ciudades, 1541 congregaciones, 57 ejidos, 81 haciendas, 3315 rancherías, 2150 ranchos, and only 135 villages. Most of the latter are situated above 800 m. in the zones traditionally called tierra templada and tierra fría. The plateau state of Mexico, with only three-fourths the population of Veracruz (concentrated in less than a third the area) had 634 villages or nearly five times as many. Tabasco offers the same picture generally with the dominance of diffuse over nucleated communities. In 1940 there were in that state 11 ciudades, 191 ejidos, 663 fincas, 165 haciendas, 1300 ranchos and rancherías, and only 50 villages or pueblos.

Northern Yucatan

No aerial photos are available for most of Yucatan so a careful analysis of community settlement patterns is not possible. The data collected from Quintana Roo, along with published maps of a few Yucatan communities, and my general observations of Yucatecan villages provide the raw materials for the analysis presented below.

In Yucatan the most common over-all settlement type is the village, invariably laid out in the typical Spanish grid pattern; even such small villages as Chan Kom possess this plan. The streets cross each other at

FIG. 9—VILLAGE PLAZA, KUNKUNUL, YUCATAN, MEXICO. (Photographed in 1928. Middle American Research Institute, Tulane University.)

right angles and generally enclose 100-m.-square blocks. In the center is the typical open square or plaza surrounded by church, municipal buildings, a few shops, and masonry houses of the wealthier families. In small villages there may be no private homes of masonry or shops. In larger communities the streets just off the square may be occupied by masonry houses almost shoulder to shoulder, but in general the pole-and-thatch house with a good-sized solar or house lot around it is the usual construction in any Yucatecan community. Larger communities may have, near the plaza, more masonry houses, along with more shops, several restaurants, a movie or two, perhaps even a hotel. Such communities fall more readily into our classification

of town and have many specialists, most of whom, however, are part-time. In Yucatan even in the largest towns most of the artisans are also farmers. One of the most important absences in Yucatecan centers is the aboriginal type of market. Markets do occur in the larger towns, but mainly for the use of the townsmen themselves, and even here most of their buying is done in shops.

Most Yucatecan solars are large, as an average at least 50 m. square, and population density is therefore low compared to that in the Mexican Plateau. Kilmartin has published (in Shattuck, 1933, pt. 2, figs. 2 and 3) two community maps, one a small village, Chan Kom, the other a large village, Dzitas. Chan Kom covered at that time 10 hectares and had a population of 197 peo-

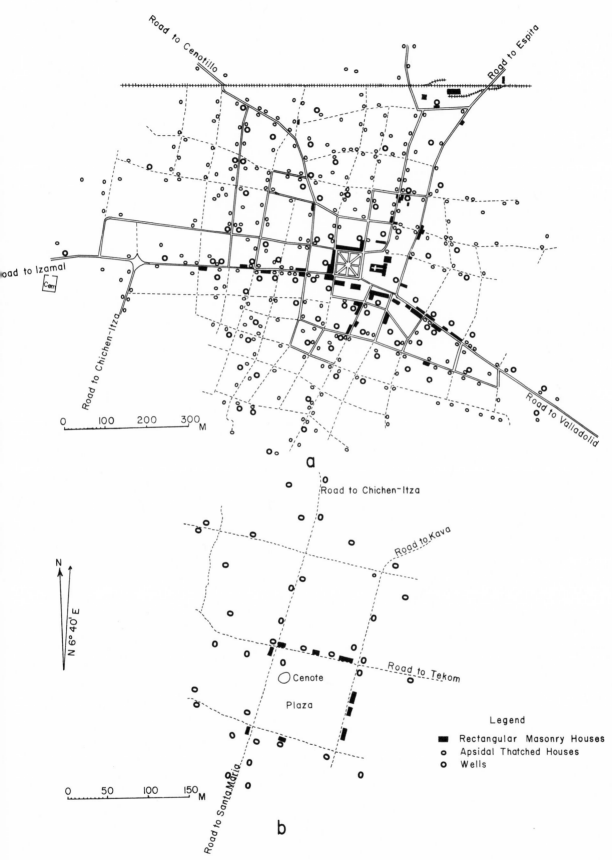

FIG. 10—MAPS OF DZITAS (ABOVE) AND CHAN KOM (BELOW), YUCATAN, MEXICO.
(From Kilmartin *in* Shattuck, 1933, figs. 1, 2.)

ple or just about 2000 inhabitants per sq. km.; Dzitas covered 80 hectares and possessed 1177 inhabitants or about 1500 per sq. km. Kantunil Kin (Quintana Roo), which I studied, covers 30 hectares and has a density of about 1800 (population 570 in 1940).

The Yucatecan communities are similar in organization and population density to the nopal-cultivation villages in the Teotihuacan Valley. In general, my impression is that these Yucatecan villages adhere much more rigidly to the Spanish grid pattern than do villages in the Valley of Mexico. The basic reason for this less compact settlement here is the tendency of the Yucateco to have a small orchard around his house.

Aside from the village and town, a high percentage of the population also live in the small hamlet type of settlement, called variously in Yucatan the rancho, paraje, or, in the case of the larger ones, the ranchería. Unlike Tabasco, the houses, although not following any orderly plan, are generally within a few score meters of each other. The settlement may be quite scattered and spread out, but there is no incentive for houses to be very widely spaced as land is not parceled. The main feature which sets off these communities from the village is the lack of plazas as centers of social orientation. If we were to extract the plaza and associated buildings from the scattered village of the Teotihuacan Valley and further reduce the size to less than 100 inhabitants, we would have the Yucatecan rancho or paraje. These settlements are generally colonies from nearby villages and very impermanent.

Haciendas are common in the central part of the state, or were before the agrarian reforms. Many place names are still listed as haciendas in the censuses, whereas they are actually now villages or combination hacienda-villages. The typical old-style henequen hacienda consisted of a large central house of the owner with a small com-

pact village type of settlement of workers nearby. The plan of the latter was the same as that found in independent villages, and today they are classed as villages in the census. With the reforms the new village received part of the old hacienda as ejido, but the original owner still holds part of his holding and many families in the village work as seasonal laborers for him.

Down on the Quintana Roo coast some of the smaller villages like Puerto Morelos have a settlement pattern of a different type. The community is strung linearly along the beach on one main street, each house being surrounded by a fairly large solar planted in coconut trees. It does, however, have the typical plaza just off to the landward side of Main Street toward one end of the village.

That part of the Yucatan Peninsula which lies within the modern borders of the Mexican republic comprises slightly over 140,000 sq. km. Within this extensive area live approximately 665,000 people or less than 5 per sq. km., one of the poorest-settled regions of the nation. Of the totals the state of Yucatan includes two-sevenths the area and five-sixths the population, with an average density of 13.4 per sq. km. (1950). The low over-all density is due to the fact that the state of Campeche and the territory of Quintana Roo are almost uninhabited. A comparison of these three political divisions is given in Table 14.

TABLE 14

	Area in sq. km.	Population	Density
Yucatan . . .	38,508	516,899	13.4
Campeche . . .	50,952	122,098	2.5
Quintana Roo . .	50,843	26,967	0.5
TOTAL . .	140,283	665,964	4.7

This tabulation shows that the Territory of Quintana Roo is one of the last demographic frontiers of modern Mexico, a huge tract of almost unpopulated tropical forest used mainly for chicle and lumber extraction and with little human occupation. This

TABLE 15

| Political Unit | Population | | | Area | Density |
	1900	1910	1940	(sq. km.)	(1940)
Yucatan					
Northern Area:					
Motul	18,756	19,001	20,791	963	22
Tixkokob	14,072	16,652	15,871	813	19
Central Area:					
Acanceh	22,677	23,456	21,290	1,537	14
Izamal	21,358	23,218	22,201	1,586	15
Western Area:					
Hunucma	18,656	22,354	22,059	2,828	9
Maxcanu	19,673	21,612	18,156	2,810	6
Southern Area:					
Peto	7,335	7,450	13,019	2,716	5
Tekax	19,757	20,160	25,063	3,012	8
Ticul	25,057	24,633	27,586	3,052	9
Eastern Area:					
Espita	10,489	12,498	14,486	2,692	6
Sotuta	9,855	10,825	12,410	2,342	6
Temax	17,058	16,437	20,543	2,710	8
Tizimin	9,174	8,523	14,468	6,330	2
Valladolid	24,740	26,399	37,431	4,449	9
Urban Area:					
Merida	60,156	79,526	118,411	961	123
Progreso	8,832	6,909	13,782	316	44
Campeche					
Campeche	...	...	28,894	2,922	10
Calkini	...	...	16,898	786	21
Carmen	...	...	13,986	15,603	0.9
Champoton	...	...	7,178	17,128	0.4
Hecelchakan	...	...	7,725	1,237	6
Hopelchen	...	...	8,045	5,151	1.5
Palizada	...	...	4,580	7,266	0.6
Tenabo	...	...	3,154	863	3.6
Quintana Roo					
Isla Mujeres	...	...	2,259	14,347	0.2
Cozumel	...	...	2,905	2,541	1.1
Felipe Carrillo Puerto	...	...	4,388	6,693	0.7
Chetumal	...	...	9,200	27,262	0.3

is even more dramatically illustrated when we note that almost half the population it does have lives in the two communities of Chetumal and Cozumel. Campeche is somewhat more populated, but most of the state is still undisturbed wilderness. The state of Yucatan, on the other hand, has a sizable population, especially in the central and northern areas, where the rural population has evidently reached a saturation point with present agricultural techniques and economies. The peninsula in general offers fascinating possibilities for a study of population expansion in tropical lowland areas, as it possesses a fairly uniform environment and all stages of the colonization process may be observed together.

Table 15 summarizes population data by small areas. In Yucatan the area is the distrito (a cluster of municipios, the cabecera of one serving as a judicial center and giving its name to the distrito), in Campeche the municipio (in Campeche of large size and comparable to the distrito of Yucatan in area), and in Quintana Roo the delegación.

The most densely populated part of the state, aside from the urban area, is the north, where henequen is more important than maize in the economy. This area in general is too dry and stony for effective maize cultivation. The western area is also a henequen region, under perhaps even more unfavorable conditions for agriculture than in the north, and the population is much less.

The central area with an average density of 14–15 is a mixed maize-henequen region; and the south and east together form what is today called "La Zona Maicera" or the Corn Belt of Yucatan. Especially favorable for maize cultivation is the southern area plus the distrito of Tizimin in the east. The rest of the eastern area is generally about as productive as central Yucatan, with a scanty soil cover but somewhat heavier rainfall.

The census data period by period offer some interesting tentative conclusions. We discover a large continuous zone in the center, north, and west of the state, in which the demographic climax seems to have been reached with present subsistence patterns (pure henequen and mixed henequen-maize). This includes the districts of Acanceh, Izamal, Maxcanu, Motul, Tixkokob, Hunucma, and the rural areas of the districts of Merida and Progreso. In some of these distritos the population has actually declined slightly since 1900–1910. This continuous zone may be considered then to be at its climax of occupation of the Yucatecan type and is the present demographic center of the peninsula. This situation undoubtedly dates from the postconquest period, even more likely from the henequen period, and probably was never true at any phase of aboriginal history. For slash-and-burn maize agriculture it is the poorest section of the entire peninsula. Its present status is probably due mainly to three key factors: (a) the development of henequen cultivation and the henequen industry, (b) its relative freedom from malaria, and (c) the urban growth of Merida, built by the Spaniards.

Hemming in this solid block of densely settled distritos to the east and south lies a continuous belt of distritos we can call the present Yucatecan demographic frontier. It is in general an area of heavier rainfall, more ample soil cover, higher maize yields, and slash-and-burn agriculture. The population is moderately heavy, running from 5 to 9 per sq. km., but is steadily increasing every census period. Individual municipios within the region have almost reached population maximum; and we can guess from their densities that it will support a concentration of 15–30 people per sq. km. with slash-and-burn maize agriculture. The main obstacles to more intensive colonization have been malaria and lack of transport facilities.

Beyond this frontier region to the east and south lie the vast, almost untouched future frontier lands of the Territory of Quintana Roo and state of Campeche. Today the interior is mainly utilized for chicle gathering and lumbering, with a few small villages of slash-and-burn maize cultivators. The only part of the two entities heavily exploited by man is the coastal beach, which is a center of coconut cultivation and fishing activities.

Actually, the picture of demographic growth of the state of Yucatan as a whole is unimpressive if we consider rural increase only. The population has grown from 309,-652 in 1900 to 418,210 in 1940; but 47,000 of this increase was urban, leaving but 30,-000 increase in rural population over a 40-year period or but 12 per cent.

For my zonal settlement pattern analysis I have selected the modern Distrito of Valladolid as a test case. My choice is based on a number of considerations. First, it is a pure slash-and-burn agricultural area inhabited by Maya-speaking peoples, and therefore the data are more pertinent to archaeological problems. The economy of central and northern Yucatan is obviously a recent one, based principally on the rise of value of henequen in the international market. Second, the area, in terms of the ecological system, is well populated. Third, we have excellent studies of the technology and economy of the agricultural system carried out by Carnegie Institution of Washington and so can relate our demographic and settlement pattern discussion to these factors. Finally, the ecology is fairly representative of the peninsula as a whole, certainly much more so than the subhumid henequen belt or the more fertile Puuc valleys.

The people of Valladolid are undoubtedly the most restless of all modern Yucatecans. The economy is one of almost pure slash-and-burn subsistence maize cultivation. Lands are divided into ejidos which are held and operated in common. This is the so-called "open ejido" system, in which each community has a large tract of land that is not divided into parcels and each farmer can sow where and as much land as he pleases.

The distrito has an area of 4500 sq. km. and a population in 1940 of approximately 40,000 inhabitants or 9 per sq. km. It probably has not yet reached its demographic limit but the instability and restlessness of the rural population indicate that the pressure is already strong. The agronomic studies made by the Carnegie staff indicate a probable maximum of 15–20 per sq. km.;

some municipios, such as Chan Kom and Chichimila, seem to be reaching this theoretical maximum. Most of the distrito has been converted to scrub forest by continuous clearing and reclearing for cultivation, and in spite of the low density of population it gives the impression from the air or on the ground of being well populated. The distrito includes the municipios listed in Table 16.

The Valladolid district, unlike most of the state, is characterized by having most of its rural population dispersed in small settlements, villages, ranchos, and parajes. In most Yucatecan municipios, especially in the henequen area, at least half and more commonly from three-fourths to seven-eighths of the population live in a single nucleated village with but a small fraction of its population living in outlying settlements. In Valladolid the reverse is true; the municipio cabecera is often rather small and contains on the average but a third of the population of the municipio. For example, if we subtract Valladolid (an urban town) from the totals in Table 16, we find that of the 32,000 or so rural population in the distrito only 10,000 live in the central villages. Six of the ten rural municipios have central villages with under 1000 inhabitants.

One is reminded of the pattern in the

TABLE 16

Municipio	Area (sq. km.)	Population (1940)	Density	Population of Cabecera
Valladolid	943	15,749	18	6,402
Tixcacalcupul	325	1,534	5	775
Chan Kom	80	1,614	20	270
Kaua	154	1,063	7	772
Tinum	291	3,028	9	1,360
Uayma	144	1,225	8	975
Kunkunul	301	922	3	.502
Chichimila	182	3,079	17	1,797
Chemax	813	4,103	5	1,573
Temozon	806	4,263	5	1,060
TOTAL	4,450	38,755	8.7	16,293

TABLE 17

Municipio	Below 50	50– 100	100– 250	250– 500	500– 1000	1000– 2000	Over 2000
Valladolid	262	6	7	6	3	1	1
Tixcacalcupul . . .	18	1	3	0	1	0	0
Chan Kom	19	5	3	1	0	0	0
Kaua	15	1	0	0	1	0	0
Tinum	25	5	1	1	1	1	0
Uayma	14	0	0	0	1	0	0
Kunkunul	9	5	0	0	1	0	0
Tekom	17	3	2	0	2	0	0
Chichimila . . .	42	4	2	0	0	1	0
Chemax	53	6	4	1	0	1	0
Temozon	113	5	2	1	1	1	0
TOTAL . . .	587	41	24	10	11	5	1

Chontalpa, but the resemblance is only superficial. In Tabasco we have a small city or town as the center of the municipio with the rural population scattered in rancherías or ranchos. In Valladolid the municipio center is simply a medium or large village, and the rest of the population live in smaller villages or hamlets. The nucleated community is the basic population unit in the Valladolid district, although usually of very small size.

Several types of these nucleated settlements may be noted. First is the "paraje," simply a clearing in the forest with 6–12 huts. These settlements are extraordinarily impermanent, often disappearing from one 10-year census to the next. The population usually consists of a number of discontented families who have left their parent village and often stay a few years and then return or move to another village or establish a new paraje. There is an inherent centrifugal force in Valladolid economy which lies behind this instability. The term "ranchería" is usually applied to the larger parajes; "rancho" theoretically refers to cattle ranches or other permanent agronomic establishments. Actually the latter is often used in place of paraje.

In Table 17 I present an analysis of community size for the district. Only six communities in this large area possess populations of over 1000 inhabitants and of these only one may be classified as a true town, the others being large villages. The rest of the population live in small villages and hamlets. Of the total population of the district only one-third live in these six large communities; this high percentage is due to the inclusion of the urban town of Valladolid. If we subtract the latter, we can say that only about one-fourth of the rural population live in large villages. Approximately one-half of the population live in communities with less than 500 people and fully one-third in communities of less than 100 inhabitants. Table 18 summarizes the data.

TABLE 18

Urban town of Valladolid 16%	
5 large villages 16%	(over 1000 population)
11 medium villages . 18%	(500–1000 population)
34 small villages 16%	(100–500 population)
628 hamlets 34%	(below 100 population)

Of especial interest is the extraordinary number of what we are calling hamlets, over 600 of them.

Several times during our discussion of Yucatecan population I have pointed out a basic restlessness and instability. Because in our area of slash-and-burn maize cultivation this is especially evident, I present here a special analysis of the municipio of Valladolid to illustrate the point.

The municipio of Valladolid occupies some 95,000 hectares of scrub forest. Within it are one urban town, Valladolid itself, and the 12 villages of Dzitnup, Ebtun, Kanxoc, Pixoy, Popola, Tahmuy, Tesoco, Tikuch, Tixhualahtun, Xocen, Yalcoba, and Yalcon. These communities may be considered as the permanent settlements of the municipio. Only one possesses over 1000 inhabitants, three between 500 and 1000, and the remaining eight between 100 and 500. In Table 17 we noted 13 communities falling within the bracket 100–500, but only 8 are classified as true "pueblos" or villages; the others are rancherías. We classified them along with the true small villages purely on a scale of population size. Actually there are two important differences between big rancherías and small villages: (a) the village has a plaza and masonry church, both lacking in the ranchería; and more important (b) the village or pueblo is a permanent settlement. No cases of actual abandonment of a village are known, whereas even large rancherías may disappear and appear frequently. These 13 communities, Valladolid and its 12 satellite pueblos, are permanent communities and the sources from which colonization proceeds.

A few families from one of these communities, or even one family, may decide, either because of dissatisfaction in personal relations or, more frequently, because of lack of nearby land, to cultivate milpa at a considerable distance from the village in fresher lands. After a few years of experiment the family head discovers the land to be more productive than the overworked land nearby and he will decide to live there for a while. He may be joined by others until the population may reach as high as a hundred or so. Within a period of 10–30 years, depending on the number of colonists, the land becomes overworked to the

same degree as around the mother village, and a number of families may return to the mother village and found a new ranch or paraje. Often the entire population moves and the spot is abandoned. After 10–20 years the spot may be reoccupied and resettled and the pattern repeats. The result is that numerous satellite communities are in a constate state of population shift; some are newly founded, some increasing in population, others decreasing, others being abandoned, and others being reoccupied. The whole pattern quite obviously relates to the technique of cultivation; the important fact about it is the presence of a restless shifting rural population with a relatively stable general demographic picture. The latter conclusion is based on the census data. The population of the municipio in 1940 was 15,749; in 1950 it rose to 18,225 but most of this growth was due to urban growth in Valladolid. The rural population in 1940 was 9349; in 1950 it rose to only 10,060, an increase of but 8 per cent. Even in the permanent villages actual increase was slight from a total of 5637 to 5982. Important for our observations, some villages declined while others grew in population, undoubtedly related to colonists going and coming from the hinterland.

Of those communities which we can class as impermanent, Table 19 summarizes their demographic history.

Today the pressure has reached the point

TABLE 19

Impermanent Communities	Number of Communities
Occupied 1940—still occupied 1950	137
show population increase	82
show population decrease	55
Occupied 1940—abandoned 1950	132
New settlements 1950	86
Occupied 1930—abandoned 1940 and 1950	40
Occupied 1930—abandoned 1940— reoccupied 1950	20
Villages (permanent communities)	12
Showing population increase	8
Showing population decrease	4

where the Valladolid district population as a whole is beginning to move out into the hinterland of the Quintana Roo–Yucatan border. Most of the new communities are of the ranchería-rancho-paraje type. There are very few foundings of true pueblos in the classic Yucatecan sense. This suggests that these smaller units, which we can call hamlets, are the natural settlement type with slash-and-burn agriculture in this type of environment. I wish also to point out for the archaeologist's benefit that a deep continuous ceramic stratigraphy at a small site in this area does not necessarily indicate a *continuous occupation*. It may indicate repeated cyclic occupation and abandonment; the periods of such are too short to be detected by the present Maya ceramic stratigraphy.

In the Valladolid area, then, with slash-and-burn agriculture, we found a pattern of true villages and hamlets rather than rancherías as the basic settlement form. However, two important differences should be emphasized in comparing this area with the Valley of Mexico. First, there are many more small communities, especially hamlets in northern Yucatan; and second, the communities are much more widely spaced. The difference is obviously correlated with the difference in the intensity of land utilization. The highway from the ruins of Chichen Itza to Valladolid, crossing the heart of this zone, passes through only the following communities: Xcalakop (ranchería) 164 inhabitants, Kaua (village) 772, San Diego (ranchería) 70, Kukunul (village) 502, Ebtun (village) 300, and finally Valladolid (town) 6402. The distance is approximately that of our transects from the Valley of Mexico—30 km. (from Xcalakop to Valladolid). Aside from the urban town of Valladolid none of the communities have over 1000 inhabitants, and the average distance between communities is 8 km. or four times that of the Teohihuacan Valley. The linear population density is but 274 per km. even

including the town of Valladolid; the rural density is only 60.

The single community of Valladolid overbalances the picture as it is the only large community in the distrito and is the center of an area much larger than the Teotihuacan Valley. Even so, the linear density for the latter is almost double that of the former and if only rural densities are considered and we exclude the towns in both areas, it is seven times.

Highland Guatemala Patterns

The final test area to be discussed is that of highland Guatemala. McBryde in his study of southwestern Guatemala (1947) summarized the settlement pattern of the area in detail. First of all he separates communities into two functional types, town and village, which correspond to our Valley of Mexico types. His distinction between them was easier, however, than ours, since in Guatemala we find a basic social cleavage between Ladinos and Indians, of which the former seem invariably to have been the town-building group. Therefore he was able to sort out towns simply on the basis of the presence of a minimum of 500 Ladinos in communities of over 1000 inhabitants as his criterion. As in the Valley of Mexico, the gross size of a community does not always determine the status of a community. Santiago Atitlan with over 5000 inhabitants is still a village.

Large villages and towns in the area seem to adhere fairly closely to the Spanish grid pattern of streets. Smaller communities usually have only a few central streets laid out gridwise, the system breaking down on the peripheries. However, there are notable exceptions. Santiago Atitlan, in spite of its large size, has a more haphazard street arrangement. The internal density of Atitlan population was 8000 per sq. km., similar to the lakeshore villages in the Valley of Mexico. Atitlan is a lakeshore village in an area of limited level land and with a more intensive system of agriculture than practiced in most of the Guatemala highlands.

In Guatemala the unit of settlement in many cases is the municipio rather than the village or town. In the Valley of Mexico we find municipios but as administrative, not settlement, units. Usually they include a town or big village as the cabecera or administrative center, plus several small villages as dependent communities; but each of them is a separate, permanent residence unit and a small definable in-group, as we have pointed out.

In Guatemala, in some municipios, we find the Mexican pattern; in others the center, whether village or town, partakes of the character of a ceremonial center. In some municipios there is a central town or village laid out on the grid plan, occupied by a small Ladino resident population who are full-time craft, political, or trading specialists. The Indian population which makes up the bulk of the population lives scattered on isolated farms, in our typical ranchería pattern. The rural population gathers in the center for trade or religious ceremonies. Here the Indians often have houses which they use during these visits but occupy only a fraction of the time. Tax (1952a) calls these "Vacant Towns," Borhegyi (1956a) "Concourse Centers." There are communities which one might class as intermediates, that is, most of the Indian population live in the centers permanently, some migrate from town to farm.

In southwestern Guatemala McBryde (1947) points out that these Vacant or Dispersed Towns are common in the high valleys of Totonicapan and Quezaltenango. Typical of the Mexican village and town are those communities on the shores of Lake Atitlan. In general the highland population of Guatemala tends toward the dispersed type of settlement.

Factors pointed out by McBryde as affecting the nucleated or Mexican type of settlement are (a) water supply, (b) sur-

face features, (c) situation with respect to trade routes, (d) specialized occupations including truck gardening, (e) availability of remunerative employment, and (f) historic precedent. Atitlan, for example, combines all these factors: it is located near one of the main water sources; it is clustered on a small terrace on the volcanic slopes; it is on one of the major trade routes; the people are specialized horticulturists, canoemen, middlemen, and craftsmen; the village is within a short distance of escarpment coffee plantations; and finally, there has always been a clustered settlement there even in preconquest times.

The Quezaltenango and Huehuetenango valleys are flat extensive plains and, McBryde feels, are natural areas for the dispersed pattern of settlement. I can not agree with this conclusion, because the same conditions are met in the Mesa Central, where the dispersed type of municipio is completely absent. Even in these more open highland valleys in Guatemala we find a number of factors such as water supply, trade route position, and craft specialization, which cause the development of nucleated communities, at any rate of the town, if not the village, type.

Borhegyi (1956a) discusses these communities and suggests the following typology: (1) Compound Village, the true permanent nucleated community, possessing a true plaza and equivalent to our Mexican towns and villages. (2) Dispersed Village, with or without plazas. Here we find a planned center, occupied by not more than a few dozen families with the rest of the population scattered over the valley and slopes. The center was evidently an artificial unit set up in the 16th century by the Spaniards to nucleate the population for conversion. As the priestly control weakened, Borhegyi feels, the population reverted to the original scattered patterns. (3) Concourse Centers with well-defined plazas. This is Tax's "Vacant Town" in which a small fraction of the population live in a central community permanently and the rest live on their farms in our ranchería type of settlement pattern. It differs from No. 2 in that the population have town houses also and reside in the central community part of the year during religious ceremonies. In other words, the central community has an important social function even though not occupied all year round.

CONCLUSIONS

The data from our Valley of Mexico test areas, West's data from Michoacan, and my general observations of the Mesa Central indicate that subsistence farmers in that area generally live in nucleated communities of the village type. Rancherías and commercial agriculture communities such as ranchos and haciendas do exist but only a very small fraction of the population reside in them.

The average size of communities is linked with the productivity of the agricultural system. In the Chinampan area, with the most intensive system of farming and highest crop return, we find more large villages than in the Teotihuacan Valley. San Gregorio Atlapulco, as an extreme example, had a population of 6000 in 1950; it is a subsistence village, not a town. Hamlets are few in number and a very small percentage of the population of the Valley of Mexico reside in that type of settlement.

The zonal distribution of communities, i.e., the number and size of communities per linear or areal unit, is also clearly related to agricultural productivity. A less easily explained correlation is that between community density and agricultural technology. The greatest densities are achieved in Chinampa communities, followed by irrigation villages in the Teotihuacan Valley, then dry-farming villages in the same valley; the scattered villages and rancherías occur in stoney hillside areas in the Teotihuacan Valley. The compact, but low density, nopal villages of the Teotihuacan Val-

ley show a clear correlation between community density and the agricultural system. Scattered villages probably occur wherever Palerm's calmil-barbecho system of agriculture is practiced. This seems to be the case in the few examples in the Teotihuacan Valley, and certainly is true in Palerm's northeast Puebla test area. This system of cultivation is carried out in dry-farming areas in the highlands of Mexico and apparently is widespread in the Guatemala highlands (Stadelman, 1940). Each family has a relatively large house lot, which is planted in maize and intensively cultivated (calmil). The land is never rested since it is continuously fertilized by refuse from the house and its occupants. Each family also holds a number of larger fields outside the residential area of the village, which are not fertilized but alternately rested (barbecho). The size of the calmil is limited by the amount of refuse available. It is not certain how close a correlation exists between calmil cultivation and the scattered village. Certainly all calmil villages must be scattered villages, but the converse may or may not be true.

The very high density of Chinampa villages may be an extreme situation related to the great demographic pressure and scarcity of agricultural land. My general impression is that the normal population density for villages in the Central Plateau with intensive agriculture is closer to the figures for irrigation communities in the Teotihuacan Valley.

In the Teotihuacan Valley, all but very few of the villages are on the edge of the valley floor in generally marginal locations with respect to agricultural land use. A string of villages lies on each side of the valley, at least seven on the south side and nine on the north side. Three others are on isolated hills in the plain, four on the archaeological site of Teotihuacan (a marginal agricultural area also). Only three villages are within the area of good agricultural land. With the limited amount of good agricultural land and very dense population, this is evidently due to the need to preserve for strictly agricultural use the better land.

In the southern Valley of Mexico a similar string of villages is arranged along the old shoreline of Lakes Xochimilco and Chalco. The position of the villages here is clearly related to two factors: (a) the need to be as close as possible to the chinampas, and (b), before the draining of the lakes, their use for transport. Nearly all the lakeshore villages are large, usually exceeding 2000 people. Behind the lakeshore villages and on the sloping mountain wall bordering the Valley of Mexico to the south is a similar parallel string of villages. These have as their subsistence base dry-farming, maguey cultivation, and woodworking; throughout the history of the area they have been in close trading symbiosis with the lakeshore villages.

One of the characteristic features of highland Mesoamerican ecology is complex environmental zoning. With the extreme variations in altitude, belts of strikingly different climates, soils, vegetation, and resources are likely to lie within a few miles of each other. This feature must always have acted as a powerful stimulus to trade, community specialization and economic symbiosis. Furthermore, within such general zones, exists considerable subzoning based on variation of specific geographical features such as angle of slope, flat versus sloping terrain, lakes versus nonlake areas, slight variations in soil, presence of permanent streams, and locations of specific resources such as wood, lime, volcanic stone, and metal. In the southern Valley of Mexico the distribution of communities can be understood only in these terms. Wolf and Palerm (1955) have described in detail a similar situation in the district of Texcoco, with ecological differentiation between lakeshore, plain, piedmont, and mountain strips. McBryde's classic study of southwestern Guatemala indicates that this is a key factor with respect to set-

tlement patterns all over highland Mesoamerica.

In most of the communities studied in the Valley of Mexico we find characteristically a central plaza with associated public buildings (church, shops, municipal offices); settlement is distributed evenly in all directions from this civic center. I am inclined to agree with Borhegyi that the plaza civic center probably derives from pre-Hispanic settlement patterns rather than Hispanic and is exceedingly ancient in the Valley of Mexico. With the exception of large communities (generally towns rather than villages) the Spanish grid street pattern is not really characteristic of plateau communities. In a few cases villages with regular grid street patterns occur (Tecomitl in the Chinampa area), but in most villages only a few main streets conform to the strict geometric pattern; most streets are winding alleys. One has the impression that the Spanish grid is a partially successful superimposition over an aboriginal street pattern. Characteristically the larger better-made houses tend to cluster near the plaza.

The environment, agricultural systems, and settlement patterns of the Gulf Coast and northern Yucatan contrast sharply with the Valley of Mexico. Subsistence agriculture is everywhere of the slash-and-burn type. In order to use this system a large quantity of land in various stages of fallowing is needed for each unit in actual production. The precise percentage of land in use to fallow land, however, varies enormously. Certainly the agricultural system tends to promote either a scattered settlement pattern of the ranchería type or the small nucleated settlements like the Valladolid hamlets. The former, of course, has the mechanical advantage of reducing time and energy spent getting to and from the milpa. The house of each family is relatively permanent, their holding is relatively compact, small, and conveniently near at hand. It is divided into a number of fields which are cultivated in succession. The hamlet has the advantage of more expanded social interaction along with relative convenience of house-to-field location. In terms of land tenure the ranchería seems to correlate with parceled ejido and private ownership systems, the hamlet with the open ejido system. Larger nucleated settlements of the village type would seem to involve too great a sacrifice of convenience to be a common settlement type in this ecological system. Villages are very rare on the Gulf Coast plain; the ranchería is everywhere dominant.

This is not to state that villages, even large villages, can not exist with slash-and-burn agriculture, as data from northern Yucatan invalidate such a generalization. Our argument is that the ecological factor favors a more dispersed pattern. Other factors of a nonecological nature such as warfare, political or religious integration, or simply improved transportation may operate in favor of a village settlement pattern.

In the case of northern Yucatan the situation seems clear. All the archaeological and documentary data from the 16th century indicate that the pre-Hispanic settlement pattern was one of ceremonial centers (Borhegyi's modern Concourse Center in highland Guatemala) and hamlets. This settlement pattern was intentionally modified by the Spaniards to facilitate religious conversion, so the hamlets dependent on the ceremonial center were moved to the center to form large nucleated communities. The fact that in Yucatan communities today adhere much more faithfully to the Spanish grid plan than in the Valley of Mexico is one indication that they are not aboriginal communities in type. The census lists for the 16th century from northern Yucatan demonstrate that the Spaniards had considerable difficulty in keeping these artificial centers intact. Population decline immediately after the founding of such communities seems to have been general; none of the sources ascribes the decline to the epidemics of the 16th century as was the case for central

Mexico. Apparently the kind of segmentation we describe for modern Valladolid was a common event as villages attempted to return to the normal settlement pattern with respect to the local ecology. Once such villages were established and at least partially accepted by the Indian population, numerous advantages would be evident; and with a strong religious institution to safeguard the new pattern, the village has become in time not only a normal part of Yucatecan life but the peasant has developed strong values to live in larger communities. One secondary factor which tended to give the new settlement type its stability was improved methods of transporting produce from field to house. In the 16th century the introduction of Spanish draft animals and in recent years commercial buslines have facilitated the cultivation of fields at distances of as much as 30–40 miles from the community.

It is of great significance in terms of the previous arguments that settlement patterns in central and northern Yucatan are strikingly different from those in our Valladolid district. To illustrate, we present below an analysis of settlement patterns in Izamal and Acanceh. These two districts lie in the demographic center of modern Yucatan, in a region where demographic growth since 1900 has come to a standstill. They are contiguous and are characterized by moderate rainfall (800–1000 mm.), scanty soil, and scrubby bush cover. The region is ideal for henequen cultivation and is marginal with respect to slash-and-burn cultivation. It is the only part of the demographic center of the state where maize can be effectively grown, and the economy is characterized by two subtypes: (a) fully commercial plantation henequen economy, and (b) village economy based on ejidos with both henequen and maize.

The two districts together in 1940 comprised 3100 sq. km. and had 43,000 people with an average of 14 per sq. km. They include the municipios listed in Table 20.

84

TABLE 20

	Area	Population	Density	Population of Cabecera
Acanceh:				
Abala	264	2747	10	632
Homun	245	2634	11	1783
Tecoh	396	5654	14	2709
Cuzama	161	1563	10	960
Seye	188	3543	19	2496
Anaceh	207	3867	10	2293
Timicuy	76	1868	25	1212
Izamal:				
Tahmek	99	1792	18	1544
Hoctun	166	2402	21	1868
Xocchel	70	1322	19	1227
Tekanto	88	2831	32	2067
Izamal	358	8737	24	5305
Tepakam	108	1824	17	1210
Sudzal	497	1007	2	498
Kantunil	250	2286	9	1350

The region is one of two basic settlement types, the nucleated village and the hacienda. The usual pattern is for each municipio to be composed of a single large village with over 1000 inhabitants, which serves as the cabecera or center, and with the rest of the population living in henequen haciendas. The latter split up sharply by size into subtypes: those with less than 50 inhabitants and those with 100–500, a few giants even exceeding the latter figure. In general small haciendas are owned and worked by people from the neighboring village; the bigger ones are owned by families who live in Merida.

Table 21 shows that almost all communities with an excess of 1000 inhabitants are nucleated municipio cabecera villages and almost all those with less than 1000 are henequen plantations. The exceptions are indicated. The other types of communities found in Yucatan, such as parajes, ranchos, rancherías, or small villages, are very rare in this area.

In the entire region but one community can be classed as a true town: Izamal. This lack of local urban development is due to the virtual monopoly that Merida, the state capital, holds on the henequen industry, thus aborting incipient urban development in the smaller communities in the henequen area. In 1950 Izamal possessed 5305 inhabi-

TABLE 21—COMMUNITY SIZE BY POPULATION

	Below 50	50–100	100–500	500–1000	1000–2000	2000–3000	Over 3000	Depopulated
Abala	2	0	5	2 (1-V)	0	0	0	6
Honun	25	0	3	0	1 (V)	0	0	19
Tecoh	7	2	7	2 (1-V)	0	1 (V)	0	0
Cuzama	7	1	2	1 (V)	0	0	0	10
Seye	22	1	4	0	0	1 (V)	0	10
Acanceh	10	2	4	1	0	1 (V)	0	1
Tahmek	3	0	2	0	1 (V)	0	0	25
Hoctun	8	0	3	0	1 (V)	0	0	5
Xocchel	12	0	0	0	1 (V)	0	0	4
Tekanto	4	0	4	0	0	1 (V)	0	1
Izamal	21	4	2 (1-V)	4 (All V)	0	0	1 (T)	3
Tepakam	5	2	3	0	1 (V)	0	0	11
Sudzal	13	3	2	0	0	0	0	4
Kantunil	4	0	0	1 (V)	1 (V)	0	0	8
Timicuy	0	1	2	0	1 (V)	0	0	2
TOTAL	143	16	43 (2-V)	11 (8-V)	7 (All V)	4 (All V)	1 (T)	109

Key: 2 (1-V) means one is a village, the other a hacienda; 1 (V) means all are villages; (T) means town.

TABLE 22

Live in town of Izamal 12%	
Live in 11 big villages 46%	
Live in communities with more than 1000 inhabitants 58%	
Live in 10 small and medium villages 15%	
Live in nucleated villages or towns 73%	
Live in 41 large haciendas 20%	
Live in 159 small haciendas, ranchos, etc. 7%	
Live in haciendas, ranchos, etc. 27%	

tants, one of the eight largest communities of the state.

All those communities not indicated as villages are in the main henequen haciendas, with a few ranchos and parajes. In our selected area, then, we find 143 small haciendas, ranchos, and parajes; 57 large henequen haciendas; 3 giant haciendas (over 500 population); 2 small villages (under 500 population); 8 medium-sized villages (500–1000); 11 big villages (over 1000); and one town, Izamal.

By comparing the number of communities in each category one might assume that the bulk of the population lives in small and medium-size henequen haciendas. Actually this is not the case if we compare the actual total population living in these divisions. We summarize these data in Table 22. Approximately 75 per cent of the population lives in villages, well over 50 per cent in villages with over 1000 inhabitants. Approximately 63 per cent of the population lives in the 15 municipio cabecera villages.

In general we find that each municipio consists of a single big village with over 1000 inhabitants and a constellation of small and large henequen plantations. Of the municipios only Tecoh, Kantunil, and Izamal possess more than one village, and of the seven extra villages five are in the single municipio of Izamal.

A glance at the final column of Table 21 offers some interesting data for speculation. Some 109 small ranchos, haciendas, and parajes were abandoned between 1930 and 1940. It indicates clearly that even in this area of permanent henequen cultivation the smaller population units are extremely fluid. The villages themselves are permanent as well as the larger Merida-owned plantations, but in the smaller communities the restless, shifting character of Maya farming is present even here in the center of the state.

REFERENCES

Borhegyi, 1956a
Gamio, 1922
Kelly and Palerm, 1952
Lumholtz, 1902
McBryde, 1947
Palerm, 1954, 1955
Reina, 1960
Sanders, 1956

Shattuck, 1933
Stadelman, 1940
Starr, F., 1899
Steggerda, 1941
Tax, 1952a
West, 1948
—— and Armillas, 1950
Wolf and Palerm, 1955

5. Indian Economies

MANNING NASH

THE ECONOMIC ORGANIZATION of the Indians of Middle America ranges over a wide gamut.[1] It runs from the virtual isolation, little trade, and almost no money of the tribal remnants of the Lacandon in the Peten to complete market interdependence of specialized communities producing for cash returns in an impersonal and competitive economic organization. There are all kinds of subtle gradients and variations between these extremes, but without doing violence to the ethnographic reality, it is feasible to sort the economic complexity of the region into three major types, each tending to be structurally, and frequently regionally, distinct. Each type carries with it some differences in the social structure and cultural pattern of which the economy is but a subsystem. The social and cultural correlates, concomitants, and prerequisites of the varying economic organizations may form the basis for providing important indices to the dynamics of social change and stability among the Indians of Middle America.

The three kinds of economic organization in Middle America are:

1. *The regional marketing system.* Communities are linked into a system of rotating markets. In its most developed form the rotating markets look like a "solar system." A major market center is in daily operation. To it flow commodities produced throughout the region, goods from all over the nation, and even items from international trade. Around the major market are a series of market places which have their special days. Each of these market places tends to specialize in a given produce or commodity and to carry a reduced selection of the goods available in the central market. Goods, buyers, and sellers move around the solar system in terms of the days of the week when market activity centers in a particular market place. Such solar systems of regional interdependence are characteristic of the western highlands of Guatemala (where they are most highly developed), the valley of Oaxaca, central Mexico, Michoacan, and eastern Guatemala among the

---

[1] This paper draws heavily on monographs and articles not directly cited and lists only the chief sources. I am indebted to June C. Nash for the idea of costume serving as a brand device, and to the Chiapas project of the University of Chicago for access to manuscript material.

FIG. 1—TAKING PIGS TO MARKET AT SAN FRAN-CISCO EL ALTO, GUATEMALA. (Photographed by Matilda Gray, 1935. Middle American Research Institute, Tulane University.)

Chorti and Pokomam. Without the marked solar qualities, regional market interdependence is found in the highlands of Chiapas among the Tzeltal and Tzotzil and in parts of the Alta Verapaz in Guatemala and a pattern of intense daily markets in the Isthmus of Tehuantepec. The regional marketing system is "money economy organized in single households as both consumption and production units with a strongly developed market which tends to be perfectly competitive" (Tax, 1953, p. 13).

2. *The adjunct export economy.* Communities produce chiefly for home and local consumption, but tend to have one or a few commodities produced for cash and market exchange. Specialization is rare; from community to community the products, skills, and economic organization are homogeneous. The economy is pecuniary, but there is much exchange of items for other items, albeit in terms of price-money equivalents. The market and the market place tend to

88

be in the hands of non-Indians, and the Indian is more seen as seller than buyer. This sort of economy varies from the coffee growers of Sayula (Guiteras Holmes, 1952a) who are mainly concerned with the export of a cash crop, or the vanilla growers of the Totonac region around the major market of Papantla (Kelly and Palerm, 1952) to the coffee, melon, and citrus growers of the Sierra Popoluca (Foster, 1942). Another axis of variation is toward the paid labor role of Indians on plantations where the export economy is organized in the hands of non-Indian entrepreneurs. The paid labor, or Indian rural proletariat (Mintz, 1953), often coexists with communities growing the basic subsistence crops. In the Yucatan peninsula (Redfield, 1941) the henequen plantations approach this; in parts of the Verapaz in Guatemala, and in the coastal regions where Indians are workers on coffee, sugar, rice, or banana plantations, there occurs the extreme form of the adjunct export system.

3. *The quasi-tribal system.* Economies are concerned chiefly with meeting locally defined demands. Economic effort is directed toward subsistence needs with handicrafts for home use, and attention to the crops of the milpa. Money is part of the daily life but tends to be scant, and transactions are not a daily occurrence. The Indians with this kind of economic system tend to be in remote or not very accessible upland regions, or to be remnants of former unintensive village agriculturalists. The economic type is found among the Cora and Huichol, the Tarahumara, the Tepehuan, the Mayo, and other groups of northwest Mexico, and, except for the Lacandon of the Mexico-Guatemala border, does not exist south of Mexico City, and is absent from Guatemala (except possibly for the Kekchi around Lake Izabal, Dr. Nancy Solien de Gonzales reports).

The three types of economies are different in scale, in the number of Indians they include, and in the areas where they are able to function. All the economies are tied, more or less tightly, to the national and international economies; none is free from the effects of national and world fluctuations. Everywhere the Indian and his communities are enmeshed in a network of economic relationships well beyond the local ethnic unit. Even the very isolated groups like the Lacandon or the Tarahumara, or the Xcacal of Quintana Roo get involved with the passing agents of the larger economy.

The quasi-tribal system is the least complicated and hence most easily accounted for. In the southern Sierra Madre Occidental, between the states of Jalisco and Nayarit, are the Cora and the Huichol. The 2000 or 3000 Cora settled in pueblos of 200–300 persons, with their mixture of plow agriculture on bottom lands and digging-stick cultivation on the slopes, and the Huichol, where 4000 or 5000 Indians live in scattered ranchos by digging-stick agriculture (Vogt, 1955), are exemplars of the quasi-tribal system. In the first place, access to the region is difficult. The paucity of usable roads encourages few persons regularly to penetrate into the depth of Indian country. Second, the natural ecology of the area does not provide a basis for much agricultural differentiation; what is grown in one part is grown in another. Finally, what small economic opportunity exists for peddling, trade, and other commercial activities tends to be in the hands of Mexicans rather than Indians. Though there are craftsmen who make artifacts of wood (stools, chairs, and guitars) and of fibers (mats, bags, and nets), and a few potters (who do not meet local demand), specialization in economic activity is not great, nor are whole communities dependent on trade relations (Grimes, 1961). The Huichol are chiefly growers of milpa and keepers of cattle. The maize grown is for home use; if there is a small surplus, it is used to buy cattle. Maize is supplemented by beans, squash, melons, fruits, and some orchards and vegetable gardens. The Huichol are near the Middle

FIG. 2—PANCACHE MARKET, GUATEMALA. (Photographed by Matilda Gray, 1935. Middle American Research Institute, Tulane University.)

American extreme in self-sufficiency, meeting most of their own requirements through their own production. Cash comes to them by paid-labor service as herdsmen for Mexicans, or work on tobacco farms or through begging or performing in towns like Tepic. A market structure is absent; buyers and sellers seek each other out as transactions need to be made. Prices tend to be in terms of what things are selling for in the stores and towns of Mexicans.

In this tribal-like setting, buying and sell-

FIG. 3—FODDER VENDOR, CHIANTLA, GUATE-MALA. (Photographed by Matilda Gray, 1935. Middle American Research Institute, Tulane University.)

ing is a small part of daily life and reaches a market-like arrangement only during times of ceremonial festivities involving whole communities. Land and other valuable productive resources are nominally communal, and with the low level of technological development, a family can exploit only a few acres, so there is no land market and no land shortage. The peak work periods in the agricultural cycle require more labor than is available to the household units, which are also the economic units. So, within a locality or settlement there is a form of exchange: unpaid, cooperative farm labor. Thus there is an economy oriented to the needs of the local community (the scattered ranchos tied together by kinship and

marriage) or the compact settlement sort, with near food self-sufficiency, household units of consumption and production, no markets, primitive technology, little cash, and exchange as extraordinary rather than everyday. The chief uses of wealth are festal and ceremonial, and there is communal pressure on the wealthy, with the possibilities of envy and witchcraft directed against them, to share their goods with the needy. Hunting and gathering and fishing supplement the milpa and cattle keeping.

Like the Cora and the Huichol, the Tarahumara (Bennett and Zingg, 1935) or the remnants of the Cahita peoples (the Yaqui, Mayo, and Tepehuan) exhibit the same general features of a milpa-agriculture system with supplemental products, exchange as a rarity, cooperative farm labor, and general demands on wealth by the needy and through the festal cycle. These economies do not transcend a householding aspect and show little dynamism or change. Isolation, relative lack of ecological variation, a reduced political and social organization, few specialists, and household attempts at self-sufficiency account for the major contours of this sort of economy.

In the western highlands of Guatemala, the solar marketing system of economic organization exists in its most highly developed form. Tax (1952c, 1953, 1957a) has summarized the chief features of this form, and the discussion here follows his guidelines. Lake Atitlan dominates the physical geography of the midwest highlands. Ranged around the lake are 14 *municipios* (the municipio is the administrative unit of Guatemala, and is here virtually identical with ethnic units). Each municipio is distinct in costume, dialect, mythology, and economic specialty (Tax, 1937). In small compass lies a tremendous variety of cultural, social, and economic features. The economic variation is a condensed example of that occurring throughout western Guatemala (McBryde, 1947, especially Map 19 which shows the distribution of Indian mar-

Fig. 4—SOLOLA, GUATEMALA, MARKET GROUP. Santa Catarina men (Lake Atitlan) selling tiny lake fish on bunchgrass stems. (From McBryde, 1947, pl. 22,*e.* Middle American Research Institute, Tulane University.)

kets in southwest Guatemala). The ecological possibilities of the municipios around the lake account, in part, for agricultural diversity. The variation in altitude, in possibilities of irrigation, in natural resources, and in available arable land underlies crop diversity. All the communities grow some maize, but a few are maize exporters and hence may be said to specialize in growing maize, whereas others are net importers of the basic foodstuffs. The physical basis of specialization is further augmented by the juxtaposition of highland and lowland regions, with a consequent interchange of agricultural products of the temperate and cold country with those of the *boca costa* and the coastal hot lands. But specialization in the region is broader than agricultural diversity or the kinds of commodities produced; it extends to the way whole communities earn a livelihood and to trades and industries as well as agricultural products. In general the Indians of the area are nearly as dependent as modern urban dwellers on the exchange of products. Economic specialization of a community is a facet of its general cultural distinctiveness, and communities that have economic specialties likewise are individualized in other aspects of culture and society.

Around the lake, Panajacheleños grow onions and other vegetables and exploit the resources of the lake hardly at all (at least by traditional Indian canoes; with motor launches they are orienting more to the lake). In Santiago Atitlan, besides maize, canoes are produced, and the Atitecos are the leaders of the western end of the lake in navigational skills. They also provide many *commerciantes* who truck in the exchange of products between the *boca costa* and the highlands. San Pablo is a rope-

91

FIG. 5—BRINGING POTTERY TO SOLOLA MARKET FROM CHICHICASTENANGO AND TOTONICA-PAN, GUATEMALA. (From McBryde, 1934, fig. 17. Middle American Research Institute, Tulane University.)

FIG. 6—SOLOLA, GUATEMALA, MARKET GROUP. Indians of Santa Cruz selling tomatoes and limes to men from Chichicastenango. (From McBryde, 1934, fig. 16. Middle American Research Institute, Tulane University.)

92

making center, as is San Pedro across the lake. And as if to underline the cultural basis of specialization, San Pablo not only buys maize (from Santiago and San Pedro) but imports a good part of maguey from San Pedro, where it grows luxuriantly. San Pedro also produces a cash crop of chickpeas. Santa Catarina, only 2 miles from Panajachel, the municipio of tablón onion gardens, grows few vegetables but develops the lake resources of fishing and crabbing. The citizens there are as sensitive to the vagaries of the lake resources, as the Panajacheleños are insensitive.

The communities around the lake are integrated into market exchange via the major market at Solola, and a smaller solar center at Atitlan, the only daily market on the lake itself. Not only do the communities in the region participate in the regional rotating market center and in the local markets, but they are geared into other solar systems with interchange of products, and the emergence of full-time Indian *commerciantes,* who live from the profits of product interchange between markets.

There is another solar market system center around Quezaltenango and its broad open valley, and another around Huehuetenango. The regional markets around Quezaltenango serve and draw on other groups of specialized communities. Totonicapan makes pottery on the wheel, produces lumber, and weaves *huipiles.* Neighboring Chichicastenango makes no pots but uses its pine forests for lumber. Momostenango produces blankets and woolens, San Francisco mines lime, Salcaja turns out woven skirts and tie-dye materials, Cantel provides corn and cotton yard goods from electric mills, Almolonga and Zunil grow vegetables, and so on around the roster of economic specialties. Examples could be indefinitely multiplied. The points to be made are two: (1) A regional marketing system based on economic specialization moves products among communities in a solar system with a major central market (like So-

lola or Quezaltenango) and a subsidiary market (like Atitlan or the mushroom wholesale market of San Francisco El Alto, where every Friday thousands of Indians converge on a cold windswept town to turn it into a bustling center) and other smaller markets which have their special days. The system has grown up over time; it is not planned or regulated, but reflects the Indian response to economic opportunity. (2) The marketing system is an aspect of general cultural differentiation. It is not that individuals or families are so different from each other, but rather that whole communities have cultural traditions which vary from each other in endless small ways. Among these ways are the special crops, trades, and industries that come to economic actors because they happen to be members of one rather than another local society.

The facts of ecological variation, the proximity of highland and lowland, are the physical basis for the cultural and economic diversity of the region. It is the occurrence of distinct local societies, however, with strong endogamous tendencies, which inclines to restrict handicrafts, trades, and industries to a single community. The present distribution of agricultural patterns, handicrafts, and special skills is the result of the operation of comparative advantage over a long time, and shifts do take place. Apparently shifts in kind of crop (other things equal, like land availability) take place more easily and rapidly than the cultural incorporation of a new handicraft or industry. This, of course, is tied to the facts of enculturation, since a handicraft or industry passes from father to son, or mother to daughter, whereas an agricultural specialty will pass from adult to adult. In addition, Indians work for each other as agricultural laborers across community lines (as they work for Ladinos) and hence are able to learn agricultural techniques more readily. But even crop shifts in a community's inventory are not easily undertaken. Indians

93

FIG. 7—POTTERY VENDOR ON WAY TO MARKET, TENANGO, CHIAPAS, MEXICO.
(Middle American Research Institute, Tulane University.)

must compete with the already established way of making a living in their own community and with the reputation of the other producing communities in the market place. For example, potatoes of Todos Santos are less valued in the Quezaltenango region than potatoes of Nahuala, or the vegetables from Zunil are thought to be the best. Indians from these communities wear their distinctive costumes, which serve as "brand" identifications; and the customers assume that a man in the Todos Santos striped pants is selling his own potatoes, or that the blue-skirted Almolongera is selling her own vegetables, though this is often not the case. So there is some stickiness even in the transfer or diffusion of agricultural techniques and products. Specialties, of course, are subject to competition from both Indian and non-Indian producers. Many handicrafts have been lost, like the hat making of Aguacatenango which could not compete with factory-made hats, or the reduction in palm-leaf rain capes with the spread of cheap plastic tablecloths used as ponchos. Conversely, new things are stimulated through competition and contact: tourists who visit Chichicastenango favor a sort of risqué pattern on napkins; the Ladinos of Chiapas are the consumers of large pottery flowerpots. Skills and agricultural patterns change over time and in response to changing market conditions, in the context of possibilities of technique transfer and development among communities.

If the contention that ecological variation, highland-lowland proximity, and distinct local societies with endogamously tied skills and economic pursuits are what underlie the degree of specialization and, with it, the width of the market is true, then where these factors are diminished, the intensity of market relations and economic specialization should in turn diminish. A brief view of the solar systems of Oaxaca and around Lake Patzcuaro adds depth to this generalization. There the posited factors are present, as well as the regional mar-

94

ket systems, whereas in lowland Yucatan some of the factors are absent as they are among the Totonac or the Popoluca, and there the solar marketing system is also absent. The strength of the above variables changes from regional system to regional system, and thus the market patterns also shift. In the valley of Oaxaca, the city Oaxaca is the major sun around which the markets of Ocotlan, Tlacolula, are secondary planets, with satellite markets at Etla, Zimatlan, Totlapa, Atzompa (where real barter does in fact take place, as is also reported from the Cuchumatanes where corn is exchanged for pots, the amount of corn depending on the size of the pot), and other communities in the valley. The market system integrates the economically specialized communities and cultural variation among speakers of Zapotec, Mixtec, and Mixe (Malinowski and De la Fuente, 1957).

Around Patzcuaro (Foster, 1948c), Tzintzuntzan, and Santa Fe are pottery producers; Quiroga and Paracho specialize in wood and wood products, Janitzio and Ihuatzio in reed mats and fire fans, Jaracuaro in palm hats, Nahuatzen in cotton, and Santa Clara in copper. The regional interdependence is organized in the periodic market system, and the market shows the same features of being free, open, competitive, and hence very sensitive to fluctuations in supply and demand, with the corresponding changes in prices and price levels. The market system of Patzcuaro, like the other regional systems, is tied into the national and international markets, and its operation reflects price movement within this broader context. Around Patzcuaro, however, local societies are less distinct than in Guatemala or Oaxaca, and hence endogamy is less, and crafts pass more readily from adult to adult across community boundaries.

The distribution of specialized occupations and crops in the Chiapas region also confirms the generalization about the occurrence and intensity of market relations.

Fig. 8—SEMANA DE DOLORES FAIR, SOLOLA, GUATEMALA. Women selling bees' honey from Antigua. (From McBryde, 1947, pl. 4,b. Middle American Research Institute, Tulane University.)

Amatenango is a pottery-making community, where every woman who grows up in the community knows how to, and does, make pots. The neighboring community of Aguacatenango does not make a single pot, but keeps pigs as a supplement to its agricultural activities. The Chamulas are active traders and have a roster of handicraft spe-sheepherders; Tenango makes a different cialties; the Zinancantecos are farmers and sort of pottery from that of Amatenango. The ecological diversity, the highland-lowland proximity, and the distinctiveness of the local societies, maintained by high rates of endogamy, give rise to economic speciali-

95

Fig. 9—WOMEN SCRAPING SALT, SACAPULAS, EL QUICHE, GUATEMALA. (Photographed by Matilda Gray, 1935. Middle American Research Institute, Tulane University.)

zation and trade. But a solar market system is not found as it is now in parts of Tehuantepec. The markets tend to be in Ladino towns (like Las Casas, Teopisca, Comitan), where Indians come to buy and sell. Local markets occur in Indian communities on special festive occasions and only a few times a year in any village. The absence of solar markets may be attributed to the difficulties of communication between Indian communities (but the great extent to which Indians in Guatemala overcome difficulties of terrain in their treks to and from the market gives little weight to this contention), or it may lie in historical factors (like the greater and more recent political and ethnic unrest in Chiapas), or it may lie in some set of social and cultural features too broad to be caught in the net of variables here proposed.

The market, as an institution, rests on the free interplay of buyers and sellers, with price established through the interaction of buyers who are not large enough to set price and sellers who do not control enough

of the supply to affect the price. There is also the feature of impersonality in an open market system. Entry (as buyer or seller) is not restricted. Anyone who pays the small tax can enter the local markets and set up a stall, though in the city markets there are some larger installations requiring more outlay than many of the vendors can muster. The interaction between buyer and seller shows indifference to person, with attention only to price. In these markets, haggling and bargaining are characteristic but they are the means of establishing the going price, and shopping is the way of getting price information where price is not posted or advertised. Vendors of similar products are usually grouped together, and from the bids of buyers and the asking of sellers a price is quickly reached. The price prevails until there is some change in the supply and demand factors. Bargaining in any single transaction reflects the state of the market place as a whole, and the market place as a whole reflects the operation of the entire regional and national markets.

Fig. 10—NAHUA MASK MAKER, TUXTLA, GUERRERO, MEXICO. (Photographed by Donald Cordry, 1941.)

Looked at closely, these markets are a series of buyer-seller transactions, an exchange of money for goods. Except for some of the food sellers, some of the medical suppliers, and a few of the stores in the market or in the towns where markets are held (and to which people may be tied by credit), there does not exist a clientele for any seller, or a body of loyal customers for any purveyor of commodities. The market relationships are truly dyadic contract and fleeting (Foster, 1961a). This characteristic of the market is a symptom of a prevailing fact of the economic organization of Indian communities, a fact with far-reaching structural and economic consequences. Indian buyers and sellers in the market place are members of households, and they act as members of households. These households are economic units in only one of their aspects, and they tend to see the economic sphere as only one of the areas in which maintenance needs may be met. Households are limited in the numbers and kinds of persons they can recruit, the capital and savings they can command, the sort of economic opportunity to which they can respond. Given the fact that households, not firms, are the economic organizations around which the market economy is built, the limits of planning, continuity, scale, and technological complexity in economic life become readily apparent. What makes these economies different from a modern, dynamic economy with a built-in drive toward economic and technological develop-

97

Fig. 11—POTTERY AND KILN, CUERNAVACA, MORELOS, MEXICO. (Photographed by Hugo Brehme, date unknown.)

ment is thus clear. They do not lack economic rationality, the matching of means and ends for best outputs; they do not hedge economic activity with a host of traditional barriers; they do not despise wealth and hard work; and they exhibit the free market where each man follows his own economic interest. Thus they have the values, the markets, the pecuniary means of exchange, the ability to calculate, and the interest in economic activity. (In Mitla, Parsons [1936] complained that it was a "ritual of price" that marked these Zapotec, Malinowski and De la Fuente [1957] have spoken of a "commercial libido," and others have reported the keen interest in price and economic activity.) What is lacking is the social organization of an entity like the firm, an autonomous, corporate group dedicated to and organized for economic activity.

That such social organizations have not grown up in Indian communities is tied to the larger social structure and cultural pattern. The specialized communities with their distinctive cultural and economic cast, maintained through endogamy and organized around a variant of the civil-

religious hierarchy (Cámara, 1952c; Wolf, 1955b; Nash, 1958b), are not conducive to a social entity based strictly on economic ends. The communities are organized to protect their corporate existence and as such have specialized controls over the free use of accumulation of resources and mechanisms to insure a democracy of poverty. In the social structure of communities like Panajachel, Cantel, Santa Eulalia, or Santiago (Wagley, 1941) in Guatemala, or Amatenango, Aguacatenango, Zinacantan in Chiapas, or Mitla, Yalalag and others in Oaxaca, there operates a leveling mechanism. The leveling mechanisms (Wolf, 1955b; Nash, 1961) operate to drain the accumulated resources of the community for noneconomic ends, and to keep the various households, over generations, fairly equal in wealth. They are mechanisms to keep economic homogeneity within the community, so that socially important heterogeneity—age, sex, previous service to the community, control of or access to the supernatural—remains the basis of role differentiation. They militate against the rise of social classes based on wealth and economic power distinctions. The leveling mechanism rests on the following interrelated aspects: (1) Low level of technology and limited land, so that absolute wealth and accumulation are small in virtue of poor resources in relation to population and a technology which is labor intensive and not highly productive. (2) Fracture of estates by bilateral inheritance. Whatever is in fact accumulated in capital goods is scrambled among sons and daughters in nearly equal shares. Almost everywhere in the region bilateral inheritance prevails. The few places with patrilineal descent groups do not vest property rights in a corporation, but exhibit a pattern of division among the patrilineally related families. (3) Forced expenditure of time and resources in communal office. The posts in the civil and religious hierarchies require some loss of work time, and the higher the post the more time is lost and the more direct costs in taking on the post. (4) Forced expenditure by the wealthy in ritual. Those who have been skilled or lucky and have accumulated wealth must expend it for communal ends, chiefly in feasting and drinking, so that the wealth is consumed.

The leveling mechanism keeps the fortunes of the various households nearly equal and serves to ensure the shift of family fortunes from generation to generation. The sanctions behind the operation of the leveling mechanism are generally supernatural, with witchcraft as the means to keep the economic units oriented to the communal drains and claims on their wealth. These economies, then, are market—competitive, free, open—but set into a social structure without corporate units dedicated to and able to pursue economic ends. Working with a cultural pattern forcing the accumulation of wealth into noneconomic channels, and buttressed by a system of supernatural sanctions against those who do not use their wealth, they show a lack of dynamism, a technological conservatism almost equivalent to that of the most isolated communities, and an inability to seize and exploit or create economic opportunity.

This combination of features presents a startling social fact: the presence of markets, economic rationality, and money form a single complex, but in addition firms, credit mechanisms, deliberate technical and economic investment are needed for economic dynamism. The latter features are part of a social structure not found in the corporate peasantry of Middle America, and their coexistence in a single society (like our own) appears a historical precipitate rather than a functionally linked set of social characteristics. Experience in other parts of the world where the market economy is set into a social structure that is not modern in the sense of organizations dedicated to purely economic ends (i.e., the bazaars of the Arab world, the regional markets of Africa, or the peasant markets of Java and Haiti) leads to the expectation that such organizations do not develop from the dynamics of internal social and economic life but are a product of social change induced by pressures or privileges generated in the modern economy.

This survey of the broad type of economy in the regional marketing areas of Middle America has been taken from an aerial view, a height which may give rise to misunderstandings. The tendency toward economic homogeneity, for example, does not indicate that a given community or village is, at any one time, virtually without wealth differences. Lewis (1947) describes a three-class wealth division for Tepoztlan and relates it to the types of land and technology that different families own. Tax (1952c) finds a wealth division into quarters convenient for Panajachel, and describes the functions of wealth in officeholding, marriage choice, and prestige. Similarly, the emphasis on households as economic units appears to play down the role of the community as a property holder. Nowhere is land fully communal; nowhere is it fully in individual hands. Some lands (often the

99

Fig. 12—POTTERY MARKET, VERACRUZ, MEXICO. (Photographed by Hugo Brehme, date unknown.)

monte, scrub land, pasture land, or firewood land) is owned by the community and open to use by all members. Frequently there are means to prevent the sale of land from Indians to Ladinos (as in many communities in Chiapas). But the communal control of productive resources in the form of ownership was everywhere eroded and destroyed by the middle of the 1800's, and one of the persisting problems of the corporate communities has been to hold on to their territorial base. (In some respects the ejido program in Mexico has strengthened Indian communities, and in others, by introducing non-Indians into the community, has weakened it.)

Such studies as these on consumption patterns in corporate communities (Tax, 1957a), however, reinforce the contention that the Indian economic pattern, in terms of production, consumption, and organization tends to be discrete from the Ladino or Mexican. Even if a Mexican or a Guatemalan Ladino is poorer than an Indian, his style of life is the eroded version of a national culture, whereas the Indian contin-

ues to implement wants and tastes embedded in a local society. Some Indian societies have gone a long way toward economic Ladinoization and its attendant changes in life style and social structure; and places like Totonicapan in Guatemala, Tzintzuntzan and Tepoztlan in Mexico, may point the way to an understanding of how Indian economies get transformed into regional examples of the national economy, whether or not the process of economic modernization is carried very far.

If the quasi-tribal economies owe their structure to isolation, relative ecological homogeneity, and a reduced cultural tradition based on unintensive agriculture, and if the solar systems take their form and function from the factors outlined above, the third major type—the adjunct export economy—is more heterogeneous as are the forces underlying it. The adjunct export economies, from the viewpoint of the Indians, is an addition to the basic business of milpa agriculture. The milpa agriculture, touching self-sufficiency (as among the Popoluca and the Totonac), is not primarily a

100

market crop and forms the chief agricultural activity of the economic units. In addition to the growing and consuming of the milpa crops, there is, however, a cash crop, some item like coffee in Sayula, or vanilla among the Tajin Totonac, or sugar cane, or rice which is grown for the export economy. This is grown by adaptations of the basic, simple technology, with the same sorts of economic organizations, to be sold to Mexican or Ladino middlemen. The economic type is called adjunct to the export economy for obvious reasons. The cash crop is an overlay on the fundamental subsistence agricultural activities; the organization, processing, marketing, and profit making lie largely in hands other than the Indian producers (in and around Papantla the Totonac face a virtual monopoly among buyers and thus do not get a "fair" share of the proceeds of the vanilla trade, whereas in Sayula the coffee proceeds have got into the domestic economy at a much greater rate, with correspondingly greater social changes). The farmers operate in a dual economic frame, one part oriented to maintenance, the other to the export economy. In situations where crops can be rotated on the same fields (as can maize and vanilla) there are not many economic strains. Where fields can be used alternately for subsistence or for cash cropping there is often conflict among the local inhabitants. The cash cropping means stricter property rules and sometimes a full private-property emphasis, with permanent use of the fields and with permanent title, a custom sometimes in conflict with a more communal, rotating use of milpa lands based on usufruct rights.

The adjunct export economy can turn in various directions: (1) the stable dual sort as with the Totonac; (2) a movement toward a commercial peasantry, as with some of the Popoluca; (3) the development of a rural proletariat, as with the henequen workers of the Yucatan Peninsula. It is clear that the adjunct export economy is most likely to experience wide economic swings, and that movement, at least in economy, toward the rural variant of national culture is most likely here. Further voluntary organizations like the cooperative, or the labor union, and perhaps credit societies, are more likely to take root here.

Three major types fairly adequately encompass the major economic organizations of the Indians of Middle America. Each type is a distinct social form, with its own ecological, cultural, and economic setting, and each has its own dynamic and conditions of maintenance. The overriding presence of money, markets, economic calculations of actors, the concern with price, and the interest in and desire for expanded economic opportunities do not, however, as yet move any of the Indian economies into the category of a modern economy. It is the social and cultural context of economic operations which keeps the forms of Indian economic organization more or less distant from modernity. Perhaps the shift to modernity, the fracturing of corporate or quasi-tribal organization for the exploitation of economic opportunity, implies the loss of those mechanisms capable of sustaining the social structure in which a distinct Indian heritage is transmitted. Or, perhaps, and just as likely, people who have kept a cultural heritage alive through nearly five centuries of contact with a technologically and politically superordinate society may discover how to blend parts of their cultural heritage with those aspects of economic modernity now absent.

101

REFERENCES

Bennett and Zingg, 1935
Cámara Barbachano, 1952c
Foster, 1942, 1948c, 1961a
Grimes, 1961
Guiteras Holmes, 1952a
Kelly and Palerm, 1952
Lewis, 1947
McBryde, 1934, 1947
Malinowski and De la Fuente, 1957

Mintz, 1953
Nash, 1958b, 1961
Parsons, 1936
Redfield, 1941
Tax, 1937, 1952c, 1953, 1957a
Vogt, 1955
Wagley, 1941
Wolf, 1955b

6. Contemporary Pottery and Basketry

GEORGE M. FOSTER

The contemporary pottery of Mesoamerica represents, collectively, a product of Hispano-Indian acculturation. A typological spectrum can be defined, one end of which is represented by purely indigenous techniques, the other end, by purely Spanish techniques. The great bulk of production, however, represents a fusion of both Indian and European traits. Recent research makes it possible to tell, with a fair degree of accuracy, which are Indian and which are Spanish elements. Basketry likewise represents the product of acculturation, but our data are less complete, and it is less easy to say with certainty what are native American and what are Hispanic origins. Mesoamerican Indian artisans make both pottery and basketry; but perhaps in terms of total production more is produced by Mestizos than by Indians. How, then, should the scope of an article for an Indian Handbook be defined? By origin of the trait, or by the language and culture of the producer? There is no easy answer. Arbitrarily I have decided to include all basketry—the data are very thin at best —and all pottery other than that which represents the Spanish end of the typological spectrum, which will be described below.

POTTERY

For variety in pottery-making techniques and in materials, forms, styles, and economic importance, few places in the world rival Mesoamerica and, particularly, Mexico. Technical and stylistic proliferation is explained by the historic fusion of vigorous Spanish and native American pottery traditions, and the commercial importance of the work is a function of both a developing economy in which metal is still relatively expensive, and a deep-seated value judgment that says food cooked in pottery tastes better than food cooked in enamel ware or aluminum.

Pottery-making techniques, to which I give primary emphasis in this account, can be described most economically by breaking the process into a series of traits identified by historic origin and then discussing the combinations, distributions, and implications of these traits. The setting can perhaps best be grasped by considering the natures of the two basically distinct pottery

103

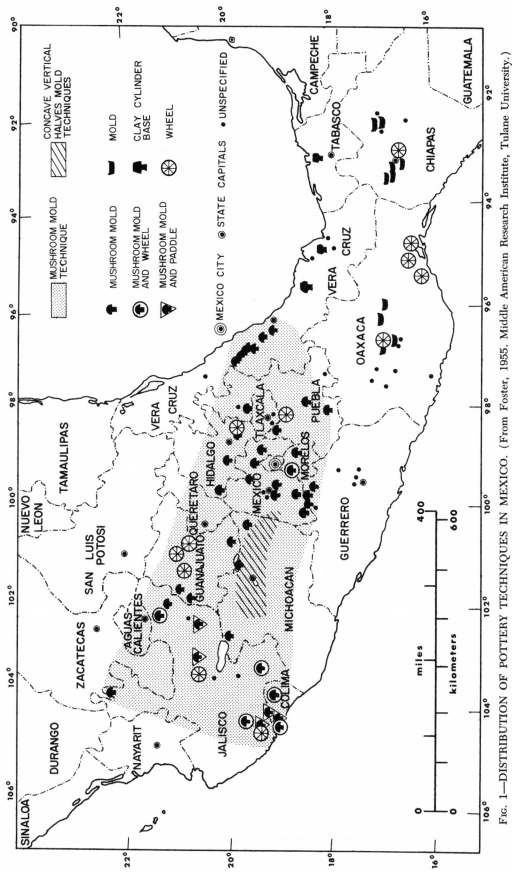

Fig. 1—DISTRIBUTION OF POTTERY TECHNIQUES IN MEXICO. (From Foster, 1955. Middle American Research Institute, Tulane University.)

FIG. 2—INDIAN WOMAN MAKING POTTERY, CIVACA, CHIAPAS, MEXICO. (From Blom and La Farge, 1927, fig. 298. Middle American Research Institute, Tulane University.)

traditions—Old World Spanish and New World Indian—that fused to give the present picture. In Spain male potters using the wheel produced simple glazed and unglazed utilitarian ware as well as artistic majolica and other more sophisticated types. In addition to the wheel two-piece molds of pottery, composed of concave vertical halves, and three-piece plaster of Paris molds were used. Large wine and olive jars were built up by coiling, and simple, pivoted turntables were known. Paste usually was prepared by levigation, but sometimes two earths were ground and mixed. Red slipped ware was burnished before firing, litharge and other glazes presumably were ground in tanks in which heavy boulders were dragged by animal power based on the *noria* wheel-and-sprocket system, and many mineral colors were used. Black oxygen-reduced finishes were known. Women participated in painting and decoration, but not in basic production, which often was carried on in small workshops. Firing of simple ware was accomplished in the primitive, circular open-topped Mediterranean kiln, which permits temperatures in the range of 900–1000°C., and majolica was fired in larger, domed kilns. A money economy had facilitated a system of naming and measuring sizes of vessels, and artistry had developed to a high point, with polychrome-glazed motifs of animals, birds, and flowers which continue to be reproduced to this day.

We can assume that in indigenous Mesoamerica female potters made most ware, forming vessels by hand modeling, by segmental building, with convex molds, and sometimes with a wooden paddle in conjunction with other techniques. These methods often were combined with the mobile base to facilitate work, and in Yucatan and adjacent areas this base probably had developed into the foot-turned *kabal*. Clays often were mined damp, and temper of sand, ground potsherds, ground rock, or, occasionally, vegetable fiber (cattail fluff in

105

some places, animal dung in others) was added. Metate-ground mixtures of two dry earths probably also were known. Real glazing was unknown, but burnished and unburnished polychrome slips were common, and the black oxygen-reduced technique was known. In marginal areas women produced for their kitchens and perhaps for a few neighbors. In populous areas a lively commerce existed, and this may well have stimulated men to take a major part in productive processes, particularly in the central Mexican mold-using area, where the family workshop may have existed. Men may also have made effigy ware. Kilns were unknown, and all firing was in the open. Concave vertical-halves pottery molds were used in Guatemala for effigy ware, but the technique probably was not used at all for utilitarian production.

Examples of both pure Spanish and pure Indian technologies survive in Mesoamerica: on the one hand, the wheel-made polychrome majolica of Puebla and other cities, and, on the other, the simple ware of the Seri, Mayo, and Popoluca. But more often blending in varying degrees has occurred, producing recognizable distribution areas characterized by clusters or associations of traits which, typologically, form a spectrum from Spanish to Indian. This is not a straight line spectrum, however, for the variety of combination of traits is such as to defy simple classification. For expository purposes I have singled out five basic techniques, all of which combine in a variety of ways with associated traits; I describe these techniques and then discuss their associations, distributions, and possible origins. (True wheel throwing is omitted, since it almost always is a non-Indian commercial-workshop urban enterprise.) These basic techniques are: (1) segmental building, (2) hand modeling from a lump of paste, (3) the mobile base, (4) convex pottery molds, and (5) concave vertical-halves pottery molds.

Segmental Building

In the simplest form of this method a rough saucer is shaped by hand to serve as a pot bottom, and the sides are built by the addition of daubs or coils of paste. In most cases the base rests in a pottery saucer or on a board so that the vessel may be turned as it is built. This technique usually, although not exclusively, characterizes marginal peoples and is associated with other simple pottery traits. The Seri coil pots in a dish (Kroeber, 1931, p. 17), the Mayo start with a clay cone punched into shape as a base to which coils are added (Beals, 1945a, pp. 39–41), and the Tarahumara rest the pot on a cloth over a sand-filled bowl while building (Bennett and Zingg, 1935, pp. 83–87). In Comanja and Cocucho, Michoacan (Tarascan), the bottom of the vessel rests in the open mouth of a broken pot, on which it is turned (West, 1948, p. 63). Mixe potters press out a clay base, place it in a pottery saucer, and finish the object with coils (Beals, 1945b, pp. 118–20). In Chinautla, Guatemala (Pokoman), the initial rough saucer is formed over the bottom of an old pot in a fashion that has been compared to the Southwestern *puki*, and the sides are built with coils (R. E. Smith, 1949, pp. 58–61). The usual make-the-bottom-first method is varied in Tajin, Veracruz (Totonac), where a cylinder is built of coils, the walls are expanded to final shape, and after drying the vessel is inverted and the paste drawn together to form the bottom (Kelly and Palerm, 1952, p. 217). Some of the big water-storage jars of the Rio Balsas look as if they have been made in this way.

In all these examples, which constitute the unchanged, aboriginal pottery base line, potters are women, a single clay tempered with sand, ground potsherds, or dung is used, glaze is absent, and firing is in the open. Forms are relatively few, usually limited to cooking pots and water-storage and carrying jars. Except in rare instances such

FIG. 3—SANTA MARIA ATZOMPA, OAXACA (ZAPOTEC). *a,* Beginning a large water jar; vessel supported on concavo-convex mobile base mold. *b,* Applying coils. *c,* Smoothing interior. *d,* Flat disc *molde* on unturned pot, for hand-modeling casseroles.

as in Guatemala, the Tzeltal communities of Amatenango and Tenango, the Tojolobal of Comitan, and Chinautla, production is very limited—for immediate use in the local area.

Coiling is also used in more sophisticated contexts, such as to finish vessels whose bottom part has been formed over convex molds or in association with mobile bases. The green-glaze water jars of Santa Maria Atzompa, Oaxaca (Zapotec), illustrate the latter method. A disc of paste of up to 45 cm. in diameter is placed in a large concavo-convex plate called *molde* (it is not strictly a mold in the usual sense), which revolves easily, and the sides are built up to the maximum height which still permits the potter to reach to the inside bottom fig. 3,*a–c*). The interior glaze for these big jars is prepared by men, using a Spanish type of man-powered grinding pit in which boulders are dragged over the litharge to pulverize it, and firing is done in the common Mexican kiln (Foster, 1955, pp. 4, 23–24). The coiling, however, is done by women; offhand I can think of no place in Mesoamerica where men engage in this activity.

It may be noted that in all examples except the Totonac and, perhaps, the Balsas Basin, the potter remains in one position, turning the vessel as she works it.

Hand Modeling from a Lump of Paste

This method, which may be used for a complete pot, is often combined with coiling and with mobile base techniques. In Oteapa, Veracruz (Aztec), the female potter places a sand-tempered paste cylinder on a leaf on a wooden stool. Then she rests her thumbs on the outside and presses down inside with her fingers to open the center. Next, with the left hand inside and the right hand outside, she backs continuously in a clockwise direction around the stationary vessel, pushing out the walls and smoothing them with a corncob. She does not mold the pot to full size until the fol-

lowing day, to prevent the moist paste from sagging. These pots, native American by every other test, are kiln-fired (Foster, field notes).

In Santa Apolonia, Guatemala (Cakchiquel), the female potter makes a cylinder of paste on the ground, opens it to the bottom, walks backward clockwise around it while forming the top half, inverts it, and closes the bottom. For larger pots the bottom is built up with a couple of coils. Firing is in the open (Arrot, 1953, pp. 3–10). A very similar technique is found in Guatajiagua, El Salvador (Lothrop, 1927b). Chorti women potters hollow a ball of paste, sometimes adding coils to build up the neck, and fire in a primitive circular kiln with cow dung, straw, and wood (Wisdom, 1940, p. 167).

Often in hand modeling, especially of larger vessels, it will be noted, the pot remains stationary and the potter works around it.

An unusual variant of hand modeling is found in Tres Zapotes, Veracruz; Tapotzingo, Tabasco (Chontal); and Soteapan, Veracruz (Sierra Popoluca). In the last-named place a female potter places a sand-tempered paste cylinder on a banana or berijao leaf resting on the ground. The top two-thirds of the cylinder is hollowed out to form the vessel, leaving the bottom third as a pedestal, which is hand-turned. When the vessel is formed it is inverted, the pedestal is cut off with a machete or maguey fiber, and after drying the resulting pot is open-fired (Foster, 1955, pp. 3, 22, 32).

Except for the occasional use of a kiln, all hand-modeling techniques appear to be purely aboriginal.

The Mobile Base

In Yucatan, Campeche, Chiapas, Oaxaca, and in Acatlan, Puebla, a hand- or foot-turned mobile base is used in conjunction with segmental building and/or hand modeling. In its simplest form this *molde*, as it is called in Oaxaca and Chiapas, is a pot-

Fig. 4—POTTERY TECHNIQUES. *a–c,* San Bartolo Coyotepec, Oaxaca (Zapotec). *a,* Pair of *moldes,* supporting finished vessel. *b,* Doña Rosa Real working with *moldes. c,* Don Maximino Mateo making a large mescal olla on *moldes. d,* Tzintzuntzan, Michoacan. Doña Natividad Peña making a plate on a mushroom mold. *e,* Acatlan, Puebla. Detail of *kabal*-like foot-turned *parador.*

tery or wooden plate or saucer which turns easily so the potter may remain in one position as he or she works. One form already has been mentioned for Santa Maria Atzompa, Oaxaca. In the same village a second form is a pottery disc of up to 40 cm. in diameter, which is balanced by a female potter on the bottom of an upturned pot. A lump of paste big enough for the vessel is patted into a thick disc, laid on the molde, and the sides curved up around the potter's hand to form a casserole (fig. 3,*d*). All the

time the potter rotates the molde so she can work all sides of the vessel (Foster, 1955, p. 24). In Ocozocoautla, Chiapas (formerly Zoque), the molde is a circular board which rests on a second board in such fashion that it turns easily. The female potter places a lump of paste on the molde, digs the inside out with her fingers, discards this paste, and proceeds to finish the vessel. Similar techniques are used in nearby Ocuilapa (Zoque) and Beriosabal (formerly Zoque). Women appear to be the potters in these

109

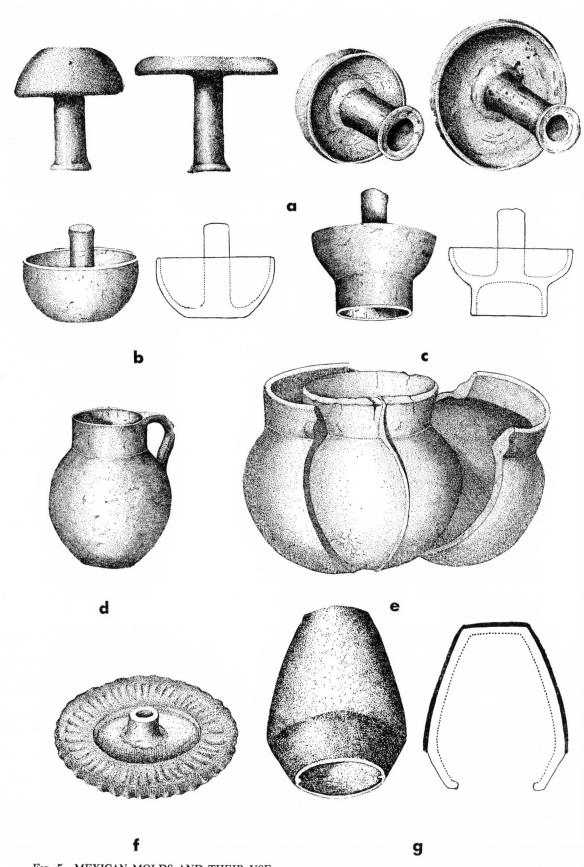

FIG. 5—MEXICAN MOLDS AND THEIR USE

a, Mushroom molds from Tzintzuntzan, Michoacan. *b-d*, Metepec, Mexico. *b*, Mushroom mold for base of pot; *c*, for upper half; *d*, the completed pot. *e*, Concave vertical-halves molds from Tzintzuntzan. *f*, Texcoco, Mexico, showing nubbin handle. *g*, Cuernavaca; mushroom-type mold without handles; section shows clay placed to form base and sides. (After Foster, 1948b, figs. 1–5.)

villages, but common kilns are used, showing Spanish influence (Foster, 1955, pp. 25–27).

The molde reaches its most astonishing development in San Bartolo Coyotepec, Oaxaca (Zapotec), where a pair of concavo-convex saucers balanced on the convex sides (fig. 4,*a*) permit routine rotation at speeds of 60 rpm and, in the case of Doña Rosa Real (fig. 4,*b*), up to 90 rpm! Small vessels are made from a single lump of paste, punched out to approximately the form of an unblocked felt hat, and then placed on the molde for finishing and smoothing. Large jars, such as 25-liter mescal containers, are built up from the same base with coils (fig. 4,*c*). The high speeds, in which centrifugal force is noteworthy, are reached only in finishing the rims and necks; the result, needless to say, is difficult to distinguish from wheel-thrown pottery (Foster, 1959a; Van de Velde and Van de Velde, 1939).

The Mayan *kabal* also must be classed as a variant of the basic southern Mexican molde. Although brief accounts of this foot-turned base have intrigued anthropologists for over half a century, it was not until R. H. Thompson's fine monograph (1958) that a complete description was placed on record. In its classic form, the kabal is a wooden cylinder 10–16 cm. in diameter and 6–10 cm. high (*ibid.*, fig. 18). The potter sits barefooted on a low stool, turning the kabal with his feet (and occasionally his hands) as he forms the vessel. Segmental building, direct modeling, and a combination of the two techniques are used, although not all in the same village (*ibid.*, figs. 20–25). Temper usually is a pulverized unconsolidated limestone. Both men and women use the kabal, but there are village distinctions. The highest speeds appear to be in the 10–30 rpm range.

A variant kabal, a heavy shallow pottery bowl on which a wooden disc rests, replaces the standard form in Mama; it is used in the same fashion as the kabal in other villages (*ibid.*, fig. 18,*h,i*). This kabal is nearly identical to the *parador* and *ladrillo* combination used by male potters in Acatlan, Puebla (formerly Mixtec). Coiled ware is made in Acatlan on the parador (= Mama kabal) in much the same fashion as in Yucatan (fig. 4,*e*), but other vessels are first formed over heavy convex molds of the approximate size and shape of the finished pots (fig. 6,*a,b,c*) (Foster, 1960b). Until the 1958 discovery of the Acatlan parador, the kabal was thought to be purely Mayan. Its wider distribution is now apparent, and we must assume that formerly it was used in intervening areas.

Historically the kabal, molde, and parador probably represent evolutionary developments from a common ancestor. In many parts of the world simple unpivoted mobile bases of pottery or wood are used as pottery-making aids. In southern Mexico this widespread tool has developed well beyond its usual limits, producing on the one hand the kabal-parador and on the other the fast-spinning Coyotepec molde. In spite of the kiln generally found associated with the mobile base, the basic techniques certainly are preconquest. Not surprisingly, kabal-made pottery has been compared to wheel-made pottery in appearance and symmetry (e.g., Brainerd, 1946, 1949). Since with the kabal, however, centrifugal force plays little or no role in shaping vessels, analogies with the wheel are misleading (Shepard, 1956, pp. 60–63; R. H. Thompson, 1958, pp. 139–44; Foster, 1959b).[1] On the other hand, maximum speeds of the Coyotepec molde fall within the range of those of the wheel, and in the formation of necks and rims centrifugal force plays an important role. On the basis of this, and much other evidence, I have suggested that the potter's wheel may well be the result of an evolu-

[1] E.g., "The *kabal* is not a primitive potter's wheel but an unpivoted mobile pottery support which is turned by the feet. The *kabal* is unique only because no other case of a foot-turned mobile pottery support is known in the New World" (R. H. Thompson, 1958, p. 144).

a   b   c

FIG. 6—ACATLAN, PUEBLA. *a,* First step in use of potlike mold. *b,* Smoothing paste over the mold. *c,* Mold and paste set in sand in *parador* prior to removal of mold.

tionary sequence beginning with some unknown fast-spinning base similar to the Coyotepec molde (Foster, 1959b, pp. 115–16).

Convex Pottery Molds

In a widespread area in central Mexico (fig. 1; recent data extend the area north to Durango) the most common pottery technique is to shape a paste tortilla over the exterior of a convex pottery mold. Small and medium-sized molds usually have a handle, which gives them their characteristic "mushroom" appearance (fig. 5,*a,b*). The potter holds the mold by the handle in the left hand, drops the paste tortilla over with the right, makes the paste conform smoothly with a wet stone scraper, and then trims the surplus with a maguey fiber or horsehair, one end of which is held with the teeth (fig. 4,*d*). This type of mold can be used only for forms in which the mouth is at least as wide as the widest interior diameter of the pot or partial pot; otherwise it could not be withdrawn. Incised designs on the top of the mold produce bas-relief de-

signs on the inside bottom of vessels so made, so this type of mold is particularly useful in making grinding bowls *(molcajetes).* Plates, saucers, bowls, casseroles, and tortilla griddles *(comales)* commonly are made with this mold; they can be formed completely in one operation and need only smoothing before firing.

This technique is used also to form the bottom of vessels which will be finished by one of several other techniques, including the use of coils, additional molds, the paddle, and the wheel. In Tzintzuntzan, Michoacan (formerly Tarascan), casserole walls frequently are raised with a single roll of paste, and in Ocoyoacac, Mexico, the base of a 40-cm.-tall unglazed water jar is formed over a handleless pottery mold while the remainder is formed by coiling (Foster, 1955, p. 4).

In such important pottery towns as Metepec and Texcoco, Mexico, two halves cast from the same mold are stuck together, their rims moistened to facilitate joining. Then a circular hole is cut in the top, and the neck and rim are added by hand or, occasionally, by a special neck mold. More often in the state of Mexico the top half is formed with a distinct mold (fig. 5,c) which requires a crescent-shaped rather than a circular paste slab. Pulque jars usually are made in this way (fig. 5,d).

A second major type of convex pottery mold has been recorded in Acatlan, Puebla (Foster, 1960b; also mentioned above), San Anton barrio in Cuernavaca, Morelos (Foster, 1955, pp. 14–15), and San Jose Tateposco, Jalisco (P. S. Taylor, 1933a). This is a full-size vessel that resembles a completed pot (fig. 6), sometimes with decorated rim or shoulder, but heavier than a normal pot to support the stresses of molding (fig. 5,g). These molds are inverted on the ground while paste tortillas are placed and made to conform as far down as the shoulder. Methods of completion vary greatly in these three towns. In Acatlan the molded form is placed upright in a sand-filled parador and finished by hand (fig. 6,b). In San Anton small vessels so made are placed on a wheel for finishing; large vessels rest upright on the ground and the potter walks around them. In Tateposco the paste is made to conform to the upturned mold with a *talache,* a pottery, anvil-like tool with hooked handle. The semiformed vessel dries a day and then is placed right side up on a *yagual,* a cylindrical pottery stand, and finished with a paddle-and-anvil technique in which the potter's left hand serves as anvil. Curiously, the talache, a ready-made anvil, is never used as such. The potter, always a woman, backs clockwise around the vessel as she works.

The technique of using a wooden paddle with the hand as an anvil to finish the top of moldmade sections is also reported in Colima and Paticajo, both in Colima state, and Tonala, San Ignacio Cerro Gordo, and Pueblo Nuevo (old Cuautitlan), all in Jalisco. Depending on the town, either men or women or both use the paddle. This technique, with a limited west-central Mexican distribution (fig. 1), is probably indigenous,

even though it is associated with Spanish-introduced elements such as the kiln. The nearest distributional occurrences are in the American Southwest, with much simpler basic techniques.

In roughly the same geographical area, moldmade pot bottoms are also finished on a simple kick wheel. In the cities of Colima and Aguascalientes, and in Tonala, Autlan, Tuxpan, and Encarnacion, in Jalisco, mushroom-molded bottom halves are placed on a wheel and finished with coils. In 1955, before I appreciated the difference between true wheel-throwing and simple turning, I classified this as wheelwork. But the wheel is not used in this context to throw pots and serves simply as a greatly improved mobile base to finish more rapidly pots previously constructed in traditional fashion. The overlapping geographical distributions suggest the possibility that the mold-and-wheel technique in some places has replaced the mold-and-paddle technique, but there is no sure evidence (fig. 1).

The kick wheel is also used to finish pots in Ixtaltepec, Oaxaca (Zapotec), in the Isthmus of Tehuantepec. Here a rough hat-shaped vessel is punched out of a lump of clay, in the same way as a pot is begun in Coyotepec. This is then placed on a bat, in turn placed on the wheel, which is turned in both directions at varying speeds while the potter finishes the object (Foster, 1959b, pp. 111–12). It must be emphasized that the pot is not "thrown" but merely finished off. But, as is true for wheel-thrown pottery, only men use the wheel in these contexts.

Handleless convex pottery molds have been found in Mexico, so the trait is certainly preconquest. Further evidence comes from archaeological specimens that have an interior horizontal weld-mark which was not removed when two molded sections were joined.[2] I suspect more molds and

[2] The forms and implications of weld-marks on archaeological and modern ware are discussed by Foster, 1955, pp. 6–8.

113

a   **b**

Fɪɢ. 7—INDIAN WOMEN FIRING POTTERY, CHINAUTLA, GUATEMALA. (Photographed by Middle American Research Institute, Tulane University, 1937.)

Fɪɢ. 8—FIRING POTTERY, AMATENANGO, CHIAPAS, MEXICO. (From Blom and LaFarge, 1927. Middle American Research Institute, Tulane University.)

114

mold fragments than are recorded actually have been dug up, since most archaeologists are little aware of the variety of forms they take. Archaeologists with Mesoamerican experience, to whom I have shown Acatlan molds without revealing their function, have told me they would describe them as pots; they were surprised to learn their true purpose. Because of its apparent absence among archaeological specimens, the handle which gives the mushroom shape appears to be a postconquest innovation, although not necessarily a Spanish importation, since this form is not found in that country.[3]

The use of convex molds and associated techniques permits more rapid production than hand modeling or coiling. Perhaps because of this, and attendant market demands, both men and women usually use them. Spanish techniques, particularly the kiln and glazing, usually are also a part of this type of work.

Concave Vertical-Halves Pottery Molds

In highland Michoacan, with a western extension to Tonala, Jalisco (fig. 1), a pair of concave pottery molds joined vertically is used for the most common ware (fig. 5,e). The process is most thoroughly described by Foster (1948a, pp. 81–84). Shield-shaped tortillas of paste are pressed into each half, smoothed into shape, and trimmed at the edges. Then the halves are joined, the paste smoothed inside, and after brief drying the molds are removed. The rough outside ridge left by the juncture of the molds is then polished off and the weld-mark nearly or entirely disappears. Vessels so made are finished in a variety of ways with handles and glazes. As in the use of convex molds— also common in these villages—both men

---

[3] The possible lines of evolution of New World molds, from molding over upturned pot bottoms on one hand, and from pottery anvils that grew beyond normal sizes on the other, are discussed by Foster, 1948b, pp. 360–67.

and women use vertical-halves molds. Although this technique is particularly associated with the Tarascan area (Patamban, Santa Fe, Tzintzuntzan) and although this type of mold is known archaeologically from Guatemala, the modern technique is almost certainly Spanish: none of the archaeological ware from this region which I have examined shows the characteristic weld-marks; no archaeological molds have been found; the system is known in Spain; Spanish-type glaze is used wherever the technique is known; and firing is in the primitive Mediterranean kiln—this is a region in which many Spanish arts and crafts were early introduced and intensively fostered.

Diagnostic Criteria Other than Mode of Manufacture

Although mode of manufacture seems to me to be the most significant diagnostic criterion in Mesoamerican pottery making, mention must be made of other features to complete the picture of the process. It has been noted that for the most primitive techniques—segmental building and hand modeling—there is usually a single clay tempered with sand, crushed rock, or crushed potsherds. Vegetable temper is found in two forms: horse, burro, or jackrabbit dung among the primitive Mayo and Seri potters, and *plumilla* (cattail fluff) among the sophisticated potters of Riotenco San Lorenzo, Metepec, Texcoco, and San Sebastian Teotihuacan, all mushroom-mold users in the state of Mexico. In most of central Mexico as well as in some marginal areas, it is customary to mix two earths, frequently a reddish and a whitish one, first crushing them with boulders and either grinding them on a metate or sieving them. Water is then added and the paste is prepared much like bread dough. When two earths are mixed, granular or other temper per se usually is not added. Only clay for the simplest pottery techniques is mined damp. Levigation, a common Spanish technique, is used but sparingly in Mexico, and then usually only in association with the wheel and workshops.

Of modern wares, the most ancient finishes appear to be a white-buff-light-brown slip with simple red-brown-coffee decoration; they are found on the Rio Balsas jars, and in other marginal areas such as Oteapa, Veracruz. Usually but not invariably this ware is fired without a kiln. The more sophisticated moldmade wares of central Mexico, when not glazed, are likely to be red-slipped, sometimes burnished and kiln-fired. Oxygen-reduced black ware, on which a design is burnished with metal or chert, has long been the trademark of Coyotepec, and recently it has been taken up in other towns such as Acatlan, Puebla, and Tzintzuntzan, Michoacan, largely in response to tourist demand. In Tzintzuntzan the black color is obtained by taking a red-hot red-slipped vessel from the kiln and covering it for a minute or two with a mixture of sawdust and horse dung. Glazing techniques are all Spanish in origin, and usually are applied to mold- and wheel-made ware, rather than to the more primitive forms. But there is much overlap, as evidenced by the beautiful green interior glaze of large coiled water jars and hand-modeled casseroles of Atzompa, Oaxaca. Most, if not all, of the common transparent red-brown glaze is a commercial litharge mixed with a chalky binder. Various other commercial colors are used to obtain different finishes. Perhaps the most unusual Mexican finish is that of the wheel-made "Mitla" design of Oaxaca, where a lacquer-like technique is used. A white slip over a brown base is allowed to dry, and is then excised to the original brown base, leaving the design in mosaic-like white and brown bas-relief similar to Mitla walls (Foster, 1955, fig. 7,c–d).

Open firing, without a kiln (fig. 7), is found in marginal areas associated with simple segmental building and hand model-ing. Firing time averages from one-half to one hour, and low temperatures make a fragile ware. The primitive Mediterranean kiln early introduced from Spain permitted temperatures of up to 1000°C., which in turn allowed the introduction of good-quality glazes. The most widespread kiln is circular, from 1 to 1.5 m. in diameter, with the firebox sunk 0.6 m. into the ground. An excavation on one side permits access to the firebox door. The grate, of fused stone supported on a central pillar, is at ground level, and the pot chamber rises another 0.6–0.7 m. above ground. In some places, such as Metepec and Texcoco, Mexico, the entire kiln is above ground and, rarely, as in Coyotepec, it is below ground. A few kilns, such as those of Acatlan, Puebla, have no grates, so that what results is little more than an open fire in which the heat is reflected by the walls.

Unglazed ware is fired once in kilns, beginning with a very slow fire and building up over six hours to maximum temperature. Cooling requires another six hours or so. Glazed ware is fired a second time at a higher temperature. Less time is spent in heating the kiln, since moisture already has been expelled from the pots, but the hottest of fuels must be used to bring the ware to a near white-hot transparency. Most firing occurs at night when kiln temperatures can readily be estimated by the color of the flames that escape through the potsherd cap that is placed over a kiln. A glaze firing is considered complete if when a white-hot vessel is removed with a stick and tapped it rings like a bell.

Spanish influence is reflected in important central Mexican pottery-making towns by a system of nomenclature which distinguishes size. This system is described for Tzintzuntzan (Foster, 1948a, pp. 84–88). Briefly, it is based on the price of the vessel at some far-back time in terms of the Spanish *real*, the eighth part of a peso. The largest vessel is a *de a 2 reales*, i.e., a two-real size, followed by the *de a medio*, or

116

half-real. Smaller sizes are *de a 4, de a 6, de a 8,* and *de a 10,* indicating the number that could be purchased for a half-real.

This elaborate naming system points up an important characteristic of much Mexican pottery: it is made in enormous quantities for the market, and presumably this has been true since before the conquest. The importance of the market suggests certain revisions in beliefs about pottery which were stated in earlier anthropological reports. Specifically, handmade pottery was often assumed to be the work of women and wheel-made pottery that of men. The rationale was that the invention of the wheel made possible vastly increased production, with consequent market development. The woman potter, who previously produced for her kitchen, was unable to keep up with the new technique developed by men, so she abandoned the field to them. I am inclined to believe, however, that this hypothesis may have the cart before the horse. Potters are notoriously conservative; they change techniques only under duress. It is possible that growth of a pottery market preceded the invention of the wheel, thereby stimulating potters to improve techniques. Segmental building and hand-modeling methods cannot completely supply a vigorous market. Production with the use of molds and wheels is much faster. Hand throwing on primitive, poorly balanced wheels was perhaps too strenuous for women, so they gave up the wheel in a new market economy. But in Mexico, without the wheel, both sexes took to molds, and today in major pottery towns where this technique predominates, both sexes are potters. Sex division in pottery is perhaps a function of a market demand rather than exclusively a function of technique.

BASKETRY

Mesoamerican basketry is reasonably homogeneous with respect to materials, techniques, forms, terminology, and uses. Batalla (1945) identifies the most common Mexican materials, which include a variety of plants of the Gramineae family commonly called *otate* and including *Arthrostylidium racemiflorum* Steud., *Arundinaria longifolia* Fourn., and *Bambusa arundinacea* Roxb.; *carrizo* reeds such as *Arundo donax* L. and *Phragmites communis* Trin.; tules of several varieties of the Ciperaceae family; the common willow; and great numbers of "palms," such as *Chamaerops humilis* L., *Acanthorhiza mocinni* (H.B.K.) Benth. et Hook., *Brahea dulcis* (H.B.K.) Mart., *Carludovica palmata* R. et Pav., *Beaucarnea inermis* (Wats.) Rose, and *Dasylirion acrotriche*.

In Mesoamerica proper, the most common weaving techniques are twilled, wickerwork, and open coil. Checkerwork has a more limited distribution, and twined work appears sporadically. Tight coils appear only in northwest Mexico, where they represent an extension of Southwestern United States occurrences. Baskets of the general Apache-Pima-Papago type are found among the Seri (fig. 9,*a,* center), Yaqui, Mayo, and archaeologically as far as the Tarahumara. The technique appears to be a splint foundation with simple interlocking coils. Alternating light and dark brown sewing material gives designs similar to those of the American Southwest. Figure 9,*b* shows modern plain twined work from Cañon de Manteca, Baja California; this represents a southern limit of more northern techniques. Plain twined work is used sparingly in the Lake Patzcuaro area (Michoacan) in weaving tules in human forms and as bottle covers. O. T. Mason (1904, p. 526) says the technique is used for slings in Tlaxcala and is known archaeologically in Coahuila, and I have seen examples from Tlamacasapa, Guerrero. The wrapped-twine method is used for baskets of dyed palm in Juchitan, Isthmus of Tehuantepec (Zapotec); Kelly and Palerm (1952, p. 225) report the same technique among the Tajin Totonac to fasten cross-pieces to fence and house posts.

117

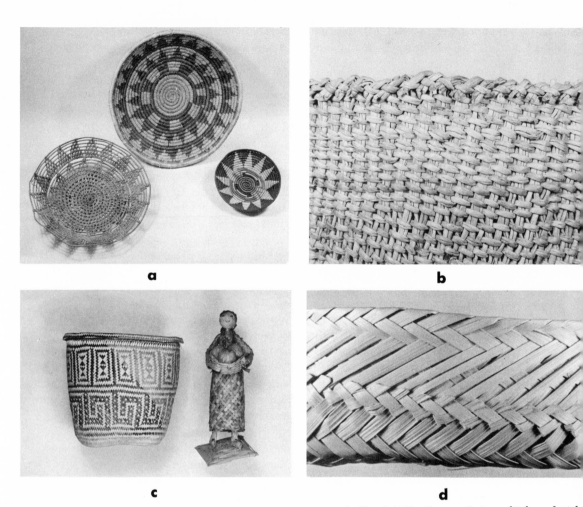

FIG. 9—BASKETRY. *a,* Coiled basketry. *Left:* Mayo, open coil, No. 3-3190. *Center:* Seri, multiple rod tigh coil, No. 3-3159. *Right:* (probably) Toluca, polychrome tight coil, No. 3-22413. *b,* Cañon de Manteca, Baj California, plain twined detail, No. 3-15329. *c,* Puebla palm weaving. *Left:* pliable twilled basket. *Right:* check erwork human figure. *d,* Arechuyvo, Chihuahua (Warihío [Guaraheo]), diagonal overlay twill, No. 3-13046. Speci men numbers are those of the Robert H. Lowie Museum of Anthropology, University of California, Berkeley.

Wisdom (1940, p. 162) speaks of a "fine type" of twined basketry made by Ladinos and a few Indians near San Juan Hermita (Guatemala), which he footnotes as identical to that LaFarge and Byers (1931, p. 60) call "twined" in Jacaltenango, but which in the latters' diagram appears to be twilled. Palm, tule, and carrizo reeds appear to be the most common twined materials.

Checkerwork, used particularly for palm and tule, seems best adapted for human

FIG. 10—BASKETRY. *a,* Central Mexico style, carrizo wickerwork warp strips in bottom of circular *canasto,* No. 3-22561. *b,* Soteapan, Veracruz (Popoluca), south Mexican-Guatemalan style carrizo wickerwork warp strips in basket bottom, No. 3-14967. *c,* Soteapan, Veracruz (Popoluca), warp strips intertwined just before release. *d,* Soteapan, Veracruz (Popoluca), beginning the weaving. *e,* Soteapan, Veracruz (Popoluca), completing the basket. *f,* San Juan del Rio, Queretaro, willow wickerwork market basket with three-strand warp border, No. 3-522.

118

a

b

c

d

e

f

FIG. 11—MEXICAN FIRE FANS. *Upper left:* Tlamacasapa, Guerrero, double weave twill in dyed palm, No. 3-22562. *Lower right:* Lake Patzcuaro, Michoacan (Tarascan) simple twill in tule, No. 3-22565. *Lower left,* No. 3-22563, and *upper right,* No. 3-22567, twilled work in palm from central Mexico.

where very pliable waste-basket shapes and *petate* mats are woven with attractive designs in red, green, purple, and yellow (fig. 9,*c*, left). Single weaves predominate, but double weaves occur sufficiently often to show the technique is widely known: e.g., Yaqui, Huichol, Tepehuane, Tarahumara (Bennett and Zingg, 1935, p. 87), fire fans from Tlamacasapa, Guerrero (fig. 11, upper left), and a curious variant type from Arechuyvo, Chihuahua, in which one element is doubled back over the completed section to form a diagonal overlay design (fig. 9,*d;* O. T. Mason, 1904, p. 526, pl. 237 for Yaqui). In the more common double twill the strips, one of which may be dyed, remain parallel so that a design appears on one side of the object while the other is plain.

Twilled weave is used generally for petate mats of palm and tule, for most fire fans, for hats, both when woven in one piece and when sewn from plaits, and for the ubiquitous nesting palm baskets with tight-fitting covers. Many small circular baskets, of the type called *tascal* in Tarascan, are of coarse herringbone weave in split carrizo reed, and are used primarily to store the day's supply of tortillas. The same material and technique also work well for much larger general-storage baskets.

Wickerwork, either of split carrizo reed or willow, is the common technique used for market baskets, carrying baskets, and general-storage baskets. Carrizo containers usually are circular with flat or flattish bottoms and straight or outward-slanting sides. Warp elements are formed by the opened stiff shell of the carrizo, and weft elements consist of narrow strips of the same material. At first glance nearly all carrizo wickerwork looks as if it might have come from the same place. Inspection reveals, however, a major geographical subdivision in the way the warp is started. In central Mexico warp strips simply are laid across each other (fig. 10,*a*). In southern tropical Mexico (e.g., Sierra Popoluca) and Guatemala they are intertwined under tension (fig.

and animal figures, as woven in the states of Puebla (fig. 9,*c*, right), Oaxaca, and Michoacan. Coarse fiber fans in tropical Mexico and Guatemala also are done in this fashion. Checkerwork probably is limited in use because for most things a far more attractive effect can be obtained, with essentially the same degree of skill, with the twill technique.

I have examined specimens or read of twilled work all the way from the Mayo-Yaqui area to the Chorti of Guatemala. Perhaps the finest is the dyed-palm work from Chimecatitlan and Tepeji, Puebla,

120

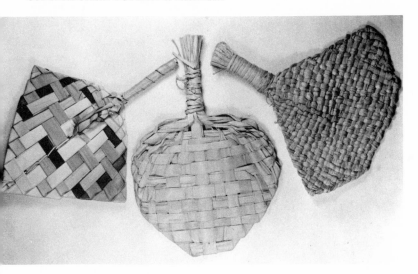

FIG. 12—MEXICAN AND GUATEMALAN FIRE FANS. *Left:* Ixtepec, Oaxaca (Zapotec), combination checkerwork and twill in dyed palm, No. 3-22564. *Middle:* Veracruz, plain palm checkerwork, No. 3-22566. *Right:* San Antonio Agua Caliente, Guatemala, plain checkerwork, No. 3-120.

10,*c)* so that when they are released a tightly locked star-shaped warp pattern results (fig. 10,*b).* Figure 10,*d,e* shows the further weaving of this specimen.

Willow wickerwork most commonly takes the form of the flat-bottomed, flaring-sided bail-handle European market basket, best known in Mexico from San Juan del Rio, Queretaro, specimens. In a common type the rim is finished by turning the warp elements to the right to form what O. T. Mason (1904, p. 262) calls a "three-strand warp border." These elements continue downward, and then turn upward to the right before terminating, to form a flounce of the same construction (fig. 10,*f).* In some baskets design elements are obtained by dyeing some of the willow, but more often today gaudy, tasteless designs are smeared on in paint after the basket has been completed.

Mexican open-coil work is known to all tourists who visit the Toluca market. Generally it is woven on a thick splint foundation with palm sewing to completely wrap the foundation. Every several wrappings the weaver goes to the adjacent coil, and then returns to wrap this extension in a kind of half-hitch before going on (fig. 9,*a,* right). This ware, made in much of central Mexico, often is ornamental, design elements being obtained both by varying the color of the wrapping palm, and by varying the spacing of the half-hitch tying (fig. 9,*a,* left). I do not know if coilwork of any kind extends into Guatemala.

Basketry types are called by many local Indian names, but a few words and concepts are ubiquitous. The term *chiquihuite* (Nahuatl *xiquihuitl*) is used generally in Mexico and Guatemala for a variety of objects in both Indian and non-Indian communities. Redfield (1928, p. 36) and Parsons (1936, p. 32) describe it as splint-coiled work; Hendrichs Pérez (1945, pp. 55–57) reports its use as a fish trap in the Rio Balsas; De la Fuente (1949, p. 47) describes it as round and of carrizo, a material usually used in wickerwork rather than coiling; and in the Lake Patzcuaro area it is carrizo wickerwork. In both Mexico and Guatemala a *canasta* must have a handle whereas a *canasto* does not.

In addition to baskets and mats, fire fans, known as *aventadores* and *sopladores,* and hats may be noted. Fans usually are twilled of various types of palm, the finest of which is the ornamental double-twilled work of Tlamacasapa, Guerrero (fig. 11, upper left). Each weaving center has a favorite handle

121

FIG. 13—SERI INDIAN BASKET MAKER, PUNTA CHUECA, SONORA, MEXICO. She is using the traditional tool, a bone of a mule deer. (Photographed by Donald Cordry, 1963.)

type: bail, single, double, triple or, occasionally, no handle at all. Diamond-shaped fans from southern Mexico and Guatemala, sometimes with a truncated tip, have a single handle projecting from one corner. These, and the crude Veracruz fans woven from a single palm frond, usually are in checkerwork (fig. 12). In tule territory, such as Lake Patzcuaro and the Toluca Valley, fire fans are of this material (fig. 11, lower right).

A few hats are palm-twilled, blocked from a single mat, or formed in two pieces, of crown and brim. Most hats, however, are made from twilled palm strips subsequently sewn together either by hand or, increasingly, by machine. In Colima, my field notes show, the finest plaits have seven or eleven strands, whereas in the Balsas Basin, Hendrichs Pérez (1945, pp. 101–03) reports that the finest have seven, but, owing to the demands of commerce, more rapidly produced three-strand plaits are used increasingly.

122

F_{IG}. 14—ZAPOTEC BASKET MAKER, TLACOLULA, OAXACA, MEXICO. (From F. Starr, 1899, pl. 86.)

Basketry styles have changed greatly over the past 50 years. Hat crowns have become much lower and brims less wide. Open-coiled-work basketry has proliferated, and increasingly gaudy designs are used. Many fire fans have acquired handles of angels or human beings, for the tourist trade, and around Lake Patzcuaro woven tule Christs are affixed to crosses. Ornamental petates likewise join traditional sleeping mats and those used to wrap and transport merchandise. Unlike palm, tule is rarely if ever dyed, so design depends on variations in the twilled technique commonly used.

Both men and women are hat and basket weavers. Beals (1945a, p. 36) reports that men make mats and baskets and women hats among the Mayo; Bennett and Zingg (1935, p. 88) say women are the Tarahumara weavers; in the central highlands of Mexico both sexes appear to participate about equally; in Chan Kom men are the exclusive hat makers (Redfield and Villa, 1934, p. 69); in the Rio Balsas women weave hat braids and men sew them to-

gether (Hendrichs Pérez, 1945, p. 57); Chorti women twill mats (Wisdom, 1940, p. 164); in Jacaltenango men make all baskets (LaFarge and Byers, 1931, p. 60). Obviously, as with pottery, in Mesoamerica the need to meet market demands and to utilize available hands is more important than mere custom in determining who makes basketry.

Which, if any, techniques are European? The sewn-hat technique probably is: this method is widely used in Spain not only for hats, but for round mats whose sides often are turned up to form baskets. Oval, wickerwork, willow market baskets with handles may very well be European, but at least some indigenous influence must occur in other types of wickerwork. Twilled, twined, and tight-coil work presumably is native American. Open coils may be a fairly recent development; similar methods are common in Spain, so it is likely there has been transatlantic influence, but in which direction we do not know. In baskets, to a greater degree than in pottery, we are dealing with

123

limited possibilities, so that without minute comparison of techniques and designs it is risky to speculate about origins.

In both Spain and Mesoamerica basketry types are diffused through the custom of teaching prisoners to weave during their jail terms; in both areas I have encountered competent weavers who took up the trade during periods of enforced incarceration.

REFERENCES

Arrot, 1953
Batalla, 1945
Beals, 1945a, 1945b
Bennett and Zingg, 1935
Blom and LaFarge, 1927
Brainerd, 1946, 1949
Brand, 1951
De la Fuente, 1949
Foster, 1948a, 1948b, 1955, 1959a, 1959b, 1960b
Hendrichs Pérez, 1945
Kelly and Palerm, 1952
Kroeber, 1931
LaFarge and Byers, 1931

Lothrop, 1927b
Mason, O. T., 1904
Parsons, 1936
Redfield, 1928, 1930
—— and Villa, 1934
Shepard, 1956
Smith, R. E., 1949
Starr, F., 1899
Taylor, P. S., 1933a
Thompson, R. H., 1958
Van de Velde and Van de Velde, 1939
West, 1948
Wisdom, 1940

7. Lacquer

KATHARINE D. JENKINS

LACQUER is a tough, glossy coating applied to objects to protect or to enhance them. It is built up in layers by successive applications of an oily or resinous medium having qualities that will bind earths and colorants to the surface and, on drying, become hard and impervious to moisture and stains. So defined, the term can be applied to a variety of productions, from waterproofed gourds of primitive peoples to synthetic coatings of modern manufacture, as well as to the exquisite lacquers of the Orient. Differences lie in the materials found and exploited in various parts of the world and in the degree to which the art has been developed.[1]

In Middle America a lacquering art was known at the time of the Spanish conquest, and archaeological evidence suggests that it was well developed and widespread several hundred years earlier (Covarrubias, 1954, pp. 117–19; 1957, p. 95).

The Spanish, arriving in the 16th century, were impressed by the beauty and durability of the paint on *jícaras (xicalli)*,[2] the vessels of many sizes and shapes, made of "calabashes" of vines *(Lagenaria)* or trees *(Crescentia)*, for a variety of purposes from simple dippers to ceremonial bowls (Mendieta, 1870, p. 404; Sahagún, 1956, 3: 143). Although neither the decoration nor the technique is described in detail by the early historians, the materials are mentioned in various places and, as they are the same as those used in modern Mexican lacquerwork, we can assume that the basic technique was similar.

The colonists had the Indians apply their *pintura* to wooden articles of European form—chests, work-boxes, writing-cases, lecterns—whereas gourd-painting has continued to the present as an important part of the industry, satisfying a continuing demand.

[1] This survey is based on the large but poorly integrated literature, supplemented by personal observations in Michoacan and by unpublished data furnished by Mary L. Foster and Dorothy Leadbeater. I wish to thank Bodil Christensen and Irmgard W. Johnson for their constant help in making inquiries and obtaining publications for me.

[2] Kiddle (1944) quotes the early historians with reference to meaning and uses of the word *jícara*. There are many other names for both tree- and vine-gourds *(cuautecomate, luch, güira, guaje, bule, tole)*, but the Nahuatl *xical*, adapted to *jícara* by the Spanish, is the generic name mostly widely used.

125

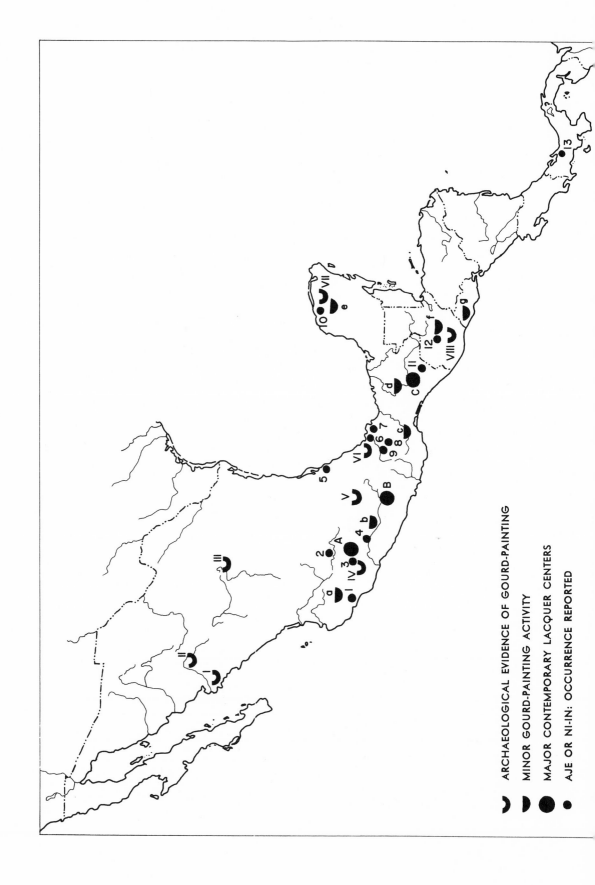

ARCHAEOLOGICAL EVIDENCE OF GOURD-PAINTING

MINOR GOURD-PAINTING ACTIVITY

MAJOR CONTEMPORARY LACQUER CENTERS

AJE OR NI-IN: OCCURRENCE REPORTED

Fig. 1—GOURD-PAINTING, LACQUER AND THE OCCURRENCE OF AJE OR NI-IN (FAT OF A SCALE INSECT)

ARCHAEOLOGICAL EVIDENCE OF GOURD-PAINTING*

◗ Sites yielding gourd fragments with adhering paint, or remains of paint in form indicating that it had once coated gourds or other perishable material.

I. GUASAVE, SINALOA (Ekholm, 1942, pp. 91–96).

II. RIO FUERTE, CHIHUAHUA (Zingg, 1940, pp. 54–56).

III. CANDELARIA, COAHUILA: Cueva de La Paila (Aveleyra Arroya de Anda, 1956, pp. 190–95).

IV. APATZINGAN, MICHOACAN (Kelly, 1947, pp. 145, 216).

V. TLAPACOYA, MEXICO (Barbo de Piña Chan, 1956, p. 109).

VI. CERRO DE LAS MESAS, VERACRUZ (Drucker, 1943, pp. 13, 21–23).

VII. CHICHEN ITZA, YUCATAN: Cenote (Ekholm, 1942, p. 94).

VIII. KAMINALJUYU, GUATEMALA (Kidder, Jennings, and Shook, 1946, pp. 100–102).

*This includes any kind of painting technique—not necessarily "paint cloisonne"—although this technique has been recognized in association with gourds in several sites: Guasava, Candelaria, Apatzingan, Cenote of Chichen Itza. At Rio Fuerte, Zingg reported "paint cloisonne" on gourds; but subsequent examination made this identification uncertain (Ekholm, 1942, p. 95). In the remaining sites, technique is not specified. Sites of paint-cloisonne on *pottery only* are *not* included.

MODERN SURVIVALS OF GOURD-PAINTING AND LACQUERWORK

◗ *Minor gourd-painting activity reported:*

a. JALISCO: Ayotitlan, Sayula, Tlaquepaque (Kelly, 1944, pp. 113–23).

b. GUERRERO: Acapetlahuaya (Brand, 1943b, p. 229).

c. OAXACA: Guienagate (near Ixtepec), Isthmus of Tehuantepec (Kamar Al-Shimas, 1922, p. 99).

d. CHIAPAS: Copainala, Ocozocoautla (Cordry and Cordry, 1941, pp. 35–36).

e. YUCATAN PENINSULA (Dondé Ibarra, 1884, p. 204; *La Naturaleza*, 1884, p. 382).

f. GUATEMALA: Rabinal (McBryde, 1943).

g. EL SALVADOR: Izalco (Hartman, 1910, pp. 136–38; Standley and Calderón, 1925, p. 102; Osborne, 1956, pp. 91–93).

⬤ *Major contemporary lacquer centers, products well known, widely distributed:*

A. Uruapan-Patzcuaro, Michoacan

B. Olinala, Guerrero

C. Chiapa de Corzo, Chiapas

AJE OR NI-IN: SCALE INSECT, *Llaveia axin*, AND ITS FAT—PAINTING MEDIUM AND UNGUENT†

⬤ *Reported localities:*

1. Comala, Colima (García Pérez, 1863, p. 475).
2. Penjamo, Guanajuato (Dugés, 1891).
3. Paracuaro, Michoacan (N. León, 1921, p. 335).
4. Huetamo, Michoacan ("El Guajal") (*La Naturaleza*, 1884, pp. 372–74; Storm, 1939, pp. 386–87).
5. Papantla, Veracruz (Llave, 1832, p. 149).
6. Tlacotalpam, Veracruz (*ibid.*; *La Naturaleza*, 1884, pp. 377–78).
7. San Andres Tuxtla, Veracruz (*ibid.*).
8. Dist. de Choapam, Oaxaca (Mexico, 1884, pp. 16–18).
9. Dist. de Villa Alta, Oaxaca (*ibid.*, pp. 41–43).
10. Northern Yucatan: Izamal (U.S. Dept. Agriculture, 1869, p. 270); Temax (Mexico, 1884, pp. 70, 93).
11. San Bartolome, Chiapas (Venustiano Carranza) (F. Starr, 1900–02, pt. 2, p. 129).
12. Rabinal, Guatemala (McBryde, 1943).
13. Chiriqui Lagoon Dist., Panama (B. L. Gordon, 1957).

†These are places where the insects have been collected or reported to grow, or where the extracted fatty substance has been obtained, regardless of whether the place produced quantities for distant markets, or only enough for local use, and regardless of the stated uses of the substance, whether as unguent (medicinal or cosmetic), or as a painting medium.

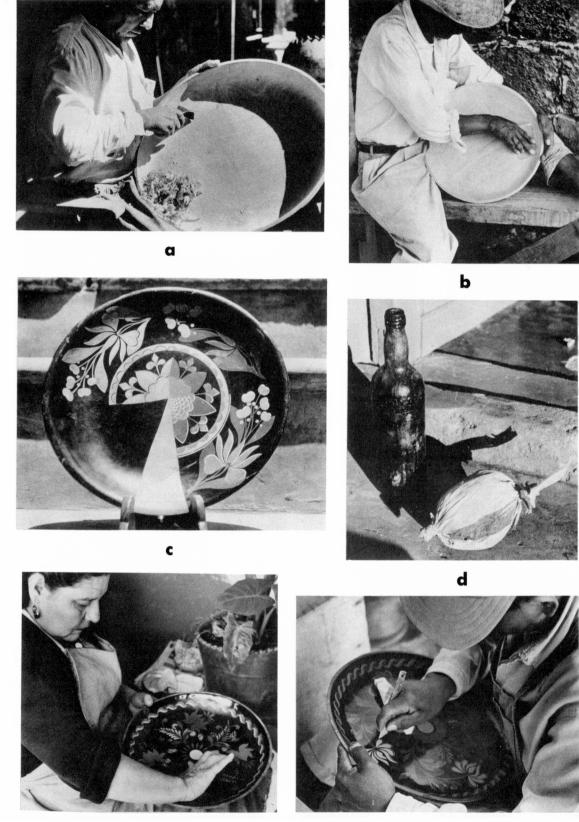

a

b

c

d

e

f

The lacquer industry has been most highly developed in Mexico, where it became concentrated in three distinct regions: (1) the Tarascan highland of Michoacan, embracing Periban, Uruapan, Patzcuaro and Quiroga; (2) Guerrero, with Olinala as the famous center and Acapetlahuaya less important; and (3) Chiapas, with an active industry surviving at Chiapa de Corzo.

Although we do not know where or when this art first appeared in America, or how it came to be centered in these areas, there is much debate about an Asiatic origin (Zuno, 1952). We must, therefore, mention briefly the materials used in Oriental lacquers before discussing those of Middle America.

Oriental lacquers are of two sorts. The "true lacquer" of China and Japan is the sap of a tree (usually *Rhus verniciflua*) which is simply tapped, the juice needing only to be gently heated to remove excess water, stored in airtight containers, and strained before use. It is applied in many thin coats, over a base prepared with a size made with a white earth, each resinous coat being hardened in a moist atmosphere and polished before the next application (Li Ch'iao-p'ing, 1948, pp. 104–12). The *lac* of India and Ceylon is the gum resin known as shellac, produced by a coccus insect *(Lacifer)* living on trees with gummy juices (such as *Ficus*) and secreting the resinous substance as a protective coating around itself and its young (Hill, 1952, pp. 159–60).

An American lac insect *(Tachardiella)* in southwestern United States and Mexico has not been reported to have been exploited for painting by the indigenous peoples (Colton, 1943).

In Mexico, the lacquering mediums known to have been used are seed oils and an insect fat, mentioned separately in the 16th century but commonly combined in the best of today's lacquers.

The seed oil may be: (1) the traditionally used *chía (chian)*, from a native *Salvia*, widely cultivated; (2) *chicalote (xaté,* in Tarascan), from a wild prickly-poppy *(Argemone);* or (3) *linaza* (linseed), introduced from Europe and now a commercial product commonly substituting for the native oils, which are troublesome to produce by the methods described by Francisco de P. León (1939, pp. 41–42).

Chía, long cultivated for food, drink and oil, is mentioned in many tribute lists and *Relaciones* (e.g., Asuchitlan, Papeles Nueva España, ser. 2, vol. 7, suppl. [6], p. 42). As a drying oil in painting *chía* is considered superior to linseed because it does not darken light colors. *Chicalote,* better known for medical uses, has been used in Michoacan lacquerwork, but is rarely used now (N. León, 1921, pp. 334–36; Brand, 1951, p. 168).[3]

The insect fat, called *aje* (from Nahuatl *axin)* in most areas, or *nij (ni-in)* in Maya areas, is derived from a coccid now indentified as *Llaveia axin* (Llave).[4] Like the lac insect, it sucks the sap of trees but, unlike

---

FIG. 2—MICHOACAN: TECHNIQUE. *a,* Scraping the inside of a large, deep *batea. b,* Smoothing the wood with sandpaper. *c,* "Sampler" showing stages in inlaid lacquerwork: smoothed wood, black *maque* applied, lacquer removed from areas of figures, spaces filled with color, outline details cut and filled with white. *d,* Ball of *aje* wax, wrapped in cornhusks, with quart bottle of oil. *Aje* is usually melted and blended with oil (*chía* or linseed), to which a small amount of white earth is added to make the basic size. *e,* Filling in the colors. The oily mixture is dabbed on with the fingers, color dusted on with a rag, then rubbed with the heel of the hand, the process being repeated until the design area is level with the background. *f,* Cutting fine details to be filled with white for final accent.

[3] Maximino Martínez (1959, pp. 198–206) summarizes data on *chía* and *chicalote* and gives bibliographies.

[4] Pablo de la Llave (1832) named the insect *Coccus axin,* the name still used in much of the literature. It was renamed *Llaveia axin* (Llave), by Signoret (1875, p. 370), and put with related genera in a new tribe, Llaveiini, of the Coccid family Margarodidae, by Morrison (1928, pp. 179–95).

The tribe ranges from western Mexico to Peru and it is possible that several species may furnish a useful wax (Morrison, personal communication, 1960).

the lac, it does not produce a resin, its body fat (extracted by cooking and crushing) being the substance used. *Aje* is an animal fat having the unusual characteristics of a drying oil (Bloede's analysis in U. S. Dept. Agriculture Report, 1869, pp. 268–69). It has a yellow color, the texture of a medium-soft cheese, and a characteristic odor reminiscent of rancid butter. It is marketed in the form of rectangular cakes, or balls wrapped in cornhusks, like *tamales* (fig. 2,*d*). On exposure to air the mass forms a brown crust on the outside. It has a melting point of 120°F., but once melted will remain in semifluid state at a temperature of about 80°F. It is not soluble in alcohol, but is soluble in turpentine and blends well with the seed oils.

The substance was known to the Maya of Yucatan (Landa, 1959, p. 125) and to the Aztecs (Sahagún, 1956, 3: 130, 143, 152–53).[5] It was used as an ointment (medicinal, protective and cosmetic) and as an ingredient of chewing gum, as well as for gourd-painting. Sahagún, describing the "unguent" and telling how it was produced, indicates that the insect was cultivated in the 16th century. Cultivation in recent times consists in storing the eggs in gourds or cornhusks during the dry season, then, at the beginning of the rains, placing them on suitable host plants (*Spondias, Jatropha, Acacia,* and *Cassia* being the genera most often mentioned), harvesting the mature insects and cooking them, to extract the wax, toward the end of the rainy season (A. Herrera, 1884, p. 199).[6] *Aje* has been cultivated in southern Veracruz, Yucatan, Chiapas, Guatemala, and Panama; but at Huetamo, Michoacan (Middle Rio Balsas), which traditionally has supplied *aje* to the Tarascans, the insects were reported to grow naturally (Storm, 1939, pp. 386–87; 1945, p. 321).

The insect wax and the seed oil appear to be complementary in lacquerwork as they are used together in Michoacan and Chia-

pas. However, in Guerrero, for which we have only one detailed description of the technique of Olinala (Meave, 1791), *chía* is mentioned but *aje* is not. Nicolás León, noting this omission, stated that he had seen *aje* used there (N. León, 1921, p. 417). Others ignore this discrepancy, or assume that the two substances are interchangeable, and assert that only seed oil is used in Guerrero (Tibón, 1960, p. 32).

In recent years the commercial "japan drier" or shellac, used with linseed oil, has been replacing the native materials, especially in Quiroga (Brand, 1951, p. 168).

The white earths, essential to all lacquerwork, as fillers and extenders for colors, are not always identifiable from reports of different regions.

In Michoacan, two white earths are used: the grayish-white *tepútzchuta*, identified as dolomite, a double carbonate of magnesium and lime (Herrera y Gutiérrez, 1891, p. 397), and the yellowish-white *igüétacua*, a ferruginous lime (Brand, 1951, p. 168). *Tepútzchuta* is added to a mixture of melted *aje* and oil, to make the basic size (*sisa* in Spanish, *nimácata* in Tarascan), and, as dry powder, is mixed with all colors. *Igüétacua* is used with *tepútzchuta* to make white and to brighten colors. *Yeso* (gypsum), available commercially, is used as a substitute for these white earths, but is regarded as an adulterant. The red and black earths used at Quiroga have been analyzed and

[5] I have found no early reference to the use of the insect fat among the Tarascans, although *aje* is traditionally associated with *chía* in the lacquerwork of Michoacan, and gourd-painting was sufficiently important in the 16th century to warrant the appointment of a supervisor of gourd-painters (*urani-atari*) (Relación de Michoacán, 1956, p. 178).

[6] This and other articles on *aje* or *ni-in* were collected and published in *La Naturaleza* (1884, 6: 198–210, 283–84, 293, 372–84), most of the material being published also in *Trabajos de la Secretaría de Fomento sobre el Axe* (Mexico, 1884), which included correspondence concerning the Mexican government's attempt to develop *aje* cultivation on a commercial scale.

found to contain considerable organic matter (Brand, 1951, p. 168).

For Olinala, five earths with Nahuatl names were mentioned in the 18th century: *tezicaltetl, toctetl, tecoxtli, tlalxococ,* and *texotlali* (Meave, 1791, p. 175). Recent writers (Armillas, 1949, pp. 240–41; Tibón, 1960, pp. 94–95) do not agree on identifications, and samples have not been analyzed. The first three, with modified names, *tesicalte, tolte,* and *tecoxtle,* appear to serve the same purpose as the two whitish earths of Michoacan.

In Chiapas, only one white earth is mentioned: *tizate (tizatl)* (F. Starr, 1900–02, pt. 2, p. 128; Olvera, 1956, p. 39; Duvalier, 1960, p. 715).

Colors, with a few exceptions, are commercial pigments, replacing the native colorants from plants, the insect cochineal, and earths. Red earths are still used, especially for undecorated surfaces, and black may be made with earth, soot-carbon, or charcoal. All pigments and earths are finely ground on a special, smooth *metate (tlalmetate)* and used as dry powder.

Procedures for building up the lacquer coating (called *maque* in Michoacan, *tlapetzole* in Guerrero) vary, but the basic technique consists in applying the oily mixture and dry materials alternately, in successive layers, dusting the powdered earths and pigments over the annointed surface, in sufficient quantity to absorb the oil, rubbing well after each application.

There are three distinct decorative techniques: (1) inlaid *(embutida* or *incrustada),* (2) cut-out *(recortada* or *rayada),* and (3) applied *(aplicada)* or brush-painting.

Inlaying lacquer in lacquer involves engraving the design in the *maque,* removing the lacquer from the figures, and filling in these cleared spaces with contrasting color, applied in layers as before, until the figures are built up to the same level as the background. Fine details can be cut out and filled as final accents (fig. 2,*c,e,f*). Inlaying

is traditionally associated with the lacquers of Michoacan, but was probably more widespread in the past. An old piece found in Chiapas, and a statement by Ximénez that the Indians colored *jícaras* and *toles* in "mosaic style," indicate that the inlaid technique was used there in the colonial period (Olvera, 1956, pp. 38–39). Archaeological evidence of inlaid lacquer was recognized in the paint remains (from decorated gourds) found at Guasave, Sinaloa (Ekholm, 1940; 1942, pp. 91–96), at Apatzingan, Michoacan (I. T. Kelly, 1947, p. 145) and at Candelaria, Coahuila (Aveleyra, 1956, pp. 190–95). Paint found at Cerro de las Mesas, Veracruz (Drucker, 1943, pp. 23, 70), showed a design which might have been inlaid, although this is not suggested in the report. Inlaid technique, called "paint-cloisonné," is also found in unfired paint decoration of archaeological pottery (Covarrubias, 1954, pp. 117–19; 1957, p. 95).

The technique called *recortada* (cut-out) or *rayada* (grooved) involves a second lacquering of contrasting color, over the background lacquer, "grooving" the design in the top coat, then removing this lacquer from around the figures to reveal the color of the lower layer as a background for the figures, which remain in low relief. Occasionally as many as four colors may be used in this technique. *Recortada* decoration is especially associated with Olinala wares. This cut-out technique has its counterpart in the "stripped painting" of archaeological pottery (Kelly, 1944, p. 122).

Aplicada decoration is usually brush-painting applied to the finished lacquer, using pigments or metallic powders mixed with seed oil, but it may include applications of gold- or silver-leaf laid over an adhesive applied with a brush. Brush-painting, developed in the colonial period, permitted greater decorative freedom but, inevitably, was used in imitation of European and Oriental styles. Some brush-painting

131

FIG. 3—MICHOACAN: DESIGN STYLES. *a*, Old *batea* (17th- or 18th-century Periban?). Inlaid lacquer. Preconquest stepped-fret motif in borders, double-headed eagle in center. Diam. ca. 50 cm. Frederick Davis Coll., Mexico. *b*, Modern *batea*, Patzcuaro, inlaid with old floral pinwheel design of Uruapan type. Diam. 35 cm. *c*, Modern *batea*, Patzcuaro, brush-painted color and applied goldleaf, depicting old Michoacan legend in 18th-century "Chinese" style. Diam. ca. 50 cm. Made at Casa Cuca Cerda, Patzcuaro, ca. 1956. *d*, Nineteenth-century tray, Patzcuaro, brush-painted gold and red, on black. Length ca. 35 cm. Frederick Davis Coll., Mexico. *e*, Detail. Modern *batea*, Patzcuaro. Brush-painted color and goldleaf on white. Diam. ca. 55 cm. Casa Cuca Cerda, Patzcuaro. *f*, Modern gourd bowl, Uruapan, inlaid, in traditional stylized floral design. Diam. 25 cm.

now is done in all Mexican lacquer centers and, in Quiroga (Michoacan) and Chiapa de Corzo, it is the sole technique used.

LACQUER CENTERS AND THEIR CHARACTERISTIC WARES

In Michoacan the articles lacquered are chiefly *bateas* or trays, most often round, made of light wood such as *aile (Alnus)* or *tzirimu (Tilia)*. Boxes and novelties are sometimes lacquered, but chests and furniture are no longer a part of the industry. Periban, once so famous for its inlaid lacquer that the name *peribana* was applied to all fine *bateas*, retains no trace of the industry. Uruapan has continued the tradition of inlaid lacquer with stylized flower designs, despite the lowering of quality by the excessive use of adulterants (figs. 2,*c,e,f*; 3,*f*). At Patzcuaro, where elegant brush-painted styles using gold paint and showing European and Oriental influences were developed in the colonial period, the art died out in the 19th century, but was revived in the 1920's during Mexico's general renascence. Inlaid, painted, and gold-leaf decorations are used now on pieces inspired by old models (fig. 3,*b,c,e*). Quiroga, never so famous for fine lacquer, is known for its black *bateas* with gaudily painted flowers, produced in quantity with cheap materials, and painted chairs, not classifiable as lacquer.

The industry at Quiroga has been thoroughly investigated by Brand (1951) and some of his data apply to Michoacan in general. The various lacquer styles are described and illustrated by F. de P. León (1939) and Enciso (1933); Romero de Terreros y Vinent (1918, 1923, 1951) and Genaro Estrada (1937) describe colonial pieces.

In Guerrero, gourd-painting once flourished in the Rio Balsas area but gradually diminished, although it was reported in Acapetlahuaya in the 1940's (Brand, 1943b, p. 229; Weitlaner, unpublished notes). At Olinala, in the Sierra Madre del Sur, the industry is the main activity of the people (Armillas, 1949); the products, widely marketed, include chests, small boxes made of the fragrant wood *linaloe* (of the Burseraceae), wooden trays, and *jícaras*, toys and novelties, made of the fruits of both *Lagenaria* and *Crescentia*. In the colonial period both the cut-out technique and brushwork were used in decoration. In the 19th century the cut-out technique was abandoned, but was taken up again in the 1920's (Toor, 1939, p. 86). Both techniques are used now, in distinctive styles notably different from those of other areas. The cut-out designs are often a maze of vine-stems and foliage, all spaces filled with figures of scampering animals, birds, people, or just spots (fig. 4,*d*). Painted decoration is largely pictorial (scenes, portraits, animals, birds, flowers, or patriotic emblems) which, although freely painted, is organized in definite zones or panels (fig. 4,*b,c*). Sometimes both brush-painting and cut-out work are used on the same piece. Olinala is most famous for its *baules* (chests), well described by Molina Enríquez (1928); its *jícaras* are less celebrated but are commonly used all over Mexico (fig. 4,*a,e*).

In Chiapas old specimens show that lacquer was used on a variety of objects (trays, boxes, niches for saints, toys and rattles, as well as gourds) through the 19th century, but that the art declined after the revolution (Duvalier, 1960). Now lacquer is used chiefly on *jicalpextles* (large vine-gourds) which are decorated with oil-painted flowers (fig. 4,*f*). These are widely marketed in southern Mexico and Central America but are used most conspicuously in Tehuantepec.

Similar *"jecapezles"* were reported to be made at Santa Maria de Guiniagate (Guienagate), Oaxaca, in 1918 (Kamar Al-Shimas, 1922, p. 99).

In Yucatan, in the 18th century, wooden objects were given a durable coating of a "paste" and over-painted with the same (Santos, 1716, 2: 475) and in the 19th century this paste was described as made of *ni-in (aje)*, *creta* (white earth), and colors. The insect fat was said to be used also for finishing guitars (Dondé Ibarra, 1884, p. 204).

In southern Veracruz, where *aje* was known to be cultivated in the 19th century, "drinking cups and trinkets" were said to be painted with better "taste" than those of Yucatan (Schott in U. S. Dept. Agriculture Report, 1869, p. 270).[7]

At Rabinal, Guatemala, *jícaras* (of *Crescentia*) are lacquered by rubbing with *aje* (from cultivated insects) and soot-carbon from pitch pine, and are then incised. *Achiote* (annato, *Bixa orellana*) is sometimes used to make orange-red *jícaras* (McBryde, 1943).

Among the Zoque of Chiapas, similar gourd treatment—rubbing with a fat (unspecified) and blackening in smoke over the brazier or staining with *achiote*—has been reported (Cordry and Cordry, 1941, pp. 35–36).

The black *jícaras* of Izalco, El Salvador, less lacquer-like than those of Rabinal, are dyed with *cascalote*, with no indication of the use of *aje* or *chía* (Standley and Calde-

---

[7] Modern literature on lacquer, with passing references to Yucatan, Veracruz, and Oaxaca, adds nothing to these data, and there are no descriptions.

FIG. 4—GUERRERO AND CHIAPAS. *a*, Olinala. Four *jícaras* (of *Crescentia*). Diam. ca. 15 cm. *Jícara* at left has *recortada* decoration, black over red. Bodil Christensen Coll., Mexico. *b*, Olinala. Small wood *batea*, painted. Diam. 25 cm. Frederick Davis Coll., Mexico. *c*, Olinala. Small chest painted in a style characteristic of larger chests of the 19th century. Length ca. 28 cm. Frederick Davis Coll., Mexico. *d*, Olinala. Small round-topped chest with *recortada* decoration, in black, green and yellow over orange. Length ca. 32 cm. Frederick Davis Coll., Mexico. *e*, Olinala. Gourd bowl, with *recortada* decoration, blue over yellow. Diam. 22 cm. *f*, Chiapas. *Jicalpextle*. Large gourd lacquered yellow, with painted flowers in vermilion, rose, white, blue, and green. Diam. 49 cm. Dwight Mcrrow Coll., now at Museo Nacional de Antropología, Mexico.

rón, 1925, pp. 102–03; Hartman, 1910, p. 138).[8]

Aje wax (from cultivated insects), combined with soot-carbon or *achiote*, is used by the Guaymi of Panama for black or red face-paint, not gourd-painting (B. L. Gordon, 1957).

At the opposite geographical extreme, Jalisco, gourds have been given a waterproof lining with *chía* oil and red earth (Kelly, 1944).

These scattered references to gourd-painting and the use of *aje* or *chía*, combined with earth or colorants, outside of the recognized lacquer-making centers, suggest that comparative studies based on a more complete survey might provide clues to the evolution of the lacquering art in Middle America, especially if occurrences could be related to archaeological evidence and historical references.

Addenda

Since this paper was written (1961) several articles on Mexican lacquer have appeared. Although none have provided new material for the history of the technique, the summary given by Rubín de la Borbolla, in Artes Populares de México (a special issue of Artes de México, 1963) should be cited as a more recent publication on the general subject than those already mentioned. In a study of the Mixteca Nahua-Tlapaneca of Guerrero, published by the Instituto Nacional Indigenista, the lacquer industry of Olinala is described with more details than have been published before (Muñoz, 1963, pp. 100–02).

Continuing research into the history, with emphasis on materials (particularly those which might have served as mediums in primitive painting) and on their natural distribution in Mesoamerica, considered in

relation to regional variations in surviving techniques, confirms the opinion that Mexican lacquer developed from indigenous gourd-painting, but suggests that it represents a fusion of different techniques, developed separately, on the basis of materials available locally.

Sixteenth-century sources mention such different mediums as pulverized *zapote* pits and roots of the epiphyte *zauctli* (Hernández, 1959, 2: 91, 117, 118), as well as *chía* seed oil and *aje* insect fat—all mentioned, individually, as useful for binding colors to gourds or wood. References to combinations of these mediums have not been found. *Chía* and *aje* are the ones which have survived in lacquerwork; but they are not necessarily used together and reports of the use of one without the other (e.g., *chía* in Jalisco and in Guerrero, *aje* in Guatemala) show a geographical separation of techniques.

The distribution of *chía* has not been mapped, but many sources indicate its abundance in the western areas. *Aje*, which might be found in hot country from Colima to Panama, is most often mentioned in areas of southern Mexico and Guatemala. (See map and Jenkins, 1964). Recent observations of lacquer techniques showed that, even where *aje* and *chía* are used together, proportions of the two ingredients vary regionally. *Chía* is the chief medium of highland Michoacan, where *aje*, though considered essential and brought from *tierra caliente*, is used sparingly; in Chiapas the lacquer is built up with *aje*, with small amounts of linseed oil, cooked with *aje* for the final coating only, or used in the brush-painted decoration. In Guerrero, where this matter has not been investigated, most reports emphasize the use of *chía*, definitely excluding *aje*; others say that *aje* is used; and one (Armillas, 1949, p. 241) mentions *chía* and "other things" not specified, because they were "secret."

Chía, being merely a very good drying

---

[8] Hartman, in his study of calabashes (*Crescentia*), their treatment and uses in Central America, does not mention the use of *aje* in any of the finishes. The resist-dyed decoration is done with other waxes, usually beeswax.

oil, like linseed, may require additives to produce a lacquer-like film. *Aje* is a more nearly complete lacquer-making medium. Recent, unpublished analyses, by James Cason and Michael Archerd in the College of Chemistry of the University of California at Berkeley, show that the substance is an unusual animal fat (not a wax or resin), with some components which polymerize with extreme rapidity and another which acts as a plasticizer, keeping the film pliable, so that it is an ideally balanced natural medium. Other oils would not be needed, except as diluents or to facilitate application. *Aje* added to the *chía* technique would be an improvement.

If *aje* is considered the diagnostic of Mesoamerican lacquer, Brand's opinion (1943a, p. 60) that "Mexican lacquer art originated in the Tierra Caliente of the Gulf of Mexico coastlands," and that it was "carried across Oaxaca" to the Balsas Basin, "whence it spread to the Tarascan highlands," may have some validity, although it does not explain the western emphasis on the use of *chía*, or the persistent reports, especially from Guerrero, that *chía* is the sole medium used. If *aje* was necessary to the development and continued execution of elaborate decorative techniques, such as inlaying or "paint cloisonné" (as exemplified in archaeological remains found at Guasave, Apatzingan, and Candelaria), we need evidence that the insect was exploited in the west, or that the substance was available in trade. Early references to *aje* in the western areas have not yet been found.

References and reports which accumulated since the map (fig. 1) was made do not change the patterns of distribution very much, but a few fill in gaps and seem significant.

Archaeological evidence of gourd-painting: Tikal, Guatemala, where remains of two "stuccoed" red-painted gourds were found in Burial 167, dated about 25 B.C. (W. R. Coe, 1965, p. 1413).

Minor gourd-painting activity reported: In Balsas Basin, Guerrero. Painted gourds seen by Elinore M. Barrett, in 1965, at Altamirano and Tlapehuala, Gro., were said to have been made at San Miguel Totolapan and at *unspecified localities between* Cuetzala and Olinala (personal communication). It should be noted that in the 16th century painted gourds were paid in tribute by several towns of the area, such as Tlacoçautitlan (Barlow, 1949, pp. 83–84) and Tepequaquilco and Tlapa (Scholes and Adams, 1957, pp. 45, 46).

Occurrence of aje or ni-in. Early references to medicinal use of "agi" at Amatlan, Oaxaca (near Miahuatlan) in 1609 (Papeles de Nueva España, ser. 2, 4: 315), and "axin" at Ataquizaya, El Salvador (near Aguachapan at Guatemala border) in 1576 (García de Palacio, 1860, pp. 50–51). Early references to *aje* mention its medicinal uses more often than its use in painting, but any use shows knowledge of the substance.

REFERENCES

Armillas, 1949
Aveleyra, 1956
Barbo de Piña Chan, 1956
Barlow, 1949
Bennett and Zingg, 1935
Brand, 1943a, 1943b, 1951
Coe, W. R., 1965
Colton, 1943
Cordry and Cordry, 1941
Covarrubias, 1954, 1957

Documentos relativos al axe o ni-in, 1884
Dondé Ibarra, 1884
Drucker, 1943
Dugés, 1891
Duvalier, 1960
Ekholm, 1940, 1942
Enciso, 1933
Estrada, 1937
Garcia de Palacio, 1860
García Pérez, 1863

Gordon, B. L., 1957
Hartman, 1910
Hernández, F., 1959
Herrera, A., 1884
Herrera y Gutiérrez, 1890, 1891
Hill, 1952
Jenkins, K. D., 1964
Kamar Al-Shimas, 1922
Kelly, 1944, 1947
Kidder, Jennings, and Shook, 1946
Kiddle, 1944
La Naturaleza, 1884
Landa, 1959
León, F., 1939
León, N., 1921
Li Ch'iao-p'ing, 1948
Llave, 1832
McBryde, 1943
Martínez, 1959
Meave, 1791, 1831
Mendieta, 1870
Mexico, 1884

Molina Enríquez, 1925, 1928
Morrison, 1928
Muñoz, 1963
Olvera, 1956, 1959
Osborne, 1956
Papeles de Nueva España, 1609, 1946
Pérez García, 1956
Relación de Michoacán, 1956
Romero de Terreros y Vinent, 1918, 1923, 1951
Rubín de la Borbolla, 1963
Sahagún, 1956
Santos, 1716
Scholes and Adams, 1957
Signoret, 1875
Standley and Calderón, 1925
Starr, F., 1900–02
Storm, 1939, 1945
Tibón, 1960
Toor, 1939
U. S. Dept. Agriculture, 1869
Zingg, 1940
Zuno, 1952

8. Textiles and Costume

A. H. GAYTON

THERE IS PROBABLY no aspect of Middle American culture in which the past and present are so dynamically expressed as in weaving and dress. The flamboyant beauty of Aztec and Mayan costume, repressed by the conquest, found new outlets in the styles of Spain and the strange fibers silk and wool. Only representative examples of these arts can be mentioned here.

Native white and brown cottons are still spun and woven; the brown, once favored for its warm tone, is diminishing in Mexico and Guatemala. Where cotton once was or still is handspun the preparatory steps are essentially the same: seeds removed by the fingers; masses of fiber whipped with wands into pads of roving (Cahita: Beals, 1943, p. 27; Chilacachapa: Weitlaner, 1941, p. 265; Totonac: Kelly and Palerm, 1952, p. 228; Chinantec: Bevan, 1938, p. 80; Zoque: Cordry and Cordry, 1941, p. 104; Guatemala: McBryde, 1947, p. 62; O'Neale, 1945, p. 7; Boruca: Stone, 1949, p. 16). In spinning by native method, the spindle is supported in a gourd, bowl (fig. 1), or sherd; the Chinantec addition of a distaff is unusual. Factory-made yarns obviate these tedious processes, though at times such yarns are opened and respun by hand (Huichol: Museo Nacional de Artes e Industrias Populares [hereinafter MNAIP], 1954, p. 31, Totonac: Kelly and Palerm, 1952, p. 228) or respun or doubled on a spinning wheel (Tarascan: West, 1948, p. 64; Guatemala: O'Neale, 1945, p. 10). Consequently, although handweaving persists, the yarns used are increasingly of commercial types.

Maguey, a native agave, provides fibers for durable cordage, utility cloths, and occasionally mantles (Otomi). The stripping of fibers, spinning by spindle or rope-twister, netting or weaving of maguey is usually men's work (entire process, typical also for Mexico: O'Neale, 1945, p. 20).

Of new fibers, wool made the greatest impact. The entire preparatory method was adopted and is essentially the same in Mexico and Guatemala. Processing includes washing, carding (carding absent, Tarahumara, Mayo; bow-fluffing, Mayo), spinning by spindle (Tarahumara, Mayo, some Guatemalan villages) or, more often, by the hand-turned spinning wheel (Tarascan villages, Yalalag, Mitla, Momostenango).

138

a

b

Fig. 1—CHINANTEC GIRLS SPINNING (ABOVE) AND WEAVING (BELOW), SAN JUAN ZAUTLA. (From F. Starr, 1908, p. 208.)

139

FIG. 2—MIXE WOMAN WEAVING, IXCUINTEPEC. (From F. Starr, 1899, pl. 96.)

(Bennett and Zingg, 1935, p. 90; Beals, 1945a, p. 27; 1946, p. 35; O'Neale, 1945, pp. 14, 240; McBryde, 1947, p. 64.)

Warping boards, creels, and reels for skeining or measuring warp lengths also are introduced tools used with cotton or wool yarns when great lengths are needed.

Silk weaving and sericulture, quickly established by the Spanish, familiarized central and southern Mexicans with the processing and uses of this fiber, even stimulating the collection of wild silk cocoons in coastal Oaxaca, Tehuantepec, and Chiapas (Borah, 1943, pp. 102, 114). Today, commercial silk yarns are purchased in markets and employed mainly for embroidery in Mexico and for brocading in Guatemala. Rayon yarns, in 1936, still were not liked as a substitute (O'Neale, 1945, pp. 17, 19, 60, 72).

Of the formerly important native dyes— indigo, cochineal, purpura—only indigo is still generally used (with urine mordant, Cahita, Mayo, Cheran: Beals, 1943, p. 27;

1945a, p. 28; 1946, p. 35; other mordants, Zoque: Cordry and Cordry, 1941, p. 124; Guatemala: McBryde, 1947, p. 65; O'Neale, 1945, p. 28). Whether of natural or aniline source, blue is the most frequently employed color. The red-producing insect, cochineal *(Coccus cacti),* was still being reared in Jocotenango in 1936, mainly for Momostenango wool weavers (O'Neale, 1945, p. 29); Mitla weavers obtained cochineal in Oaxaca and Tlacolula (Parsons, 1936, p. 45). The secretion of a mollusc *(Purpura patula)* produces a unique purple, obtainable only at the warm coastal source. Purpura-dyed yarns, once traded far inland, now are dyed chiefly for local consumption (Oaxaca Chontal, Amuzgo: Norman, 1959, p. 24; Boruca: Stone, 1949, p. 17; Nuttall, 1909; McBryde, 1947, p. 62; Born, 1937; Gerhard, 1964).

Aniline dyes are rapidly replacing natural sources. Of some 30 Tarascan weaving communities, all use commercial forms (West, 1948, p. 64); in other cases aniline

140

Fɪɢ. 3—MAYO INDIAN SERAPE WEAVER, HUATABAMPO, SONORA, MEXICO. (Photographed by Donald Cordry, 1939.)

FIG. 4—BACKSTRAP LOOM WITH SINGLE-FACE BROCADING IN PROGRESS, TAC-
TIC, GUATEMALA. One web of a 3-breadth huipil; web width 36 cm. Specimen 1861,
Department of Decorative Art, University of California, Berkeley. (From O'Neale, 1945, fig.
76,*d*.)

FIG. 5—TORTILLA CLOTH, PLAIN SINGLE-FACE BROCADE, HUAVE, CHIAPAS. Woven length 48.5 cm., width 51 cm. G. M. Foster Coll., Berkeley. (Photo, William Ricco.)

and natural dyes are both used (Mitla: Parsons, 1936, p. 45; Salcaja: O'Neale, 1945, p. 24). The availability of factory-dyed yarns is reducing home dyeing; it remains, rather, a specialized craft as at Salcaja in Guatemala.

Spot-dyed yarns (jaspé) are widely used in Guatemala, more rarely in Mexico, as at Tenancingo, Aguas Calientes, and Zimapan (O'Neale, 1945, pp. 25, 30; Start, 1948, pp. 77, 83, pl. 8). Cloth tie-dyeing, with areas reserved from the dye by knotted and/or stitched threads, survives among the Otomi of Zimapan and, highly Hispanicized, at Vi-

ground (Tarahumara: Bennett and Zingg, 1935, p. 91; Cahita, Mayo: fig. 3; Beals, 1943, p. 27; 1945a, p. 29; Opata, Huichol: J. B. Johnson, 1950, p. 16). The backstrap loom (fig. 4), still widely used in Mexico, Guatemala, and Costa Rica, is the traditional form associated with domestic weaving by women. One warp beam is fastened to a high support, the other to the weaver by means of a strap around her hips. Both this and the ground loom have a heddle made by looping a thread continuously over a rod and around alternate warps (Tarahumara: a heavy cord instead of the rod). The remaining warps are controlled by a flat or round shed stick. (Descriptions of the backstrap loom and its manipulation: Kelly and Palerm, 1952, p. 230; Christensen, 1947, *passim;* Cordry and Cordry, 1941, p. 117; O'Neale, 1945, p. 47.) Its occurrence is too frequent to specify, but may be spot-listed for Tarahumara, Huichol, many Tarascan villages, Nahua and Otomi in the Sierra de Puebla, Totonac, Chinantec (fig. 1), Zapotec of Oaxaca, Zoque and Tzotzil of Chiapas, most of Guatemala, and Boruca of Costa Rica.

The introduced treadle loom, whereon frame heddles are shifted by foot attachments, is operated generally by men to produce wool or cotton yardage or serapes for sale. These are more often located in cities or towns. They may be the only type in use (Quiroga), be used for wool while backstrap looms continue for cotton (several Tarascan villages), or fail to be established at all (Yalalag) (Brand, 1951, p. 174; West, 1948, p. 64; De la Fuente, 1949, p. 100). Draw looms, once necessary for the complicated Spanish silk weaves, seldom function today in home industry (Borah, 1943, p. 33; O'Neale, 1945, p. 38).

Hybrid looms resulted from native and foreign types. The small table with treadled heddles, but warp length attached to the weaver's belt and a distant post, is found in Totonicapan for weaving headbands (Start, 1948, p. 48, pl. 5). A European framed slat

FIG. 6—BELTS. *Left:* Twilled tapestry-weave belt. Mayo, Sonora. Woven length 221 cm., width 9.5 cm. Specimen 3/3428, Robert H. Lowie Museum of Anthropology, University of California, Berkeley. *Center:* Plain twill belt with warp fringes still uncut. Mayo, Sonora. Woven length 241 cm., width 10 cm. Specimen 3/3341, Robert H. Lowie Museum of Anthropology, University of California, Berkeley. *Right:* Belt of ribbed weave. Popoluca, Veracruz. Woven length 125 cm., width 8 cm. G. M. Foster Coll., Berkeley. (Photo, William Ricco.)

zarron de Montes for wool skirts (Start, 1948, p. 99, pl. 16; Katharine D. Jenkins, photographs).

Looms differ by region and product. The native horizontal loom has two beams lashed to two logs or four posts close to the

144

FIG. 7—TWILL-WEAVE PLAID BLANKET, MAYO, SONORA. Woven length 198 cm., width 139 cm. Specimen 3/3333, Robert H. Lowie Museum of Anthropology, University of California, Berkeley. (Photo, William Ricco.)

heddle controls the warps on narrow back-strap looms for belts (Jalieza: Start, 1948, p. 98, pl. 15; San Pedro Sacatepequez: O'Neale, 1945, p. 36).

Plain weaves (square count, warpface,

weftface), tapestry (fig. 6, left), twill (fig. 6, center), pattern weave, gauze, and brocade (plain, plucked) (fig. 5) are native construction techniques currently persisting in Mexico and Guatemala, though one or

145

F<small>IG</small>. 8—TAPESTRY-WEAVE SERAPE, TEOTITLAN DEL VALLE, OAXACA. Woven length 196 cm., width of each web 73 cm. Specimen 3/15730, Robert H. Lowie Museum of Anthropology, University of California, Berkeley. (Photo, William Ricco.)

more are favored in specific localities. Spanish colonial culture brought fine woolens, damasks, velvets, and laces; such fabrics, as well as Oriental textiles coming by galleon trade, may have stimulated further developments of already known techniques. Tapestry weave creates the serapes of the Mayo and such famous centers as Saltillo, Aguas Calientes, Texcoco, and Teotitlan del Valle (figs. 3, 8, 9). Warpface and twill wool skirt lengths are made in Michoacan, the Sierra de Puebla, and Mitla; blankets in plain and twill weaves come from the Tarahumara, Mayo (fig. 7), and Guatemalan Momoste-

146

Fig. 9—SALTILLO-STYLE TAPESTRY-WEAVE SERAPE. Hemmed length 236 cm., width of each web 67 cm. Specimen 3/2382, Robert H. Lowie Museum of Anthropology, University of California, Berkeley. (Photo, William Ricco.)

FIG. 10—JASPÉ-PATTERNED WOOL BLANKET, MOMOSTENANGO, GUATEMALA.
Woven length 228 cm., width of each web 84 cm. (From O'Neale, 1945, fig. 84,c.)

nango (Bennett and Zingg, 1935, p. 93; Beals, 1945a, p. 31; Cordry and Cordry, 1940, p. 48; O'Neale, 1945, p. 240). Double-cloth bags and belts are a speciality of the Huichol, Otomi, and Zapotec (MNAIP, 1954, p. 32; Start, 1948, pp. 86–98); the weave perhaps is not native and appears to be absent in Guatemala. Brocade, once generally popular, is still so in Oaxaca and Guatemala, and the original plucked variation may have been reinforced by Spanish confites and velvets (Kelly and Palerm, 1952, p. 231, pls. 29–31; O'Neale, 1945, pp. 59, 73; Start, 1948, pp. 66, 68, pl. 11). The florescence of jaspé, prevalent in Guatemala (fig. 10) and exquisitely refined in Tenancingo rebozos (fig. 11), implies a re-stimulus from galleon trade imports (O'Neale, 1945, pp. 25, 30; Start, 1948, pp. 49, 77, 83, pl. 8).

Certain techniques are highly specialized. Yalalag huipiles and Popoluca belts (fig. 6, right) have a ribbed weave owing to warp/weft manipulation (Start, 1948, p. 70, fig. 29; G. M. Foster Coll.). Crêpe weft stripes appear in Sierra de Puebla quexquemitls (Altepec, Huachinango, Cuetzalan) and Guatemalan huipiles (San Juan Chamelco, Quezaltenango), and weft-veneering is reported for Quezaltenango (Start, 1948, pp. 35, 61, 64, fig. 11; Bird, 1953, p. 30; G. M. Foster Coll.). Sprang (twine-plaiting), undoubtedly native, like gauze may have received an impetus from European examples or lace materials (Ichcateopan: I. W. Johnson, 1958). Unique is the curved weaving by the Otomi (Christensen, 1947); weaving with feathered yarns survives in Chiapas (I. W. Johnson, 1957). Otomi and some Guatemalans produce weft-looped fabrics, and pile rugs with cut weft-loops are made at Aldea Oboton (Dewar, 1957, p. 106; O'Neale, 1945, p. 73; McBryde, 1947, p. 65, pl. 37).

Textiles superior in quality and design are, as in the past, primarily costume items. They may be woven at home for family use as in Cuetzalan, Yalalag, and much of Guatemala. However, many fabrics, especially skirt lengths, serapes, and blankets, are woven in towns such as Nahuatzen, Quiroga, Mitla, Salcaja, and Momostenango for extended trading (West, 1948, p. 65; Brand, 1951, p. 175; Parsons, 1936, p. 45; O'Neale, 1945, p. 239; McBryde, 1947, p. 52). Quite generally, commercial muslin is replacing not only handwoven cotton but, by double acculturation, handwoven woolens because of the cost of the latter (Tarahumara: Bennett and Zingg, 1935, p. 109; Sierra de Puebla: MNAIP, 1951, p. 55). Decoration on bought yardage can only be by post-weaving methods, hence the increased use of embroidery, beading, ruffles, and lace, e.g., Huichol, Totonac, and the Cantel area in Guatemala.

Costume of men, once so rich as shown by codices, archaeological evidence, and murals at Teotihuacan and Bonampak, has become almost uniform in two stages: first, the adoption of trousers, shirts, and hats in colonial times; and second, the current acceptance of factory-made garments. The latter, catrín, Ladino, Euro-American styles are prevalent in or near cities. The former style continues throughout rural Mexico and Guatemala: white cotton, flyless trousers supported by a handwoven sash, white or colored cotton shirt with turn-over or band collar and sleeves gathered into wristbands, a wide-brimmed plaited palm hat, and sandals with leather straps and soles from rubber tires. A wool mantle, or short or long open-sided, slot-necked wool cloak (jorongo, serape), completes the daily dress. Minor variations mark local styles, as: cerise sashes at Tzintzuntzan, truncated-cone hat crowns in Cheran, heeled sandals at Yalalag, or jorongos with jaspé stripes in Zimapan. A normal addition to men's dress in Mexico and Guatemala is a large, over-shoulder bag of maguey fiber or fine cloth (both, Otomi: Start, 1948, pl. 13).

The least acculturated men's styles occur in northern and southern Mexico. The Tarahumara, with two cotton squares tied as a breech-loin covering, a wool belt, a large mantle, and their long hair confined by a headcloth, preserve a primitive simplicity. Muslin shirts and straw hats are occasional additions. Distinctive Huichol features are embroidered muslin trousers and shirt, embroidered triangular scarf, a series of doublecloth bags and a wool sash at the waist, and a flat straw hat adorned with appliqué and tassels. In Chiapas, Lacandon men continue to wear the big Mayan tunic (as seen in reliefs and the Bonampak murals), while the Huistec have full, white cotton breechclothes (also old Mayan), a wool mantle

149

F ɪ ɢ. 11—JASPÉ-PATTERNED REBOZO WITH MACRAMÉ FRINGE, TENANCINGO, MEXICO. Woven length 201 cm., fringe length 36 cm., full width 83 cm. G. M. Foster Coll., Berkeley. (Photo, William Ricco.)

a

b

12—GUATEMALA INDIAN COSTUMES. *a,* San Martin Chile Verde, Sacatepequez. *b,* San Cristobal, Alta Vera-. (Photos, Middle American Research Institute, Tulane University.)

draped in a loop across the chest over a cotton shirt, and a "pancake" straw hat or cloth headband. As late as the 1930's men in several villages of Yucatan and in Amatenango, Chiapas, wore a knee-length cotton cloth wrapped around the hips. Likewise, in Guatemalan Solola, Santa Cruz, and Panajachel, men wore small plaid wool kilts. Although cotton shirts and trousers were also worn, these hip-cloths seem to be vestiges of the ancient Maya kiltlike loincloths (Bennett and Zingg, 1935, pl. 7; Toor, 1947, pl. 25; MNAIP, 1954; Shattuck, 1933, pls. 11D, 13A, 17C, 22C, 23D, 34D, 35A, 36B,C: Leche, Gould, and Thorp, 1944, figs. 2–4; McBryde, 1947, p. 49; Osborne, 1935, figs. 5, 7).

Perpetuation of styles evolved in the colonial period are found in Chichicastenango and Tuxtla Gutierrez. The former has a costume of wool, with pullover jacket and knee-breeches of 17th-century cut, enlivened by foliate silk embroidery and fringes; a brocaded headcloth, red sash, sandals, and huge shoulder bag complete the outfit. In Tuxtla Gutierrez there are leather pants (short, and split at the sides), which have woolen counterparts in Todos Santos Cuchumatan and Solola (alcaldes); all are worn over cotton trousers (O'Neale, 1945, pp. 256, 302, figs. 55, *b,g,* 130,*f;* Cordry and Cordry, 1941, p. 94, fig. 23, pl. 19). On the whole, men's dress in Guatemala has pre-

151

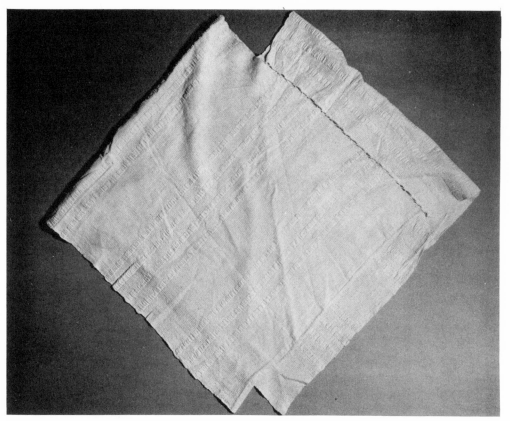

FIG. 13—GAUZE AND CREPE WEFT-WEAVE QUEXQUEMITL, SIERRA DE PUEBLA.
Web widths at shoulder folds 48 cm. G. M. Foster Coll., Berkeley. (Photo, William Ricco.)

served or added to colonial conventions more idiomatic liveliness than in Mexico by using jaspé cottons (Solola, Santiago Atitlan) or brocaded cotton shirts and trousers (Santa Maria de Jesus, Todos Santos Cuchumatan).

Women's dress in Middle America roughly falls into the same categories as men's yet, aside from the Euro-American clothes, the amalgamated and primitive styles are far more varied. As domestic weavers, women have continued more traditional features and devised adaptations of new materials and techniques with great ingenuity. The least native rural dress is a cotton blouse, long-sleeved, often having a peplum, and adorned with embroidery or lace, accompanied by a cotton skirt gathered onto a cord or waistband and usually ruffled at the bottom. Both garments seem more 19th century than colonial Spanish in derivation. Seri, Tarahumara, Mayo, Cora, Huichol, and Tehuana women, as well as others sporadically in Mexico, wear this dress. Yet the Huichol add the quexquemitl, many others the rebozo, and Tehuanas make a huipil-like, sleeveless blouse of red and brown printed muslin. Some Guatemalans, as at Coban and Quezaltenango, gather yards of treadle-loom, jaspé cotton cloth onto a cord at the waist in non-native style, but top this skirt with a huipil of traditional design. Rebozos, which in Mexico are worn even with store-bought dresses, are replaced in Guatemala with many varieties of handwoven, squarish shawls which serve the same purposes of headcover, baby and bundle carrier.

The Tarascan styles at Cheran and Tzintzuntzan are stabilized adaptations of post-

152

FIG. 14—CROSS-STITCH EMBROIDERED PLAIN-WEAVE QUEXQUEMITL, SIERRA DE PUEBLA. Web widths at shoulder folds 41 cm. G. M. Foster Coll., Berkeley. (Photo, William Ricco.)

conquest garments. A blouse of muslin with square neck, tiny sleeves, and embroidery around these apertures, is generally worn in central Mexico. At Cheran a muslin petticoat, embroidered at the edge, and a dark wool skirt several meters wide are held in place by wool belts. Excess widths of both skirts are arranged in many small pleats across the back, and excess lengths extend above the belts to fan out over the hips. The belts are wound in layers, producing a horizontal flange at the waist. An embroidered apron is worn for "polite" occasions. A handwoven blue rebozo may be draped in many graceful ways. Here, as generally for women, the feet are bare. The hair, arranged with center part and two pendant braids, exemplifies the basic coiffure of all Middle America. The man's hat and woman's apron have prestige significance: to appear without either is unthinkable. (This costume, its variations and changes, are described by Beals, 1946, p. 38, and Foster, 1948a, p. 43.)

Wool skirts with embroidered blouses of the above type clothe Tepehua, Otomi, Nahua, and Totonac women of the Sierra de Puebla, but here are accompanied by quexquemitls of many varieties, e.g., fine gauzes (Pahuatlan), brocaded and embroidery-encrusted types (San Gregorio, Pantepec), airily cross-stitched ones (Acaxochitlan), and thick, round-cornered forms (San Pablito, Santa Ana Hueytlalpan; figs. 13–16).

153

FIG. 15—WOOL EMBROIDERED QUEXQUEMITL, TULANCINGO, HIDALGO. Web widths at shoulder folds 41 cm. Specimen 3/558, Robert H. Lowie Museum of Anthropology, University of California, Berkeley. (Photo, William Ricco.)

FIG. 16—QUEXOUEMITL WITH WOVEN CURVED CORNER, SANTA ANA HUEYTLAL-PAN, HIDALGO. Web widths at shoulder folds 37 cm. Specimen, A. H. Gayton, Berkeley. (Photo, William Ricco.)

Nahua of Cuetzalan place a second quex-quemitl on their headdress of bulky wool cords (Christensen, 1947; MNAIP, 1951; Cordry and Cordry, 1940, p. 40).

Wool skirts, like preconquest cotton ones, are usually made of two lengths seamed together horizontally, the two breadths making the hip-to-ankle length; the ends may be seamed or merely overlapped. The arrangement of the excess circumference is locally conventionalized; usually a great double fold is made across the back and a few large pleats in front (Tepehua: Gessain, 1953, p. 196; Nahua, Cuetzalan: Cordry and Cordry, 1940, p. 49; Zapotec of Mitla and Yalalag: Parsons, 1936, p. 36; De la Fuente, 1949, p. 69). Unique is the Zoque cotton skirt, with its excess length and width twisted into a pendant loop (Cordry and Cordry, 1941, p. 82, fig. 19, pl. 17). Wool clothing rarely has been adopted by Guatemalan women, save for belts (Chichicastenango).

The huipil, a native blouse of cotton, rectangular and sleeveless, is retained in southern Mexico and Guatemala. In Mexico its dimensions are large, of tunic proportions, and it is worn outside the skirt; Guatemalan huipiles except those for ceremonies are hip-length or shorter and tucked inside the skirt. At Coban they are too short and wide to stay tucked in. Chinantec and Amuzgo huipiles are three-breadth and lavishly brocaded (fig. 17) or embroidered. The Yalalag dress is a pure white huipil with ribbed shoulders, a brown and white striped cotton skirt, a white rebozo, and a huge turban of black wool cords. Yucatan women make huipiles of white muslin adorned with European-style floral embroidery. (Bevan, 1938, p. 81; Start, 1948, pp. 67–73, pl. 12; Cordry and Cordry, 1940, pl. 9; Morley, 1946, pl. 26,c,d.)

Traditional purity of line is retained at Santiago Atitlan where a long, tightly wrapped skirt, narrow huipil, slender scarf over one shoulder, and hair bound in a long tape distinguish the women from other Guatemalans. Chichicastenango skirts, while tight, are very short; a bulky brocaded huipil, jaspé shawl, thick glass bead necklaces, and a two-braid coiffure complete this top-heavy costume. (Complete roster of Guatemalan dress: O'Neale, 1945, pp. 105–216, 249–306; McBryde, 1947, plates.)

A wrap-around skirt as the sole garment is the most primitive style, and still exists in a few areas where climate or custom do not enforce covering the upper half of the body (Popoluca: G. M. Foster, verbal information; coastal Guatemala: McBryde, 1947, p. 51, pl. 2,b,d.)

Aberrations such as the woman's wool shirt (Tlatauqui), ruffled berthas of lace (Totonac), starched lace huipiles (Tehuana), or concentrically stitched and ruffled yokes (Jacaltenango) occur sporadically as isolated developments, yet all indicate a continuing independent inventiveness.

The specialized Charro outfit for men and its feminine equivalent, the China Poblana dress, are colonial derivations which once had a legitimate place in Mexican culture, but now are donned for festive display as artificial symbols of "national" costume.

In native habits of weaving and dress Mexico and Guatemala are essentially one, differentiated by variations subordinate to the Middle American whole. The ground loom links with Pima, Papago, and Maricopa types to the north, yet the backstrap loom is common to the Pueblos to the north, all of Middle America, and Andean South America, as are the basic weaving techniques for cotton (Kent, 1957, p. 483). Wool weaving was adopted everywhere, and silk was sought for embellishments; preferred styles in designs and uses mark the differences. Women's simplest dress of wrap-around skirt and scarf was supplemented in preconquest times by a quexquemitl or huipil. The occurrence of the latter garments may have been mutually exclu-

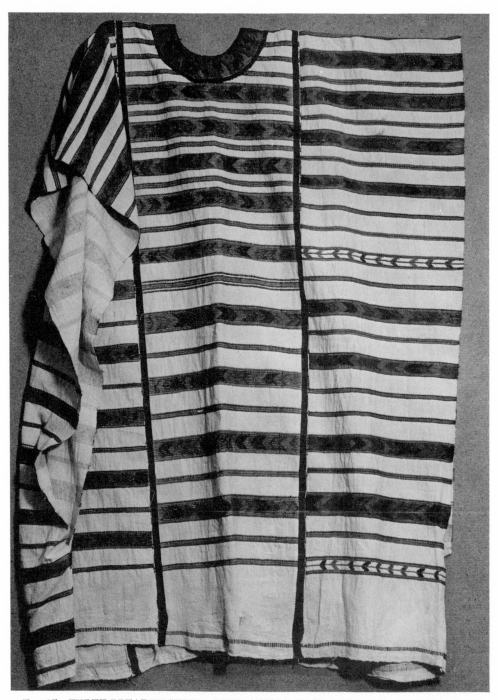

Fig. 17—THREE-BREADTH HUIPIL WITH SINGLE-FACE BROCADE, MIXTECA ALTA. Web widths as viewed: left 34 cm., center 39 cm., right 35 cm. Length from shoulder fold to bottom edge 83 cm. Specimen 3/15729, Robert H. Lowie Museum of Anthropology, University of California, Berkeley. (Photo, William Ricco.)

sive, according to Irmgard W. Johnson (1953). Adaptations and amalgamations of introduced and native fashions redeveloped as local styles; the Spanish ingredients have been analyzed by George M. Foster (1960a, p. 95). Known changes in recent times, such as the diffusion of headdresses from Oaxaca to Guatemala, or of Tehuana styles in Oaxaca and Chiapas, exemplify the vitality manifest by Middle American costume from ancient times to the present (Morgadanes, 1940; Cordry and Cordry, 1941, p. 75).

REFERENCES

Beals, 1943, 1945a, 1946
Bennett and Zingg, 1935
Bevan, 1938
Bird, 1953
Borah, 1943
Born, 1937
Brand, 1951
Christensen, 1947, 1953
Cordry and Cordry, 1940, 1941
De la Fuente, 1949
Dewar, 1957
Foster, 1948a, 1960a
Gerhard, 1964
Gessain, 1953
Johnson, I. W., 1953, 1957, 1958
Johnson, J. B., 1950
Kelly and Palerm, 1952
Kent, 1957

Leche, Gould, and Thorp, 1944
Lumholtz, 1902
McBryde, 1947
Morgadanes, 1940
Morley, 1946
Museo Nacional de Artes, 1951, 1954
Norman, 1959
Nuttall, 1909
O'Neale, 1945
Osborne, 1935
Parsons, 1936
Shattuck, 1933
Starr, F., 1899, 1908
Start, 1948
Stone, 1949
Toor, 1947
Weitlaner, 1941
West, 1948

9. Drama, Dance, and Music

GERTRUDE PROKOSCH KURATH

ALTHOUGH the performing arts of Middle American Indians have changed in form since the 16th century, they have maintained a basically religious motivation. Some surviving native rites are addressed to native deities for success with crops or hunting, or for therapeutic effects. Hispano-American dramas render homage to the Virgin Mary, Christ, or a patron saint, sometimes in fulfillment of a vow, sometimes in supplication for agricultural success.

To the Indian the fiesta is the peak occasion in community life and a break in its routine. Certain rural, native dances engage the entire community, bedecked in regional costumes. Other rituals include a cast of special male (rarely female) performers, who are surrounded by admiring spectators. The actors, in special costumes and often in masks, perform on a sacred hill, on a street corner, or in a village or church plaza.

Popular, recreational dances often conclude religious fiestas in rural outdoor or indoor settings. Again, they may provide entertainment in urban homes or on theater stages. Such secular dances are almost always for couples of men and women, dressed in regional attire or in modern Euro-American clothes.

Fiesta Calendars

The dances, which are legion, have traditional places in annual calendars of festivals, ecological, ecclesiastical, or secular.

The ecological cycle refers mainly to peoples of the northwestern sierras of Mexico, but it includes some mountain and jungle tribes throughout Middle America. The ecclesiastical cycle was adopted by village and city people who were subjected to Spanish soldiers and missionaries. The new calendar was a substitute for the native calendar, but it sometimes coincided with the ecological dates, as in the Tarahumara planting rituals. Our discussion of events in the ecological calendar follows a regional arrangement, because of great differences in local practices. On the other hand, events in the ecclesiastical calendar subordinate regional variations to the four widely distributed Catholic festivals (see F. J. Hernández, 1946; Toor, 1947).

Ecological Calendar

Maya of Quintana Roo: offerings for rain and

158

FIG. 1—DANZA DE LOS VIEJITOS, PATZCUARO, MICHOACAN, MEXICO.

crops, especially the "Okotbatam" of August and September.

Quiche of Guatemala: seasonal agricultural ceremonies, Volador or Flying Pole fiestas (fig. 2).

Lacandon, Tzotzil, and Tzeltal of Chiapas: cave ceremonies for planting.

Chinantec and Mixe of Oaxaca: planting and rain ceremonies.

Mixtec of Guerrero: June 13 rain, September 12 harvest, October 26 late harvest fiestas.

Tepehua of Huehuetla, Hidalgo: April-May rain ceremonies.

Otomi of Sierra de Puebla: Volador at various times (Chila, February 10–17, Pahuatlan, Easter); Acatlaxqui in Santa Catarina Nopochtla, November 25–26.

Totonac, Veracruz: harvest ceremonies in October.

Huastec, Tamaulipas, and San Luis Potosi: fall hunt dances.

Huichol, Jalisco, and Nayarit: January 27 deer dance, rain rituals; November, Hikuli ritual.

Southern Tepehuan, Durango, and Nayarit: Mitote in January, May for sowing, October for harvest, formerly with deer dance.

Tarahumara, Chihuahua: Rutuburi and Yumari at March planting, rain fiesta, September

FIG. 2—VOLADORES, SANTO TOMAS CHICHICASTENANGO, EL QUICHE, GUATEMALA. (Middle American Research Institute, Tulane University.)

159

FIG. 3—EIGHTEENTH-CENTURY VOLADORES. (From Clavigero, 1807, fig. 17.)

FIG. 4—EIGHTEENTH-CENTURY ACROBATS AT VOLADOR CEREMONY. (From Clavigero, 1807, fig. 18.)

Green Corn festival, formerly harvest Kuvala.

Seri, Sonora: In May, men's dance for animals, women's round for plants.

Papago, Sonora: Wiikita harvest-cure at midwinter and midsummer.

Ecclesiastical Calendar

Carnival:

Merida, Yucatan: Xtoles, Cintas (Ribbon) dances.

Zaachila, Oaxaca: battle of devils and priests.

Cuautla, Tepoztlan, Yautepec, Morelos: Chinelos.

Tecalpulco, Guerrero: Moros y Cristianos, Concheros, Tecuanes, Vaqueros, Las Tres Potencias.

Chilpancingo, Guerrero: Tlacololeros.

Santa Maria Atlihuatzia, Tlapalita, Santa Ana Chiautempan, Tlaxcala: Morisco, Arcos, Catrines or Cihuames.

Tepeyanco, Tlaxcala: Paragueros.

Amecameca, Mexico: Moros, Concheros, Pastorcitas.

Huejotzingo, Puebla: drama of Agustin Lorenzo, with Zacapoaxtles, Zuaves, Apaches, and other groups.

Tuxpan, Jalisco: Huichol bull burlesque.

Merida, Progreso, Yucatan; Oaxaca City, Veracruz, Acapulco, Mazatlan, other cities: floats, bailes, sometimes bull burlesque.

Holy Week and Easter:

Chimaltenango, Guatemala: Deer, Bull dances.

Oxchuc, Chiapas, Ixtapalapa, D.F., Tzintzuntzan, Michoacan, other towns: Passion Play.

Pahuatlan, Puebla: Volador, Santiagos (figs.
4, 18).

Tarahumara, Huichol, northern Tepehuan:
Matachini, Pascol.

Cahita, Sonora: Passion Play with Matachini,
Pascolas, Deer, Coyotes.

Corpus Christi:

Papantla, Veracruz: Volador, Moros y Cristianos, Quetzales, Santiagueros, Negritos.

Huehuetla, Hidalgo: Tocotines, Santiagueros, Tambulan with Malinche, Pastoras;
evening Huapangos.

Tzintzuntzan, Michoacan: Moros, Viejitos,
procession of fishermen.

Tuxpan, Jalisco: Moros, Sonajeros.

Advent and Epiphany:

Most Guatemalan towns: Loas.

Tepoztlan, Morelos: December 16–24, January 5–10, Pastoras.

Texcoco, Mexico: Coloquios of Wise Men,
regional dances.

Taxco, Guerrero to Tepic, Nayarit: Christmas Posadas.

Tuxpan, Jalisco: also Danza del Heno.

Pichataro, Capacuaro, Michoacan: December 16-January 6, Pastorelas.

Paracho, Michoacan: Huananchas.

Chicomoztoc, Zacatecas: January 8, Pastorela.

Many larger cities: children's Posada processions, and plays of Wise Men.

There are many other Catholic holidays:
with dances, as Candlemas, February 2, in
Tzintzuntzan and in San Juan de los Lagos;
and without dances, as the Día de Muertos,
November 1, in Janitzio and other places.
Each village celebrates its saint's day. Numerous towns hold festivals for the Virgin
Mary, for the Assumption on August 15, or
for a miraculous image. At Chalma a miraculous image of Christ is honored by a series
of pilgrimages, which are set for specific
areas: Otomi of state of Mexico, January
1–7; Tehuantepec, February 2; Guerrero
and Tlaxcala, first Sunday in Lent; Mexico,
D.F., Pentecost; Xochimilco, August 28; un-
assigned groups, September 29.

FIG. 5—AZTEC FEAST OF XOCOTL HUETZI. Codex
Matritense.

The Moros y Cristianos and the Pastorelas have a wide diffusion, but other dances
are regional specialties, as the Chinelos of
Morelos and the Danza de Plumas (fig. 6)
or La Conquista of Oaxaca. The Pluma is
danced January 15 at Zimatlan, January 27–
28 at Cuilapan, the Sunday before Corpus
Christi at Zaachila, and July 8 and 25 at
Teotitlan del Valle. The Chinelos calendar
forms part of an elaborate regional calendar of the towns clustered near Tepoztlan,
Morelos, and the barrios of Tepoztlan. Here
each place has its specialty, but intervisit-
ing brings the specialties to various fiestas.
At the January 16 fiesta of Santa Catarina
groups converge from several pueblos, at
the May 8 fiesta of Ixcatepec Apaches attend from San Juan and Santiago. The only
specialty which does not migrate is the
drama of El Tepozteco in Tepoztlan on
September 8 (Redfield, 1930, pp. 103–32).

At the Tzintzuntzan festival for the Señor
del Rasgate (Ecce Homo), as part of the

161

Fig. 6—AZTEC TOXCATL CEREMONY. Codex Matritense.

places. The fourth Sunday in Lent they converge on the village of Acopilco, D.F., from Mexico City and San Miguel de Allende. Pilgrim groups worship two miraculous Virgins: September 1–8 at Los Remedios, December 12 at Guadalupe, Mexico. The great Conchero festival at San Miguel de Allende, September 28–29, is a more regional celebration, attended by nearby groups (Kurath, 1946).

Secular Calendar

Just as native and ecclesiastical dances sometimes overlap, secular events may take place on a religious occasion. Ceremonies often conclude with regional bailes. In Tehuantepec and other large towns religious fiestas are likely to concentrate on the Zandunga and similar dances. Though church holidays, February 2 and March 4 schedule secularized or popular dances and music.

February 2, Candlemas—villages of Michoacan: Viejitos, Las Sembradoras.
March 4, Crucifijo de la Veracruz—Taxco, Guerrero, Torito. Salinas, San Luis Potosi: balls.
March 18–31, Antiguo Morelos, Tamaulipas: Huapangos, cockfights, horse races.
May 5, national holiday—everywhere regional dances or balls, parades.
May 15–25—Juchitan, Oaxaca fiesta: Zandunga, parades, bullfights.
Week after July 16—Guelaguetza at Cerro del Fortin, Oaxaca: religious and secular dances (Conquista, Jarabes) for public.
September 16—Independence Day, regional dances, balls, parades, speeches.
October 17–24—Alvarado, Veracruz: Huapangos, fair.
New Year's Eve—Tehuantepec and other cities: parades, bailes, Mass.

Secular dances also celebrate crises of life—baptisms, weddings, sometimes wakes. They enliven anniversaries like birthdays, dedications of schools and other buildings, or welcome for distinguished guests. The Sierra Norte de Puebla Indians have special songs for life crises; the Indians of Michoa-

Passion drama, visiting dancers include the Santiagos from Patzcuaro, a Pastorela from Zipiajo, and the Old Men or Viejitos (fig. 7) from Cucuchucho (Carrasco, 1952b, p. 25; Foster, 1948a, p. 208). It is common practice to engage expert groups from neighboring villages, especially if the celebrating village no longer can supply local dancers (Kelly, 1953, p. 184).

Perhaps the groups that travel farthest are the Concheros, alias Apaches or Chichimecas. At the great Candelaria festival of San Juan de los Lagos, Jalisco, Concheros travel long distances in box cars, for instance from Mexico City. For the carnival at Tecalpulco, Guerrero, they travel from Tenancingo, Mexico, and more distant

FIG. 7—HUICHOL SQUASH FIESTA, LA MESETA, NAYARIT, MEXICO. (Photographed by Donald Cordry, 1938.)

FIG. 8—HUICHOL HIKULI DANCER, NEAR RA-TONTITA, MEXICO. See also fig. 9. (From Lumholtz, 1902, 2: 279.)

can have these and also a girls' Iguiris dance for guests (see Secular Celebrations below).

TYPES OF DANCES AND DRAMAS

To a large extent the calendar types coincide with two other classifications, according to function and provenience. Religious dances conform to the ecological and ecclesiastical calendars; recreational dances celebrate secular holidays. In the ritual category, only certain native survivals follow the ecological cycle. But native rituals and

164

Hispanic bailes may take place on Catholic holidays. In fact, the Catholic holiday is likely to be a conglomerate of many events. To complicate the situation, no sharp division exists between native dances and blends of Indian and European traditions. Also, it is not always feasible to label an element as native or imported, because of the analogies between customs on both sides of the Atlantic.

Despite overlapping, the following classification helps clarify the religious and artistic acculturation.

1. Native rituals and their composition
   a. Native survivals in the ecological calendar
   b. Native survivals in the ecclesiastical calendar
2. Blended ritual dramas
   a. Colonial ecclesiastical introductions
   b. Postconquest creations
3. Secular celebrations

Native Rituals and Their Composition

NATIVE SURVIVALS IN THE ECOLOGICAL CALENDAR. The Mixtecs of Guerrero make a series of supplications to native deities, the largest one on April 25 to Nusavitche, the supreme aquatic deity (P. A. W., 1951, pp. 156–61). The procedures reduce to the following essentials:

1. Preliminaries: begging procession by ceremonial officials for food for a feast; transportation of the deity's idol to a sacred hill.
2. Ritual action: on the hill, after assembly of the people, offerings of prayers and flowers by priests to the four directions, a dance with contortions before the idol.
3. Communal dance: Chilena by men and women, holding boughs and flowers, men improvising steps near the idol, women in the background, wind instruments to one side.
4. Ritual action: sacrifice of animals by priests and officials; general offering of copal, eggs, aguardiente to the four directions.
5. Feast: communal consumption of food and ceremonial drinking of pulque, followed by prayer.

Fig. 9—HUICHOL HIKULI DANCE NEAR RATONTITA, MEXICO. (From Lumholtz, 1902, 2: 274.)

6. Secular dance: couple dance, Fandango, to lively "sones" of wind instruments, amid increasing inebriation.

7. Postlude: homeward procession past crosses with idols, principals dancing before crosses on the road.

The main features of this structure fit other surviving native festivals, in preparation, dedication and offering, dance and feast. The Fandango is certainly a recent addition; the Chilena appears to be native, in spite of the name. The structure also applies to the much more complex pre-Columbian Aztec ceremonies, notwithstanding the difference in time and environment. For instance, the Aztec ceremony of the fifth month, Toxcatl, against drouth follows a similar order:

1. Preliminaries: preparation of an impersonator of the god Tezcatlipoca, and preparations for a feast.

2. Ritual action: processional invocation by priests.

3. Ritual dance: solemn circuit by nobles.

4. Ritual action (fig. 8): sacrifice of the impersonator and other human victims, offerings of maize to an image of Huitzilopochtli.

5. Feast: communal consumption of tamales.

6. Communal dance: serpentine by warriors and girls, with self-accompaniment of song.

7. Postlude: next day, self-sacrifice by a priest (Anderson and Dibble, 1951, pp. 9–10).

The *Mitote* remains the ritual dance of the southern Tepehuan and other tribes of the Sierra Madre Occidental—the Tepecano, Cora, and Huichol. Men and women skip in a counterclockwise circle, five circuits one way, then five the other. A shaman accompanies with native songs, assisted by a musical bow on a gourd resonator. Formerly a deer dance followed the rounds.

165

FIG. 10—TARAHUMAR YUMARI DANCE. (From Lumholtz, 1902, 1: 340.)

In both name and style the Mitote appears related to the ancient Aztec Mitotiliztli, or profane dance (J. A. Mason, 1948, p. 298).

The *Hikuli* or peyote dance, held in November, follows Huichol and Tarahumara pilgrimages for peyote buttons. The dance of the Huichol is the more ecstatic (fig. 9). After consumption of the trance-inducing buttons, men and women leap jerkily and twist their bodies, in a counterclockwise progression. The men flourish deer tails and the women carry bamboo sticks, both representing serpents, to indicate the hunting and fertility potency of the ritual. A shaman sings songs in irregular meter, to the accompaniment of two deer bones scraped against each other (Lumholtz, 1902, 1: 276).

The *Rutuburi* is the typical ritual dance of the Tarahumara for three agricultural festivals—rain, green corn, and harvest—and for death and memorial rites. After tri-

ple invocations by a shaman, the women cross the dance space six times, then circle counterclockwise, holding hands and leaping with a stamp from left to right foot. The shaman's songs, with gourd rattle, often address the turkey. Just before sunrise men join the women in the *Yumari* dance for the deer (fig. 10). The men zigzag across the patio with the shaman, while the women circle. This dance is gay and accompanied by intoxication, but it concludes with offerings (Bennett and Zingg, 1935, pp. 273–75; Lumholtz, 1902, 1: 330ff.).

These unquestionably native dances share the features of offering, dance, feast, and intoxication, with final offering. They follow the same type of circuit, on a special outdoor space. They are for all men and women, though accompanied by special priestly singers. Thus they resemble the final dance of Toxcatl rather than the Aztec cir-

166

Fig. 11—ACATLAXQUI DANCE, SANTA CATARINA, HIDALGO, MEXICO. (Photo, Bodil Christensen.)

cuits by exclusive groups of priests or nobles. They are, after all, rituals of democratic, rural peoples rather than of an urban society.

NATIVE SURVIVALS IN THE ECCLESIASTICAL CALENDAR. The Sierra Madre Oriental also has native survivals. The *Acatlaxqui* dance certainly is pre-Cortesian, despite the trousers and bandannas worn by the dancers. It is a specialty of the municipality of Pahuatlan, Puebla. Otomi Indians of Santa Catarina Nopochtla perform it on November 25 (fig. 11). Ten or more young men dance in two rows inside the church, then in one row in front of the entrance. Then they encircle a Maringuilla, a boy dressed as a girl, holding a wooden snake. They lift her on a small platform. At the climactic moment each man flings the acatlaxqui, a strong reed with small ones attached in such a way as to slide out. This forms a canopy over Maringuilla's head

(Christensen, 1937). Though performed on St. Catherine's Day, the dance is native in style and doubtless in purpose, with fertility and probably harvest symbolism.

The *Quetzales* share fiestas with the Voladores and with several groups of Euro-colonial actors, for instance, at the Totonac village of Papantla, Veracruz. They are named after the resplandores, disc head-dresses formerly of quetzal feathers but now of raffia. They are also called Huahuas. With simple two-steps and raising of alternate knees, the dancers walk or skip through longways figures. They advance, retire, cross over, and weave in and out in a snakelike "vibora." The formations resemble those of European longways dances, but the steps are quite native. So is the music of flute and drum. And so is a concluding trick of revolving on a trapeze-like contraption (Amezquita B., 1943, pp. 75–78).

The *Voladores* or Flyers are widespread

167

FIG. 12—QUETZALES, SIERRA DE PUEBLA, MEX-
ICO. (Photo, Bodil Christensen.)

in the Sierras, appearing for instance on
the saint's fiesta of Chila, Puebla, February
10–17. The dancing and flying have ritual
preliminaries. In Papantla and Tajin, four
Totonac men, symbolizing the cardinal
points, dance a "cadena" or chain around a
pole seven times, then climb to the top and
seat themselves on a framework, while the
drummer-flutist dances on a small platform.
They tie a rope around their waist and
launch themselves into space head first. To
special tunes they spiral with 13 revolutions. The 4 times 13 represent the Aztec
cycle of 52 years. The flyers represent sun-
birds, also the descent of rain. Local variants include hawk costumes among the
Huastec; among the Otomi, six flyers, in-

cluding a transvestite Malinche, dance in
turn on the pole (Larsen, 1937; personal
observation).

The spectacle is limited to the eastern
sierras and the states of Hidalgo and San
Luis Potosi, but is also known in Guatemala, as a probable Toltec importation around
A.D. 1100. The Quiche at Joyabaj have further variants. Two men descend, while two
called "micos" or monkeys guide the ropes,
then slide down. On the ground a dozen
men hop to the music of a marimba (Termer, 1931).

The feat was reported by early 16th-cen-
tury writers as a specialty of the Totonac,
Huastec, and Mixtec (Dahlgren de Jordan,
1954, pp. 279ff.). It was associated with an
arrow sacrifice and an acrobatic stunt, "Juego de los Huahuas. The stunt is still performed by the Huahuas on the same occasion as the Volador. The Aztecs of Tenochtitlan knew the arrow sacrifice and a
simpler version of the pole sacrifice. In the
feast of Xocotl Huetzi (the fruit falls), in
August, a pole was surmounted by an idol
of dough. After sacrifices, young men
climbed after the idol (fig. 15; Anderson
and Dibble, 1951, pp. 17–18). Sometimes a
priest or noble flung himself from the pole
as a self-sacrifice to the rain gods.

Blended Ritual Dramas on Catholic Holidays

COLONIAL ECCLESIASTICAL INTRODUC-
TIONS. The semiurban ecclesiastical fiestas
include three types of dance-dramas: Moriscas (Moros y Cristianos, Santiagos, Matachini, and related plays); Passion plays;
Posadas, Pastorelas, and Guatemalan Loas.
These are often true dramas, with dramatis
personae and dialogue as well as dance and
music. The dialogue may be in Spanish or
in the native language, or it may mix Spanish and Nahuatl (Horcasitas Pimentel,
1949, p. 157).

Moriscas abound during carnival but also
occur at Corpus Christi, during pilgrimages
to San Juan de los Lagos or Chalma, on the

Fig. 13—VOLADORES CEREMONY, VILLA JUAREZ, PUEBLA, MEXICO.
(Photo, Bodil Christensen.)

village saint's day, especially for Santiago on July 25. In the drama of Moros y Cristianos two factions tangle in arguments and battle mime, with ultimate victory of Christians over Moors and the conversion of the latter. The contestants wear bearded masks and gaudy costumes with helmets and turbans; they wield wooden swords. A buffoon jumps about in ragged attire, molesting the combatants or spectators with a desiccated squirrel. The performance is casual and puppet-like, without any dramatic build. To a vapid, medieval tune of flute and tabor, the opponents slide, hop, pivot, and cross over in two lines.

In the variant termed Santiagos, the Christians are led by St. James on a hobby-horse (fig. 18). In the Sierra de Puebla the vanquished party is at times identified with Pilate in the plural. In the Conquista or

169

FIG. 14—SANTIAGUITOS DANCE, CHILA, PUEBLA, MEXICO. (Photo, Bodil Christensen.)

Danza de las Plumas of Oaxaca and in the Guatemalan version, the Spaniards vanquish Moctezuma and his Indians. Usually all combatants wear gorgeous garb, but in Juquila, Oaxaca, Cortés and his soldiers are ludicrously dressed, whereas the Indians, including two girls, are magnificent in plumed headdresses. This drama has two parts: a scene with Indian court dances, including a maypole dance, and a scene with combat (F. Starr, 1908, p. 30).

The Yaqui of Potam enact a vigorous battle on Tiniran, Holy Trinity. Blue fiesteros (festal society members) entrench themselves in the church as Christians. Red fiesteros, with crescent headdresses, encamp as Moors on the plaza. After relay racing by youngsters with banners, the two factions struggle and pull amid the audience, laugh-

ing, shouting, and shoving. Finally the reds are rushed to the altar and "baptized" (Spicer, 1954, pp. 145–46).

A Cahita votive society performs Matachini dances with solemn zest and precision. They stylize the battle to the opposition and interweaving of two lines. A monarca leads the intricate, syncopated Indian steps. A small transvestite Malinche in white dress copies him. The Matachini wear mitre-like headdresses with ribbon and mirror ornaments. They manipulate feathered tridents and tufted rattles in time with harp and fiddle music.

The Matachini dance forms part of the Cora, Tarahumara, and New Mexico Pueblo church pageantry, among the Pueblos with a battle of old man clown and bull masker (Kurath, 1949, pp. 92–94). Variants to the south bear different names, as Santia-guitos in Chila, Puebla (fig. 14), and Los Malinches in San Dionisio del Mar.

Name, costume, and music show European provenience, though the steps may be Indian (Robb, 1961, p. 91). Spain, Portugal, Austria, England, and Roumania retain various types of Moriscas. The Renaissance Matachini and the related Seises of Seville cathedral are confined to dancing; other forms emphasize pageantry and dialogues. They favor carnival and Corpus Christi fiestas. The splendor is fading in Spain, in contrast with the flourishing English Morris. A spectacular drama has lasted from 1276 to the present day, in Alcoy, Alicante. It pays homage to St. George, who miraculously leads Christians to victory (Foster, 1960a, pp. 223–24).

Combat has its aboriginal counterpart in several types of Aztec ceremonial battle. The spring festival for Xipe Totec features gladiatorial combat between sacrificial victims and knights of the Eagle and Jaguar orders (fig. 22). The harvest festival for Toci included skirmishes between old and young priestesses and a symbolic feud between deities of warmth and ice (Anderson and Dibble, 1951, pp. 48–50, 110–14).

A warriors' contest forms the theme of the Rabinal Achi—a rare remnant of prehistoric Guatemalan drama, in the Quiche language. A brave youth of Rabinal vanquishes a warrior of the Quiche. After much dialogue, round dancing, and performance of ritual acts, the prisoner is sacrificed to 12 priestly anthropomorphic eagles and 12 jaguars (Monterde, 1955).

In every case the combat was associated with sacrifice. In the Aztec ceremonies, fertility and vegetation symbolism was paramount. In the European contests, the origin reached into pre-Christian rituals, reinterpreted by the church. The same process repeated itself in Middle America.

Mexican *Passion plays* usually follow European patterns. In Tzintzuntzan, Michoacan, the Tarascans enact the biblical story,

FIG. 15—SANTIAGO AND HORSE, STATE OF PUEBLA, MEXICO. (Middle American Research Institute, Tulane University.)

with spoken words (relatos) and realistic action but without dancing or music. The whole village participates under the direction of the priest. After preparatory rites and parades of "centurions," the drama of Christ's suffering unfolds in the church and church plaza.

171

a **b**

FIG. 16—SANTIAGO DANCES, STATE OF PUEBLA, MEXICO. *a*, Rey Santiago. *b*, Santiago. (Middle American Research Institute, Tulane University.)

1. Thursday evening, enactment of the Last Supper.
2. Betrayal by Judas, capture of image of Christ by moonlight.
3. Trial, with populace reacting in passionate protest.
4. Friday morning, procession to Calvary, with four falls.
5. Afternoon, crucifixion and burial of the image.
6. Midnight, the Virgin's search for her Son, during procession of self-torturing Penitentes.

The Yaqui Easter fiesta emphasizes the struggle between spirits of good and evil,

while ceremonial groups present the Passion and Resurrection symbolically. Preliminaries begin on Ash Wednesday, when the Chapayekas clown society takes over the management. The main events on Easter weekend are:

1. Friday afternoon, carrying of an empty bier on a circuit of the stations of the cross, church societies and chanter attending the bier, Chapayekas cavorting on the sidelines or molesting the worshippers.
2. Inside the church, descent of image from the cross and symbolic burial in the bier, with mourning by altar women and girls,

172

Fig. 17—DANCE OF THE MOROS, IXTAPALAPA, D. F., MEXICO. (Middle American Research Institute, Tulane University.)

and massed stamping by evil groups—Chapayekas and black-robed Pilatos.

3. Saturday morning, another stampede, symbolizing attack on church.
4. Great surge from the church and burning of Chapayekas masks and Judas.
5. For the rest of Saturday and all night, dancing in a special "profane" ramada by animal mimes—Deer, Pascolas (fig. 21), Coyotes—and in the almost empty church by the Matachini (Spicer, 1954, pp. 78–93; personal observation).
6. Sunday morning, joyous processionals and running by maidens with the Virgin's image; approach and merging of two processions across the huge church plaza, with images of Christ and the Virgin, symbolizing the "Encuentro."

The Yaqui unconsciously enact the ulti-mate Mediterranean symbolism of spring-time contest, death, and rebirth, and blend this drama with dancing by overtly pre-Jesuit ceremonial groups.

Posadas and *Pastorelas* are episodes of the Christmas-time Coloquio de los Pastor-es (Englekirk, 1957, p. 28). They are most popular in southern and central Mexico, New Mexico, and Texas. The Posadas are now generally processions by city boys and girls, who go from house to house ask-ing for gifts and lodging and singing spe-cial hymns. Youngsters also dance qua-drilles of Pastores and Pastoras on Holy Night, symbolic of the shepherds who came to visit the infant Jesus (Toor, 1947, pp. 247–50).

On January 6 the Three Kings come to

173

Fig. 18—DANZA DE PLUMAS, ZAACHILA, OA-XACA, MEXICO. (Model by Enrique Alférez. Middle American Research Institute, Tulane University.)

worship the infant Jesus in a drama, El Auto de los Reyes Magos. They are often joined by other characters. In addition to dancing and music, these Autos call for long tirades, which have been shortened because of impatience in the audience.

There are many local variants of the danced Pastorelas and acted Autos. Tepoztlan and neighboring villages present attractive candle-light Pastorelas winding to the church (Redfield, 1930, p. 132). In Huehuetla nine boys and nine girls dance in rows to the music of a violin, guitar, and three teponaztli or native drums (Gessain, 1953, p. 203). In Paracho, Michoacan, the Huananchas, girls in charge of the image and altar of the Virgin, two-step through elaborate evolutions (Kaplan, 1951). In Cheran the pre-Christmas processions, December 14–24, include masked savages, Apaches, old men, and Negroes; Christmas events feature a dance of Negros and Pastoras; at Epiphany comes a dance of Viejitos. The Pastorela of Pichataro starts with a dance of three devils–Luzbel, Sin, and Cunning—then proceeds to the adoration by shepherds, a ranch boy and girl, a hermit, and angels. In Capacuaro a devil's play is followed by a Pastorela of shepherds, angels, Europeans, and hermit-buffoons (Beals, 1946, pp. 144–55).

Guatemalan *Loas* have a wider range than Pastorelas in both date and content. Correa (1958a, p. 5) defines a Loa as "a short dramatic work of religious character, designed for presentation on the days of the Immaculate Conception, the Virgin of Guadalupe, the patron saint, and Christmas, or during Holy Week." Performed on street corners during processionals, Loas aim to entertain the populace as well as to praise the Virgin. In addition to the Nativity and Three Kings, the topics include allegorical figures of Hope, Faith, and Charity, like morality plays in the Valley of Mexico. Angels dance longways in a Baile de las Flores (*ibid.*, pp. 41–43). Ten Devils and Death argue, dance, and finish by praising the Virgin in a Baile de Diablos y Muerte (Correa, 1958b). The Marian cult combines with the Morisca in Historia entre Moros y Cristianos para celebrar la Purísima Concesión de la Madre de Dios (Correa, 1958a, p. 37). In short, themes range from Paradise to modern homey scenes, with humble people, Ladinos, Germans, and the like.

In place of the Rabinal Achi, the village of Rabinal performs some mixtures of native, Spanish, and Greek themes. In the Baile de San Jorge, St. George miraculously appears to save a virgin offered to a dragon, because she appeals to the Virgin Mary. The Devil betrays St. George to the girl's father, an emperor; St. George is condemned to death by flaying, but is saved by an angel. All are converted and praise the Virgin (ibid., p. 32). In the Baile de los Animales y Tiradores, figures of a lion, ox, deer, jabali, monkey, tiger, coyote, and dog plot against a hunter, who is after them; but they all unite in a eulogy of the Virgin dieval patterns. Sahagún likened the Aztec festival, Toxcatl, to Easter (Anderson and Dibble, 1951, p. 9), but in structure and cast it differed from the Passion plays of the 15th–17th centuries (Foster, 1960a, pp. 178–88). Posadas, Pastorelas, and Loas resemble not the Aztec festivals to the mother and conclude with a cheerful dance.

The liturgical dramas clearly follow medeities, Toci and Ilamatecutli, but the former Spanish autos de nacimiento, as the Pastorcillos de Belen (ibid., p. 205) and the thriving Austrian peasant Schäferspiele (Kretzenbacher, 1952). Penitente rituals, acceptable because of pre-Cortesian penitential customs, derive from the medieval Italian and Spanish brotherhoods (Kirstein, 1935, pp. 123–27; Kurath, 1950, pp. 851–52). The exploitation of humorous, homely situations was a characteristic of the European entremés.

The dramas were introduced by early Spanish missionaries, who noticed the native love of dance and mime (Acosta, 1590,

FIG. 19—DANCE OF THE MOORS COSTUME. CHINAUTLA, GUATEMALA. Dance performed during the *fiesta titular*. (From Reina, 1960, fig. 17. Middle American Research Institute, Tulane University.)

p. 508), and who soon taught their converts Moriscas, Autos, and alabanzas (Mendoza, 1956, p. 13). In 1538 padres produced La Destrucción de Rodas in Tenochtitlan, in 1539 they put on a vast pageant for a Tlax-

175

FIG. 20—DANCE OF THE CONQUEST, TACTIC, ALTA VERAPAZ, GUATEMALA. (From Bode, 1961, fig. 1,*c*. Middle American Research Institute, Tulane University.)

FIG. 21—DANZA DE LOS MOROS, CHICHICASTENANGO, EL QUI-CHE, GUATEMALA. (Photographed in 1928. Middle American Research Institute, Tulane University.)

calan peace treaty and Corpus Christi celebration. La Conquista de Jerusalem dramatized the victory of Spaniards and Christian
Indians over Moors, with the help of Santiago and the Archangel Michael (Steck,
1951, pp. 160–66). The padres and their literate converts wrote texts for the Temptation of Our Lord; for St. Francis preaching
to the birds, calming an ugly beast, and
summoning demons to carry a drunkard off
to hell; and for the Fall, with a paradise of
fruit trees, flowers, birds, ocelots, and other
animals. The Guatemaltecans, as inventive
as the Mexicans, produced La Conquista in
Antigua by 1642 (Reynolds, 1956, p. 32).

In time the texts, paraphernalia, and
characters changed, through the efforts of
anonymous authors and occasionally named
playwrights (Englekirk, 1957, pp. 18–29).
Many original scenarios have been created.

POSTCONQUEST CREATIONS. The Altepe-
ilhuitl, or drama of El Tepoztecatl, may replace an old September harvest festival, but
it has a postconquest plot. A chief, Tepozteco of Tepoztlan, a convert to Christianity,
defends his fortress from four neighboring
village armies. He defeats them after skirmishes and long declamations in Nahuatl
(Redfield, 1930, pp. 227–31).

In a Lenten fiesta at Acopilco, Mexico,
men and boys in ordinary white shirts and
calzones enact a quaint play, with dancing
and fiddle music but without dialogues.
Arrieros (mule-drivers) wander through
mountains. At the end of a weary day they
eat, dance, gamble with dice, and lie down
to sleep. During the night they are attacked
by bandits, but they appeal to the Lord and
are miraculously rescued (Kurath, 1947).

Another bandit story is enacted by a
medley of characters in fantastic costumes
and masks. The Huejotzingo carnival drama concerns a famous bandit, Agustín Lorenzo, who abducts the daughter of a rich
hacendado, and is attacked by groups of
federal soldiers during his wedding celebration (Toor, 1947, pp. 194–97).

The Concheros are a highly organized

FIG. 22—TLACAXIPEUALIZTLI GLADIATORS. Codex
Magliabecchi 18.¨

votive dance society. They take long pilgrimages to appear in many fiestas, from
Taxco, Guerrero, to Queretaro. Their preliminary rituals and alabanza songs are addressed to the four winds and the Virgin
of Guadalupe. Their processions include
mythological figures of the primal Aztec
deities, Oxomoco and Cipactonatl, and devils. In San Miguel de Allende the associated
Rayados dance out the christianization of
Chichimecas after a battle of 1531 (Fernández and Mendoza, 1941, pp. 12–17).
The Concheros dance in a circle with steps
partly Indian, partly European. The leaders
accompany themselves, while dancing, on
conchas, lutelike stringed instruments made
from armadillo shells; they use European
harmonies and Indian rhythms. The society
appears as a nativistic complex for men and
women of all ages in search of Indian tradition (Kurath, 1946).

Secular Celebrations

Ritual and secular categories often overlap. The Tarascan Viejitos dance has become secularized, the Yaqui Pascol ensemble loses ritual functions from year to year.
Again, many ceremonies conclude with jo-
vial social dancing, as the Mixtec April cer-

177

Fig. 23—DANCE OF ANIMALS AND HUNTERS, ACATLAN, PUEBLA, MEXICO.
(Middle American Research Institute, Tulane University.)

Fig. 24—JAGUAR DANCE MASKS, STATE OF GUERRERO, MEXICO. (Middle American Research Institute, Tulane University.)

emony and the series of Tarahumara fiestas. In Tehuantepec the feast of the barrio saint ends with regional dances, waltzes, and Danzón to brass band (Covarrubias, 1947, pp. 365–70). Urban carnival celebrations consist of parades with floats and masked balls, as in Merida, Guadalajara, and Mazatlan (Vázquez Santana and Dávila Garibi, 1931, pp. 67, 81, 99–100). In the city of Oaxaca masked comparsas gad about every Sunday the month before carnival, in a competitive spirit. Near the city of Oaxaca, on Cerro del Fortin, the Guelaguetza, formerly a religious festival, includes ritual dances as well as couple dances; it has become a secular affair (Millán Maldonado, 1942, pp. 41–46).

Crises of life often give an excuse for a church-sanctioned night of social dancing, which is usually the regional type. In some locations they require a special dance or song. A girl's dance, the Canacuas, honors a Tarascan bride and groom. The Puebla mountain Aztecs celebrate baptisms with songs of the flower pole, Xochitl Cuahuitl, and weddings with flower rain, Xochi-pitzahua (Amezquita B., 1943, pp. 22–25).

In form the regional, secular dances are distinct from the rituals. Except for the circular mitote types, they are all for parejas sueltas, couples who do not touch. Their variant names and forms are legion, and are only partly covered in the large literature (Sedillo Brewster, 1935; Kurath, 1949; Mooney, 1957; Lekis, 1958, pp. 39–40). Among the best known are the Jarana Yucateca, the Zapotec Zandunga and Llorona, the Chiapanecas, the Huapangos of the East Coast, and regional Jarabes, as the Jarabe Yalalteco, Tlaxcalteco, Michoacano, and Tapatío. Guatemalans call their regional variant Zarabanda (Wagley, 1949, pp. 109–10). The Huapango is termed Fandango in the Mixteca and in Popoloacan. Sometimes the theme of flirtation or female coyness blossoms forth in humorous interludes. In the Vaquería of Chan Kom the girls act like bulls, chasing the boys with lassos. The

FIG. 25—JAGUAR DANCER, GUERRERO, MEXICO. (Model by Enrique Alférez. Middle American Research Institute, Tulane University.)

179

Fig. 26—YAQUI DEER DANCE, SONORA, MEXICO. Accompanied by water drum and notched sticks. (Photo, Bodil Christensen.)

boys counter with humorous refrains called bombas (Redfield and Villa Rojas, 1934, pp. 153–54). Contests of bomba improvisations also contribute to the merriment of the Veracruz Huapango.

All regional dances are blends of European and native steps and styles, and all use European or European-derived instruments and tunes. Some, as the Jarabe Tapatío, urban Huapangos, and Danzón, are so European as to fit into the Mestizo rather than the Indian category. Nevertheless, Indians do enjoy them and give them a native flavor. Even the Chiapanecas contains hops with back-pulls alongside waltz steps. The

Sierran Huapango dancer takes a bowed posture. Like the Jarabe Michoacano, the Pueblan Huapango has music in changeable meters (Amezquita B., 1943, pp. 33–35). The accompaniments are: in the south, marimba; in the center, fiddle and guitar; in the cities and villages, brass band. Sometimes there are songs in Spanish or mixed Indian and Spanish. Mestizos sometimes dance to mariachi ensembles of guitars, a harp, and sometimes a cornet.

The origins must usually be deduced from the style. Mendoza (1956, pp. 83–88) suggests Andalusia for the Zandunga, the Flamenco Fandango for Huapangos, and the Jota Aragonesa for Jarabes. However, zapateados are omnipresent, and the Austrian waltz, Slavic polka and mazurka are mixed into most routines. These arrived in the mid-19th century. The alemana and contrapás, brought by early colonists, have lost popularity.

Animals and Clowns

Animal mimes and clowns greatly enliven the fiestas. Often, but not always, they are identified.

Termer (1930a, p. 662) separates the two categories in his listing of Guatemalan dances. Yet the monkey is comic, and the Toro clowns are animals. Serious animal maskers perform in the Rabinal Achi and the Loa, Los Animales y el Tirador. The Deer Dance of San Marcos retains native ritualistic features. After ritual preliminaries, shamans are in steady attendance. The owners of the animals, Old Man and Old Woman, correspond to the primal deities of the Concheros. A lion, a jaguar, and six monkeys mime realistically, but the chief actors, three deer and six hunters, act symbolically and wear strange colonial costumes. The accompaniment is marimba music (LaFarge and Byers, 1931, pp. 104–06). The Cil-Marimba, or Deer Dance, of Jacaltenango parodies this drama with ragged clothes (Cil) and humorous dialogue (*ibid.*, pp. 109–11).

Tigers (tecuanes) are generally comic, for instance, in the Conquista of Juquila, Oaxaca (F. Starr, 1908, p. 34), and in the agrarian Tlacololeros drama of Chilpancingo, Morelos (Vázquez Santana, 1940, pp. 184–89). Contests of toros and cowboys are always farcical, in Chimaltenango, Guatemala (Wagley, 1949, pp. 117–20), in the Mixtec Pachecos (Toor, 1947, p. 358), and the rowdy Huichol carnival of Tuxpan, Jalisco (*ibid.*, p. 201). Assorted beasts cavort during the carnival of Huixquilucan, Mexico, as Visionudos. They mask as wolves, turtles, dogs, rabbits, turkeys, and donkeys (Mérida, 1940, pl. 3).

FIG. 27—YAQUI DEER AND PASCOLA DANCERS, SONORA, MEXICO. (From colored lithograph by Carlos Mérida, *Danzas de México.*)

The Cahita clowns of the Easter and other fiestas have zoomorphic attributes. The Chapayekas, or long-noses, have long-eared, horned hide-masks. They leap, wriggle their hips, rattling deer-hoof belts, and click sticks against serpentine staves. They also engage in reverse, antinatural and irreverent parodies characteristic of clown societies. The Pascolas (old men of the fiesta), also called Macho Cabrillo or he-goat, have bearded black masks; they leer and caper. They are ritual hosts, initiating and closing the ceremony with exorcism gestures and with greetings to woodland animals. They amuse the crowd with obscene raillery in Yaqui or Mayo (Beals, 1945a, pp. 127–28). Chiefly they are dancers. Unmasked they

181

a

b

c

FIG. 28—INDIAN MUSICIANS, GUATEMALA AND MEX-ICO. *a*, San Martin Chile Verde, Guatemala. (Foto-Sport, Guatemala.) *b*, Mexico: slit drum (toponaztli) and flute. *c*, Mexico: laced double-headed drum and flute. (*b,c*, Middle American Research Institute, Tulane University.)

dance, one at a time, with fleet Spanish tap-steps (zapateados) to harp and fiddle jig tunes. Then each man dons his mask and thumps toe and heel to the accompaniment of flute and drum. The Pascolas gang up on Maso, the Deer; they imitate him clumsily, leap to the ceiling, then fall flat. The Maso also dances alone, to deer songs, water drum, and notched sticks (fig. 27). With a headdress of a real deer head, he steps gingerly and shivers, then bounds lightly. All dancers wear butterfly-cocoon anklets and jingling belts; Maso shakes two large gourd rattles, and the Pascolas strike a sena'asom rattle with copper discs against the palm of their left hand. In alternation with this group, three Coyotes slink back and forth in unison outside the ramada. They wear coyote skins surmounted by feathers, and they straddle and brush a bow in hypnotic rhythm. Their songs are about Coyote Brother. They are not clowns, but belong to a warrior society.

The Pascol, but not Deer and Coyotes, have diffused to the Tarahumara. They appear along with Matachini and with Chape-ones clowns at the Easter and Death fiestas (Bennett and Zingg, 1935, pp. 243–44, 315). The entire performance traveled with Yaqui to Arizona settlements, but the animal clowns are losing prestige, in contrast with the Matachini society. The ancient shaman-istic and hunting rites are fading before the Marian cult (Beals, 1943, pp. 13–18, 70; Kurath, 1949, p. 92).

Anthropomorphic clowns disguise themselves frequently as Viejos, old timers, or as White bourgeoisie. At all fiestas buffoons cavort singly or in pairs with a larger ensemble, or as a separate company. A curious group of Gracejos dances La Culebra in Santo Tomas Chichicastenango, Patzaj, Santa Cruz Quiche, Momostenango, and Totonicapan, Guatemala. Up to 20 ragged men pirouette in lines and cry out from time to time. They wear ridiculous wooden masks, blond or black, precious or ferocious; some lean on canes or wield whips.

Fig. 29—DRUMMER AND HELPER, CHINAUTLA, GUATEMALA. Beating of the drum heralds beginning of all rituals here. (From Reina, 1960, fig. 10. Middle American Research Institute, Tulane University.)

They engage in lascivious mime with two transvestites. Late in the day each snatches a snake from a vessel in the "woman's" hands, places it in his shirt, and urges it to exit from his pantaloons. The performance includes ritual preliminaries in Quiche and improvised dialogue in Spanish (Termer, 1930a; Reynolds, 1956, pp. 33–34).

The Tarascan dance of Los Viejitos is at home on the shores of Lake Patzcuaro, in native patios or in hotels. In grinning masks of wood or pottery, broad-brimmed hats and serapes, the mimes stumble and lean on canes. To crisp chords of a jarana, a small guitar, they perform Spanish zapateado steps and original hops and taps. One step is La Cruz, a cross formation, recurring three times in zapateados or jumps.

In 1897 Starr saw a less tidy comparsa than the modern Viejitos. In Corral and Santa Fe de la Laguna, the clowns strolled through the streets, in ragged and dirty suits, or in brilliant robes, in wooden and clay masks, with wigs of cornhusk. Each band tried to outdo the other (F. Starr, 1908, pp. 71–72). During the 1900 carnival he saw an even more motley collection in the Aztec town of Huauchinango. The Huehuetes (old men) represented gentlemen, an Englishman, a lady, a devil, and other characters (ibid., p. 243).

Parodies of dandies and tourists are carnival favorites. In the state of Tlaxcala, men ridicule Catrines, dandies. In Santa Ana Chiautempan they sport top hats, mustached masks, formal suits, and parasols. In Santa Maria Atlhuitzia they mince about as women, Cihuames, in pink simpering masks, short cotton dresses, and bonnets (Vázquez Santana and Dávila Garibi, 1931,

183

FIG. 30—OTOMI VOLADOR MUSICIAN, PAHUA-TLAN, PUEBLA, MEXICO. (Photo, Bodil Christensen.)

pp. 49–52; Mérida, 1940, pls. 7, 10). They improvise silly rhymes and hop in disarray.

The medieval Devil, Diablo, capers alongside carnival mummeries or other comparsas, as the Concheros. He also appears in the plural, along with Death, in Loa dramas. He is black or red, has a tusked and horned mask, a tail, and often a pitchfork. Ushered in by fireworks, he clatters about and makes crude jokes, when not eulogizing the Virgin. Sometimes he trills in a high falsetto. Death is more grotesque than fearsome, despite his disguise of skull and ribs (Mérida, 1940, pl. 2). Some devil antics resemble the Chapayekas Easter fray, as the battle of devils and priests in Zaachila, Oaxaca (Toor, 1947, pp. 199–200).

Most of the animal and clown mimes seem to have native provenience. The Gua-

temalan Deer Dance and Culebra, and the Yaqui dancers have a few superficial European traits. Termer (1930a) relates the Culebra play to the Aztec serpent juggling in the festival of Atamalcualiztli and to the Hopi Snake-Antelope ceremony. Some of the now comic beasts used to be symbolic or even sinister, especially the jaguar or tiger. Jaguar appears as the predatory earth god in numerous ancient artifacts, often in connection with the eagle (e.g., Covarrubias, 1947, p. 103). He appears in this capacity in the gladiatorial combat for Xipe Totec and in the sacrificial end of the Rabinal Achi. The monkey was the culture hero Hunah Pu (Gómez, 1944, p. 84). Less sinister were the impersonations as bats, birds, and other creatures during the Aztec feasts of Teotleco and Atamalcualiztli (Anderson and Dibble, 1951, pp. 120, 163).

There was also much humorous animal mime and clowning. Comedians participated in Aztec and Maya ceremonies and secular amusements. At the fiesta for Quetzalcoatl clowns represented the wounded, blind, and otherwise disabled, partly for therapeutic, magical reasons (Durán, 1951, 2: 123). Clowns and jugglers entertained Moctezuma and his court (Anderson and Dibble, 1951, p. 30). Ancient artifacts show the Maya and Tarascans as great caricaturists (Morley, 1946, pl. 88; Médioni, 1952, figs. 2, 24; Krickeberg, 1956, p. 500).

On the other hand, many kinds of animals and clowns have been discontinued; others, like the bull, have been brought from Europe. Europe had its share of beasts and clowns (Kirstein, 1935, pp. 96–97, 114) and still revives these figures in Alpine regions (Wolfram, 1951, pp. 54–55). The great chthonian buffoon, the Devil, cavorted through many a carnival and liturgical drama, in the same guise and capacity as in the New World (Kirstein, 1935, pp. 77–78). Death sometimes danced with Devils or enacted his own gruesome ballets (*ibid.*, pp. 83–89). Some Spanish villages still have

184

FIG. 31—ZOQUE MUSICIANS, TUXTLA GUTIERREZ, CHIAPAS, MEXICO. Flutist and four drummers at the fiesta of San Roque. (Photographed by Donald Cordry, 1940.)

their comparsas of devils, though they are vanishing (Foster, 1960a, pp. 209–11). Devils of Majorca have a demonic mien (Parsons, 1930, pp. 589–603).

Such horned demons would have appeared familiar not only to the Yaqui but to southern peoples. Sahagún (1956, bk. 3, 1: 19–20) speaks of the god of the underworld as "el diablo que se decía Mictanteculti" (the devil called M). Other prototypes are the underworld aspect of Quetzalcoatl as the buffoon, Xolotl (*ibid.*, bk. 8, 2:28); and the Maya bat god, Zotzilaha Chimalman, god of darkness, who opposed

the sun god, Kunichachan (Verrill, 1929, p. 103).

NATIVE AND EUROPEAN COMPONENTS

The profusion of native, colonial, and post-colonial forms shows many gradations of mixture. Very few dances are free of European influence. Even the Yaqui deer dancer wears a woman's rebozo instead of a kilt. On the other hand, even the most Hispanized popular dances differ in posture from their Spanish prototypes. Quadrilles of the Old World appear only in parties of pure-bred Spaniards, and Sevillanas in

185

FIG. 32—FLUTIST, CHAMULA, MEXICO. (Middle American Research Institute, Tulane University.)

nightclubs or on the stage. The unraveling of native and foreign elements is difficult but not entirely nebulous. Though many traits are common to natives and conquerors, yet the two types of movement and music can be distinguished (Kurath, 1952, 1958). The components can be briefly analyzed.

Dance Styles and Forms

The posture of the Indian dancer seems the most conspicuous link with the past. In contrast with the proud, erect bearing and high tension of the Spanish dancer, he has a forward-tilted torso, forward motion of the knees, and a relaxed, pulsating style. Even in the Mestizo Jarabes and Fandangos the dancers flex their spines, and the men cup their hands behind their backs (Guiteras Holmes, 1952a, pp. 126, 130, and pl. 15,b). Among the tribal variations in bearing, the Maya posture is erect, the Aztec is humble, the Yaqui free and vigorous Campobello and Campobello, 1940, pp. 21, 223, 158).

Some steps have a local or mimetic character, as the Yaqui deer step, but many can be called Pan-Indian—certain stamps, pulsating runs, trots, brushes, back-pulls, and toe-heel patterns. These may turn up even in popular dances. In contrast are the obvious imports, as the vals and zapateado, notwithstanding modifications in quality. The deviation from Spanish prototype is less marked in the bouncy Jarabe Michoacano than in the flat-footed unmasked Pascola. Some steps, however, are common to conquered and conqueror. Concheros perform a succession of Indian brush-hops, Spanish pas-de-basques, and steps of uncertain provenience (Kurath, 1946). The Santiaguitos of Chila, Puebla, use side shuffles that could descend from Otomi dance or Renaissance branle.

The ancient Maya and Aztecs evidently used ritualistic gestures. Maya gestures were elaborate (Villacorta and Villacorta, 1933), whereas Aztec hand positions were limited and codified (Vaillant, 1940). Of this symbolic art nothing has remained. Dancers now let their arms dangle, or they manipulate a sword, trident, skirt, or other object, as do most Spanish folk dancers. In Spain, sinuous arm movements belong exclusively to Flamenco dance art.

Circular formations prevailed before the conquest but are now scarce, except in processional circuits. Concheros dance in stationary circles. Voladores encircle the pole.

Fig. 33—PLAYING HARP AND VIOLIN, MEXICO. (Middle American Research Institute, Tulane University.)

Seri women dance in multiple, concentric circles (Coolidge and Coolidge, 1939, pp. 226–34).

In many ceremonial and secular fiestas Aztec and Maya men and women held hands and ran in serpentine courses. Sahagún (1956, bk. 2, 4: 50) compared the serpentines in Aztec palatial patios to the popular dances of Castilla la Vieja. He did not encourage their preservation. They have disappeared in Middle America, but have become increasingly popular on the former periphery of Mesoamerican culture, as the Snake dance of southeastern Woodland Indians, the Creek and their neighbors (Kurath, 1956, p. 296). J. B. Griffin (1949, pp. 91–97) and Beals (1944a,b) are among the champions of diffusion to the periphery. Gladwin (1937, pls. 152, 157) reproduces 1000-year-old sherds with dances resembling both the Aztec and Creek chains (Kurath and Martí, 1964, pp. 153–56).

The serpentine occurs in a more complex form as the "vibora" of the Quetzales and the "cadena" of the Voladores. However, the elaborate formations suggest European provenience. Certainly the European longways dance inspired the interweavings of the Matachini and of the Paracho Huananchas, as also the less involved maneuvers of the northern Tepehuan Easter dance (J. A. Mason, 1952, pp. 49–50; Burt Bascom, personal communication). Only simple double-line patterns, as in Moriscas, resemble the facing ranks of contestants or the multiple files of Aztec ceremonies.

Also suspect are the Arcos and Baile de Cintas. The Arcos recall the Acatlaxqui arch formation—performers carry half-hoops covered with flowers and manipulate them in decorative patterns, in Tlaxcala (Vázquez Santana and Dávila Garibi, 1931, pp. 33–36) and Oaxaca (Toor, 1947, pp. 357–78). However, the steps, music, and costumes are all European. The Baile de Cintas or Maypole dance is a feature of some Yaqui Matachini fiestas and of the Yucatecan carnival. Clavijero described (1807)

187

it in Yucatan soon after the conquest. The diffusion and problems are fully presented in Fortún de Ponce (1957, pp. 104–08).

The provenience of couple dancing raises no questions. Couple dancing is a Central European idea but a common European grouping. It is true that Aztec ceremonies often concluded with social dances for men and women, pairing off within the dance line; but that is quite different from parejas sueltas, where each man concentrates on one girl and pursues her, whether she ignores him or encourages him with coquettish smiles.

Instruments, Songs, and Texts

Dance movements are perfectly adapted to musical accompaniment: aboriginal dances to percussion and song or flute; colonial rituals to flute and drum, perhaps small rattles, homemade string instruments or marimba; bailes to strings, marimba, brass band, or singing. Native music is distinguished by duple or irregular meters and phrases, tunes in scales of five tones or less; Mestizo music prefers triple meters, regular phrases, tunes in diatonic scales or church modes, and often harmonies. But there are many doubtful instances and many blends.

Rattles are mostly native, as the large gourd of the Maso and the Tarahumara shaman chanter; so are deer-hoof belts, bells, cocoon anklets worn in action. Their antiquity is testified by reports and by ancient artifacts, as the maracas on Bonampak frescoes and anklets on Tlatilco figurines (Martí, 1955, pp. 58, 39). Nowadays they are often of modern materials. Commercial sleighbells have replaced Aztec copper and gold bells. The Pascola sena'asom derives from the Egyptian sistrum, but it may have had a native prototype in a rattle like the Aztec chicahuaztli. More like the chicahuaztli is the Jaliscan Sonajero wooden stick rattle, with metal disks dangling in tiers of hollows (Kurath, 1960).

Drums are indispensable. For dancing,

the Aztecs beat a horizontal, tuned, wooden, carved teponaztli; for ritualistic action they played a booming, vertical panhuehuetl with bare hands. Now many drums are double-headed and laced like European drums (Martí, 1955, pp. 23–28, 34, 197, 201). The large drum with a flared metal chirimía derives from the same combination of Spain and Majorca. The Maya tunkul drum is replaced by the marimba, which may derive from the African sansa (Kurath, 1963, p. 293).

Masters of the one-man, native flute and drum hold both in the left hand (fig. 30). The Pascola musician brushes a stick along the hide surface. The Volador and Quetzales player beats a tiny drum in triple or duple time. With his cane pito he conjures forth a stream of ethereal melodies. The tunes follow a definite, traditional sequence, for the Volador entrance, chain dance, ascent, dances on the platform, descent, and recessional (Martí, field notes). They differ somewhat in each location. None of the modern flutes can play harmonies, as did many of the ancient multiple clay flutes. For highly ceremonial occasions, modern European metal trumpets have replaced native clay trumpets and conch shells (Martí, 1955, pp. 47–62, 131–41).

Certainly native are the Maso's drum—a half-gourd floating on water—scraping sticks of the Yaqui and Huichol, turtle shells which Zapotecs scratch with antlers, and two kinds of bows—the Tarahumara earthbow which is struck, and the Yaqui Coyotes' bow which is scraped.

True stringed instruments are certainly of European inspiration, though they have evolved some original forms. Lacandones use gourd resonators, Conchero musicians use the shells of armadillos. Huichol and Tarahumara violins are tiny, homemade objects; Seri fiddles have one string (Martí, 1955, pp. 145–51). The fiddlers hold them below the left shoulder and play their own variants on jig tunes. Except for the Matachini and Concheros, stringed instruments are associated with secular affairs. The modern mariachi ensembles are typically Mestizo. They are a long way from the Aztec ensemble of rattles, drums, flutes, and conches, played by trained priestly musicians.

The pulsating songs of Maso and Hikuli contrast with the modal Gregorian chants and diatonic, harmonized popular songs. One may compare the Maya Xtoles with a Jarana song (Michel, 1951, pp. 99–104). Most of the current songs are compositions by Indians on Spanish, Italian, or Austrian patterns. Huastec singers interpolate yodel-like falsetto calls reminiscent of the Alps. La Bamba and other Veracruz Huapangos suggest Negro influence in their lively syncopations. Vocal harmonies are typically in thirds, and guitarists use dominant-tonic harmonies.

The Indians sing alabados for the Passion, alabanzas for the Virgin, and Posada hymns. Ritual songs are termed sones or villancicos. But a huge repertoire is for secular occasions—romances, tonadillas, corridos, cradle songs, children's games. These are very European in style and belong to a study of Ladino arts (Mendoza, 1956, Ex. 63–231). In purpose, they have aboriginal precedents, for the Aztecs sang narratives (Simmons, 1960), and the Seri told legends in epic songs (Coolidge and Coolidge, 1939). But that is where the resemblance ends.

The sentiments expressed in song words also show changes, from the indigenous texts to the native or mixed-language words with triple-time jigs, to the Hispanic verse and refrain ballads. Contrast, for instance, a Yaqui Deer dance song with a Yaqui alabado:

> yo'ota pa'aku welama [The spirit walks in the meadow.]
> Venid, pecadores, venid con su cruz,
> Adorar la sangre, y dulce Jesus. [Toor, 1947, p. 381.]

Compare a chant to the Aztec Mother goddess, Cihuacoatl, with an alabanza:

> The maize is our hands and feet in the field of the god, who resteth upon her rattle board. [Anderson and Dibble, 1951, p. 211.]
> Bendita sea tu pureza y eternamente lo sea. [Mendoza, 1956, Ex. 40.]

Compare a native modern Aztec and Ladino Zapotec love song:

> Xochipitzahua del alma mía, que ante la virgen me das tu amor. . . . [Wedding Huapango in Toor, 1947, pp. 426–27.]
> De que me sirve la cama, ay llorona,
> Si tu ne duermes conmigo. [Llorona dance *ibid.*, pp. 443–44.]

CONCLUSION: CONTINUITY VS. ALIEN INFLUENCES

Indigenous festivals contrast with colonial religious dramas and secular celebrations in composition and style. The purest native forms survive in mountainous, remote regions; the most Europeanized forms flourish in the urban centers of ancient civilizations, among mixed bloods. But there are many blends, new developments, and local gradations between the extremes. Virtually all Indian dance or music shows some alien influence, but also native qualities persevere even in some popular Mestizo forms.

Influences from Spain were strongest during the 16th century, due to colonial policies (Beals, 1952). They transformed the entire repertoire in the centers of high culture. Ritual types, Moriscas, Pastorelas, Diablos were widespread in Europe at that time, including Austria and the Balkans. Later on France also provided topics for dramas and Italy for songs. In the mid-19th century Austria and Poland brought the vals, polka, mazurka, and yodel. On the west coast Chilean commerce brought the Cueca under the name of Chilena. On the east coast Negro influences via Cuba pro-

189

duced the Huapangos. In the 20th century North American jazz became popular.

To an extent historical and prehistorical research can suggest prototypes both sides of the Atlantic; analysis can disentangle native and foreign components. But these processes also reveal many analogies which facilitated acculturation and thus complicate interpretation.

REFERENCES

Acosta, J., 1590
Amezquita Borja, 1943
Anderson and Dibble, 1951
Barker, 1957
Beals, 1943, 1944a, 1944b, 1945a, 1946, 1952
Bennett, J. W., 1944
Bennett, W. C., and Zingg, 1935
Bode, 1961
Campobello and Campobello, 1940
Capmany, 1931
Carrasco, 1952b
Christensen, 1937
Clavigero, 1807
Coolidge and Coolidge, 1939
Correa, 1958a, 1958b
Covarrubias, 1947
Dahlgren de Jordan, 1954
Dieseldorff, 1930
Durán, 1951
Englekirk, 1957
Fernández and Mendoza, 1941
Fortún de Ponce, 1957
Foster, 1948a, 1960a
Gessain, 1953
Gladwin et al., 1937
Gómez, 1944
Griffin, J. B., 1949
Guiteras Holmes, 1952a
Hernández, F. J., 1946
Horcasitas Pimentel, 1949
Kaplan, 1951
Kelly, 1953
Kirstein, 1935
Kretzenbacher, 1952
Krickeberg, 1956
Kurath, 1946, 1947, 1949, 1950, 1952, 1956, 1958, 1960, 1963
—— and Martí, 1964
LaFarge and Byers, 1931

Larsen, 1937
Lekis, 1958
Lumholtz, 1902
Martí, 1955
Mason, J. A., 1948, 1952
Médioni, 1952
Mendoza, 1955, 1956
Mérida, 1940
Michel, 1951
Millán Maldonado, 1942
Monterde, 1955
Mooney, 1957
Morley, 1946
Parsons, 1930
Redfield, 1930
—— and Villa Rojas, 1934
Reina, 1960
Reynolds, 1956
Robb, 1961
Sachs, 1933
Sahagún, 1956
Sedillo Brewster, 1935
Simmons, 1960
Spicer, 1954
Starr, F., 1908
Steck, 1951
Stresser-Péan, 1953
Tax, Sol, 1952a
Termer, 1930a, 1931
Toor, 1947
Vaillant, 1940
Vázquez Santana, 1931, 1940
—— and Dávila Garibi, 1931
Verrill, 1929
Villacorta and Villacorta, 1933
W., P. A., 1951
Wagley, 1949
Wolfram, 1951

10. Play: Games, Gossip, and Humor

MUNRO S. EDMONSON

At first glance the linking of games with gossip and humor may appear both arbitrary and misleading. Certainly one could make a good case for discussing games, say, in relation to ritual, gossip in relation to village organization, humor in relation to folk literature or linguistics. Taken together, however, the three topics have a certain coherence peculiarly relevant, perhaps, to the Middle American Indians: in many languages of Middle America they are called by the same word. To "laugh with" (or "at" or "over") somebody is to play with him, to mock him, or to amuse him (Nahuatl *uetzca,* Yucatec *cheeh*). Play is probably a protean concept in most cultures; in Middle America it covers a range of things from highly organized and heavily ritualized games, through children's pastimes, toys, horseplay and joking, to the subtler forms of humor—literary or informal.

The Middle American Indian, with his somber religious ideology and his often tragic history, has an even more established reputation for humorless sobriety than the British, the Germans, or his North American Indian cousins. This is largely undeserved.

Middle American Indians pun; they tell dirty stories; they are inveterate and vivacious gossips; they have an extensive repertoire of games and amusements. It is nonetheless true that the context of play is not everywhere the same, and in Middle America it is often strikingly different from that in other traditions. There is, for example, no humor whatever in any of the great literary works of these Indians: the *Popol Vuh,* the *Books of Chilam Balam,* or the *Annals of the Cakchiquel.* On the other hand, their folk plays and ceremonial pageants frequently include clowns, sometimes syncretized with European comic figures, sometimes overwhelmingly Indian. It is unfortunate that much of the playful activity of any people lies in the area of culture least accessible to the "outside observer." Even a highly competent ethnographer is usually lost when his informants begin to joke among themselves. In consequence, it may be that there is no area of Middle American culture on which we have less adequate data. The survey which follows must be taken as only the crudest outline of the probable cultural reality; even if it could exhaust the rather scattered sources, it would still be a danger-

191

FIG. 1—LAUGHING TOTONAC. (From Spratling, 1960, pl. 17.)

ously partial and selective glimpse of the Middle American Indian at play.

Like most peoples, those of Middle America enjoy themselves by feasting, dancing, singing, and "playing." The context of these activities is predominantly religious. Many aspects of them consequently present a serious side somewhat at odds with the European conception of diversion, recreation, or amusement. Such activities are nonetheless meant to be enjoyed within the framework of that harmony of spiritual forces that lies at the heart of Middle American religions, and the concept of play as a special aspect of life is well developed in gossiping and joking, sports, games, gambling, and toys.

FEASTING

Before the conquest, feasting, drinking, smoking, and using narcotic drugs tended to be reserved by the Indians for special occasions of a religious nature, during the great calendar ceremonies of cities, towns, and villages, or the life crises within a fam-

ily or small group. Because of the variety of foodstuffs available, Middle America may be said to have possessed the nucleus of one of the world's great cuisines, notably less varied, perhaps, than French or Chinese cookery but incomparably more attractive than the primitive diet of many areas of the world. The menu for a typical aboriginal feast might be:

Atolli
Uexolotl ica Chilmolli
Chilacayotl   Tamalli
Auacamolli   Xitomatl
Tlaxcalli

Chia
Chocolatl   Posolli
Xocotl   Nopalli   Meocuillin
Octli   Popocani

Corn Mush
Turkey in Chile Gravy
Baked Squash   *Sweet Bean Rolls*
Avocado Whip   *Sliced Tomatoes*
Corn Bread

Honey Seeds
Chocolate   *Corn Drink*
Custard Apple/Cactus Pear/Maguey Grubs
Wine   *Cigars*

This menu has been selected to indicate the kinds of foods regarded as festival fare. Some were ordinary items to the Indians, but the inclusion of meat (game or turkey), the preparation of the chocolate-based chile gravy, baked squash or special tamales made it a festive meal; addition of chocolate or tobacco made it an occasion; and addition of beer, wine, or pulque converted it into a ceremony. The implication of traditional courses is, of course, facetious, but all these foods and preparations were well established in all nuclear Middle America, and it is quite likely that this exact meal has confronted many an Indian noble. Peripheral areas often lacked parts of this tradition: avocadoes, chocolate, tomatoes and chirimoyas, for example, were not grown north of central Mexico, and the north Mexican plateau had no agriculture at all. A number of alcoholic drinks were concocted from the sap, fruits, and flowers of various cacti, but usually only one was favored by each group. Tobacco, generally known and widely used, often ceremonially, was smoked in both cigars and pipes. For special purposes the hallucinogenic mushrooms, peyote cactus buttons, or locoweed were used by various groups.

Dancing

Important pre-Hispanic ceremonies were usually accompanied by dancing. Usually this was ritual and commemorative in character, though the dances covered a broad range of types, and at least in small communities were sufficiently spontaneous to border on social dancing. The masked dances of colonial and modern times (see Article 9) are not infrequently obscure descendants of the ritual dances of the preceding period, and they have certainly preserved their essentially ritual character. Modern Indian populations "enjoy" these dances or dance-plays and will sometimes go long distances to see them, but despite their frequent inclusion of clown figures, these performances are not primarily recreational, being now endowed with ritual and didactic functions of both Indian and Christian character.

Music

Preconquest dancing was normally accompanied by music: singing, or playing on drums, flutes, rasps, rattles, bows, whistles, horns, or pipes. This formal and ritual use of music was (as the dance was not) matched by extensive informal use as well, and most or all of these instruments serve for purely personal enjoyment or even as toys. Singing, humming, whistling, stamping, clapping, and whooping are common among most groups. (See Article 9.)

Play

Play as such may be differentiated in Middle America into (1) verbal play, (2) sports, (3) games, (4) gambling, and (5) toys. These activities range from very casual and only slightly patterned behavior requiring no special equipment or even company, to highly elaborated and ritualized team play involving whole communities and considerable capital investment. Our survey summarizes our present knowledge of the occurrence and distribution of these things in Middle America and their relation to comparable things in North and South America and the Old World. Rarely can we have much confidence in a negative finding, for many aspects of play have engaged only the most peripheral attention of the occasional ethnographer.

Our sources on the classic ball games of Middle America are Acosta and Moedano Koer, 1946; Amsden, 1936; Blom, 1932; Corbett, 1939; Crawley, 1914; Fernández, 1925; Kelly, 1943; Krickeberg, 1948; Mendner, 1956; Schuller, 1935; Stern, 1950; Swanton, 1929; J. E. S. Thompson, 1941b, 1943; and Toscano, 1945. Other humor, games, and sports have only very rarely been investigated for themselves: Beals and Carrasco, 1944; Caso, 1924–27, 1932; Ibarra, 1942; Mateos Higuera, 1930; Mena, 1930; Zingg, 1932. The only general summaries are by Peterson (1959b), Beals (1932), and Toor (1947); the latter two are fragmentary, being mainly concerned with other things. Scattered information can be found in ethnographies of the Tarahumar (Lumholtz, 1902), Cahita (Beals, 1943), Acaxee (Beals, 1933), Tarascans (Brand, 1951; Foster, 1948a; Beals, 1946), Zapotec (Parsons, 1936); Quiche (Edmonson, 1961; Burgess and Xec, 1955), Miskito (Conzemius, 1932), and Boruca (Stone, 1949); these sources can be supplemented from early dictionaries of Cahita (Buelna, 1890), Nahuatl (Molina, 1880), and Yucatec (Martínez Hernández, 1929; Solís Alcalá, 1949). The materials from these sources are here compared with the very useful North and South American summaries by Culin (1907) and Cooper (1949). More

193

occasional references are noted in the text.

VERBAL PLAY

Plays on or with words (Zapotec *tichaco-quite*, Zoque *otong-si-cuy*) are undoubtedly commonplace in Indian tradition. Puns of various types can be documented, perhaps the most famous being the Nahuatl one proposed by Caso (1936): *quetzal-coatl*, 'feathered serpent' versus 'precious twin.' The Mayan languages particularly lend themselves to punning: Yucatec *cho* 'cactus' versus *chop* 'lizard' (Barrera Vásquez, 1948, pp. 204ff.), Quiche *av a* 'your thighs' versus *a va* 'your face' (Mace, 1957). The tonal languages of the Mixtec-Zapotec area use "whistle speech" in a humorous fashion closely akin to punning, particularly in a courtship vein. Some ritual plays on words are more poetic, e.g., 'old man with nine children' for 'big toe' or 'light of the Peten' for 'honey' (from which the *balché* drink is made) in the slang of the Yucatecan apprentice priest (Barrera Vásquez, *loc. cit.*). Similar usages can be found in the "war language" of the Apaches of northern Middle America.

Anecdotal narratives—about humorous events which really happened—are a major theme in Indian conversation. Jokes, on the other hand—about imaginary or contrived situations—are not found in the aboriginal tradition; the modern types are of Spanish origin. In the nature of things, anecdotes are tied to modern rather than traditional situations. A single example may suffice: a Quiche informant told me with great relish a story about a minor panic among the Indians over a rumor that a large labor party that had been collected at the Quezaltenango airport for work on the field were to be decapitated and their heads used to surface the runway. Someone had overheard the engineer in charge calculating how many *cabezas* he was going to need.

Most of Middle American humor is similarly context-bound. The folk tales are rarely witty, although they may include broadly humorous situations, particularly in a trickster vein, as when Deer borrows Rabbit's shoes (in a Cora story) and disappears to "try them out" but unaccountably fails to return (Preuss, 1912). Pranks of this sort are enjoyed in real life as well as in tales. Chorti boys are reportedly fond of sprinkling powdered velvet-beans on groups of their elders, producing a skin irritation—and, presumably, howls of laughter.

Nicknames are common throughout the area and are frequently critical or derisive. A Chorti woman became known as *tintini-nica*, because that's what she always sang to her children. Quiche nicknames are not infrequently obscene and may be leveled at groups as well as individuals. People from Rabinal call those of Joyabaj *ch'oil*, literally 'rats,' secondary meaning 'female genitalia.' The Quiche consider obesity to be hilarious, and have a rich vocabulary for alluding to it with ridicule, although this and kindred insults possibly productive of real strife can be countered with pat retorts like, "Oh, I didn't know you left your heart at home," implying that one's tormentor doesn't have all his wits about him. In Quiche as in Zapotec there are also stock joking retorts intended to jolly someone out of a momentary pique (Zapotec *tibeepechanijlàchia*). Name calling and banter shade easily into ridicule and gossip about character and morals. Perhaps the most serious subject of gossip everywhere is witchcraft. In these connections the element of humor is apt to be lost, and public squabbling may result. Cursing is reported from Middle America (notably Yucatan) and may well be pre-Columbian, but the techniques of open insult are little elaborated, and it would seem that backbiting, slander, and covert factionalism were more characteristic modes of interpersonal relations throughout the area. Joking relationships are reported to be lacking (Guiteras Holmes, 1952b). Singing, rhyming, and counting games are generally

FIG. 2—TARAHUMARAS RACING BY TORCHLIGHT. (From Lumholtz, 1902, 1: 285.)

lacking in Middle America, but one naming game *(matirilirililong)* is reported from Mitla. Even the name is Spanish.

SPORTS

A variety of bodily exercises requiring no equipment were widespread in Middle America: running, jumping, hopping, fighting, tumbling, catching and finding, and swimming are all reported. The most famous runners are the Tarahumar (fig. 2), whose name for themselves *(rarámuri)* means 'runners.' Ceremonial races (Nahuatl *paynatotoca)* are recorded for the Aztec, Huichol, Tarahumar, and probably Coahuiltec. Representative individual Tarahumars have performed prodigies of distance running under close observation (Toor, 1947). Running as a contest of both speed and endurance is probably universal. So, most likely, is follow-the-leader (Tarascan *matatiro).* Jumping exercises are reported to have been part of the training of Aztec warriors and were probably general. Leap-

frog is reported only among the Tarascans, who call it *burro.* One hopscotch game (fig. 3) called *peleche* is reported among the Tarascans, and another among Zapotec boys. The game is reported in South but not in North America, so it is possible that Michoacan may have been near its northern limit. Mock fighting is probably found among all peoples, usually as a wrestling contest. Team wrestling and boxing are both reported from South America but not from Middle or North America. Tumbling and acrobatics were highly developed in nuclear Middle America, including headstands, hand-walking, and contortions (fig. 5), recorded principally among Nahuatl-speaking peoples. They are unknown elsewhere in the Americas. Catching and finding games—tag, blindman's-buff and hide-and-seek—are probably worldwide. Tug-of-war games are not reported, unless the Yucatecan *tzolom bat* (?'line fight') be such a game. The "tiger game" of South America, in which the tiger on all

195

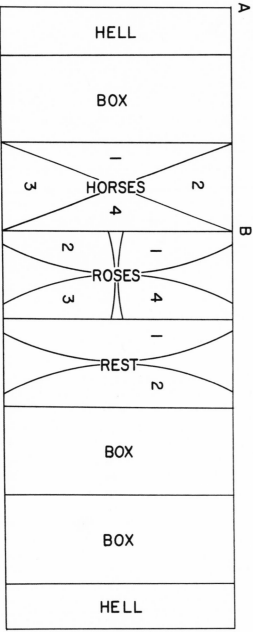

A

B

FIG. 3—TARASCAN HOPSCOTCH. (From Foster, 1948a, fig. 34.)

both of the latter groups call it "onion picking" in Spanish. It may be cognate with the North American "wolf game." Somewhat similar are the circle games in which the object is to break into or out of a circle, as in Tarascan *coyotito*. Favorably situated tribes usually excel in swimming and diving. Miskito boys played water tag games called *wli* (turtle) and *ilili* (shark); in the latter the person who is "it" tries to pinch the others under water and still get away. With or without water there are breathholding contests. Sweatbaths (Nahuatl *temazcalli*, Quiche *tuh*) were taken throughout the area both for diversion and for curing. Contests over the speed and volume of eating are not reported from aboriginal America. *Malacatontzin* was an Aztec circle game with two circles of players going in opposite directions; bets were laid on how many turns they could take before getting dizzy. The same name was later applied to a drinking game in which bets were made on how many times a man could revolve after a stiff drink without falling down. Some kind of hand game is mentioned among the Zapotec *(tiquiteñaaya)* and Yucatec *(etzya)*, but we have no description.

Games

A wide variety of pastimes requiring a certain amount of equipment may be differentiated as games. Like sports, they are typically organized as contests with more or less determinate rules, although they may vary from solitary amusements to highly ritualized social events. Collecting objects of a particular type, such as dirt or potsherds (Nahuatl *nitlallotinemi, nitapalcayotinemi*) is probably a universal children's pastime, as are games centering on the finding of hidden objects such as coins, toys, counters. Games involving manipulation of objects are legion, and in Middle America the accent is on dexterity rather than strength, endurance, or daring. Balls and similar objects may be thrown, caught, vol-

fours, or on his feet and one hand, or hopping, tries to capture the last of a line of linked children while the head of the line tries to outmaneuver him, is reported among the Miskito, Quiche, and Tarascans;

leyed, rolled, slid, pitched, bounced, kicked, batted, bowled, or juggled, and specific games may specify particular combinations of these as legitimate. Often a target is designated, and the object—ball, arrow, knife, pebble—is thrown, pitched, or slid towards a hole or line. The Tarahumar *rixiwátali* or *cuatro* (Nahuatl *cocoyocpactolli*), in which pits or stone discs are pitched at a hole, is typical of these games, which are probably worldwide. A special form is that in which one's counters are directed against those of his opponent in order to hit them (Nahuatl *chinchina*), knock them out of a given area (as in marbles), or break them (as in tops). Both marbles and tops are found throughout Middle America. Among the Tarascans, marbles are shot in a square or triangle; among the Quiche, in a circle. Native tops are made from gourds or large seeds. Humming tops, noted in South America, are not reported farther north. A game similar to tiddlywinks is played with wax pellets or discs by the Boruca *(cuepas)* and Quiche *(juego de cera de Semana Santa)*, and may be cognate with the Nahuatl *chinchina,* or 'burning' game. The discs are thrown hard from directly above an opponent's disc. Bowling games may have existed, like the Zapotec *tochijcuàya 'jugar bola o bolos.'*

Ring-toss (Nahuatl *totoloque*) or hoop-and-pole games like the chunkey of North America were almost certainly widespread in Middle America, but have not been extensively reported (though they are known to have existed in South America). Ring-and-pin games, in which a ring, loop, or hoop is tossed and caught on a stick (fig. 6,*a*), pin, or arrow held in the hand, are found throughout the Americas. The *barril* of modern Middle American markets is probably representative of the aboriginal form in this area. The sliding "snow-snake," hoop rolling, and wheel-and-stick (in which a stick or arrow is slid or bounced at a rolling hoop) were almost certainly represented in Middle America, being reported

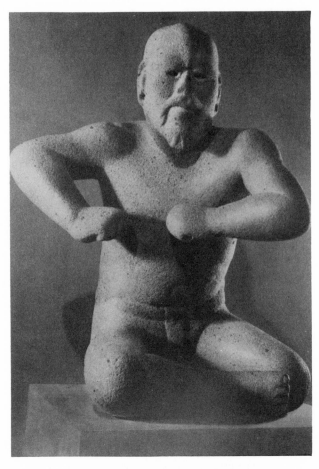

Fig. 4—OLMEC "WRESTLER," UXPANAPAN, MEXICO. (From Peterson, 1959a, pl. 11. Photo, courtesy of Museo Nacional de Antropología e Historia, Mexico.)

to the north and south, but have not been observed. Hoops *(bate)* are mentioned among the game implements of the Quiche in the *Popol Vuh,* and hoop racing is a woman's sport among the Tarahumar *(rowemala).*

A stick game is reported (Yucatec *colomche,* Zapotec *quija, yaga*) in which a seated player tried to catch or bat (with a small bat) a series of sticks thrown at him by a standing one. In Yucatan this was part of a dance.

Marksmanship with the various implements of war and hunting was a widespread object of both childish and adult

197

Fig. 5—TLATILCO CONTORTIONIST. (From Anonymous, 1958, pl. 24.)

recreation. The principal weapons were the bow and arrow, the blowgun (and bean-shooter), the slingshot, club, axe, and shield. Miskito and Sumo children are reported to have played war with knobbed or wax-pointed arrows; doubtless most other children played similarly. Fighting games are also attested for the Zoque *(quipp-cuy)*, Zapotec *(tiquitea)*, and Aztec. The Honduran Ulwa engaged in an endurance game with a quarterstaff reminiscent of Robin Hood, but stickfighting as such is not reported and may not have occurred. Zapotec boys are reported to have engaged in ash-, mud-, or excrement-slinging, *tonipetèea.* Weight-lifting was part of the exercise in

198

the Aztec Calmecac, but is not reported elsewhere.

Relay racing, reported in South America, is not recorded in Middle America as a sport, though the famous courier system of the Aztecs attests that the idea was known. Kick-ball (Tarahumar *ralá hipá*) and kick-stick, stick-ball or hoop racing, known in Southwestern North America, are restricted to northwestern Middle America (Opata, Pima, Yuma, Cahita, Tarahumar, Acaxee, and northern Sinaloa). An equivocal instance is reported from the Coahuiltec area. The Tarahumar had marathon races, kick-ball races, kick-stick races, and women's races in which the ball was propelled by a forked stick (fig. 7) or replaced by hoops propelled by straight sticks. In one type the "ball" became two stubby rods loosely tied together (fig. 8) to be easily caught by the toes and kicked along.

A rope swing for teaching infants to walk and a swing for older children are reported among the Tarascans. Swings are also depicted in Tajin figures from the Totonac area. Stilts are reported among the Aztec *(icxitl)*, Miskito *(umas)*, Tarascans, Yucatec, and Quiche *(tik)*. They are also reported from both North and South America and many parts of the Old World. The impressive "flying pole" (Nahuatl *teocuauhpatlan-que)*, found from Nicaragua to central Mexico, is to be considered a dance or ceremony (see Article 9) rather than a game or sport. A "windmill" game *(aspas)* of ceremonial type with two vertical wheels on a horizontal axis is reported from (apparently) someplace in central Mexico. The dancers climbed onto the four-armed wheels, grabbed their feet with their hands and took a predetermined number of revolutions. Balancing games are not reported aside from stilts, though the Yucatecan *tippcuzam* (?'elevated') could be a reference to some such pastime.

Juggling, like acrobatics, was something of a specialty of central Middle America (Nahuatl *tapayellalaca,* Zapotec *penipià-*

hui). The log juggling (Nahuatl *quauhilaca* or *xocuaxpatolin*, Yucatec *cuculbil chéob*) was particularly spectacular, but balls, roses or other flowers, shuttlecocks and other objects were also used. Juggling or volleying games using flowers or the cornhusk ball or shuttlecock was particularly a woman's pastime among the Aztecs, but ruggeder forms of keep-it-up employing more stringent rules and a harder or heavier ball are found as men's games throughout the Americas, usually as part of the elaborate ritual ball games. Rag-ball keep-away is reported among the Tarascans and may have been widespread.

The formal ball games of Middle America may be divided into three main types: handball, stick-ball, and hip-ball. All three were widely popular. Handball is reported for the Nahuatl *(nematotopeuiliztli)*, Zapotec *(tigaapayapitípi)*, Tzental *(pax* or *pox)*, Mixtec *(pelota mixteca)*, Tarascans *(apantzaqua)*, possibly Yucatecans, and various parts of South America. Gloves (Nahuatl *mayeumatl*, Quiche *pach q'ab*) are sometimes found in relation to the ball games and suggest handball.

Stick-ball games were various. Racket games related to lacrosse were played as far south as the Cahita and northern Sinaloa. Hockey games with J- or L-shaped sticks and comparable to South American games or to North American shinny are reported for the Cahita, Tarahumar *(tákwari)*, Acaxee and Tarascans. Bat games comparable to those of South America are reported as far north as Guasave (*male*; fig. 10) and the Tarascans.

A variety of balls were used in Middle America: the leaf or rag or cornhusk ball in volleying games and sometimes in hockey (Nahuatl *totopetli*), wooden pucks, marbles or bowling balls (Nahuatl *momotla*), a hide or hair ball for throwing and catching games (Nahuatl *telolotli*), the juggling ball of wood, rubber, stone, or clay (Nahuatl *tapayolli*), and the rubber balls in handball and hip-ball games (Nahuatl *olli*,

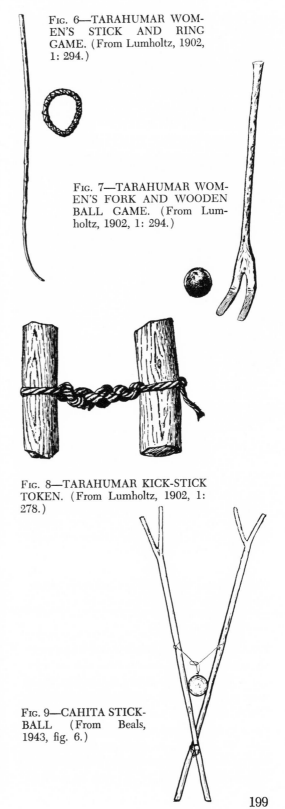

FIG. 6—TARAHUMAR WOMEN'S STICK AND RING GAME. (From Lumholtz, 1902, 1: 294.)

FIG. 7—TARAHUMAR WOMEN'S FORK AND WOODEN BALL GAME. (From Lumholtz, 1902, 1: 294.)

FIG. 8—TARAHUMAR KICK-STICK TOKEN. (From Lumholtz, 1902, 1: 278.)

FIG. 9—CAHITA STICK-BALL (From Beals, 1943, fig. 6.)

199

Fig. 10—GUASAVE *MALE* PLAYERS, BADIRAGUATO, SINALOA, MEXICO. (From Ibarra, 1942, p. 44.)

Cahita *ulin*, Tzental *chich*, Yucatec or Quiche *k'ik'*, all meaning 'blood, sap, rubber'). A particularly remarkable ball of slow-burning maguey roots was used for night hockey games among the Tarascans, showering sparks when hit.

Tlachtli

The ball game of Middle America is the hip-ball associated with the stone ball courts of the ceremonial centers (Nahuatl *tlachco*, Nayarit *taste*, Tarascan *querétaro*, Quiche *hom*, Cahita *batey*, Acaxee *vatey*, Yucatec *pek*, Otomi *mexei*, Zapotec *queya*). The ball courts are found as far afield as Haiti, southern Arizona, and northern South America. The game itself may have been

even more widespread. Its most general features were the use of a rubber ball in a volleying team game on a marked-off playing court with rules interdicting the use of the hands (and usually of the head and feet as well). This is the Nahuatl *tlachtli*, Tarascan *taránduqua*, Zapotec *láchi*, Quiche *tzalatz*, Yucatec *pok*, Tzental *pitz*, Zoque *pecspa*, Nayarit-Sinalea *hulama*, and Huastec *mule*. The early Spaniards called it *batey*, apparently an Antillean name for it, by which it was later known in Cahita and Acaxee. The game was played in postconquest times as far north as Guasave and possibly Tamaulipas and among the Otomi and Guachichil of the north Mexican plateau. It may have affinities with the ritual handball game of the Natchez and the *pillma* of the Araucanians of Chile. A number of North American keep-it-up games permitted kicking; the South American games did not (except in handball). Rules permitting the use of the feet are reported among the Isthmus Zapotec and Tzental. Most of the Middle American players stuck to the Aztec rules, in which the player (Nahuatl *ollamani*) wore a leather apron (Nahuatl *quezeuatl*, Nayarit *chimal*) down to his knees and could hit the ball only where he was covered by the apron (i.e., with his thighs or buttocks). The ball, though rubber, was hard and heavy and, even with the protective apron, often left severe bruises; we may imagine that the players did not often foul intentionally. Quiche players protected their heads with helmets and face masks. Court ball was often an intertown game (Acaxee), played with 2-, 4-, 6-, or 8-man teams (Cahita), and dedicated to its own god (7 Flower), the god of games in general (5 Flower), or other deities such as Xipe, 1 God (Aztec). The object of the game was to keep the ball in play without a body fault, without permitting it to strike or go over the wall one was defending, and without permitting it to die on one's own side of the court. It could not be struck twice in succession and had to be returned past the centerline. A lapse of any of these points gave points to one's opponent while simultaneously subtracting points from one's own score. Knocking the ball through one's opponent's stone ring at the side of the I-shaped court was an automatic win, but did not happen often. Although the game was essentially ceremonial, heavy betting was involved among both players and spectators. It has not been played in central Mexico since early colonial times, but it hung on until the present century in Sinaloa and Veracruz and, possibly, among the Quiche, who had a traditional Good Friday game that may have been the old ball game under altered rules.

It is altogether likely that the ball courts of Middle America were used for more than one game. Not only did the rules of the game vary from time to time and from place to place, but they were also subject to alteration by mutual agreement. In some areas, handball was played on a rectangular court; it is quite possible that most groups used the great I-shaped courts for a variety of games. A Teotihuacan mural is said to depict players in a classic court with clubs or bats. Illustrative of the variations are the Tarascan ball games *uayukuni* (a team hockey using J- or L-shaped sticks), *akúperani* (the same game played by two individuals), and *atáukuni* (a similar game between two teams but using two balls). Other Tarascan ball games used bats (fig. 11) and possibly even rackets. Probably most of Middle America could present at least as extensive an inventory if our data were more adequate. The Tarascan games are now played in the streets. Many such games may well have been played in the *tlachtli* courts in former times.

GAMBLING

The Indians were dedicated gamblers. Sports and games of skill were (and still are) almost always the subject of betting both for stakes and forfeits and as much among children as among adults. A typical

FIG. 11—POTTERY FIGURINE, NAYARIT, MEXICO. Variously interpreted as depicting a ballgame player or a warrior. (Photograph by Giselle Freund.)

case is the Aztec *titotlalalqualtia*, apparently a juggling game in which the loser had his mouth crammed with food or some less pleasant substance. The Acaxee made endurance wagers over not flinching as their eyelashes were pulled out or chili was passed across their eyeballs. Most of the amusements already mentioned were usually played for stakes, particularly racing, searching games, pitch, ring games, marksmanship, and above all the ball games. A similar devotion to gambling appears to be general to the American Indians. It is the more noteworthy that nowhere in the Americas are the Indians reported to bet on future contingencies or nesciences. That, after all, is what divination was for. In Middle

201

FIG. 12—TARAHUMARAS PLAYING QUINZE. (From Lumholtz, 1902, 1: 279.)

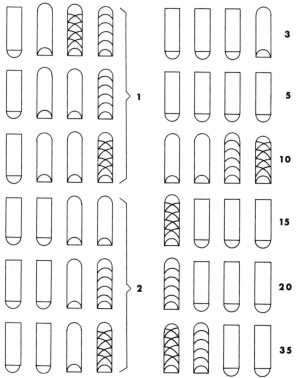

FIG. 13—TARASCAN STICK-DICE SCORES. (From Beals and Carrasco, 1944, fig. 5.)

202

America there is a general lack of guessing games. Riddles are reported, but appear to be rare. (See, however, Peterson, 1959b; Toor, 1947.) The hand games, straw games, stick games, and moccasin games of North America are not reported south of the Rio Grande; the shell and pebble games of South America are not recorded north of Panama. Word-guessing (as from the initial syllable) might be expected—in relation to "whistle speech," for example—but is not reported.

Patolli

Games of chance employing bone and stick dice were probably universal in Middle America: Spanish *quince* or *coyote*, Nahuatl *patolli*, Yucatec *bul* or *baac*, Cahita-Acaxee *patole*, Tarascan *kolia atárakua* (stick dice, *romálaka*), Quiche *baq*, Tarahumar *romavóa*. The Boruca are said not to gamble, and dice are "practically unheard of" among them, but this is probably acculturational. The modes of scoring stick dice among the Tarascans and bone dice among the Tarahumar are illustrated in figures 13 and 14. Dice of shell, reeds, and seeds are reported elsewhere in the Americas but not in Middle America. None of the simpler dice games have been described, but the elaborate "board game" of *patolli* was very widespread and is well known. It was very closely related in at least some cases to the calendar and the divination system. Apparently it was a woman's game among the Acaxee; everywhere it was reserved for ceremonial occasions and accompanied by heavy betting. It is remarkably similar to the *moncalla*, draughts or *parchisi* of the Old World, and may be related to the Chacoan *tsúka* in South America. No comparable complex game has been reported from North America, although the Hopi stick-dice game is called *patol*, and an acquaintance of mine once turned up with a game virtually identical with the Egyptian *moncalla* which he had learned from Oklahoma Indians. The historical background of Middle American *patolli* is still a riddle.

In addition to multiple dice, *patolli* requires a cruciform four-track board with 12 "houses" on each side of each track plus four in the middle, for a total of 52 spaces, representative of the 52-year cycle. (Quiche diviners also arrange their divining beans in "houses" in a closely related pattern.) Beans or other seeds, pebbles, or sticks are used as counters, commonly five to each player among the Aztecs (for the god 5 Flower), and four among the Tarascans. One moves his counters around the board in accordance with the throw of the dice, and wins when he gets all of them to the center. The second counter to land in a space "kills" the first, which must then start over. The Aztecs were likely to *cenquiça* (shoot the works) in their excitement.

Toys

Prevocational play with miniature replicas of adult equipment—cooking utensils, agricultural implements, weapons, and the like

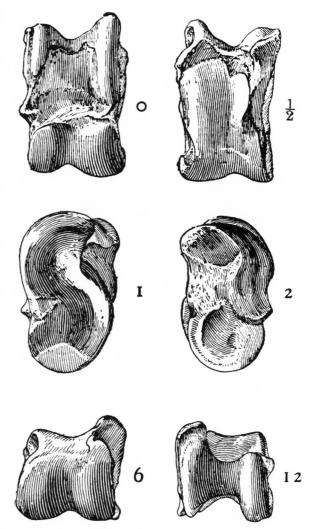

Fig. 14—TARAHUMAR KNUCKLE-BONE GAME VALUES. (From Lumholtz, 1902, 1: 278.)

—must surely be found among all children. It can be endlessly documented in Middle America. "Playing house" with dolls, mud tortillas, toy animals, and other children is doubtless equally general. In Middle America it can be very realistic. Little girls in Yucatan played *alam* ('childbirth') or joined little boys in *tamacaztal* ('mock intercourse'). Tarahumar children got their dolls drunk on *tesgüin* from acorn cups, in imitation of their parents. The appeal of pets is similarly universal. In Middle Amer-

203

FIG. 15—STONE PATOLLI BOARD FOUND AT TULA, HIDALGO, MEXICO. (From Acosta, 1960, pl. 23.)

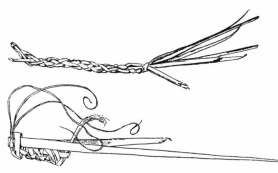

FIG. 16—TOTONAC LEAF-STRAND TOYS. Snake (above) and grasshopper (below). (From Kelly and Palerm, 1952, fig. 53.)

ica this meant puppies, and in central Mexico *etzcuintli* ('dog') has passed from Nahuatl into Spanish as a pet name for 'my child.' Wild animals were also captured and kept as pets by many Indian groups.

Toys are not abundant in Middle America by European standards, but a great many types are made by both adults and children, and they are found everywhere: Zoque *muetzi*, Cahita *ilichi*, Yucatec *baxal*, Quiche *etz'ebal*, etc. Dolls and animals are commonly made of clay, wood, cloth, twigs,

or straw. Tops (Miskito *purmaya*), kites (Miskito *istapla*) and marbles are found everywhere. Kite-fighting is reported only for the Tarascans. Cat's cradle and string figures, used for divination among the Aztecs, were also children's amusements throughout the area. Leaf-strand figures comparable to those of South America have also been found—an accordian among the Chorti, "snails" among the Quiche, a palm-leaf trumpet in Yucatan, a snake and grasshopper among the Totonac (fig. 16). Fingerstalls are not reported. Aztec children played *mapepena*, a form of jacks. Yucatecan children blew soap bubbles from *pomolche* sap. Tarascan children made hot-air balloons from oil-soaked paper. Possibly the most exotic toys of all were the little wheeled figures excavated in Veracruz (fig. 17) representing the only known anticipation of the wheel in aboriginal America. Children of many areas played with flowers, personifying them, arranging them, or weaving them together. A number of musical instruments were also found as toys: buzzers, bullroarers, rattles, whistles, pipes, flutes, and drums.

CONCLUSIONS

Among the Spanish diffusions to Middle America may be counted: volleyball, basketball and soccer, bullfighting and bull-baiting, the horse and horse games (including races), a large number of card games, chess, checkers, bingo, jumping rope and lassoing, the cowboy sports, riddles, circuses, "soldiers," "cops and robbers," "enchantment" (a tag game in which one must "freeze" when tagged but can be freed by someone else not yet caught), rhyming games, counting-out and some circle games, the reed flute (*chirimía*), wind toys, and possibly kites, leapfrog, and spiral hopscotch.

Aboriginal pastimes of probable worldwide occurrence include: feasting, dancing, music, anecdotal humor, kidding, gossip, plays on words, running, jumping, hopping, fighting, catching and finding games (including tag, hide-and-seek and follow the leader), collecting, throwing, catching and pitching games, marksmanship, the ball, handball and volleying games, gambling and dice, playing house or other parent-imitating games, pets, dolls, string figures, buzzers, bullroarers, rattles, whistles, and flower games and toys. Although not universal, stilts, hoop-and-pole, wheel-and-stick, the spear and spearthrower, the bow-and-arrow and slingshot, stick-ball, tops, and marbles probably reached Middle America from the Old World via North America.

Probably of American origin are: the "tiger game," the blowgun and beanshooter, American soccer (*tlachtli*), and hopscotch (*peleche*), bat-, racket- and stick-hockey, and perhaps kick-ball and kick-stick racing, humming tops, pipes, the wax game (*chinchina*) and leaf-strand figures. The most distinctively Middle American elements would appear to be whistle speech, tumbling, acrobatics and juggling, the ball court, and *patolli*. On present data it is impossible to sketch the subareas of Middle America in relation to the present topic. Doubtless the most distinct region would be the northern plateau, from which information is altogether lacking. Very tentatively, the northwestern desert and sierra can be aligned with the Southwest of North America, principally in relation to racket hockey, kick-ball and kick-stick racing, and perhaps ritual clowns. The central plateau is somewhat distinct for tumbling and juggling, and may be the northern limit of the blowgun, leaf-strand figures, the wax game, and the tiger game.

Notably absent or unreported in Middle America are: dart games, tossing in a blanket, jokes, rhymes and counting games, tongue twisters, skipping, finger games or finger snapping, shadow games, rope walking, log birling or other balancing games (except for stilt-walking), vaulting or high jumping, pledging future acts or playful

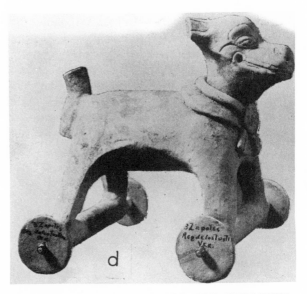

FIG. 17—TOTONAC WHEELED TOY, VERACRUZ, MEXICO. (From Medellín Zenil, 1960, pl. 56.)

vows, betting on future contingencies or past but unknown ones (like the weather or someone's father's name), tugs of war, yodeling, rib skates, the spring-action beanshooter, the Spanish astragalus-dice game *taba*, and whistling with hand or fingers. Riddles and guessing games seem rare but are reported by Peterson (1959a) for the Aztecs.

Childhood in Indian Middle America is today brief and pressured by poverty. In former times it may have been longer but pressured by primitivism. The general evidence certainly suggests much less elaboration of children's play and toys than is found in European culture. Scattered scraps of information nonetheless confirm the conclusions from our direct observations of these children: that they play richly and imaginatively with whatever comes to hand, and that they play largely in the pattern they are taught—by adults and by other children.

Adult play and recreation are no different. The particular elements in the play of Middle American Indians have their several histories in and out of the area. Like the

205

recreation of other American Indians, the pattern is deeply intertwined with the rest of culture, and particularly with the brooding religiosity, the aloof dignity that stands for good manners, the formalism that converts games into ceremonies and sports into sacrifices—all the values, in short, that set the tone of Middle American cultures. But we can also see here the eruption of spontaneous gaiety and squalls of violence, the normal eventful absurdities that make life in the social state nasty and delightful by turns.

It is too soon to attempt a sociology, let alone a psychology, of Indian humor and play. However, even the extremely scanty data we possess may justify the supposition that the effort would be rewarding. It is clear that in this area of culture, as in so many others, Middle America is or has been the highly complex center of a most varied and distinctive part of general history.

REFERENCES

Acosta, 1960
—— and Moedano Koer, 1946
Amsden, 1936
Anon., 1958
Barrera Vásquez, 1948
Beals, 1932, 1933, 1943, 1946
—— and Carrasco, 1944
Blom, 1932
Brand, 1951
Buelna, 1890
Burgess and Xec, 1955
Caso, 1924–27, 1932, 1936
Conzemius, 1932
Cooper, 1949
Corbett, 1939
Córdova, 1942
Crawley, 1914
Culin, 1907
Edmonson, 1961
Fernández, 1925
Foster, 1948a
Guiteras Holmes, 1952b
Ibarra, 1942
Kelly, 1943
—— and Palerm, 1952

Krickeberg, 1948
LaGrasserie, 1898
Lumholtz, 1902
Mace, 1957
Martínez Hernández, 1929
Mateos Higuera, 1930
Medellín Zenil, 1960
Mena, 1930
Mendner, 1956
Molina, 1880
Parsons, 1936
Peterson, 1959a, 1959b
Preuss, 1912
Schuller, 1935
Solís Alcalá, 1949
Spratling, 1960
Stern, 1950
Stone, 1949
Swanton, 1929
Thompson, J. E. S., 1941b, 1943
Toor, 1947
Toscano, 1945
Wisdom, 1940
Zingg, 1932

11. Kinship and Family

A. KIMBALL ROMNEY

N THIS review of available data on kinship and family in Middle America, major attention is devoted to kinship systems. Discussion of kinship terminologies is organized by major linguistic groups: Uto-Aztecan, Macro-Oto-Manguean, Mayan, and others. The references are arranged by language groups and contain the main sources. Previously unpublished terminologies are presented in the appendix.

Kinship systems considered here were chosen to give the most balanced areal coverage within the limits of the data. Of the several hundred terminologies published on Middle American groups, the majority are so incomplete and so internally inconsistent as to preclude any meaningful analysis. Therefore, I have been selective and have presented only those systems that are fairly complete and consistent.

Residence patterns may be characterized as "loosely" patrilocal. Variations from strong patrilocality can be measured in two dimensions: (1) the distance married couples live from the husband's family, and (2) the percentage of couples who live closer to the husband's family than to the wife's family. Although these two features vary greatly, I found no documented cases in which the majority of newly formed couples live matrilocally.

Both nuclear and extended families are common. The question of the distance the new couple lives from the husband's or the wife's family is closely related to family composition. If the new couple lives with one of the sets of parents, an extended family automatically results. In general, there tend to be more nuclear families than extended families. Family composition, like residence, shows wide variability and some exceptions. For example, among the Chorti bilateral extended families are more characteristic than nuclear families. It is quite common throughout the area for a newly formed couple to reside with one or the other set of parents for a fixed period of time or until a new house can be built close by. In outlying areas among the Macro-Oto-Manguean groups, related families occupy their own dwellings within a compound. The compound forms a loose extended family. The nuclear family tends to have economic independence, however, and

207

	Direct		Collateral		Collateral Affinal		Direct Affinal	
	male	female	male	female	male	female	male	female
+2	GrFa	GrMo	GrPaBr	GrPaSi	GrPaSibHu / SpGrPaBr	GrPaSibWi / SpGrPaSi	SpGrFa	SpGrMo
+1	Fa	Mo	Un	Au	PaSibHu / SpUn	PaSibWi / SpAu	SpFa	SpMo
0	ElBr / YrBr	ElSi / YrSi	Co		CoHu / SpCo(male)	CoWi / SpCo (female)	SpBr / SiHu	SpSi / BrWi
-1	So	Da	Ne	Ni	SpNe / NiHu	SpNi / NeWi	DaHu	SoWi
-2	GrSo	GrDa	SibGrSo	SibGrDa	SpSibGrSo / SibGrDaHu	SpSibGrDa / SibGrSoWi	GrDaHu	GrSoWi

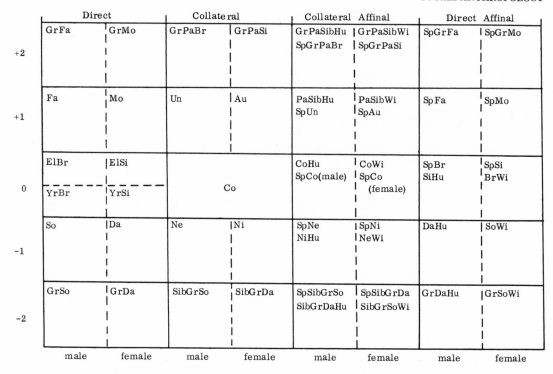

Fig. 1—KINTYPES AS REPRESENTED IN STANDARD DIAGRAMMATIC FORM

each married woman maintains an independent cook shack (Romney and Romney, 1963).

In general, the area is devoid of any special highly institutionalized kinship behavior patterns such as mother-in-law avoidance or strong joking relations. There are no reports whatsoever of either matrilateral or patrilateral cross-cousin marriage. Bilateral cross-cousin marriage may have been practiced among the Maya in former times (Eggan, 1934). Polyandry was and is unknown. Polygyny was probably almost universal in aboriginal times. At present, it occurs rather commonly in the more unacculturated sections. The sororate once was very general, as elsewhere in North America, whereas the levirate is nonexistent or extremely rare (Beals, 1932, p. 121). Marriage of one sibling group with another is preferred among the Chorti (Wisdom, 1940) and is common in the genealogies of the Tzeltal (field notes). The village or local community is almost always endogamous.

The diagrams that follow do not represent a componential analysis or any other formal structure analysis. They are laid out in a five-generation format. Generation differences are represented by horizontal lines (fig. 1). Generations are arranged in descending order. Direct relatives, placed to the left of the diagram, are defined to include ancestors of ego, full siblings of ego, and direct descendants of ego. Collateral relatives are to the right of the direct relatives. In many of the diagrams only consanguineal relatives are given since information is lacking on affinals. In charts that include affinal relatives, these kin types are placed to the right of the consanguineals.

Solid lines in the diagram represent major social principles of classification, e.g., direct vs. collateral. Broken lines represent simpler distinctions, such as relative age or sex. The space occupied by kin terms separated only by broken lines refers to all kin terms within that space, i.e., enclosed in solid lines. For example, if in the second ascending generation there is no solid line, it is to be assumed that grandparental terms are extended to grandparents' siblings. Similarly, if no solid line separates direct from collateral in zero generation, all sibling terms are extended to cousins. If a term is self-reciprocal, the word "self-reciprocal" is placed in the corresponding descending generation area. For example, if the same term is used self-reciprocally for grandparent and grandchild, the word "self-reciprocal" occurs in the minus-two generation. Absence of data is marked by "n.d."

Major or primary kin types are indicated. Each cell in the diagram represents a term in the kinship terminology, represented both by the space occupied and by the notation, according to the abbreviations: x, male speaking; o, female speaking; Fa, father; Mo, mother; So, son; Da, daughter; Br, brother; Si, sister; Hu, husband; Wi, wife; Sp, spouse; Pa, parent; Ch, child; Gr, great or grand; Sib, sibling; Co, cousin; El, elder; Yr, younger; ( ), alternate term.

Uto-Aztecan Kinship Systems

Uto-Aztecan groups for which data are satisfactory are (in crude geographic order from north to south): Papago, Pima, Opata, Tarahumara, Cahita, Tepehuane, Cora, Huichol, Huitziltepec, and Aztec. The structure of each is shown in figures 2–11.

These systems are characterized by certain features: (1) Hawaiian cousin terminology, within which there is a distinction between elder and younger relatives; (2) a distinction between direct and collateral relatives in plus-one and minus-one generations; (3) four grandparental terms that distinguish each of the grandparents and merge grandparent siblings with the respective grandparents; (4) frequent use of self-reciprocal terms for grandparent, grand-

	Direct		Collateral	
+2	FaFa	FaMo	MoFa	MoMo
+1	Fa	Mo	FaElBr / FaElSi ; MoElBr / MoElSi ; FaYrBr / FaYrSi ; MoYrBr / MoYrSi	
0	ElSib ; YrSib			
−1	xCh ; oCh		ElBrCh / ElSiCh ; YrBrCh / YrSiCh	
−2	xSoCh	oSoCh	xDaCh	oDaCh

FIG. 2—PAPAGO. (Underhill, 1937; Dolores, 1923.)

child, and collateral relatives in plus-one and minus-one generations; (5) a recurring pattern in which ascending kinsmen are distinguished on the basis of sex of relative, whereas kinsmen in descending generations are distinguished by sex of speaker.

The figures representing the Uto-Aztecan systems reveal that geographically central groups have more of the characteristic features than do the more peripheral groups. The northernmost groups—Papago, Pima, Opata, Tarahumara, Cahita, and Tepehuane—distinguish relative age of the connecting relative for collaterals in plus-one and minus-one generations. Since Shimkin (1941) finds this feature in Proto-Uto-Aztecan, it might be assumed that the southernmost groups—Cora, Huichol, Huitziltepec, and Aztec—have lost this feature since early times.

The extreme northern groups—Papago, Pima, and Opata—show further specializations. They have developed nonreciprocal

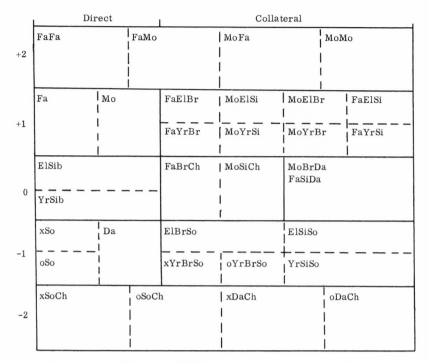

Fɪɢ. 3—PIMA. (Parsons, 1928.)

	Direct		Collateral		Direct Affinal	
+2	FaFa FaFaSib	FaMo FaMoSib	MoFa MoFaSib	MoMo MoMoSib		
+1	xFa oFa	Mo	FaElBr FaElSi FaYrBr FaYrSi	MoElBr MoElSi MoYrBr MoYrSi	SpPa	
0	ElBr YrBr	ElSi YrSi	Co		SpBr SiHu	SpSi BrWi
-1	xSo oSo	xDa oDa	ElBrCh YrBrCh	ElSiCh YrSiCh	DaHu	
-2	SoSo BrSoSo SiSoSo SoDa SiSoDa BrSoDa		xDaCh xSibDaCh	oDaCh oSibDaCh		

Fɪɢ. 4—OPATA. (J. B. Johnson, 1950.)

210

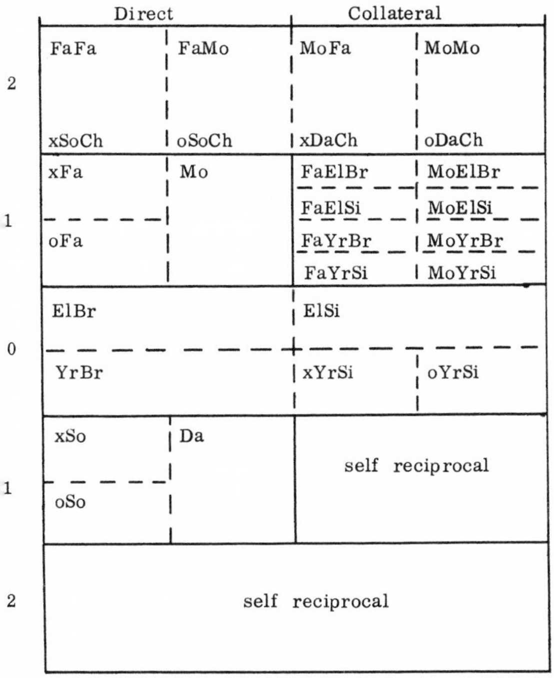

Fig. 5 — TARAHUMARA

	Direct		Collateral	
2	FaFa	FaMo	MoFa	MoMo
	xSoCh	oSoCh	xDaCh	oDaCh
1	xFa	Mo	FaElBr	MoElBr
			FaElSi	MoElSi
	oFa		FaYrBr	MoYrBr
			FaYrSi	MoYrSi
0	ElBr		ElSi	
	YrBr		xYrSi	oYrSi
1	xSo	Da	self reciprocal	
	oSo			
2	self reciprocal			

FIG. 5—TARAHUMARA. (Bennett and Zingg, 1935.)

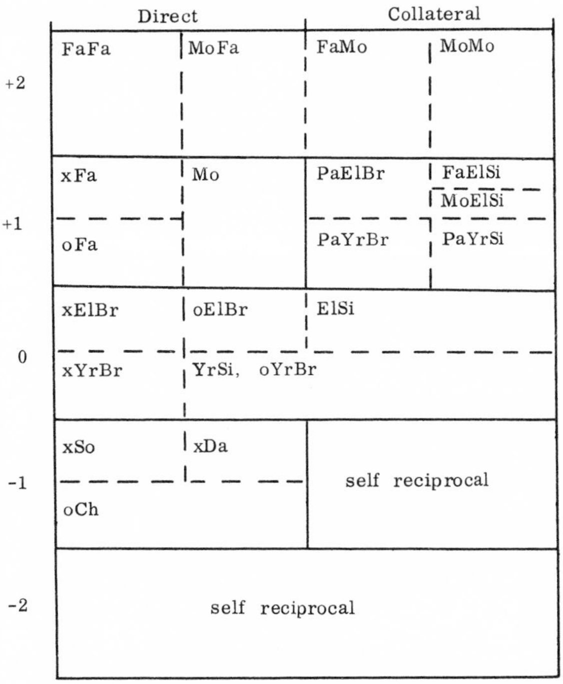

Fig. 6 — CAHITA (MAYO)

	Direct		Collateral	
+2	FaFa	MoFa	FaMo	MoMo
+1	xFa	Mo	PaElBr	FaElSi
				MoElSi
	oFa		PaYrBr	PaYrSi
0	xElBr	oElBr	ElSi	
	xYrBr	YrSi, oYrBr		
-1	xSo	xDa	self reciprocal	
	oCh			
-2	self reciprocal			

FIG. 6—CAHITA (MAYO). (Beals, 1943.)

terms for grandchildren and first descending collaterals. This specialization may be a result of contact with Yuman groups. In addition, Pima and Opata are the only two groups that distinguish cousins from siblings. Pima resembles Yuman groups in that it makes further distinction between cross and parallel cousins. The extreme southern groups—Huitziltepec and Aztec—appear to have much simplified bilateral systems and probably represent recent influences of acculturation.

Cora and Huichol share only one cognate term, a surprising fact since they have traditionally seemed to be rather close relatives within the Uto-Aztecan family.

MACRO-OTO-MANGUEAN KINSHIP SYSTEMS

The discussion of these kinship systems follows Hamp's (1963) rearrangement of Tax's (1960) linguistic classification. Hamp's outline follows:

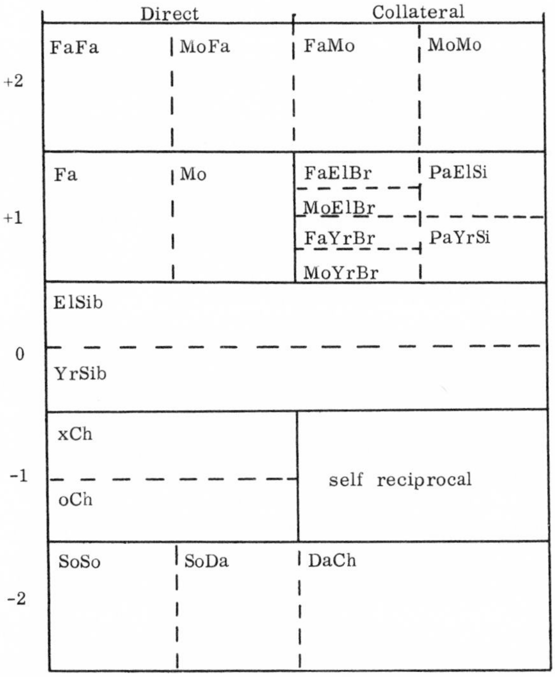

Fig. 7 — TEPEHUANE

	Direct		Collateral	
+2	FaFa	MoFa	FaMo	MoMo
+1	Fa	Mo	FaElBr	PaElSi
			MoElBr	
			FaYrBr	PaYrSi
			MoYrBr	
0	ElSib			
	YrSib			
-1	xCh		self reciprocal	
	oCh			
-2	SoSo	SoDa	DaCh	

FIG. 7—TEPEHUANE. (Radin, 1931.)

211

Fig. 8 — CORA table:

	Direct		Collateral		Direct Affinal
+2	GrFa ... xGrCh		GrMo ... oGrCh		n. d.
+1	Fa	Mo	Un	Au	SpPa
			Ne	Ni	ChSp
0	ElBr / YrSib		ElSi		xWiBr | oSpSib, xWiSi
-1	xCh / oCh		self reciprocal		self reciprocal
-2	self reciprocal				n. d.

Fig. 8—CORA. (Hinton, see Appendix.)

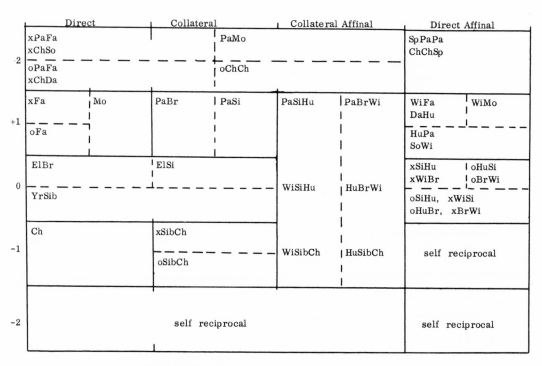

Fig. 9 — HUICHOL table:

	Direct		Collateral		Collateral Affinal		Direct Affinal	
2	xPaFa, xChSo / oPaFa, xChDa		PaMo / oChCh				SpPaPa, ChChSp	
+1	xFa / oFa	Mo	PaBr	PaSi	PaSiHu	PaBrWi	WiFa, DaHu	WiMo
							HuPa, SoWi	
0	ElBr / YrSib		ElSi		WiSiHu	HuBrWi	xSiHu, xWiBr	oHuSi, oBrWi
							oSiHu, xWiSi / oHuBr, xBrWi	
-1	Ch		xSibCh / oSibCh		WiSibCh	HuSibCh	self reciprocal	
-2	self reciprocal						self reciprocal	

Fig. 9—HUICHOL. (Grimes and Grimes, 1962.)

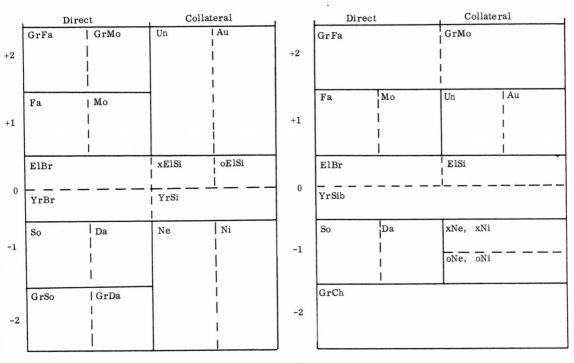

FIG. 10—HUITZILTEPEC. (Weitlaner, Velásquez, and Carrasco, 1947.)

FIG. 11—AZTEC. (Radin, 1925.)

Macro-Oto-Manguean

  I. Proto-Popoloca-Manguean
      A. Proto-Amuzgo-Mixtecan
          1. Proto-Mixtecan
             a. Mixteco
             b. Cuicateco
             c. Trique
          2. Amuzgo
             a. Amuzgo
      B. Proto-Popolocan
          1. Popolocan
             a. Chocho
             b. Popoloca
             c. Ixcateco
          2. Mazatecan
             a. Mazateco
      C. Chiapaneco-Manguean (no kinship information)

  II. Otomian
      A. Otomi
      B. Mazahua
      C. Ocuiltecan
          1. Matlatzinca

      D. Pamean
          1. Chichimeca-Jonaz
          2. Pame
  III. Chinanteco
  IV. Zapotecan
      A. Zapoteco
      B. Chatino

The first three systems—Mixteco, Cuicateco, and Trique—form a homogeneous subgroup. Mixtec is shown in figure 12, Trique in figure 13; Cuicatec is virtually identical to Mixtec and is not illustrated here. All three systems are characterized by the merging of collateral consanguineals and collateral affinals, by Hawaiian cousin terminology, and by special terms for direct affinals. There are three terms for siblings and cousins: male-speaking brother, male-speaking sister, and cross-sex sibling. Direct relatives are distinguished from collateral relatives in first ascending and first descending generations. There is great variation among and within various Mixtec systems

213

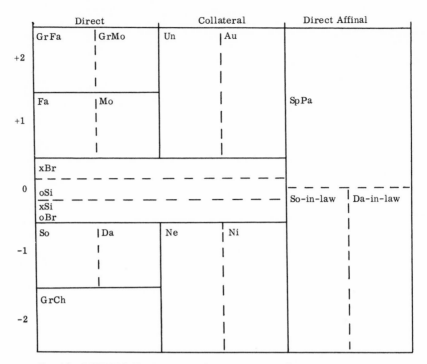

Fig. 12—MIXTEC, JUXTLAHUACA. (Romney and Romney, 1963.)

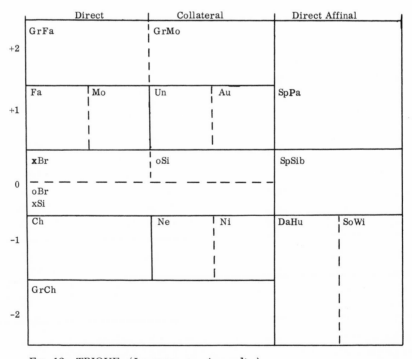

Fig. 13—TRIQUE. (Longacre, see Appendix.)

	Direct		Collateral		Direct Affinal	
+2	GrFa	GrMo	Un	Au		
+1	Fa	Mo			SpFa	SpMo
0	Br		Si		Br-in-law	Si-in-law
					DaHu	SoWi
-1	So	Da	Ne	Ni		
-2	GrCh					

Fɪɢ. 14—MAZATEC. (F. H. Cowan, 1947.)

as to whether grandparents' siblings are classed with grandparents or with aunts and uncles.

The Mazatec have basically the same system (fig. 14). We have no kinship data from the Chiapaneco-Manguean language families. Popoloca (fig. 15) is a variant on the same basic pattern. Mazatec and Popoloca indicate sex of sibling only and thus have two sibling terms instead of three as among the Mixtec and Trique. In the Popoloca system, as reported by Ann F. Williams, sibling terms are not extended to cousins, but cousins are merged with nephews and nieces.

All the Proto-Popoloca-Manguean groups for which we have information, except Amuzgo, form a single type (with Popoloca as possibly the most variant), of which Mixtec and Trique are examples.

Amuzgo presents one example of a genuine divergent type within the Proto-Popoloca-Manguean group. As reported by W. C. Stewart (personal communication), Amuzgo has the unusual feature of merging siblings with all collateral relatives regardless of generation. Affinal relatives are generally referred to by descriptive terms and appear not to be merged with consanguineal relatives. These features and the recognition of relative age set the system apart from close linguistic relatives such as Mixtec and Trique. A comparison of the Amuzgo system in figure 16 with those in figures 12, 13, and 14 illustrates the magnitude of the differences. The Amuzgo system is very much like that among the Chinantec and Zapotec groups.

The Chinantec-Zapotec system is best represented in the Papantla Chinantec kinship terminology (Merrifield, 1959). It has two main structural features (fig. 17): (1) a distinction between affinal and consanguineal relatives, and (2) an extension of sibling terms to consanguineal-collateral relatives in all generations. Both these fea-

215

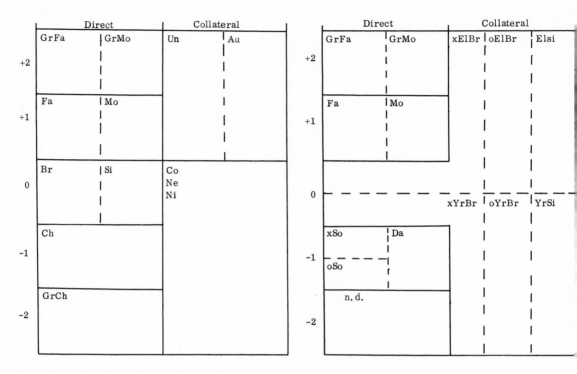

FIG. 15—POPOLOCA DE PUEBLA. (Williams, see Appendix.)

FIG. 16—AMUZGO. (Stewart, see Appendix.)

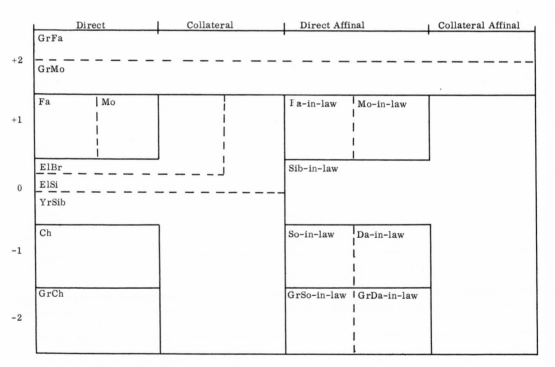

FIG. 17—CHINANTEC. (Merrifield, 1959.)

216

tures, however, are ignored in the second ascending generation, where all senior relatives are merged with grandparents.

This system is also found among the Zapotec and is represented (fig. 18) in clearest form in the conservative town of Juquila (L. Nader, personal communication). In more acculturated Zapotec towns, this merging of collaterals with siblings is being dropped, and, in general, Spanish terms are borrowed for the collateral relatives such as uncle and aunt, nephew and niece (see, for example, De la Fuente's report of Yalalag Zapotec in fig. 19, and Nader's on Talea Zapotec in fig. 20). An alternative development is seen in Yatzachi el Bajo Zapotec (Nader), where descriptive terminology is used for the collateral relatives (fig. 21). This is shown in the diagram by the + symbol, which indicates, for example, that the term for uncle consists of the term for father plus a descriptive suffix.

This Chinantec-Zapotec type system is thus found in three of the four branches of the Macro-Oto-Manguean stock. It is also found among nearby but apparently linguistically unrelated groups of Mixe and Sierra Popoluca. It is also present among the more geographically distant and unrelated Mayan group, the Tzeltal of Aguacatenango.

The fact that this rather anomalous system occurs among groups separated both linguistically and geographically indicates that the system has some historical depth and some special functional significance. My own speculation is that the family organization which is characterized by loose bilateral extensions produces a situation in which ego's parents (and, by reciprocity, ego's children) are the only relatives that require differentiation. During the age of socialization, all other relatives are roughly equivalent, e.g., those who are around the compound but do not have authority over ego.

A third structure type within Macro-Oto-Manguean is found among the Otomian

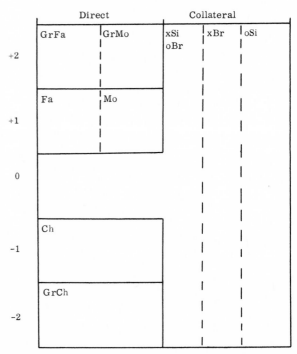

FIG. 18—ZAPOTEC, JUQUILA. (Nader, see Appendix.)

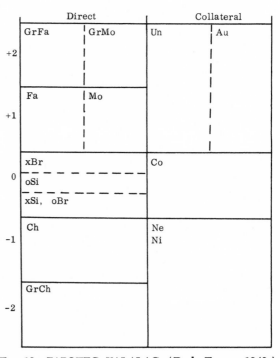

FIG. 19—ZAPOTEC, YALALAG. (De la Fuente, 1949.)

217

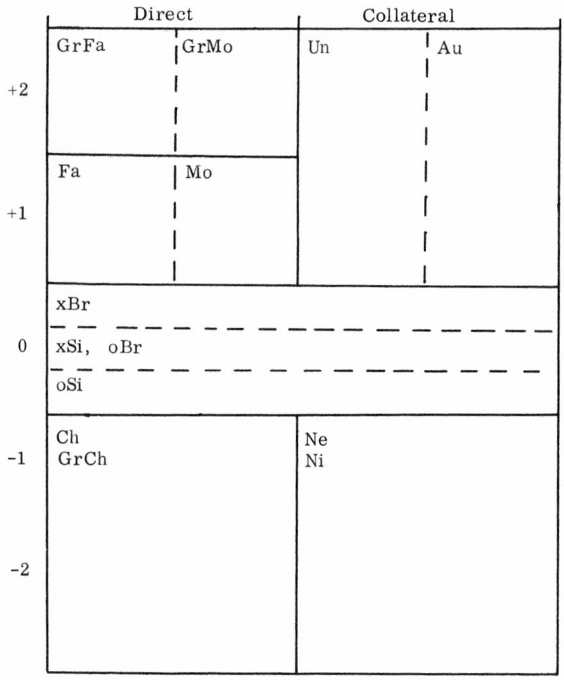

	Direct		Collateral	
+2	GrFa	GrMo	Un	Au
+1	Fa	Mo		
0	xBr / xSi, oBr / oSi			
−1	Ch GrCh		Ne Ni	
−2				

Fig. 20—ZAPOTEC, TALEA. (Nader, see Appendix.)

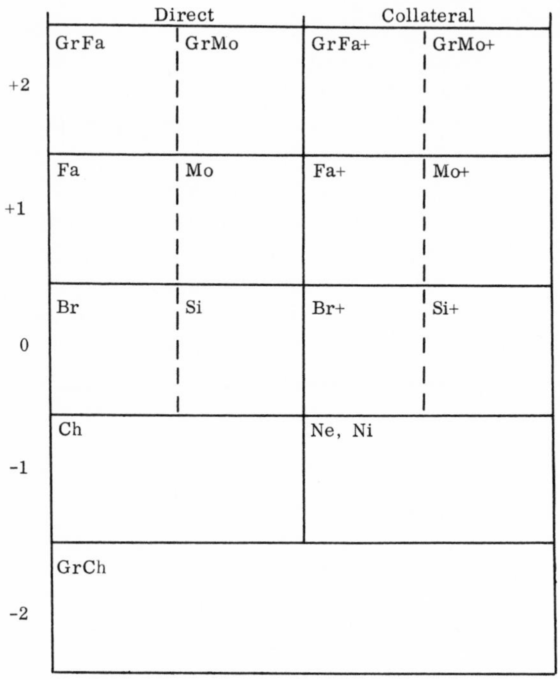

	Direct		Collateral	
+2	GrFa	GrMo	GrFa+	GrMo+
+1	Fa	Mo	Fa+	Mo+
0	Br	Si	Br+	Si+
−1	Ch		Ne, Ni	
−2	GrCh			

Fig. 21—ZAPOTEC, YATZACHI EL BAJO. (Nader, see Appendix.)

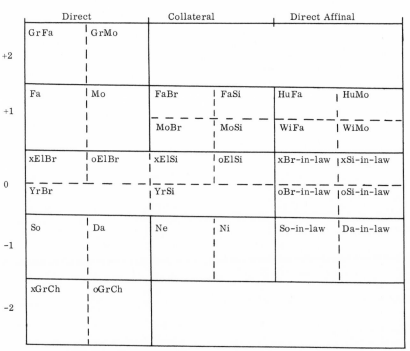

Fig. 22—OTOMI. (Ecker, 1930.)

218

groups. Insufficient data preclude giving variations in detail, but the degree of differentiation is greater in Otomi than in the groups discussed above. This increased differentiation results in a greater number of kin terms and in recognition of more distinctions among kin types. Figure 22 shows the most complete system of Otomi terms. Note the great number of distinctions recognized (relative age, sex of relative, sex of speaker, sex of intervening relative, etc.) as compared to other Macro-Oto-Manguean systems reported earlier.

KINSHIP SYSTEMS OF UNAFFILIATED AND REMOTE GROUPS

These groups are either unrelated to any of the three major linguistic stocks in Middle America, such as Tarascan, or too distantly related for verification, such as Mixe and Zoque. The latter may be related to Uto-Aztecan or Mayan as part of the Macro-Penutian superstock.

Mixe, Zoque, Popoluca, and Huave

Mixe, Zoque, and Popoluca of Veracruz form a linguistically related enclave between Oto-Manguean and Mayan groups. Among both the Mixe and the Popoluca are systems very similar in structure to those discussed above among the Chinantec, Zapotec, and Amuzgo.

Figure 23 shows the structure of the Sierra Popoluca (Foster, 1949). Since this basic structure has been found to recur in several groups, its possible functional significance was noted in the discussion of Macro-Oto-Manguean systems. Foster's reasoning follows (1949, p. 333):

The kinship terminology is functionally suited to the present social organization of the Sierra Popoluca. There are no clans, and though Soteapan—and probably the other larger villages—is divided into two barrios, they appear to be non-functional as far as relation to kinship is concerned. Family affiliation and descent appear to be completely bilateral, and

Direct		Collateral
GrFa	GrMo	
Fa	Mo	
ElBr		
ElSi		
YrSib		
So	Da	
GrCh		

(rows marked +2, +1, 0, −1, −2)

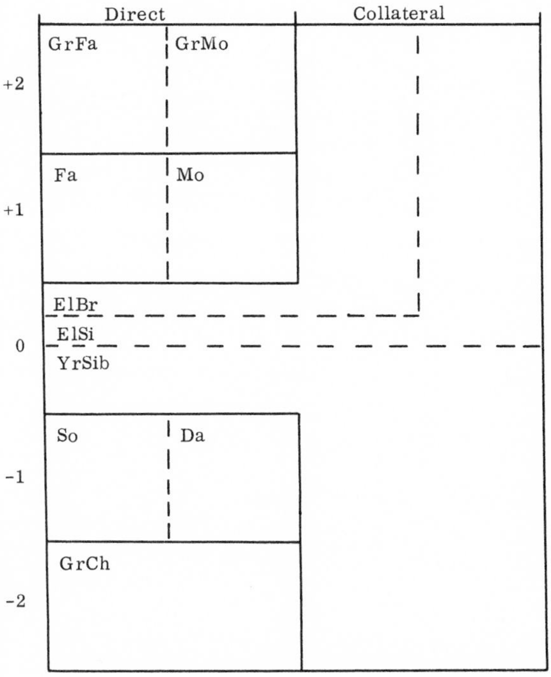

FIG. 23—SIERRA POPOLUCA. (Foster, 1949.)

marriage between cousins is forbidden. Households are elementary in composition. A numerically small but sociologically significant number of families are polygynous. Sometimes this institution is of the sororal type, in which case the two or three wives live in the same house. When it is non-sororal the wives tend to live in separate houses not parts of the same patio cluster. Lack of distinction between male and female lines is in accordance with the bilateral family organization. The lumping of all older collateral relatives with older brothers and sisters, depending on sex, is a device admirably suited to coping with the confusion created by many other collateral step-relatives, i.e., the relatives of one's father's other wives. This also holds true for the equating of younger siblings with all younger collateral relatives.

The Mixe of Coatlan have a very similar system (fig. 24). The only departures are distinction of sex of speaker for elder brother and extension of grandparental terms to collateral relatives in second ascending generation. Foster reports on an earlier terminological system, published in 1733 and di-

219

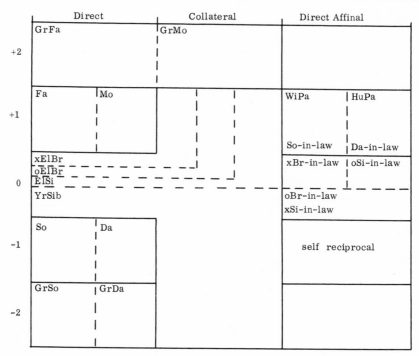

FIG. 24—MIXE, COATLAN. (Hoogshagen and Merrifield, 1961.)

agrammed here in figure 25. This structure does not resemble the contemporary system reported by Hoogshagen and Merrifield (1961), a difference that might be taken as tentative evidence that the merging in several generations of collaterals with siblings is a recent development.

The atmosphere of the Zoque system (Roy Harrison, personal communication) is similar to that of English. Consanguineal relatives are all classed as in English with the exception of sibling terms. Relative age and sex of elder siblings are recognized, producing three sibling terms: one for elder brother, one for elder sister, and one for younger sibling. The original terms are given in the appendix.

A more distant linguistic relative of the Mixe-Zoque is found in the Huave. The Huave (A. R. Diebold, Jr., personal communication) exhibit the most thoroughgoing descriptive system of any encountered. There are 13 basic nondescriptive terms, in-

cluding affinal as well as consanguineal. These root terms are reported in the appendix. Terms for such relatives as uncles, aunts, nieces, nephews, cousins, are formed descriptively from these root terms.

Coahuiltecan

R. C. Troike (personal communication) has discovered a remarkably complete set of Coahuiltecan kinship terms recorded by Fray Bartolomé García in a confessional published in 1760. (Because the Coahuiltec are extinct, this discovery is important.) Coahuiltec is unique in the extent to which various kinsmen are distinguished. These terms are given in the appendix. The total inventory is probably the greatest in Middle America. There are, for example, four parental terms since both sex of relative and sex of speaker are recognized. There are eight aunt and uncle terms since sex of relative, relative age, and sex of intervening relative are all regularly distinguished. Similarly, there are eight sibling terms since relative age, sex of relative, and sex of speaker are consistently distinguished. The distinctions appear to be made in a bilaterally symmetrical way and thus show no evidence of a lineal bias.

Tequistlatec

Perhaps the simplest terminological (fig. 26) system is found in Oaxaca among the Tequistlatec (Olmsted, 1958). In ascending generations direct relatives are distinguished from collaterals, and sex of relative is distinguished within each of these categories. One term serves for all ego's generation, and all descending relatives are merged in a single term. Possible similarities in kinship structure between Tequistlatec, which is a Hokan language, and its distant relatives such as Seri, Coahuiltec, and Yuman were sought without success.

Seri

The Seri have a complex terminological system. Kroeber's data (1931) are not clear at all points, but the main features may be seen in figure 27. The Seri are at the opposite extreme from the Tequistlatec in number of terms in the respective systems. In this respect, Seri resembles Coahuiltecan. Structurally, the Seri most resemble the Cocopa of the Yuman linguistic family, their Hokan neighbors to the north.

Seri regularly recognize sex of relative in ascending generations and sex of speaker in descending generations (they recognize both in own generation). They also recognize relative age (as do Yuman groups to the north) and sex of intervening relative.

Tarascan

Although there are many mentions of Tarascans in the literature (e.g., Radin, 1925; Beals, 1946; Pimentel, 1874–75), it is impossible to reconstruct a viable native system from the published sources. Modern systems are well known from the work of

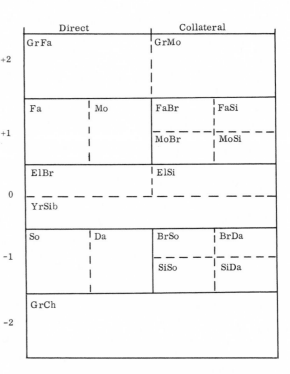

Fig. 25—MIXE, 1733. (Foster, 1949.)

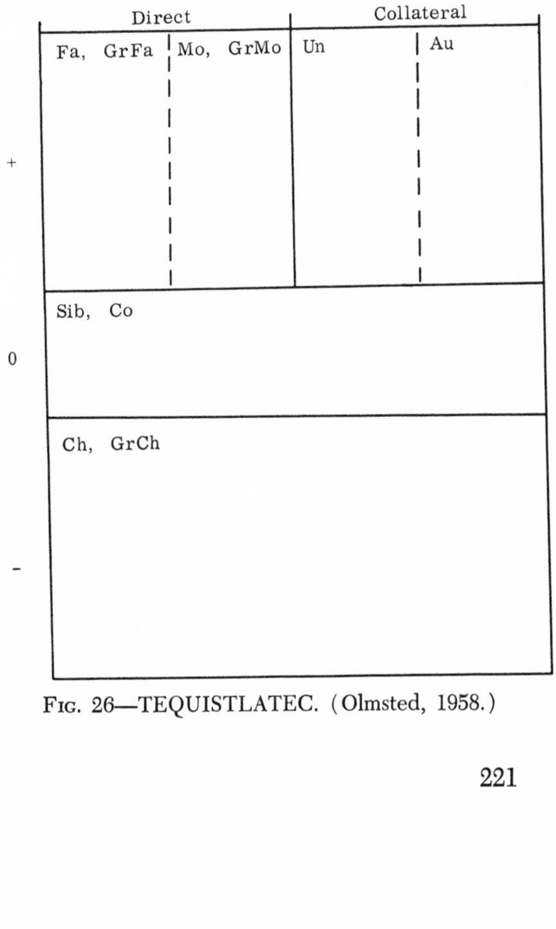

Direct		Collateral	
Fa, GrFa	Mo, GrMo	Un	Au
Sib, Co			
Ch, GrCh			

Fig. 26—TEQUISTLATEC. (Olmsted, 1958.)

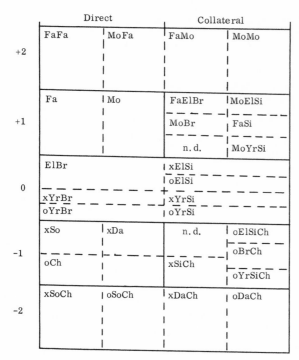

	Direct		Collateral	
+2	FaFa	MoFa	FaMo	MoMo
+1	Fa	Mo	FaElBr	MoElSi
			MoBr	FaSi
			n. d.	MoYrSi
0	ElBr		xElSi	
			oElSi	
	xYrBr		xYrSi	
	oYrBr		oYrSi	
-1	xSo	xDa	n. d.	oElSiCh
				oBrCh
	oCh		xSiCh	
				oYrSiCh
-2	xSoCh	oSoCh	xDaCh	oDaCh

Fig. 27—SERI. (Kroeber, 1931.)

Beals (1946), but they include so many Spanish terms that it would be unsafe to infer a pure Tarascan system.

Totonac

There are no complete modern reports on Totonac. According to Palerm (1953, p. 172), the ancient Totonac practiced polygyny, the levirate, and the sororate. Kelly (1953, p. 181) reports the occurrence of the latter two customs among modern Totonac and distinguishes highland monogamy from lowland polygamy.

There is one fairly complete terminology from 1752 (Radin, 1931). It is characterized (fig. 28) by a direct-collateral distinction except at second removed generations. Relative age and sex of speaker are recognized only for siblings.

MAYAN KINSHIP SYSTEMS

The Mayan linguistic stock has been classified by McQuown (1956) as follows:

Mayan
  A. Huastecan
      1. Huastec
          a. Veracruzano
          b. Potosino
      2. Chicomuceltec
  B. Cholan
      1. Chontal of Tabasco
      2. Chol
      3. Chorti
  C. Tzeltalan
      1. Tzeltal
      2. Tzotzil
      3. Toholabal
  D. Chuh
  E. Kanhobalan
      1. Jacaltec
      2. Kanhobal
      3. Solomec
  F. Motozintlec
  G. Mamean
      1. Mam
      2. Aguacatec
      3. Ixil
  H. Quichean
      1. Rabinal
      2. Uspantec
      3. Quiche
      4. Cakchiquel
      5. Tzutuhil
  I. Kekchian
      1. Kekchi
      2. Pokonchi
      3. Pokomam
  J. Maya proper
      1. Yucatec
      2. Lacandone
      3. Itza
      4. Mopan

"A less cautious sub-grouping would combine B and C, D and E, F and G, and H and I," says McQuown (1956).

Despite extensive work among the Mayan groups, detailed information on their kinship systems is very spotty. The variability among these systems is much greater than among those of any other parts of Middle America. For the Yucatec Maya, Eggan (1934) reconstructs a "Kariera-type" ter-

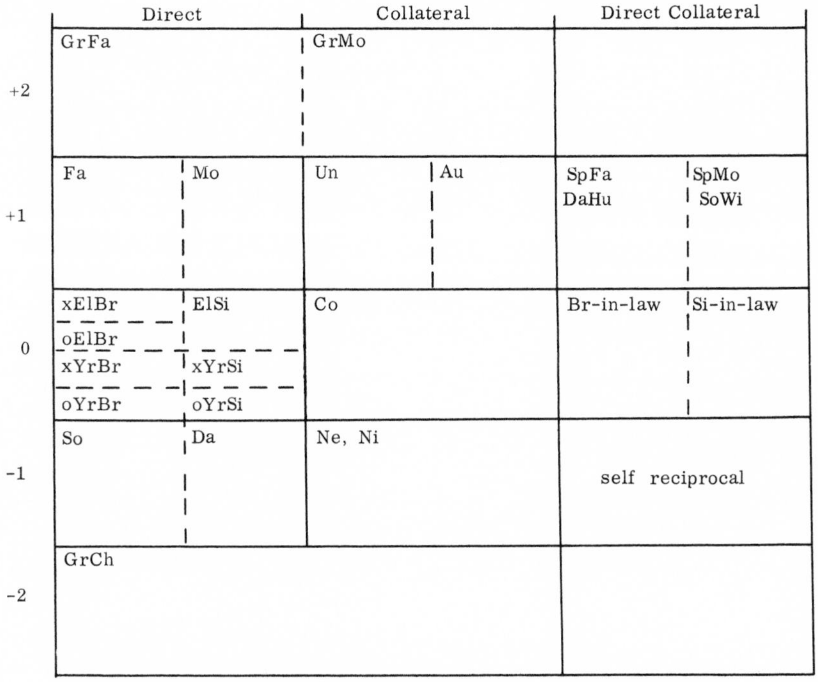

	Direct		Collateral		Direct Collateral	
+2	GrFa		GrMo			
+1	Fa	Mo	Un	Au	SpFa DaHu	SpMo SoWi
0	xElBr / oElBr / xYrBr / oYrBr	ElSi / xYrSi / oYrSi	Co		Br-in-law	Si-in-law
-1	So	Da	Ne, Ni		self reciprocal	
-2	GrCh					

FIG. 28—TOTONAC, 1752. (Radin, 1931.)

minological system with bilateral cross-cousin marriage. More recently, Lounsbury (personal communication) confirmed Eggan's findings and added precision to the analysis. If true, this is the only documented example of a preferential cousin-marriage rule in Middle America. The Mayan family contains many other examples of terminologies and practices which are unique for Middle America.

Because of this wide variability, it is impractical to attempt a coherent picture of a unified Mayan system or family of systems. Therefore, each system is discussed separately in the order it occurs in the linguistic outline above.

Huastec

We have information on two Huastec systems: one (Radin, 1931) is from the 1700's, deriving from Potosino, the second is modern Veracruzano (Guiteras Holmes, 1948).

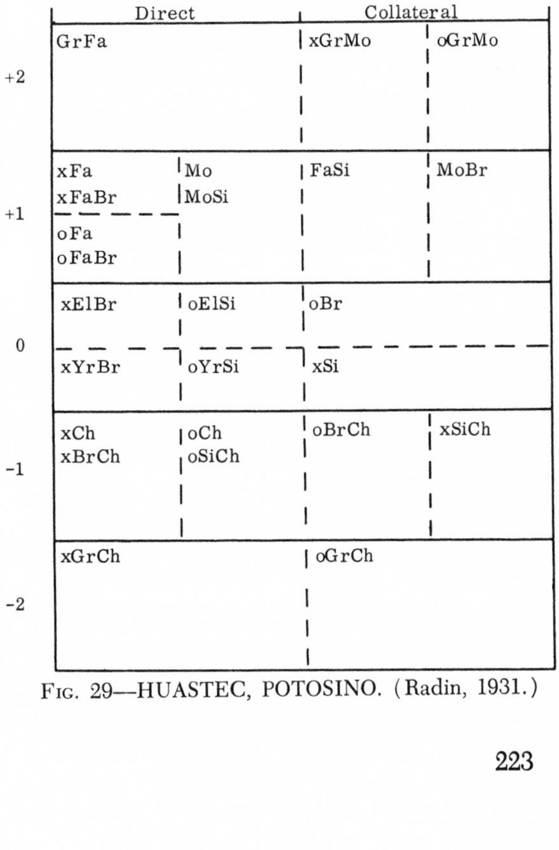

	Direct		Collateral	
+2	GrFa		xGrMo	oGrMo
+1	xFa xFaBr / oFa oFaBr	Mo MoSi	FaSi	MoBr
0	xElBr / xYrBr	oElSi / oYrSi	oBr / xSi	
-1	xCh xBrCh	oCh oSiCh	oBrCh	xSiCh
-2	xGrCh		oGrCh	

FIG. 29—HUASTEC, POTOSINO. (Radin, 1931.)

223

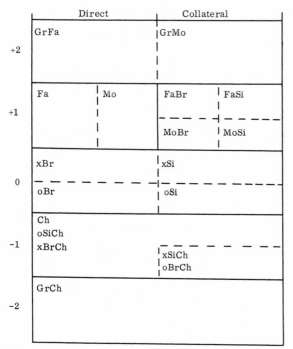

	Direct		Collateral	
+2	GrFa		GrMo	
+1	Fa	Mo	FaBr	FaSi
			MoBr	MoSi
0	xBr		xSi	
	oBr		oSi	
-1	Ch oSiCh xBrCh		xSiCh oBrCh	
-2	GrCh			

FIG. 30—HUASTEC, VERACRUZANO. (Guiteras Holmes, 1948.)

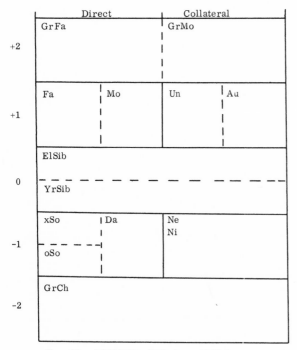

	Direct		Collateral	
+2	GrFa		GrMo	
+1	Fa	Mo	Un	Au
0	ElSib			
	YrSib			
-1	xSo	Da	Ne Ni	
	oSo			
-2	GrCh			

FIG. 31—CHORTI. (Wisdom, 1940.)

The early data (fig. 29) are characterized by bifurcate merging terminology with extensive use of the distinction of sex of speaker. Siblings are classed with cousins; relative age is recognized for same sex siblings and ignored for opposite sex siblings. The distinction between direct and collateral relatives is consistently ignored.

Among noteworthy features of modern Huastec (fig. 30) are four terms for first ascending collaterals. The terminology in the first descending generation is somewhat unusual; children are merged with parallel nephews and nieces, and a distinct term exists for cross-nephews and nieces. Distinct terms are found for direct affinal relatives (although they are descriptive for first ascending generation). Collateral affinals are merged with consanguineals.

A comparison of the two systems shows the modern one to be considerably simpler than the earlier one. It has, for example, 15 terms rather than 20. The bifurcate merging has become bifurcate collateral, and relative age distinctions have been lost in zero generation. In addition, recognition of sex of speaker has been dropped for several categories of relatives.

Chorti

The system of consanguineal kinsmen among the Chorti (fig. 31) is characterized by Hawaiian cousin terminology that recognizes relative age and ignores any sex distinctions. Direct and collateral relatives are merged in second ascending and descending generations. In first ascending and descending generations, direct relatives are distinguished from collaterals. Collateral affinals are merged with consanguineals except in own generation. In ego's generation, there is one term for all collateral affinals. Special terms exist for direct affinals in own and adjacent generations. Wisdom (1940) presents a rather complete account of the family and kinship among the Chorti and points out that there is a good functional fit between the practice of sibling exchange between unrelated families at marriage and the terminology.

Tzeltal and Tzotzil

In highland Chiapas there are several dozen Indian towns comprised mainly of Tzeltal- and Tzotzil-speakers. Adjacent to the highlands are Zoque, Chol, and Toholabal. The variation in kinship systems among the Tzeltal and Tzotzil villages probably is equal to that among all the remainder of Middle America. It offers some problems for comparative analysis. For example, in this area are found the only examples of Omaha systems in Middle America. It also includes towns that are completely bilateral and show no lineal bias whatsoever. Still other towns exhibit various intermediate stages between the Omaha and bilateral types. Such a distribution raises the obvious historical question as to the direction of change. This is still an open question.

The best example of a thoroughgoing Omaha system is found in the Tzotzil town of Chalchihuitan (Guiteras Holmes, see appendix). In this system, all of the males in mother's line are merged (except in second ascending generation where grandparental terms are used for all senior relatives). Thus, mother's brother, mother's brother's son, mother's brother's son's son, and mother's brother's son's son's son are all called by a single term. Similarly, females in mother's line (with the exception of a special term for mother) are merged in a single term. In own and adjacent generations, children of females in ego's line are merged. Thus, father's sister's children are classed with sister's children. Mother's lineage is diagrammed in figure 32.

Guiteras Holmes (n.d.,*b*) has compared the Omaha system of Chalchihuitan with an intermediate system as found in the Tzotzil town of Chenalho. Chenalho is marked into three divisions, northern, central, and southern. Usages in the southern division are distinct from those in the central and northern divisions. Guiteras Holmes interprets non-Omaha Tzotzil groups as having changed from an earlier Omaha form and toward a bilateral form. Thus, she sees Chenalho as changing from Omaha to bilateral. A third town brought into her comparison is Chamula. Figure 33 compares the four systems for selected diagnostic relatives, from the Omaha system in Chalchihuitan through the intermediate systems of Chenalho to the bilateral system of Chamula.

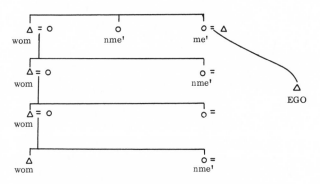

FIG. 32—MOTHER'S LINEAGE IN TZOTZIL, CHALCHIHUITAN. (Guiteras Holmes, see Appendix.)

The same progression from an Omaha type of system to a bilateral type of system is seen among the Tzeltal groups. Thus, as one moves from Oxchuc through Tenejapa to Chanal and Aguacatenango, the progression is from Omaha to bilateral. There is one important difference between the Tzotzil and Tzeltal cases, however. Among the Tzotzil groups, the bilateral systems closely resemble the Spanish systems, whereas among the Tzeltal the bilateral system is very different from that of the Spanish.

Figure 34 shows Cancuc (Guiteras Holmes, 1947), a Tzeltal system which is intermediate between Omaha and bilateral. One unusual feature is the use of a self-reciprocal term for the following relations: mother's brother, mother's brother's son, male-speaking father's sister's child, and male-speaking sister's child.

Aguacatenango represents the best example of a bilateral Tzeltal system that does

225

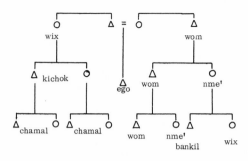

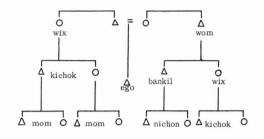

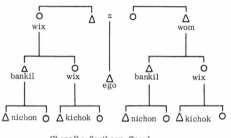

Chalchihuitan

Chenalho Northern Capul

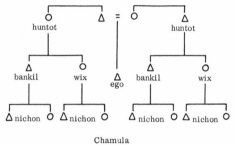

Chenalho Southern Capul

Chamula

FIG. 33—PROGRESSION FROM OMAHA TO BILATERAL TYPE SYSTEM IN TZOTZIL FOR DIAGNOSTIC RELATIVES, MALE EGO ONLY. (From Guiteras Holmes, n.d.,b.)

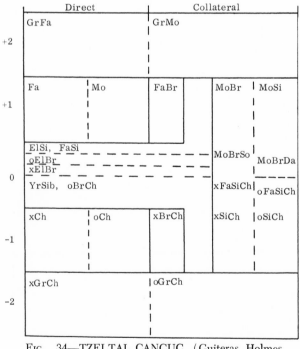

FIG. 34—TZELTAL, CANCUC. (Guiteras Holmes, 1947.)

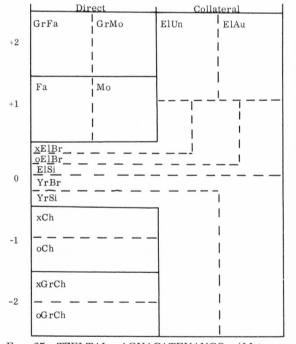

FIG. 35—TZELTAL, AGUACATENANGO. (Metzger, see Appendix.)

not closely resemble the Spanish system. The merging of collateral relatives in several generations with siblings is characteristic of the structure presented in figure 35 (Metzger, n.d.). This structure is reminiscent of examples presented earlier from the state of Oaxaca including Amuzgo, Zapotec, Chinantec, Mixe, and Popoluca. The main difference is the recognition of age relative to parent. Siblings of parents older than parent are referred to by aunt and uncle terms; parents' siblings younger than parent are referred to by elder sibling terms. All collateral relatives in descending generations are referred to by younger sibling terms.

Jacaltec

LaFarge and Byers (1931) describe a simple system for Jacaltec (fig. 36). It contains the only example of generational type aunt and uncle terminology in Middle America.

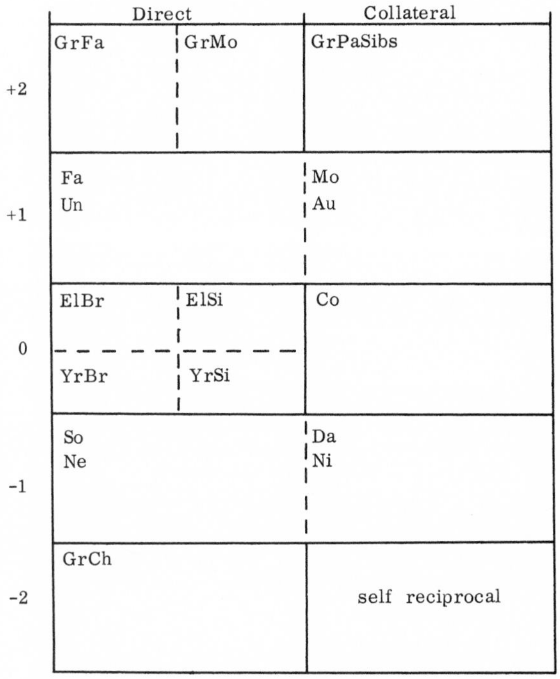

Cakchiquel

Tax (1946) has presented complete data for the Cakchiquel terminological system (fig. 37). It is characterized by Hawaiian cousin terminology and lineal aunt and uncle terminology. It makes thoroughgoing use of sex of speaker distinctions in own and descending generations.

Pokomam

Pokomam kinship terminology (Gillin, 1951) presents several puzzling complexities (fig. 38). It illustrates the inadequacies of simple, categorical, descriptive statements. For example, in the first ascending generation are three terms: one for father and father's brother, another for mother and father's sister, and a third for mother's sister and mother's brother. Thus, for males, avuncular terminology is bifurcate merging in traditional nomenclature. However, for females, the merging of mother with father's sister, with a separate term for mother's

Direct		Collateral	
GrFa	GrMo	GrPaSibs	
Fa Un		Mo Au	
ElBr	ElSi	Co	
YrBr	YrSi		
So Ne		Da Ni	
GrCh		self reciprocal	

FIG. 36—JACALTECA. (LaFarge and Byers, 1931.)

Direct		Collateral	
GrFa	GrMo	GrPaBr	GrPaSi
Fa	Mo	PaBr	PaSi
xElBr oElSi		oBr	xSi
xYrBr oYrSi			
oSo	xSo	oDa	xDa	xSibSo	xSibDa	oSibCh
xGrCh	oGrCh		oSibGrCh

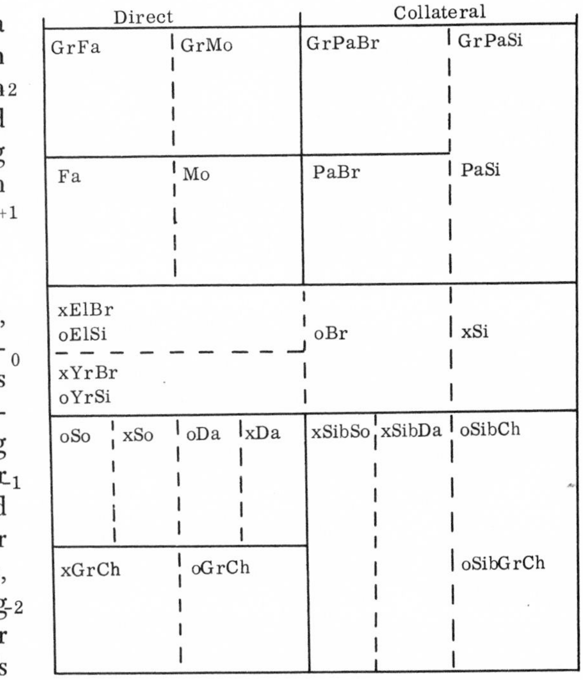

FIG. 37—CAKCHIQUEL. (Tax, 1946.)

227

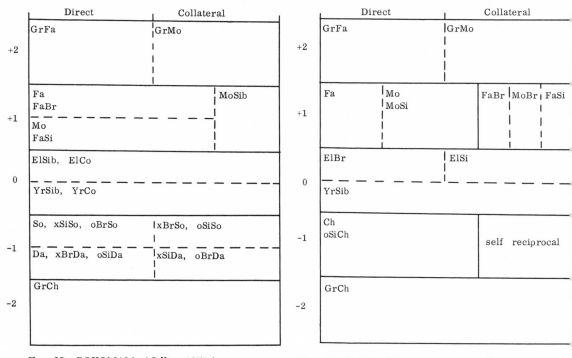

FIG. 38—POKOMAM. (Gillin, 1951.)

FIG. 39—YUCATEC, X-CACAL. (Villa Rojas, 1945.)

sister, fits none of the traditional categories. The situation is even somewhat more complex in the first descending generation. Here, the term for son is extended to cross-nephews, the term for daughter is extended to parallel-nieces, parallel-nephews are classed separately, and finally, there is a separate term for cross-nieces.

Yucatec

The X-Cacal (Villa Rojas, 1945), is presented in figure 39. The merging of mother and mother's sister without the corresponding merging of father and father's brother is unusual. The other aunt and uncle terms are completely and precisely self-reciprocal, taking into account sex of speaker and ignoring sex of relative in the descending generation. No distinction is made between collateral affinals and consanguineals. Distinct direct affinal terms are present except

for the first ascending generation where spouse's parents are merged with own parents.

CONCLUSIONS

There are still serious gaps in our knowledge of Middle American kinship systems. Fragmentary data are available for virtually every group. The need is for more complete reports on a greater number of groups.

More study is needed on the functional interpretation of individual systems. Even though most of the systems are relatively simple, there are many challenging puzzles within individual ones, as pointed out above.

Historical reconstructions are probably possible and would be most useful for each of the major linguistic groups. The classified references below may serve in this respect.

APPENDIX

This appendix consists of previously unpublished terminologies. I owe a great debt of gratitude to a number of people who responded to requests for new materials, especially Roberto Weitlaner, who led me to dozens of sources and people that otherwise would not have come to my attention. His frequent appearances in the references also attest to his contributions in the field. Others to whom I am indebted are: Brent Berlin, A. Richard Diebold, Jr., Lawrence Ecker, Lorna F. Gibson, Roy Harrison, Thomas B. Hinton, Calixta Guiteras Holmes, John Hotchkiss, Eva Verbitsky Hunt, Robert Longacre, Duane and Barbara Metzger, Laura Nader Milleron, Manning Nash, Robert Ravicz, W. Cloyd Stewart, Evangelina Arana de Swadesh, Rudy C. Troike, Bill Upson, and Ann F. Williams. Contributions to Chiapas materials were also made by the "Man-in-Nature" Project of the University of Chicago under the direction of Norman A. McQuown.

AMUZGO, Xochistlahuaca, Guerrero (W. Cloyd Stewart).

1. tsotya tsaⁿtkie	GrFa
2. tsondyotsaⁿtkie	GrMo
3. tsoty	Fa
4. tsondyo	Mo
5. ti'jndaya	xSo
6. ñejndaya	oSo
7. nomjndaya	Da
8. ti'šio	xElBr, xUn, xGrPaBr
9. ñešio	oElBr, oUn, oGrPaBr
10. nomšjo	ElSi, Au, GrPaSi
11. ti'tyjo	xYrBr, xNe, xSibGrSo
12. ñetyjo	oYrBr, oNe, oSibGrSo
13. nomšjo	YrSi, Ni, SibGrDa

COAHUILTECAN (Rudy C. Troike)

Terms in parentheses are from variant dialect. Main dialect is from San Antonio, Texas, and variant, from near Rio Grande. All terms are from a confessional by Fray Bartolomé García, 1760.

1. puc'al	FaFa
2. cuan	MoFa
3. caca	FaMo
4. cis (macis)	MoMo
5. mama (janai)	xFa
6. t'anague	oFa
7. tai	xMo
8. leish (tzaguaj) (tai)	oMo
9. jat'al	xElBr
10. cuanitap (t'atal)	oElBr
11. tal (quital)	xElSi
12. tzaal	oElSi
13. matzan	xYrBr
14. macutzan	oYrBr
15. yat'an	xYrSi
16. tzutzan (matzutzan)	oYrSi
17. pam	So
18. palum	xDa
19. q'uia	oDa
20. ha	SoCh
21. mat'an	oDaSo
22. tzat'an	oDaDa
23. cuant'an	xDaCh
24. cou	FaElBr
25. cuanaj	MoElBr
26. macit'an	FaElSi
27. tache (taish)	MoElSi
28. cochtan (cotstan)	FaYrBr
29. cut'an	MoYrBr
30. jotal	FaYrSi
31. chal	MoYrSi
32. mamou	Male Co
33. mamocham	Female Co
34. tala (talt'an)	xElBrSo
35. mijal	oElBrSo
36. tzojal	ElBrDa
37. p'ai	xYrBrCh
38. pchatzjop	oYrBrCh
39. jont'an	oElSiSo
40. cant'an	xElSiCh
41. apjaisht'an (apjat'an)	oElSiDa
42. jc'ou	xYrSiCh
43. ptaj	oYrSiCh
44. pujuai	StepFa

229

45. tapai	StepMo	
46. pam	StepSo	
47. palum	xStepDa	
48. q'ui	oStepDa	
49. cham	HuPa, SoWi	
50. pacuan guaco	WiFa	
51. pamacis guaco	WiMo	
52. yagua	DaHu	
53. aptajai	SpElBr	
54. taish guaco	SpElSi	
55. no data	ElSibSp	
56. pacuatzo	SpYrBr	
57. michal guaco	SpYrSi	
58. no data	YrSibSp	

CORA (Thomas B. Hinton, personal communication)

1. ya šu	GrFa, xGrCh
2. yak' wa	GrMo, oGrCh
3. tah'ta	Fa
4. na'na	Mo
5. nank'	Un, Ne
6. ti'	Au, Ni
7. ha'	ElBr
8. ah ku'	ElSi
9. hu'	YrSib
10. péri	xCh
11. yo'	oCh
12. ah mu'	SpPa, ChSp
13. yo' o re	xWiBr
14. hí i ta	oSpSib, xWiSi
15. ʔug	Wi
16. kng	Hu

HUAVE, San Mateo del Mar (A. Richard Diebold, Jr.)

1. téàt	Fa
2. mí m	Mo
3. šéèč	GrFa
4. nčéy	GrMo
5. kóh	ElSib
6. číìg	YoSib
7. kwál	Ch
8. ntáh	Wi
9. òkwáàc	WiPa
10. nóh	Hu
11. píw	HuPa
12. kùnyádà	xSpSib, xSibSp
13. híy	ChSpPa

All other terms are formed descriptively from above.

PAME (Lorna F. Gibson)

1. rawé	Fa
2. rawi	Mo
3. rabbéoʔ	MoBr, PaBrWi
4. ncʔok	FaSi, MoBrWi
5. rahiŋ	GrFa, xGRCh
6. rattoi	GrMo, oGrCh
7. hweo	Sib, Co
8. naʔi	Ch
9. ʔywáŋ	Hu
10. ʔiaʔa	Wi
11. légŋ	SpPa
12. waʔe	DaHu
13. waŋkhao	SoWi
14. akkwa	xBr-in-law
15. kommo	xSi-in-law, oBr-in-law
16. tochao rawéʔ	FaBr
17. tochao rawi	MoSi
18. čhi rabbeoʔ	xSiCh
19. tochao naʔi	xBrCh, oSibCh

POPOLOCA, San Felipe Otlaltepec in Puebla (Ann F. Williams)

1. tačiʔna	GrFa
2. načiʔna	GrMo
3. ʔapanaa (tʔanaa)	Fa
4. ʔamanaa (nʔanaa)	Mo
5. sʔonaa	Br
6. thakhoonaa	Si
7. čaʔna	Ch
8. čandʔinaa	GrCh
9. čiʔninaa	Un
10. khvaʔna	Au
11. čauvʔe	Co, Ne, Ni

TRIQUE (Robert Longacre)

1. dukụʔ	Ne, CoSo
2. dugwačiʔ	Ni, CoDa
3. nika	Wi (Hu)
4. n·ižičeh	SpMo, SpMoSi, SpFaSi
5. dreh žičeh	SpFa, SpPaBr
6. žako	xBrWi, xCoWi, PaBrWi PaCoWi
7. dinïʔ	xBr, xCo (male)
8. daʔnï	PaBr, PaCo (male)
9. žugweh	opposite sex Sib and Co
10. ɸɸn·i	Mo
11. dreh	Fa
12. duʔwi	PaSi, PaCo (female)
13. ži	GrFa, GrPaBr
14. žugwạ̃ʔạh	GrMo, GrPaSi

15. da²ni   Ch
16. da²nizïnï   GrCh, NeCh, NiCh
17. da²ni zna²u   So (zna²u = male)
18. da²ni žana   Da (žana = female)
19. ϟ zigatah   xSibHu, xCoHu, PaSiHu, PaCoHu
20. ziče   SpSib
21. žugwih   oSi, oCo (female)
22. da²ni žako²   SoWi
23. da²ni sigatah   DaHu

TZELTAL, Aguacatenango (Duane Metzger)

1. č'in tata   FaFaBr, FaSiHu, FaBr, MoSiHu, MoBr,
                            xSiHu, xWiSiHu
2. tata   FaFaBr, xFaFaBrSo, FaBr, Fa, MoBr
3. č'in nana   FaFaSi, FaBrWi, FaSi, MoSi, MoBrWi
4. muk'ul tat   GrFa
5. muk'ul me²   GrMo
6. bankil   xFaFaBrSo, xFaFaSiSo, FaBr, MoBr, xEl
                            male Sib, xEl male Co
7. wiš   FaFaSibDa, FaSi, MoSi, El female Sib,
                            El female Co
8. ²ih'ȼin   YoSib, YoCo, Ne, Ni, all –2BKTs with
                            exception of lineals, oSiChSp, xWiBrCh
9. ši²lel   oElBr, oFaFaSibDa
10. nana   FaSi, Mo, MoSi
11. tat   Fa
12. me²   Mo
13. nič'an   xCh
14. ²al   oCh
15. mamanič'an   xGrCh
16. ²ilal   oGrCh
17. mamalib   oHuFa
18. me²lalib   oHuMo
19. mamanial   xWiFa
20. menial   xWiMo
21. mu   oHuBr, xBrWi, xWiSi, oSiHu
22. hawan   oHuBrWi, oBrWi
23. mamalal   oHu
24. ²inam   xWi
25. ²alib   xSoWi
26. nial   xDaHu

TZELTAL, Chanal (Barbara Metzger)

1. mam   GrFa, FaFaBr
2. yahme²   GrMo
3. wiš   FaFaSi, FaFaSibDa, FaSi, MoBrWi,
                          ElSi, El female // Co
4. mehuk   FaMoSi (probably me²hun)
5. me²hun   MoFaSi, FaBrWi, MoSi
6. tahun   FaFaBrSo, FaMoBr, MoFaBr, FaBr, MoSiHu
7. ²ičan   MoBr, FaMoBrCh, MoFaBrCh, MoMoSibCh,

	FaSiCh, MoBrCh, FaSiChCh, SiCh,
	// female CoCh, MoBrChCh
8. bankil	ElBr, El male // Co, FaFaSiSo
9. ?ih'ʧin	YoSib, Yo // Co
10. nič'un	BrCh, male // CoCh
11. mamtak'	GrCh
12. bal	FaSiHu
13. tat	Fa
14. me?	Mo

Tzeltal, Oxchuc (Barbara Metzger)

1. mam	GrFa, FaFaBr
2. yame?	GrMo
3. wiš	FaSi, ElSi, female // Co
4. tahun	FaBr, MoSiHu
5. me?hun	MoSi, FaBrWi, MoBrDa
6. tat	Fa
7. me?	Mo
8. ?ičan	MoBr, FaSiCh, xoMoBrCh, FaBrDaCh,
	MoSiDaCh, xSiCh
9. bankil	xElBr, xEl male // Co
10. ?ih'ʧin	YoSib, Yo // Co, oBrCh
11. ši?lel	oElBr, oEl male // Co
12. ?al	oCh, oFaSiCh, oSiCh
13. ?alhun	oFaSiCh, oSiCh, oHuBrCh
14. nič'an	xCh
15. nič'un	FaBrSoCh, MoSiSoCh, xBrCh, xWiSiCh
16. činmam~mičun	all −2 gen. w/ exception of MoBrChCh,
	MoBrChChCh terms not given
17. kalmamal	oHuFa
18. kalmel	oHuMo
19. nialmamal	xWiFa
20. nialmel	xWiMo
21. bal	xSiHu, xWiBr
22. mu	xBrWi, oHuBr, xWiSi, oSiHu
23. hawan	oBrWi
24. ?alib	xSoWi
25. nial	xDaHu, oSiDaHu
26. mambal	oHu
27. ?inam	xWi

Tzeltal, Tenejapa (Brent Berlin) male ego

1. mam	GrFa, GrPa male Sib, −2 gen., FaSiDaCh
2. me?čun	GrMo, FaMoSi, MoPa female Sib
3. muk'ul wiš	FaFaSi
4. tahun	FaFaBrSo, FaBr, MoSiHu
5. wiš	FaFaBrDa, FaSi, ElSi, El female // Co
6. ?ičan	FaFaSiSo, MoBr, FaSiSo, MoBrCh,
	FaSiSoCh, MoSiDaCh, MoBrChCh,
	MoBrChChCh?, xSiSo, FaBrSiCh
7. tat	Fa
8. me?	Mo

9. ʔanȼiʔal   FaFaSiDa, FaSiDa, xSiDa
10. bankil   xElBr, xEl male // Co
11. šiʔlel   oElBr, oEl male // Co
12. ʔih'ȼin   Yo male Sib, Yo male // Co, oYo female Sib,
                     oYo female // Co
13. nič'hun   BrCh, FaBrSoCh, MoSiSoCh
14. nič'an   xCh
15. ʔal   oCh
16. bal   xWiBr, FaSiHu
17. hawan   oHuSi
18. muʔ   SpSib
19. ʔalib   xoSoWi ?
20. nial   xDaHu

Tzotzil, Chamula (Brent Berlin) male speaker

1. muk'tot   GrFa
2. huntot   GrPa male Sib, Un
3. hunmeʔ   GrPa female Sib, Au
4. yaya   GrMo
5. bankil   male Ch of GrPaSib, ElBr, El male Co,
                     xWiBr
6. wiš   female Ch of GrPaSib, ElSi, El female Co
7. ʔi'ȼin   YoBr, Yo male Co
8. ʔišlel   YoSi, Yo female Co
9. tot   Fa
10. meʔ   Mo
11. huničon ('ȼeb)   Ne, Ni
12. nič'on   xCh
13. ʔol   oCh
14. mom   GrCh
15. bol   xSiHu, xWiBr
16. muʔ   xBrWi, xWiSi
17. ʔahnil   xWi
18. muni   xWiFa
19. meni   xWiMo
20. ʔalib   xSoWi
21. niʔ   xDaHu
     Unattested
22. muk   oYoSib, YoCo
23. šibel   oElBr, El male Co
24. hunʔol   oBrCh

Tzotzil, San Pablo Chalchihuitan (Calixta Guiteras Holmes)

1. moltot   GrFa
2. yameʔ   GrMo
3. wiš   FaSi, FaBrElDa, ElSi, MoSiElDa,
                  MoBrDaElDa, MoBrSoDaElDa
4. huntot   FaBr, MoSiHu
5. tot   Fa
6. meʔ   Mo

7. hunmeʔ	MoSi, FaBrWi, MoBrDa, MoBrSoDa, MoBrSoSoDa
8. wom	MoBr, MoBrSo, MoBrSoSo, MoBrSoSoSo
9. ʔičokʹ	xFaSiCh, xSiCh, xFaBrDaCh, xMoSiDaCh, xMoBrDaDaCh
10. hunʔol	oFaSiCh, oSiCh, oFaBrDaCh, oMoSiDaCh, oMoBrDaDaCh
11. bankil	xFaBrElSo, xElBr, xMoSiElSo, xMoBrDaElSo, xMoBrSoDaElSo
12. ʔiȼʹin	xFaBrYoSo, xYoBr, xMoSiYoSo, xMoBrDaYoSo, xMoBrSoDaYoSo
13. šibel	oFaBrElSo, oElBr, oMoSiElSo, oMoBrDaElSo, oMoBrSoDaElSo
14. muk	oFaBrYoCh, oYoSib, oMoSiYoCh, oFaBrSoCh, oBrCh, oMoSiSoCh, oMoBrDaYoCh, oMoBrSoDaYoCh, oMoBrDaSoCh
15. ʔišlal	xFaBrYoDa, xYoSi, xMoSiYoDa, xMoBrDaYoDa, xMoBrSoDaYoDa
16. huničʹon	xFaBrSoCh, oBrCh, xMoSiSoCh, xMoBrDaSoCh
17. ničʹon	xCh
18. ʔol	oCh
19. čʹamal	FaSiChCh, (−2 gen. of all // Co and of Patrilateral xCo)

Tzotzil, Chenalho, San Pedro (Calixta Guiteras Holmes), center and northern calpuls

1. moltot	GrFa
2. yameʔ	GrMo
3. mukʹtot	GrPa male Sib
4. mukʹtameʔ	GrPa female Sib
5. wiš	FaSi, ElSi, female // Co, MoBrDa
6. tahun	FaBr
7. wom	MoBr
8. bankil	xElBr, x male // Co, xMoBrSo
9. ʔičokʹ	xFaSiCh, xMoBrDaCh
10. hunʔol	oFaSiCh, oMoBrDaCh
11. šibel	oElBr, x male // Co, oMoBrSo
12. mom	FaSiChCh
13. huničʹon	xMoBrSoCh
14. muk	oMoBrSoCh
15. momničʹon	xGrCh
16. momol	oGrCh

Tzotzil, Chenalho, San Pedro (Calixta Guiteras Holmes), southern calpul

1. moltot	GrFa
2. yameʔ	GrMo
3. mukʹtot	GrPa male Sib
4. mukʹtameʔ	GrPa female Sib
5. wiš	FaSi, female Co, female Sib
6. tahun	FaBr
7. wom	MoBr

234

8. bankil	x male Co, x male Sib
9. ʔičok′	xFaSiDaCh, xMoBrDaCh
10. hunʔol	oMoBrDaCh, oFaSiDaCh
11. šibel	o male Co, o male Sib
12. hunič′on	xFaSiSoCh, oMoBrSoCh
13. muk	oMoBrSoCh, oFaSiDaCh
14. momnič′on	xGrCh
15. momol	oGrCh

ZAPOTEC, Juquila (Laura Nader Milleron)

1. šoʷzaʔgul	GrFa
2. šnaʔagul	GrMo
3. šoʷzaʔ	Fa
4. šnaʔa	Mo
5. zanaʔ	xSi, xAu, xGrPaSi, oBr, oUn, oGrPaUn
6. buǏčaʔ	xBr, xUn, xGrPaBr
7. rǰilaʔ	oSi, oAu, oGrPaSi
8. rǰiʔnaʔ	Ch
9. rsuaʔ	GrCh

Note: All affinals are distinguished from all consanguineals. Modifiers to indicate relative age are commonly used as follows: bIi is younger than ego, ngul is older female, and buIni is older male.

ZAPOTEC, Talea (Laura Nader Milleron)

1. šozaʔgul	GrFa
2. šnaʔagul	GrMo
3. šozaʔ	Fa
4. šnaʔ	Mo
5. buǏčaʔ	xBr
6. rǰilaʔ	oSi
7. zanaʔ	xSi, oBr
8. rǰiʔnaʔ	Ch
9. rsnaʔ	GrCh
10. tio	Un
11. tia	Au
12. primo kiuʔ	Co
13. sobrinukinʔ	Ne, Ni

ZAPOTEC, Yatzachi el Bajo (Laura Nader Milleron)

1. šagulaʔ	GrFa
2. šnaʔgulaʔ	GrMo
3. beni plus GrFa	GrPaBr
4. beni plus GrMo	GrPaSi
5. šaʔ	Fa
6. šnaʔa	Mo
7. beni plus Fa	Un
8. beni plus Mo	Au
9. bišaʔa	Br

10. bizangul	Si
11. bišiblaʔa	male Co
12. zanblaʔa	female Co
13. rjininaʔ	Ch
14. birjinaʔ	Ne, Ni
15. rIswaʔ	GrCh

ZOQUE (Roy Harrison)

1. ndataj (tataj)	Fa
2. nanaj	Mo
3. njaya'une	So
4. nyomo'une	Da
5. mbotso	YrSib
6. atsi	ElBr
7. ŋgose	ElSi
8. ŋgañchu	GrFa
9. apaj	GrMo
10. oko'une	GrCh
11. mo'ot	DaHu
12. ndzu'si	xSoWi, xChSoWi
13. sake	oSoWi, oChSoWi
14. ndzʌni	PaBr
15. eme	PaSi
16. ndzʌni'une	Ne
17. eme'une	Ni
18. ndzʌñdyʌwʌ	Co
19. mbini	xSiHu, xWiBr
20. ŋgapay	oSiHu, oHuBr, xBrWi, xWiSi
21. ojya	oBrWi, oHuSi

REFERENCES

AGUACATEC: Andrade, 1946a.
AMUZGO: F. H. Cowan, 1947.
AZTEC: Biart, 1900; Ecker, 1930; McQuown, 1942; Monzón, 1949; Radin, 1925; Redfield, 1930; Sapir, 1913, 1915; Schoembs, 1949; Shimkin, 1941; F. Starr, 1901–02; J. E. S. Thompson, 1930; Vaillant, 1941; R. J. Weitlaner, 1941; —— and Johnson, 1943; ——, Velásquez, and Carrasco (Huitziltepec), 1947; Whorf, 1946.
CAHITA (Mayo): Beals, 1943.
CHIAPANECA: F. Starr, 1901–02.
CHICHIMECO: Angulo, 1932; Hrdlička, 1903.
CHINANTEC: Angulo, 1925; Bevan, 1938; Merrifield, 1959; F. Starr, 1901–02; I. Weitlaner, 1936; R. J. Weitlaner, 1940, 1951; —— and Castro, 1954.
CHOCHO: Angulo, 1925; Orozco y Berra, 1864; F. Starr, 1901–02.
CHOL: Aulie and Aulie, 1953; Joyce, 1929.
CHONTAL (Tequistlatec): Angulo, 1925; Olmsted; 1958; Scholes and Roys, 1948; F. Starr, 1901–02.

CHONTAL (Tabasco): Harris, 1946.
CHORTI: Wisdom, 1940.
CHUJ: Andrade, 1946a.
CORA: Cervantes, 1732; Lumholtz, 1902; Monzón, 1945; Preuss, 1932b, 1935; Radin, 1931.
CUICATEC: Adán, 1922; Angulo, 1925.
CUITLATEC: Hendrichs Pérez, 1939.
HUASTEC: Guiteras Holmes, 1948; Larson, 1953; Meade, 1942; F. Starr, 1901–02; Staub, 1919, 1940.
HUAVE: Radin, 1916; Starr, 1901–02.
HUICHOL: Fábila, 1959; Grimes, 1959; Grimes and Grimes, 1962; Klineberg, 1934; McIntosh and Grimes, 1954; Zingg, 1938b.
JACALTECA: Andrade, 1946a.
KEKCHI: Andrade, 1946c.
LACANDON: Andrade, 1946a; Baer and Baer, 1949; Blom and Duby, 1949; Tozzer, 1907.
MAM: Andrade, 1946a.
MATLATZINCA: García Payón, 1942.
MAYA: Basauri, 1931; Brinton, 1882b; Butler, 1935;

Ecker, n.d.; Eggan, 1934; Gann, 1918; Gann and Thompson, 1931; LaFarge, 1947; —— and Byers, 1931; Morley, 1947; O'Neale, 1945; Radin, 1925; Redfield, 1941; —— and Villa Rojas, 1934; Roys, 1933, 1943; Scholes and Roys, 1948; J. E. S. Thompson, 1927, 1930, 1954; Tozzer, 1907; Villa Rojas, 1945.

MAZATEC: Angulo, 1925; F. H. Cowan, 1946, 1947; G. M. Cowan, 1952; J. B. Johnson, 1939a, 1939b; F. Starr, 1901–02.

MIXE: Angulo, 1925; Bauer, 1915; Beals, 1936, 1945b; Foster, 1949; Hoogshagen and Merrifield, 1961; Mann, 1958; Radin, 1916; F. Starr, 1901–02.

MIXTEC: Angulo, 1925; Caso, 1942; Dahlgren de Jordan, 1954; Romney and Romney, 1963; F. Starr, 1901–02.

OPATA: Balcastro, 1931; J. B. Johnson, 1950; Radin, 1931.

OTOMI: Basauri, 1930; Carrasco, 1950a; Christensen, 1953; Ecker, 1930; Henning, 1911; J. Jenkins, 1946; Pimentel, 1903; Radin, 1931; J. Soustelle, 1937; F. Starr, 1901–02.

PAPAGO: Dolores, n.d.; Hoover, 1935; Joseph, Spicer, and Chesky, 1949; J. A. Mason, 1950; Underhill, 1937.

PIMA: Parsons, 1928.

POKOMAM: Andrade, 1946c; Gillin, 1951; Miles, 1957.

POPOLUCA: Foster, 1940, 1943, 1949; León, 1905.

QUICHE: Andrade, 1946b; Brinton, 1885a.

SERI: Ascher, 1962; Kroeber, 1931; McGee, 1898; Pimentel, 1874–75.

TARAHUMARA: Basauri, 1929; Bennett and Zingg, 1935; Ferrera, 1920; Passin, 1943.

TARASCAN: Beals, 1946; ——, Carrasco, and McCorkle, 1944; Bourke, 1893; Corona Núñez, 1946; Ecker, 1930; Foster, 1949; León, 1903, 1934; Noguera, 1942; Pimentel, 1874–75; Radin, 1925; Rendón, 1941; F. Starr, 1901–02; Swadesh, n.d.

TEPECANO: J. A. Mason, 1917; Radin, 1931.

TEPEHUAN: Cerda Silva, 1943; Gamiz, 1948; J. A. Mason, 1912a; Radin, 1931.

TEPEHUAS: G. M. Cowan, 1952.

TOJOLABAL: Basauri, 1931.

TOTONAC: Aschmann, 1946; Williams García, 1953; Kelly, 1953; Kelly and Palerm, 1952; Krickeberg, 1918, 1933; Palerm, 1953, 1954; F. Starr, 1901–02.

TRIQUE: Comas, 1942; F. Starr, 1901–02.

TZELTAL: Andrade, 1946a; Basauri, 1931; Cámara B., 1952b; Guiteras Holmes, 1947; F. Starr, 1901–02; Villa Rojas, 1947.

TZOTZIL: Guiteras Holmes, n.d.,b; 1960; Pozas A., 1952b; Rodoz, 1723; F. Starr, 1901–02; Weathers, 1946.

YAQUI: Beals, 1944a.

ZAPOTEC: Adán, 1922; Angulo, 1925; Bauer, 1915; Caso, 1942; Covarrubias, 1947; De la Fuente, 1947c, 1949; Mendieta y Núñez, 1949; Orozco y Berra, 1864; Parsons, 1936; Salas, 1928; F. Starr, 1901–02; Toro, n.d.; Velasco, 1929.

ZOQUE: Cordry and Cordry, 1941; F. Starr, 1901–02.

ZUNI: Swadesh, n.d.

12. Compadrinazgo

ROBERT RAVICZ

COMPADRINAZGO forms an essential part of many Middle American social organizations. It is characterized by proliferation, by certain formal variations, and by the significance of its role in the social structure as a guide in interaction.[1] An integral aspect of European culture (Mintz and Wolf, 1950; Foster, 1953a), the compadrinazgo diffused during the early years of the conquest primarily through the priests, who used it as a significant part of the Catholicizing process.[2]

[1] The term *compadrinazgo* is used here (1) to cover the joint aspects of this dual system, since single terms such as *compadrazgo* are inadequate; (2) to take the place of "ritual" or "ceremonial" kin, since *compadres* do not think of their relationship as kinlike and the system is therefore not a kin grouping; (3) to state more specifically for Middle American cultures the idea of "ritual kin" in other cultures.

I wish to acknowledge my indebtedness to Dorris L. Olds and Francisco Portilla Pliego for their assistance in the preparation of this article, and to Clyde K. M. Kluckhohn and A. Kimball Romney, who have contributed significantly to my perspective.

[2] Evidence for preconquest sponsorship is found in Redfield and Villa R., 1934, pp. 189–90; J. Soustelle, 1935b, pp. 106, 112; Pérez de Ribas (1645) *in* Beals, 1943, pp. 66, 67; Landa, 1938,

FORM

In response to sacraments and other church ritual, kinlike ties *(padrinazgo)* are established between a child *(ahijado/a)* and a man and woman *(padrino* and *madrina)* who serve as its *padrinos* (godparents).[3] In turn, a relationship—*compadrazgo*—is ritually formed, binding the padrinos and the parents as compadres (coparents; the term

---

p. 118; Sahagún, 1956, 1: 224; Robelo, 1911, p. 332. The presence of padrino in early conquest times is suggested in the drama "Coloquio de la Nueva Conberción y Bautismo de los Quatro Ultimos Reyes de Tlaxcala en la Nueva España" (in Rojas Garcidueñas, 1935, pp. 181–221), which Castañeda (1932) refers to as "the first American play." The author and date of composition are unknown, however, and Gibson (1952) suggests that the "kings" may not have been baptized at all.

[3] To express the somewhat greater emphasis on the male godparent in Middle America, the term *padrino* is used here. Ordinarily, phonologic alterations in Spanish (e.g., *kumali: comadre*) or terms descriptive of compadrinazgo (e.g., mother, child of water; compadre of the heart) in indigenous languages express the relationships. Indigenous linguistic terminology not derived from Spanish or compadrinazgo is used in Palantla toward child's padrinos and child's spouse's parents (Merrifield, 1959, pp. 878–80); son-in-law/father-in-law compadrazgo terms occur (Cerda Silva, 1943, p. 108).

of address and of reference is *compadre,* male; *comadre,* female). With the child as basis[4] for both relationships, relations within each are marked by mutual rights and responsibilities. Among these, the formalized actions contained in the concept of respeto[5] emphasize the ritual nature of the dual system and its crucial significance in the social structure. For many cultures, a considerable part of their total ritual is built around the compadrinazgo.

Chosen by the parents,[6] the padrinos confer on the child its first status, introducing it to society at the baptismal font.[7] By becoming ritual parents of the child, the padrinos add this position of social relatives to their other social statuses. At that time the child receives a double identification: a name from its parents and the name of a saint. Although baptism is the child's introduction to the church, its significance is

expressed primarily in terms of his eventual (1) relations with all padrinos, (2) participation in church *cargos,* e.g., *mayordomías,* and (3) compadrinazgo activities.

Ideally, the padrinos will socialize the child in the world of the church; actually, they provide a living frame within which the child learns and practices rules that reflect respeto, one of the fundamental values of Middle American cultures. Respeto builds respect for age and for ritual experience, promotes participation in other rituals, and repeatedly emphasizes the compadrinazgo itself.

The compadrazgo opens a range of patterned activities and sentiments whose uniqueness is extension to new sets of individuals. A new social identity commences for those who call each other compadre. As with the padrinazgo, the compadrazgo signifies the achievement of a new status and an increase in the total number of statuses of an individual. Nevertheless, satisfaction for the individual lies in the kind of relationship involving the new obligations and rights, rather than in the position as rank. The twofold importance of the compadrazgo rests on the satisfaction felt by the individual participating in a thoroughly desirable relationship and on the network of relationships of this kind that are societywide. Of the two sets of relationships, the compadrazgo is the more important.[8]

Obligations of the padrino commence with little ceremony at baptism. He pro-

[4] The ultimate ritual basis for the ties lies in baptism, considered the duty of someone other than the parents. Although kin may serve—as noted elsewhere in this article—the selection of non-kin is by far the dominant diagnostic for indigenous compadrinazgo patterns. Relative frequency of this and other criteria varies considerably in rural and urban aggregates; multiple and varying factors must be adduced as explanatory: residence, inheritance, quality or tone of interpersonal relations, interaction frequencies, value emphases (Kluckhohn and Strodtbeck, 1961, pp. 256, 257), diffusion, subsistence, and others. This study could well be undertaken, using *emic* propositions as an analytic methodology; a study of a changing compadrinazgo system along the lines of a decision-making model might better elucidate the changes than do other models of culture change used in acculturation or folk-urban continuum studies.

[5] *Respeto* connotes an honorific; it is characterized by patterned modes of action and attitudes which create respect and affection while maintaining distance and avoiding conflict.

[6] This is the typical pattern of compadrinazgo; variations are discussed below.

[7] Baptism is frequently performed without benefit of priest or church. If the child is ill, the rite is conducted in the house of parents or padrinos. Baptism may be performed by a native curer instead of a Catholic priest; with the former, who occupies an important position in the social structure, the compadrinazgo takes effect (Holland, 1963a, p. 49).

[8] This is contrary to the restrictive tendency in the selection of sponsors (Foster, 1953a, pp. 3, 4) and to the weakening of its influence (Mintz and Wolf, 1950, p. 352) in southern Europe. Some obligations of the padrino seem to be of lesser import in Middle America and probably reflect considerable time depth, possibly to the time of the conquest. Specifically, concern with the Christian education of the ahijado is secondary to the relationships of compadrazgo, if not totally neglected; this is consistent with the Middle American emphasis on organization of ritual to the neglect of its theological premises. Holland (1963a, p. 50) remarks that responsibilities toward ahijados are not practiced by Larrainzar Tzotzil.

vides new clothes at that time and later has a role in the ahijado's marriage. If the child dies, the padrino assumes responsibility for the expenses of funeral and burial. He is obliged to see that the child learns cultural values. Expected to punish the child when necessary, he may reward it when he chooses or on ritual occasions. Parents call on the padrino for advice relating to the child, and he offers them advice when he thinks it necessary. Any friction between parents is referred to the padrino by the ahijado. The padrino may care for the ahijado if its parents die.

That there is and should be more respeto for padrinos than for parents is commonly stated. Deference and obedience are manifest by the ahijado. Upon meeting, the ahijado bows his head, often touching one knee to the ground as he kisses the hand of the padrino. He does not tease, mock, or disobey the padrino. On specified occasions and during a surplus of food, he takes gifts of food to the padrino. These customs are taught by the parents, observed in the actions of others, and practiced with agemates.

Compadre status is ritually established by a fiesta[9] provided by the ahijado's father. The reciprocal term "compadre" comes into use, overriding kinship terms and personal names. In speaking of one's child to a compadre, one says "your ahijado"; when speaking of one's wife, one says "your comadre." Compadres consult on private and public matters. The padrino is expected to help resolve disputes between his comadre and compadre. When in difficulty, a man turns first to his compadre. He prefers to borrow from compadre than from kin, since this could lead to trouble within the family whereas there can be no difficulties between compadres; further, the obligation to repay the family is not bind-

ing as it is toward the compadre. Compadres give mutual aid[10] in agriculture and its ritual and in house construction, and they provide support in political and religious matters. The considerable expenditures which are part of the compadrinazgo obligations are one of the few means by which wealth is distributed; consequently, the system provides one of the sanctioned modes of wealth accumulation.[11]

Respect is prescribed in the compadrazgo. Compadres remove hats when they meet, greet each other with the term and use it repeatedly in conversation (fig. 1). Speech and attitude reflect the quiet reserve of respeto; the nature and emotional intensity of the relationship may be measured by the absence of external display, such as contact or excessive vocalization.[12] Sexual relations,[13] or references to them, and marriage

---

[9] Fiesta refers to the Middle American rite symbolizing approval by society. It is the ultimate sanction for many statuses: compadrazgo, marriage, mayordomo.

[10] A common expression for this is "dar la mano." In neighboring Zapotec communities, "gozon" (dar la mano) characterizes compadrazgo in one, while in the other respeto proscribes the mutual assistance in the fields or in house construction (personal interview with Gonzalo and Alfredo Bautista, Talea, Oaxaca, July 1959). Reciprocal workdays are worked out with neighbors, not compadres (M. Nash, 1958a, p. 51).

[11] In many societies the expenses of the compadrinazgo rank second only to household costs.

[12] Contact occurs during hand-kissing or a light touch of the hands, when greeting. Hand-holding, such as prevails among young male friends, is not practiced, nor do compadres look directly into the eyes. A compadre and comadre avert the eyes during an entire conversation, not looking at each other at all; the compadre holds the hat slightly raised above his head (Ravicz, 1965). More extreme ritual avoidance characterizes whole groups during the hand-washing ceremony, when members of the parents' and padrinos' companies have no interaction with those of the other group, though in the same room (Ravicz, 1966). A. W. Pausic (personal communication, 1960) notes that when mounted compadres meet, they dismount, leaving their rifles in the saddle and plunging their machetes into the ground; such is their confidence in each other that on parting they mount and ride away without a backward glance.

[13] Gamio (1922, 2:243) reports compadrazgo sexual relations to be worse than murder; De la Fuente (1949, p. 169) ranks the taboo on marriage and sexual contact between compadres as stronger than between affinal and consanguineal

Fig. 1—COMPADRE GREETING, SAN MIGUEL (MIXTECA), OAXACA, MEXICO. (Photographed by R. Ravicz, 1961.)

are prohibited within the compadrazgo. Padrinos, ahijados, and compadres should not drink together.

The intimacy and high regard between compadres is thus expressed in formal and objective patterns which provide a model for all interpersonal relationships. Since a position in the compadrazgo is potentially available to all members of society, and since it is the only ritual status of which such is true, its importance in the status network becomes apparent. Its key role—through respeto—as the most significant social model in mirroring the quality of desirable interpersonal relationships helps to explain its range of occurrence and variation in Middle American culture.

Asymmetry occurs in the compadre status-pair. The direction assumed in respeto is discerned in the phrase "hay mucho respeto para el compadre," which indicates a slight imbalance favoring the padrino, further evidence of the importance of his original service. Whereas the obligations of

the padrino tend to weaken after the marriage[14] of the ahijado, the relationship of compadres continues through life, increasing in affect and confidence.

Compadrinazgo acts to bring separate families together in special relationships of a pseudokinship nature. Terminology approximates but does not parallel that of the kinship system. The padrinazgo reproduces the nuclear family in terminology and partially in function. It supports the child with affection through benevolent, unquestioned authority; by thus exemplifying the desirable, it offers the child an opportunity for learning. In return, the padrino receives a maximum of respect. By serving as the model parent-child surrogate, the padrinazgo mitigates strains within the family. Families are not linked through the padrinazgo; rather, problems may be alleviated through the exercise of ritually sanctioned authority as a mechanism for family stability.

Based on the padrinazgo, a ritual form of nuclear kin group, it is the compadrazgo

relatives. Studies relating to population genetics could consult baptismal records and compadrinazgo customs in addition to genealogical and marriage data.

[14] This refers to baptismal, not marriage, padrinos.

which effects bonds between families, but bonds different from those of kinship. The compadrazgo bears no resemblance to the family or other kin group, in organization, terminology, or behavior. Reflecting lack of resemblance to family structure, terminology differentiates only by sex. Generation differences are collapsed, accompanied by emphasis on horizontal extension and the near-disappearance of lineality and differences of authority. The compadrazgo thus does not create a family situation among compadres, nor does it attempt to create kinship relations in its image.

As a social control, the compadrazgo acts to channel conflict. The essence of the compadrazgo is the observance of respect relations; in establishing them, it represents a model for social interaction at all levels, emphasizing the patterned, valued behavior of respect between individuals. It follows that the compadrazgo is characterized by absence of conflict. With the compadrazgo society-wide, however, the suppression of conflict in the compadrinazgo network implies the channeling of aggressiveness and tensions into other, patterned outlets such as the family. Covertly, then, the compadrinazgo may be a source of potential conflict.

Through the compadrinazgo, regional, ethnic, and local ties are established. When one is traveling, the padrino or compadre in another community may be counted on for food, shelter, and information. Indigenes and nonindigenes[15] share these relationships, thereby further extending control in areas of actual or potential friction. Identification with the locality as the locus of secure relationships receives reinforcement through individuals and families of a community linked in bonds of affection and responsibility through the compadrinazgo. In this sense, the system operates as a factor restricting migration.

ELABORATION AND VARIATION

As with other aspects of Middle American culture, there are variation and elaboration

in the compadrinazgo.[16] With few exceptions (Foster, 1953a, pp. 23–24; Pozas, 1959a, p. 44)[17] its distribution is universal. Although variation occurs in nearly every element, nowhere is the system unrecognizable. The system relates primarily to individuals, but also functions in the entire society. It may emphasize either sacred or profane aspects of culture.

Selection of the padrino is generally made by the parents, but services may be volunteered (Wagley, 1949, p. 18; Weitlaner and Castro, 1954, p. 152). Although the most frequent padrino forms include baptism, marriage, confirmation, and first communion (the latter two in the presence of a priest), they vary in significance (De la Fuente, 1949, pp. 168–70).

Baptismal compadrinazgo is always the most important (Paul and Paul, 1952, p. 182) in that it creates the strongest and most durable bonds (Weitlaner and Castro, 1954, p. 152) and demands the greatest responsibility from the padrinos (Redfield and Villa R., 1934, p. 99). It is common to ask the padrinos to serve for three (Parsons, 1936, p. 395), several (Wagley, 1949, p. 18), or all (Bunzel, 1952, p. 161) children of a family, or to choose separate pairs for male and female children (Bunzel, 1952, p. 161). The association of the destiny of a child with its godparent (Paul and Paul, 1952, p. 180) occasions the selection of another padrino for the next infant, should the first child have died (Beals, 1946, p. 103), although this custom is variable. Emphasizing the significance of baptism is the choice of

[15] Including Ladinos, Mestizos, gente de razon, and other varying, national ethnic elements. Less permanent residents (traders, anthropologists) have been known to participate. Negative attitudes reflecting racial differences are absent in Middle America, but social and cultural differences do exist and for these the term "ethnic" is used here.

[16] Only major variations are considered here.

[17] Nowhere is the system entirely absent. That this absence among the Tzeltal, for example, is only partial is indicated by Hotchkiss (1959, pp. 1, 2, 21) and D. Metzger (1959a, pp. 19, 20). Possible explanations of variations are offered below.

grandparents as padrinos since "only if one is compadre with one's father and mother will one meet with them in heaven" (Redfield and Villa R., 1934, p. 99); they may serve for only the first child.

Sanctions for the newborn child are sought from the native as well as the Christian tradition. Along with the protection afforded by the padrino through baptism, the child receives the protection of an "*animal-companero o animal-tono*" (Aguirre Beltrán, 1958, pp. 141, 142). The baptismal madrina sponsors *hetzmek*, an aboriginal Maya ritual ". . . to make sure that the child is endowed with the faculties and skills essential to a useful adult life" (Villa R., 1945, p. 144).[18] If the saint's name is changed, the male child will become perverse, the female will never marry (Haro, 1944, p. 258).

Padrinos de vela (or *de iglesia*) take a sick child to church, burn a candle for him, give him a ribbon or medal (Parsons, 1936, p. 69); another set of padrinos de vela provides candles for the wedding. *Padrinos de la casa* take the cross for a new house to the church to be blessed and later the padrino throws cigarettes from the roof to those below. Among the Chorti, the padrino sprinkles the new house inside and out with water from a sacred spring; the wives of several padrinos decorate the house with paper and buy fireworks for the affair; all is aimed at driving evil spirits from the house (Wisdom, 1940, p. 131). In Mitla the *madrina de comunión* gives the child the candle he holds as he kneels at the altar rail. The *padrinos de confirmación* pay the church fee and treat the ahijado to sweets. At marriage, the same madrina becomes the *madrina de metate* by giving the bride a grinding stone (Parsons, 1936, p. 99) or a broom (Madsen, 1960, p. 101). On Christmas Eve, a madrina of the Christ Child takes the image first to the house of the mayordomo, then to the church (Parsons, 1936, p. 283),

while *madrinas del Niño* dance to observe the same occasion (Pozas, 1959a, p. 167). Parsons notes (1936, p. 228) the *padrino de los cuates* (double ears of corn), who dresses the corn as a child to help ensure good crops for the owner. The *padrino de la nueva canoa*, bedecked with flowers, enters the new canoe to paddle it on its first voyage (Weitlaner, personal communication, 1960). Sponsors appear in competitive situations. Five *madrinas de listones* present ribbons to the victors at a basketball match; others act as *madrinas de banda* at a horse race (Parsons, 1936, pp. 249, 278). *Madrinas de calenda* participate in a public fiesta by carrying flowers or contributing to it. Neither form establishes the padrinazgo or compadrazgo relationship, however (De la Fuente, 1949, p. 174). Parsons (1936, p. 55n.) speaks of the "cleansing" by a padrino of his ahijado, using salt and candle, to prevent the ahijado's return to jail. The *padrino of twenty-four hours* is usually a stranger selected by the child to hang the scapulary, a passerby chosen to perform the same duty if a person is near death, or one who breaks in a mule for the owner (Madsen, 1960, pp. 99–103).

Compadrinazgo may be established through the saints. In Cheran a *padrino de la corona* takes the child to the image of a saint wearing a crown and places the crown on the child's head, paying a small fee to the custodian-owner of the house; the padrinos for church images do not call each other compadre (Beals, 1946, p. 103). The *compadrazgo de la corona* may be considered mainly an Indian trait where the adults regard themselves as compadres (Foster, 1948a, p. 263). A strong compadrazgo is effected by the erection of a family shrine for saints; non-Christian clay images are termed compadres (J. Soustelle, 1935b, pp. 105, 114).

The *padrino de miscotón* and the *padrino de medida* provide the child with a sweater and a ribbon as protection against illness (Lewis, 1951, p. 351).

---

[18] Baptismal padrinos are distinct from the hetzmek pair in Maya Chan Kom (Redfield and Villa R., 1934, pp. 98, 99).

Padrinos de evangelio[19] and *de rosario* occur in Ojitlan (Rubel, 1955, p. 1039) and in Jamiltepec (S. Drucker, 1959); those of evangelio in Tepoztlan (Lewis, 1951, p. 351). The medium may be a rosary, candle, or tree branch which a parent requests someone to expose to a church altar in another village, particularly when a child is ill. On the person's return, the rosario compadrinazgo takes effect (Ravicz, 1958, p. 113). In the evangelio form, marriage proscriptions and terminology are invoked. The number of evangelio padrinos is unlimited. Accompanied by an adult relative and the child, the padrino—preferably a woman with a "hard heart" (Lewis, 1951, p. 351)—says a prayer, blesses the child, leaves a candle in the church, and gives a few coins to the child. The first padrinos of this class are chosen by the parents, but selection of successive ones is the right of the child. Although lacking access to the compadre status, the child may thus enter the padrinazgo through his own choice; many children have 10 or more padrinos of this form. For the rosario form, a child might have 15 padrino pairs by age 10 (De la Fuente, 1949, p. 169). Conversely, in Mam-speaking Chimaltenango the only padrinos are those of baptism (Wagley, 1949, p. 17), and for the Cora the only compadres those of marriage (Cerda Silva, 1943, p. 108). In Larrainzar, padrinos and compadres derive from baptism, the only sacrament practiced (Holland, 1963a, p. 49).

Religious specialists serving the entire village may be termed padrinos. Among the Chorti (Wisdom, 1940, pp. 374–77) they perform rain-making and agricultural ceremonies and they care for the village patron saint. The more malicious of them are regarded as drought-makers. Representing the community during a civil ceremony at the church prior to baptism, the padrino in Chichicastenango explains to the child how to prepare himself to be a good citizen, thus emphasizing individual responsibility to community well-being (Bunzel, 1952, p. 81).

From a ceremonious beginning, the mutual obligations of padrinazgo are multiple and cover several years. Padrinos' support is primarily manifest through their presence, advice, and gifts. Padrinos among the Chorti act in every way as second parents, giving help as the child matures. If the child is orphaned, the padrinos will adopt him (Wisdom, 1940, p. 293); padrinos will rear an ahijado if the parents are financially unable (McClendon, 1961, p. 26). Exceptions to the rule occur (Bunzel, 1952, p. 163; Rubel, 1955, pp. 1039, 1040; M. Nash, 1958a, p. 51). S. Drucker (1959) mentions that more Mestizo than Mixtec padrinos rear an orphaned ahijado, whereas prestige-conscious Ladinos will rear their ahijados but not as equals in the family (Gillin, 1951, p. 62).

Padrinos may be chosen after the child is born (Redfield and Villa R., 1934, p. 98), before (Wisdom, 1940, p. 291), or either way (Garibay K., 1957). The request may be made by the parents in person in a formal speech of praise (Villa R., 1945, p. 142) or through the gift of a chicken (Wisdom, 1940, p. 291), by the mother of the new father (Lewis, 1951, p. 350).

Ritual activities and ceremonial expenses due to fiestas and gift-giving characterize the relationship. The parents take gifts of food and candles to the new padrinos to show respect (Villa R., 1945, p. 142); the padrinos reciprocate by placing a coin in the food-wrapper (*ibid.*, p. 143). To announce the birth ritually, hens and corn are taken by the father to the padrino, who brings clothes for the child. The Chorti (Wisdom, 1940, p. 291) announce the birth by sending a cooked chicken, as they had done for the invitation, to the padrinos. The padrino of Tusik (Villa R., 1945, p. 143) travels to another village to ascertain the name of the saint the child will bear and pays the fee. A few months after baptism,

[19] This refers to Roman Catholic practice, not to the Protestant Evangelical sect.

the madrina provides ceremonial food and is offered a respect ceremony in return. Six months after the birth of the child, the Chorti parents send a chicken to the padrinos, followed by a feast given by the madrina (Wisdom, 1940, p. 292).

Since the padrinos frequently serve all future siblings of the ahijado, they assume an enduring and expensive set of obligations, although the parents also bear other expenses. The parents pay for the services of an older man as intermediary during the requesting ritual and for gifts of rum and cigarettes. After the padrinos sponsor two or three of their children, the parents offer them a fiesta marked by food and gifts (Redfield, 1941, p. 224; Villa R., 1945, p. 143; Weitlaner and Verbitzky, personal communication, 1955) and of which the essential element is the ritual washing of the padrino's hands by their compadres.[20] The ceremonial cleansing represents appreciation and great respect for the padrinos. Should this obligation be neglected, the padrinos would have to spend time in hell after death (Villa R., 1945, p. 143) or eat buzzard rather than turkey in heaven, since they were not cleansed of the sins they assumed at baptism (Ravicz, 1958, p. 124).

Following baptism, the parents serve a meal for the padrinos (Redfield, 1941, p. 225). In Cheran the padrino provides chocolate, bread, and soap, but he eats the ritual meal in his own house, where it is sent by the parents (Beals, 1946, p. 171). The padrinos send an article of clothing to the child after baptism, and the parents send a chicken and drink to the new compadres; the chicken must not be killed, for then the child would die[21] (D. Metzger, 1959a, p. 19). The padrino brings atole, bread, and liquor to the compadre's house, where he is fed eggs, chili, and tortillas (Dyk, 1959, pp. 188, 189).

The father's choice determines the location of the post-baptismal feast; if he takes the child to the padrino's house prior to baptism, the meal will be held there, but if he has the padrino come for the child, the meal will occur in the father's house (Ravicz, 1959). After confirmation, the parents provide a meal of chocolate and mole for padrinos (Parsons, 1936, p. 90) at the child's home or send food to the padrinos. Baptismal padrinos provide the trunk for the bride in Mitla (ibid., p. 99). The bolo[22] occurs (Rojas G., 1943, p. 203; Josefina Rodríguez, personal communication, 1960) as nonindigenous (Parsons, 1936, p. 90).

The padrinazgo is related to other rites of passage. A padrino is sought when death seems imminent or has occurred (G. Soustelle, 1958, p. 168). Yaqui baptismal padrinos dress the body of a deceased ahijado. They are consulted for advice if a child is ill, and special padrinos sponsor the child's entrance into a ceremonial society (Spicer, 1954, p. 60). An ahijado may bury the padrino (Weitlaner and Castro, 1954, p. 152). That confirmation padrinos must give a wedding blessing and advice about married life is related to the belief that the soul of the ahijado conducts the souls of padrinos de comunión and de confirmación to the next world; in the present world, the ahijado gives the padrinos his labor (Madsen, 1960, p. 95). *Padrinos de*

[20] The ritual seems to have considerable Mexican distribution (Ravicz, 1961).

[21] This sympathetic element seems to characterize many aspects of the belief systems of past and present-day Middle American cultures, being found in man-man and man-nature relationships. Its projection in the compadrinazgo may be diagnostic for the Middle American relationship.

[22] In many places, the padrino is expected to provide bolo immediately on leaving the church after baptism. This consists of dispensing coins to children who are eagerly awaiting his exit. In the upper classes, the distribution is usually restricted to family or of friends, distribution generally being made during the baptismal fiesta at the home of the parents. In Chiconcuac, state of Mexico, the padrino distributes small coins to all children who appear at the home of the baptized child. Following the meal, the padrino distributes a somewhat larger sum to the cook and those who have served the food; the sum paid to the adults is considered as part of the bolo (interview with Josefina Rodríguez, Chiconcuac, Mexico, 1960).

levantar la cruz are boys and girls who serve for one day (Lewis, 1951, p. 416), as does the padrino of the Chinantla (Weitlaner, personal communication, 1960).

Although baptismal padrinos aid during marriage negotiations by advice to the compadre (Redfield and Villa R., 1934, p. 99) or in the petition to the father of the girl (Weitlaner and Castro, 1954, p. 157), marriage padrinos often pay the cost of a large part of the activities and act as advisors to the couple. In Mitla the padrinos provide the bridal dress, the money for the church service, the wedding breakfast, candles for the church service, and the silver chain which the padrino lends to the groom (Parsons, 1936, pp. 102–03). The ostentatious display of wealth at the wedding (Beals, 1946, pp. 180–92) involves multiple expenses and interactions of marriage and other padrinos.

The role of madrina is specific. Baptismal madrinas sometimes receive special attention from compadres and ahijados. They are adorned with paper and ribbons and are given cigarettes; they lead the dancing and are the first to drink (Beals, 1946, p. 185), after a signal from the marriage padrino (E. V. Pike, 1948, p. 222). F. Starr (1900–02, p. 17) notes that the wedding feast commences when the madrina and padrino feed a morsel of food to the bride and groom.

Cleansing of the bride in preparation for marriage may be done by the baptismal madrina[23] of the groom at a sacred spring (Rubel, 1955, p. 1038) or by washing the hair of the bride jointly with the marriage madrina; the baptismal madrina of the bride is in charge of washing the head of the groom, for which she provides water, soap, and comb. The same items are provided by the marriage madrina for the bride (E. V. Pike, 1948, pp. 219–21). A representative of the marriage madrina ritually cleanses with flowers the relatives of the bride and groom after the marriage padrinos have been similarly cleansed by the

mother of the groom (G. Soustelle, 1958, p. 132).

Soap for the ceremonial sweat bath of the new mother is provided by the baptismal madrina of the child; the baptismal padrinos, providing clothing for the child, accompany it and its mother to *sacamisa*[24] (Redfield, 1930, p. 137).

The compadrazgo is effected in a number of ways. It takes effect when the couple agrees to serve as padrinos (Villa R., 1945, p. 90). After the baptism, members of the families of parents and padrinos, led by the latter pairs, become compadres by kissing the hands of those of the other family (Garibay K., 1957); hand-shaking signals the marriage compadrazgo between relatives of the bride and groom (Covarrubias, 1947, p. 351). After an embrace and the exchange of the compadre term in a brief ritual phrase, a kneeling ceremony effects the relationship in Cheran (Beals, 1946, p. 103) between various relatives of the bride and groom.

FUNCTION AND SYSTEM

Three padrinazgo forms emerge, with an irregular distribution. There may be separate padrinos for baptism and for marriage (Redfield and Villa R., 1934, p. 192; Parsons, 1936, p. 69; Beals, 1946, pp. 102, 103). Marriage padrinos may become baptismal padrinos to the offspring of their marriage ahijados[25] (Madsen, 1960, p. 93; C. Conde,

[23] In a Mestizo community the sisters of the groom wash and dress the bride (Beals, 1946, p. 190).

[24] The *sacamisa* is rare among the Otomi, occurring for the first child, if at all (Garibay K., 1957). A *madrina de los cuarenta dias*, rather than the baptismal madrina, takes the mother and child for sacamisa among Mestizo elements of the Amuzgo area (Ravicz, 1960).

[25] At that time, the marriage padrinos and ahijados become compadres. Conde (interview with Camilo Conde, Cuauhtenco, Contla, Tlaxcala, 1961) phrases it: "once he [padrino] and I are compadres, I no longer must kiss his hand" and "in order not to continue kissing his hand, I give him

personal communication, 1961). The same padrinos may serve in baptism and marriage[26] (De la Fuente, 1949, p. 169).

The compadrazgo varies in the range of individuals it relates. Baptismal compadres (fig. 2) may include child's parents, padrinos and parents and older siblings of each (Weitlaner and Castro, 1954, p. 151) or all siblings of each as well as padrino's offspring[27] (Ravicz, 1958, pp. 118, 119). Emphasizing lineality, Yalalag padrinos and parents and grandparents become compadres with parents, grandparents, and great-grandparents of the ahijado[28] (De la Fuente, 1949, p. 168). In more restricted fashion, relations are established between two married pairs (D. Metzger, 1959a, p. 19).

The social structure is affected by compadrinazgo through the linking of status-

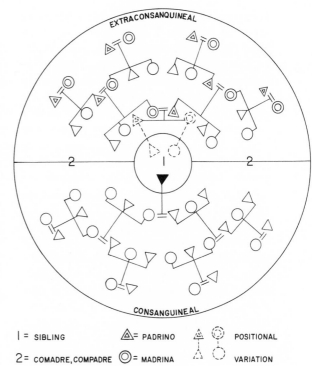

I = SIBLING   △ = PADRINO   POSITIONAL

2 = COMADRE, COMADRE   ◎ = MADRINA   VARIATION

Fɪɢ. 2—MODEL OF COMPADRINAZGO TERMINOLOGY

---

a child of mine [to baptize]." An individual may be padrino and compadre to another; an (adult) ahijado (de comunión), on meeting his padrino, greets him appropriately, following which, through the baptism of the ahijado's child, they exchange the compadre formalities. The same procedure characterizes each meeting of the two (Ravicz, 1960.)

[26] Commonly, a couple is selected to serve in important padrino forms; for Mitla, Parsons (1936, p. 104) remarks that two marriage pairs may be selected, each set bearing different duties. Among the Amuzgo, parents decide whether separate marriage padrinos or baptismal padrinos will serve at marriage (Ravicz, 1960). Tenejapa Tzeltal appear to select a single baptismal sponsor: padrino or madrina (Metzger and Ravicz, 1966).

[27] Padrino's offspring will serve as padrino should his father die, and he is thus called padrino by the ahijado (often rendered as "segundo papá de mi papá"). Since anyone whom a child calls padrino must be father's compadre, padrino's child is included in the compadrazgo. Padrino's parents are also considered padrinos (sometimes called padrino or compadre grande). Elsewhere, padrino's offspring may be called by the sibling term.

[28] Here, parents and grandparents of the padrinos are not considered as padrinos of the ahijado.

[29] The extensions of these bonds contradict the edict that compadres develop from baptism and confirmation only, and that witnesses of a marriage do not enter the compadrazgo, in Paredes' *Promptuario Manual mexicano* (1759, pp. 256, 257; prepared for Nahuatl-readers or -speakers by use of the terms *comadreyotl, compadreyotl).*

classes. Thus, in Larrainzar, *me'santo*—the most important curer—is preferred over the Catholic priest to officiate at baptism as me'santo and the child's parents thereby become compadres (Holland, 1963a, p. 49).

Marriage enlarges the compadrazgo network by uniting: two families (Parsons, 1936, p. 101); parents of the bride and groom, and the brothers, sisters, and first cousins of the parents (Beals, 1946, p. 103); all padrinos of the bride and groom as well as the parents of the young couple (Redfield and Villa R., 1934, p. 192); all friends, neighbors, and visitors who may choose to attend the fiesta[29] (Ravicz, 1958, p. 130). At the very least, the compadre term links only father-in-law and son-in-law (Cerda Silva, 1943, p. 108) or parents and padrinos of bride and groom (Merrifield, 1959, pp. 878–80).

The compadrazgo operates strongly in

247

assistance. Compadres of the wedding padrinos assist them in the festivities (Parsons, 1936, pp. 69, 106). Marriage compadres accompany each other during obligations involved in a wedding, mayordomía, or house-moving (Beals, 1946, p. 103). A compadre's request for money would rarely be refused (Lewis, 1951, p. 351), but Manning Nash (1958a, p. 51) notes that compadre bonds do not encourage borrowing or lending. Compadres of the padrino of the deceased accompany him during an all-night vigil (G. Soustelle, 1958, p. 168). House construction receives compadre aid. Transmitting special information may characterize the relationship. For instance, a man may learn from his compadre an auto-suggestive technique enabling him to communicate with spirits perceived in auditory or visual hallucination (Ravicz, 1962-65).

In others parts of the life and annual cycles, control and aid are provided. Compadres of baptism, confirmation, and corona act together to pacify an irate father whose daughter their ahijado has kidnapped (Beals, 1946, p. 103). At the time of death, compadres dig the grave and serve as pall-bearers (Wagley, 1949, pp. 47, 48). During Todos Santos, compadres visit the altar at the home of the deceased, receiving food in return (Parsons, 1936, p. 281), while an exchange of gifts is marked by the visit of the parents to the padrino's house (G. Soustelle, 1958, p. 179). Compadres aid in constructing the family shrine (oratorio) and organize the fiesta corresponding to the saint (J. Soustelle, 1935b, pp. 106–07). Compadrinazgo assistance marks farming and its rituals. Compadres may plant a field jointly, equally providing seed and labor and sharing in the crop; if one provides the field, the other does the clearing (Ravicz, 1965). During the ceremony requesting rain, marriage padrinos may help kill the sheep used as offering to the rain deity, skin and carve up a rabbit for the family altar as a further offering, and witness the pouring of a libation by a curer on the floor

at the foot of the altar and in the doorway. A madrina or comadre assists at the ceremony in skinning the sheep and preparing food; if the woman of the house is ill, a comadre or madrina assists the daughter or assumes major responsibility, working through the night (Ravicz, 1962-65).

The compadrazgo characteristically reflects a number of functions. The *compadrazgo de voluntad* prevents aggression in barrios (Mintz and Wolf, 1950, p. 357) and in commerce (Toor, 1947, p. 94). The *compadrazgo de rosario* relates compadrazgo to the saints (S. Drucker, 1959). The *compadrazgo de pollito* gives children a chance for participation and expression through animals (*ibid.*, p. 5) and in daily play[30] (Ravicz, 1958, p. 114). The compadrazgo established at a time of death provides emotional support (G. Soustelle, 1958, p. 169).

Through folklore, the compadrazgo serves to sanction the rule against incest (Erasmus, 1950, p. 45; Redfield, 1941, p. 212; Wagley, 1949, p. 19);[31] to express underlying feelings of hostility toward the compadre (J. E. S. Thompson, 1930, pp. 156–57; W. S. Miller, 1956, pp. 120–22); to maintain harmony between the living and the dead (Wisdom, 1952, pp. 120, 122); to emphasize the quality of assistance in the compadrazgo (Parsons, 1936, p. 355), allegorically by use of animals (Ecker, 1939, p. 229); to explain and reinforce a myth-based regional bond (Parsons, 1936, p. 336).

Other ways of effecting the compadrazgo

---

[30] In play, children act the roles of the compadrazgo, using terms and observing the formal demeanor, respect, and gift-giving of adults. The game is carried on mostly with agemates but also with adults.

[31] A myth recounted by Redfield (1941, p. 212) ranks incest in this decreasing order of seriousness: compadre-comadre, father-daughter, mother-son. Redfield remarks that breach of the taboo does occur in the compadrazgo. That nonobservance of the taboo occurs in other relationships is undoubtedly true, although infrequently mentioned in the literature.

are through the exchange of bread by people from different towns, in Campeche (Y. Guemes, personal communication, 1961); the selection, among the Tlapanec, of a person one likes and wishes to call compadre[32] (Zavaleta, personal communication, 1961); the cleansing of a child with the new corn: *compadrazgo de pepentli* (Williams García, 1955, p. 35).

Although no longer common in certain cultures (Lewis, 1951, p. 351; De la Fuente, 1949, p. 172), elaborately respectful greetings (F. Starr, 1900–02, p. 65) within the compadrinazgo persist: verbal greeting and removal of the hat; bowing (Parsons, 1936, p. 89); hand-kissing (Gamio, 1922, p. 243; Parsons, 1936, p. 89) while the knee of the ahijado touches the ground (Pausic, personal communication, 1960); requesting a blessing (*pedir el santo*) of the padrino while standing with folded arms or by bringing the padrino's hand to the forehead (Ravicz, 1960).

The numbers of individuals connected through the compadrazgo are considerable. The parents and grandparents of a child aged 10 might be compadres with up to 60 people (De la Fuente, 1949, p. 169); most people in Cheran have 20 or 25 compadres. The most popular marriage arranger claimed 100 compadres through baptism (Beals, 1946, pp. 100–04). The padrino with 1000 ahijados (Redfield, 1941, pp. 222, 223) would have wide compadre bonds.

The compadrinazgo is a selective factor in mating. Although its rule on sexual relations within the system promotes harmony (as Erasmus notes, 1950, p. 46), its rule proscribing marriage is equally important, since compadrinazgo governs the attitude of a large proportion of the people. Whereas the rule for local exogamy is relatively infrequent in Middle America, system exogamy can be expected where the compadrinazgo flourishes (Ravicz, 1965, pp. 147, 149). Both rules, then, restrict and define the range of potential sexual partners.

Socio-cultural and psychological factors determine selection and participation in the compadrazgo.

1. Status.
1.1. Class (Redfield, 1941, pp. 63, 64).
1.2. Worldly position (D. M. Taylor, 1951, p. 92).
1.3. Numerical increase in membership: to enlarge the network (Rubel, 1955, p. 1038); to give leadership potential (Lewis, 1951, p. 350); to increase prestige (Redfield and Villa R., 1934, p. 99).
2. Wealth (Redfield, 1941, pp. 222–23; Gillin, 1951, p. 62; Lewis, 1951, p. 350; Beals, 1946, p. 103).
3. Age/generation (M. Nash, 1958a, p. 50; Redfield, 1941, pp. 63–64; Wisdom, 1940, p. 373; Lewis, 1951, p. 299).
4. Skill.
4.1. Curing (Paul, 1942, p. 92; S. Drucker, 1959).
4.2. Labor, exploitation (Gillin, 1951, p. 62; McClendon, 1961, p. 26).
4.3. Teaching, influence (Beals, 1946, p. 103; S. Drucker, 1959).
4.4. Knowledge/wisdom (Redfield and Villa R., 1934, p. 99; Wisdom, 1940, p. 373; Holland, 1963a, pp. 49, 50).
5. Aid.
5.1. Based on available candidates (Foster, 1948a, p. 263).
5.2. Hospitality (S. Drucker, 1959).
5.3. Social, economic, political (Lewis, 1951, p. 350).
6. Friendship.
6.1. Negative criterion (M. Nash, 1958a, p. 51).
6.2. Positive criterion (Lewis, 1951, p. 351).
7. Kinship.
7.1. Positive criterion (Solien, 1960, p. 150; Villa R., 1945, p. 90; D. Metzger, 1959a, p. 19.
7.2. Negative criterion (Wagley, 1949, p. 18; Beals, 1946, p. 103; Nader, 1960, p. 7).
7.3. Alternative (Weitlaner and Castro, 1954, p. 152; De la Fuente,[33] 1949, p. 168; Redfield and Villa R., 1934, p. 99).

[32] Since it is not a relationship based on respeto, its superficial nature is expressed by the phrase *compadrazgo de totomoxtle* (cornhusk).

[33] The more urbanized of the population select kin (p. 173), whereas the indigenous element generally chooses non-kin (p. 168).

8. Personality/character (M. Nash, 1958a, pp. 50, 51; Wisdom, 1940, p. 377; Beals, 1946, p. 103).
9. Conflict (M. Nash, 1958a, pp. 50, 51).
10. Sexual avoidance, preselection (Wagley, 1949, p. 18).
11. Sex of ahijado (Bunzel, 1952, p. 161; G. Soustelle, 1958, p. 131; Foster, 1948a, p. 263).
12. Ethnic/urban, sometimes cross-cutting other criteria (Lewis, 1951, p. 350; 1959b, p. 40; Gillin, 1951, p. 62; Paul, 1942, p. 92).

CONCLUSIONS

The importance of the social and psychological functions of the compadrinazgo helps to explain its acceptance, its retention (often in virtually unchanged form) for over four centuries, and its variety.

Acceptance of the compadrinazgo provided new statuses for channeling order and respeto to replace those lost through the Spanish conquest; in this sense, it forms a mechanism for reintegration through stabilization. By collapsing differences in the adult generations to some extent, it substitutes an equalizing factor for the former stratified society.

Since access to the compadrinazgo is open to all, social differences are minimized. In providing for the distribution of wealth, surplus is controlled and channeled and thus further restricts intragroup differentiation. The ideal and the observance of respeto form the basis for numerous kinds of social control, preventing conflict which could be disruptive for these small-scale societies; in many of them, compadrinazgo affords one of the few dependable peace-maintaining mechanisms.[34]

Basically, compadrinazgo provides a model for all interpersonal relationships and an organization to set them in action. By joining large numbers of individuals in respect-relations, it gives security and satisfaction to the participants. Where ethnic or status differences are present, it helps to bridge the cultural and socio-economic problems. There is thus vertical and horizontal[35] structuring of relationships.

There is cost in the system. Although suppressed within the compadrinazgo, conflict is directed elsewhere, often into overloaded systems like the family. Whereas it restricts social distance, it may permit abuses by superordinate ethnic elements. In directing expenditure of wealth, it is a factor in slowing the acceptance of new cultural items: medicine, clothing, technology.

No single culture or region shows the entire range of compadrinazgo proliferation. Some varieties occur in one or in widely separated cultures. The terms may be extended to include relationships connected only secondarily with compadrinazgo (Wisdom, 1940, pp. 373–74; Bunzel, 1952, p. 81). It is characteristic of much of Middle American culture to substitute or to elaborate a theme rather than to develop structural differences in form; thus, community padrinos may represent what elsewhere are termed *principales sabios* or *ancianos*. There is clear syncretism of compadrinazgo and Nahuatl culture (illustrated in G. Soustelle, 1958, p. 168). For the historical accident, Kroeber's view on "play" as a factor in social organization is suggested by the great variety in the system. The term *ahijado* is used by the Mazatec for the ritual hallucinogenic mushroom.

Cultural, social, and environmental factors explain some of the instances. Thus, in the less acculturated, impoverished, single ethnic communities there are fre-

[34] De la Fuente's view (1949, p. 172) that certain overt forms of the compadrinazgo seem to be lost with the decreasing importance and loss of the system of elders probably holds true for many cases. There is evidence, however, that emphasis on the compadrinazgo may, instead, increase, to reinforce authority for this loss of the status and authority of the elders.

[35] Terms used by Mintz and Wolf (1950, p. 348) in discussing godparents and compadres in medieval France.

quently fewer forms and relatively fewer individuals involved in any set of compadrinazgo relations. In ethnically mixed societies compadrinazgo is a mechanism for sanctioned competition (Ravicz, 1958, pp. 131–32).

Where the system shows less elaboration, factors of kinship cohesion may be involved. Where compadrinazgo does not occur (Pozas, 1959a, pp. 44, 46), community integration and the modes of assistance elsewhere provided through the compadrinazgo rest on "la familia extendida o la parentela."[36] In a related culture (D. Metzger, 1959a, p. 20) an attenuated compadrinazgo primarily involves kin. Compadrazgo terms alone override[37] kin terms, incest rules covering only compadres and padrinazgo responsibilities are weak. Although terminology might weaken, existing consanguineal and affinal bonds might be tightened; also, it creates a kinlike relationship with Ladinos. In Cantel (M. Nash, 1958a, p. 51), "the padrinos function as a weaker version of the biological uncle"; "the compadre relationship is restricted largely to salutation and a greater concern than for a complete stranger"; and "compadres take their tone from the vague and indefinite duties ascribed to consanguineal and affinal kin."

In general, then, the form of compadrinazgo appears to reflect the degree to which expected rights and responsibilities are fulfilled by another system. It may relate to the form of the kin grouping, taken in conjunction with the relative emphasis on other factors prevailing in the society, e.g., wealth and class differences, conflict-producing situations, social mobility, and ritual elaboration.

To an extent, compadrinazgo may provide an index of urbanization. Although simplification and breakup[38] tend to occur in urban areas (Redfield, 1941, pp. 222–23, 225–26), the compadrinazgo operates effectively, with some modifications, within an integrated community of urban slum dwellers who have little outside contact (Lewis, 1959b, p. 14).

The occurrence of compadrinazgo in other Middle American urban social strata suggests that it may withstand the onslaught of modern market and secular conditions, its form signaling the absence of other systems to satisfy needs created by such conditions, as well as mirroring the nature of the needs.

The compadrinazgo serves as a complementary form in the social structure. It operates by reinforcement of existing forms or by substitution, providing for relationships and activities that are failing or lacking in existing forms. It does not arise to displace or to duplicate functioning forms. Adaptability and flexibility are apparent in the variety of functions it subserves and in the varying degree of its florescence in different social organizations and subcultures.

---

[36] "Constituido por los hermanos varones del padre y los hijos varones casados" (Pozas, 1959a, p. 46).

[37] As mentioned by Redfield and Villa R. (1934, p. 99), the kinship terms are retained. Residence seems to be the determining factor.

[38] Redfield concludes that the relationship has only nominal meaning under such conditions. The loss is in spiritual meaning and ritual observance, e.g., "compadre" becomes a general term for intimacy; there is reduction in maintaining sentiments of respect, rather than disappearance of the system.

REFERENCES

Aguirre Beltrán, 1958
Beals, 1943, 1946
Bunzel, 1952
Castañeda, 1932
Cerda Silva, 1943
Covarrubias, 1947
De la Fuente, 1949
Drucker, S., 1959
Dyk, 1959
Ecker, 1939
Erasmus, 1950
Foster, 1948a, 1953a
Gamio, 1922
Garibay K., 1957
Gibson, 1952
Gillin, 1951
Haro, 1944
Holland, 1963a
Hotchkiss, 1959
Kluckhohn and Strodtbeck, 1961
Landa, 1938
Lewis, 1951, 1959b
McClendon, 1961
Madsen, 1960
Merrifield, 1959
Metzger, D., 1959a
—— and Ravicz, 1966
Miller, W. S., 1956
Mintz and Wolf, 1950
Nader, 1960

Nash, M., 1958a
Paredes, 1759
Parsons, 1936
Paul, 1942
—— and Paul, 1952
Pike, E. V., 1948
Pozas, 1959a
Ravicz, 1958, 1959, 1960, 1961, 1962–65, 1965, 1966
Redfield, 1930, 1941
—— and Villa, 1934
Ribas, 1645
Robelo, 1911
Rojas G., 1935, 1943
Rubel, 1955
Sahagún, 1956
Solien, 1960
Soustelle, G., 1958
Soustelle, J., 1935b
Spicer, 1954
Starr, F., 1900–02
Tax, 1952a
Taylor, D. M., 1951
Thompson, J. E. S., 1930
Toor, 1947
Villa R., 1945
Wagley, 1949
Weitlaner and Castro, 1954
Williams García, 1955
Wisdom, 1940, 1952

13. Local and Territorial Units

≡◱◱◱◱◱◱◱◱◱◱◱◱◱◱◱◱◱◱◱◱◱◱◱◱◱◱◱◱◱◱◱≡

M. EVA HUNT and
JUNE NASH

LOCAL GROUPS and territorial units in Middle America have two dimensions: as demographic, administrative, or political units first of the Spanish colonial government and then of independent national states; and as means of ordering social interaction and giving community identity. Although at times the two dimensions coincide, variations result from regional, state, and national differences in the use of terms and of historical and demographic factors.

As administrative units of the national government, the *municipio* and its subunits —*pueblo, paraje, aldea, colonia, barrio,* and *cantón*—are comparable entities. However, their degree of autonomy and internal cohesion vary from region to region and even from town to town in the same region. The sense of community (which we here consider as a group of people having a sentiment of belonging) contained within territorial limits and characterized by functional integration (MacIver and Page, 1949; Redfield, 1941, p. 15; Howenstine, 1963) may embrace the entire municipio, as in the western highlands of Guatemala, or may be limited to a single barrio. A few local units are not here discussed in detail because they have significance only for the state, not for the Indian, even though he may recognize their existence.[1] Other units, such as

[1] Among the Tarascans there are several such units. The *tenencia,* for example, is a municipal subdivision for administrative purposes, which may be identified with an Indian pueblo, but it also may cut across it (Mendieta y Núñez, n.d.). In Quiroga the town is divided into *cuarteles,* beyond which are outlying settlements of ranches and old haciendas. The cuartel, however, divided into *manzanas* (blocks), cuts across the old barrio divisions of the Indians, within the town, and does not exist outside the town itself (Brand, 1951, pp. 1–52). The other divisions of the municipio such as ranches, rural barrios, and tenencias, are not endogamous, nor are they congruent with the limits of the Indian community. Fincas are large private landholdings which are owned by Ladinos or non-Indians but contain a population of Indian workers.

The *sección,* a term often used in Mexico for the administrative unit which overlaps the barrio, is in other cases a separate subdivision, which cuts across the barrio. In Yalalag the sección is the new name of the old barrio, in Sayula the sección has replaced the barrio division, and in Tepoztlan (where it is also called *demarcación*) secciones and barrios are equal in number, but their limits do not coincide. The Indians themselves do not know in which demarcación they live, but they do know their barrio.

253

rancherías, ranchos, pueblitos, agencias municipales, are not territorial units by themselves (although they may coincide with an indigenous unit) but a classification of settlements by size of population created by the government for administrative and political purposes.

Indian territorial units may be called in Spanish by different names according to where they occur in Middle America. The paraje, the small hamlet, is equivalent to the Guatemalan aldea, to the Tarascan pueblito, or to the Mexican government classification of ranchería. The barrio, called cantón in southwestern Guatemala, may refer to the division of a nucleated pueblo or a municipio as a whole, or may be a rural enclave within a municipio. One of the problems of analyzing such units lies in the fact that because the terminology is in Spanish, we cannot always determine when these divisions are recognized in the Indian languages, what is the native's definition of them, and to what extent they overlap with superimposed Spanish colonial divisions and with present government nomenclature.

THE HOUSEHOLD

The peasant Indian establishes in his household and landholdings the minimum territorial group. The domestic group, or household, combines the principles of descent and marriage with the principle of association in terms of spatial propinquity. In Middle America the household is the focus of primary identity for the individual. Through his attachment to his home, his milpas, his gardens and orchards, the Indian is attached to a series of widening territorial units (Wisdom, 1940, p. 258).

Physical Dimensions

The physical dimensions of the domestic establishment vary throughout the area. Some authors define the domestic type by the buildings. In Tepoztlan (Lewis, 1960) there are jacales and adobe homes, occupied mostly by Indians, and western-type homes of the rich. In other places the domestic unit is a sitio: one or more buildings and a yard surrounded by a low fence, the milpa located elsewhere. Common in the nucleated communities of Chiapas, this is the standard "home" in the pueblos in the Valley of Mexico and other sections of Middle America. In the paraje settlements, however, each domestic unit may contain not only the huts and yard but also a garden, and the milpa will be adjacent to it, none of it being clearly demarcated.

Romney and Romney (1963) have pointed out the difficulty of distinguishing the physical boundaries of the domestic unit, even in communities where the houses are arranged in a Spanish street pattern (Juxtlahuaca). The most reliable identification is the separate cooking fire, part of each separate production and consumption unit. Sometimes a separate kitchen building or a granary (*troje*) may be added. The physical limits of the domestic group as a local unit may be symbolized. In Santa Eulalia family, home, and landholding are symbolized in the *kurus ko-mam,* the ancestral cross; wherever it is placed, the family is said to be "planted." Even when the family moves, the members return to pay their respect to this ancestral cross. The heads of subordinate families make their own crosses, and as their families become detached from the original domestic unit these crosses are elevated to the status of ancestral crosses. The complex concept of birthplace, cross, and family center, with special reference to the soil, is called *lobol* (LaFarge, 1947, p. 24). Other symbolic elements which define the household may include the household altar, a cross in the top of the hut, or a cross in the yard. In Zinacantan the house yard and its cross duplicate the sacred arrangements in the ceremonial center (Vogt, 1961).

Household Ceremonies

The unity of the household is expressed in rituals that take place within the house. Throughout Middle America occur ceremonies of housewarming (De la Fuente, 1949, pp. 55, 209; Hunt, 1962; J. Nash, 1959b; Guiteras Holmes, 1961; Hermitte, 1958–60). The house is thought to have a soul or guardian spirit which exercises discipline over its occupants by causing illness. In Chichicastenango ancestors are the guardians of the house they occupied in their lifetime and continue to live there. Here their power and discipline over their descendants is greatest (Bunzel, 1952, p. 39).

Transfer of house ownership requires sacrifices to the house spirit, both old and new owners participating (Cantel—M. Nash, 1953–54). All household residents take part in curing ceremonies, to which is added an offering to the house spirit (Amatenango—J. Nash, 1960b; Chorti—Wisdom, 1940, p. 133).

In some cases the dead are buried within the house itself (Tenejapa—Medina, 1961–62) or in lands owned by the household (Oxchuc—Villa Rojas, 1946). All household members observe the Day of the Dead, November 1 in the Catholic calendar. Offerings are made in both house and cemetery not only for the direct ascendants of the family, but for all household residents.

Household Composition

The core of the domestic unit is the nuclear family, which may be enlarged by addition of other kin, the rules of membership varying from community to community. Before marriage, membership in a particular domestic group is primarily by birth in the household of one's parents. Children may be attached to a domestic unit through a sponsor there who is not one of the parents (e.g., grandparents, primary collaterals, nonkinsmen) but who has taken charge of their socialization and maintenance.

At marriage several alternative cycles of domestic development are open. In general, the norm throughout Middle America is virilocality for women and patrilocality for men. Men may, however, reside with their fathers for only a short time until they receive their own land (Aguacatenango); there may be a period of bride-service or groom-service (fincas of Ocosingo); new domestic groups may be formed immediately after marriage with just minor emphasis in patrilocal proximity (San Bartolome—Hunt, 1963; D. Metzger, n.d.; Montagu, 1960–61; Díaz de Salas, 1960–61). The rules of residence seem to correlate not only with the descent system but with other important social variables, such as the market value of woman's labor input and the availability of agricultural lands through the agnatic group. Thus, where the family unit in the household is larger than the nuclear family, the links of kinship and affinality may vary.

The survival of any group as a kinship unit beyond the household seems to depend on whether or not any land is held in common. In most communities the nuclear family, with any accessory members attached to the household, is the primary functioning kinship group within the community. However, many men after marriage are dominated by their fathers if the latter still hold the land (Wagley, 1949, p. 17).

In most communities it is the man with the greatest landholdings who is able to keep his married sons near him (Redfield and Villa Rojas, 1934, p. 91; Wagley, 1949, p. 11; Hunt, 1962; Gillin, 1951; LaFarge, 1947, pp. 23–24; Kelly and Palerm, 1952, p. 60). In communities where the agnatic emphasis has given way to "ambilateral" or "bilateral" ties, however, and where women contribute to the household income by their marketable labor, residence after marriage and the existence of joint households depend on which spouse's parents have more land, so that both married daughters and married sons may remain with parents and form joint households (J. Nash, 1959b, 1960b; Tax, 1953, pp. 203–06; Pozas, 1959a, p. 51).

Economic and Political Functions

Throughout Middle America the household is the basic unit which controls production, consumption, and recruitment of labor. Since most Indian communities are composed of peasants subsisting on maize, each household is in a sense a small family farm, attempting to support itself throughout the whole year, and to provide for extra cash, in times of emergency, through the use of household labor. In exceptional households (Panajachel—Tax, 1953, p. 18) the members may keep their earnings and property separate, but usually the household is a small "corporation," and even in exceptional cases cooperation for work on a noncash basis is a household function. Moreover, whenever the community has an economic specialization such as pottery or a cash crop, the production is handled by each household as a separate small "factory" or productive unit (M. Nash, 1961). The household is also an economic unit in that taxes are levied by household rather than by individual.

The household functions as a political unit in the corporate Indian communities where the political system is based on a civil-religious hierarchy, in which power is vested in household heads, and where the political personnel is recruited by household. In order to become a community officer a man has to be married and be the head of his own household (except for the posts at the bottom of the hierarchical ladder).

PARAJE AND CANTON

The term *paraje* has been applied to three functionally distinct territorial units: (1) a named geographical unit, (2) a group of

256

agricultural plots, and (3) a small settlement of households.

In the first usage, a paraje may be a segment of the landscape recognized by and named after a landmark. The Yalaltec designated any such territory, or even a section of a river bed, by the old Zapotec term *yoosh* (or the new *paraj*), translated as paraje or lugar (De la Fuente, 1949).

Paraje as applied to clearings in the monte where the community cornfields lie is used by the Zapotec, the Mixe, and the Aztec in early colonial times. Each nucleated Zapotec village has several parajes cleared by communal labor and divided equally among householders (Schmieder, 1930). The system of paraje-milpa forces most householders to control small plots in several parajes of the community, whereas no one paraje is controlled by a single family unit. Thus the system fosters, first, the atomization of landholdings and, second, the unity of the village community as a physical aggregate. Since each household works plots in scattered areas, the pueblo itself rather than the milpa becomes the most convenient place of residence (*ibid.*).

The third type of paraje, a hamlet of a few households which control the agricultural plots and have primary rights of usufruct, is typical of communities of highland Chiapas (Zinacantan, Oxchuc, Cancuc, Chenalho, Tenejapa) and of some highland Guatemala communities (Chichicastenango, Cantel, Santiago Chimaltenango), where it is called a cantón. In these examples the paraje or cantón is recognized by particular landmarks, but its boundaries are fluid because of shifting agricultural practices.

The residential paraje is an ancient pattern of settlement. In highland Chiapas, the parajes in preconquest Pokom-Maya communities, the *kokomak* or *pajuye* was a political, religious, and economic unit, dependent on the center and having only low-level officials and priests in residence (Miles, 1957, p. 769). The paraje as the locus of an exogamous patriline was characteristic of the Otomi (Caso, 1954; J. Soustelle, 1935b); the Chinantec (Bevan, 1938) and the Mixe (Schmieder, 1930) were similarly organized.

The residential paraje, although primarily a territorially defined rather than a kinship-defined group, may be identified with an extended family group. In highland Chiapas, the localization of descent groups (patrilines) in parajes is found only in communities with unilateral kinship structure (Oxchuc, Tenejapa, Chenalho, San Pedro Chalchihuitan) and is absent in parajes of bilateral kinship communities (Chamula). Whether or not the agnatic descent unit (patriline) is localized in the paraje does not affect the paraje structure. The patriline is exogamous, but the paraje is not necessarily so.

It is important to notice, however, that descent-group bonds and paraje bonds are not in opposition but may be juxtaposed. If a man needs land and cannot find it available within his paraje, he may obtain permission to cultivate more easily in the land of a paraje controlled by households of his same Spanish name-group than in a paraje of another name-group. In those communities in which membership in a paraje is determined by descent as well as by residence, as in Tenejapa (Medina, 1961–62), a family may still claim membership in a paraje after moving out. They may continue to pay taxes to the paraje of father's origin, and it usually takes two or three generations to switch loyalties from the paraje of origin to the paraje of residence. The determination of loyalties and membership is also complicated by the rights over land obtained through inheritance which lies in some other paraje than that in which one resides. It will be a man's choice, determined by a series of circumstances, to which paraje he pays taxes and of which he considers himself a member. In Chanal (McQuown, 1959) it is stated that a man working land outside his paraje

of origin has to contribute taxes to that paraje as well.

The residential paraje is not only a territorial subdivision of the community but, in some areas, is an administrative and political subdivision and a ritual unit. A group of officials nominated from the household heads of the paraje organize and perform rituals and services without the immediate participation of each household.

The officials associated with ritual affairs of the paraje in both Tenejapa and Oxchuc are called *cabildos*. In both communities, the paraje symbolizes its unity by rituals performed by the cabildos de milpa, which are dedicated to sacred spots within its boundaries (the Calvario, the water holes, a cave or great rock) and carried out in the interest of better crops. In Tenejapa these sacred spots are named *anhel,* and each paraje is said to have a minimum of 13 (a sacred number among the Maya) although the actual figure varies. Several times a year, in crucial periods during the agricultural cycle, the cabildos de milpa, together with the paraje musicians, travel over the paraje visiting the anhels, praying and presenting offerings to the paraje guardian spirits who are said to reside there. In Oxchuc the cabildos de milpa carry out similar functions (Villa Rojas, 1946, p. 27). These officers are in charge of collecting money for the ritual performances from householders of the paraje.

The cabildos de milpa of Tenejapa may act as middlemen between the parajes when two parajes share a particular anhel. The cabildos de milpa of one paraje may visit the anhels of another paraje to pray for special petitions, and they may be asked by another paraje to perform special ceremonies.

When the paraje observes community-wide fiestas separately, officials may be designated in the paraje. During Carnaval, in Tenejapa the cabildos de carnaval are the paraje representatives in rituals for the occasion, distinct from the mayordomos de carnaval who are delegates at the community level (Medina, 1961–62).

Religious items owned by householders may become the object of pride and devotion for the paraje as a whole. Such it is in Tenejapa with the Talking Saints, images said to talk miraculously and give advice about sickness and other misfortunes (*ibid.*). The mayordomos of the Talking Saints, or householders who "own" them, give fiestas for the saints which are the focus of great communal activity until the saints are said to have lost their power and are sold to another paraje.

A number of civil officials are links between the paraje and the municipal center. They are communication agents, carrying news and commands from the center to the paraje and back; they are tax collectors; and they are recorders of demographic information. These officials are called *fiadores* in Tenejapa, Chenalho, and Oxchuc (*ibid.*), but they may be called by a more general name such as principales (Chichicastenango) or mayores. There is some evidence that in the past the cantón officials may have had more power than they do now. In Cantel's oldest cantón, Estancia, the principal has independent authority in handling disputes, whereas in the rest of the cantones he is merely an official agent under the central hierarchy (M. Nash, 1953–54).

Some new officers, such as president of the school committee or ejido agent, which have been recently introduced at the paraje level, may also serve in a general capacity as leaders of the local group, and alternate in leadership functions with the old local officials (Villa Rojas, 1946; Siverts, 1964). But the new leaders do not derive their power from territorial allegiances, as do the cabildos de milpa and fiadores. In Tenejapa both the cabildos and the fiadores form groups, each one with a *jefe* or chief; the new officials do not. The jefe of the cabildos changes through time from paraje to paraje, whereas the jefe of the fiadores is always from the same paraje, that which

is said to be at the exact territorial center of Tenejapa. The location of jefes ties up symbolically with the functions of these local officials: jefes of the cabildos are dispersed through the land, but fiadores, whose main job is that of centralization of communication, are always from the center of the community.

Ritual officials differ from civil officials in that the former unite parajes to each other; the latter tie the paraje to the cabecera. The existence of offices at the paraje level allows for the dispersion of political power at the same time that centralization is maintained.

When the community includes a large population with dispersed settlements, such as Tenejapa, the number of political and religious posts at the community level are not sufficient to maintain a democratic distribution of *cargos* among the male population. This may lead to a monopoly of cargos, as in Chichicastenango or Zinacantan (Cancian, 1965) and may cause resentment among those who cannot participate in the community government. By allowing the smaller community subdivisions to keep their own internal offices, the danger of fission and decentralization is, if not avoided, slowed down. In Zinacantan, where a tendency toward political monopoly is well under way, parajes whose members feel left out of the political-religious control of the community tend to try to become autonomous by creating their own political-religious hierarchies. They have refused to pay their taxes or to send men to service at the center (Cancian, personal communication).

The paraje is a territorial subdivision rather than an autonomous territorial unit. As such, its boundaries are fluid, and its social functions are an adaptation to the structural demands of the larger community of which they form a part. The paraje is a segment of the community in a manner analogous to the lineage segment as a part of the lineage. Parajes function within the community through the principle of segmentary opposition. Primary loyalties, rights, and duties are maintained within the paraje; primary rivalry with equivalent segments occurs with other parajes. But just as lineage segments function as a unit at the lineage level, parajes function as units at the level of the barrio or the municipio of which they form the building blocks. As we shall show later, it is beyond the community that territorial units become differentiated and specialized.

The Aldea

Aldea is the term applied in Guatemala to a population aggregate within the municipio limits which is dependent on the political administration of the center. The boundaries of the aldea are not always marked, but are usually known to the people who reside in it. There is no single pattern of settlement of aldeas even in the same municipio: in Cantel, for example (M. Nash, 1958a), two have nucleated and three scattered residential patterns. The aldea is generally equivalent in function to the paraje, with one definite difference: aldeas, although not endogamous by prescription, tend to be so in fact.

Within the aldea, as within the paraje, all life-cycle ceremonies are held, in addition to those rituals connected with the agricultural cycle. But, although the paraje has only natural ritual places, the aldea may have a ceremonial house.

In the organization of the economy, it can be said that the aldeas are the point of production in the municipio and the center is the point of distribution. The exceptions lie in specialized, nonagricultural production. In Cantel the center was differentiated from all the rural barrios by having more development of specialization than in any of the five aldeas, where, in fact, specialization was practically lacking (M. Nash, 1958a).

There is some interchange between aldeas of the same municipio, particularly if they are at different elevations above sea level, which allows for crop variation. The same may be true for parajes (Wagley, 1941; Wisdom, 1940).

There is a great deal of variance in the degree of autonomy accorded each aldea. Among the Chorti, where the center of the community tends to be dominated by Ladinos, the Indians maintain their independence by withdrawing to the aldea (Wisdom, 1940, p. 26). But where the Indians run their own affairs in the center (Santiago Chimaltenango—Wagley, 1949), the aldea is equivalent to the paraje in that it is a subordinate sector of the community.

The strong sentiment uniting the Chorti within the aldea seems to be related to the fact that the center is dominated by Ladinos. Although the towns of the area (Zacapa, Chiquimula, San Esteban, and San Jacinto) are preconquest sites, the population today is predominantly Ladino; the Indians have withdrawn more and more to the aldeas. In San Luis Jilotepeque, which is another large Ladino-Indian population mixture, Tumin (1952, p. 103) noted that the Indians of the aldea give the impression of being far more outgoing, expressive, and free from restraint than are the pueblo Indians.

The officers of the aldea are called *auxiliares* and *comandantes* instead of cabildos and fiadores, but they may also have policemen who take posts in the community civil-religious hierarchy. As in the paraje, these officers have internal functions in settling local disputes and are also contacts with the administration at the cabecera of locally originated action.

Territorial Dependencies

Colonias, Rancherías, Caseríos, and Rural Barrios

Many of the communities include smaller local units which are not a part of the community from their point of view, or from the point of view of those who identify themselves as members. These local en-

259

claves are for the most part ethnically different immigrants from other communities. These enclaves may at times be found within pueblos or towns, forming peripheral neighborhoods or barrios, somewhat separated from the main community settlement. The members of these settlements are usually looked upon by the community as inferior foreigners; ordinarily they do not participate fully in the political life of the community.

The process of breaking off and reorganizing territorial units has been repetitive and historically continuous. Throughout Middle America one may find local enclaves of this sort, at different levels of development called *colonias, caseríos, rancherías,* or rural barrios, and in some cases *agencia municipal* (when they are enclaves within a municipio community). They usually do not have an internal political structure of their own, but have one or two officers, who are selected not by the residents but by the community government, to whom alone they are responsible.

THE BARRIO

The Spaniards applied the word *barrio* to several distinct indigenous territorial units as well as to divisions of towns in which they lived in the New World. The indigenous units which have been translated as barrio include (1) the Aztec *calpul*, (2) the Maya *cuchteel* of Yucatan, and (3) *molom* of Pokom-Maya, divisions of larger communities. The formation of barrios in postconquest times resulted from (1) the *parcialidades* or separate Indian communities drawn into a single center, (2) small settlements of Indians devoted to agriculture and attached to larger colonial towns,[2] and (3) neighborhoods of large towns based on the Spanish Old World pattern.[3] Barrios in the Spanish colonial towns included ethnically and economically segregated territorial units, whose distinctiveness was symbolized in religious and political places, symbols, and offices.

Indigenous Preconquest Barrios

THE CALPUL. The principles of descent and locality are incorporated in the ancient calpul, which Zurita (quoted in Waterman, 1917, p. 253) defined as "... a barrio inhabited by a family, known as of very ancient origin, which for a long time owns a territory of well-defined boundaries, and all the members of which are of the same lineage." The Aztec calpulli functioned as (1) land tenure units, (2) ritual units each with its own gods and ceremonies, (3) specialized economic units, each with its own craft, (4) segregated wealth classes, with the nobility residing in separate barrios from the commoners, (5) kinship units in that each barrio or calpul contained a localized descent group (Bandelier, 1880a; Carrasco, 1950b, p. 91; Kirchhoff, 1955; Monzón, 1949) identified today as a clan, although it is not clear whether it was exogamous and unilineal or endogamous and ambilateral, (6) military units, the members of which formed separate companies with their own leaders and emblems, and (7) political and administrative units, with separate officials who dealt with internal affairs, tribute, and service payments to a central political organization (Monzón, 1949; Redfield, 1928). Present-day barrios retain more or less the same characteristics except for the military leadership and the presence of nobility.

The Aztec calpul seems to have been extended to other people under the domination of the Toltecs and the Aztecs (Totonacs—Krickeberg, 1918, p. 1055; Chiapas—

[2] This type of barrio is more frequently called paraje or pueblito in Mexico; its occurrence (Tarrascan pueblos—Brand, 1951) is discussed in the sections on parajes and aldeas. The term cantón denotes this type of territorial unit in much of Guatemala; wherever it is not used, the terms aldeas and caseríos have certain rural territorial extension (R. N. Adams, 1957b, p. 343).

[3] In central and western Guatemala, the term cantón is applied to this unit, but the term barrio is more common in the east (R. N. Adams, 1957b, p. 343).

Villa Rojas, 1946, pp. 366, 376; Calnek, 1961; Guiteras Holmes, 1947; 1951, pp. 199–201; Tlaxcala—Nutini, 1961). Barrio, or calpul, representatives functioned as the basis of local government under the Spaniards up to the mid-18th century. The calpul survives today in some of these same areas, but with limited functions. In the Chiapas highlands, the calpulli introduced by the Aztecs merged with the pre-existing localized agnatic groups. In San Pablo Chalchihuitan the barrio or calpul retains both territorial and descent bases as a territorial division where the members of different agnatically related families inhabit a certain locality. The land belongs to the calpul which assigns it to patrilines, and land cannot be sold to anyone of another lineage unless the whole lineage dies (Guiteras Holmes, 1951, pp. 199–201). The tie between the individual and his calpul territory is reinforced at birth and at death: the pregnant woman of San Pablo goes to her own calpul to give birth, and the sick man returns to his calpul lands "where he ought to die and where he should be buried" (ibid., p. 202). Each lineage within a calpul is linked with a hill, a cross, or a tree. The functions of the calpul in San Pablo are extensive. The pasados of each calpul carry out religious ceremonies concerned with the crops and with health. They settle conflict cases and handle the management of communal works.

The calpulli of San Pedro Chenalho are similarly effective in maintaining the link between descent and locality. They hold communal lands, and informants can still indicate the mythical place of origin of each of the lineages (Guiteras Holmes, 1961, p. 69). Each calpul has its own sacred water hole, crosses, and senior mountains in its neighborhood, and these are the sites of religious ceremonials (ibid., pp. 65–66). The calpul in Oxchuc is defined territorially only in the ceremonial center, where an imaginary line drawn east-west through the church divides the village

into northern and southern halves (Siverts, 1960, p. 19). The functioning of the calpul here is related to ceremonial events; all fiestas are in the charge of capitanes, elected from each of the three calpulli (Villa Rojas, 1946, pp. 366, 376). Here the patrilineal extended family of the same Indian surname is the largest landholding unit, and there is no larger localized kin-group holding land (ibid., p. 148). In Chanal, formerly part of the township of Oxchuc, the same group holds land in common (McQuown, 1959). The institution of territorially linked clans was maintained in Cancuc, but there was called culibal (Guiteras Holmes, 1947).

CUCHTEEL. The preconquest Yucatan Maya towns of any size were divided into cuchteel, the smallest organized political unit which was governed by an ah cuch cab. This official was later called a principal or regidor by the Spanish, or chunthan (chief speaker) by the Maya. Unlike the calpul, the cuchteel was not a descent group, and members of the same name group could be distributed in several of these "barrios." The barrio had some autonomy and was given veto power in the town council (Roys, 1957, p. 7).

MOLOM. The Molom, or Pokom-Maya localized descent group, has been equated with barrio or parcialidad, but Miles (1957, p. 759) points out that "it is doubtful that town wards and clans were entirely coincident."

Postconquest Barrio Formation

When separate Indian settlements of highland Chiapas were concentrated into nucleated centers, the original communities retained their separateness in barrio organization (Calnek, 1961; Villa Rojas, 1961, pp. 25–29). Each barrio retained its name (as did Aguacatenango, which in colonial days was called the pueblo of Aguacatenango formed by the parcialidades of Aguacatenango and Quetzaltepeque) and its separate political officers. In these

261

Indian communities the barrio forms a named[4] semi-autonomous social group limiting marriage to the barrio members. Both Aguacatenango and Amatenango retain this pattern of separateness and independence (Hunt, 1962; J. Nash, 1960b).

In the Mestizo-dominated towns barrios of distinct groups of people drawn into a center tended to become dependent sub-neighborhoods, with less political and social autonomy than in the Indian-dominated communities. The Indian barrios of large towns tended to be located on the peripheries of the pueblo, with the Ladinos in the center barrio (Guatemala—R. N. Adams, 1957b, p. 332; Merida—Hansen, 1934; Redfield, 1941; Villa Carranza—Day in McQuown, 1959; the Mixtec towns of Juxtlahuaca and Tlaxiaco—Romney, 1963; San Luis Jilotepeque—Tumin, 1952, p. 101). Where the ethnic division between center and peripheral barrios is strong, the Ladinos may feel that there is a separate community, as in Panajachel (Tax, 1953, p. 188) and Teopisca (Hotchkiss in McQuown, 1959). Indians may feel it is to their advantage in maintaining in-group privacy and political independence (Tumin, 1952, p. 101). A contrary tendency, that of Indians dominating the center with impoverished Mestizoized barrios on the peripheries was noted in Amatenango, Chiapas (J. Nash in McQuown, 1959), and Sayula (Guiteras Holmes, 1952a).

Dual and Multiple Barrio Systems

The classification of barrios as dual or multiple systems is based on function, not on number. The dual system may have more than two barrios, but they are grouped into two sets (Yalalag, where four barrios form two sets—De la Fuente, 1949, p. 28; Mazatec of Huautla, where five barrios form sets of two and three—Villa Rojas, 1955; Tepoztlan, where seven barrios occur in two sets—Redfield, 1930; Oxchuc, where 12 parajes are grouped in two calpulli—Villa Rojas, 1946). The Tarascans usually had

262

four or eight barrios (Uapatzequa—Brand, 1951, p. 35), but the archaeological remains of Quiroga have only two *yacatas*, or "temples" *(Ibid.,* p. 11).

The dual system is a native division of old standing and occurs usually in Indian-dominated communities, especially the less acculturated ones, whereas the multiple system is more often followed in Mestizo or in acculturated Indian communities. The dual barrio system has been equated with moieties,[5] but we prefer the designation of dual barrio.

The location of the barrios differs for the dual and the multiple barrio systems. In the former, an imaginary line across the central plaza of the head town divides the community. Any settlement on either side of the line, both in the center and in the outlying parajes, forms part of the barrio on the same side (Tzeltal and Mixtec towns). Variations of the dual barrio occur in the Mixe town of Atitlan, where the two barrios are about one-half kilometer apart, and in Totontepec, where there are no clear boundaries (Beals, 1945b). In the multiple barrio system, the pueblo has a central nucleus, usually called the centro, where

[4] In most instances the names are those of the patron saint of the barrio, but in dual barrios they may be called by the native terms for "above" and "below." Foster (1960a, p. 34) suggests that this division into upper and lower is "modeled after Iberian prototypes," but sometimes they may have overlapped pre-Hispanic moiety divisions. In Tepoztlan, Redfield (1930) indicates that each barrio had a Nahua name for some animal, which was explained by informants as a result of the abundance of these animals in the district or the inhabitants' resemblance to such animals. There seems to be no totemic affiliation.

[5] Murdock (1949, p. 47) has pointed out that this creates terminological confusion because membership is not determined by descent, although the barrios may regulate marriage and be endogamous. But if one accepts Beals' definition of moieties (1945b, p. 33) as "non-exogamous institutions concerned with ceremonial and political problems and little or none at all with kinship," the dual barrio system qualifies. In communities where barrios do correspond to clans (Cancuc—Guiteras Holmes, 1947) Murdock's criterion for moieties is met.

the church, central plaza, government offices, and stores are situated. Grouped around it are the barrios, some on the periphery of the town, some separate (Teopisca—Hotchkiss, 1960–61; San Bartolo, Tlaxiaco—Marroquín, 1954; Juxtlahuaca—Romney and Romney, 1963).

The feature distinguishing multiple from dual barrio systems is the designation of membership. In communities with a dual barrio system, membership in the barrio nearly always depends on descent. This standard is reinforced by rules of endogamy which are followed with more or less rigor according to population size, degree of acculturation of the community, and other preferential rules regulating marriage. The occurrence of endogamous rules in the least acculturated of Indian towns is consistent enough to suggest that this type of barrio is of pre-Hispanic origin. The converse does not hold, since nonendogamous barrios may have been Spanish administrative units but may also have been indigenous towns which have lost this ruling.

In the highland Chiapas areas where residence and marriage have been carefully studied, statistics on barrio intermarriage indicate that the endogamous regulation is realized in a high proportion of marriages (Aguacatenango, 86 per cent—Hunt, 1962; Chanal, 90 per cent—Hunt in McQuown, 1959). Even with intermarriage in towns with preferential virilocal residence, the patrilines retain their barrio of birth identity. Among the dual barrio towns, two have exceptions to the regulation of barrio endogamy, but the two sets of barrios are each endogamous. In Chamula two barrios of one set intermarry, but the only barrio of the second set is endogamous (Pozas, 1959a, pp. 33–34).[6] Among the Mazatec, where the dual system operated by barrio sets, the barrio itself was not endogamous,

but the sets to which the barrios belonged were. In the town of Tepoztlan (Lewis, 1960) only 42 per cent of marriages are barrio endogamous, but 50 per cent are between adjacent barrios. At the time of Redfield's study (1928) barrio membership was hereditary, particularly for the eldest son, who was bound to keep his father's place. The church tax paid in a barrio was symbolic of "a perpetual pledge to the Santo, irrevocable, and binding on a man's family after his death." Residence alone did not give membership rights in a barrio (Redfield, 1928, p. 288). At the time of Lewis' study 20 years later, however, owning a house site in a barrio gave rights of membership there.

Descent as the principle on which barrio residence rests has been weakened with the loss of barrio control over lands. In the traditional pattern of dual barrios, men can obtain land and reside only within the barrio of birth. With the introduction of sale of land and rental of houses, these rules have been relaxed.

The territorial base of the barrios is frequently emphasized in those towns in which it is found by burial of the dead in barrio cemeteries, or in community-wide cemeteries in which the arrangement of plots follows the barrio pattern of the living community in orientation and spatial arrangement (J. Nash, 1960b).

In the multiple barrio communities there are neither rules of membership based on descent nor stated endogamous restrictions. Intermarriage within the barrio seems to follow the convenience of "marrying the girl next door" (Teopisca—Metzger, NSF II) rather than any norm. In multiple barrio Mestizo communities, the Indian barrios may retain barrio endogamy because of ethnic endogamy rather than barrio endogamy (Mixtec community of Juxtlahuaca; Teopisca in Chiapas—Hotchkiss in McQuown, 1959).

Exceptions to the claim of barrios as territorial units occur in a few cases. Pozas

[6] Pozas (1959a) gives economic reasons for the exchange of marriage partners of the two barrios which specialize in one product and for the barrio of the second set.

(1959a) maintains that the three barrios of Chamula are not territorial units because their boundaries are not clearly demarcated. This may have resulted from the fact that at the time of his study the two barrios on the same side of the dual division were in the process of merging, a situation which appears to be occurring in Cancuc (Guiteras Holmes, 1947, p. 6). Another exception is the Nahua town of Contla, where Nutini (1961) maintains that the barrio is an exogamic unit regulating marriage and is nonlocalized. The territorial unit, called there a sección, cut across barrio lines. Each barrio has a fixed number of name-groups belonging to it, but after two or three generations, when individuals move out of their regular territory, a name may appear in two different barrios. Here again the principles of descent and territory appear to have merged.

Political Functions of the Barrio

In communities with the dual barrio system, one of the most characteristic features is the division of political responsibilities, rights, and duties between the barrios or sets of barrios. This balance of leadership may be achieved by an oscillating incumbency in the top posts and an equal number of officers from each side in the lower posts serving simultaneously or taking turns (Yalalag—De la Fuente, 1949, p. 29; Oxchuc—Villa Rojas, 1946; Mixe—Beals, 1945b; Chanal—Metzger in McQuown, 1959) or in equal representation of each barrio at the same time (Amatenango— J. Nash, 1960b; Aguacatenango—Hunt, 1962).

In addition to participating in the community political structure, each barrio may have its own internal officers, either formally or informally elected (Lewis, 1960, p. 51). In Sayula each barrio had its own jefe whose principal mission was to take care of the cleaning of the barrio and the public work projects (Guiteras Holmes, 1952a, p. 111). Among the Mazatec each barrio has

its own principales, older men who form a council charged with the responsibility for cleaning the barrio territory and running the court system (Villa Rojas, 1955).

Political power may become concentrated and monopolized by one or a few barrios, particularly in the case of multiple barrio towns with a large Mestizo population. In Tepoztlan all municipal presidents between 1922 and 1944, and the ejido authorities, came from the three larger barrios (Lewis, 1960, p. 52). In Venustiano Carranza, Chiapas, the Indian barrios have a single councilman representing them in the government, which is in Mestizo hands (McQuown, 1959). When Ladinos are a large part of the population, even if they are a minority, their political connections with the state government and the economic power within the community make it possible for them to monopolize power.

Differentiation of political power is also tied up with differences in wealth and population between barrios. Because political posts are not paid, poorer and smaller barrios tend to avoid participation in the government. When each barrio is forced to contribute an equal number of men, smaller barrios are at a disadvantage, and the adult male population is forced to take posts more often (De la Fuente, 1949, p. 211).

Differences in political power and competition for political control are among the main forces behind community fission along barrio lines. Because the status of municipio gives the greatest degree of political self-determination locally for a community, political conflict between barrios tends to split the communities; barrios with lesser power may migrate en masse to form a separate village. Thus the Mixtec town and municipio of Santa Cruz Etla was formerly a barrio of San Pablo Etla and obtained its political independence after lobbying for about 20 years in Mexico City (Bailey, 1958; see also Chan Kom in Redfield and Villa Rojas, 1934.) The traditional way in which fission has been avoided in Indian communities is through the creation of independent internal political posts within the barrio. In some of the Maya communities of highland Chiapas, until the end of the 18th century, each barrio had a completely separate government hierarchy and functioned as independent political communities (Calnek, 1962). Since the failure of the Indians in the War of the Castes to achieve political independence from Ladinos, the struggle for self-determination has become a battle of each community to obtain municipal status, thus achieving independence from Ladino control. Current policies which counter barrio fission are the appointment of community-wide officials for new tasks, such as the education committee (Villa Carranza, Teopisca—Metzger in McQuown, 1959).

Economic Functions of the Barrio

The barrios of Indian communities are not economically specialized, but in Mestizo communities economic specialities tend to be distributed along barrio lines. This may reflect the guild system of the Old World (San Cristobal, Chiapas—Calnek, 1962, p. 40; Montagu, 1959) or it may reflect a distinction between Indian barrios of agricultural workers and Mestizo barrios of landlords, craftsmen, and service workers.

Barrios may provide the basis for a division of labor in the communal work of road repair, maintenance, building or repairing official buildings. In Yalalag (De la Fuente, 1949) each barrio cares for a bridge within its territory, cleans one section of the village market place, and builds one side of the corral for bullfights. In Soteapan, a Popoluca town (Foster, 1942), each barrio has a *jefe de manzanas,* who is in charge of the *faena,* or communal work. Barrios may be responsible for cash tribute for public construction projects and may have a special officer who collects the money.

In large towns, each barrio may have its own market, as in Tlaxiaco, but in the smaller Indian villages, barrios may share a market place in which each has a section which "belongs" to it; that is, the barrio is responsible for its maintenance. The barrio may be a corporation in the sense of a unit having rights over scarce goods or resources. Barrio land tenure is found in Aguacatenango (Hunt, 1962), and among the Amuzgos, Trique, and Mixtec of Oaxaca (Marroquín, 1954, p. vi). In some cases separate barrio tenure has split the community in two, as in Ihuitlan, Oaxaca, or accentuated rivalries between the Mestizo-dominated center and rural Indian peripheries, as in Tlaxiaco (*ibid.*, p. 11). Usufruct rights may similarly be limited to barrio members. In Aguacatenango only members of the barrio can gather palm or berries within its boundaries; in neighboring Amatenango members of either barrio of the center gather clay (found in only one area), but they collect wood and wild products only in the hills of their own side of the dual division.

Exclusive rights to property and products within the boundaries of the barrio may stem from the earlier calpul system, or from a barrio which was a landholding corporation. Breakdown of exclusive rights over land has resulted from early grants by the Spaniards of communal land to whole communities, as well as to postrevolutionary grants of ejido land to all members of the community. Inheritance of land by widows in cases of inter-marriage between barrios has blurred barrio limits to privately owned plots. The Mixe, in order to maintain barrio control of land, permit the widow to retain land for her children only if she remarries a man of the same barrio as her first husband (Beals, 1945b). Other factors leading to the breakdown of barrio land tenure are the introduction of land sales for cash and of sources of income other than agriculture, the increasing tendency toward bilateral inheritance, and the new rights of women over land combined with the breakdown of barrio endogamy. Exclusive rights of barrios to land based on 16th-century titles is not

265

supported in modern courts since, from a national point of view, barrio separation fosters constant friction and conflict within pueblos (Aguirre Beltrán, 1954).

Religious Functions of the Barrio

One of the most characteristic barrio distinctions throughout Middle America, in Indian and Mestizo communities, is the patron saint complex. The patron saint not only gives the name to the barrio but has its own chapel, an annual fiesta, *cofradías* (brotherhoods), and *mayordomías* responsible for carrying out religious functions surrounding the worship of the saint as well as for the maintenance of the religious buildings and the sacred objects "owned" by the barrio. Church cleaning, alms collecting, and worship of special saints are thus divided along barrio lines. Moreover, there may be nonwestern religious symbols, objects, and "spirits" which are barrio-controlled. Among these are sacred stones, hills which "belong" to the souls of particular barrios, and protective animal spirits or *nahuales*.

The cofradía system may formerly have been organized in terms of barrio divisions as in Coban, Alta Verapaz, Guatemala. Here the seven cofradías formerly corresponded to the seven barrios of the town. Each cofradía had its own lands on which corn was grown for sale (Goubaud Carrera, Rosales, and Tax, 1947).

The religious activities within the barrio may be left in the hands of specialists (sacristanes, Catholic priests) or they may be redistributed within the barrio population (e.g., in Contla, a Nahua town, sponsoring of cofradías for the principal saints alternates among name-groups; Nutini, 1961) with certain time limits. But the saint and the activities around the sacred possessions of the barrio are symbolic of the unity of the social group, and every member is a participant in the celebrations, which, outside those for town saints, are the most important social affairs in the year.

This religious complex has both pre-Hispanic and Spanish origins, in the Aztec calpul and in 16th-century Spanish towns and neighborhoods. The coincidence of the two traditions has ensured that this function of the barrio is universal in Middle America, in both Indian and Mestizo communities (Redfield, 1928; Monzón, 1949; Foster, 1960a).

Esprit de Corps: Solidarity and Rivalry

The unity of the barrio as a territorial group is expressed not only in its functions but in repetitive aspects of social interaction within the barrio and between barrios.

Barrios tend to form unified factions in political struggles joining the same party (e.g., the Sayula war of the barrios of 1917, Guiteras Holmes, 1952a, pp. 112–13). During interpersonal conflict people tend to side with the party from their own barrio.

As the local communities were drawn into national political networks in Guatemala after the revolution of 1944, barrios sometimes became the bases for political party support, as in Magdalena Milpas Altas, where one barrio supported the government party and the other the opposition party (R. N. Adams, 1957b, p. 15). A great deal of pride is taken in the "efficacy" of the barrio saint versus the saints of the other barrios; during the fiestas all members of the barrio act as host to residents of other sections of the community. According to Beals (1945b, p. 33), the barrio is the rallying point for community feeling.

The other side of the same coin is the constant expressions of inter-barrio rivalry and hostility. Barrios divided communities during the Mexican revolution by siding with different agrarian and nonagrarian groups. They compete in the display of wealth and merrymaking during fiestas. They have nicknames and effigies of the residents of other barrios; witchcraft accusations, stonings, and personal fights during drunkenness are very likely to occur between members of different barrios;

TABLE 1—BARRIO TYPES

Administrative Status	Primary Political Control	System	Subsystem	Examples
Subdivision	Indian	Dual	Two barrios	Aguacatenango (Tzeltal) Atitlan (Mixe) Copala (Trique) Magdalena Milpas Altas (central Guatemala)
			Two sets or sections	Tepoztlan (Nahua) Yalalag (Zapotec) Huautla (Mazatec) Chamula (Tzotzil) Sayula, historically (Popoluca)
		Multiple		Sayula, at the present time (Popoluca)
	Mestizo	Dual		None
		Multiple		Mixtec barrio of Juxtlahuaca, Oaxaca Tzotzil barrios of San Bartolome, Chiapas
Dependency	Indian	Dual		Santa Cruz Etla, before it became independent of San Pablo Etla (Mixtec) San Antonio barrio (Tepelolutla)
		Multiple		
	Mestizo	Dual		None
		Multiple		Barrio Septimo of Tlaxiaco, Oaxaca (Mixtec) The Uapatzequa of historical times, Quiroga, Morelia, etc. (Tarascan)

competitions for efficiency in communal work are frequent between barrios; competitions during special holidays, such as Carnaval, between dance groups of *comparsas* (groups of men who sing or dance in costume) are widespread. In Chiapas the failure of crops may be frequently attributed to the sorcery of members of the opposite barrio. Sometimes the barrio struggle has taken on bloody proportions, amounting to small, community wars. The competition and hostility which are the daily expression of "segmentary" opposition (e.g., refusing to sell household products to members of other barrios) may also indicate real community conflict which may split the community, especially when it involves politics or land rights.

Traditionally, rivalry is just another expression of in-barrio esprit de corps. Rules such as the balance of power in the distribution of political posts keep hostility at a low level. In cases of conflict, it is likely that the lines of fission will follow the issues

267

which divide the community, and barrio antagonism acts as a safety valve. Barrios will be solidary, however, when external trouble threatens the whole community. Intra-community strife expresses barrio rivalry. In mixed ethnic communities barrios may represent different ethnic groups or economic interests; hence, during the Mexican revolution of 1920 Mestizo barrios supported the government while Indian barrios (especially those suffering from land shortage) became *agraristas*. This, however, cannot be considered basically a barrio characteristic, but rather a product of class and ethnic identity differences. In whole Indian towns, the social, political, and economic conditions of each barrio are very similar to those of other barrios in the community. Small differences between barrios may stem from degrees of acculturation (Tepoztlan—Redfield, 1930), a slight variation in wealth caused by the quality of the agricultural lands in the control of the particular barrio, or a tendency toward a concentration of specialists in one barrio (e.g., charcoal burners), but usually these minor variations do not create sufficient difference in interest to divide loyalties to the community of which they are a part.

The Indian barrio may be characterized as a community subdivision, with secondary political, economic, and religious functions, with a certain degree of internal solidarity, with rules of residence and/or endogamy regulating membership, and with an overall orientation towards the larger territorial or social unit which is the total community.

THE VILLAGE

The term *pueblo*, or village, represents not only the physical conglomerate of homesteads and public buildings but also the people who live there. This amalgamation of settlement and inhabitants occurs in the terminology of Spain (Pitt-Rivers, 1954) and of pre-Hispanic Middle America. The Zapotec of Yalalag use the single term *yež*

for the village conglomerate of houses and the human inhabitants (De la Fuente, 1949, pp. 209–10).

All municipios of Middle America include a *cabecera,* or head village, and some may include other villages. The cabecera is recognized by the national government as a civil administrative center, and by the Catholic Church hierarchy as a religious center. The Indians of some areas think of the cabecera not only as a civil and a religious center but as the hub of the world (M. Nash, 1953–54).

Early Spanish documents record the presence of towns throughout the Maya area. Landa (1938) indicates that the Maya of Yucatan were town dwellers. The Pokom-Maya-speaking people of northwestern Guatemala as a whole probably did not live in nucleated centers, but some lived in fortified settlements, the *tenamit* (Miles, 1957, pp. 751, 769). Vogt (1961, p. 139) argues that Zinacantan, which controlled five subject towns (Calnek, 1962, p. 5), represents the basic Maya settlement of a ceremonial center with scattered parajes. Robert M. Adams (1961), however, found in the same area many archaeological remains of nucleated settlements on hilltops, possibly occasioned by military uprisings and the need for fortified cities. Surveys of lowland Maya archaeological remains suggest that some of the supposed vacant towns were really large population aggregates (Willey, 1956a, p. 113). Where dispersed settlements existed, revolving residence of civil and religious officials provided a convenient integrative device (M. D. Coe, 1965, p. 112).

The Spanish policy of *reducciones* did not always draw the scattered rural population into new centers but sometimes into old ones. Large pre-Hispanic centers were found among the Totonacs (Kelly and Palerm, 1952, p. 33), the Tarascans (Tzintzuntzan—Foster, 1948a; Quiroga—Brand, 1951, p. 53), in the Cuchumatan mountain range of Guatemala (Jacalte-nango, San Miguel, and Santa Eulalia—LaFarge, 1947, p. 131), the Valley of Mexico (Carrasco, 1950b; Vaillant, 1941, pp. 1–12) and in the numerous small chiefdoms in the Mixtec-speaking area (Achiutla, Titaltongo, Tezacoalco—Aguirre Beltrán, 1954). The Zapotecs distinguished the old poblados of long standing, *yedsh-goēl*, from new ones of Spanish creation, *yedsh-kōb*. Schmieder (1930, p. 22) states that old poblados were in every way superordinate to the newly created centers, controlling more land and wealth, and having a "higher degree of civilization." Today old towns look down upon the new ones.

Other Indians, however, never had nucleated settlements until the Spaniards applied their policy of reducciones. The Mixe were congregated into villages only after 1600; since then the villages have become again vacant or semivacant ceremonial centers. Small settlements tend to be stable, but "like amoebae [they] divide and form new communities" (Schmieder, 1930, p. 71). The Mazatec also, at the time of Villa Rojas' study (1955), were mostly organized in vacant-town arrangements. People had two houses: one in their fields where they lived most of the year, and one in the center for holidays and other important occasions. Quintana Roo Indians live today in scattered villages which represent smaller population aggregates than their pre-Hispanic counterparts (Redfield, 1941).

In other cases, the Spaniards relocated their population in new settlements. Calnek (1962, p. 113) indicates that many highland Maya villages were formed by incorporating more than one pueblo into parcialidades or barrios of a single new one.

The village arrangement of a central plaza with public buildings from which extended a grid pattern of streets was a Spanish introduction (Foster, 1960a, pp. 34–49). These villages were created in an attempt by the colonial administration to facilitate control by the Church and State and to organize activities within the population (Jones, 1940, p. 145; Simpson, 1934; Villa Rojas, 1961, pp. 28–29; Wolf, 1955a). Wherever Spanish control was weak and wherever the reducciones did not fit the native pattern, the village organization failed to persist in its original or ideal form. Indians forced to come into villages were hard to hold (Miles, 1957, p. 751) and were decimated by epidemics and death (Kelly and Palerm, 1952, p. 8).

Some nucleated settlements succeeded as a stable territorial arrangement, becoming culturally and functionally integrated local units. These villages, with whatever landholdings they retained during the 17th and 18th centuries, formed the defensive territorial nucleus of the corporate peasant community of today (Wolf, 1955a). The persistence of these nuclear towns, even when they had no pre-Hispanic antecedents, must involve other factors than historical continuity. One such factor seems to have been the ecological potential of the immediate surrounding lands. The Maya of both Yucatan and highland Chiapas cluster around water holes or *cenotes* wherever these are the only supply of water (Chan Kom—Redfield, 1941). Larger nucleated settlements are made possible by irrigation ditches conducting streams from surrounding hills, as in Amatenango in the valley region of highland Chiapas (J. Nash, 1959b). This could have been accomplished in preconquest times, but another adjustment making for larger population concentrations—well-digging—was introduced by the Spanish (Redfield, 1941, p. 4).

Functions of the Pueblo

The pueblo is the locus of most social life and of all important community events within the municipio. The cabecera in the vacant ceremonial center, and the village in nucleated municipios, serve as the locus of

269

ceremonial, administrative, political, and economic functions of the municipio as a whole. The presence of a plaza, in some but not all towns, with cabildo, church, and market, marked the village as a political, religious, and economic center.

The village in Middle America tends to retain some rights over land. This is historically tied up with the grants of land given to the nucleated settlements created during the reducciones (Wolf, 1955a). In dispersed municipios, each village may have a traditional share of the agricultural plots granted to the municipio as a whole. Increasing population has led to constant lawsuits in national courts over boundaries of communal land earmarked for each village, strife which seems to have had pre-Hispanic antecedents (Caso, 1954, pp. 72–79).

Contention over land is at the core of the territorial organization of the corporate Indian communities because the basis of the corporations lay in the communally controlled land system. The fission and fusion of territorial units as communities are directly tied to the changes in agrarian law and the redistribution of lands by the state and national governments, affecting the relative share of Indians and of the finqueros or hacendados in the fertile land. Among the Zapotec, Schmieder (1930) mentioned two types of villages based on land rights: (1) villages having enough or more than enough land, which tend to be defensively organized against neighboring settlements, and (2) villages with little land, which tend to be expansive, constantly involved in presenting new claims over land through lawsuits, and encroaching on other villages' lands. Lawsuits over land are endemic in the village. For every Middle American community one can find historical or contemporary evidence of the land struggle in the Archivo General de la Nación in Mexico.

As a form of landholding corporation, the village contrasts not with the municipio but

with the hacienda (Wolf, 1962, ch. 10). Municipios and/or villages may have identical rights over communal lands, but, because most land titles following national independence and new ejido grants were reallocated for municipios, most villages in Mexico try to become legally defined as independent municipios. In this way, rights over land are reinforced by political control.

Concern over land rights is reflected in the treatment of land titles as sacred objects. They are never shown to strangers and are hidden or reluctantly disposed of when new titles nullify the legal value of previous ones. Emphasis is placed on the symbolic aspects of land rights and community integration where village boundaries are ceremonially visited, where the four cardinal directions are marked off by calvarios or crosses, and where caves on the borders of village land are said to be the dwelling places of the ancestral founders of the pueblo and the guardians of the village territory and villagers' morals. Other such symbolic boundaries may be water holes, or shrines placed in small hills (Vogt, 1961, pp. 32–38; Beals, 1945b, p. 91; Bevan, 1938; M. Nash, 1958a; Tumin, 1952, p. 38; Bunzel, 1952; Guiteras Holmes, 1961, p. 87; Wagley, 1949; Tax, 1946, p. 35).

It is rare to find a Middle American village without a church. The most important event of the year is the fiesta of the village patron saint. When the village is the cabecera of a municipio, the fiesta is also the most important event for the whole municipality. Even if there are other shrines or chapels in the municipio, the church of the head village is the largest and most imposing. In dispersed settlements, if the parajes are closely dependent on the cabecera, their own local saints may also be housed in the cabecera church (Wagley, 1949; Vogt, 1961; M. Nash, 1958a; LaFarge, 1947).

In those municipios which have a visiting or a resident priest, the church draws reg-

270

ular attendance at weekly Masses. The rockets, church ornaments, and marimba, violin, or chirimía music which accompanies either occasional or regular gatherings give to the center the reputation of being gay and sophisticated, whereas smaller local groups are pitied by both town residents and themselves as leading a dull life.

The center as the locus of religious life is the stage on which the ceremonies marking life crises or communal fiestas are enacted. The streets surrounding the plaza are the reference points for regularly staged rituals such as processions, for races, or for funeral marches. These special shrines and sacred places adjacent to the plaza stimulate the traffic from scattered hamlets to the center.[7]

The center is host not only to ceremonial visits from the parajes in some towns but also to visits from saints of neighboring towns. Zinacantan's central church receives visits from saints of three neighboring towns, thus preserving a ritual link which reinforces the trading pattern (Vogt, 1961, p. 140).

The town as a civil and religious center stimulates the kind of traffic which makes it a natural location for a market. Mass days and fiesta days are always good days for markets, and the market is an added incentive for attending the fiesta. During these times law cases from the hinterland may be brought into the cabecera, to be dealt with by the ayuntamiento officers.

When the village is not a head town, its

functions are the same except that they are performed for the benefit of the residents and do not integrate the surrounding local units. Thus small villages which are not cabeceras may have smaller and less visited fiestas, and the local government does not deal with cases from outside the village unless complaints are brought against village members.

In the corporate villages most legal cases are handled by local village officials. It is a characteristic of all the local units of Middle America that they tend to keep the regulation of crime or conflict within bounds through settlement by the local authorities. It is only in unresolved or unsatisfactorily settled local cases that the inhabitants may resort to the jurisdictional powers of a larger territory and a more powerful set of officials.

One of the means by which distinctive village character and control over communal resources is maintained is the high degree of endogamy. This is true of other smaller territorial units, except those composed of localized exogamous descent-groups, but endogamy is more clearly associated with a village than with any of the smaller units. Even non-Indian towns in Middle America tend to be highly endogamous.

Sentiment of Identity

From cradle to grave the Indian is tied to his village by a series of life-crisis rituals. A child is identified with his local settlement physically from the moment he is born and spiritually from the moment he is baptized or given a name in a native ceremony. A pregnant woman, if for some reason far from her village, makes every attempt to return home before the birth of her child, and will return at the first opportunity if the child should be born before term. It is felt that the danger of soul-loss is far greater for the newborn away from his home village (Amatenango—J. Nash, 1959b).

Baptism establishes the child's position

[7] In Cantel the entire village becomes a stage for the re-enactment of the Passion of Easter week. The Last Supper takes place in the calvario, the "Judios" seek the Lord in local bars and, on finally catching him, put him in jail. At a certain spot before the cabildo the cross is raised and the image of Jesus is crucified. On Easter Sunday the stations of the cross are marked out in the plaza, and the story of the ordeal of Jesus and his suffering at each place is recounted by a prayermaker (M. Nash, 1958a). In Chamula the plaza before the church is sanctified ground, and crosses mark the observation of certain repeated rituals (Pozas, 1959a).

271

as a member of the community. Until baptized, the child is not shown to any stranger outside the nuclear household, but at the baptismal ceremony he is revealed to godparents, relatives, and friends of his parents.

During any serious sickness the Indians away from their pueblo try to return, either to effect a cure there where they feel they can regain their health more quickly, or to be buried in familiar surroundings where their soul will not wander. In Tenejapa, where baptism is not practiced, return to the village is linked with the three-day ceremony after birth when the child is tied to the earth, and at death when the ceremony ensures that the earth will receive the soul back. The earth is personified as the Holy Earth which watches over each member of the community, and so in sickness the Indian returns to receive this protection (Medina, 1961–62). In the fincas of Ocosingo there is a "sickness" called the "rejection of the earth" (*rechazo de la tierra,* or *bal luminal* in Tzeltal), which attacks people who say that they are going to a particular territory to found a new village and then fail to (Montagu, 1960–61). Lewis has reported (1957, p. 243) that even the urbanized Tepoztecas return from Mexico City to their village during extreme illness.

Along with drawing the living population together in nucleated centers, the Spaniards created communal cemetery plots. The preconquest pattern was probably similar to that surviving in Oxchuc, where there are patrilineal, patrilocal name-groups located in parajes and where members of the lineage are buried (Villa Rojas, 1946).

The cemetery is an important index to community sentiment; burial in a community-wide cemetery, typical of nucleated settlements, points to the cohesiveness of the community. In dispersed settlements the paraje may have its own cemetery or there may be family burial plots (Chanal, Oxchuc, Quintana Roo) or the dead may even be buried in the house (Tenejapa).

The *panteón* is the locus of a yearly ceremony on the Day of the Dead in homage of the deceased inhabitants of the settlement.

The community of the dead is in some villages a re-creation of the community of the living, as in Amatenango (J. Nash, 1960b). Here the graves of the principales are placed in the center, around a large cross, their position symbolic of the location of the ayuntamiento in the center of the village. Around this center people are buried according to the barrio or paraje in which they had lived, here in the cemetery oriented in the same compass directions. Neighborhood clusters are recognized within these larger territorial groups, so one is buried near all the people with whom one had lived. This put the soul at rest so that it was not forever bothering the community of the living by trying to return to familiar territory.

MUNICIPIO

The municipio has emerged as the most significant territorial group since its definition, by Tax (1937), as the unit of ethnographic investigation and as the outermost limit of community sentiment and cultural homogeneity. Dialectical boundaries,[8] costume, and endogamy regulations coincide with municipal limits. The Indian is conscious of the unity and uniqueness of his municipio. Tax (1937) originally pointed this out for the western highlands of Guatemala; since then, the same observation has been made for most of the Indian communities of Mexico (Aguirre Beltrán, 1953). The municipio has been defined as the "functional resource unit" for the Indian (Lewis, 1960, p. 46), and its economic, political, and religious functions have been spelled out.

[8] Dialectic markers are extremely important in that they are congruent with municipio and community boundaries. Among the Mazatec there are 23 municipios corresponding with 23 dialect areas.

Although boundaries of other minor territorial groups may be vague or changing, municipal limits are clearly established. Tax observed that in vacant-town municipios it is the outermost borders that are significant, whereas in nucleated municipios it is the boundaries of the center, or cabecera.

Whether the strongest sentiment of belonging is focused on the municipio or on smaller territories—pueblo, paraje, aldea, or barrio—depends on certain variables: (1) the history of the community in postconquest times, especially in relation to political autonomy and corporate rights over land, and whether or not there is continuity with preconquest territorial and social groups; (2) the settlement pattern: in municipios with a vacant-town ceremonial center the focus of primary attachment may be the local hamlet; in municipios coincident with a nucleated pueblo, the pueblo itself, rather than outlying rural settlements, may be the locus of community identity; (3) ethnic diversity: if there is a large Mestizo population living in the municipio controlling the affairs in the cabecera, the Indians may withdraw from the center and strongly identify with their local settlement, multiplying the functions of their local officials. Hence, although the Ayuntamiento Constitucional in Mexico is the governing body of a municipio, Indian villages within a municipio controlled by Mestizos may maintain their own unofficial ayuntamiento (Gillin, 1951; Tax, 1937).

Tax (1937) spelled out for the western highlands of Guatemala the two major types of municipio organization based on settlement pattern and functional distinction: (1) the vacant political and religious center with a scattered rural population, and (2) the nucleated residential center. A third type represents a mixture of these. Borhegyi (1956a) introduced the added criterion of historical origin, and subdivided Tax's first type into municipios with a functioning ceremonial center in pre-Hispanic times and municipios with a center defined by a plaza but existing only as a creation of Spanish administrative efforts.

The territorial arrangement in small ethnic units and *señoríos* is an ancient preconquest pattern (Villa Rojas, 1955; Lewis, 1960, p. 46; Carrasco, 1950b, p. 106). The dialect differences between many municipios had been developed long before the municipio as a unit was officially recognized (McQuown, 1959). Sometimes, such independent señoríos or ethnic units were granted as *encomiendas* and after independence became independent municipios (Villa Rojas, 1955).

Political Functions

As administrative units of the national government, the municipio and its subdivisions—pueblo, paraje, aldea, colonia, barrio, and cantón—are comparable units. The degree of autonomy and internal cohesion of these subdivisions, however, varies from region to region and even from town to town in the same region. The effectiveness of the civil authority in administering the internal affairs of the municipio depends on (1) the amount of competition of other local authorities, e.g., aged leaders of the patrilineal group, or principales of the aldeas or parajes; and (2) the proportion of Indians to Ladinos. When the center has a greater number of Ladinos, the Indians turn to the aldea or paraje officials to settle differences between Indians; the Ladino officials of the center are resorted to only in Ladino vs. Indian disputes (Tumin, 1952, p. 150; Wisdom, 1940, p. 235).

In the western highlands of Guatemala the political community is coincident with the municipio (Wagley, 1949; Tax, 1937; M. Nash, 1958a), but in the eastern highlands, in the Chorti area, the aldea emerges as a significant and in many respects an independent unit (Wisdom, 1940). In some of the municipios of the Chiapas highlands of Mexico the paraje competes with the center in many of the social control

273

functions as well as in ceremonial affairs and lineage activities (Villa Rojas, 1946). A few of the municipios contain intrusive populations which exist apart in aldeas, colonias, or rancherías. In some municipios there is a head town with smaller villages around it (Villa Rojas, 1955); in others there is a division in sections represented by councilmen (e.g., Contla—Nutini, 1961). Among the Tarascans subdivisions vary according to size, from villas to rancherías, and include enclaves of haciendas or private ranchos (Brand, 1951).

The municipio may be equivalent to one village or to a large territory composed of loosely structured subunits such as parajes and a ceremonial center (Tenejapa—Medina, 1961–62; Mixe—Beals, 1945b). From the national point of view, municipios of Mexico are distinguished from other territorial units by the size of their population and their degree of administrative independence (Caso and Parra, 1950). From the native point of view, the municipio is the outermost limit of ethnic identity, and any territorial unit which forms a community, such as barrio or pueblo, may aspire to become an independent municipio. Whether or not they do depends on local conditions, average size of the municipio in a particular state, restrictions of the national government on size of population necessary to acquire such status, and the kind of land interests involved.

The independence of the municipio and the local and territorial units formed by Indians are directly related to proximity to national centers of political and economic control, and to the degree of acculturation which increases the needs for goods and forms of organization of capital and labor which come from outside the traditional Indian system. In Tepoztlan local independence of the traditional municipio system broke down with the revolution and the opening of the road, coupled with the entering of Tepoztlan people into the na-

tional market. The same was true for Sayula (Guiteras Holmes, 1952a, p. 120) and Yalalag (De la Fuente, 1949, p. 254) in relation to Villa Alta. The Sayula municipio of today is tied up with the nation directly through the regional political figures. The municipio is politically and economically subordinate to the nation. Schools and electricity are considered "presents" from the governor or the president. Guiteras Holmes (1952a) points out that the political destiny of Sayula is decided outside the municipio by state political leaders.

The Municipio as a Landholding Unit

Communally-held land is an ancient tradition in Middle America, and the persistence of communal landholding has made possible the survival of the corporate Indian community as a more or less independent economic unit. Although rights of usufruct of particular parcels may have been given to householders, among the Maya of Yucatan and the Aztec the land was primarily controlled by the authorities of the village or the calpul, and the ultimate distribution of parcels was conditional on the approval of such authorities. Nobles of the Yucatan provinces held parcels which were cultivated by commoners in return for services (Roys, 1957, pp. 8–10), or because they represented religious brotherhoods or military organizations or officerholders (McBride, 1923, p. 116). Otherwise, although fruit trees, cacao groves, or maize crops were privately owned, the land itself could be held individually only for as long as it was cultivated by the man who had permission to plant there. When a man had no heirs to his rights, the land reverted to the territorial unit which controlled its distribution.

Communal landholdings by town were also an old Castillian trait, and as the Spaniards moved into the New World they extended their own system of *propios, ejido, pastos comunes,* and *montes* into the old communal lands of the pre-Hispanic communities (McBride, 1923, pp. 104–23; Simpson, 1934, pp. 3–42). The new pattern thus fitted in with the old concept of communal landholding and contributed to the preservation of the community and to its permanence and identity during the colonial period by providing an economic base for the Indians. Wherever communal lands were lost because of Spanish or Creole expropriation, so was the collectivized settlement with its political and administrative nucleus, as happened among the Totonac (Kelly and Palerm, 1952, p. 46). The same occurred whenever the land became part of the haciendas, in which case the Indian community became a dependent population within the haciendas (Zavala and Miranda, 1954; Wolf and Mintz, 1957). Where tribal forms of political relations were retained, as in Quintana Roo, the Indians did not think of owning the land in terms of having titles, such as in the nucleated villages and municipios, but they did persist in claiming their rights over the territory adjacent to their settlements, by virtue of their residence there (Redfield, 1941, p. 53). The desire to attain municipio status is tied to the desire for independent control of agricultural lands. This has been solved in some cases by the community becoming an ejido rather than a municipio. Among the Tarascans the old established corporate communities, which had their own land, had no interest in the revolution of 1920, whereas the hacienda Indians participated very actively in the agrarian wars and later became ejidos (Carrasco, 1952b).

These communal landholdings and ejidos made possible organization of the municipio as a self-sufficient economic unit, and ensured the preservation of the civil-religious hierarchy which controlled its ultimate disposal. In many Chiapas settlements the ejido redistribution provided for an allocation of lands in both highlands and lowlands for the same municipio, thus expanding the range of crops and making possible two harvest periods so that the community could depend on its own crop production (Hunt, 1962).

Even when land is not communally owned, and the ejido functions in agreement with the agrarian laws and not with the traditional Indian system of land distribution and usufruct, municipio lands are ritually united under the patron saint, who is said to be the protector of the municipal territory. Maintenance of traditional agricultural ritual ties the Indians to the civil-religious hierarchy.

Religious Functions of the Municipio

The municipio is not only an administrative local unit but also a single religious community under the guardianship of the patron saint. A series of lesser saints are the responsibility of the religious cofradías. These saints and the Holy Family are thought of as local personages (M. Nash, 1958a; Tax, 1946; Wagley, 1949). They protect the crops, property, and life of the residents, but just for their own municipio. When Indians leave their municipio, they ask for the protection of the saints in their travels (Hunt, 1962; Wagley, 1949). Foreign Indians who rent agricultural lands outside their municipio give a contribution to the patron saint of that municipio, since whatever crop they harvest is thought to be due to his good graces (Panajachel—Tax, 1946). The relationship between Indians and patron saint is more formalized than that between the family and its saint because of the symbolic status of the former in the community as a whole (Wisdom, 1940, p. 417).

The municipio may also have its "native" guardians (i.e., other than Catholic saints), such as owners of the mountains, which are said to watch over municipio welfare. These may be identified with natural phenomena, cultural heroes, or historical persons. The older men of the municipio who form part of the principales' council, or local shamans and curers, perform ritual to these guardians (Hunt, 1962; LaFarge and Byers, 1931, p. 149; Oakes, 1951, p. 58; LaFarge, 1947; Redfield, 1941; Wagley, 1949, p. 85; Tax, 1946). Such guardians may be given a role in the civil-religious hierarchy and occupy a named office such as that of the dzunubiles (Oxchuc—Villa Rojas, 1946).

Whether pagan deities or Catholic deities represent the community as a whole depends on the level of acculturation of the municipio. Beals (1945b, p. 84) has said that the Catholic ritual is the major concrete expression of community cohesiveness among the Mixe, and the pagan ritual centers about a number of sacred shrines which are not community-wide. Guiteras Holmes (1961, p. 94), on the contrary, notes that in the highland Chiapas community of San Pedro Chenalho the pagan ritual is for the community and the saint's ritual is for the individual and household. In most cases, however, there has been a syncretistic identification between saints and other native spiritual powers, and the dichotomy is not a native distinction.

The sense of unity for the municipio as a religious unit is reinforced by a series of ceremonies occurring regularly in the annual cycle of events. All Middle American Indian communities observe the fiesta of the patron saint. The annual fiesta is an event for which members of the municipio who have left to work on the finca or for some other purpose try to return. Other fiestas such as Carnaval, Santa Cruz, or particular saints other than the patron associated with the municipio, also provide such occasions.

REGIONAL INTEGRATION

Relationships beyond the municipio are mediated through participation of the Indian in governing administrative centers, regional markets and ceremonial centers, and through the Mestizoized "cultural

brokers" between the Indian community and the nation (Wolf, 1956). The social insulation characteristic of the Indians' interaction with Ladinos or foreign Indians limits the effect of these centers on acculturation or social change (Reina, 1960, p. 102; Tax, 1941; Tumin, 1952, p. 51). Specialization of production by communities has created some regional trade areas with focal market centers, but there is no pan-Indian political organization linking towns together. As Gillin (1951, p. 197) has pointed out, "The Indian universe is spatially limited and its horizon typically does not extend beyond the limits of the local community or region."

The primary area where there was strong preconquest regional integration was the Aztec. The Aztecs welded an "empire" out of the original three-cities coalition, extending from the Grijalva River to the Tarascan area, and governed it for over 50 years before the Spaniards arrived. Large urban areas such as Teotihuacan must have demanded a unified hinterland to support a concentrated population in previous periods.

During the colonial and independent periods, the region lost some of its importance, and the strong corporate village, with an inward orientation, developed as the typical social unit (Wolf, 1962). Regional interaction is hindered by mistrust, rivalry, and hostility between communities, competition about land in particular, and also by a desire for noninterference which protects the community interest against the outside world at large. Some of these phenomena are the result of historical events; some, of the nature of the corporate community (Gibson, 1955; Wolf, 1955a, 1957, 1962). Even under these conditions, regions can be distinguished as territorial units of interaction, especially if they coincide with ethnic and linguistic boundaries.

The region is integrated primarily in the economic realm through internal market systems, based on exchange between municipios having specialized products. It is in specialization in crops and handcrafts that some division of labor between municipios exists.

The degree of economic integration varies from the midwestern highlands of Guatemala, where there is a developed solar market system based on crop and handcraft specialization, to the Chiapas highlands, where there is some specialization but also market exchanges through Ladino centers, except for pueblos on the border of Tenejapa and nonmarket trading between Indians, to Yucatan, where both crop and handcraft specialization is lacking. Specialization alone does not make for regional integration. In Yucatan specialization in cash crops raised for a national or international market does not serve to integrate the region and may even add to the isolation of the villages.

Despite these exchanges, there are no regional economic organizations. De la Fuente (1949) indicates that intervillage hostility, based on competition over the same market, stops the formation of regional cooperative institutions. Among the Zapotec, attempts to form an *ixtle* cooperative for the region, including Yalalag, failed on the basis of such competition. Wolf (1957, pp. 5–6) has pointed to the function of such "local centrism" in preserving community identity.

In regional trading the identity of the town is reinforced rather than broken down. First, a space is marked out in the market place for Indians of the same town or municipio, regardless of the product they are selling (De la Fuente, 1949; Beals, 1945b, p. 123; Marroquín, 1954 [description of the Juarez market]; Reina, 1960). Second, Indians of the same town or municipio may be taxed as a group (Marroquín, 1954). Third, the seller's costume brands the item being sold.

Some municipios and towns of the Chiapas highlands have attempted to preserve their independence from a regional market by acquiring ejido land grants at a lower altitude, where they can grow a second crop of corn which will yield a harvest at a time when the supply grown in their own milpas is ordinarily exhausted (Amatenango, Aguacatenango).

Other forms of economic interaction outside the market are primarily concerned with labor exchanges. The Zapotec sometimes transact *gozonas* (labor exchanges) between villages, but even if it is for communal benefit (such as building a hospital for the region), the Indians may refuse to participate if the work is outside their own village. Yalalag has carried on gozonas with many neighboring towns, but only with those inhabited by Zapotec-speakers. The most common gozona consists in the exchange of musicians for fiestas, but it has no official or economic importance. Such intermunicipio exchanges are rare, but all Indians have contact with Indians of other municipios in the fincas where they work and live together (Tax, 1941, p. 30).

Negative economic relations take the form of economic blockades between antagonistic villages. The Zapotec and the Chinantec do not sell their products to villages which have had land fights with them (Bevan, 1938, p. 20).

Noneconomic Regional Ties

Neighboring towns are tied together by a number of interchanges which are not primarily economic. These may grow out of and reinforce the ties stemming from economic exchanges. Vogt (1961, pp. 139–40) has pointed out that regional pilgrimages in Chiapas between the lowland neighboring towns of San Lucas, Ixtapa, and Salinas with highland municipios such as Zinacantan follow the exchange of goods specialized in the different ecological zones. Guiteras Holmes (1961, pp. 18, 19) states that in Chenalho healing and witchcraft dealings develop in the wake of long-established trading relations. Amatenangueros seek diviners outside the local

277

community in the lowlands, where they go to work in the fincas and to exchange their pots for lowland fruits, textiles, and other products. These trading centers are often the source for Ladino compadres of baptism between established patron-client relations (Guiteras Holmes, 1961, pp. 18, 19; J. Nash, 1960b; Hunt in McQuown, 1959).

Belief in the talking saints, which in the latter part of the 19th century were a powerful force in linking the Indian municipios of Chiapas in a movement to overwhelm the Spanish oppression, exists today and stimulates visits to the villages in which they reside. Their power is limited to influencing personal, not political, decisions and to divining answers to the questions put to them. Certain special religious figures in Guatemala, such as the Black Christ of Esquipulas and the esoteric cult figures of Judas, draw both Indians and Ladinos from the farthest limits of the nation on their fiesta days.

Regional fiestas are set throughout the calendar year so that nearby towns do not have their fiestas on the same day and can be visited by the inhabitants of other villages or municipios. Villagers travel to consult diviners. They take advantage of religious peregrinations to combine worship and economic exchange in the fiesta market. These religious markets are thus arranged in a cyclical calendar which moves throughout the region, in a manner similar to the *tianguis*, or weekly cyclical market of the Mixtec and Nahua (Marroquín, 1954).

Fiesta peregrination may be individual or may be formalized between villages. Some of the Tarascan towns send delegations carrying their own saints to visit other saints in their towns (Mendieta y Núñez, n.d., p. 163). Dancers and other religious officials may also be sent in delegation.

Interchanges between communities which are not politically or administratively dependent on each other are rare. They may come about in the search for lost cattle or delinquents, but this kind of communication usually occurs through state or federal agencies. Most land disputes are not carried on directly between villages or municipios, but between intermediaries of the national government. Regional wars of limited extension have occasionally resulted from unresolved land disputes. Mixe and Zapotec fought along ethnic lines in the 16th century (Beals, 1945b, p. 18), and towns which owned land *de mancomún* carried on warfare against each other (Schmieder, 1930, p. 68). This was true among the Tarascans during the 1920 revolution and other parts of Mexico (Carrasco, 1950b). In most cases, however, land disputs are handled by specialized state and federal agents.

To what extent the Indians themselves recognize the existence of a region is difficult to determine. The Zapotec have a name for themselves as an ethnic group, another for their village community, but no name for the region (De la Fuente, 1949). The Chinantec distinguish two regions of Chinantec-speakers, the Valle Nacional *(hu-me)* and the region of Cohapam *(wah-mi)* (Bevan, 1938, p. 5). In most cases the evidence is lacking; in others it tends to indicate that the Indians recognize, outside their own community, only the boundaries of common language or those imposed by the state, whose functioning they do not clearly understand.

The regional territorial units such as the Distrito de Oaxaca may be named only by the national government and be ignored in terms of Indian social organization. Such political and administrative subdivisions uniting regions have little or no significance for the Indian, because they are arbitrarily imposed from the outside.

The lack of data which hinders our understanding of regional integration results from our focus on the community as a unit of study, the ethnographer following the limits of the Indian world view. Mc-

Bryde (1947) called for studies of ecological regions, and Palerm (1956) stressed the need for regional studies. But from the existing data, it is evident that Middle America has a low regional integration. Specialization and market exchange have produced high integration in only a few areas. Even in areas where specialization exists, production is a function of internal needs rather than extra-municipio market demands.

Conclusion

In Middle America we find that the sentiment of community is intimately tied to occupation of a defined territory. All territorial units recognized by the Indians serve to define some sense of community identity, but this depends primarily on historical and demographic factors, the extent to which the territory is coterminous with extra-familial kin groups, the degree of political autonomy of the social group, and the ethnic composition. The municipio is consistently recognized as the outermost limit of this sense of belonging.

Relationships and social groupings in territorial units within the municipio vary according to the size of the group and the settlement pattern. The size of the territorial unit seems to affect social relationship in several ways: the smaller the group, starting with the household, the higher the intensity of interaction; reciprocal expections are implicit rather than stated, and obligations of long standing are permitted; the sanctioning system functions through consensus, social ostracism, and witchcraft.[9] The larger the local group, the lower is the degree of interaction between members; reciprocal expectations are explicit

and short-term or of definitely stated duration; and the sanctioning system relies more on external than internal social control mechanisms.

Within the municipio, specialization of production and exchange is limited to those municipios in which extremes of altitude affect the maturing of crops and make for crop diversity (Santiago Chimaltenango, Chorti). Households, parajes, and barrios reflect the same form and function in the ritual, political, economic, and social life of the Indians.

The lack of a division of labor among units in the municipio produces a system of territorial subdivisions based on mechanical solidarity. The equivalence of these local units is expressed in the local governing body or bodies when equal representation is accorded to each side of a dual division or in the democratic principle of succession to office of all household heads of the community.

The democratic principle in the political hierarchy imposes a maximum population size on the municipio for efficiency of operation. Sometimes this has resulted in a tendency for smaller territorial units within the community to separate and acquire independent political status, as in the parajes of Zinacantan and barrios of the Mixtec. To control the process of fission, several devices have been invented: (1) an increase in the number of offices available through development of new cofradías or new posts in the ayuntamiento; (2) elaboration of barrio or paraje offices to create local positions for those left out of the cabecera posts; (3) monopoly of offices by a group of elite families, a solution possible only when there are marked wealth differences in the population or where the local government is controlled by a cacique.

If, on the other hand, there is a reduction of the size of the town by epidemic or emigration, the existing political structure may make too many demands on the reduced

---

[9] Lewis (1960, pp. 40–41) indicates that identification, pride of in-group, feeling, knowledge of the unit geographically and in terms of its functioning, and interaction rates move in inverse ratio with the size of the unit. Hence, the smaller the local unit is, the more clear its functions and the identification of its members with it.

population, resulting in impoverishment and loss of land, as in San Antonio Palopo (Tax, 1937, p. 41). For such population decrease or for economic impoverishment, two remedies have been worked out: (1) reduction in the scale of celebrations and cargos around certain cofradías, thus creating a kind of hierarchy of cofradías based on elaborateness of ritual (Panajachel—Tax, 1946); here the duty to the town can be fulfilled by poorer members of the community serving in lesser cofradías which do not require as great an expenditure of money; (2) reduction in the number of cofradías, as in Cantel, which lost some of its cofradías during the depression (M. Nash, 1953–54).

Community solidarity is expressed in symbols and rituals centering around the church in the Catholic cycle of saint's fiestas and around sacred natural sites in the hills, caves, and water holes in the cycle of agricultural rituals. These rituals may be duplicated in all the territorial units within the municipio. Titles establishing municipios, maps, and grants are treated as sacred objects, and the boundaries of the community may be ritually visited in annual celebrations.

Solidarity within the community may be expressed in rivalries over land and in competition in fiestas with neighboring communities, in cultural trait and dialect differentiation, in endogamous restrictions on marriage, and in refusal to permit the sale of land to outsiders. The existence of such factors and their effect on internal cohesion vary from region to region in Middle America. Segmentary opposition of territorial units is found in dual barrio organization, an opposition built into the political and religious administration.

The status of the municipio as a landholding unit has been the basis for its organization and its survival as an independent political and economic unit, and has set in motion the processes of fission which have characterized the history of

community organization in Middle America.

Relationships beyond the municipio are qualitatively different from those of the territorial units within the municipio. The "division of labor" between municipios with specialization in crops or handcrafts, trade within a regional market system, and the ancillary activities which come in the wake of these have made for a sort of organic unity. Regional integration ranges from the high interaction in a solar market system of the midwestern highlands of Guatemala and Tlaxiaco to the low degree of exchange in Yucatan. The degree depends on municipal specialization, which is a function of ecological variation within an area resulting in crop specialization, on the tradition of handcraft specialization passed on in household production from father to son or from mother to daughter within the same community, and on the type of market system developed within an area.

Economic specialization has not resulted in economic or political organizations of Indians beyond the municipio. The few services the Indians seek outside their local group are a supplement rather than a complement to what they find within. Market centers, except in the midwestern highlands of Guatemala, are Ladino- or Mestizo-dominated economic units, and the Indian pattern seems to be a rotating trade circuit between equivalent trading towns.

The communities of Middle America usually control a definite territory over which they have exclusive corporate rights maintained through semi-autonomous political bodies recognized as legal representatives in state and national levels of political control. Territorial and local units smaller than the community are either subdivisions of the community with ritual and/or political functions or dependencies which form separate enclaves. The subdivisions are tied to the municipio through the civil and religious hierarchy with political power distributed among them. The dependencies, on the other hand, do not participate directly in the civil and religious organization and are usually subordinate in social and political activities. In preconquest times the kinship units were linked to territorial units through ownership of agricultural lands by clans and lineages. These kinship groups have given way to exclusively territorial units as the basic building blocks in the social structure in most areas.

REFERENCES

Adams, R. M., 1961
Adams, R. N., 1957a, 1957b
Aguirre Beltrán, 1953, 1954
—— and Pozas, 1954
Bailey, 1958
Bandelier, 1880a, 1880b
Beals, 1945b
Bevan, 1938
Borhegyi, 1956a
Brand, 1951
Bunzel, 1952
Calnek, 1961, 1962
Cámara Barbachano, 1952a
Cancian, Frank, 1964, 1965
Carrasco, 1950b, 1952b
Caso, 1954
—— and Parra, 1950
Chávez Orozco, 1943
Coe, M. D., 1965
Cowan, G. M., 1954
De la Fuente, 1948, 1949
Díaz de Salas, 1960–61
Felipe Segundo, 1573
Foster, 1942, 1948a, 1960a
Gay, 1881
Gibson, 1955
Gillin, 1951
Goubaud Carrera, Rosales, and Tax, 1947
Guiteras Holmes, 1947, 1951, 1952a, 1961
Hansen, 1934
Hermitte, 1958–60
Hotchkiss, 1960–61
Howenstine, 1963
Hunt, 1962, 1963
Instituto Nacional Indigenista, Memoirs
Jones, 1940
Kelly and Palerm, 1952
Kirchhoff, 1955
Krickeberg, 1918
LaFarge, 1947
—— and Byers, 1931
Landa, 1938
Lewis, 1957, 1960
McBride, 1923
McBryde, 1947

MacIver and Page, 1949
McQuown, 1959
Malinowski and De la Fuente, 1957
Marroquín, 1954, 1956
Medina, 1961, 1961–62
Mendieta y Núñez, n.d.
Mendizabal, 1928
Metzger, D., n.d.
Miles, 1957
Miller, F. C., 1959a
Mintz and Wolf, 1950
Montagu, 1959, 1960–61
Monzón, 1947, 1949
Murdock, 1949
Nash, J., 1959b, 1960b
Nash, M., 1953–54, 1958a, 1961
Nutini, 1961
Oakes, 1951
Olson, 1933
Palerm, 1956
Pitt-Rivers, 1954, 1963
Plancarte, 1954
Pozas, 1959a
Radin, 1920
Redfield, 1928, 1930, 1940, 1941, 1960
—— and Villa Rojas, 1934
Reina, 1960
Relación de las Ceremonias y Ritos, 1869
Reyes, 1963
Romney, 1957
—— and Romney, 1963
Roys, 1957
Schmieder, 1930
Silvert, 1954
Simpson, 1934
Siverts, 1960, 1964
Soustelle, J., 1935b
Stanslawski, 1950
Starr, B. W., 1954
Tax, 1937, 1941, 1946, 1947a, 1950, 1952c, 1953, 1957b
Tumin, 1952
Vaillant, 1941
Villa Rojas, 1946, 1955, 1961
Vogt, 1961

Wagley, 1941, 1949
Waterman, 1917
Weitlaner and Castro, 1954
—— and Verbitsky, 1956
Willey, 1956a, 1956b

Wisdom, 1940, 1952
Wolf, 1955a, 1956, 1957, 1962
—— and Mintz, 1957
Zabala Cubillos, 1961
Zavala and Miranda, 1954

14. Political and Religious Organizations

FRANK CANCIAN

THE CHARACTERISTIC politico-religious institution in Middle American Indian communities is the civil-religious hierarchy. It is a system in which adult males serve in a series of hierarchically arranged offices devoted to both political and ceremonial aspects of community life. This institution, the core of a community-wide social structure, has received notice from almost every ethnographer who has reported on this area. In general I shall not attempt to credit the author who first published a specific interpretation, but a number of general articles deserve mention. Tax (1937) set down guidelines for the study of the hierarchy in his treatment of the Guatemala midwestern highland system. Cámara (1952c, p. 143) distinguished communities that are "traditional, homogeneous, collectivistic, well integrated" and have obligatory service in political and religious offices (centripetal organization) from communities that are "changing, heterogeneous, weakly integrated" and have voluntary service (centrifugal organization). The centrifugal community is the more Ladinoized. The centripetal, or conservative, community is my principal concern here. Wolf includes such communities in his general typology of Latin American peasantries (1955b), and specifically compares them with similar "closed corporate" communities in Java (1957). M. Nash (1958b) interprets more fully those features of the hierarchy which tend to maintain the closed character of Guatemalan Indian communities.

Carrasco (1961) has added an important historical dimension to the interpretations. Other valuable material on Spanish and native elements in present-day hierarchies comes from Carrasco (1952b) and G. M. Foster (1960a). Vogt (1961 and 1963) has offered hypotheses about the organization of ancient Maya society based on his analysis of modern cases; I have used similar reasoning to make alternative suggestions (1964). In the following discussion I am concerned with the 20th-century forms of the hierarchy.

This article is divided into three parts: (1) a general picture of the civil-religious hierarchy, focusing on the prototypical form in conservative communities and variations within this form; (2) a review of the interpretations of the functions (conse-

283

quences) of the traditional hierarchy in the Indian community, and proposals for modifying these interpretations; (3) the breakdown of the traditional form, and the changes that take place as Indian communities move into the national cultures of Mexico and Guatemala.[1]

CIVIL-RELIGIOUS HIERARCHY

The basic features of the civil-religious hierarchy are summarized in many places (Tax, 1937, pp. 442–44; M. Nash, 1958b, p. 67; Carrasco, 1961, p. 483). It consists of ranked offices taken for one-year terms by the men of the community. The offices are ranked in two ways: first, they are arranged in levels of service, whereby a man must serve on the first level before he is eligible for service on the second level, and so on; second, authority tends to be concentrated in the top levels, making a hierarchy of authority as well as a hierarchy of service. It is often called the "ladder" system.

The individual office is called a *cargo*. It is customary for a man to have what might be called a cargo "career." He begins with a low office, usually before he is married, and, with years of rest between terms of service, occupies a number of offices during his lifetime. Those who pass through all the levels of the hierarchy become the elders, or *principales,* of the community. They are usually exempt from taxes and communal work, and have great influence in community decision-making.

The hierarchy usually includes offices from both the civil or political and the religious or ceremonial sides of community life. As traditionally conceived by Middle Americanists, progress through the hierarchy involves some alternation between the civil and the religious sides as the indi-

vidual develops his career. Characteristically, there are only one or two offices at the top, many at the bottom, giving the hierarchy a pyramid shape. All the men of a community are expected to serve in the hierarchy, at least at the bottom level; social pressure on those who hesitate is great. Service is without pay and, in religious cargos, may involve very substantial expenditures by the incumbent.

In communities with *barrios* or other local subdivisions, officials are often chosen so as to distribute them evenly over these subdivisions.

This summary is only an approximation. Regarding the midwestern highlands of Guatemala, Tax (1937, p. 443) pointed out that, "There are almost as many variations . . . as there are municipios. . . ." Economic and demographic factors, actions of Mexican and Guatemalan governments, and a conglomeration of events which now must be called historical accident have produced many variations on the basic pattern.

References to sources describing some of these variations are given in the text below. General sources are discussed in the Appendix, where there is also a tabulation of traits as distributed over eight communities.

Civil and Religious Sides of the Hierarchy

In many communities natives do not distinguish civil and religious offices when discussing service to the community. This is a distinction made by the ethnographer (M. Nash, 1958b, p. 67). In other communities —apparently where national governments have recently imposed a new system of civil offices—the differentiation is clear, and the civil offices may even be excluded from the formal hierarchy of service (Cancian, 1964). If so, the old civil offices (stripped of civil powers) may be retained because of their old religious duties and thus become purely religious offices, which are called *regidor* or *alcalde* (Carrasco, 1952b, p. 30). In Mexico the new civil offices are usually called *presidente, síndico, regidor*

[1] I am grateful to my wife, Francesca Cancian, and to Evon Z. Vogt for comments on earlier drafts of this article.

My research in Zinacantan was supported by grants M-2100 (the Harvard Chiapas Project directed by Evon Z. Vogt) and MPH-17,719 from the National Institute of Mental Health.

and *alcalde* (*juez*). Some communities integrate the new civil officials into the old hierarchy system (Guiteras Holmes, 1961).

The conceptual distinction made by anthropologists refers to differences in duties. The civil side is responsible for: (1) representing the community in relations with the Ladino world outside, and (2) administering justice within the community. The religious side is concerned with care of the saints of the Catholic Church, with maintaining the church and celebrating the saints' days or fiestas. Integration of civil and religious functions is closest in offices at the top level; lower offices are ordinarily specialized on the civil or the ceremonial side.

Types of Offices in the Civil-Religious Hierarchy

As a male goes from boyhood to old age he receives different kinds of responsibilities in the hierarchy of his community. Some people serve only at the lowest levels and never complete a career. Even for those who complete service and become elders, however, the number of cargos served varies from community to community. The individual may serve from four to a dozen cargos, depending on his community, but there is great consistency from community to community regarding types of cargos and order of service. The four types of cargos in virtually every hierarchy may be labeled *alguacil, mayordomo, regidor,* and *alcalde* (Carrasco, 1961, p. 483). These terms describe the ideal career in Chichicastenango (Bunzel, 1952, p. 188); most other communities use some of them. There are subtypes and other names, but the basic duties remain the same. Two positions related to the hierarchy are those of *principal,* a man who has completed his cargo career, and *sacristán,* a man who may serve outside the hierarchy as an alternative to service in it.

1. ALGUACIL. Typically, at marriage or at age 21 a young man becomes a member of the tax-paying community of adults. Before this he serves at least one cargo of the alguacil type: janitor for public buildings, errand boy for higher officials, and policeman. Each community has many such cargos; the larger ones have more. The service is performed in groups for a year, normally two groups which alternate week-long tours of duty. This is sometimes called a carefree time when the young man enjoys himself and "learns to drink." These cargos normally do not require any cash outlay for ceremonies. Sometimes, young men who behave badly are appointed to alguacil as a corrective and punitive measure.

Many communities have separate alguacil cargos for the civil and the religious sides of the hierarchy. "Alguacil" is a term normally applied to the civil cargos, which may also be called *mayor, policía,* and *topil.* The religious cargos of this type may be *caxal, escuelix, chajal,* and *topilillo.* Frequently there are two types of civil cargos, e.g., a group of "alguaciles" and a group of "mayores." One is ranked lower than the other; this lower one may be ranked above the errand boys of the church or may be equivalent to them and considered an alternative to church service. Where these lesser groups are ranked, the ideal is service in both of them before attainment of the higher civil cargo. Almost all youths serve at least one of the lower cargos. The higher civil cargo may rank above the lowest of the second type of cargo, the mayordomo.

2. MAYORDOMO. Once married and established as an adult, a man becomes eligible for mayordomo cargos, which are almost always completely religious. They involve sponsorship of fiestas and care of saints. Often the incumbent has a saint's image or other sacred objects in his home during the period of service and is responsible for seeing that candles and other offerings are placed before the altar on which they rest. In some communities he practices sexual abstinence before important rituals. His service usually demands substantial

expenditure for the drink and food consumed at fiestas by fellow cargo-holders and by members of the community.

Usually there is more than one level of such cargos in a community. That is, a man is expected to serve a series of mayordomo cargos on his way up the hierarchy. Other names for this office include *capitán, pasionero, alferez,* and *cofrade.* Cofrade is a term limited to those communities that have a *cofradía,* an organization of sodalities devoted to individual saints. Usually these communities have one cofradía in charge of burial of the dead. Where there are cofradías they may be ranked, and there may be further ranking of positions within each cofradía. An individual moves up through the ranks of his particular cofradía, or moves from cofradía to cofradía in order of their rank. In other communities the mayordomo cargos are ranked as independent units, and a man must take one from each level as local custom dictates.

Although service in this cargo usually begins as a young adult, it sometimes extends into very old age, and men who are almost elders of the community serve in the top mayordomo cargos. Service in the third type of cargo may overlap with service as a mayordomo.

3. REGIDOR. Cargos of the third (and fourth) level usually combine civil and religious duties in accommodation to the needs of the national government. In Mexico the duties are predominantly religious; in Guatemala they have retained civil aspects, and some communities exert pressure to eliminate religious obligations altogether (e.g., M. Nash, 1958a). Nevertheless, this office has common characteristics throughout the area.

The officeholders, mature men with experience as mayordomos, are called regidores. Their tasks are administrative—collecting taxes, supervising communal work, and settling conflicts between members of the community. The regidores are responsible for knowing who is eligible for

lower cargos and capable of holding them, and they are otherwise involved in the appointment of cargo-holders. In most communities a man serves only one cargo at the regidor level, but in other places the first of the ranked group of regidores may be chosen from men who have already served as regidores. In general, the regidores are part of the local administration directed by the alcaldes, the fourth type of cargo.

4. ALCALDE. The alcaldes are the chief executives of the civil-religious hierarchy. Wherever another form of civil government has not been imposed in recent years, they are the principal authority on which Ladino government officials must call for contact with the Indians, and the ultimate native court of appeal in disputes within the community. Often they appoint others to cargos; they usually bear certain responsibilities towards the saints and supervise the installation of new cargo-holders and the accompanying transfer of paraphernalia of the saint. In most communities there are one or two alcaldes; where there are two they are ranked as first and second, the first being the chief authority. The alcalde is sometimes expected to be the ideal type of good man. He tends to be a conservative who has an excellent record of performance in his previous cargos. He also tends to be a rich man, because the numerous cargos required to reach this office cause great expense.

5. PRINCIPAL. When a man has passed alcalde (or sometimes a very high mayordomo), he becomes a principal, a respected elder of the community. These men, by virtue of their service to the community and, it seems, their ability to climb the hierarchy, are often the permanent locus of authority. All communities have their past alcaldes, who may be called *pasados* or *ancianos,* as well as principales. However, there is a basic distinction between communities that have a formal group of principales, limited in number and selected from among past alcaldes, and communities

that have an informal group of principales who are simply elder statesmen participating in policy making according to their inclinations and abilities. Chimaltenango, for instance, has four *principales del pueblo* (Wagley, 1949, p. 95), who constitute a formal council of elders and are distinguished from other past alcaldes. They serve as long as they live and are self-perpetuating. Other communities have no formal offices beyond that of alcalde. Sometimes, the principales, rather than the alcaldes, have the chief power and responsibility for appointing others to cargos.

6. SACRISTÁN. Many communities have a sixth type of post, sacristán, that is not formally part of the hierarchy but is closely associated with it. The sacristanes are ritual specialists associated with the mayordomo cargos and are usually five or fewer. They may be assistants to a resident or a visiting priest. In many communities this is a life-time position that frees the incumbent from serving in the regular hierarchy. It thus offers an alternative type of service for the man who is religiously inclined and who does not have the financial reserves or the personal qualities necessary to pass through the civil and religious sides of the hierarchy.[2]

The Individual and the Hierarchy

In most communities the exact cargos and levels that must be passed to become alcalde are not rigidly set, though many ethnographers report that older informants have an ideal of a cargo career as it was or as it should be. Individuals often skip levels and repeat levels as they are defined by the community. It appears, however,

that almost every man who becomes a principal passes at least one cargo in each of the four types discussed above. The rigidity of the system may vary with the balance of population and cargos available as well as with the inclinations of individuals.

As I see them, the salient features of the civil-religious hierarchy, as exemplified by the types of cargos defined above, are: community service for all at the lowest level (alguacil); expensive religious service for those who want the respect of their fellows and aspire to leadership in the community (mayordomo); service in administrative positions of responsibility for those who have demonstrated their commitment to the community and its values by serving as mayordomos (regidor); and, finally, service in a position of ultimate formal authority for a limited number of those who have proven themselves in lower offices (alcalde). All these positions are for one-year terms until service as alcalde opens the way to status as an elder. Sacristán offers an alternative to the individual who is not inclined to compete in the hierarchical system.

Cargo Career and the Family Group

Usually it is the adult male who moves through the offices of the hierarchy, but his family is nearly always involved in his service. In most communities a man must be married before he can participate in cargos above the alguacil level. Sometimes his wife is given a formal role in the ritual, and nearly always she takes part in preparation of ritual meals. Beyond the informal or formal help of his wife, each cargo-holder has assistants who gather flowers, serve meals, and run errands. These people may come from the larger kinship group.

The nuclear family is usually the unit considered for recruitment into the cargo system. That is, if one member of a nuclear family is serving a cargo, all others are regarded as drawn into it and are not eligi-

[2] A special sort of temporary ritual adviser and spokesman attached to a particular cargo-holder at important ceremonials, especially change of office, is found in some communities (Beals, 1946, p. 133; Cancian, 1965; Parsons, 1936, p. 187). In Zinacantan these men enable cargo-holders who have financial resources, but little ritual knowledge and speaking ability, to hold cargos of the mayordomo type.

ble to serve other cargos. Thus a son is exempt from service as alguacil if his father is currently a mayordomo. The prestige that accrues to a man through service in the hierarchy usually extends to his wife.

Recruitment for Service in the Hierarchy

Individuals may be appointed by the alcaldes and regidores in office at the time, or by the principales responsible for creating new cargo-holders. The ordaining individuals use their official and personal power to insure that the appointees will accept the duty, and are aided by strong social pressure from the community. In many communities, outgoing cargo-holders are responsible for suggesting their own replacements.

In the northwest highlands of Guatemala communities have an official calendar priest who holds office for life. This man divines whether the candidate suggested by the principales will have a successful year of service if he is appointed (Wagley, 1949, p. 87ff.). Since he has power to reject a candidate, the priest is, in this area, a significant addition to the usual appointers.

Volunteering is a second type of recruitment for service in the hierarchy. In Zinacantan (Cancian, 1965) men who want to serve cargos present themselves before the assembled alcaldes and regidores and request the cargo of their choice. There may often be previous requests for the same cargo so the man's name is recorded on a list that may extend as much as 20 years into the future. When a man with appropriate financial resources does not volunteer for a cargo, he is appointed by the regidores and alcaldes in a manner similar to that in other communities. This type of volunteering differs from the voluntary (non-obligatory) service done by cargo-holders in some of the more Ladinoized communities where the "modern" sector is allowed to forego service in the hierarchy (Cámara, 1952c). The situation in Zinacantan seems to be a temporary adaptation to expanding population and economic growth.

In conservative communities, all men are expected to serve, and virtually all men do serve at least one cargo.

Cost of Cargos

Everywhere religious fiestas cost money. Candles and fireworks are expended "for" the saint; new clothes may be purchased for the image. At great feasts in the name of the saint quantities of food and liquor are consumed. These expenses are paid (Carrasco, 1961, p. 484): (1) with earnings from community-owned land or animals, (2) by collection of an equal amount from each of the village families, or (3) with funds provided by the individual cargo-holder who is sponsoring the fiesta. The third method is the most important in modern times.

The expenditures often represent very substantial outlay by the sponsor. Tax (1953) shows that the most expensive cargo costs considerably more than a man could earn in a full year of wage work. Beals (1946, p. 85) notes expenses that represent about two years' wage work. In Zinacantan (Cancian, 1965), the most expensive cargo costs the equivalent of ten years' wage work. Guiteras Holmes (1961, p. 58) records the most expensive cargo relative to local wages: "One of the lesser religious offices . . . implies an expenditure which is the equivalent of . . . between three and four years of a man's daily wages. Higher positions demand that the Pedrano expend four or five times the above amount." It is easy to see why most ethnographers report that the cargo positions are often great economic burdens to those who pass them.

In most communities the wealthy take the most expensive posts, the poor man passes less expensive ones. Alguacil cargos normally do not impose any significant expenditures (e.g., Tax, 1953, p. 179). According to data from Tax and Guiteras Holmes, even cargos on the mayordomo level carry varying costs. Those of the regidor and alcalde grade, it seems, are most expensive in traditional communities where they necessitate sponsorship of important fiestas, i.e., where they entail important "religious" duties.

In addition, of course, service in any cargo takes much time which might otherwise be devoted to economic activities.

The cargo system as a whole, as contrasted with the cargo career of an individual, may also be a real burden for the community, draining a substantial part of the economic surplus of the community. This fact has been discussed by Tax (1937, p. 443; 1952c, p. 57f.) and many others.

Variant Political and Religious Organizations

Variant political and religious organizations lying outside the general characterization of the hierarchy mostly appear to be remnants of civil-religious hierarchies that have broken down. They are usually in Ladinoized communities (Cámara, 1952c). Others include the organization among the conservative lowland Maya of east-central Quintana Roo (Villa Rojas, 1945). This seems to be a peculiar pattern resulting from isolation and an unusual history of contact and conflict. The Huichol, in the northern part of Middle America, have most of the features of the prototypical hierarchy (Zingg, 1938b); the Tarahumara, who are outside the area, show the influence of Spanish contact, but do not have the annual change of alcaldes so crucial to the civil-religious hierarchy (Bennett and Zingg, 1935, p. 205; Aguirre Beltrán, 1953, p. 81).

THE HIERARCHY AND THE COMMUNITY

Three features of the civil-religious hierarchy should be kept in mind as we examine its consequences for the social structure of the community: (1) virtually all adult males participate in some degree; (2) service in all but the lowest positions imposes substantial financial investment; and (3) prestige and positions of leadership and respect are achieved through service in

the hierarchy. Most of the interpretations of the functions or consequences of the hierarchy have much in common, and later ones explicitly build on earlier ones (Tax, 1953; Wolf, 1955b, 1957; M. Nash, 1958a, 1958b; Carrasco, 1961). Nash has distinguished between manifest and latent functions of the hierarchy, i.e., between the intended or direct and the unintended or indirect consequences.

Manifest Functions

Nash's observations for Cantel (1958a, p. 100) provide a concise statement:

From the public point of view, the hierarchy entailed the manifest functions of caring for the administrative order of the community, providing police protection, dispensing justice, caring for the church, housing the saints, discharging the community's responsibilities to the supernatural by seeing that important feast days were celebrated by a duly constituted organization, and providing the body of elders who were the actual government of the Pueblo.

The hierarchy is the link between the local community and the nation, on the one hand, and between the local world view and the Catholic Church, on the other. The requests and demands of the Guatemalan national government are transmitted to local Indian societies through officials of the hierarchy.

He also gives an excellent summary elsewhere (1958b).

Latent Functions

The hierarchy sponsors ceremonials that bring the people of the community together in common rituals. This is especially important in towns which have dispersed settlement patterns, for the people may not see each other at any other time (Vogt, 1961).

The hierarchy permits the symbolic reassertion of "the strength and integrity . . . [of the community] structure before the eyes of its members" (Wolf, 1955b, p. 458; see also Aguirre Beltrán, 1953, p. 131). And it allows for individual expression of commitment to the community.

289

It also provides a clear definition of community membership. Nash (1958b, p. 68) says, "The ordinary operation of the civil-religious hierarchy defines the limits and membership of the local society. A person is a Panajacheleño, or a Chimalteco, or a Cantelense, or a Maxeño, only in so far as he is eligible for and participates in the hierarchy."

Nash also points out (*ibid.*, p. 69) that the hierarchy serves as "a channel for the socially controlled modes of personal display" and that it "is an efficient device for . . . marking clearly the paths and methods for achieving respect and political say in a local society."

Wolf (1955b, p. 460) has emphasized the role of "institutionalized envy" in keeping individuals to the traditional patterns of behavior in the closed corporate community. Fear of witchcraft may be seen as an inducement to participate in the hierarchy. On the other hand, participation is a public manner of declaring good intention for those who have accumulated great wealth and are concerned about the envy of others.

As Wolf (1955b) has pointed out, all these consequences of the hierarchy may be considered integrating from the point of view of the community. Their net effect is a strengthening of bonds within the Indian community against the surrounding Ladino world.

Two further interpretations of latent consequences are, in some degree, conflicting. The first emphasizes equalization of economic status through the operation of the hierarchy, i.e., the "leveling" consequences; the second emphasizes separation into multiple social statuses, i.e., the "stratifying" consequences. Other writers have emphasized the first interpretation and the tendency towards socio-economic homogeneity in traditional communities with hierarchies, but in my study of Zinacantan, I have emphasized the latter and the patterns of socio-economic stratification. The contrasting positions tend to bring different kinds of evidence to bear, though each attends to both economic and social factors.

THE EQUALITARIAN COMPLEX. The interpretation of the hierarchy as a "leveling mechanism" says that, "By using the income and resources of individuals and of the community the hierarchy keeps any one family from accumulating very much cash or property" (M. Nash, 1958b, p. 69; see also Tax, 1953, p. 206; Carrasco, 1961, p. 493). This view is based on the fact that religious cargos are serious economic burdens for individuals, and on "the low absolute wealth of the community. Although relatively rich, the wealthiest families are not far above the subsistence level. They have little margin of safety, and a series of bad times (sickness, drunkenness, etc.), may send them down. . . . Further, nobody is rich enough to establish his descendents . . ." (Tax, 1953, p. 206).

Wolf (1955b, p. 457) and Nash (1958b, p. 69) specifically emphasize the role of traditional technology and marginal land; the latter mentions an inheritance pattern that usually fragments family lands. Tax notes (1953, p. 206) that in Panajachel the economic value of women also militates against the development of wealth-tied social classes, for men seek out wives who are good workers rather than women from wealthy families; but this pattern is not common in the area.

Given the essential poverty of the community, the hierarchy helps to maintain socio-economic homogeneity. Furthermore, Wolf (1955b, p. 458), Nash (1958b, p. 69), and Carrasco (1961, p. 493) regard this leveling effect as an important integrating influence; and they imply or state that internal social and economic differentiation, which the hierarchy tends to check, would disrupt the corporate structure of the community.

The second aspect of the equalitarian complex emphasizes social rather than economic factors. Nash (1958a, p. 68) states this most strongly: "All the families are age-graded according to which rung in the ladder they have reached, and at the same time fill a general position of respect due to the past services given. At any one point, then, all of the families in the community are graded according to age and ranked in prestige through the operation of the hierarchy."

Weitlaner and Hoogshagen (1960) have labeled the age groups in the hierarchy in Oaxaca as "age grades." Connected with this age-grading idea are the statements that *all* adult males are expected to move through the hierarchy and become principales in their old age (Nash, 1958a, p. 69) and that the hierarchy is simply a way of spreading the burden of community service over all men (Carrasco, 1961, p. 493). Tax (1953, p. 206) and Carrasco (1961, p. 484) note that this happens only in small populations. Tax and Nash state that the wealthy normally reach the status of principal faster because it is easier for them to make the economic outlays necessary to move up the ladder. In sum, however, age is seen as the independent variable, prestige as the dependent variable, and the hierarchy as the mechanism for expressing the relationship between them.

THE STRATIFICATION COMPLEX. The stratification complex emphasizes social differentiation resulting from operation of the hierarchy. Although the writers who stress the equalitarian complex also recognize the stratification complex, they seem to think it less important. In my work in Zinacantan (Cancian, 1965) and my reading of factual records on other communities I have found it to be more important (1) because the formal structure of the hierarchy inevitably differentiates people, and (2) because there is considerable evidence for economic differentiation within the communities in question.

First, as Carrasco notes (1961, p. 483), the hierarchy has many positions at the lower levels, few at the top. Regardless of other factors, this pyramid produces social

differentiation, since not all who serve can reach the top. Only one man each year can attain ultimate social position as first alcalde. If the population is small, this one man will represent a higher proportion of the adult men than he could in a larger community. As a result, the smaller community might be said to be less stratified, because its group of past alcaldes will be less exclusive relative to the population as a whole.

In Zinacantan, until very recently, virtually every man had to serve one of the 34 first-level cargos. On the second level there are positions for only 12 of these 34 men, on the third level positions for only six of the 12, and on the fourth and final level one first alcalde and two other positions (Cancian, 1965). Thus, many begin but few reach the top. Social differentiation is inevitable.

In his report on Panajachel, one of the smallest of Indian *municipios* (population about 800), Tax says, "Every man can expect to become alcalde eventually" (1953, p. 206). Given the population of Panajachel (or even Tax's data on age distribution in the population, p. 9), it is hard to see how this can be true. Calculating roughly on the basis of the life expectancy of Indians in Middle America,[3] one male will reach age 45 each year for every 160 people in the population. Thus, in Panajachel about five men turn 45 each year. Only one of them can be first alcalde. In all likelihood others of them have not served all the cargos preliminary to alcalde in any case. Even in such a small population, then, the operation of the hierarchy can significantly differentiate the adult males.

Given these facts, it is clear that the age-grading function of the hierarchy, the social aspect of the equalitarian complex, cannot

[3] This calculation is made from the Survivors Within Age Groups tables published by the United Nations (1956, p. 78f.). I assume a life expectancy at birth of 50 years, probably something of an overestimate (see United Nations, 1954, p. 39).

be as important as its proponents state. However, the first and most important aspect, economic equalization, may not be so easily dismissed. Whether it does or does not coexist with social differentiation is an empirical question. A number of communities show significant economic differentiation. Because of this, I conclude that the hierarchy is often ineffectual as an equalizer—as a mechanism for keeping the community economically homogeneous.

In Zinacantan the evidence for economic differentiation is clear. Cargos involve expenditures ranging from 50 to 14,000 pesos in a community where an average man is fortunate to clear 1,000 pesos (80 dollars) yearly after having put aside part of his corn and bean crops to feed his family. Yet the rich take a number of expensive cargos and tend to reach the top of the hierarchy, whereas the poor barely manage a single less expensive cargo. The rich obviously spend more than the poor, both because they take more cargos, and because they take more expensive individual cargos. This is leveling in some sense, but in fact the rich seem to be so rich that they do not lose their relative standing. To a statistically significant degree, sons of men who have taken expensive cargos also take expensive cargos (Cancian, 1965). Not only do individuals maintain their economic standing during their lifetimes, but many even manage to pass it on to their descendents.

For other communities there are three kinds of evidence that point to the existence of similar economic differentiation. First, the great variation in the cost of cargos *within* a number of communities (see the first section of this article) suggests that there are significant differences in the economic capacities of individuals in the communities. Second, evidence for significant economic differences is explicitly given by Wagley (1941), and certain ethnographers report native distinctions between "los ricos" and "los pobres" (e.g., Wagley, 1941, p. 77; Beals, 1946, p. 89). Third, available

figures on ownership of land show wide ranges of wealth. Wagley (1941, p. 72) notes the differences: ". . . some 12% of the 253 men held 36% of the total land." Beals (1946, p. 60) gives data from a single page of the tax rolls: among 58 landowners the average holding is 5.1 hectares; the range goes from 0.5 hectare to 32 hectares. Tax's careful calculations for Panajachel (1953, p. 68) show that the top 5 per cent of the population owns about 20 per cent of the land; the top 20 per cent of the population owns more than 50 per cent of the land. Granted that the norm of equal distribution of land among all children might fragment some holdings, these differences seem substantial to me.

As Wagley has pointed out for Santiago Chimaltenango (1941, p. 81), there is not "the great gulf between a Rockefeller and the clerk in his offices." No leisure class exists. Some men hire helpers, and others do not, but all work in the fields. Manual work is respected by Indians, and this respect is converted into social standing when a man demonstrates his success by serving an expensive cargo.

Ethnographers are impressed by the fact that there seems to be little "undue" display of wealth (Wagley, 1941, p. 79; Beals, 1946, p. 86), but Wagley's Diego, although perhaps not conspicuous about it, has a larger house, eats better food, and uses his economic advantages to satisfy his sexual desires (1941, p. 79). Economic differentiation exists in Indian communities and is important to Indians, even if by some standards the richest Indian is a poor man hoeing a row of corn.

In summary, in terms of the *internal* relations in the community, the hierarchy does socially stratify the population, and in a number of cases it is not an effective economic leveler but only a way of making public and acceptable the economic differentiation that does exist in the community.

The two foregoing interpretations—leveling and stratifying—are most clearly in conflict when one attempts to see both sets of consequences as strengthening community integration. Such a view of the leveling consequences depends on the theory that differentiation is disruptive. Such an interpretation of the stratifying consequences depends on the theory that differentiation is (or can be) integrating. I argue (at greater length elsewhere, Cancian, 1964, 1965) that the social differentiation is integrating in this situation because it rewards more highly those who perform better according to shared values on industry, accomplishment, and community service. This differential reward reaffirms these Indian values and is thus integrating.

From the point of view of *external* relations, i.e., relations with the non-Indian world, the consumption of wealth may be seen as integrating in a manner independent of the conflicting interpretations reviewed above. As Wolf (1955b, p. 458) has pointed out, "The corporate structure [with the hierarchy] acts to impede the mobilization of capital and wealth within the community in terms of the outside world which employs wealth capitalistically." That is, cargos require that wealth be used in an Indian way, and prevent its use in a way that might bring foreign elements into the community. This, however, does not imply that the community is socially and economically homogeneous (undifferentiated), but rather that it is homogeneously Indian when compared with the outside world.

Economic and Demographic Factors

All the interpretations of the consequences of the civil-religious hierarchy for the community depend on the existence of a certain balance between the supply of wealth and personnel in the community and the demands of the hierarchy for these resources. As this balance varies, so may the consequences of the hierarchy. The variation may be found in different communities at one time, or it may take place in one community over time.

Tax (1937, p. 443) has noted that smaller communities which support relatively large hierarchies tend to be made poor by the ceremonial expenses. And, as he (1953, p. 206) and others have pointed out, the hierarchy tends to stratify the population more in larger communities. Both of these generalizations imply the fact that the hierarchy varies less in size, arrangement of offices, and expense than do the populations and wealth of the communities in which it exists.

Over time in the same community a variation in the balance may bring about a change in the consequences of the hierarchy, assuming again that the hierarchy will tend to vary less than the population and wealth of the community. Both population and wealth have increased in Zinacantan (Cancian, 1965) since the turn of the century, and the hierarchy has not changed enough to balance these increases. There is an overdemand for cargos. The hierarchy no longer is as inclusive of the total population as it was in the past. The cargos remain a very substantial financial burden to individuals who serve them, but the number of individuals capable of serving them is increasing. Thus, there is a corresponding reduction of the burden on the entire community. If the increase in wealth and population continue without much modification of the hierarchy, the traditional consequences of the hierarchy will disappear.

BREAKDOWN OF THE CIVIL-RELIGIOUS HIERARCHY

The social structure of most Indian communities in Middle America has been and is changing; the traditional civil-religious hierarchy is breaking down. In his study of both traditional and modern or changed communities, Cámara says (1952c, p. 163):

The process of acculturation in Mesoamerica consisting of "mestizoization" or "ladinoization" has accelerated in the last few years. Where this occurs, it is possible to point out the following changes in religious and political organization: (a) formal and functional separation of the native religious and political bodies; (b) greater acceptance and significance of religious events than of political events; (c) substitution in the political organization of native officials by Ladino or Mestizo officials; (d) preeminence of festivities in the cabecera over those of other ecological units; (e) subordination of native religious and political organization to the standards of the Ladinos; (f) tendency toward secularization of the important fiestas (patron saint, carnival, semana santa, etc.); (g) greater acceptance of secular events and their consideration as a form of recreation and enjoyment independent of religious duty; (h) disintegration of the group religious organization and the beginning of religious events held in the family or among friends; (i) decline of these religious organizations and preponderance of political groups; (j) absorption and control of both on the part of the state and the church.

My principal concern here is the process by which the hierarchy changes. Adams has noted that the hierarchy is more than a simple trait which changes with others as a community moves toward Ladinoization. It is crucial to the maintenance of the traditional Indian community. He says (1957b, p. 48) that with change in the socio-political structure, "the Indian's resistance to culture change began to disintegrate. His insulation was gone."

Three aspects of the change are discussed separately below, but often appear in a given community simultaneously.

Ladinoization

The Ladinoization of Indian communities in Middle America is a long-standing process. Reina (1960, p. 101) even suggests that much of the change he records for Chinautla may simply be "the result of a natural process continuous since the Conquest." New factors, however, seem to be accelerating change. Expanding systems of roads and schools are bringing the Indian populations closer to the national cultures of Mexico and Guatemala. Communications

are radically improved. Laws protecting Indians from much of the exploitation widespread in the past have no doubt encouraged them to wander more freely into the Ladino environment. In general, alternatives to the traditional life in the Indian community are rapidly increasing.

The fact that very expensive religious cargos are an essential feature of the traditional system provides, I think, great potential for disruption. As long as the traditional norms are held by all in an Indian community, and the alternatives to being an Indian are unattractive, the hierarchy would seem to be a very satisfactory way of converting economic surplus into social position. However, when the norms weaken and the non-Indian environment becomes less hostile, the expense of cargos may only add to individual motivation to reject the traditional system.

Paul and Paul (1963) have recorded two ways in which the strength of the traditional cofradía system was undermined in San Pedro la Laguna. The success of Protestant missionaries reduced the number of men available for religious service. Whatever the strain that allowed the Protestants a foothold in the community, their success further divided community opinion on the worth of traditional religious activities. Completely independently, the call to national military service again reduced the number of men who would participate. Those who returned from the military could argue—even according to the traditional norms—that they had already done service to the community and should not be called on to serve in the hierarchy.

Old trends towards Ladinoization in their accelerated form have weakened attachment to the Indian way of life, and at the same time the non-Indian world has made itself more attractive to the Indian. In this situation the repelling economic aspects of the traditional system have further opened the breach through which alternatives may enter the life of an Indian.

Direct Political Action

All the Indian communities considered in this review exist as formal political entities (on the municipio level or below) in Mexico and Guatemala. National government policies have important effects on their political organization and, by extension, on the civil-religious hierarchy. Since government policies have been different in the two countries, they will be considered separately below. Despite differences in political action, effects have been somewhat similar. The religious and political sides of the hierarchy have separated, and the traditional manner of achieving political power by proving oneself in expensive religious service has been undermined.

The actions of the national government in Guatemala have been reviewed in a symposium (Adams, 1957b). "Prior to 1936 the principal officers were the departmental *jefes políticos* (governors) who were appointed by the president and who were responsible for all the municipios in their respective department" *(ibid.,* p. 4). The jefe político controlled selection of officers of the municipios, but it seems that in communities with entirely Indian population the offices could be filled in the traditional way as long as those chosen met with the satisfaction of the jefe político. The Indian communities were isolated, and contact with the larger governmental system was limited. As Wagley has noted for Chimaltenango (1949, p. 96), a conservative man who spoke little Spanish was preferred by the people as alcalde, for he could have little contact with Ladinos. Similarly, Bunzel (1952, p. 174) notes that the Indian government in Chichicastenango (before 1936) was kept relatively independent of Ladino influence "by regularly choosing as alcalde a man who speaks no Spanish."

Under the *intendente* system which was introduced in 1935, an appointed official, usually a Ladino from outside the community, was the head of every municipio (Adams, 1957b, p. 4). As far as I can tell, this change in government required no major change in the traditional hierarchy. It brought the Ladino controlling agent closer, but allowed the Indian to continue traditional ways.

The important changes came after the revolution of 1944 when the intendente system was abolished. Adams says *(ibid.,* p. 6), "Elected mayors and town councils were re-established, but with the difference that the elections were intended to be competitive. Towards this end, political parties were promoted." Political parties, like Protestant religion, provided an opportunity for formal expression of differences within the community. Elements dissatisfied with the old system had open and enthusiastic support from outside the community (see papers in Adams, 1957b), and the old system was undermined.

In Mexico the change, though less sharp, had many of the same results. Carrasco's historical study (1952b) of Tarascan communities shows the effects of both church and state policies since the conquest. About 50 years ago a new system of political offices consisting of presidente, síndico, and regidores *(Ayuntamiento Constitucional)* replaced the traditional alcaldes and regidores as top officials *(Ayuntamiento Regional)*. Since the new offices were political, however, the religious authority of the old alcaldes and regidores was not directly threatened. The old offices could be maintained alongside the new, an adaptation not possible in Guatemalan communities where new selection procedures for the old offices were introduced.

Some communities have attempted to integrate the new officials into the old ladder system (Guiteras Holmes, 1961), but the requirement that the new officeholders speak Spanish and deal with the Ladino world made it difficult to recruit them consistently from among those who already had appropriate service in the lower level of civil and religious posts. Other communities have kept the old and the new separate. In Zinacantan (Cancian, 1965), for instance, no attempt has been made to appoint presidentes who have proved themselves in religious posts. Civil posts are filled by relatively young men who, on important issues, are controlled by the political bosses of the community. These bosses tend to be elders who have respectable careers in the religious hierarchy, but similar religious service may not be necessary for their successors a generation from now.

De la Fuente's description (1949, p. 214) of the three principal leaders of Yalalag (until 1944) illustrates the continuum from the old type of leader who was respected for the sacrifices he made in service of the community to the modern leader who must be able to handle Ladino language and Ladino law. The first was a rich and rustic individual knowing little Spanish; the second, a Spanish speaker of moderate means; the third, a poor man fluent in Spanish and informed in Ladino law.

Both countries have changed the manner of selecting the top formal political authorities responsible to the larger governmental system. In both countries, for different reasons, appointment to high political office no longer requires previous service in expensive religious cargos. Thus, one of the basic features of the civil-religious hierarchy was destroyed.

Economic and Demographic Factors

Serious imbalance between the demands of the hierarchy for wealth and personnel and the supply of these in the community may create internal strains that lead to the breakdown of the hierarchy. If a community and its citizens lose major sources of income, then the burden of cargo service may become so great that the arguments of reluctant individuals become accepted; as has happened in many communities, the cargos go unfilled and eventually disappear. If there is an overabundance of wealth, service in the hierarchy may fail to consume the

surplus and individuals will seek alternative ways to spend it, thus opening the community to influences from the Ladino world. In addition, excess wealth not devoted to community service may lead to envy and witchcraft.

Change in population may similarly affect the economic balance: reduction may bring too heavy a burden of cargos on each individual; increase may result in too few cargos to consume community resources. Simple population growth, independent of the economic variable, may mean that all individuals can no longer be included in the system of community service.

It is in viewing the community as such a system in balance that the effect of Ladinoization and demographic and economic factors may be best seen. Insofar as a shift to Ladino values reduces the willingness to commit surplus income to the hierarchy or reduces the number of people who will participate in the traditional system, it upsets the postulated balance in a manner very similar to direct change in wealth or population.

SUMMARY

This article describes the civil-religious hierarchy as the characteristic political-religious organization in Middle American Indian communities. It has examined the traditional hierarchy and its basic features, reviewed interpretations of its functions in the community and argued for more emphasis on its stratifying consequences, and, finally, seen the breakdown of the hierarchy as the result of several factors working simultaneously. Direct political action by national governments undermines the combination of religious and political service characteristic of the traditional hierarchy. Both Ladinoization and demographic and economic factors threaten the other two features essential to the traditional system: the economic burden of service and participation by all members of the community.

APPENDIX

Generalizations in the text are based on the following sources for the groups indicated: Beals (1946) and Carrasco (1952b) for Tarascan; Beals (1945b) for Mixe; Parsons (1936) and De la Fuente (1949) for Zapotec; Guiteras Holmes (1961) and Cancian (1965) for Mexican Maya; Wagley (1949), Bunzel (1952), Tax (1953), M. Nash (1958a), and Reina (1960) for Guatemalan Maya. Valuable material is also found in Zingg (1938b) for Huichol; Leslie (1960a) for Zapotec; Pozas (1959a) and Zabala Cubillos (1961) for Mexican Maya; Wisdom (1940), LaFarge (1947), Oakes (1951), and McArthur (1961) for Guatemalan Maya. Studies of hierarchies in many other areas do not include enough information to support or contradict these generalizations.

The distribution of some important traits across eight communities is tabulated below.

In the tabulation X indicates presence, O absence, of a trait. A capital letter indicates a clear statement in the monograph cited; a small letter means that my rating is based on ambiguous evidence, or on no evidence in a situation where the trait in question almost surely would have been mentioned if present. A blank indicates insufficient evidence for a decision. In a few cases, most of them evident from the ordering of the list, the blank means that the "question" does not apply.

The list parallels the exposition in the body of the article.

	Monograph	Community
A.	Carrasco, 1952b	Tarascan (historical)
B.	Beals, 1945b	Ayutla
C.	Parsons, 1936	Mitla
D.	Guiteras Holmes, 1961	San Pedro Chenalho
E.	Cancian, 1965	Zinacantan
F.	Wagley, 1949	Santiago Chimaltenango
G.	Bunzel, 1952	Chichicastenango
H.	Nash, 1958a	Cantel

Trait	A	B	C	D	E	F	G	H
ALGUACIL								
First service before marriage	X	X	X	x	X	X	X	x
Janitor, errand boy, policeman	X	X	X	X	X	X	X	X
Service done in groups		X	X	O	X	X	X	X
Carefree time					X	X	x	
Two groups		X	X	O	X	X	O	X
Alternate one-week service		X	X	O	O	X	O	X
No substantial expenditures		o	x	x	X	x	x	x
Appointed for bad behavior				X	X			
Separate civil and religious posts		X	X	o	O	X	X	X
Two types of civil alguaciles		X	X	X	O	X	X	X
Lower civil above religious		X	X			O	O	X
Virtually all youths serve	X	x			O	X	X	X
High alguacil above low mayordomo		o	O	O	O	O		X
MAYORDOMO								
First service after marriage	x	x	x	X	X	x	X	X
Completely religious	x	x	X	X	X	X	X	X
Sacred objects in incumbent's house	x		X	X	X	X	X	
Sexual abstinence practiced		X		X	O	X		
Substantial expenditures	X	X	X	X	X	X	X	X
More than one level	X	X	X	X	X	x	X	X
Cofradías	X	O	O	O	O	O	X	X
Old men may serve		x	X	X	X		X	X
Some served after regidor cargo	o	x	X	X	X	O	X	X
REGIDOR								
Combine civil and religious duties	X	X	X	X	x	X	x	x
Mature men	x		X	X	X	X	X	

297

Trait	Community							
	A	B	C	D	E	F	G	H
Passed a mayordomo cargo	X	X	X	X	X	x	X	X
Have administrative tasks	X	X	X	X	X	X	X	x
Involved in appointments		X	X	X	X	X	X	
Serve only once		X		x	X	O	x	x
ALCALDE								
Chief religious leader	x		x	o	X	x	x	X
Chief civil leader	x	x	x	x	O	X	X	X
Official contact with Ladino world		x	x	x	O	X	X	x
Ultimate native appeal in disputes			x	x	O	X	X	X
Principal powers as appointers	o	o	x	x	X	O	O	O
Specific ritual responsibilities	X			x	X	X		X
Supervise installations		X	x	x	X	o	X	X
One of them	X	x	x	x	O	X	O	O
Usually rich men			X		X	X	X	X
PRINCIPAL								
Passed high-level cargo	X	X		x	X	X	X	X
Permanent authority in community	X	X		x	O	X	X	X
Formal group		O		x	O	X	X	o
Life service				x		X	X	
Self-perpetuating				x		X	X	
Informal group	X	X		X	X	X	X	x
Power in appointments	X			o	O	X	X	X
SACRISTÁN								
Not formally in hierarchy		X	X	X	X	X	X	O
Ritual specialist		x			X	x	X	O
Associated with mayordomos		o	o	X	X	o	o	
Five or less of them		X	X	X	X	x	O	X
Assistants of priest		X	x	X	X	x	X	X
Long-term position		X	X	x	X	x	X	O
Incumbent free from other service		X			X	x	X	X
No substantial expenditures		X	x	x	X	x	X	
RECRUITMENT								
Alcaldes principal appointers	o	o	x	x	X	O	O	O
Principales principal appointers	X	o	o		O	X	X	X
Volunteering	X	o	X	o	X	o	o	o
All expected to serve		X	X	X	X	X	X	X
Most do serve		X	x	x	X	X	X	X

REFERENCES

Adams, R. N., 1957b
Aguirre Beltrán, 1953
Beals, 1945b, 1946
Bennett and Zingg, 1935
Bunzel, 1952
Cámara, 1952c
Cancian, Frank, 1964, 1965
Carrasco, 1952b, 1961
De la Fuente, 1949
Foster, 1960a
Guiteras Holmes, 1961
LaFarge, 1947
Leslie, 1960a
McArthur, 1961
Nash, M., 1957b, 1958a, 1958b

Oakes, 1951
Parsons, 1936
Paul and Paul, 1963
Pozas, 1959a
Reina, 1960
Tax, 1937, 1952a, 1952c, 1953
United Nations, 1954, 1956
Villa Rojas, 1945
Vogt, 1961, 1963
Wagley, 1941, 1949
Weitlaner and Hoogshagen, 1960
Wisdom, 1940
Wolf, 1955b, 1957
Zabala Cubillos, 1961
Zingg, 1938b

15. Levels of Communal Relations

ERIC R. WOLF

Much of the recent history of Middle America may be summed up as a major effort to disestablish the twin foundations of the old social order, represented by Indian community and hacienda, and to ring in a new order, unhampered by the narrow social boundaries and unbreachable cultural barriers of the past. Each Indian community, supported in its autonomy by a grant of land, charged with the autonomous enforcement of social control, constituted a small, closely defended island, securing the social and cultural homogeneity of its members within, struggling to maintain its integrity in the face of attacks from without (Redfield and Tax, 1952; Wolf, 1955b, 1957). The other integrative institution of the past, the hacienda, similarly exercised a monopoly over the labor force within its social and economic precinct. Using the mechanism of peonage to turn community-oriented peasants into a disciplined labor force capable of producing cash crops for a supercommunity market, the hacienda nevertheless imprisoned its workers in a tight little social world, circumscribed by its boundaries, lorded over by the hacienda owner who, concentrating in his hands social, political, and judicial as well as economic power, became chief arbiter of their life and chief buffer between them and higher levels of integration (Wolf, 1959, pp. 203–11).

Indian community and hacienda both had in common that they interposed institutional barriers between local group and outside, containing their personnel within narrow limits, and causing communications from the outside to pass through the hands of special agents, the members of the civil-religious hierarchy in the Indian community, the hacienda owner or his managers on the hacienda. The Mexican revolution of 1910, as the Guatemalan revolution of 1945–54, has been an attempt to break open these monopolies of men and resources, to set the captive peons free to seek new attachments within their communities or to enter into new alliances beyond their communities. But it has also launched a major effort to subvert the protective barriers of the Indian towns, to render them effective components of a larger, more embracing social and cultural structure.

The concept of levels of communal relations or levels of socio-cultural integration

299

Fig. 1—COMMUNAL WORK ON CHURCH ROOF, JACALTENANGO, GUATEMALA. (Photographed in 1927. Middle American Research Institute, Tulane University.)

is especially useful in the analysis of this type of change, since it illuminates the manifold processes of conflict and accommodation which take place when the components of a socio-cultural system are rearranged to answer new needs, or taken up into more embracive systems. The concept itself, as old as St. Thomas Aquinas who spoke of five such levels—family, village, province, kingdom, and the empire of Christendom—has had its most fruitful application and development in anthropology at the hands of Julian Steward (1950, pp. 106–14; 1951). Steward emphasized three major levels: the level of the nuclear family; the level of the multifamily socio-cultural system coordinated through a supra-

family organization, sometimes referred to as the "community" or "folk" level; and the state level of integration, bringing several multifamily aggregates into functional dependence on another within a still larger system. At the same time, he acknowledged clearly that "there are probably several levels of socio-cultural integration between the family and the folk society which should be distinguished. And above the folk society there are many significantly different levels of integration" (Steward, 1951, p. 382).

The term "integration" taken by itself signifies the social and cultural processes by which the part-processes characteristic of a plurality of social and cultural units are coordinated into a social system. Integration may be either "horizontal" in that such coordination takes place among units of approximately the same form and scale; or it may be "vertical" in that coordination is accomplished by a group of decision-makers, organized into a social unit superordinate and embracive of previously existing units. It is in the second case that we may speak of "levels of integration." Integration may, however, be weak, if the participating units coordinate only a few of their processes or do so ineffectively. It may be strong, if the coordinating units interfere effectively with a wide range of processes.

In applying the concept of socio-cultural levels to Middle America, we must include both major levels and sublevels to construct a series which would appear as follows: nuclear family, kindred, *barrio* or ward, community, constellation of town center with dependent communities, constellation of regional capital with satellite towns (given institutional form in Mexico as states, in Guatemala as departments), and, finally, state (Aguirre Beltrán, 1955; B. W. Starr, 1954).

Passing these levels in brief review, we may say that the nuclear family appears to be present everywhere in Indian communities, though it is usually embedded in a constellation of friendly families related through ties of descent, affinity, or ritual kinship. In most parts of Middle America, these constellations of families form bilateral noncorporate kindreds, and the few surviving cases of unilineal corporate organization, such as those of Oxchuc in Chiapas (Villa Rojas, 1947) are undergoing a process of rapid social erosion. A number of bilateral kindreds form a barrio or ward. These units may vary locally from religious sodalities mobilized only on special occasions (e.g., at Tepoztlan, Morelos; see Lewis, 1951, pp. 19–26) to units with enduring loyalties towards members and antagonisms towards other similarly constituted units. In some cases, these groupings may split the community into halves, with each half represented equally in the civil-religious hierarchy, as in unilineal Oxchuc (Siverts, 1960, pp. 19–20) or bilateral Amatenango in Chiapas (J. Nash, 1960b). Or they may take on the characteristics of factions, as in Zapotec-speaking Yalalag, Oaxaca, where a wealthier, more conservative Barrio Santiago opposes a poorer, more "progressive" Barrio San Juan (De la Fuente, 1949, pp. 28–29, 245–46). Important as these barrio divisions may be in concrete cases, however, the community usually exercises a decisive formal overright which includes all families within the boundaries of its communal jurisdiction. Such integration is based on a tendency to defend land and resources against outsiders, to curtail the extensions of the network of affinal kin beyond the communal boundaries, to administer its own internal affairs, to exercise social control against individuals who deviate from established custom, and to maintain an autonomous religious cult involving mechanisms of wealth-distribution which ensure a measure of socio-economic equality among the members of the community.

Although these features of organization ensure the jurisdiction of the community over its members, they also create a gulf between the community striving for separate identity and the higher levels of integration of region, province, or state. This article focuses specifically on the question of how the community is integrated into these higher levels in the realms of economics, social organization, politics, and religion, in three Middle American areas: the Zapotec-speaking area of Oaxaca, the Tarascan-speaking area of Michoacan, and the Peninsula of Yucatan. An attempt will then be made to generalize the results obtained to the area as a whole.

It is incumbent on us to warn the reader to view this material with caution. Areas inhabited by Indians are by definition marginal, and not representative of regions in which the ties between community and state have been strong. The Indian population has been permitted to continue its patterns of culture either because the state was too weak to effect a major transformation, or because the economic and political gains to be expected from such transformation did not warrant the expenditure of effort involved (Monzón, 1947). Unfortunately, the anthropologist has centered his research primarily on Indians, thus neglecting to give us data which would apply to other than marginal areas. Furthermore, the material indicating the nature of ties between levels of integration is still rudimentary. Our data are especially deficient in tracing the ties between region and superordinate state. This is especially true in the political realm, where, of course, the real workings of power are rarely visible to the outside observer.

THE VALLEY OF OAXACA AND ITS ZAPOTEC-SPEAKING HINTERLAND

When we examine the mechanisms of integration of the Valley of Oaxaca and its Zapotec-speaking mountain rim in the economic realm, we find, first, that integration is effected largely through the mechanisms of distribution rather than through the mechanisms of production. The Valley of Oaxaca, in contrast to the Valle Nacional, has never been an area of extensive latifundia, and what large estates massing labor power beyond the capacities of the individual household existed in the past have been divided up and redistributed in the course of the agrarian reform. An example of such redistribution is the Hacienda de Xaaga, near Mitla, which has been divided up among the Spanish-speaking sharecroppers of Mixtec origin (Parsons, 1936, p. 54, note 46) who inhabited it. The mountain country, on the other hand, has never witnessed the aggregation of large productive units. Thus distribution vastly overshadows production as a force of integration, and the three institutions which are relevant in this connection are (a) the market, (b) the commercial network beyond the market, and, to a lesser extent, (c) the offer of specialized services by members of one community in another. Since the market system of the valley has received ample treatment elsewhere (Malinowski and De la Fuente, 1957), little need be said here except to underline the transcendental importance of such an institution in which individuals participate segmentally as buyers or sellers of produce, yet do not allow their tangent economic contact to bear directly on other realms of socio-cultural interaction. Economic interests are thus served without jeopardizing the autonomy of the local culture-bearing units. From this point of view, the market plays a distinctly dual role. Integrative in one sense, the economic, it yet emphasizes the opposition of the various participant segments to each other.

Goods are distributed not only through the market, but also through a network of commercial relationships in which commercial travelers explore the hinterland of the valley in search of gain. This activity involves both carrying goods to the hinterland and bringing goods from it. The area covered by the traveling merchants extends not only into the immediate hinterland, but may reach as far as neighboring Veracruz, often providing commercial contacts for regions in which no market system exists. The

goods distributed may of course come not only from the Valley of Oaxaca, but from as far away as Mexico City or the Isthmus of Tehuantepec, and the goods obtained in the hinterland (especially coffee) may be returned to these far-off places through a marketing chain which transcends regional limits. Individuals from different communities may also offer specialized services to men living elsewhere, as when Mixe- or Zapotec-speakers from Lachirioag hire out to carry burdens for the commercial travelers, or Mixe-speakers from Yacochi, Mixistlan, and Chichicastepec are sought as curers of *espanto* in Yalalag (De la Fuente, 1949, p. 321; see also Parsons, 1936, p. 129). Although many transactions in the market are between small-scale producers who in a few cases exchange goods directly (Malinowski and De la Fuente, 1957, pp. 124–32) or indirectly by converting goods into money and money back into goods, the market is also a place in which buyers from outside collect produce with the purpose of shipping it elsewhere or offer goods for sale which have been manufactured beyond the limits of the region. The market is thus characterized not only by horizontal relationships between individuals or communities, but also contains the vertical channels through which commercial institutions operating at levels higher than the community tap the supplies or the purchasing power found at lower levels. Similarly political institutions operating at the level of market-town, state, or republic use both horizontal and vertical exchanges as means of extracting revenues through taxes. The taxing power is on occasion used to forcibly divert produce which might go into horizontal exchanges into the channel of vertical exchange (Malinowski and De la Fuente, 1957, p. 75). The commercial network beyond the market, moreover, does not set up a systematic exchange between opposing participating sections, but represents essentially a continuation of the vertical network of exchange into the marketless hinterland.

F<small>IG</small>. 2—VILLAGE ELDERS, TENANGO, CHIAPAS, MEXICO. (From Blom and LaFarge, 1927, fig. 313. Middle American Research Institute, Tulane University.)

Everywhere in this region we find that in the smaller rural settlements ties of affinal kinship tend to remain confined within the local group, or—as we have phrased it above—within the local section counterpoised in systematic opposition to like groups within the horizontal market. The Zapotec-speaking hill towns are largely endogamous. The district of Choapan is an exception to this rule, but relations of affinity do not extend beyond the local circuit. In Yalalag, maize emporium of the *bene xon*, however, marriage within the locality is preferred, but affinal relations extend to Betaza and Villa Alta within the highlands, to Oaxaca City, and even to Mexico City; and Mitla, great trading town that it is, does not put up local defenses against immigration or marriage with outsiders (Parsons, 1936, pp. 178–81). We thus note a widening of affinal ties beyond the community as one goes from the localities which are the passive recipients of traded goods to the active purveyors of produce. Neverthe-

less, we must also note that affinal connections remain predominantly on the same level of integration, and even where permitted, only a few such ties reach beyond the community level to personnel operating on the level of state or federal institutions.

The same generalization may be extended to ties of ritual kinship. Compadre ties from Yalalag, for instance, extend to people of Spanish descent, as well as to Zapotec- and Mixe-speakers of the region, and beyond to Catemaco and Otatitlan (De la Fuente, 1949, p. 171). The main function of these extracommunal ties appears to lie in securing already existing lines of horizontal and vertical exchange, but there is no record of such ties which would allow an individual to maneuver into levels transcending the limits of the economic region. Moreover, the tie of ritual kinship, like kinship itself, is particularistic; it centers on the individuals involved and does not guarantee security against other members of the compadre's communities. An example in

303

point is the killing of a man from San Pablo Cuatro Venados by men from Cuilapan, where the murdered man had compadres and friends (Steininger and Van de Velde, 1935, pp. 21–22).

The importance of particularistic ties and the stress on relationships operating on the same level is also evident, however, in the migration patterns followed by people from one community when settling elsewhere. Primary reliance is always on kin and friends, beyond that on compadres, beyond that on people from the same region or sub-region. This leads to the formation of ethnic enclaves (De la Fuente, 1949, pp. 17, 35) and to the maintenance of opposing segments within the larger structure.

The primary importance of local issues is also evident in the political realm. There is, by and large, a reluctance on the part of local authorities to resort to powerholders operating on the next higher level, beyond the community. Charles Leslie has shown, for Mitla, that this reluctance is motivated by unwillingness to be humiliated by outside power figures; by the high cost of bribery paid to ensure the receipt of a favorable decision from these power figures; by foreknowledge that outside authorities will not understand the complicated history of disputes in the community; by uncertainty that favorable decisions will be forthcoming even if adequate bribes are paid; and by fear of vengeance from opponents within the community (Leslie, 1960a, pp. 33–34).

Nevertheless, communal disputes often have a way of becoming state or federal concerns. This is largely due to the existence of factions which align themselves with political parties operating on the level of state or nation, and which are thus able to convert a purely local matter into a matter of much wider concern. Mitla has studiously and successfully avoided the formation of such units by "maintaining a dispersion of conflicts within their town" (ibid., p. 35). This is accomplished by taking a hands-off attitude towards private disputes

that involve violence and turning one's back on any event which might bring about the crystallization of interest groups within the community (ibid., pp. 25–36). While such avoidance of public intervention prevents appeal to the jurisdictional level beyond the community, it also renders impotent the appointed officials of the town. Such withdrawal from active intervention, however, is therefore rare and may be dictated by the wish to avoid friction and maximize the commercial transactions for which Mitla is known throughout the region. More frequent is the formation of groups which rally around active leaders, and back up their support through the use of arms. Such groups may have their origin in trivial incidents, as at Yalalag, where rivalry first began around the end of the 19th century over control of a local tavern (De la Fuente, 1949, p. 239, note 37). Very quickly such groups drape themselves in the symbolisms of state or nation-wide political groupings. At Yalalag, the factions were first "Greens" (progressives) and "Reds" (conservatives), after the model of the state capital; later "Constitucionalistas" (pro-Carranza) and Soberanos; still later agraristas and anti-agraristas. Since the real strength of a faction leader lies in his armed followers, factional fights must be aimed at killing or exiling the leader and on destroying or expelling his armed following. De la Fuente notes six such killings of political leaders in Yalalag between 1935 and 1945. Killings within the village strengthen the loyalty of the killers to their leader, since their feats of arms commit them increasingly to his person. At the same time, every murder immediately sets up a quest for vengeance which sooner or later adds fuel to the flames. In a community like Yalalag where at least 80 of 850 taxpayers may be credited with blood delicts (De la Fuente, 1949, p. 244), feuding remains an ever-present possibility. Moreover, when armed followers of one man are expelled and granted asylum in a nearby community, relationships

304

Fɪɢ. 3—VILLAGE AUTHORITIES, CANCUC, CHIAPAS. (Photographed in 1925. Middle American Research Institute, Tulane University.)

between the communities involved tend to deteriorate.

The logical development of the factional fight which ends in the elimination of a faction is the rule of the victorious group and, through the victory of this group, of one boss. Boss rule, it must be noted, can exist side by side with the more traditional authorities of the indigenous population. Ralph Beals has given us one of the very rare pictures we possess of such a man among the Mixe. The Colonel, Daniel Martínez, of Mixe origin, risen in the military hierarchy of the outside world and acquainted with its language and ways, returned to the Mixeria to become its *Jefe de Defensa.* Supported at one time by the intervention of federal troops and basing himself locally on a small armed force, he became a fountainhead of advice for people who seek aid against the local authorities as well as for the authorities who come to ask

him for help in problems they cannot solve themselves, as well as a promoter of public works, roadbuilding, and schools (Beals, 1945b, pp. 19–20, 34–37, 133). One may speculate on whether such a principle of boss rule or dominant personal influence is not at odds with the traditional basis of the civil-religious hierarchy. The hierarchy is appointed through processes of consensus-management that involve the entire community. The positions contained within it may be achieved through appropriate participation and behavior, yet are shorn of the attributes of individual power. The main functions of the hierarchy are to maintain the internal equilibrium of the community; it accomplishes this by keeping the outside world at arm's length. In contrast, the position of the boss is gained by dividing the community and by establishing the dominance of one section over another, perhaps to the point of excluding the competi-

305

tors. His power is maintained by giving preferential treatment to some over others that cannot be matched by a potential rival. Even where a boss is absolute, therefore, the possibility for feud always exists, for he can never be sure that a rival will not arise, better fitted than himself to give protection and offer help. One of the effects of this is that he must always seek support outside, to strengthen the foundations of his rule inside. His connections with a higher level of integration thus would appear necessarily to threaten the traditional distribution of power within the community.

A similar challenge to the constituted authority of the civil-religious hierarchy is represented by the rise of newly rich merchant-entrepreneurs in towns such as Mitla. Thus Leslie has written of how at Mitla an individual's status was less and less determined by town service, more and more by individual achievement. "By 1929–33, for instance, men did not receive any special recognition for having completed their town service, and the offices of fiscales, traditionally occupied by men in their final year of servicio, were not of high rank. Money competed with sacred rituals and kinship in defining social relationships . . ." (Leslie, 1960a, p. 14).

The social dominance of the merchant is also evident at Yalalag, where power is located in a great family whose trading and manufacturing members have achieved considerable position (De la Fuente, 1949, p. 214).

Yet feuding not only persists in communities, it also persists between communities. These feuds sometimes have their origins in fights over land or access to resources like a forest from which people derive an income as charcoal burners. Such fights have been recorded, for instance, in different parts of the Valley rim, between San Pablo Cuatro Venados and Cuilapan (Steininger and Van de Velde, 1935, pp. 18–22); Santa Cruz Etla and San Felipe de Agua (Bailey, 1958, pp. 20–21), and Ayutla and Tlahuitoltepec (Beals, 1945b, pp. 16–18). Fights have developed between Yalalag and San Mateo, San Francisco and Zoochila, over the granting of asylum to armed members of a defeated faction, or between communities ranged on opposing political sides, as between Yalalag on the one hand and Zoochila, Yatzachi, Betaza, El Bajo, San Mateo, and San Francisco on the other (De la Fuente, 1949, pp. 252–53). Such disputes often may be terminated with a ceremonial exchange of musical bands and mutual visiting, a mechanism also used to stress peaceful relations in less clouded times (Parsons, 1936, p. 190).

Beyond the economic encounters in the market place or in the commercial network, and beyond the tenuous ties of affinity and friendship and occasional exchanges of bands, there are few formal organizations linking the various communities. A Unión de Campesinos Serranos Villaltecos, sponsored by progressives and schoolteachers (De la Fuente, 1948, p. 403; 1949, p. 25), exists to put pressure on the state or federal government in the interests of the hill people, but its effectiveness appears to be limited. A similar organization has been set up in the Mixeria, under the leadership of a new political boss, successful rival to the Colonel, with headquarters at Zacatepec. Its functionality remains to be determined. The atomism of local communities in Oaxaca has increased, if anything, in recent years, since the passage of the law of 1938 granting communities greater administrative autonomy from their regional centers. In some cases this measure has robbed formerly more important administrative towns of their specialized functions, while increasing commercial prosperity has often allowed their former charges to overtake them in economic status and education. An example of this is the relation of declining Villa Alta to its former hinterland (De la Fuente, 1948, pp. 402–03).

Fig. 4—MAXEÑOS ON WAY TO MARKET, CHICHE, EL QUICHE, GUATEMALA. (Photographed by Dan Leyrer, 1937. Middle American Research Institute, Tulane University.)

In the religious sphere, again, communal integration is dominant over higher levels of integration. In both Yalalag and Mitla, the local folk religion operates in relative independence of the higher ecclesiastical institutions. "The Yalaltecos," says Julio de la Fuente, "generally show a tendency to have their own Church—as they also have their own municipality and other institutions,—and to maintain priests who yield before what they wish or indicate" (1949, p. 272). The same is characteristic of Mitla. In both communities, it must be noted, increased wealth has gone to finance an increase in the local institutions that sponsor and carry on religious festivities, though increasingly with a secular emphasis (De la Fuente, 1949, p. 363; Leslie, 1960a, p. 58).

Since such ceremonial expenditures act to drain off and destroy economic surpluses, they operate as mechanisms which retard the process of capital investment and inhibit the formation of new vertical economic channels. Their persistence, therefore, tends to strengthen communal autonomy, and to create barriers to wider socio-cultural integration.

Communities as equivalent segments within a horizontal system interact further through the mechanism of religious pilgrimages, which often accompany the trips to the weekly rotating markets or wider commercial journeys. Thus Yalalag carries on pilgrimages to towns in the Mixeria and in the nearby Zapotec-speaking zone. Only occasional pilgrimages to Oaxaca City and

Mexico City take the worshippers to shrines that represent—on the symbolic level—the existence of wider levels of integration.

THE TARASCAN-SPEAKING AREA OF MICHOACAN

The Tarascan-speaking area resembles the Zapotec-speaking region of the Valley of Oaxaca in a number of ways. Here as there, the individual relies on the particularistic network of affinal relations and on compadre relationships to stabilize his position in the world. Here as there, the individual is a member of a community, active in maintaining community membership and influenced by it. As in Oaxaca, so in Tarascan Michoacan communities specialize in various products, and men from different communities meet to exchange goods in weekly rotating markets. As in Oaxaca, also, Tarascan-speakers engage in trade beyond the market, going as traveling merchants from town to town, and communicating coast with highland. As in Oaxaca, moreover, religious attendance and pilgrimages build a network of relationships across the Tarascan-speaking area, as from Tzintzuntzan to Morelia, to Patzcuaro, and—formerly—to San Juan Parangaricutiro.

Again, as at Mitla, growing commercial involvement and the development of wealth based on sources other than land have created a new group of aspirants to status and power. This is most clear at Paracho, the landless sierra town specializing in the manufacture of wooden artifacts of all kinds, where production has transcended the scope of the individual craftsman to reach the level of organization of the large shop with 8–30 workers. Such an establishment no longer funnels its produce into the local markets or into the network maintained by traveling merchants, but sells to urban distributors. Here control of credit by the wealthy has resulted in a monopolization of productive equipment and distributive outlets that underwrites a social and economic

dominance easily translatable into political terms even where the formally elected figures are other than the men who hold the reins of economic power. In a community like Paracho, therefore, the owner of the large craftshop or the wealthy merchant comes to stand between the individual members of the community and the higher levels of organization beyond (Kaplan, 1953).

The Tarascan area further resembles Zapotec Oaxaca in its political factionalism, but it far surpasses the Zapotec-speaking region in the intensity and the ideological orientation of its political strife. As in Oaxaca, there were few large estates to divide, with the exception, perhaps, of the southern edge of Lake Patzcuaro and the vicinity of the Zacapu marsh. Yet the slogans of agrarian redistribution found a receptive echo, with the result, however, that land to stake the landless claimants to property was generally taken from small holders rather than from wealthy landowners. Redistribution of land in the sierra was complicated, moreover, through the existence of subleasing arrangements so that the resultant reshuffling of titles hurt not only the original owner but also all those who made a living off his land through leasing land from him (Aguirre Beltrán, 1952, pp. 152–53; Carrasco, 1952b, pp. 20–21).

The struggles between agraristas and anti-agraristas in consequence caused here deep and bitter schisms. In Durazno, Paul Friedrich counted 23 cross-checked politically motivated homicides and several times more woundings and armed encounters for the years between 1937 and 1939 (Friedrich, 1958, p. 28). Cheran, taken over at the height of the agrarian movement in Michoacan by some 30 agraristas, in 1939, killed a dozen and expelled the rest (Beals, 1946, p. 112). In 1938 most of the agraristas who had taken over Charapan were killed; a handful of families found refuge in Paracho (Aguirre Beltrán, 1952, p. 153; Kaplan,

FIG. 5—GUATEMALA HIGHLAND INDIAN MARKET. (Photographed by Dan Leyrer, 1937. Middle American Research Institute, Tulane University.)

1953, p. 26). In Nahuatzen, the agraristas defended their seizure of the town commons against the inhabitants of the town in what proved to be a Pyrrhic victory. Santa Elena and Huecato near Chilchota, on the other hand, passed entirely into the hands of the agraristas who expelled their opponents (Kaplan, *ibid.*). These developments have in general weakened the authority of the traditional civil-religious hierarchies, and produced here as elsewhere the phenomenon of the political boss who comes to power through the leadership of a political faction. The "real" boss of Cheran rose to his position by organizing the fight against the agraristas. His influence apparently extends over a wider area, well beyond Cheran (Beals, 1946, p. 113).

Such factions are linked, through the informal ties of loyalty or the formal ties of organization, to political organization operating on the regional or national level, such as the *Confederación de Trabajadores Mexicanos,* or to the clerically oriented, protofascist Sinarquist Party. In general, the agrarista factions gained political control during the presidency of Lázaro Cárdenas and have since been displaced or pushed back by groups with Sinarquist or quasi-Sinarquist affiliations. Certain towns have in this struggle emerged as focal points of agrarismo, others as focal points of Sinarquismo. Tzintzuntzan, studied by George Foster (1948a) was heavily under Sinarquist influence. Paul Friedrich, on the other hand, has drawn an excellent picture (1958, p. 27) of the political constitution of an agrarista town to which he gives the name of Durazno, and shown how ties of kinship, affinity, ritual kinship, and friendship are all mobilized to support the position of the local political boss and his armed following. People say that this town specializes in politics the way other towns specialize in making hats or pots.

Durazno leaders have occupied numerous formal positions at higher levels owing to the salient informal role of the tiny pueblo in the intrigue, violence, and heartfelt radicalism of Michoacán politics. Politics and the cultivation of political leaders have in fact become a sort of communal specialty in Durazno. Durazno caciques founded and held numerous offices in the state-wide peasant League of Agrarian Communities; they have been municipal presidents three times, state congressmen three times, and, once, substitute to a national congressman. They have always formally controlled the important "Regional Committee," the regional organ of the National Peasant Confederation. While highly atypical with respect to this prominence, Durazno does exemplify the role that tough, sophisticated and land-controlling Indian caciques can play in regional and state politics.

Pedro Carrasco (1952b) provides an excellent study of the contradictory trends in integration of community and higher levels within the Tarascan-speaking area. The agraristas stood not only for a different distribution of land and resources but also for "atheism," meaning minimally disestablishment of the church as a holder of property, restrictions on the number of activities of the clergy, the establishment of secular education. At Urapicho, for instance, where the agraristas remained dominant, the church was never rebuilt, and at Tzutumutaro and Puaca churches and the priests' houses were

turned into social centers and schools. Cargos and fiestas were forbidden (Carrasco, 1952b, p. 32). The church, on the other hand, pursues a policy of upholding priestly authority and ecclesiastical education; yet it similarly wishes to put an end to the autonomy of local civil-religious hierarchies or religious sodalities which threaten to make the "little tradition" of the folk an autonomous system of its own, independent of the larger system of the church (see, for instance, Kaplan, 1951). Conservative Tarascans are thus often pulled two ways. They see in agrarista anticlericalism an attack on sacred symbols and associate the reaction against the agrarians with the defense of these symbols. Yet the church to which they belong also demands that they yield their autonomous religious jurisdictions to the proper ecclesiastical authorities. "The conflict between conservative and disruptive tendencies goes on," says Carrasco (1952b, p. 58), "and a stable integration can not be attained."

YUCATAN

If Michoacan and Oaxaca show a basic similarity of patterns and trends, but for the sharpening of the agrarian conflict in Michoacan and the consequent accentuation of ideological involvements, Yucatan differs from these two regions in two major respects. For where the Tarascan-speaking area lay on the margins of the hacienda country in Michoacan and where Zapotec Oaxaca never faced directly the problems of the voracious large estate, Yucatan developed the hacienda system in all its florescence. The hacienda fulfilled both productive and distributive functions. As a productive system, it integrated the labor supply into a community. Yet it also erected its characteristic social barriers between laboring community and higher levels of integration. The hacienda, not the individual small producer, marketed its crop of henequen. If Yucatan differed from the two cases pre-

Fig. 6—MEN FROM SACAPULAS, GUATEMALA, SELLING CANDY AND TUMPLINES. (Photographed by F. Webster McBryde about 1935. Middle American Research Institute, Tulane University.)

viously discussed in possessing extensive haciendas, it also lacked the marketing system characteristic of Oaxaca, Michoacan, or other areas of Middle America. Buying and selling is here done through stores or ambulant traders; ultimately, as Redfield put it (1941, p. 156), here "the city makes the trade." Exchanges of locally produced goods include maize, minor foods, brown sugar, hammocks, and baskets, but the amounts exchanged are small and unimportant (ibid., p. 381, note 3). It is this commercial network without Indian markets which links the two major regions of Yucatan: the henequen-producing northwest and the maize-producing southeast. Henequen is exported beyond the confines of the peninsula, whereas the maize-producing zone raises its produce largely to satisfy its own needs and to feed the henequen-producers.

The agrarian revolution, here as elsewhere, went through several successive phases. Peonage was abolished in 1915, giving great impetus to population movements and to the extension of affinal ties beyond the local level. It was following this liberation of the labor supply from its local ties, for example, that Chan Kom, founded on the frontier of the maize area, doubled its population (Steggerda, 1941, p. 9). Yet the large henequen-producing estates—owned largely by upper class residents of Merida, but worked by Maya-speaking laborers—were not broken up until 1937, and their importance as processing centers for newly founded ejidos, for small private holders, and for their own residual estates persists to this day. Plans to dispossess their decorticating plants were prepared but never put into effect. The hacienda cores thus continue to exercise considerable influence in the countryside, even though they must share power with government-installed or -supervised agencies. Between 1937 and 1955 this government-sponsored

311

peak organization was *Henequeneros de Yucatan,* since divided into three separate autonomously functioning bodies.

In a study of such a henequen-producing hacienda, near Merida, called Mukui-il by the author, Shirley Deshon has shown that the paternalistic boss with personal interest in his workers is still addressed with formalized respect. Though he no longer distributes food to his workers, he grants them the privilege to raise crops on residual estate lands, a privilege which he can withdraw and which thus constitutes an important indirect sanction at his disposal, together with the right to fire workers altogether. He extends loans both to individuals and to the local ejido society. He no longer has any judicial rights over his workers, but he continues to hear complaints, and he may intervene for workers in search of medical aid at the relevant public agencies. He encourages the formation of formal marital unions over consensual arrangements, may contribute to weddings, and may sponsor workers' children in baptism. He has also encouraged the visits of a catechist and contributes to the annual fiesta (Deshon, 1959, pp. 98–101). Thus, the owner "remains an important force because of social and economic conditions peculiar to Mukui-il, and to the extent that the Mukui-ileños' material needs, economic security, and local prestige continue to be based on their relationships with the owner" (p. 101). The foreman, intervening between owner and workers, moreover, constitutes another important middleman between community and higher levels. A member of the community and the ejido society, he wields his power to allocate henequen fields and residual plots to eligible workers, to contract workers from elsewhere, together with his influential kin relationships to overseers and labor contractors to maintain a complex balance of factions in the community (p. 103). In contrast, the ejido is riven by multiple cliques based on kinship and opposing interests

and can rarely achieve clearcut leadership (pp. 103–05).

Unlike most Maya communities in the bush, individuals and families from Mukui-il have kinsmen in nearby towns and on neighboring haciendas whom they visit and in whose life-cycle events they participate. They also shop or sell in the towns. A significant development is the growth of reciprocal assistance in the preparation and carrying out of religious ceremonies between sodalities located in Mukui-il on the one hand and T-Town (another pseudonym) and Tizimin on the other. Pilgrimages extend to Tizimin and Izamal (pp. 93–97).

In contrast to Mukui-il where the shadow of the past still hangs heavy over the present, Chan Kom in the maize zone has "chosen progress" (Redfield and Villa, 1934; Redfield, 1950) and established successful links with higher levels of integration. The first settlement in the area was founded at the end of the last century, but the community did not gain prominence till the revolution of 1915 abolished debt peonage and released a great flood of migrants as colonists to the southern area. Chan Kom began its revolutionary career as a dependency of nearby Ebtun, but soon came into conflict with the dominant town over the requirement to carry out there compulsory labor at public improvement. In its attempt to shake off this hegemony, it became a bastion of the Socialist Party in the southeast in its battles with the conservative *Liberales.* This affiliation stood Chan Kom in good stead. The *Liga de Resistencia* organized in Chan Kom was the main instrument in securing recognition from the state leadership for the little settlement in the bush. In 1926 Chan Kom became the first community in the area to receive an ejido grant, and in 1934 it became an independent municipio.

In its phase of growth, Chan Kom exhibited a pattern characteristic of other Maya-speaking villages. The struggles between

Liberales and Socialists on the state level in 1923 involved it in conflicts on the local level with the neighboring communities of Yaxcaba and Sotuta. When these attacked X-Kopteil, friendly to Chan Kom, Chan Kom made war on them and accepted Socialist refugees from Yaxcaba.

Thus was expressed in violent form [says Redfield, 1950, p. 11] that endless struggle among the Maya settlements: a factional dispute within a settlement is resolved by the victory of one party; those of the defeated party take refuge and establish residence in some neighboring village that has given aid to their party for reasons arising from the rivalry between the two settlements . . . a mechanism whereby the bold and vigorous settlement, the settlement that defends itself and takes up the interests of its friends in other settlements, grows strong at the expense of its rivals.

Thus Chan Kom has prospered, while older towns like Dzitas, formerly important because of its location on the railroad but now displaced by new highways, have tended to stagnate.

Chan Kom has, in fact, become wealthier and more powerful than many villages surrounding it. Here, as in Paracho, Mitla and Yalalag, the full-time merchant is a rising figure of social, economic, and political importance. Livestock raising has become a major source of income, and livestock raising damages the milpas of the hinterland, involving Chan Kom in disputes and hostile relations with outlying hamlets, with many of which Chan Kom is related through affinal ties and visiting patterns. Communities that have no livestock and that face an increase in population without adequate resources in land to absorb it, view the prosperity of Chan Kom with misgivings. These motives came into play when Chan Kom was riven by internal dissensions, due to a split between families that became Protestants and other kindred who went back on their original conversions. As internal dissension mounted, hamlets in the orbit of

Chan Kom began to question Chan Kom's authority over them and to pull away in the direction of neighboring communities which, in turn, were doing their best to foment trouble. The tug-of-war was settled first by the intervention of federal troops and later by the withdrawal of most Protestants from Chan Kom to a nearby hamlet, leaving Chan Kom once more substantially homogeneous in its religious affiliation.

Again we witness the formation of factions, first with respect to politics, and later —when the early goals of material security and political independence were won— around the issue of religious denominationalism. The results of this religious struggle are not entirely clear. Redfield suggests (1950, p. 112) that the appearance of Protestantism in a number of local communities may foreshadow the development of a Protestant society which transcends the community level. Such a growth would be spurred by the need, among other factors, to find mates who belong to the faith. On the other hand, the local folk religion continues in its ancient ways, captained by its characteristic leaders, the *maestro cantor* and the *h-men*.

Conclusions

On the basis of these three regional cases we may note the existence of the following processes:

(1) The market system where it exists appears to be the main institution perpetuating the links of horizontal integration between communities. The extramarket commercial network, functioning side by side with the regular market among the Tarascans and Zapotecs, alone in Yucatan, appears to be the main carrier of vertical exchanges, and links lower to higher levels of integration. As these channels bear increasingly heavy flows of products, there is also a tendency for the successful merchant-entrepreneur, singular or plural, to become a major intermediary between the community and higher levels. Nevertheless, it

313

would appear that increased wealth flowing through the channels as such does not of itself subvert the relative autonomy in economic values imposed by the community. Thus increased wealth may also mean increased expenditure for ceremonial ends. Up to a point, therefore, increased participation in the outside commercial network may accentuate the integrity of the community in other cultural aspects, unless changes in the field of values keep pace with changes in economics.

(2) In the field of social ties, involving ties of descent and affinity, ritual kinship and friendship, one may note that endogamy is strongest and the circle of acquaintances outside the community narrowest in the communities least involved in economic and political struggles, widest in communities that have dealings with institutions representing a wider level of integration. Although the material on extracommunity relations of kinship and friendship is exceedingly scanty, it may be worth our while in this context to stress the importance of these ties in societies in which many economic and political transactions follow the lines of kinship and friendship. Hacienda system and Indian community prevented the formation of such wider range of ties; the demise of the hacienda and the opening up of Indian communities to more extensive outside contact permit their formation. Not all members of a community, however, can take equal advantage of this new opportunity. One may surmise that it is the successful political leader or the successful merchant-entrepreneur whose circle of kin and friends is largest, and more than that, embraces personnel operating at the next higher level of integration. Where this is true, we witness the conversion of ethnic groups into classes (Harris, 1959). Conversely, such participation in the class system of the larger socio-cultural system acts as a device in differentiating the personnel of a community or region and in selecting the agents

within it who will become the "brokers" between community and state.

(3) In the political sphere, we observe a tendency on the part of factions formed on the basis of wholly communal issues to take on the trappings of political parties on the state level of integration. This process undermines the autonomy of the community perhaps more effectively than any other, and may furnish the chief mechanism for the penetration of the community by the state.

(4) In the religious sphere, the processes of integration appear contradictory. Everywhere in Indian Middle America there is a tendency to carry on the religion of the folk, the "little" religious traditions of the folk, in independence or separation from the "great tradition" of Catholic religion, through specialists or semispecialists who are not members of the ecclesiastical hierarchy and often in opposition to them. This tendency towards autonomy may be explained in part through the fact that the myths and rituals of the little tradition are functionally a component of the religio-political system through which the political autonomy of the community was preserved, and of its wealth-distributing mechanisms which maintained the internal homogeneity of its members. It has a further explanation, stressed by Richard Adams (1957a, p. 353), in the great wave of anticlericalism of the 19th and early 20th centuries which reduced the number of priests in the country districts and otherwise heavily curtailed the ability of the Church to maintain contact with the Indian hinterland. One may predict therefore a general increase in interference with the native folk traditions and popular religious practices wherever the Church appears to be in the ascendancy. This is most clearly evident in the Tarascan-speaking area. To the extent that these efforts at reforming the popular religion are successful, they curtail ceremonial expenditures through the traditional *mayordomías*

314

and may have pronounced effects on the internal economic differentiation of the communities and on the degree of integration of the community into wider levels of integration. Such efforts may thus have directly or indirectly the same effects as the abolition of costly sponsorships by the anticlerical agraristas or by Protestants. On the other hand, one may expect, under such renewed clerical tutelage, a decrease in pilgrimages to regional shrines associated with local popular saints, a pattern which in the Tarascan and Zapotec areas reinforces horizontal integration of the Indian markets, and an increase of visits to shrines located in the state or federal capital, such as the Basilica of the Virgin of Guadalupe, representative of the national level of integration (Wolf, 1958). To the extent, furthermore, that the individual ecclesiastics or ecclesiastical organizations support a political faction, as they have done in the Tarascan area, such support further speeds the disintegration of communal autonomy, and integration with organizations operating on a higher integrative level.

These conclusions, arrived at through the comparison of Mexican materials, are also applicable, *pari passu,* to conditions in highland Guatemala. Here, also, we find as the dominant institution of exchange the market in which individuals belonging to various communities exchange their products in horizontal fashion. The system of exchange is paralleled by a system of pilgrimages. These mechanisms appear to have remained relatively intact, even where a factory has invaded the local setting, as in Cantel (M. Nash, 1958a). There the wages paid by the factory have served, in part, to sustain the expenditures essential to the maintenance of the ceremonial system.

The greatest change in Guatemala appears to have occurred rather in the political sphere, where the revolution of 1945–54 produced, on the local as well as the national level, the sudden growth of political groupings and voluntary associations with a political slant. These groupings served as transmission belts for the government in its attempt to overcome the inertia of the autonomous communities and to breach local defensive barriers. Elections or appointments of officials regardless of previous communal service did much to undermine the traditional civil-religious hierarchies. It is likely that this phenomenon is irreversible, despite the political changes which have taken place in Guatemala since 1954. As Adams has summed up (1957b, p. 38), "political action, initiated outside the community, brought about a destruction of or violent alterations in the socio-political structure (whether purely Indian or Ladino-Indian) and with this change, the Indian's resistance to culture change began to disintegrate. His insulation was gone."

In the religious realm, we may note again the persistence of what Adams has termed "a reformation of activities on a non-priest dominated basis" (1957a, p. 353). Indians and Ladinos maintain separate sodalities and religious celebrations (p. 356). Where there are priests, they have inveighed against traditional Indian folk cults. The reform government of 1945–54 followed an outright anticlerical line; there has been an upswing in clerical influence since 1954 (p. 353). To these contradictory influences has been added the weight of Protestant conversions by individuals who wish to break the cycle of drinking and poverty associated with the traditional folk religion or to avoid the expenditures required by full participation in the brotherhoods, or who wish to take advantage of the social service benefits extended through the missions, or who are spiritually unsatisfied by the traditional rituals of Catholicism (J. Nash, 1960a). Here, as in the three Mexican cases cited above, anticlericalism, formal Christianity, and Protestantism join hands in discrediting the principles of recruitment

315

underlying the traditional civil-religious hierarchies and point the way to other alternative modes of political and social recruitment which will tie the communities more completely to the wider level of the state.

REFERENCES

Adams, R. N., 1957a, 1957b
Aguirre Beltrán, 1952, 1955
Bailey, 1958
Beals, 1945b, 1946
Blom and LaFarge, 1927
Carrasco, 1952b
De la Fuente, 1948, 1949
Deshon, 1959
Foster, 1948a
Friedrich, 1958
Harris, 1959
Kaplan, 1951, 1953
Leslie, 1960a
Lewis, 1951
Malinowski and De la Fuente, 1957

Monzón, 1947
Nash, J., 1960a, 1960b
Nash, M., 1958a
Parsons, 1936
Redfield, 1941, 1950
—— and Tax, 1952
—— and Villa R., 1934
Siverts, 1960
Starr, B. W., 1954
Steggerda, 1941
Steininger and Van de Velde, 1935
Steward, 1950, 1951
Villa R., 1947
Wolf, 1955b, 1957, 1958, 1959

16. Annual Cycle and Fiesta Cycle

RUBEN E. REINA

MIDDLE AMERICAN economic and social life is oriented toward agriculture. Only a narrow margin remains from the business of making a living, which demands foresight, calculation, and careful use of natural resources. This needs the development of a rhythm, which, once the balance is found, must be sustained rigorously. In contrast with the rhythm of city dwellers, these people live by a work rhythm largely dependent on nature. For the purpose of this study, the Indians' efforts to subsist throughout a calendar year constitute what we are here calling the annual cycle.[1]

Among the heavily populated countries of Latin America fiestas take up approximately one-third of the year, in addition to holidays at other times. Celebrations "tend to implicate the whole community or the whole extended family . . . and draw at least the presence, if not the active partici-

pation, of everybody in the community and its environs" (Salz, 1955, p. 98). There has been a marked change since the colonial period. The Spaniards "did not comprehend that, for the Indian, no work was worth doing which was not infused by ceremonial symbolism. . . . work was punctuated by ritual and festive occasion; work itself was ceremonially performed" (Kubler [1947, pp. 392–42] in Salz, 1955, p. 97). Among the Indians little affected by Spanish rule—very few—the seasonal habit of work is almost inseparable from religious ceremonialism. The impact of acculturative pressures in the 16th century, especially under Christian influence, divided work from religious festivities. Religion and work are not as closely interrelated nowadays, so that fiestas may be distractions instead of integral parts of the total effort.

Let us examine the relationship between these two areas of activity. The fiesta cycle embraces scheduled religious holidays believed to benefit all members of the group. Activities springing from individual initiative (baptisms, weddings, funerals, Mass, family saint celebrations) are mentioned only in passing. Only indirectly do we draw

---

[1] I extend my sincere appreciation to graduate students and members of a Middle American seminar, conducted in 1960 at the University of Pennsylvania, for their discussions and assistance in the search for raw material; and also to those colleagues who answered my questionnaire.

317

Fig. 1—BRINGING OUT BANNERS FOR CARNAVAL, JACALTENANGO, GUATE-MALA. (Photographed in 1927 from LaFarge and Byers, 1931, fig. 26. Middle American Research Institute, Tulane University.)

attention to the ability of the Indians to support both cycles. The crucial question is whether one is carried on at the expense of the other, and to what extent. We further consider matters related to timing, discipline, degree of mass participation, motivation, and willingness, as well as continuity of the annual and fiesta patterns when people are under stress.

The picture can be pieced together from only a very few complete field studies. Because their methodology has varied during the last 30 years and their publication has been highly selective our data are uneven. Furthermore, it is unsatisfactory to generalize from relatively few and frequently very small groups to regions in which there are many thousands of individuals whose histories have been differently linked and affected. Unfortunately, study of a single community frequently reveals the workings of the two cycles within the smaller context of a village, whereas the total calendar cycle often goes beyond such limits. This is often suggested only. To know wherein a community is representative and wherein distinctive forms a difficult problem.

Gaps in full listings of fiestas, size of attendance, role of community interrelations, population roles, relationship with the non-Indian population, effect of national events on both cycles, sources and amount of money for celebrations, and fiestas related to work and leisure all had to be considered in the preparation of this article.

NORTHWEST HIGHLANDS

Most of the annual activities for subsistence in the northwest highlands of Guatemala begin during February. For two months all attention is turned to burning and clearing *milpa* plots in preparation for planting corn. Although the amount of time spent in the milpas varies with the variety of corn produced, a family with 40 *cuerdas* works approximately 135 days of the year in this alone. In April potatoes are planted; from May through December fields are cleared and wheat is cultivated.

The harvest of early corn begins in mid-September as does the cutting of wheat and the gathering of potatoes and beans. At the same time the late corn is bent, and harvest in the *siembras* (fields) of *ayotes*

318

and *chilacayotes* is begun. This marks the end of the rainy season in the area. In mid-November the late corn is harvested.

After the crucial moment in the care of the milpa passes in late September, only a few members of the extended families (those who live on distant milpas) are left to care for the fields; the rest migrate to the Boca Costa in search of work in coffee plantations. The combination of producing basic crops, acquiring cash through marketing of surpluses, and laboring in coffee plantations rounds out the annual subsistence activities. Very little time is left between the end of these and the first of February when the burning of the milpas is begun again, and the preparation of the fields for the planting initiates a new cycle. Constant economic activity allows little leisure.

Of the whole agricultural cycle, October is the least busy month. Work continues but requires fewer individuals per field; it is also less oppressive since the growing season does not demand constant attention. Therefore, from some communities[2] one-third of the population leaves for the coffee plantations. March also affords a few days of leisure, either before or after the seeding. The time is used for the erection or completion of houses begun during the dry season.

In contrast, all of August and part of September are crucial. Daily inspection of the fields is maintained, and milpa owners become anxious about crop damage from heavy rain, high winds, or hail. During this period of anxiety people go to *chimanes*, who perform rituals to assure successful crops. To augment the ritual, sex taboos are observed, and during the ritual candles, *copal*, and prayers are offered in field and church.

The religious activities constitute only

[2] Since this article was submitted, and too late to make extensive revisions in proof, I have reconsidered the concept of the term "community" and prefer that the term "town" or "village" (whichever is appropriate) be substituted therefor throughout this article.

FIG. 2—EASTER CELEBRATION, CHINAUTLA, GUATEMALA. Apostles and their assistants in churchyard on Holy Thursday. (From Reina, 1960. Middle American Research Institute, Tulane University.)

part of the entire fiesta cycle of Indian communities, for seldom does a month pass without a fiesta of some kind. There are three types. One is *costumbres,* including the aforementioned rituals conducted by chimanes. The second is the *fiesta de costumbre,* which includes the celebration of saints conducted by appointed individuals in *hermandades* and *cofradías.* The saints have no popular appeal and frequently hold only a minor position in the Catholic hierarchy. The third type comprises those fiestas organized by the religious groups, the *pueblo,* and the civil-political units, and are called *fiestas patronales or fiestas titulares.*

Most important in the area are the celebrations of Candelaria, San José, Virgen del Rosario, San Francisco, Todos Santos, Santa Cruz, Corpus Christi, Santiago, Natividad, San Ildefonso, San Antonio Abad, Santa Eulalia, and Santo Tomás. Some of the saints in a community are honored in a fiesta patronal; the same saints in other communities are assigned to one of the fiestas

319

Fig. 3—EASTER CELEBRATION, CHINAUTLA, GUATEMALA. Washing apostle's feet. (From Reina, 1960. Middle American Research Institute, Tulane University.)

de costumbres. The fiesta patronal requires from three to five days and attracts individuals from various communities and *aldeas*, most of whom come as merchants and pilgrims.

The few communities studied in the region fail to show specific patterns and therefore cannot be correlated with the annual cycle. However, a report in the files of the Instituto Indigenista de Guatemala states that the highest concentration of fiestas patronales comes in July and August during the rainy season and again during November, December, and January in the dry season. The fact that agricultural duties are very demanding from March through May suggests a correlation between the annual and fiesta cycles for this area, but it is difficult to establish a correlation in terms of leisure. During these months of frequent celebration the people are busy, but they are also racked with anxiety, for they will soon know whether their crops will succeed or fail.

MIDWESTERN AND EASTERN HIGHLANDS

In the midwestern and eastern highlands similarities in the individual cycles are more significant than differences, and so these areas are considered together. In these lower altitudes wheat and potatoes are replaced by *siembras* of fruits and vegetables.

After the harvest of corn in January, agriculturalists concentrate on preparing their fields by burning or by clearing without burning. The fields are seeded and, with the coming of rain, are weeded diligently. Farmers with fields of 20 or more cuerdas attend their crops full time during the growing season, seeking temporary work on fincas only during October and November. Many communities of the midwestern and eastern highlands are known for their textile, charcoal, and pottery industries, which absorb much of the free time during the dry season, although production continues on a small scale throughout the year. Where water is available and irrigation is practiced *huisquiles* (pear-shaped fruit) and other fruits and flowers are grown, making a fully agricultural cycle for the entire year.

During the dry season, the pottery centers are intensely active, men mining the clay and women shaping and firing the pottery. The Indians also make tiles and adobe bricks, and repair and build houses. Those who are unable to find sufficient work during this period seek employment on a finca or in urban centers where houses are being constructed.

Throughout the area rituals are conducted, by individuals or by leading families, for the control of the elements affecting the agricultural cycle. Some Chorti proceed with the rain-making ceremony about April 25th, use the *padrino* to induce the Chicchans to send rain, spread the blood of a turkey on the ground, prepare a planting festival on May 4th, and perform rites to the wind gods on May 15th. The Pokomames of Chinautla prepare a pilgrimage to an important hill to request rain.

Fig. 4—CAPITANAS LED BY TUTAHPISH IN RITUAL, CHINAUTLA, GUATEMALA. (From Reina, 1960. Middle American Research Institute, Tulane University.)

Anthropological literature indicates an equal distribution of community fiestas throughout the year, the fewest occurring in January, February, August, and September. But a generalization from this literature alone will be incorrect. Data collected by the Instituto Indigenista for the fiesta titulares showed the highest concentration of religious activities during January, February, June, July, and December, and fewer in August, September, and November. The same distribution applies to the eastern area, except for a total lack of fiestas titulares in May and September. Only one community had celebrations in January, April, October, and November; the peak of fiesta activities is in February, July, August, and December.

The administration of the fiestas falls into the hands of the members of the cofradías, who are in turn assisted by *sacristanes* and other religious practitioners. In the Pokomam community of Chinautla the *tatahpish* and the *tutahpish* (fig. 4) supervise and manage the action of the cofradías and direct much of the native religious life.

Among the fiestas patronales and fiestas de costumbres are Esquipulas, Holy Week, Ascención, Corpus Christi, Santa Cruz, San Juan, Santiago, San Miguel, Dolores, Todos Santos, San Andres, Concepción, and Natividad. Because the fiestas de costumbres come at a busy time of year, they are attended only by members of the religious organizations, but the rest of the inhabitants, heeding the urgent economic demands of the season, are aware of the activities, know all the steps as they are announced through rockets, participate at a distance, and serve as a forceful pressure on the members (*mayordomos* and *capitanas*) representing the pueblo. The rest of the population proceeds with the imperative demands of the season. The fiestas patronales are scheduled at times of diminished agricultural work, frequently after harvest, and so community interrelations are intensified. The Instituto Indigenista reports an average of five communities attending one fiesta. The head municipio attracts as pilgrims aldea inhabitants, whose important images in some cases are brought

321

F𝑖ɢ. 5—EASTER CELEBRATION, CHINAUTLA, GUATEMALA. Apostles on way to church to spend 24 hours with Christ. (From Reina, 1960. Middle American Research Institute, Tulane University.)

to join in the celebration. In addition, merchant groups rotate with the religious calendar of the area, marketing fiesta foods.

Chiapas

Here, as in the previously mentioned regions, the annual agricultural cycle and much of the rhythm in the economic activities are governed by the sharp distinction between the rainy and dry seasons. Variations in altitude do not permit a uniform beginning, but February and March mark the start of agricultural work. During April and the next three months weeding and watching the growth of the crops absorb the workers' time. While milpa is growing, other crops, particularly frijoles, are planted along with the corn. After the bending of the corn from September through November, Indians migrate to the large fincas where they seek employment. One responsible person per family is left behind to watch the fields until harvest, which takes place late in November and in December and can be extended over a long period and completed with relatively few workers.

The land dries out in January under the intense heat, and, as an informant said, "there is no need to pray for rain now." But at the onset of the rainy season the fields

receive a final clearing, a *misa de la milpa* is held, and people proceed confidently with seeding. Families also may offer prayers independently during or after harvest.

The ethnographic accounts indicate that during each month of the year religious rites are conducted by the mayordomos, stewards of saints for fiestas de costumbres. The fiestas patronales, however, or other public rituals are held during January, February, and March, all dry months. A long period without religious activities follows until July and August, after which celebrations diminish again until December. The pattern corresponds to that of the highlands of Guatemala.

The following saints are held in very high esteem: San Sebastián, San Juan, San Antonio, San Miguel, Santiago, San Lorenzo, and Santo Tomás. Celebrations which may be classified as fiestas de costumbres are Holy Week, preceded by the Carnavales, Santa Cruz, Corpus Christi, San Juan, San Pedro, Virgen del Rosario, Santa Catarina, San Antonio, Natividad, Santa Lucía, All Souls' Day, and New Year's Day.

It appears that the fiesta cycle in Chiapas is maintained through intercommunity participation. Duplication of ritual could weaken the enthusiasm needed to carry on a

322

large fiesta, so nearby communities join in the celebration and may have representatives in the brotherhoods of another community. Although this pattern exists to some degree in other areas, it is highly prominent in Chiapas. Zinacantan, for instance, draws thousands of people from Chamula, San Andres Larrainzar, Ixtapa, San Lucas, Chiapolla, and San Cristobal de las Casas. Ixtapa and San Luis Indians bring their town's saints; as in Zinacantan, religious officials have a welcoming ceremonial for these visitors, who remain in town for two or three days. Those individuals who come without a saint are marked, because they are at a religious celebration for economic or social reasons and only to a small extent for religious ones. The people of Zinacantan attend the fiesta in Ixtapa and San Luis as devout religious participants but travel to Chamula and San Andres in the role of merchants.

The elaboration of fiestas of first importance is characterized by the dramatization of the religious theme. This draws large crowds of spectators.

Maya Lowlands

Included in the Maya lowlands are the Yucatan Peninsula, Belize, and the Peten. Although the annual cycle is geared to the rains, which cause two distinct seasons, there is no time of year when Yucatecans are not involved in the production of either the first milpas in the rainy season or chance crops and siembras in the dry season. The cycles of work include clearing the *monte* of timber, burning, planting, weeding, the *doblada,* and harvesting. During the rainy season, while the milpa is growing, men from the Peten and Yucatan gather *chicle* for *contratistas.* During the dry season they find employment with house builders, with oil companies, with government road construction, or with small businessmen. These opportunities encourage a great deal of migration from villages to the areas of work.

In the milpas weeding is intensive during June and July because of the heavy May rains. Men accomplish this by returning from the chicle camps for a few days at a time. In August the first *elotes* (ears of corn) are gathered and the rest ripen rapidly; by September the harvest is in full swing. The uncertainty of a successful crop causes much anxiety. Each person can recount his unfortunate experiences with droughts, winds, and animals which at one time or another destroyed his milpa. Because rains are not totally absent in January, a second milpa is possible in the lower regions of the Peten, though this is becoming rather rare because of its relatively poor return.

Redfield and Villa Rojas speak a great deal about the offerings to the milpas: the-dinner-of-the-milpa, the-dinner-of-the-thub, the rain ceremony to *chaac,* and the first-fruit ceremonies. The people of Soccotz conduct their *primicias* and make offerings to the wind deities. The inhabitants of San Jose, Peten, once performed these rituals in the past, but now feel that *secretos antiguos* are too strong for today and, if practiced, might ruin one's life. Therefore, in order to avoid self-destruction they no longer conduct secretos (Reina, 1961).

Fiestas of community importance for the area are Lent, San Marcos, San Bernardo, Santa Cruz, San Juan, All Souls' Day, Virgen de la Concepción, Natividad, San Diego, Ascención, San Luis, and San Antonio. Most of the fiestas have public appeal, and participation in them during the burning and weeding periods is no less than after the harvest. Milperos and chicleros spend much time during the growing and gathering seasons away from their communities, but the fiestas are occasions of homecoming. San Jose, Peten, is a case in point. The fiesta of November 1st and 2nd, next in importance to the fiesta patronal of San Jose, takes place at the peak of the chicle-gathering season. Large numbers of men return for the festivities, but because they cannot be present for the organization and prepa-

323

Fɪɢ. 6—ZOQUE DANCES, TUXTLA GUTIERREZ, CHIAPAS. Fiesta of San Roque. (Photographed by Donald Cordry, 1940.)

ration of the fiesta this duty has become the responsibility of the women, old men, and young people. The lack of cofradías brings a different style to the celebrations. Instead, one family becomes the "owner" of the day and prepares the fiesta under the leadership of the *prioste*. Fiestas patronales are not as important as in the aforementioned areas, but, if held, each lasts nine days.

SOUTHERN MEXICAN HIGHLANDS

In the southern Mexican highlands the rainy season may begin any time between February and April. June and July are months of anxiety because of the threat of too much moisture for the crops. The rains are expected to end in September or October; from then on the weather is cold, with frost frequent in January.

Preparation of the land for seeding begins in January, and by April all crops are planted in both the lowlands and the highlands. Fields are weeded carefully because of possible droughts. Harvest months are November and December.

The climatic division between quite cold and warm allows a variety of crops. There is a scale of temperate to tropical products in the area, which favors much market activity. The differences in climate facilitate constant growth of similar products throughout the year. So a particular crop that is planted in February in the warm areas is planted in May or June in the colder zone.

A generalization for the area is risky. There are outstanding differences from group to group in the same geographic area of the southern highlands and coastal region. The Mixe, for instance, are very near to the digging-stick level. "They spend long seasons in provisional ranches near their clearings, often as far as ten miles from the villages, settlements that in time grow and become new villages. They grow much corn, beans, squash, and chile, enough for themselves and export, and in the lowlands they cultivate some coffee, sugar cane, pineapples, and other tropical fruits. They raise cattle, fowl and turkeys, and distill liquor in primitive stills. Little is known of Mixe ceremonial life and customs" (Covarrubias, 1947, p. 52). The Zoque are at about the same stage; the Huaves make their livelihood through fishing, principally from June through November.

Trading is brisk in the southern highlands of Mexico and with the coastal area. During the dry season the salesmen travel extensively, reaching as far as Chiapas.

There is some specialization in crops. For example, the Chinantec currently grow coffee and bananas for export and raise corn and beans only for their own consumption.

Some of the rituals related to agricultural activities seem to be in the nature of church ceremonials, to which people bring seed and, after placing them before the saints in small piles, offer prayers (rezos). In the more conservative groups, offerings are made to the lightning and to the wind, and on such occasions a turkey may be sacrificed in the fields before sowing.

The fiestas patronales attract thousands of people from communities as far away as a day's walk. The most common fiestas are Santiago, Holy Week, Candelaria, Corpus Christi, and All Souls' Day (an incomplete list because taken from a very small community sample). They are sponsored by cofradías, and full participation of all members and guests is expected. Merchants, pilgrims, and curious observers flock to the celebrating towns.

Other fiestas, conducted by the cofradías alone in the name of the community, include San José, Ascención, Santa Cruz, San Isidro, San Juan, San Antonio, Virgen del Carmen and del Rosario, San Francisco Xavier, Virgen de Guadalupe and Soledad.

Of interest is the fact that fiestas of greater significance come after the clearing of the fields, just before harvest, and in the dry winter months. Among the Huaves of the coastal area, fiestas are held before and after the fishing cycle. The celebrations last for three or four days and sometimes are accompanied by dramas with religious or political themes. The participation of the priest is minimal and upon invitation, as it is in all the foregoing areas.

CENTRAL MEXICAN HIGHLANDS

The rainy season starts late in May in the central Mexican highlands and continues until the end of October. August and September are the most important months for the success of the corn crop. The classification of the topography into *tierra fría, templada,* and *caliente* is relevant to the growth of the crops, and therefore harvest time varies by weeks from the low to the high land. During January people are busy producing charcoal and storing corn in bins, but after this the agricultural activities fall off rapidly until March, when the land is prepared for seeding. Not until May, however, is constant rainfall certain. When the seed has been blessed by the priest, planting begins; cultivation and weeding follow and continue through August. The first harvest of fruits is ready in September; in October the milpas are weeded for the last time. The leaves from the corn plant are harvested in early December. While awaiting the corn harvest, farmers spend September and Oc-

325

tober picking fruit throughout the Valley of Mexico. After harvest many people migrate from their villages to haciendas, where they are employed until March or April. Those left at home continue making charcoal and rope or building houses for the duration of the seven-month dry season.

Because data on the fiesta cycles of the Totonac and Otomi are limited, we must rely primarily on information from the Nahuatl group. The Catholic celebrations are to honor the popular saints already mentioned for other areas, the heaviest concentration being in January, June, August, and December. The other months each have one celebration, but it is large and attracts many people from surrounding communities and lasts for several days. Fiestas are held for Santo Domingo, San Sebastián, Santa Cruz, San Pedro, San Miguel, San Isidro, Virgen del Carmen, San Juan, San Pedro, and San Pablo, Santiago, Virgen de Natividad, All Souls' Day, Christmas, and Lent. The last two are highly dramatized.

The reports indicate that hundreds of people attend the important fiestas since they are open to community participation. Many of the visitors are merchants, who do not take part in the religious rites unless a *promesa* has been made to the particular saint of a town. The organization of the fiestas is in the hands of the men, assisted by the women in the domestic chores. The minor fiestas, conducted primarily by the brotherhoods representing the community, are not open to everyone. In this region the church seems to participate more formally in the celebrations; possibly the community does not act as independently as in other areas, although it is still responsible for the celebration.

Here no exact pattern is discernible. Fiestas take place throughout the year regardless of leisure and crops. Where the religious factor is important, fiesta cycles pertain to the individual community. Communities in this area are related primarily by commercial interests and only secondarily by religious ones.

WESTERN MEXICO

The agricultural activities of the Tarascan people of western Mexico are also governed by the two seasons. The rainy season extends from May to September, "when all the eight hundred millimeters of moisture fall in afternoon drizzles, or dangerous electric storms accompanied by tropical deluges of rain and hail" (Friedrich, 1958). The natives are occupied with growing corn, beans, chili, squash, and, to a lesser extent, wheat, barley, oats, potatoes, and fruits.

Beals (1946, p. 21) gives the Tarascan farming cycle as follows:

January: Little to do; second plowing of maize lands may begin.

February: Second plowing of maize lands.

March: Maize planting begins.

April: Maize planting; first cultivation of early maize at the end of month; planting of vegetables and maize in *solares*.

May: Wheat harvest; second cultivation of maize.

June: Second cultivation of maize; some wheat threshing (continued in dry weather throughout rest of year).

July: Fairly free month; weeding of maize begins; second cultivation of maize continues.

August: Plowing for wheat.

September: Planting for wheat; cutting maize fodder.

October: Plowing for maize; rains usually end; cutting maize fodder; wheat threshing nearly finished.

November: Maize harvest (if lower lands planted); plowing.

December: Maize harvest on higher lands; plowing.

Commercial activity on a scale from most to least intensity takes place in this order: December, September, and April; May, March, and October; January, February, and November; August, July, and June. Pottery making is at its height in January

FIG. 7—RELIGIOUS PROCESSION, MILPA ALTA, MEXICO. Fiesta honoring the Virgin of the Assumption. (From Madsen, 1957. Middle American Research Institute, Tulane University.)

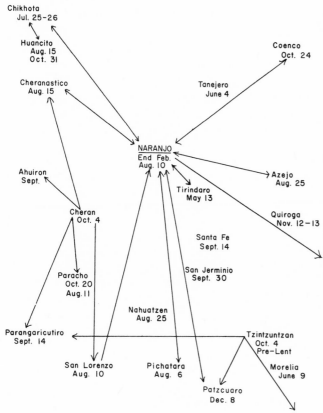

FIG. 8—TARASCAN FIESTA DATES AND ATTEND-
ANCE OF NEIGHBORING TOWNS. (Based on information supplied by Paul Friedrich.)

but diminishes rapidly after March. Fishing
is also keen at this time of the year. The
people of the Sierra plow the land twice a
year, but people outside this area plow only
once, this before the rains. Altitude causes
some degree of specialization and therefore
a slight variation in the annual cycles.

In the few Indian communities known to
ethnographers major fiestas are held in all
months except April, June, and July. The
religious societies conduct other fiestas,
which fill in the year with festivities. Cele-
brations are offered for Santos Reyes, Padre
Jesus, San José, San Anselmo, Santa Cruz,
Corpus Christi, San Antonio, San Juan, San
Pedro and San Pablo, Santiago Apostol,
Asunción, San Bartolomé, San Luis, San
Miguel, Virgen del Rosario, San Francisco
Assisi, San Rafael, All Souls' Day, San Di-

ego, Inmaculada Concepción, Virgen de
Guadalupe, and Christmas.

Figure 8 reveals the intercommunity
movement motivated by religious holidays.
It is significant that a large market is held
in the celebrating communities simultaneously with the fiesta.

For the fiesta of Padre Jesus at the end
of February, Naranjo attracts approximately 5000 individuals, but during minor celebrations virtually no outsiders and less than
half the community are present (Friedrich,
1958). The *carguero* religious organization
is in charge of all celebrations. Among the
Tarascan communities the larger fiestas occur after harvest or in times of more leisure,
particularly March, May, and June.

By a unique arrangement the celebrations of Corpus Christi and Holy Week
were at one time rotated among five pueblos—Azejo, Zipiaja, Tirindaro, Naranjo, and
Tanejero—so that each played host once
every five years. The pattern was disrupted,
however, during the agrarian reform of the
twenties (Friedrich, personal communication). In all cases the church remains in the
background and participates by invitation
in the celebration of the Masses during the
fiestas titulares.

Changes in the calendar itself were few
despite the Mexican revolution, agrarian reform, radicalism, and government with anticlerical orientation. As a consequence there
has been a reduction in size of all religious
fiestas, diminishing numbers of pilgrims,
and less intercommunity cooperation.

Northwest Mexico

Northwest Mexico, home of several groups
of less developed people, is high, rugged,
and accessible in some parts only on horseback. The high altitudes bring frost to the
valleys and snow to the mountain peaks.
The dry and rainy seasons determine the
activities of the people. For the Tarahumara
the annual agricultural period begins in
March, when the fields are plowed and
seeded. Cultivation continues throughout

June and July, looking toward harvest in November. Afterwards, migration tends to warmer *barrancas* until March. The Tarahumara agricultural cycle is accompanied by costumbre ritualism, in which the *matachines* dance ceremoniously.

The Sonora desert, inhabited by Papago and Pima, affords a long growing season but has erratic precipitation throughout the year. During the annual cycle of the previous generations, planting took place in June and July, harvest in October. The Kickapoo, on the other hand, chose a hunting subsistence and looked to the nearby hills for their livelihood. Droughts threatened their attempts at growing grains and raising livestock. Yaqui people subsisted on agriculture. After the summer rains flooded the Yaqui river planting took place in the silt land during August and September, making harvest possible by the end of November and the beginning of December. The condition of the soil frequently permitted a second crop between February and June. "Today, however, the two harvests cannot be counted on as certain" (Spicer, 1954, p. 41).

In the area in general, the costumbre rituals to rain, first fruits, and the sprouting of corn were elaborate and interesting. Catholic practices were comparatively few.

The list of fiestas is again incomplete, for much depends on the memory of the people. April and September had no fiestas to Catholic saints. Important fiestas patronales were held in March, July, October, and December; celebrations to saints and virgins occupied the other months. Santa Cruz was widely celebrated as were San Juan, All Souls' Day, and Virgen de Guadalupe. Carnaval before Lent was held as in Chiapas.

For the Cora group of Jesus Maria in Nayarit, the largest fiesta of the year is Holy Week, followed by approximately 12 fiestas of secondary importance; that is, the number of participants is very small. Thomas B. Hinton (personal communication) reveals that there is a very strong tendency to remain within one's village since each community celebrates the same saint, which, interestingly enough, ties in with the fact that there are very few Cora merchants. Concurrently, celebrations are carried on almost independently by the Indian population; on some occasions a priest may come to offer a Mass and to perform some of the church rites. The Indian government and those with a *cargo* are in charge of the celebrations. The impression here is that fiestas come at a time of less economic urgency, though the little information available does not permit a direct correlation.

RECAPITULATION

It is evident that in the annual cycle the Indian would like to be fully occupied by *milpa* and *siembra*, but scarcity of land or technology or both prohibit this. Private agricultural enterprise cannot be a full-time occupation—though it has priority among the individual's alternatives—and fills little more than half the calendar year. Sufficient cash can be acquired only by trade, employment on fincas or haciendas, and other semiskilled work, in addition to farming activities. At certain times of year intensive trade keeps merchants busy covering large areas of the country. Skilled work such as carpentry, construction of houses, and production of pottery, charcoal, and lime occupies many persons between the end of harvest and the beginning of milpa chores. Others are employed on fincas and plantations or as laborers in towns. To be at work every day of the year is distinctive of the Indian population. The women, too, alternate between domestic duties, assistance in the milpa, production of pottery and textiles, and marketing. One can hardly say there is leisure at any time of year; work is allotted for every day.

Fiestas have an extraordinary importance in the social life of all groups. Indians frequently state that they have been engaged in intensive trading, household industries, or other employment for days, months, and even one-year periods before a fiesta which they sponsor either on their own initiative or by appointment. Cash earned by such special activities is dedicated to the celebration. Fiestas de costumbres undertaken by mayordomos and capitanas, and the fiestas titulares or patronales absorb large sums of money in comparison to the costumbre rituals.

In the costumbre rituals, one finds less participation by the Catholic church and more traits of a native origin. The Lacandon rituals are more purely native than in the other areas, where acculturation had been intense after the 16th century. Here are found costumbres such as the "dinner to the milpas," rain ceremonies, thanksgiving rites and others primarily initiated by individuals. They follow the rhythm of agricultural work alone. They do not constitute a fiesta but appear to have about the same importance as grace before meals.

The fiestas de costumbres are celebrations of religious holidays conducted by small groups representing the community. These individuals with a *cargo* are under strong community pressures because the celebration is important not only to the participants but to all members of the village or town. Those fiestas appear in the midst of the agricultural season and at crucial points of the year *(tiempos delicados)* when there is much work and a high degree of anxiety over success in agricultural pursuits. If they seem to be distributed throughout the year rather than specifically related to other factors such as leisure or weather conditions, it is not surprising. The religious organizations or individuals *encargados* can take care of the celebrations at any time of the year; they are fiestas for the saint rather than for saint and town combined. This is a main difference between the fiestas de costumbres and the fiestas titulares or patronales.

In contrast the fiestas titulares do not have a random occurrence. For the most part they are concentrated during the time of year when rains are not too heavy and when many people are in town; they are most likely to appear before and after the agricultural cycle, seldom in the midst of it.

The Instituto Indigenista reports that for all the municipios of Guatemala whose Indian population is 50 per cent and above, the total annual expenditure for fiestas titulares reaches $81,500 and the attendance is estimated at 1,200,000 persons. Most of this money is collected from members of religious organizations and only partly supplied by municipalidad and community contributions.

From the over-all point of view, religious activity ranges from celebrations with native elements to those acceptable within the Catholic church. The pervasive character of Roman Catholicism in the structure of fiestas, however, is clearly recognized. In both Yucatan and northern Mexico, Holy Week and Lent, numerous celebrations to the saints, and All Souls' Day are marked by rites; simultaneously, these two areas are most active in the native ceremonialism.

Throughout Middle America the same days are celebrated as fiestas patronales and fiestas de costumbres: Santa Cruz, All Souls' and All Saints' Days, San Pedro and San Pablo, San Francisco Xavier, San Juan, Natividad, and Holy Week. Among the most common dramatizations presented in celebrations are the reenactment of the birth and death of Christ. One can only speculate as to why certain days become a fiesta; explanations may be found in the folklore of miraculous events. The greater the reputation of the saint, the more elaborate and higher the cost of the fiesta. Furthermore, the emphasis on certain saints can be related to the priesthood order which favored certain saints over others. San Franciscans certainly favored Santa Cruz, whereas the Dominicans were partial to the cults of Santo Tomás, Virgen del Rosario, and Santo Domingo.

Because the physical geography is not uniform, the beginning and end of the agricultural cycle differ for each area. Lack of detailed information on seasonal migration, adoption of temporary work outside the communities, marketing, and cash surplus make it difficult to establish correlations, but it is clear that seasonal migration does not coincide with the fiestas patronales. The religious organizations of the communities, however, are always sufficiently representative to carry on the fiestas de costumbres regardless of the number of people currently in the village or town and amount of work.

The occurrence of major fiestas and the conditions of weather are surely related. Important community fiestas tend to be omitted during June and August, when rains are heavy. Transference of the fiestas patronales to the dry season, or to times when the rain is highly predictable, is not uncommon.

There is a sprinkling of fiestas de costumbres around harvest time and around planting time. One is tempted to generalize that this may be an accident explainable in terms more of the Catholic calendar than of the annual cycle of the area. Fiestas de costumbres appear in a near-random distribution maintained by the religious organizations, as previously noted. As a tentative conclusion, it may be said that as the difference between Indian and Ladino becomes more pronounced (particularly in more Ladinoized communities), the correlation of fiestas with the annual cycle is less significant; celebrations could be set for almost any time of year. So far, costumbres rituals among Indians show the closest tie to the annual cycle.

The religious activities and the economy of the people based on agriculture and subsidiary industries reinforce each other. The financing of the fiestas titulares and the fiestas de costumbres requires much of the cash surplus from those with cargos. But the enthusiastic devotion to the maintenance of a cult to a saint justifies all effort; it is not necessarily viewed as an economic burden.

The fiesta complex speaks of the careful treatment accorded Catholic saints in order to bring general well-being. The "purchasing" of success and the amelioration of tristeza is an obvious exchange made through the fiestas. In treating this point the people suggest that to alegrar los santos is part of the bargain. In return the saints bring alegría to human beings through protection and blessings. The degree of protection and blessing is relative to the amount offered, but most of all to the person's voluntad. The fear of misfortune is intense, warranting at least one large celebration annually. Costumbre, as a philosophical concept, is strong, and once the saints become acostumbrado to celebrations, the obligation cannot be overlooked because they will become wrathful.

While the "owners" of the fiestas are primarily motivated to exchange religion for well-being, the community guests find both economic and social pleasure. The fiesta guests seem to be in the majority; pilgrims and other religious participants are not numerous. The gathering of people as an opportunity for market activities is a primary concern.

Currently there is an increasing number of individuals attending fiestas patronales in villages where they had formerly been residents. They use the fiesta as a day for homecoming to relatives and friends left behind. In a personal communication Arden King states that fiestas in Alta and Baja Verapaz are considered homecoming events. They certainly seem to be in the more rapidly developing areas of Middle America, in contrast to the less developed areas where visiting remains within the neighboring centers of population. The participation of guests at the fiestas is generally on the periphery, sometimes carrying out a promesa. The hosts organize and direct the celebration.

Redfield (1941, p. 220) summarized: "The fiestas no doubt include piety, local and personal pride, desire for relaxation

331

and play, sociability, commercial interests, and fear of misfortune which might follow if an obligation regarded as traditional should be neglected."

As to the question of the annual and fiesta cycle in the midst of socio-cultural changes, it is predictable that as long as the annual cycle remains basically rural the fiesta patterns outlined will continue. Even though the form and rhythm of the fiestas could continue in the face of economic changes, the meaning and psychological orientation of the ceremonialism would be severely affected.

REFERENCES

Alvarez, 1955
Arciniega, 1944
Baer and Baer, 1949
Basauri, 1929
Beals, 1945b, 1946
Beesley, 1943
Bennett and Zingg, 1935
Berlin, 1951
Bernal and Dávalos Hurtado, 1953
Bevan, 1938
Brand, 1951
Bunzel, 1952
Calendario de las Fiestas, 1959
Cámara B., 1946a, 1946b
Carrasco, 1952b
Caso, 1944
Castetter and Bell, 1942
Cline, 1952
Corona Núñez, 1946
Covarrubias, 1947
Davis, 1920
De la Fuente, 1942, 1949
Doll, 1952
Drucker, 1941
Dutton, 1939a, 1939b
Ewald, 1957a
Fábila, 1940
Foster, 1948a
Friedrich, 1958
Gámiz, 1948
Gann, 1917
Gillin, 1951
Goubaud Carrera, 1935, 1949a, 1949b, 1949c
Grossman, 1871
Guiteras Holmes, 1946a
Hewes, 1935
Instituto Indigenista Nacional de Guatemala
Johnson, J. B., 1950
Joseph, Spicer, and Chesky, 1949
LaFarge, 1928, 1947
—— and Byers, 1931
Lanks, 1938
León, N., 1905

Lewis, 1951
Lincoln, 1946
Lothrop, 1927a, 1928, 1929a, 1929b, 1930
Lumholtz, 1898
McBryde, 1934
McDougall, 1947, 1955
Madsen, 1957
Mason, J. A., 1912a, 1912b, 1920, 1948, 1952
Mendieta y Núñez, 1949
Munsch, 1943
Nash, M., 1958a
Nicoli, 1885
Oakes, 1951
Pacheco Cruz, 1947
Parsons, 1936
Patiño and Cárdenas, 1955
Paul, 1950a
Recinos, 1913
Redfield, 1930, 1941, 1946a, 1946b
—— and Villa Rojas, 1934, 1939
Reina, 1960, 1961
Rojas Garciduenas, 1942
Rosales, 1949a, 1949b, 1950
Roys, 1943
Salz, 1955
Sánchez Garcia, 1956, 1958
Soustelle, J., 1935c
Spicer, 1954
Starr, B. W., 1952a, 1952b
Tax, 1941, 1944, 1946, 1947a, 1947b, 1950, 1952a
Thompson, D. E., 1954
Thompson, J. E. S., 1930, 1941a
Tozzer, 1907
Tumin, 1946
Underhill, 1938, 1940, 1946
Valladares, 1957
Villa Rojas, 1939, 1941, 1945, 1946, 1955
Wagley, 1941, 1949, 1957
Weiant, 1940, 1955
Weitlaner and Barlow, 1955
Wisdom, 1940
Zingg, 1938a, 1938b

17. Sickness and Social Relations

RICHARD N. ADAMS and
ARTHUR J. RUBEL

Tʜᴇ ᴀꜱᴄʀɪᴘᴛɪᴏɴ of illness is one of society's ways of recognizing that individuals are not always able to fulfill all the socially prescribed behaviors. When a person becomes ill he is allowed to drop many of his usual habits and indulge in other things. Diagnosis is the means by which society finds out what is wrong so that the individual may return to his regular role; curing is a specific path chosen to regain health. This article reviews the principal features of illness, diagnosis, and curing in contemporary Middle American Indian communities, and relates them specifically to the context of social relations within which they operate.[1]

With a few exceptions the sources of our data are community studies, general ethnographic surveys, and a few analyses specifically of sickness and curing. Hypotheses are suggested in the last section of the

article. We have tried to stay within the available data, even though they do not always provide entirely convincing support.

Table 1 summarizes the major sources utilized. Because the *Handbook* is concerned with Indians, we have included only a few highly Mestizoized communities, these in order to allow insight into the range of variation. Our concern here is to relate sickness and curing behavior to social relations, so we shall not attempt historical reviews or hypotheses. With this goal in mind, our definition of illness is broadened at various points to include the general state of ill-being. Were this to be followed out systematically, all manner of troubles such as crop failures, taxation, and revolutions would be included; in fact, precisely these kinds of things are often included in the same reasoning framework in many communities. Since bodily ill-being is the more common meaning of illness in our societies, our treatment has been somewhat ragged: where the material is suggestive, illness is extended to cover general ill-being; where it is not, the narrower definition—bodily ill-being—is followed.

---

[1] In preparing this paper, Rubel, working as a Pre-Doctoral Research Fellow sponsored by the National Institute of Mental Health, analyzed the Mixtec and the area north; Adams took the Zapotec and the east. The individual reports were exchanged and then combined under final review by both authors.

ILLNESS AND MAN

Illness in many forms troubles the life of the Middle American Indian. Besides the accidents common to rural dwellers—snake bites, machete cuts, broken bones, scrapes and bruises, chills, fevers, muscular aches— most of the population is still subject to a wide variety of endemic and epidemic diseases. Intestinal ailments, worms, and diarrhea are extremely common, and are contributing features to the high infant mortality. Smallpox, measles, typhus, whooping cough, "flu," typhoid, and malaria, among others, occur and recur with devastating results; to these may be added regional ailments such as onchocercosis, goitre, and kwashiorkor. Depending on the habitat, cultural practices, and resources, a given population suffers severe and recurring health problems. Only in recent years have public-health efforts begun to bring some of these conditions under control. On the basis of current data a difficult area to explore is the relation of the way people interpret symptoms to scientifically recognized etiologies and syndromes. This very central problem deserves concentrated attention.

The concept of illness is but meagerly described in the ethnographic literature of Middle America. In Chenalho, "The word for illness is *chamel,* derived from the verb 'to die,' because all illness is a step toward death, and is inflicted on man as a means to destroy the body" (Guiteras Holmes, n.d.,*b*). As suggested by this, illness is generally applied to any condition which makes a person feel bad; distinction between illnesses of organic and psychological origin is not reflected in the terminology although it is recognized in methods of treating them. The distinction, however, is not basic to the Middle American view of the subject.

The malfunctioning of man is seen in terms of fairly general views of the human body. Literature from the southern part of the area described the body as getting its strength from blood (cf. also Beals, 1946, p. 202, on the Tarascans of Cheran). The stomach and intestines occupy a general cavity in the lower abdomen, and the heart is variously located immediately above this. The lungs are in the upper back, and the kidneys thought to be either in the upper abdomen or over the hips. A single general category serves for tendons, veins, arteries, and ligaments. Pains, cramps, and strains that extend through the body may be associated with the tendon-vein-ligament (R. N. Adams, 1952, pp. 28, 63; De la Fuente, 1949, p. 312). Blood plays a central part in health and illness. A person's condition is often expressed in terms of whether his blood is strong or weak, hot or cold. In Yucatan blood may be weakened by evil winds; elsewhere it may be chilled. Blood is thought to be nonregenerative; a person is provided with a limited amount, and any loss must lead to permanent weakness. (R. N. Adams, 1952, pp. 13–16; De la Fuente, 1949, p. 312; Redfield and Villa, 1934, p. 209; Wisdom, 1940, pp. 307–08.)

Knowledge of the interior workings of the human body, however, is very general and imprecise. Intruded objects, *aire,* and other things are thought to move around inside the body with little restriction. An aire may enter one part of the body and move to another; objects may be removed from places where there is no aperture, although the use of an aperture for the purpose is also common. Most generally, in the northern part of the area, intruded objects are sucked out from the place at which the pain or discomfort seems to be localized. However, special attention is usually paid as well to the major movable joints: wrists, behind the knees, shoulders, neck. The crown of the head is also sucked to remove objects. This is true of the Tarahumara (Lumholtz, 1902, 1: 314, 317), Mixtec (Mak, 1959, p. 130), Mixe (Beals, 1945b, p. 97), Huichol (Lumholtz, 1902, 2: 239), Cuicatec (J. B. Johnson, 1939b, pp. 138–39), Tepehua (Bower, 1946, p. 682),

Nahuatl (G. Soustelle, 1958, pp. 149–51), Chinantec (Rubel, 1950), and Zapotec (De la Fuente, 1941, p. 45).

One or both of two kinds of conditions must be explored in order to interpret susceptibility to illness: one is the individual's psychophysical state, the other his social and ritual conduct. Concerning the first are two general conditions common to the Mesoamerican peoples that may be extended to all of Middle America: strength-weakness and hot-cold (Wisdom, 1952, pp. 129–30). To these must be added a third, a variety of strong emotional experience (Foster, 1953b, p. 211). A person who falls ill will frequently be said to have been overheated, chilled, too weakened (due to a number of further reasons), or suffering from a strong emotional experience. Extreme jealousy, envy, or anger will render a person susceptible to illness from the outside. Fright (*susto, espanto*) may be due to a sudden start, a fall in a lake or river, an earthquake. *La muina* is the condition of getting very angry; in this state a person is subject to being hit by aire (Parsons, 1936, p. 119, note 116). Unlike the hot-cold and strength-weakness characteristics, these emotional qualities are not seen as being on a polar continuum. Thus they are not congruent with the strength-weakness distinction although in some instances the emotional condition is said to have weakened a person.

The concept of strength is applied both to people and to natural phenomena. Rosales (1949b, p. 465) characterizes as a strong person in San Pedro La Laguna one who can stand hunger, heat, and cold; does not take sick; is physically strong and is *bravo* (psychologically dominant, aggressive). Here witches and sorcerers have these qualities, have "hot" blood, live a long life, and are not afraid. Wisdom (1952, pp. 129–30) summarizes conditions leading to weakness: "(1) abnormal bodily condition, as lack of vigor, over-exertion, excessive sweating, body exposure, wounds and blows, any sickness, and conditions of childbirth, pregnancy, menstruation, and menopause; (2) disturbed emotional states, as fear, anger, jealousy, hysteria; (3) lack of full development, as youth and infancy in persons, animals, and plants, old age, and unfinished conditions, as an object in process of manufacture; and (4) possession of bland and pleasing qualities as beauty, tameness, domestication. The opposites of these make for 'strength.' "

"Hot" and "cold," qualities historically attributable to the classical tradition of humors, are also shared with nonhuman elements of the environment. Generally involved in these is the issue of a balance: a person should not remain in either a "hot" or a "cold" state for too long a time. As has been frequently pointed out by students of this medicine, healthiness requires the maintenance of some equilibrium between the two extremes. Occasionally intermediate degrees will be distinguished, such as "fresh." Strength and weakness share a tenuous relationship with the hot-cold distinction. A person of "hot" blood is thought to be thereby rendered strong. However, where strength can sometimes protect a person from attacks of external elements (such as aire or witchcraft), hotness serves more as a condition of susceptibility.

The commission and avoidance of social and ritual error is a behavioral counterpart to weakness and strength. Whereas people are said to *have* strength or weakness, there are ways of altering the condition; a person may act in a sinful, erring or insulting manner, whether by commission or omission. However, the *post facto* quality of the two is basically the same. As is the case with judging one's strength, if a person gets sick, it may be due to social or ritual error; if he does not get sick, then whatever he may be doing can hardly be considered an error. In very traditional communities elders who have led impeccable lives are thought to have special ritual protection from illness; almost everywhere, on the other hand, infants, who are incapable of sinning, are regarded as being inherently weak.

One further set of characteristics that play a role of some importance in sickness and curing are the *souls*. This English word does not carry the variety of concepts that are current in Mesoamerica. In this short space we cannot discuss regional and local variations, but for present purposes we may say there are three different souls, usually two of them in current use. They can be called *nagual, tonal,* and soul. The nagual is a special transformation of a man into an animal, and the term helps define a witch. It acts in giving sickness, but has nothing to do with its "owner's" contracting sickness. The tonal is a companion animal or destiny; where it occurs, everyone is said to have one. The soul, essentially the Christian concept, is seen as a shadow or ghost that dwells after death in some eternal place or, in some instances, is reborn in a new body. It is either the tonal or the shadow soul that is subject to stealing, and is specifically of concern in becoming ill. This will be discussed later.

ASCRIBED CAUSES

The ascribed cause of a patient's ailments is set by two areas of knowledge. The first concerns knowledge of the patient, his physical symptoms or general syndrome, and his behavior and social relationships. These things may be known beforehand or learned during the diagnosis. The second involves a set of concepts from among which an explanation is formulated as to why the patient finds himself in this condition. Similar concepts are found scattered irregularly through most of Middle America, but their specific distribution and combination are always unique to a given community, or even to individuals and groups within a community. We cannot here explore the variations, since even such clearcut syndromes as epidemics of whooping cough or smallpox receive quite different interpretations. In the Guatemalan

336

midwestern highlands they are due to God (Rosales, 1950), in Santiago Chimaltenango to a specific spirit, Juan Noq (Wagley, 1949), and in parts of Chiapas to a witch who may be killed for having caused them (D. Metzger, 1959). The terms, the syndromes, and the concepts vary.

We shall discuss the ascribed causes in two parts. The first concerns anthropomorphic and other volitional beings and includes the entire area of ascription of sentient, animate, or volitional qualities to segments or aspects of the environment, including other people. The second, environmental and nonvolitional factors, includes those ascriptions in which portions of the environment including people are seen as following some fairly general rules wherein volition seems to have no part.

Anthropomorphic and Other Volitional Factors

Animation of the environment is strong in Mesoamerica, but the mere belief in the existence of such beings or things is not necessarily a good index to their role in illness and health. Five kinds of factors concern us here: gods and saints, spirits and sprites, ghosts, volitional aires, witches and sorcerers.

GODS AND SAINTS. God, as a dominant cause of illness, is most clearly important in the western area of Guatemala and neighboring Chiapas. In Santiago Chimaltenango Dios is almost exclusively held responsible for sickness and is said to punish people for a variety of errors and sins: the breaking of ritual custom (especially by having sexual relations on a day of ritual) brings colds and fevers; if one's grandparent laughed at a blind man, it may give one sore eyes; dysentery may result if one's grandfather or father stole cattle or pigs; a quarrel between husband and wife brings a stomach ache (Wagley, 1949, p. 76). In this particular community there is a wide variety of ailments that are ascribed, *post facto*, to some error committed by the individual, his father, or grandfather. Herbal remedies are used, but they must be accompanied by God's forgiveness.

Although witchcraft is also believed here, it is not practiced. It is proper, if one has been offended, to pray to God to visit punishment on the offender. It is up to God to make the decision, nevertheless, and the individual is not responsible.

In neighboring Chiapas witchcraft is commonly practiced, but God and saints play an important role in illness. In Cancuc a witch may cause a person to lose his soul or send aires to make him ill, but theoretically he cannot do so without first obtaining the permission of San Juan, the special protector of the community. The cure for such witchcraft requires learning from San Juan in which one of a number of caves the soul of the sick person is located (Guiteras Holmes, n.d.,*a*). In Oxchuc, San Ildefonso was said to have visited typhus on the town because he had been abandoned in favor of another saint (Villa R., 1946, pp. 232–33). In the Guatemalan midwestern highlands God's decision often determines if a witch's work will be fatal. The inevitability of such visitations is illustrated by a comment that malaria was sent by God so that people would not multiply so rapidly.

Just as God is displaced by witchcraft and saints in Chiapas, in Yucatan the deity is displaced by winds or aires, both god-sent and evil ones, who act on their own volition. Whereas the evil winds must catch someone in a weakened condition, god-sent winds may attack anyone who fails to observe proper ritual or social obligations (Redfield and Villa, 1934, pp. 164–67; Villa R., 1945, p. 134). In Dzitas there were special "lords" assigned to the major epidemics of smallpox, measles, and whooping cough (Redfield and Redfield, 1940, p. 67). But aside from these, deities played a minor role in sickness. The same seems to be true through almost all the rest of Middle America. A diffuse kind of "God will punish"

may be heard from time to time, but it is not central to diagnosis and curing. Perhaps illustrative is a Mitla woman who died after an earthquake. People remembered that she had earlier stated that it was better that God kill her than that the earthquake should do so, but they attributed the death to fright rather than to God (Parsons, 1936, pp. 143–44).

Farther north, in Tecospa, God is seen as a destroyer in a diffuse sense. He uses pestilence to kill people (Madsen, 1960). In the south there is some tendency to ascribe epidemics to a god or a godlike cause, although as has been indicated there are local variations.

The role of the saints is also attenuated in the rest of Middle America. Failure to keep a promise to a saint or a spirit of the dead may bring God's punishment (De la Fuente, 1949, p. 319). In Magdalena four angels—San Rafael, San Miguel, Santa Isabel, and San Gabriel—are seen as evil; they are likely to strike little children if they go into the hills (R. N. Adams, 1952, p. 32). Saints, however, where they are important are usually called into prayers concerning any kind of illness. They are sometimes seen as sprites (see next section), but more often these take other forms.

SPRITES AND SPIRITS. One kind of sentient being found over all Middle America is characterized by its dwarflike stature, light-colored skin, sometimes bearded and blond, and generally with Spanish-American, Mexicanoid, or Ladino appearance. These sprites usually occupy specific sites: to the north they usually have an underground abode or live in or near the water (Lumholtz, 1902, 1: 243; 2: 422; Lewis, 1951, pp. 280, 356; Madsen, 1960, p. 131; Foster, 1940, p. 170; Gamio, 1922, pp. 412–14; Mak, 1959, p. 128; G. Soustelle, 1958, p. 155); to the south and east they dwell in mountain caves (Beals, 1945b; J. B. Johnson, 1939b, p. 137; Weitlaner, 1952a, pp. 282–83; J. Nash, 1959a, pp. 58–59; Wagley,

1949, pp. 55–62; Gillin, 1948; 1951, pp. 108–14; R. N. Adams, 1952, pp. 29–31, 57–60). Both habitats are reported from the Mazatec, Cuicatec, and Zapotec (J. B. Johnson, 1939b, pp. 133–38; Hendrichs Pérez, 1946, 2: 41; De la Fuente, 1941, p. 45; L. Nader, personal communication), probably owing to the relative prominence of aridity and mountains in the regions. As will be noted later, in the Yucatan peninsula sprites are all but absent. Their "role" is played there by aires or winds.

The qualities ascribed to these sprites vary from downright malevolence to mere mischievousness. Like all sentient beings, they bring other kinds of trouble besides sickness: they may destroy crops and domestic animals, as well as cause accidents. In Ladino areas, however, and theoretically in some Indian communities, these or other sprites may be helpful rather than harmful. Among Ladinos they tend to become dissociated from their local residences and wander more freely. Whether localized or not, they appear under a variety of forms, from the *sombrerón* to the crying woman (Rubel, 1950; R. N. Adams, 1952, 1957a).

Characteristically these sprites attack people when in a weakened condition, or sometimes specifically as punishment for offenses to themselves. Merely going near their abode is sufficient to incur danger (see works cited above, and Mak, 1959, p. 139; Lumholtz, 1902, 2: 238). Although seldom thought to punish a person for moral or social errors, they are not without a social role in the community.

These sprites are usually seen to be the "masters" or "guardians" of the specific locales they inhabit, and their behaviors and characteristics are projections of ethnic social relations. Known variously as *chanes*, *chaneka*, *chaneca*, *chaneque*, and *chancles*, they behave towards the Indians as Ladinos or Mexicans traditionally behave, that is as masters, employers, and bosses. Sometimes a sprite takes on the characteristics and even the name of a recent or historical figure, either of local importance or in the general historical tradition (Wagley, 1949, pp. 55–62; J. Nash, 1959a, pp. 58–59; Gillin, 1951, p. 108; Rosales, 1949b, p. 653; R. N. Adams, 1952, pp. 31, 57–60).

GHOSTS. Ghosts of people play a fairly minor role in sickness. In some places they send sickness as punishment if a person forgets to provide them with the proper ritual after death, as in Yucatan (Redfield and Villa, 1934, p. 170), central Guatemala (R. N. Adams, 1952, pp. 31–32, 62–63), and Yalalag (De la Fuente, 1949, p. 319). In these cases there is nothing special about the death of the individual whose ghost is making the trouble; rather it is a matter of failure on the part of the victim. In the north, however, the dead play a more malevolent role. In Tecospa ghosts of people who died by violence are said to remain for extended periods, trying to kill people in order to liberate themselves (Madsen, 1960, p. 189). Among the Tarahumara they inflict illness on persons "that they too may die and join the departed"; the dead may also be sent or summoned by witches "to harm the people, and make them ill, but generally they come of their own accord" (Lumholtz, 1902, 1: 380; cf. Bennett and Zingg, 1935, p. 347). Similarly, among the Huichol the dead are feared and considered as malevolent (Lumholtz, 1902, 2: 244). Among the Mixtec, on the other hand, although the dead are feared as a source of contagion, they are not thought of as malevolent (Mak, 1959, p. 140).

VOLITIONAL AIRES. *Aires*, *viento*, and related forms are among the most elusive of illness concepts. Essentially, something identified formally as a kind of air or wind enters the body and renders the individual sick. Sometimes it merely strikes the body. In this sense the aire may be self-activated or it may be a vector used by a sprite, spirit, or witch. Whether or not such an agent is involved (but most significantly when there is none), aires may be classified, some involving hot-cold distinctions (such as *se pega el frío*), others being specifically bad or evil (such as *hijillo*). From the standpoint of social relations the principal variables to be noted are the degree to which the winds are regarded as acting independently or as being sent by an agent, the nature of the agent, and the degree to which they are diffused in the environment in such a way that an individual seems incapable of escaping them (cf. G. Soustelle, 1958, p. 147).

The aires play their most prominent role in sickness in Yucatan and among the Chorti. Redfield (1941, pp. 305–06) has summarized their position in Yucatan: "The concept exists both in generalized form, 'wind,' and as many separately distinguished and often semipersonified 'winds.' They are connected with wells, caves, and water generally. . . ." This suggests a similarity of association with the sprites of the rest of Middle America. Whirling winds are particularly dangerous, Redfield goes on to say. "Persons going into the bush are in special danger from these winds; so also are those who become heated from exercise, or who are tired, or who become sexually excited."

Among the Chorti, "The *aigres* are the principal substance which enters the body to cause illness, pains, aches, and malfunctioning. They are said to be somewhat like ordinary air or wind; the Indians are certain that *aigre* is not quite the same as ordinary air but have difficulty in explaining the difference. . . . *Aigre* is of three principal classes. . . . The first is of natural origin and enters the body in an accidental way. . . . The second class, acquired from contact with ritually unclean persons and objects, is more feared. . . . The third class, which is sent upon the victim by black magic, is the most feared of all. . . . The natural *aigres* may be named for their

source, where they lodge in the body, or their inherent characteristics and the bodily condition they cause" (Wisdom, 1940, pp. 317–19).

The wide variety of aire forms in Yucatan and among the Chorti is not matched elsewhere in Mesoamerica. Toward the south and east, it tends to be restricted to a specialized cause of *pasmo* in El Salvador (R. N. Adams, 1957a, p. 481) or in the form of hijillo, resulting from contact or proximity to a corpse (*ibid.*, pp. 484, 600). This noxious air quality is found over much of Guatemala (Gillin, 1951, p. 159; R. N. Adams, 1957a, pp. 366–67) and in Tequila (G. Soustelle, 1958, p. 147).

To the west and north of the Yucatan-Chorti area the role of aires is also reduced, and generally becomes subordinated as a vector of some other agent, or is downgraded to the status of a mere draft. In Panajachel and San Juan Chamelco aire or viento brings colds, coughs, whooping cough, and fever, as well as smallpox and measles (Rosales, 1950, p. 589; Tax in Carr, 1952, p. 11; Goubaud, 1949c, pp. 14–15, 44). In Panajachel the last two illnesses are punishments of God; they are brought by a local nagual type of spirit, the *characoteles*, and enter the bodies of the strong by the air they breathe and the food they eat (Rosales, 1950, p. 794a). Reports from the rest of western Guatemala and Chiapas vary in details from this general picture. A significant difference is in Oxchuc where aires left by the side of the road by witches may affect anyone who passes by (Villa R., 1946, p. 227). There seems to be little question that toward the north aires become weapons used by sprites or spirits, and have but a small volitional role themselves. In Tepoztlan aires were "mysterious forces variously thought of as winds, spirits, or little people. . . ." (Lewis, 1951, p. 280). Among the Tarahumara and Mixtec whirlwinds are specifically mentioned (Mak, 1959, p. 139).

It seems to be only among the Chorti and in Yucatan that the aires are self-activating; elsewhere they are sent by spirits or human beings, thus being vectors of sickness, or are simply drafts of air that, being constantly around, can bother people only when in a special condition.

WITCHCRAFT AND SORCERY. Witchcraft and sorcery (the two terms are used here interchangeably) refer to the ascription of special animate powers to individual human beings, specifically to those where the ascribed power is used or believed to be used by the individual so endowed to affect the behavior of and control the welfare of other people. Witchcraft concerns us here as a source of illness.

Among Middle American Indians belief in witchcraft is ubiquitous, but practice varies. In some communities its efficacy is recognized, operative within the realm of one's own social relations; in others it is believed in, but its practice is attributed to social relations other than those in which the individual participates; in still others it claims an uncertain belief but at the same time recognition that it is practiced in social relations in which the individual does not participate. The first of these attitudes is the most common, although there are important differences as to which specific social relationships are involved.

The second attitude is found in two different circumstances. In highly acculturated Indian communities in which witchcraft is still remembered from the recent past and still believed to occur the elimination of the last witch can often be cited (usually brought to notice by police action or simply by her death). In other similar neighboring communities, however, witchcraft is still known to be carried on, and the names of particular witches can often be given (R. N. Adams, 1952, pp. 34, 62; 1957a, pp. 214, 368–69, 484, 600–01). The sheer presence or absence of the practice of witchcraft, however, is no index to acculturation, for, as Redfield (1941) has clearly pointed out, it

also occurs in thoroughly nonindigenous contexts.

The other circumstance in which belief exists without practice is in specific communities where witchcraft is still greatly feared but is punished by a very strong authority that exercises jurisdiction over most of the relationships within which witchcraft usually occurs. The two instances are Tusik (Villa R., 1945) and Santiago Chimaltenango (Wagley, 1949). The theoretical significance of these communities will be taken up in the final discussion.

The third degree of belief and participation may be omitted from consideration since it occurs principally in Ladino communities where there is a recognition of neighboring Indian practice. Our discussion here will focus principally on cases of the first kind.

Communities have little obvious consistency as to whether witches are specifically identifiable or not. In the Zapotecan Talea and Juquila, in Guatemalan Panajachel and San Pedro La Laguna, and in Nahuatl Tecospa, it was easy to ascertain who were witches simply by asking (L. Nader, personal communication; Rosales, 1949b, 1950; Madsen, 1960, pp. vii–viii). Much more common are certain individuals suspected of being witches but generally not admitting to it, particularly where deaths are frequently attributed to the practice and where, therefore, the witch may be "executed." In many communities witches are identified by the very fact that they are principales, or town elders and leaders, and also that they are curers (Chiapas—F. C. Miller, 1959b, p. 132; M. Nash, 1960; Tarahuamara—Passin, 1942, p. 13; Lumholtz, 1902, 1: 322; Bennett and Zingg, 1935, pp. 264, 265, 347; Nahuatl—Lewis, 1951, pp. 281, 294; G. Soustelle, 1958, p. 151; Chinantec—Rubel, 1950; Cora—Lumholtz, 1902, 1: 515; Tepehua—Bower, 1946, p. 682; Tzintzuntzan—Foster, 1948a, p. 277). In some, such as Mitla, ordinary people are said to practice it (Leslie, 1960a, p. 37),

340

although it requires a special faculty to identify them (Parsons, 1936, p. 320). People will usually identify the witch because of some outward peculiarity or sign (Wisdom, 1940, pp. 334–36; D. Metzger, 1959, p. 10).

The major devices utilized by witches are (1) the sending of the witch's nagual to molest, to "eat," or in some other way to cast sickness or death on the victim; (2) the intrusion of foreign objects or aires; and (3) imitative and contagious practices. To these may be added a fourth, the sheer desire or strength of the witch to affect people through *envidia* or something similar to *ojo*.[2]

The nagual, and its kindred form the tonal, are classic features of Middle American witch lore. Earlier authors, Brasseur de Bourbourg and Daniel Brinton (see Foster, 1944), and recently Correa (1955) held that there was a pan-Mesoamerican witches' cult based on nagualism. Foster (1944) has demonstrated that there is little to support this view. Since curers and leaders in communities are precisely those to whom the ability to have a nagual is ascribed, they are the ones who must for this reason be most feared.

The nagual is an animal into which certain people can convert themselves, and in whose form they may become malevolent. Usually the ability to do this is restricted to curers or otherwise powerful men, but in those communities where witches do not necessarily hold important ritual status this need not be the case. The tonal is a companion animal but hardly enters the issue of witchcraft since every person usually has one in communities where it is recognized (Foster, 1944; Aguirre Beltrán and Pozas, 1954). When a witch goes out as a nagual

[2] To avoid confusion, the term for "evil eye," variously *mal ojo* and *mal de ojo* in different parts of the area, is here rendered simply as *ojo*. The difficulty in using either of the other terms is that where one is used, the other usually refers to some kind of eye infection. *Ojo* nowhere has this meaning.

he may "eat" the victim's soul and thereby kill him, or he may cast an aire or an object into the person.

This may be complicated when the witch acts as an agent for some other spirit or deity. In Cancuc the nagual (locally *lab*) of a witch can bring sickness only with San Juan's permission (Guiteras Holmes, n.d.,*a*, pp. 260–70). The characoteles of Panajachel must also have God's approval before their work will bring death (Rosales, 1950, p. 794a).

Object intrusion is another element widespread in the region, and the cure consists in ridding the person of the object, commonly a toad, lizard, snake, stone, and dirt. Foster (1951) believes that the practice of sucking to withdraw the offending object is not characteristic of Mexico; the present review does not confirm this for the region as a whole (G. Soustelle, 1958, p. 149; Mak, 1959, p. 130; Beals, 1945b, p. 97; Lumholtz, 1902, 1: 317, 2: 239; J. B. Johnson, 1939b, pp. 138–39; De la Fuente, 1941, p. 45). The objects are made to pass off through the feces or are pulled out (Wisdom, 1940, p. 350) by the curer.

Imitative and contagious magic techniques, such as sticking pins in figurines or putting something belonging to the victim in his house after being ritually treated, are quite common and blend with the use of the nagual and object intrusion. The nagual frequently is the vector for accomplishing these things. The imitative and contagious methods may be of European origin, but they are reported from various areas and seem relatively more important in the less acculturated communities (cf. De la Fuente, 1949, p. 340; Wisdom, 1940, p. 332; J. E. S. Thompson, 1930, pp. 74, 109; Rosales, 1950; Guiteras Holmes, n.d.,*b*).

In the social relations aspect of witchcraft it is possible to distinguish two quite different contexts in which witchcraft operates to cause illness. The first of these·is exemplified in Chiapas communities. In Cancuc witchcraft could be practiced only

341

on a member of one's own clan (patrilineal lineage) (Guiteras Holmes, n.d.,*a*, p. 278), as was true also in neighboring Oxchuc (Villa R., 1946, cited by J. Nash, 1959b, p. 24). In Guatemala, residents of Panajachel, San Pedro La Laguna, and San Luis consider it wise for the responsible witch to remove the spell, even though other curing techniques will accompany this. The main ingredient is to bring together victim and witch. The victim is questioned during diagnosis and cure as to what kind of social-ritual offense he may have committed, for the illness is evidence of his guilt: he may have failed in household maintenance or matrimonial or affinal obligations, committed theft, or forgotten or neglected some ritual obligation.

The second context in which illness is ascribed to witchcraft is much more common and is found over most of Middle America. Here witchcraft is attributed to someone outside of one's family or group. The witches usually refuse to admit guilt, and may be hired to practice their craft. It is also commonly involved in affinal relationships, and may initiate counter-witchcraft and even witchcraft feuds. In these situations the victim is usually regarded not so much as inevitably susceptible to the work of the witch but rather as specifically weakened by something and therefore susceptible. There is no implication of social or ritual guilt in which the community shows concern.

Environmental and Nonvolitional Factors

There are many factors in illness that seem to have little or no relation to animate volition. They are often present in conditions already described, but in many instances they appear separate and are considered as hot-cold, strength-weakness, and emotional tension.

Hot-Cold. These terms refer not to temperatures but to categories of environment. They refer to qualities, and stem from the Hippocratic humors introduced by Europeans in the colonial period. Because of the selective way in which the hot-cold distinction has survived and the wet-dry humors have been lost over the years, and because some such hot-cold distinction may have originated in Yucatan (Redfield and Villa, 1934, p. 372), the presence of an indigenous counterpart cannot be wholly eliminated.

Generally today in Middle America two degrees of "hot" and "cold" are recognized, and in various places may include intermediate states, such as "fresh." Madsen (1955b) has reported seven functioning categories in Tecospa. The classification is rationalized on different bases in different places. In Tecospa things associated with water were regarded as cold, those with the sun as hot (Madsen, 1955b); in Yalalag, water and mountain associations were cold, whereas hot climate associations were hot; in Quintana Roo, Yucatan, and Guatemala, things digestible were hot and those indigestible were cold (Villa R., 1945; Redfield and Redfield, 1940; R. N. Adams, field notes).

Although these distinctions are found everywhere, their application is especially important in sickness in Yucatan (Redfield and Villa, 1934, pp. 161–64; Villa R., 1945, pp. 132–33; Redfield and Redfield, 1940, pp. 63–64). Interestingly enough, whereas Yucatan and the Chorti share some attitudes that set them off from other parts of Middle America, in this respect they differ. Neither Wisdom (1940) nor Gillin (1951) mentions the hot-cold distinction as important in illness to the neighboring Pocomam, although both discuss the subject in other connections. The distinction is clear in most other communities but is limited as a cause of illness (R. N. Adams, 1957a, pp. 213, 363–64, 480–81, 598; De la Fuente, 1949, pp. 313–16). In more traditional Indian communities there is limited mention of it (Guiteras Holmes, n.d.,*a,b*; Villa R., 1946;

Rosales, 1950), although F. C. Miller (1959b) holds it to be of some importance in Yalcuc.

Where the distinction is cited as a cause of illness, it is usually in terms of hot as equated with strength and specifically affecting children (see discussion of ojo below), or with chills and fevers. In Yucatan, where it is most prominent, the distinction involves a balance of one against the other, with the normal condition of the body considered to be on the hot side. A person often finds himself in situations where he or she is too hot (from working hard, eating hot food, menstruating, being immediately postparturient). Such states create susceptibility for which there seems to be no standard social relational context. These conditions, however, are temporary. In Yucatan and Quintana Roo some people are said to be born with one or the other quality; if in a marriage one spouse is continually unwell, it is ascribed to the fact that husband and wife were born with different qualities and were bad for each other (Redfield and Villa, 1934, p. 163). In most cases, however, hot and cold are temporary qualities of individuals but permanent attributes of things. In Magdalena, for example, a person may be inherently strong and thus cause ojo, but he will not be thought inherently hot (R. N. Adams, 1952).

One illness frequently associated with the hot-cold issue in the southern part of the region is *pasmo*. It is mentioned in all the Yucatecan studies here reviewed (Table 1) as well as in other Central American countries (R. N. Adams, 1957a) and in Yalalag (De la Fuente, 1949, p. 314). Almost everywhere it involves an attack of cold on someone who is too hot. This etiology is also found, of course, without use of the term *pasmo*.

The currency of the hot-cold distinction over much of the Ladinoized region and its minimal use in many of the less acculturated communities suggests that the terms are brought into play when the more traditional usages are reduced. When social relations require that more illnesses be ascribed to wider relations, these qualities provide a convenient classification for conditions. Madsen (1955b) has indicated that they are convenient devices for the classification of new forms, a point more fully discussed in the final section of this article.

STRENGTH-WEAKNESS. Strength and weakness closely parallel the hot-cold distinctions but tend to be used in somewhat different contexts. Both sets of qualities vary in their permanence. Strength is often identified with hot; in Chenalho the soul of a man is stronger than that of a woman because it has more heat (Guiteras Holmes, n.d.,b). Also it is widely held that a person overheated from working is strong and can cause ojo by virtue of this. Strength in an individual is both protection for himself and danger to others who may be weak. Although some individuals are thought to be constitutionally one or the other, the terms usually refer to temporary conditions.

In the section "Illness and Man" we reviewed some of the more common characteristics associated with strength and weakness. To these can be added certain environmental circumstances such as the day of the week or the phase of the moon. In the indigenous Middle American calendars there were good and bad days for various events; today this is calculated by days of the Christian week. Tuesdays and Fridays are commonly dangerous (Redfield and Redfield, 1940, p. 62; Mak, 1959, pp. 134–35), but communities vary in this. It is Mondays and Fridays in Panajachel (Tax, 1950, pp. 2260–61), Thursdays and Fridays in San Luis (Gillin, 1951). Similarly, phases of the moon cause in men and other living things (animals, plants, trees) regular cycles of strength and weakness.

Weakness is considered inevitable among infants and children, and among people who are already sick from some other cause.

343

TABLE 1—CHECK LIST OF COMMUNITIES AND BIBLIOGRAPHIC SOURCES

Community or Region	State or Department	Country	Indigenous Languages	Sources
Ladinoized communities	various	Guatemala, Honduras, El Salvador, Nicaragua	Spanish	R. N. Adams, 1957a
Tzintzuntzan	Michoacan	Mexico	Spanish	Foster, 1948a
San Antonio	Toledo	Belize, British Honduras	Yucatecan	J. E. S. Thompson, 1930
Socotz	Stann Creek	Belize, British Honduras	Yucatecan	J. E. S. Thompson, 1930
Tusik	Quintana Roo	Mexico	Yucatecan	Villa R., 1945; Redfield, 1941
Chan Kom	Yucatan	Mexico	Yucatecan	Redfield and Villa, 1934
Dzitas	Yucatan	Mexico	Yucatecan	Redfield and Redfield, 1940
Merida	Yucatan	Mexico	Yucatecan	Redfield, 1941
San Juan Chamelco	Alta Verapaz	Guatemala	Kekchi	Goubaud, 1949c
Chorti	Chiquimula	Guatemala	Chorti	Wisdom, 1940
San Luis Jilotepeque	Jalapa	Guatemala	Pocomam	Gillin, 1948, 1951
Magdalena	Sacatepequez	Guatemala	Cakchiquel	R. N. Adams, 1952, 1955
Panajachel	Solola	Guatemala	Cakchiquel	Rosales, 1950; Tax, 1950
San Pedro La Laguna	Solola	Guatemala	Tzutuhil	Rosales, 1949; Paul, 1950b
Chichicastenango	El Quiche	Guatemala	Quiche	Tax, 1947
Santiago Chimaltenango	Huehuetenango	Guatemala	Mam	Wagley, 1949
Todos Santos	Huehuetenango	Guatemala	Mam	Oakes, 1951
Yalcuc	Chiapas	Mexico	Tzotzil	F. C. Miller, 1959b
Cancuc	Chiapas	Mexico	Tzotzil	Guiteras Holmes, n.d.,a
San Pedro Chenalho	Chiapas	Mexico	Tzotzil	Guiteras Holmes, n.d.,b
Oxchuc	Chiapas	Mexico	Tzeltal	Villa R., 1946
Amatenango	Chiapas	Mexico	Tzeltal	J. Nash, 1958a,b
Aguacatenango	Chiapas	Mexico	Tzeltal	B. Metzger, 1959b; D. Metzger, 1959
Mitla	Oaxaca	Mexico	Zapotec	Parsons, 1936; Leslie, 1960a
Yalalag	Oaxaca	Mexico	Zapotec	De la Fuente, 1949
Talea, Juguila, Yajoni	Oaxaca	Mexico	Zapotec	L. Nader, personal comunication Gómez-Maillefert, 1923; De la Fuente, 1941
San Esteban Atatlahuca, San Miguel El Grande, Santo Tomas Ocotepec	Oaxaca	Mexico	Mixtec	Mak, 1959
Juquila Mixe; Western Mixe	Oaxaca	Mexico	Mixe	Beals, 1945b
San Lucas Camotlan	Oaxaca	Mexico	Mixe	W. S. Miller, 1956
Ojitlan	Oaxaca	Mexico	Chinantec	Rubel, 1950
Jalapa de Diaz, Huautla de Jimenez, San Cristobal Mazatlan	Oaxaca	Mexico	Mazatec	J. B. Johnson, 1939b; Weitlaner, 1952a
San Jose Independencia	Oaxaca	Mexico	Popoloca	J. B. Johnson, 1939b
Trique region	Oaxaca	Mexico	Trique	Comas, 1942
Ocozotepec, Soteapan	Veracruz	Mexico	Popoluca	Foster, 1940, 1945
Otomi of Puebla	Puebla	Mexico	Otomi	J. B. Johnson, 1939b
Tecuanapa	Veracruz	Mexico	Nahuatl	Blom, 1923
Tequila	Veracruz	Mexico	Nahuatl	G. Soustelle, 1958
Tepoztlan	Morelos	Mexico	Nahuatl	Redfield, 1930; Lewis, 1951

Table 1 continued

San Juan Teotihuacan	Mexico	Mexico	Nahuatl	Gamio, 1922
San Francisco Tecospa	Federal District	Mexico	Nahuatl	Madsen, 1955b, 1960
Huehuetla	Hidalgo	Mexico	Tepehua	Bower, 1946
Zirandaro, Totolapan	Guerrero	Mexico	Cuicatec	Hendrichs Pérez, 1946
Cheran	Michoacan	Mexico	Tarascan	Beals, 1946
Tarascan (general)	Michoacan	Mexico	Tarascan	Lumholtz, 1902, vol. 2
Sierra Huichol (ca. Mizquitic)	Jalisco	Mexico	Huichol	Lumholtz, 1902, vol. 2
Sierra Tarahumara	Chihuahua	Mexico	Tarahumara	Lumholtz, 1902; Passin, 1942
Samachique	Chihuahua	Mexico	Tarahumara	Bennett and Zingg, 1935
Disemboque	Sonora	Mexico	Seri	W. B. Griffin, 1959
South Texas–northeast Mexican communities	Nuevo Leon, Tamaulipas	Mexico–U.S. border region	Spanish	Rubel, 1960

Among children the most common affliction derived from weakness is ojo. The "falling" of the fontanel in very small children is another affliction, but is especially ascribed to rough handling and not the strength of another person.

Ojo is usually the label given to any general complaint of an infant or child, and implies that the weakness of the child has left him open to harm from the outside. It does not refer to conjunctivitis or any specific eye condition, nor does the English "evil eye" correctly carry its meaning. Ojo is not the result of evil, of intentional damage, but rather it is "bad eye" in the sense that it is dangerous.

Anyone who is by nature strong (or who is temporarily strong, or hot) can, by touching, fondling, or even being close to the child, cause ojo. There is no intent necessary, although in a few cases it is mentioned as a variety of witchcraft. A witch, an angry or envious woman (e.g., a woman who wants children), a stranger, a policeman, or a soldier may cause it. In the Tarascan area, "The Tarascans do not like strangers to caress their little ones, for fear of the evil eye. The mother anxiously begs the visitor rather not to molest and irritate her child that it may remain in good health. Any illness that may befall it afterward is traced to the evil eye; there is no other cause for children's illness" (Lumholtz, 1902, 2: 423). In Chiapas and Mitla, where a child's soul is lightly held to its body, ojo is a form of soul-loss whereby the child's soul is jarred from its body by the stranger (Leslie, 1960a, p. 46).

The importance of this common belief is that ojo is apparently a pan-Middle American illness usually derived from a stranger (cf. Rubel, 1960). It thus places the mother in the position of protecting her child against the world of outside dangers, for when caused by an outsider, the illness will not be cured by him. Ojo can also be caused by a friend, but, significantly, in this case the person thought to have caused it is asked to participate in the cure. This usually requires the responsible person to wrap the child in his clothing, "pass" an egg, or perform whatever the particular local ritual is. The relative participation of the stranger-outsider and friend-insider in the cure parallels witchcraft (see Discussion).

EMOTIONAL TENSION AND EXPERIENCE. Strong emotion, whether experienced gradually or suddenly, is seen as a kind of illness in some people, and gives them qualities of strength or weakness so that they may either cause illness in others or be more susceptible themselves. Anger, frustration, jealousy, and fright are the most common forms, but simple fits of depression or exhilaration from whatever cause may also be significant. *Cólera, bilis, envidia* (not to be confused with witchcraft in San Luis, Gillin, 1951, pp. 114–16), and *muina* are common terms for these conditions; *susto* and *espanto* refer to fright.

Aguirre Beltán and Pozas (1954, p. 234) state that, "There is probably no traditional sickness more widespread in the country [Mexico] than that designated *bilis,* a popular classificatory entity consisting in the stirring up of the humors of the organism that originate in a person 'que hace muina,' that is, who experiences sensations of anger, passion, or fright." Anger causes muina in Tecospa women more often than it does in men because men can take out their frustration in beating up friend or wife, which a woman may not do (Madsen, 1960). In Dzitas, "The significance of attacks . . . lies in the fact that there are many of them, and that they are commonly connected with quarrels, and through quarrels with witchcraft" (Redfield and Redfield, 1940, p. 65). The relationships most frequently involved in this, as in witchcraft, are affinal ones.

Situations that produce sudden emotional reaction are usually regarded as fright, and are widely associated with soul-loss sickness. The soul here is either the tonal or the shadow type, never the nagual. In the southern part of the area this association is particularly prominent, but here and elsewhere the two kinds of soul may appear separately. We should distinguish between (1) soul-wandering, (2) the jarring loose of the soul by a sudden experience, (3) capture of the soul by a spirit, and (4) sudden emotional experience, fright with no accompanying soul-loss.

The soul may wander away from the body of its own accord, usually while the individual is asleep but not necessarily while dreaming. It may leave by one of the regular body openings: mouth, eyes, nose, or fontanel (Foster, 1948a, p. 266). The danger lies in the individual's waking up while it is gone; sickness and death will result if it is not brought back. These wanderings are not clearly associated with social relations (Lumholtz, 1902, 1: 435; Gómez-Maillefert, 1923; Bennett and Zingg, 1935, p. 266; Foster, 1948a, p. 266; 1951, p. 167). Soul-wandering is not common in southern Middle America. Indeed, among the Chorti the soul is of no importance after death (Wisdom, 1940, p. 402); it appears to be of no consequence in the Yucatan–Quintana Roo area during sickness, except as it may return after death to cause trouble.

The jarring loose of the soul by a sudden emotional experience is reported without soul-capture from Chiapas. F. C. Miller (1959b, pp. 138–40) specifically distinguishes soul-stealing by witchcraft from simple soul-loss. This kind of soul-loss was reported from various Guatemalan communities, as well as in Cacaopera and Izalco in El Salvador, and Dulce Nombre de Copan, Honduras (R. N. Adams, 1957a, pp. 366, 483, 599).

The soul may also be captured independently of fright, as reported from Chiapas and from Todos Santos in Huehuetenango (J. Nash, 1959a, pp. 58, 60; Oakes, 1951, p. 87). It is widely associated, however, with the commission of social or ritual error. Slipping, stumbling, and thus offending the sprite of the locale may result in the capture of the soul among the Mixtec, Cuicatec (?) of Tanganhuato, the Sierra Popoluca, the Tarascans, and the Nahuatl (Mak, 1959, p. 128; Hendrichs Pérez, 1946, pp. 42–43; Foster, 1951, p. 170; Lumholtz, 1902, 2: 422; G. Soustelle, 1958, p. 155; Gamio, 1922, pp. 412–14). Bennett and Zingg (1935, p. 259) tell of a boy who threw stones into a whirlpool and had his soul captured by the local sprite. In general the sprites that capture souls are of the type described earlier as Ladino or Spanish-American in form. Many cases (Gillin, 1948, 1951; R. N. Adams, 1952; Wagley, 1949; Hendrichs Pérez, 1946, pp. 42–43; Gamio, 1922, pp. 412–14; Weitlaner, 1952a, p. 280) make it clear that it is often a problem to convince the soul to return to his regular life and that much of the curing ritual is directed to this end.

Simple fright, with no soul-loss (and consequently no problem of capture), is widely found in Ladinoized communities and among Spanish-Americans of central and eastern Middle America. Here it may be treated as an emotional problem or with herbal remedies and the presence of a lay curer. However, this simple form is not limited to Spanish-American communities but exists also among the Chorti (Wisdom, 1940), where the concept of the soul is not important and is not associated with fright (Foster, 1948a, pp. 266–67; 1951, p. 173; Toor, 1926, pp. 31–32; Redfield, 1930, p. 161; Madsen, 1960, pp. 187–90; R. N. Adams, 1957a, pp. 213, 366, 483, 599–600).

Diagnosis, Curing, and Prevention

Although it would be desirable to relate the patterns of behavior to *materia medica* in diagnosis, curing, and prevention of the illnesses previously mentioned and to relate them further to scientifically identifiable syndromes, we lack space for the first and lack data for the second. Here we shall merely review the principal features of these activities as they pertain to some of the general conditions already studied (for further details see the bibliographical guide in Table 1).

Diagnosis

The Middle American Indian usually makes an initial diagnosis of his discomfort and applies a home remedy. Unless incapacitated by an accident, he will treat the onset of illness by some mild herbal remedy, usually a tea, and cut down on his activity in accordance with how he feels. In the early stages of an illness there is no profound analysis of causes aside from simple ascriptions in terms of immediate past events. Cuts, brief frights, chills are handled directly. If the difficulty hangs on,

however, and daily activity is interrupted by ill-feeling or real incapacity, then the individual and his family become concerned and will probably decide to consult a curer. Diagnosis may thus be said to have two phases, the second of which begins only if the illness is prolonged and/or becomes severe. If the cost of curing is too high, getting the curer may be further delayed. Nevertheless, it is with the calling in of the curer that the most socially significant phases of the diagnosis are made (F. C. Miller, 1959b, p. 141; M. Nash, 1960; G. Soustelle, 1958, pp. 142–46; Wisdom, 1940, p. 346).

The kind of curer called or visited varies with the degree of Spanish-American culture in the community. If the problem is obvious, a specialist may be sought, but more traditionally the curers tend to be general practitioners of a sort. (See section "Curing," below.)

The diagnosis of the curer varies from community to community, but seems to follow general patterns within a given community. In the half-Ladino town of San Luis a lay curer (*parchero*) will first decide whether an illness is "simple" or "serious"; and if the latter (with symptoms of appendicitis, pneumonia, ulcer), he will not try to treat them (Gillin, 1951, pp. 111–12). This kind of decision, however, takes a slightly different form in the more traditional communities where alternative medical service is frequently unavailable or not even considered. When a lay curer is called in, the first thing is to determine the nature of the illness. Is it caused by the gods or evil winds (Yucatan—Redfield and Villa, 1934, p. 170), by God or witchcraft (Panajachel—Rosales, 1950, p. 794a), by envidia-witchcraft or fright (San Luis—Gillin, 1951, pp. 111–12), or by other locally recognized causes? Along with the diagnosis may go a judgment of whether or not the individual will survive. In communities where there are few alternatively ascribed causes, e.g.,

347

either witchcraft or God, the possibility of survival is one of the immediate issues. Therapeutic steps to be taken depend on both diagnosis and expectancy of survival.

Two aspects of reasoning in diagnosis are worthy of note. First is the search for both the condition that made the individual susceptible to illness, and for the thing that took advantage of this susceptibility. Adams referred (1952) to these as the "inner" and "outer" conditions respectively, and held that they are common to much of the Maya area; the present review suggests they are to be found over much of Middle America. Depending on the community and the symptoms, the inner condition is usually a matter of being too "hot," weakened, under some emotional tension, or at fault in a social or ritual observance.

The outer condition will also vary. In traditional communities a few alternatives will suffice, whereas in a fairly highly acculturated community like Magdalena, spirits, ghosts, God, angels, witches, aires, too much sun, too much cold, the wrong kind of food, the rough life of the countryman, the strength of some other individual, and counter-witchcraft may be held accountable (Adams, 1952).

The second aspect of reasoning is the fact that it is implicitly *post facto*, as in most medical diagnoses. The kind of cause chosen, and consequently the kind of cure assigned, is completely dependent on the conceptual categories of illness causation current in the community. Since diagnoses are recognized as tentative, no curer claims to have discovered all the factors, nor does he hesitate to indicate that the situation can change. In Panajachel (Tax, 1950; Rosales, 1950) and elsewhere subsequent diagnoses have reversed opinions a number of times over. Concern over the efficacy of the diagnoses is lessened by the fact that something is being done about the patient's inability to carry on.

Whenever a person is thought to have committed a social or ritual error, a variety

of social relations are brought into play; with this, even the actual relief of physical symptoms by other means may not be regarded as a cure. A certain man with a headache found relief in aspirin but he insisted that he would not, in fact, be well until God forgave his sin (Wagley, 1949, p. 76).

The formal techniques of divination are fairly similar over much of the region (although each community has its own complex) and include feeling the patient's pulse and "passing" an egg. The egg is rubbed over some part of the patient's body, then opened and inspected for signs. A crystal offers clues among the Chorti and in Yucatan (Wisdom, 1940, pp. 334–35; Redfield and Villa, 1934, p. 170). Very commonly used in both Guatemala and Mexico but absent in Yucatan and Yalalag are grains of corn or beans, which may be counted in many ways, laid out in patterns, or dropped in water. Sometimes spiritual help is invoked: the Chorti curer receives a diagnostic message from the sun god by feeling the calf of his own right leg (Wisdom, 1940). More modern apparatus—books and playing cards—serves in Yalalag (De la Fuente, 1949, p. 325).

The socially central part of diagnosis, however, is the questioning of the patient, and sometimes his family and friends, about his recent behavior and experiences. Under scrutiny are relations within the household (possibly fighting, lack of proper care) and between affinal relations (how the wife or mother-in-law has been treated), as well as ritual observances possibly forgotten or a specific witch or potential witch perhaps offended. Over the entire area this procedure is carried on in the presence of the whole household, and thus constitutes a public confessional. If the patient cannot be found guilty of some social or ritual misdemeanor (and it is rare indeed that one cannot be found), then in some communities the lives of the patient's parents or even grandparents may be explored. (J. Nash, 1959b;

348

1959a, pp. 59–60; Villa R., 1946; Guiteras Holmes, n.d.,*a;* Rosales, 1950; Tax, 1950; Goubaud, 1949c; Gillin, 1948; R. N. Adams, 1952; Redfield and Villa, 1934; Lumholtz, 1902, 1: 314; Hendrichs Pérez, 1946, pp. 42–43; G. Soustelle, 1958, p. 158.)

Curing

In a psychological sense curing begins as soon as the first diagnostic reflection is made. In some cases the very diagnostic process is regarded as having curing qualities. The "egg cure," so-called, is often used simultaneously as a device to discover what has entered a person, and to remove it (R. N. Adams, 1952). For any serious complaint, however, the choice of a particular kind of specialist, or merely calling in a curer, will follow on some phase of the home diagnosis.

Curers in Middle America are of two general types: the limited practitioner or specialist who concerns himself with particular situations; and the socio-ritual curer who, while utilizing techniques of the specialist, is also concerned closely with the socio-psychological side of the illness. Among the limited practitioners are diviners, midwives, massagers, egg-rubbers, people who suck or pull out illnesses, medical doctors, herbalists, surgeons, bonesetters, pharmacists, and witches, all, of course, differing greatly in activity, efficacy, and skill. Which one is sought out hinges not merely on skill but rather on accessibility, familiarity through known social relations, and the diagnosis made up to that moment. To the sociologist or cultural historian a medical doctor and an herbalist represent different systems, but to the Indian their relative attractiveness depends on other factors. Few of all the specialists mentioned are available to a given Indian community; the presence of a good bonesetter or a skillful midwife varies from one place and one period to the next; medical doctors and pharmacists are relatively scarce and unobtainable in most Indian communities.

The social and ritual curers are usually men of considerable standing in a community. They may be principales, elders and community leaders, as in San Luis (Gillin, 1951) and Ojitlan (Rubel, 1950); or they may be curing specialists to whom is attributed some of the power and knowledge of a witch, as in the midwestern highlands of Guatemala and Chiapas; or they may be generally responsible for the ritual welfare of both the community as a whole and the specific welfare of its members, as with the *h-mens* of Yucatan, the Mixe, Huichol, and Tarahumara (Redfield and Villa, 1934; Beals, 1945b, pp. 90, 97; Lumholtz, 1902, 2:49, 1:354). The important feature of these individuals is that their immediate concern is with the ritual and social correctness of the patient as well as with other devices for his welfare. They tend to see the patient as a victim of his own misbehavior, and their job is to keep him an effectively behaving member of the group. Because of this it is rare that these curers charge fees; a cure they sponsor may be expensive in food, liquor, and other materials, but the fee charged by the curer is usually little or nothing. This curer, after making his diagnosis, may practice pulsing, sucking, massaging, praying, and recommend the use of the sweatbath and certain herbals.

Where the social and ritual curer shows his special position is usually in connection with the spirit world. They have naguales that they may utilize during the cure, and they know how to perform ceremonies that are especially useful in accomplishing cures, like the *santiguar* and *kex* of Yucatan.

In many communities, because of these special powers, curers have become feared, as being witches simultaneously, and people are sometimes reluctant to go to them except in very desperate cases. The witch of Tecospa insisted that he was a curer, but the community regarded him as a witch (Madsen, 1957, p. 162). Many laymen, however, are seen as having knowledge of how

349

to treat particular problems, commonly those resulting from the clash of strength and weakness, hot and cold. In these cases there is usually no attribution of supernatural powers.

The knowledge of how to treat ojo is part of the lore that every woman learns. Since it is often caused by strangers, they cannot participate in the cure. If it is caused by a strong person of the community, however, it is not unlikely that this very strength has made this person particularly knowledgeable. Curers, being strong, can cause ojo but can also cure it.

Cases of being hit by cold or getting overheated are generally curable by application of things of the opposite quality, but the balance is not simple. Whereas cold conditions often result from a person being attacked by cold when he was in a state of being overheated, the literature seems barren of cases where hotness is said to attack a person who is too cold. Rather, hotness as an illness simply comes from getting too much heat. Since most of the literature has concentrated on the curative aspect of the condition, this difference in etiology has seldom been explicit. Possibly a correlative to this (obviously not an explanation) is that cold is often associated with aires and winds; hot is seldom so associated. Night airs are cold generally, whereas genuinely hot airs are rare.

The cure for witchcraft depends on whether the sorcery arises within the group of which the victim is a member, or stems from across some group boundary. In the first instance the witch can, and is expected to, participate by actively removing the spell; in the second, the witch must be combatted since he is beyond the group's influence. When a curer steps in, there is the double problem of correcting the victim's error and of removing the evil sent by the witch. The first part is largely effected through the public confessional carried on during the diagnosis; the second necessitates a variety of complicated rituals. Simi-

larly, the cure for regaining a patient's lost soul requires reassuring him that he is necessary to the community and his family, and at the same time performing a ritual to guarantee that the sprite will let the soul go and, of equal importance, that the soul will come back to the body when released. Offenses against God, saints, spirits, sprites, and ghosts must be removed by gaining forgiveness or permission, and this can be done only through ritual.

Prevention

Prevention is regarded as control of conditions that may lead to illness and is usually realistically directed toward those conditions that may be controllable. These may be (1) where the individual is thought able to manage his own condition or conduct, and preventive measures are thus clearly indicated; (2) where the individual's condition is inevitable in the nature of things but preventive measures are taken to avoid external dangers to this condition; (3) where both inner and outer conditions are amenable to some control; and (4) where neither condition is controllable and therefore, logically and practically, no preventive measures are taken at all.

From the point of view of social relations, the first and second situations are the most significant. When ritual and social offense is at issue, preventive measures are simultaneously social control devices for the group as a whole. A number of students ascribe social control to witchcraft retribution and punishment by God (Guiteras Holmes, n.d.,a; M. Nash, 1960; Villa R., 1946; B. B. Whiting, 1950; J. W. M. Whiting, 1959). It should be noted, however, that social control varies according to which of situations 1 and 2 is pertinent. Where the accusation and curing of witchcraft occurs within a group and where curing is seen as requiring the presence of the offending witch, prevention can be accomplished by strict adherence to social and ritual norms. This is the situation that interests the authors cited above. It may be called "intra-group" witchcraft and illustrates situation 1. In the literature reviewed, witchcraft more commonly occurs in situation 2. Here the witch does not participate in the cure; he either refuses knowledge of the event or is simply inaccessible. In this "inter-group" or "extragroup" witchcraft, prevention is much more difficult because it is not predictable who on the "outside" is going to cast a spell. And since prevention is here essentially unrealistic, it is generally not attempted and therefore plays little or no role in social control. Instead, it is often positively destructive of social solidarity and integration. In San Luis (Gillin, 1951, p. 115) if the accused witch willingly comes forward to remove his spell, the group is thereby drawn together, and witchcraft is seen as preventable by proper conduct of the victim; if the witch refuses to do this, however, counter-witchcraft is practiced and the group is further torn apart.

Ojo somewhat parallels this. A child's inherent weakness cannot be changed, but presumably prevention may be practiced by protecting the child from "strong" things. But as one cannot always keep one's child out of the way of friends and relatives, it is not surprising that from time to time one of these people will cause ojo. When this happens, the same person is called in on the cure and thus serves to draw the group together. Strangers, however, cannot usually be pulled into a curing role if charged with the harm, so prevention must be especially exercised against them. This is feasible because a child is constantly in its mother's care. The material summarized in Tables 2 and 3 indicates the way these two situations work in other forms of illness ascription.

Where the individual's susceptibility is seen in terms of hot-cold, strength-weakness, or emotional experiences, prevention depends largely on its practicability. Getting overheated makes one susceptible, but a countryman's work makes overheating inescapable. If one gets overheated from overeating, however, one can refrain from going out into the cold night and thereby ward off a chill. Emotional experiences, on the other hand, are generally unavoidable, and the literature provides no examples of preventive measures against them. Many weaknesses are also uncontrollable: being sick from something else, being young, being born that way.

An important feature not clarified by the literature is the degree to which the perception of real incidence of illness affects exercise of preventive measures. Where incidence is particularly high, we might expect preventive measures to be particularly significant, as, for example, the very reduced diet given to children in the two years immediately after weaning, in an attempt to avoid foods that are too hot or too cold. This, of course, incidentally leads to malnutrition and kwashiorkor.

Discussion

An attempt to delineate features in sickness and curing common to major Middle American indigenous cultures also reveals changes in forms and in social relations.

Changes in Forms

The external forms into which Middle Americans project interpretations and meanings are confined to the natural habitat, the fairly limited material inventory of a peasant culture, and human beings themselves. These have been classified as having hot or cold qualities and having animate qualities. In major illness ascriptions there is to some degree a complementary distribution of certain dominant traits. The Yucatan–eastern Guatemala area seems dominated (in the nonhuman side) by aires; central and northern Mexico, by sentient beings. Such predominance does not mean that aires are absent from the north, nor sentient beings from the south, but that they have been differentially emphasized. Between the two areas lies the band of

351

Table 2—CHARACTERISTICS OF SICKNESS INTERPRETATIONS IN THE INTRA-GROUP CONTEXT

Sickness Interpretation	Ascribed External Cause	Ascribed Internal Cause or Susceptibility	Use of Curer	Prevention
Witchcraft (general)	A spell cast by a witch, sometimes with permission of God; witch is member of same group	A social or ritual offense (in the north social offenses are more common)	Curer must come from within the group	Social and ritual correctness
God's punishment (Chiapas, Guatemala, Yucatan)	Punishment sent by God or other deities (wind gods in Yucatan)	A social or ritual offense	Curer must come from within the group	Social and ritual correctness
Ojo (general)	Strength of person who is known and a friend	Natural weakness of infant; failure of mother to provide care	Person who caused it should participate in cure	Protection of child by the mother, especially against strangers
Ghosts of dead (mainly in south but also Tarahumara)	Punishment sent by ghosts of family dead	Failure to show ritual correctness or to provide care	None; done within family	Keeping up rituals showing respect for family dead (among Tarahumara, destroy house of the dead)
Attack by mischievous sprites (general)	Stealing of soul by sprite	Weakness of individual in craving luxuries of non-Indian life, a social offense	Curer must come from within the group	Avoidance of temptations of non-Indian life; stay close to the village

Table 3—CHARACTERISTICS OF SICKNESS INTERPRETATIONS IN THE INTER-GROUP OR EXTRA-GROUP CONTEXT

Sickness Interpretation	Ascribed External Cause	Ascribed Internal Cause or Susceptibility	Use of Curer	Prevention
Witchcraft (general)	A spell cast by a witch, either at own volition or employed to do so	Weakness of the individual, due to various reasons	Curer may come from anywhere; he needs to be strong; counter-witchcraft may be employed	No prevention possible since it is unpredictable who may cast spell
Ojo (general)	Presence of stranger, especially showing interest in child	Natural weakness of child; failure of mother to provide care	Variety of cures, some purely diagnostic	Protection of child by the mother; difficult against close family members
Winds (Yucatan, Tequila)	Winds waiting to attack a person	Person weak from work or other causes	Curers must convince winds to leave, or get rid of them	No prevention; such weakness is inevitable part of life
Fright (no soul-loss)	Sudden apparition or scare	Weakness (it would not affect a strong person)	Various	No prevention
Return of ghosts of dead for malevolent purposes (north)	Ghost needs to kill someone to gain freedom	Weakness	None	No prevention

communities from the midwestern high-lands of Guatemala through Chiapas, wherein God and a few of his saints play the main role. In all three regions witch-craft is significant (although for specific reasons it may be absent from particular towns). Thus in all areas there is a parallel ascription of illness causation to both "super-animated" human beings (as in witchcraft) and animated habitat features (aires, sprites, God).

We find adaptations of new meanings to old forms and the incorporation of new forms under old interpretations. Madsen (1955b) has pointed out how the hot-cold category classifies any new items coming into the cultures of Middle America. Al-though the present survey shows that this distinction still plays a relatively minor part in many sickness and curing interpreta-tions, there is some reason to think it will become increasingly important. This, we hold, is not because of its historical Euro-pean origin, but because it readily adapts to the increased cultural inventories of ex-panding societies. A possible aboriginal counterpart in Yucatan might help to ex-plain its peculiar prominence in that locale (Redfield and Villa, 1934, p. 372).

The ubiquitous dwarflike sprites reflect social, and especially ethnic, relations over much of the region. They are generally Spanish-American, Mexicanized, or Ladino-like (or Negro on the Gulf Coast where that ethnic characteristic is prominent) and are out to cause trouble for the Indian. They demand that he work for them while building his house and cultivating his fields, that he give them his soul, that, in short, he maintain a relationship with them essen-tially similar to the position the Indian has endured with the superordinate group the past 400 years. That these projections by the Indian are delicate and sensitive to spe-cific known relations is evident from the local variations that always reflect local conditions. This interpretation, like the hot-cold, is well adapted to most of the sorties

the Spanish-Americans make into Indian life. When in the Zapotec area a new high-way was proposed, the word quickly went around that the local sprite would re-quire the lives of 100 Indians for the work (L. Nader, personal communication). When public health workers tried to intro-duce powdered milk and other nutritional supplements into the diet of Guatemalan villages, it was regarded as a new device to fatten up the children so that they could be consumed by the outsiders, an interpre-tation stemming essentially from belief in the nagual of powerful people who are said to eat their victims (R. N. Adams, 1955).

Witchcraft practice is also incorporating new elements. This is a likely tendency be-cause witchcraft is usually handled by spe-cialists and therefore is much more subject to cultural drift, innovations of individuals who need not check their forms against those used by others. It is in antagonistic witchcraft (described below) that these in-novations are most helpful (cf. De la Fuen-te, 1949).

Finally, as pointed out by Redfield (1941) and by Rubel (1960), many of the standard forms described here are especial-ly satisfactory in helping the adjustment of the individual who must face the tensions of living in multicultural situations. They provide ready-made devices for directing aggression to scapegoat groups and individ-uals, and at the same time reaffirming the importance of the local group to the well-being of the individual. Fright, ojo, and witchcraft all are easily adjustable to this modern situation.

Changes in Social Relations

This review of social relational aspects of illnesses points up the different ways in which a given cultural form may operate if the context of the relationships changes. Two kinds of changes can be observed: first, a tendency to shift the relationship im-plicated in a sickness from a defined group necessary for the welfare of the individual, to other segments of a larger social whole; second, change in the kind of group necessary to the well-being of the individual. Thus some communities tend to associate the cause and cure of illnesses with relationships solely within the clan, the village, or the ethnic group (see Table 2); whereas in most situations, the "same" illnesses will involve relationships that specifically cut across group boundaries, and relate a person to his non-consanguineal kin, his neighbors, or members of other ethnic groups (see Table 3). Here the group necessary to the individual's well-being is principally his own consanguineal family and, even more, his own household.

These two situations in which the "same" cultural form appears we have distinguished as "intra-group" and "inter-group" or "extra-group" contexts. Both contexts appear in all societies, but societies differ in their scope or *scale* (cf. Wilson and Wilson, 1945, p. 45) (that is, of the clan or village as contrasted with consanguineal family) and the relative degree to which illnesses are ascribed to relations within these groups as opposed to relations stemming from them to other groups or more indefinite parts of the larger society.

Differences in the operation of cultural forms by social contexts are readily apparent in instances of witchcraft, fright, and ojo. When ojo is ascribed to a friend, that friend is included in the curing and draws the group together; when it is attributed to a stranger, it is tantamount to saying that the mother has not adequately cared for her child. Protecting the child from dangers and keeping it within the safety of the family is an intrinsic part of the interpretation of this illness. In some regions a witch who has been identified as responsible for a person's illness and who refuses to admit responsibility triggers counterwitchcraft and even witchcraft feuds, results which are antagonistic, aggressive, and fissive. The increase of witchcraft described first by Redfield and Redfield (1940) and later comparatively by Redfield (1941) is entirely of this second type. The personal grudge, the affinal dispute, the personal aggression, these are paramount; no one is concerned with community unity. In an occurrence of soul-loss in San Luis and Magdalena a central effort is to convince the victim that he will cease to be an Indian if he gives in to the temptations of Ladino life. This expresses community distinctiveness and sharply separates Indians from the dominant Ladinos (Gillin, 1948, 1951; R. N. Adams, 1952). And ojo, when it is caused by a stranger, cannot be cured since no one knows who did it; the moral is to avoid strangers, keep one's own group sharply separate from outsiders.

Our analysis clarifies how seemingly identical cultural traits differ by social context. The question becomes, What determines in which context a given event will occur? To this we find at present only a partial answer in the hypothesis of B. B. Whiting (1950) to the effect that witchcraft is essentially a coordinate social control mechanism; and that in any social group the importance of witchcraft varies inversely with the significance of superordinate punitive authority (cf. Lieban, 1960, pp. 141–42).

Evidence from the present study indicates that in so far as such a superordinate authority does take over the control of specific relationships, witchcraft will cease to operate in these relationships, but will not disappear from society. In Santiago Chimaltenango (Wagley, 1949) and Tusik (Villa R., 1945) witchcraft is deeply believed but not practiced. In both these communities there was a strong and rigid superordinate authority system: in the first it was Ladino controlled, and handled even affinal disputes; in the second it was handled by the military organization that had long since been set up to fight the War of the Castes in Yucatan. What evidently happens commonly in the Chiapas and

Guatemalan communities, and more isolated communities elsewhere, is that coordinate social control is part of the witchcraft system. This system operates essentially to certify, first, the sick victim as guilty (by virtue of his sickness) of some social or ritual error. This established, the community (curer and witch included) gathers around to cure him. If the victim should die, however, the witch becomes, by virtue of the death, a criminal, and the community then begins to regard him as a danger. This results in the killing of witches, a reaction that has hit an extraordinarily high pitch in some of the Chiapas communities (M. Nash, 1960) and is serious elsewhere (Villa R., 1945). Or the witch is driven out, primarily for the welfare of the community.

With the institution of superordinate punishment authority, disputes are not brought before the community for its unified action but are handled by an "impartial" authority, which serves to separate defendant from plaintiff. After this, the defendant is likely to be punished and he loses any warm feeling he might have held for the other party. Whether the establishment of superordinate authority precedes the splitting up of the community, or whether the community for other reasons was already being split up into a series of antagonistic groups and therefore requiring such an authority, doubtless varies historically from one community to another. In any event, the presence of such an authority serves to crystallize groups within the community over any issue that may come up, and thus to eliminate any social control function witchcraft might have had.

By way of summary we can identify the principal social relations that serve as dimensions of illness interpretation. Most intra-familial relations serve as mechanisms for witchcraft, God's punishment, or the punishment by sprites or volitional aires. Most common are affinal relations and relations between men or women in competition with each other in love or marriage. But parent-child relations are also important here as are also sibling relations. The role of the family's dead is manifest in trouble brought on by failure to provide them with the proper ritual.

Proper respect and provision for persons of high ritual status, especially principales, curers, and known witches, cut beyond familial lines. There are in limited regions specific corporate entities, such as clans or local communities, that provide the context for most such witchcraft and punishment. However, in these and other communities the community versus the outside is manifest in the Indian-Ladino dichotomy wherein the dangerous sprites are non-Indian, and the quality of Indianness is endangered by giving in to the desire for non-Indian things. More generalized is the friend-stranger distinction manifest in ojo ascriptions, and the similar rationale that strangers are particularly dangerous.[3]

[3] Between the preparation of this article and its publication, the following references have been published: Holland, 1963a, 1963b; Kelly, 1965; Metzger and Williams, 1963b; Rubel, 1964.

REFERENCES

Adams, R. N., 1952, 1955, 1957a
Aguirre Beltán and Pozas, 1954
Beals, 1945b, 1946
Bennett and Zingg, 1935
Blom, 1923
Bower, 1946
Carr, 1952
Caso, 1954
Comas, 1942, 1951
Correa, 1955
De la Fuente, 1941, 1949
Estudios Antropológicos, 1956
Foster, 1940, 1944, 1945, 1948a, 1951, 1953b
Gamio, 1922
Gillin, 1948, 1951
Gómez-Maillefert, 1923
Goubaud, 1949c
Griffin, W. B., 1959
Guiteras Holmes, n.d., *a,b,* 1946a
Hendrichs Pérez, 1946
Holland, 1963a, 1963b
Johnson, J. B., 1939b
Kelly, 1965
Leslie, 1960a
Lewis, 1951
Lieban, 1960
Lumholtz, 1902
McQuown, 1959
Madsen, 1955b, 1957, 1960

Mak, 1959
Metzger, B., 1959b
Metzger, D., 1959
—— and Williams, 1963b
Miller, F. C., 1959b
Miller, W. S., 1956
Nash, J., 1959a, 1959b
Nash, M., 1960
Oakes, 1951
Parsons, 1936
Passin, 1942
Paul, 1950b, 1955
Redfield, 1930, 1941
—— and Redfield, 1940
—— and Villa, 1934
Rosales, 1949b, 1950
Rubel, 1950, 1957, 1960, 1964
Soustelle, G., 1958
Tax, 1947a, 1950, 1952a
Thompson, J. E. S., 1930
Toor, 1926
Villa R., 1945, 1946
Wagley, 1949
Weitlaner, 1952a
Whiting, B. B., 1950
Whiting, J. W. M., 1959
Wilson and Wilson, 1945
Wisdom, 1940, 1952

18. Narrative Folklore

MUNRO S. EDMONSON

THE NARRATIVE FOLKLORE of Middle America, covering a broad acculturative spectrum, an aboriginal diversity in sophistication, and a large and exceedingly complex ethnographic area, presents peculiar problems of interpretation and analysis. The following survey emphasizes those general features which appear to characterize the folk literature of the area in its more aboriginal form, traces some of the lines of development during the colonial period, and presents a bibliography of textual or near-textual sources useful for a more extensive exploration of this lore.[1]

The essence of the literature of the Mexican and Guatemalan Indians lies in a cosmology and an ethic so distinctive that its flavor has survived four centuries of impingement from outside influences, and continues to present a marked contrast with other major cultural areas of the globe. This essence is embodied in a tragic fatalism which is the all but universal hallmark of

the literature despite its variation, and which is captured with singular force and beauty in the Aztec midwife's address to the newborn child:

You have come to this world where your relatives live in labor and fatigue, where there is intemperate heat, cold and air, where there is neither pleasure nor contentment. . . . We do not know whether you will live long enough to know your grandfathers and grandmothers. . . . We do not know whether you have any merits or whether perchance you have been born like an ear of corn with no kernel which is of any use; or whether perchance you carry some bad fortune which inclines you to filthy deeds and vice; we do not know whether you will be a thief. . . . Do not sigh or cry for you came greatly desired; nevertheless you will experience labor and fatigue for this is ordained. . . . [Sahagún, 1938, 2: 187.]

The contrast between this philosophy and the Western European optimism of "living happily ever after" is obviously profound. More subtly, however, the Middle American Indians succeed in transmuting and subverting the trickster motif so prominent in the coyote tales of North America, totally avoiding the moralism of the Middle East

[1] I am deeply indebted to John J. Bodine of Marquette University for the bibliographic work in this article.

357

represented in Aesop of biblical folklore, ignoring the psychological niceties of Japanese or Chinese narrative or the legalism of African tales or the heroics of European or Polynesian epic tradition. On a world scale, Middle American literature, fragmentary as it is, presents a truly distinctive world view, which attracts, repels, puzzles, or intrigues but seldom bores.

It is necessary to speak of the "essence" of Middle American folklore, because folklore has little respect for boundaries and because Middle America's boundaries are particularly problematic. Located on an isthmus narrowing to the south, the area is open to cultural influence by only one land route from that direction—via Panama—and only two from the north—the west coast route from Arizona and New Mexico, and the east coast route from the Plains, the Mississippi Valley, and the southeastern United States. To these possible routes of diffusion may be added two sea tracks—a Caribbean pathway from Yucatan through Cuba to the Antilles, and a Pacific coastal connection to South America from around Guatemala to Ecuador. The general geography of Middle America ordains that although it has no boundaries, it has a core (or rather, two cores) at which external influences converge for possible synthesis and elaboration. It is thus in part a geographical fact that the "essence" of Middle America is to be found at its double heart: the highlands of central Mexico and the triangle of Yucatan, Chiapas, and Guatemala. It is no accident that in these two crossroads areas there arose the great civilizations of Middle America, and that the Aztec and the Maya were able to accumulate and elaborate there the cultural riches which then gave distinctive coloration to a much broader, if ill-defined, area of Mexico and Central America.

If the configuration of Middle American geography dictated the complex fact of its double center, its isolation in world geography is an equally important determinant of its general culture history. By land routes, even northern Peru is more than 1800 miles away; the nearest centers of Old World civilization in north China are more than 7000 miles distant, farther than the track from Peiping to London. Geography has thus also dictated that although ideas have traveled from the Old World to the New (and probably vice versa), the civilizations of the New World necessarily developed with a higher degree of cultural autonomy than those in any other part of the globe. They are correspondingly distinctive.

Perhaps the most dramatic expression of the unique ethos of Middle America is the large-scale practice of human sacrifice. Directly or indirectly this unparalleled rite has left its mark, not only on the folklore of the Middle American Indians, but also on the scholarship of Europeans who have studied them. It is not, of course, ritual murder as such but rather the fatalistic philosophy which underlies it that is the central feature of the Guatemalan and Mexican Indian in his literary as in his religious life. This, then, is the essence, and also the central mystery, with which the Middle American folklorist must come to terms.

The most revealing expression of what human sacrifice signified for the Middle American Indians may well be the text of the Quiche *Xahoh Tun* or *Rabinal-Achi* (Brasseur de Bourbourg, 1862, pp. 1–119), a play fraught with obscurities but lucid enough on this central point. The plot deals with the epic contest of the warrior representatives of two of the leading lineages of the 15th-century Quiche kingdom. The style is wordy and repetitive, marked by the archaic parallelism characteristic of some other primitive literatures; the action is slow and ritualized. At the end of the play, however, the prince of Quiche, captured and facing death by sacrifice, achieves real poignancy as he pleads for the chance to return home for a final farewell. When this is refused, he disappears magically, says his farewells, and then returns to accept death, having demonstrated dramatically that even the powerful magic of the sorcerer-kings does not escape the unquestioned inevitability of fate. An appealing humanity shines through his wistful remark, "Would that I had lived like the squirrel on yonder branch, to die on the same bough whereon he fed." But the pride and courage of the warrior dominate even his final speeches, and it is precisely these virtues which doom him. In the end he does not achieve heroism or martyrdom. He does not even teach us a moral lesson or interest us in the psychological implications of his plight. He merely fulfills his tragic destiny.

No other product of Middle American Indian literature gives so explicit or so powerful an interpretation of the drama of life and death, but scarcely any example of it fails to convey some sense of the acquiescence in a tragic fate so vividly expressed by the prince of Quiche. When one searches even the modern tin-pan-alley songs of Mexico or Guatemala for gaiety, he is almost invariably disappointed. Even in a near-nonsense song:

Guadalajara on a plain; Mexico on a lake.
I have to eat this *tuna* even if it pricks me.

There is continuity and generality to the fatalistic tradition of the Middle American Indians, whether the language is Nahuatl, Quiche, or Spanish and whether the Indians are aboriginal, colonial, or modern. Indeed, the tradition has had sufficient force to leave its mark on Guatemalans and Mexicans who are not, by descent, Indians at all, but who have come to share the almost telluric fatalism of the region in a degree quite foreign to European tradition.

Spain, too, has its tragic sense of life, but Spain's tragedy is not bound to the immutable workings of calendric destiny. Spanish pride and Spanish passion do not permit. There is something quintessentially Spanish and totally strange to the Indies in the oft-quoted oath of fealty to the kings of Aragon:

We, who are each worth as much as you, and who together can do more than you, offer you our obedience if you maintain our rights and liberties, and if not, no. [Serrano Plaja, 1944, p. 48.]

The Spaniard rebels against a tragic fate; the Indian accepts it. There is, of course, a great deal of Spanish folklore in Middle America, and much more that is partly Spanish. In this dimension, too, Middle America has no clear boundaries. Nonetheless, in those reaches of folklore where Indian influence is strong, we invariably encounter echoes of a world view more fatalistic than Spain's and lacking in other parts of the Hispanic world. This is the contribution of Middle American Indians to the world's literature.

Chef-d'oeuvre of the literature of the region is almost unquestionably the *Popol Vuh* of the Quiche (Recinos, 1947). Probably the longest Indian narrative we possess (it runs to some 150 printed pages of Quiche text) and possibly the most literary, it is divisible into three rather autonomous parts. Part I, which opens with a syncretistic paraphrase of Genesis, describes the multiple creations of the world and the doings of the gods. It is a compendium of Quiche mythology. Part II begins with the creation of the ancestors of the Quiche lineages—the first men—and recounts the history of these founding fathers and their migrations down to the founding of the Quiche capital. This part is legendary in character, and since it is a product of the tradition of the royal lineage (Cavek), it gives that lineage's view of the origins of the tribes and of the Quiche state. The doings of its protagonists are scarcely less marvelous than those of the gods, with whom they walk and talk. Part III may be distinguished from the founding of Gumarkaah. It is mainly historical, and describes the development of the Quiche kingdom, the succession of its rulers, and the evolution of the system of ranks of its three main lineages down to the conquest. It concludes with a summary list of the lords of these three lineages, possibly as a basis for validating land claims.

Elements and episodes from the *Popol Vuh* can easily be paralleled from the less codified traditions of the Aztec, the Maya, and other groups of Middle American Indians. There can be no doubt that the cosmology of Part I and the elements of the legendary history of Part II are common to nuclear America. The multiple creations and destructions of the world, the adventures of the twin gods (Hun Ahpu and Xbalanque for the Quiche), and a somewhat equivocal reflection of the Quetzalcoatl legend are excellent illustrations of the point. Despite a general disregard for calendrical niceties (the *Annals of the Cakchiquel* are more punctilious about chronology), or for divination and prophecy (the *Books of Chilam Balam* are more concerned with time and fate), the *Popol Vuh* nonetheless reflects faithfully, even if "in the language of God, being now in Christianity," the calendrical fatalism of Middle American religion. It is startling to note that even the seemingly historical lists of kings tend to run in cycles of four reigns, with the day-name identifications of the rulers repeating cyclically and with every fourth ruler a "great man" identified with snake and death. It seems likely that the author-editor of the *Popol Vuh* was not a competent diviner, but it is equally probable that the traditions had passed through the hands of someone who was.

A basically similar framework of cyclical and calendrical cosmology was differentially elaborated among all the sophisticated peoples of pre-Columbian Middle America, and comes down to us in very fragmentary form, variously intellectualized by the diviners and priests who reworked it. The fundamental similarity, however, does not preclude considerable differences within the common frame. The *Annals of the Cakchiquel,* for example, though attentive to calendrical detail, manages to achieve a strength of historical characterization that is unique in the area. Its description of Alvarado is typical:

Since he had received nothing, Tunatiuh became angry and said to the chiefs, "Why haven't you given me the metal? If you don't bring me the precious metal in your towns, then make up your minds that I will burn you alive and hang you." Thus he spoke to the chiefs. Then Tunatiuh ripped the earrings they were wearing from three of the chiefs, an indignity which caused them considerable pain. But Tunatiuh was unconcerned, and said, "I'm telling you that I want that metal here in five days. It'll be bad for you if you don't bring it. I know my own mind." [Villacorta C., 1936, p. 265.]

Throughout the *Annals* there is a preoccupation with precise recording of events and their chronological sequence which makes them the best historical writing in Middle America's Indian literature. Other indications, such as the clarity of the day names of the kings or the similar historicity of *The Wars of Xpantzay* (Recinos, 1957), suggest that this may be related to the particular ethos of the Cakchiquel.

Despite such stylistic variations, the systemic elaboration of Middle American religion, and hence of Middle American mythology and literature, was originally calendrical and divinatory, and it is thus that the system-builders passed the tradition down in pieces to the general population and to peripheral regions. The gods and heroes of Middle America therefore tend to travel alone. A society of gods never developed, for the separate deities never became personalities who had to be accommodated to each others' existences. Similarly there was little development in Middle America of cycles of related tales centering on the character of a particular hero. We find no parallel for Anansi, Coyote, Tyl Eulenspiegel, or the Fox of the South American Toba. To the degree that they are systematized, the animal tales take their cue from the divinatory meanings of the animal day-names. Snake, Jaguar, Coyote, Monkey, or Hawk are never the wandering individualists they manage to be in North or South America, with foibles and habits. They become symbols, overlaid with secondary and tertiary mystical meanings which give them significance but not character. Animal tales are thus little elaborated in Middle America, for the importance of the animals lies less in what they do or teach than in what they pretend. (See, however, K. L. Pike, 1948–49; Kunst, 1915.) The mere appearance of an eagle on a cactus with a snake in his mouth is a dominating and brooding omen, but how the eagle got there, how he trapped the snake, where he goes next, or what he says do not concern us. Middle American thought is punctuated by these episodic images, isolated, stationary, and arresting.

Such a presence, obscurely presiding over the legends of Middle America, is the feathered serpent. Possibly no other image more deftly defines the limits of Middle American literature. Traceable affinities of the Quetzalcoatl story have been found from Bolivia to Arizona, but the specific element of the plumed serpent is unique to the double heartland of Middle America. Various traditions among different groups describe the life of the culture hero more or less vaguely identified with this image, but it is the symbol itself rather than the man or what he did that seems to command Middle American attention. Different individuals have doubtless been coalesced through the image, and the traditions have been preserved in more or less narrative form, but there is no cycle of Quetzalcoatl stories. Common elements over any very wide area come down to Feathered Serpent, white, light, and bringer of gifts (corn,

honors, wisdom), who disappears to the east, sometimes promising to return. The feathered serpent is thus a motif but not a genre of Middle American literature.

A great deal of our knowledge of Middle American folklore presents a similar problem. Legends or myths are described or reported in rough paraphrase but not recorded. We are left to guess whether or in what form an oral narrative existed, and we must frequently surmise it to have been a piecemeal "tradition" rather than a traditional story of somewhat codified style. Although our corpus of actual texts of a more or less aboriginal character is therefore small and fragmentary, it does tend to point to the domination of this literature by the religious preoccupations already noted. Like so much else in Middle American culture, this tendency reaches its peak (and its greatest obscurity) among the Maya.

It seems natural that the framework of thought which made Yucatan and the Peten the centers of mathematics and astronomy in the New World should find expression in a corresponding precocity of divination and prophecy. The note of doom which darkens Aztec literature attains a kind of mathematical certainty in the *Books of Chilam Balam*:

Year of the 9 Flood *Tun*: 9 Flood in 1 Mat. Then 5 Lord will take a name and 7 Heart-Offering will speak his word. That will be the time when the newborn will multiply and the boys will multiply; old men will engender and old women will conceive. It will be the time of deaths and the power will be destructive in all the round land of Sun Monkey, of Water Magician Monkey. It will be the rule of Tortoise-shell Staff and Roasted Music Bone, those of the sad face, of the fleshless face. Bloody will be the roads to the north and west. [Barrera Vásquez, 1948, pp. 173–74.]

The Maya were great ritualists as well as diviners, and there is a willful obscurantism to their symbolism which reinforces the impression of mysticism we find elsewhere in Middle American literature. An exceptional document apparently intended for giving instruction to novices, *The Language of Zuyua,* illustrates the pitfalls in the interpretation of this esoteric literature:

The precious blood of his daughter that he asks for is *balché;* the guts of his daughter are the little balls of honey in the hive, and his daughter's head is the new jar in which *balché* is fermented . . . and the femur of his daughter is the bark of the *balché* tree . . . and his daughter's arms are its branches . . . for that is the language of Zuyua. [Barrera Vásquez, 1948, pp. 211–13.]

The Yucatecan delight in these convoluted symbolisms never entirely diffused to other peoples, but there is a gulf of sophistication as well as ethos between the literature of the Maya priests or Aztec kings and that of the common people of Middle America, nuclear or peripheral. Even among the Kekchi, the esoterica of Yucatan are replaced by an earthy narrative form much closer to the tales of North and South American Indians:

(Sun runs away with a girl, whose indignant father kills her with a thunderbolt.) Sun was sad, but then he had an idea. He gathered up the girl's blood and put it into gourds. (When he went to open the gourds), in the first he found frogs, and in the second, snakes. In the third he found various kinds of toads who had been born there. Finally he found the girl, but she had no feet. He made her feet. She had no flesh either. Three times he spread his antelope skin over her, but it did not make flesh. Then he tried deer, but when they ran away together they had wounded a deer. So now they met their fate. Sun went back to shining, and the girl remained as the moon. [Termer, 1957, pp. 291–93.]

The Spanish conquest revolutionized the very cultural geography of Middle America. The sea axis of the treasure fleet from Manila to Cadiz, crossing Mexico from Acapulco to Veracruz and making Mexico City the true geographic heart of the viceroyalty, furnished a channel for the introduction not only of Spanish cultural influence, but of some Oriental elements as well. But although the Europeans, Orientals, and Africans who came to the New World enormously complicate the general cultural history of Middle America, their impact on the Indians was slight, gradual, and highly structured. Reliance on sea transport in part turned the isthmus inside out, and now it was the heavily populated Indian hinterland which became marginal and isolated. Thus the Indians, influenced primarily by the missionary priests, absorbed the new elements which reached them in a synthesis which remained regionally distinctive. The smoothness of this absorption and synthesis is nowhere more beautifully illustrated than in the opening passage of the *Popol Vuh:*

Until then everything had been calm; the waters stretched away peacefully; there was no wind. All was silent, motionless. The reaches of heaven were empty. This is the first thing which is told and related. There was still no person and no animal, nor bird, nor fish, nor crab, nor tree, nor rock, nor hole, nor canyon, nor meadow, nor woods. Only the sky existed. The face of earth could not be seen; only the sea and the reaches of the sky existed in the stillness. There were no groups at all, nothing that moves, nothing that crawls or runs, nothing that flies, nothing that walks. Only the sea unfolded flat into the distance; absolutely nothing existed. There was only the surface of the sea in the darkness of the night. There were only the Shaper and Former, Majesty, the Snake-Dressed, Begetter of Sons and Daughters there in the clear water wrapped in green quetzal plumes, whence they were called the Snake-Dressed. There they were and they were wise and great. Thus there was always heaven and the Heart of Heaven, for this is the name of God. [Burgess and Xec, 1955, p. 7.]

Few indeed of our sources for understanding the narrative literature of pre-Columbian Middle America lie so close to the aboriginal reality as does the *Popol Vuh.* All the native language documents are in some measure tinged with Spanish culture, if only because it was Spaniards who taught the Indians to write. A precious handful of chroniclers recorded more or less adequately the traditions which were soon to disappear into the syncretism of colonial Indian culture, and in a very few cases items of aboriginal folklore have come down to us in something like their original literary form. Almost all of these are chronicles:

CAKCHIQUEL:
Annals of the Cakchiquel (Villacorta C., 1936).
Relation of the Capital City of Atitlan (MS in Univ. Texas Library, Austin).
Wars of Xpantzay (Recinos, 1957).

MAYA:
Book of the Jaguar Priest of Chumayel (Roys, 1933).
Book of the Jaguar Priest of Ixil (Gropp, 1934).
Book of the Jaguar Priest of Kaua (Roys, 1929).
Book of the Jaguar Priest of Mani (Martínez Hernández, 1909b).
Book of the Jaguar Priest of Noh (Roys, 1933).
Book of the Jaguar Priest of Tekax (Gates, 1924).
Book of the Jaguar Priest of Tizimin (Gropp, 1934).
Chronicle of Calkini (Barrera Vásquez, 1948).
Chronicle of Chac Xulub Chen (Martínez Hernández, 1909a).
Chronicle of Oxkutzcab (MS in Peabody Museum, Cambridge, Mass.).
Chronicle of Yaxkukul (Martínez Hernández, 1926).
Language of Zuyua (Barrera Vásquez, 1948).
Notebook of Teabo (Roys, 1933).

MIXTEC:
Mixtec Chronicles (Jiménez Moreno and Mateos Higuera, 1940).

NAHUATL:
Annals of Chimalpahin (Siméon, 1889).
Annals of Cuauhtitlan (Velásquez, 1945).
Annals of Tlatelolco (Berlin and Barlow, 1948).

General History of the Things of New Spain (Sahagún, 1938).
Horrible Cruelties of the Conquerors of Mexico (Alva Ixtlilxochitl, 1938).
Legend of the Suns (Paso y Troncoso, 1903).
Memorial of Tepetlaostoc (Kingsborough, 1831–48).
Toltec-Chichimec History (Berlin, 1947).

QUICHE:
Book of Counsel (Brasseur de Bourbourg, 1861).
Lineage of the Lords of Totonicapan (Recinos, 1950).
Royal Title of Don Francisco Izquin Nehaíb (Recinos, 1957).
Quiche History of Don Juan de Torres (Recinos, 1957).
Title of the Town of Santa Clara la Laguna (Recinos, 1957).

Elsewhere in Middle America anything resembling first-contact folklore is virtually nonexistent.

Our secondary source of folklore from the region is overwhelmingly quite recent, collections of tales or plays of the 19th and 20th centuries. These have been spottily collected and almost never sifted, so that they are a mélange of data covering most of the acculturative spectrum. Some of them seem little touched by European culture; many are clearly synthetic, often so subtly so as to be unanalyzable into their original components; some are definitely within the framework of European literary or folk-literary tradition.

Typical of the problems raised by much of this material is the miracle of Tepeyac. The story of the first appearance of the Virgin of Guadalupe has definable antecedents in Indian tradition, yet it was sufficiently European to be accepted by the Church. Among most of the major language groups of Middle America, the industry of the missionary priests made available in the native languages within a century or so of the conquest a wide range of religious literature: catechism, missals, lives of the saints, and sermons. The Virgin of Guadalupe is only the most prominent example of the impact of this entirely new literary and religious medium on Indian thought. Not infrequently in writing, and much more often in oral tradition, the teachings of the church fathers were readapted to Indian culture, even at considerable cost to orthodoxy. Thus there developed the complex interchange of form and symbol through which Spanish medieval and renaissance plays came to be Indian ceremonies, and elements from biblical history came to be plays or dances. In one remarkable case (Hunter, n.d.) the Nahuatl text may be considered the *editio princeps* of a play of Calderón! Indian plays or legends came to be reworked into the romantic and postromantic forms of Mexican and Guatemalan literature.

Unfortunately the syncretistic beliefs concerning the saints have almost never been recorded in narrative form (see, however, Paso y Troncoso, 1890), despite the vast literature on religious syncretism in virtually all parts of Middle America. Yet it seems obvious that such traditions as the equation of Santiago and Tziholah at Chichicastenango must have been perpetuated in some narrative form. Much better documented are the related developments that spring from the didactic and missionary use of drama. *Los Pastores* and similar *autos* came to be known over wide areas of Middle America, sometimes disintegrating into fragments re-recorded in modern times.

Among the plays which proved most popular, those dealing with conquest and conversion stand out: *Cristianos y Moros* and the *Baile de la Conquista*. Both can be found considerably reworked by the Indians. On the northern borders of Middle America, the Sonoran Yaqui have assimilated the Christians and the Moors into their Passion Play ceremonies of Lent and Easter—in fact, into the very structure of their religious societies. Although the dance of the conquest of Mexico is often performed in the Guatemalan highlands in rhymed Spanish, there is also a Quiche version, the *Zaqikoxol* (Anonymous, 1875), in which Montezuma speaks Quiche and the *kaxlan vinak* speak Spanish. The Guatemalan Indians also have a dance of the conquest of Tecum Uman by Alvarado. These plays end with everybody happily converted, but there would seem to be something of the quasi-masochism of pre-Columbian tradition to the insistent rejection of "our gentile days" which they reiterate. Otherwise, even when they are in the Indian languages, they are much more Spanish than Indian (see Bode, 1961; McAfee, 1952; Correa, 1958a).

A similar syncretism is reflected in the Nicaraguan *Huehuence,* which has a Nahuatl and Spanish text (Brinton, 1883c). The character of the hero Huehuence, however, represents a thematically Indian comic type rather akin to the clown figures in the *Zaqikoxol* or even in the Spanish language *Dance of the Conquest.* This humor is naive and full of rather gross and simple puns and posturings, and although the allusions are often sexual, they are more earthy than obscene. The Flute Dance (*Charamiex*) of Rabinal, in a highly Hispanicized Quiche, applies this same sense of comedy by interlingual punning (Mace, 1957).

The complexity of the Indo-Spanish transculturation is even more emphatically pointed up in the subtle transformation of the Indian gods into devils. Here again we have virtually no textual material to go on, but as the cult of the mountaintop (or mountain-valley) earth gods of the Guatemalan Maya became equated with *brujería* and the day-diviners with *brujos,* an arena was defined in which the interchange of concepts could take place at very significant psychological levels (Correa, 1955, p. 59ff.). Zizimitl, a minor Aztec conception of the satanical, became a widespread mountaintop demon in Salvador, Honduras, and among the coastal Caribs, as well as in parts of Guatemala. Less formally, a wholesale fusion of elements of folk magic created a genre of witchcraft stories which is possibly the most widespread narrative form in the modern folklore. Some of these stories and anecdotes take the functional place of obscenity in modern European oral literature, as they did in the demonology of the medieval church. Otherwise there is a notable lack of such themes among the Middle American Indians. Purely secular dirty stories, like sex jokes, appear to be a Mestizo-Ladino trait. Witchcraft stories are overwhelmingly anecdotal, describing the real (or imagined) experiences of known individuals. No purely Indian examples are known, but in communities of Indian speech they not infrequently involve identifiable pre-Columbian elements (Madsen, 1957). Despite their anecdotal character, these stories are thematically quite repetitive, and often carry a specific moral such as would justify their classification as fables.

Witchcraft anecdotes shade off into a great variety of brief narratives of the supernatural and the marvelous, often felt or implied to be portentous but with no explicitly stated meaning. Animals with lights in their foreheads, buried treasure, uninterpreted apparitions, unexplained illnesses, natural disasters, and the perennial theme of secular climatic change are among the topics treated. Doubtless these reflect in some measure the aboriginal preoccupation with omens, and the conviction of periodic doom, though specific elements (la llorona, el dorado) are often thoroughly Spanish. Indeed, little that is specifically Indian remains in many of these brief tales, and they may be reworked so thoroughly as to relate to 20th-century religious, political, and social issues. Some particularly valuable examples are recorded from the Tarascan area, different versions of the same story being told by rival political factions (Carrasco, 1952b).

Some folklore traditions are available to us only in creolized forms strongly influenced by 19th-century romanticism. Even some of the earlier chroniclers, influenced by the Spanish romances, were prone to read princesses and romantic love into the Indian lore. But the figures of Popoca and Ixtaccihuatl, like the china poblana and the charro in the non-Indian lore, swallow Indian fatalism into the excesses of romantic tragedy. In a 20th-century rendition:

Sounds the teponaztli and the chirimía,
Telling of the victories that the great Popoca
Won from the foe.
But when he returns then honored and victorious
There he finds the princess he had won in battle
Dead a year ago. [Trio Los Panchos recording.]

Little is Indian in this construal but the names. An even more modern quasi-Indian development is illustrated by the canonization of Cuauhtemoc in Mexico and of Tecum Uman in Guatemala, a purely 20th-century re-evaluation of the Indian tradition generated by the nationalism and indigenismo of the non-Indian population. This would appear to be very nearly the end of the trail of Middle American Indian folklore.

Another end of the trail is displayed by the 20th-century folk literature of the Arizona Yaqui, who still preserve a genre of story in which the narrator dreams that parts of his body become detached and go on adventures of their own:

I dreamed last night that my leg came off and went on a long trip. It flew way up in the sky and came to the gate of heaven. St. Peter came to the gate and looked at it, "Guachu wan', boy? . . . Ju gotta pass, boy?" . . . [C. N. Edmonson, n.d.]

The story is told in Spanish, but St. Peter speaks straw-boss English.

One of the most vital forms of Middle American narrative folklore at the present time is the Spanish-derived corrido. Particularly characteristic of the Mestizo population of the cowboy north and west of

Mexico, these lengthy ballads are widely distributed everywhere north of Tehuantepec, though they are little developed in Central America. *Corridos* celebrate such diverse historical events as the death of Franklin D. Roosevelt or Manolete, the careers of famous bandits or revolutionary heroes, the end of the W.P.A. in the United States, local floods or other disasters, famous strikes, dance-hall brawls, feuds, or purely imaginary events. They range from songs composed for the growing popular music industry (the Juan Charrasqueado cycle) to highly traditional folk productions. Although primarily a Mestizo form, they have also been recorded in Indian towns (Redfield, 1930) and Negro villages (Aguirre Beltrán, 1958). On the Caribbean coast and in Central America these ballads tend to be replaced by the *son* and the *danzón,* lyric forms with relatively little narrative content. There does not appear to have been a native tradition of narrative poetry any place in Middle America.

It has long been accepted dogma in the study of Middle American folklore that the task of isolating the differential contributions of Spanish, Indian, and other traditions is fruitless or impossible. Certainly no one would deny that it is difficult. Nonetheless, this viewpoint is far more defensible in relation to the scholarship of a generation or so ago than it is today. Real progress has been registered in the interpretation of the cultural history of Middle America in the last few decades on a very broad research front: archaeological, sociological, historical, linguistic, analytic, and comparative. Sources for scholarly treatment of the problems of this history are more accessible than ever before; archival materials have been organized, catalogued, sifted, and sometimes published. The number of scholars working in the field has grown immeasurably. Particularly crucial among these developments is the growth of a library of materials for interpreting the culture of Spain, without which analysis of Spain's

contribution to the cultures of the New World would be truly impossible. Although, therefore, many problems of unraveling the origins of elements of Middle American culture remain unpromising on the basis of present resources, many others have now become soluble. In folklore as in other areas of Middle American culture we are in a better position than ever before to tackle these knotty problems and to gain a more precise understanding of the fusion of cultures that Middle America undeniably represents.

Conclusion

The narrative literature of the area dominated by the great civilizations of Mexico and Guatemala is overwhelmingly a religious literature. In the proportion that it is Indian rather than European it is thematically preoccupied with doom and destruction, witchcraft and calamity, conquest and salvation, which are also features of the religious life of the area. Even a cursory survey of this folklore suggests that an adequate analysis must rest on a rather careful classification of contexts. At the same time it may be observed that our corpus of textual material on Middle American folklore is still far from adequate, and that many of the relevant data are still recoverable from the wide variety of acculturative levels represented in the Middle American population. Finally, we may note that in thematic as well as in geographic dimensions, the limits of Middle American Indian influence are virtually impossible to specify, even though its nuclear elements are beginning to seem somewhat clearer.

The social context of Middle American folklore was originally dominated by the regional forms of shamanism and by the priesthoods in the urban centers. Peripheral areas which lacked the tonalamatl calendar and the diviners who went with it also share only dimly the major themes of Middle American literature. Following the conquest the dominant influences came to be those of the missionary priests, the cofradías and the surviving shamans and diviners, now equivocally transformed into brujos. In modern times the traditions are becoming secularized, politicized, reduced to symbols, or lost entirely. In one highly contemporary medium, the Indian influence on Mexican Mestizos may be placed at around 4 per cent of the image content (M. S. Edmonson, 1959). It will be a long time, however, before the stoic fatalism of the Indian tradition disappears from Mexico and Guatemala. *Primero Dios.*

REFERENCES

This list of references summarizes sources which provide us with textual or near textual materials on the narrative folklore of the Middle American Indians. It is slanted towards the inclusion of materials with a maximum bearing on the pre-Columbian narrative literature, regardless of the date at which these may have been collected or published. It is offered in the belief that the greatest value of this unique folk literature lies in the cultural autonomy of its point of departure, rather than in those processes of change and acculturation in which it parallels so many other regions of the globe.

It has proved impossible to locate any relevant sources for the folklore of many Middle American Indian linguistic groups. Numbers of these are now extinct: Chicomuceltec, Coca, Cochimi, Chiapanec, Concho, Diri, Guachichil, Jalisco, Janambre, Lagunero, Nicarao, Nio, Olive, Pericu, Sabaibo, Sinaloa, Subtiaba, Tamaulipec, Tapachula, Tebaca, Tehueco, Tepahue, Teul, Toboso, Waicura, Xixime, Zacatec, and Zoe. On the other hand, lack of materials from many of the groups can yet be remedied, in some cases easily: Aguacatec, Akwaala, Amusgo, Carib, Chocho, Coahuiltec, Cuicatec, Diegueño, Huastec, Ixil, Lenca, Matagalpa, Mazahua, Mopan, Motozintlec, Opata, Pame, Paya, Pirinda, Pokomam, Sumo, Tepehuan, Tzutuhil, Ulua, Uspantec, Xenca, and Xicaque.

GENERAL: Anon., 1945; Arias Larreta, 1951; Astrov, 1946; Asturias, 1948; R. S. Boggs, 1939, 1945, 1949; Bonilla y San Martín, 1923; Brasseur de Bourbourg, 1871; Brinton, 1882a, 1883a, 1890, 1896; Burland, 1949; Campos, 1929, 1936, 1937; Castillo Ledón, 1917; Covarrubias, 1947; Curtin, 1899; Darío, 1954; Espinosa Ramos, 1949; G. M. Foster, 1950; García A., 1942; González Casanova, 1946; González Peña, 1940; Ibarra, 1941; Lehmann-Nitsche, 1926; Lesser, 1928; Ludewig, 1858; Médiz Bolio, 1941; Pérez Estrada, 1954; Samayoa Chinchilla, 1934, 1936, 1941, 1959; Silva y Aceves, 1925; Squier, 1861; Toor, 1947; Ugarte, 1954; Yáñez, 1942.

ACAXEE: Beals, 1933.

CHAÑABAL: Anon., 1939–48; Basauri, 1931.

CHATINO: Boas, 1912.

CHINANTEC: Bevan, 1938; J. B. Johnson, 1940; Weitlaner, 1952b.

CHOL: Anderson, 1957; Anon., 1939–48.

CHONTAL: Keller and Harris, 1946; Martínez Gracida, 1910.

CHORTI: Girard, 1944; Wisdom, 1950.

CHUH: Kunst, 1915.

CORA: Lumholtz, 1902; Preuss, 1912.

HUAVE: Radin, 1929; Warkentin and Olivares, 1947.

HUICHOL: Cordry, 1947a; McIntosh, 1949; Preuss, 1932a; Toor, 1947; Zingg, 1938b.

JACALTEC: LaFarge, 1947; LaFarge and Byers, 1931; Siegel, 1943.

KEKCHI: Burkitt, 1920; G. B. Gordon, 1915; Termer, 1957; Villacorta Vidaurre, 1953.

KILIWA: Meigs, 1939.

LACANDON: Cline, 1944.

MAM: Oakes, 1951.

MAYA: Alcalá Dondé, 1954; Anon., 1863, 1952; Brinton, 1883b; Cornyn, 1932a, 1932b; Erosa P., 1932; Falcón, 1949; Hernández, 1905; Pérez Arceo, 1923, 1954; M. P. Redfield, 1935; R. Redfield, 1950; Redfield and Villa Rojas, 1934; Rejón García, 1905, 1926; J. E. S. Thompson, 1930; Toor, 1947; Xiu, 1954.

MAYO: Beals, 1945a; H. M. Taylor, 1933.

MAZATEC: J. B. Johnson, 1940; Johnson and Johnson, 1939; Williams García, 1953.

MISKITO: Berckenhagen, 1894.

MIXE: Carrasco, 1952a; W. S. Miller, 1956; Radin, 1933; Sánchez Castro, 1947; Toor, 1947.

MIXTEC: Anon., 1946; Dyk, 1959; López Ruiz and Martínez Gracida, 1906; Martínez Gracida, 1898; K. L. Pike, 1937, 1944, 1945a, 1945b, 1946, 1948–49.

NAHUATL: Anon., n.d.,*b;* Bárcena, 1862; Barlow, 1945; Boas, 1912; Boas and Arreola, 1920; Boas and Haeberlin, 1924; Castillo, n.d.; Cornyn, 1925, 1935; Cornyn and McAfee, 1944; Croft, 1957; Frias, 1907; Gamio, 1922; C. de Gante, 1921; Garibay, 1953; González Casanova, 1920, 1928, 1946; Horcasitas Pimentel, 1949; J. B.

Johnson, 1940; Law, 1957; Lehmann, 1906; Mechling, 1912; 1916; Meza, 1934; Morales Gómez, 1944; Parsons, 1932a; Paso y Troncoso, 1890, 1902; Pittman, 1945; Ramos B., 1945; Rojas, 1933; Schultze Jena, 1938; Séjourné, 1957; Seler, 1923; J. Soustelle, 1955; Toscano, 1947; Vera, 1925; Weitlaner and Johnson, 1943.

Otomi: Ecker, 1937; J. Soustelle, 1935a, 1937.

Papago: J. A. Mason, 1921.

Pima: Russell, 1905.

Pipil: Hartman, 1907; Imendia, 1951.

Pokonchi: Mayer, 1958.

Popoluca: Elson, 1947; G. M. Foster, 1945; Foster and Foster, 1948; Lehmann, 1928.

Quiche: Anon., 1875, 1932; Bunzel, 1952; Chinchilla Aguilar, 1951; Coester, 1941; Goubaud Carrera, 1935; Mace, 1957; Schultze Jena, 1933; Tax, 1949; Teletor, 1945, 1955; Termer, 1930a.

Seri: Kroeber, 1931.

Tarahumar: Basauri, 1927; Hilton, 1948; Lumholtz, 1902.

Tarascan: Anon., 1944; Carrasco, 1946, 1952b; Corona Núñez, 1957; Fernández de Córdoba, 1944; La Grasserie, 1896; Lumholtz, 1902; Ochoa, 1945.

Tepecano: Mason and Espinosa, 1914.

Tlapanec: Lemley, 1949.

Totonac: Aschmann, 1946; Oropeza Castro, 1947.

Trique: Valentini, 1899.

Tzental: Toor, 1947.

Tzotzil: Anon., 1939–48; Flores Ruiz, 1954.

Yaqui: Beals, 1945a; Dedrick, 1946; Fábila, 1940; Gamio, 1937; Toor, 1947.

Zapotec: Beals, 1935; Boas, 1912; Carriedo, 1852; Chacón Pineda, 1936; Cruz, 1935, 1946; Espejo and Barlow, 1944; Guerrero, 1944; Henestrosa, 1936a, 1936b; Maqueo Castellanos, 1936; Parsons, 1932b, 1936; Radin, 1935a, 1945, 1946.

Zoque: Cordry, 1941, 1947b; Harrison, 1952; Toor, 1947; Wonderly, 1946a, 1946b, 1947.

Unidentified Groups: Delgado, 1950, González Rosa, 1949; Padilla, 1953.

19. Religious Syncretism

WILLIAM MADSEN

THE STUDY of syncretism concerns both a process of acculturation and the resulting coalescence of traditions from different cultures. Ethnologists used to deal with religious syncretism in Middle America by simply describing the mixture of Spanish and Indian traits found in the contemporary supernaturalism of particular localities. Recently, research interest has shifted to the dynamics of syncretism which help explain why and how native Indian religions have changed in response to the influence of Christianity in Middle America. This article presents an analysis of both processes and patterns of religious syncretism among the Aztec and the Maya from the time of the Spanish conquest to the present. The analysis is limited to those areas for which the most complete historical documentation is available.[1]

Barnett (1953, pp. 49, 54) defines the process of syncretism as a type of acceptance characterized by the conscious adaptation of an alien form or idea in terms of

some indigenous counterpart. The fusion of religious forms and beliefs is cited as the type instance of syncretism. He distinguishes acceptance by syncretism from acceptance by imitation, which is an attempt to copy an alien form. Barnett's concept will be used here as the basis for discussion of religious syncretism in Middle America.

Foster's valuable work on Latin America's Spanish heritage shows that the conquerors deliberately transmitted only those essentials of their culture deemed desirable for export to the New World. Spanish missionaries implanted an expurgated Catholicism free from European pagan customs observed in Spain. Foster believes that this "stripping down process" enabled the Church to impose a relatively uniform Catholicism throughout Latin America with only nominal concessions to Indian beliefs and practices (1960a, pp. 2–4): "From the Rio Grande to Patagonia the cult of the Virgin Mary is the core of religious loyalty, the same saints are honored on the same days and in essentially the same fashion and the same mass draws the faithful each Sunday."

Generalizations about the uniformity of

[1] I am indebted to Professor Wigberto Jiménez Moreno for a number of ideas elaborated in this article and to Claudia Madsen for invaluable aid in the historical research.

369

Latin American Catholicism do not apply in full to Middle America, where regional contrasts in folk religions reflect differing kinds of syncretism with more than nominal concessions to Indian beliefs and practices. Mexico's success in interweaving Spanish and Indian traditions, particularly in the realm of religion, has been noted by Jiménez Moreno (1958, p. 87): "It is precisely this success which sets Mexico apart and makes her unique in Latin America."

Religious syncretism among two dominant ethnic groups in Middle America at the time of the conquest poses a challenging problem: Why did the Aztec and the Maya, who shared many similar religious traditions before the conquest, develop contrasting patterns of reaction to the same form of Spanish Catholicism? The Aztec abandoned pagan rites and fused their own religious beliefs with Catholicism, whereas the Maya retained paganism as the meaningful core of their religion, which became incremented with varying degrees of Catholicism. This contrast, dating from the postconquest period, today applies mainly to folk religions of the Nahuatl Indians in the Valley of Mexico and Maya Indians of the Yucatan Peninsula. To analyze the differing patterns of Aztec and Maya syncretism, we must first examine the impact of the conquest on the religions of the two groups.

The conquest beheaded Aztec religion by destroying its focal values—war and human sacrifice. Aztec war provided sacrificial victims whose blood and hearts were fed to the gods, who were thus enabled to provide men with sun, rain, crops, and all the necessities of life. Huitzilopochtli, the Aztec tribal patron who was also the god of war and sun, required enormous meals of human blood and hearts to give him strength for his daily battle with the forces of darkness. Without such meals, it was feared that Huitzilopochtli might lose his battle and plunge the world into the blackness of night (Sahagún, 1938, 2: 51–52;

Caso, 1958c, pp. 12–14). There is evidence that before the conquest there was growing discontent with the excessive demands of the priests for human sacrifices, but the Aztec people still believed such sacrifices were necessary for the preservation of the cosmic order. When the Spaniards abolished human sacrifice, tore down Aztec temples, smashed pagan idols, and displaced the native priesthood, they caused a severe disruption of Aztec values; this resulted in the eventual abandonment of the fundamental value premise that the successful functioning of the universe depended on human propitiation of Mexican gods.

Hernan Cortés never forgot that the goal of the conquest was the conversion of heathen Indians to Christianity. Even before the conquest of Tenochtitlan he began to destroy pagan idols and preach Christianity. While holding Montezuma as his hostage, Cortés overturned the principal idols in the Aztec temples and replaced them with images of Catholic saints. This deed "grieved Montezuma and the natives not a little," Cortés wrote (1908, 1: 260–62). "At first they told me not to do it for if it became known throughout the town the people would rise up against me, as they believed that these idols gave them all their temporal means and, in allowing them to be ill treated, they would be angry and would give nothing, and would take away all the fruits of the soil and cause the people to die of want."

Aztec priests told Montezuma that Huitzilopochtli and Tezcatlipoca, the god of night, were very angry and would leave Mexico unless the insulting foreigners were killed. When the Spaniards besieged the capital, the Aztec fought a determined battle of resistance and sacrificed their white captives to Huitzilopochtli. But the Aztec war god failed to keep an announced promise to defeat the Spaniards within a 10-day period and the long siege of Tenochtitlan ended in the Spanish victory of 1521. Although the Aztec continued to worship

Fig. 1—ALTAR, CHICALAJA, GUATEMALA. Stone cross at left. Broken pottery offerings in center. (Photo by G. Hurter.)

some pagan idols after the conquest, the cult of the war god was dead.

The conquest destroyed not only public worship of Aztec gods but also belief in the protection of Huitzilopochtli. Wolf (1959, p. 168) theorizes that defeat provided a visible demonstration of the impotence of the Mexican gods. It is equally likely that defeat convinced the Aztec that Huitzilopochtli and Tezcatlipoca had carried out their threat to leave Mexico. In any case, the war god ceased functioning in the Aztec universe after the conquest.

The shattering of Aztec focal values and value premises produced disruptive effects which have been perceptively appraised by Jiménez Moreno (1958, p. 81): "When it lost its own religion and the spiritual guidance of its priesthood, Mexican culture . . . lost its strength. And many of the vanquished, free of the ancient norms which had imposed upon the Mexican citizen a Spartan discipline, now abandoned themselves to drunkenness and to many other vices."

This appraisal is comparable to Barnett's analysis (1953, p. 72) of the individual's reaction to the collapse of social controls in situations of social and political upheaval, including conquest. The individual loses his orientation points because the microcosm in which he has lived has been destructuralized and is not habitable in that condition. He strains to give it some meaning and in so doing he innovates or accepts the definition of the situation offered by others or he and his associates work out a solution together.

The destructuralization of Aztec religion elucidates the distinctive nature of culture change produced by conquest. Forced inhibition of culture complexes can temporarily suppress determinants of change which normally operate when a conjunction of differences occurs. The defeated society may be denied a choice of rejecting change or accepting new elements on the basis of their utility and compatibility with the pre-existing cultural configuration. The Aztec abandoned their religion because they were

371

forced to do so, not because they preferred Christianity. Indian discontent with the burden of human sacrifice may have facilitated the inhibition of Aztec rites, but it is doubtful that they would have ceased without the use of force.

The suppression of public pagan worship did not result in the immediate acceptance of Christianity. The conquest was followed by a period of nearly ten years in which the dominant Aztec reaction to Christianity was rejection. The main causes of the initial resistance to Christianity were Aztec bitterness toward the conquerors and direct conflict between native polytheism and Christian monotheism. The full extent of the conflict between paganism and Christianity was not perceived at first by the Aztec, owing to the language barrier, but they did understand that the Christians were bent on destroying idols of all the Indian gods.

The period of rejection may be viewed in terms of Festinger's theory of cognitive dissonance (1957). Such dissonance arises when people are faced with new events, new information, and decisions. The individual may try to re-establish consonance by changes of cognition, behavior, or values, but if the discrepancy between the old and the new is too great, he may reject the new in order to maintain consonance. The discrepancy between paganism and Christianity throughout Middle America was a major reason for rejecting the new religion. But Aztec rejection of Christianity did not restore consonance because the Aztec had developed grave doubts about their old gods.

Unfortunately, there is little documentation to show precisely what happened to Aztec religious beliefs in the crucial years of despair and anxiety after the conquest, when the Indians were no longer certain which gods ordered the universe or what they expected of men. Idolatry and human sacrifice were practiced secretly around Mexico City and Texcoco until at least 1525. A cacique of Texcoco was publicly

burned to death by the Inquisition in 1539 for worshipping idols of Tlaloc, the Aztec rain god, and other pagan deities in his own home. It is significant that the worship of Indian rain gods survived the conquest, whereas the cult of the war god disappeared. Rain continued but Aztec victories stopped after the conquest.

The first missionaries were three Flemish monks who arrived in Mexico in 1522 and wisely directed their main efforts toward learning Nahuatl. The outstanding member of the trio was Pedro de Gante, who is called the father of Mexican education. The reaction of the Aztec toward the missionaries and their religion was recorded by Gante (n.d., pp. 42–47): "The common people were like animals without reason. We could not bring them into the pale or congregation of the church, nor to the doctrine classes, nor to the sermons without their fleeing from these things like the devil flees from the cross. For more than three years they fled like wild men from the priests."

The arrival of twelve Franciscans in Mexico City in 1524 astounded the Aztec because the ragged friars had walked barefoot all the way from Veracruz. When Cortés knelt before the priests as they entered the city, the Indians also fell to their knees. The Spartan self-discipline of the Franciscans and the respect they commanded from the conquerors created among the Aztec a favorable impression which endured and became a powerful influence in the conversion.

Although rejection still prevailed as the dominant Aztec reaction to Christianity, a period of limited compliance began with the compulsory education of Indian children in Franciscan schools established in 1524. This period conforms to Kelman's concept of compliance as a process of attitude change in which the agent of change possesses means of control (1958, pp. 51–60). The individual changes his behavior because he expects to gain rewards or ap-

Fig. 2—ALTAR NEAR CHICHICASTENANGO, GUATEMALA. Stone idol (at center left) and crosses (at center right). Pine boughs stuck in ground behind. (Middle American Research Institute, Tulane University.)

proval and avoid punishment or disapproval by compliance. His change of behavior does not involve acceptance of new values.

Backed by the authority of Cortés, the Franciscans ordered the Aztec to build boarding schools in Texcoco, Tlaxcala, and Huejotzingo, where Indian nobles were commanded to place their children. They obeyed this command because they feared punishment for disobedience. Each school had from 600 to 1000 pupils. The learning of Christianity began through a process of enforced imitation as the friars taught their Indian pupils how to kneel, make the sign of the cross, and recite Latin prayers (Mendieta, 1945, 3: 70–71).

Simultaneous attempts to teach Christian dogma failed because the friars had not yet learned Nahuatl and tried in vain to teach Christian beliefs by means of signs. After observing one priest waving his hands and preaching loudly in his unintelligible tongue, a group of adult Indians concluded that the poor man must be crazy. But the

diligent Franciscans quickly mastered Nahuatl and established doctrine schools for children in most of the important Indian towns of central Mexico. The friars had anticipated by four centuries Bruner's theory (1956, p. 194) that new ideas transmitted early in a child's training are most resistant to change.

Missionary methods of enforcing compliance with Christianity are described by Gante in a report on the doctrine school at the church of San Francisco in Mexico City (n.d., pp. 42–47). About 1000 young people were confined to the school, where they were not permitted to converse. "This rule was made so they would forget their bloody idolatries and excessive sacrifices," Gante wrote. "When there is a fiesta or dedication for the demons (pagan gods) the most able students are sent to forbid it. . . . Then I summon them (the idolaters) to Mexico City and they are reprimanded. Other times they are frightened with threats of justice and told that they must be punished if they

373

do it again. In this way, little by little many idolatries are destroyed and abandoned."

Adults were lined up and marched to church carrying a banner and singing religious songs on Sundays and feast days. Roll was called outside the church and absentees were later punished with six lashes on the back. Before the sermon, one of the older pupils quoted from memory some Christian doctrine, which the Indians repeated word for word after him.

While Franciscan schools administered consistent punishment for noncompliance they also offered social rewards for compliance with the teachings of the friars. The sons of the Indian nobility who attended the schools were trained to become the native ruling class and were later appointed to high civil offices. They learned reading, writing, music, masonry, carpentry, ceramics, weaving, metal working, and silk culture.

During the course of close contact in the schools, the Indian children came to respect and admire their Franciscan teachers. This warm interpersonal relationship later extended to entire communities in central Mexico, where the Franciscans doctored the sick, comforted the dying, and defended the accused before Spanish magistrates. The Indians particularly esteemed the Franciscans for their tradition of self-denial, which approached the Aztec ideal. The monks practiced mortification of the body by wearing hair shirts and lashing themselves for their faults. They went barefoot, wore coarse, torn habits, slept on grass pillows, and ate Indian food including chiles and tortillas (Braden, 1930, pp. 134–37).

The Franciscans may be credited with a great deal of practical wisdom in attempting to begin the conversion with Indian children whose values had not yet been crystallized. Although these children did not accept, or perhaps even understand, the entire Christian value system, they had made a change in their valued entities by the time they eagerly assisted the friars in

the destruction of Aztec temples, which began in 1525.

The Catholic education of Indian children created a deep value conflict between the older and younger generations in Aztec society. The basic conflict between Aztec and Christian religions was vividly emphasized by the Spanish missionaries, who tried to make paganism and Christianity as incompatible as possible. This was not hard to do. The Indians believed in many gods whereas the Spaniards taught belief in one God and denounced all Aztec gods as demons. The Christian God depended on no man whereas Indian gods required offerings of human blood in order to run the universe. The Indians believed in multiple creations and destructions of the universe whereas Christianity taught that the world had been created only once by one God. Christianity threatened punishment in the fires of hell for the soul of an individual who flouted Christian ethics whereas the Aztec did not believe in afterworld torture. Christianity emphasized salvation of the soul through perfection of the individual character whereas Indian religion valued the individual only for his contribution to collective activities designed to preserve the cosmic order. Catholicism taught that the individual chooses the path of righteousness or wickedness of his own free will, whereas the Aztec believed that a man must resign himself to the fate meted out to him by the gods at the time of his birth. The Christian value most emphasized by the friars was the salvation of the individual soul through Christianity and the corollary threat of eternal torture in hell for adherence to paganism.

The friars endeavored to teach the Aztec the Christian values as well as Catholic ritual, but it is difficult to ascertain how much Christian theology the Indians understood. New forms are relatively easy to transmit, but it is almost impossible to communicate abstract religious concepts in their entirety, as Linton has pointed out

Fig. 3—ALTAR ON SUMMIT OF INDIAN MOUND, COLOLTE, OCOSINGO VALLEY, CHIAPAS. Stone idol and pine boughs in center. (Photographed by Frans Blom, 1925. Middle American Research Institute, Tulane University.)

(1936, p. 339). When the Aztec school children began destroying pagan temples and idols, they exhibited a fierce loyalty to Christian supernaturals and a zeal for Christian martyrdom that went beyond mere compliance with the instruction of the friars. In fact it is not too farfetched to hypothesize that the Christian war against paganism replaced Aztec religious war as a focal value of the younger generation.

The circumscribed acceptance of certain Christian values by the school children was a reflection of their identification with the Franciscan agents of change. In the process of identification, as defined by Kelman (1958, pp. 51–60), the individual accepts influence in order to establish or maintain a satisfying, self-defining relationship to the agent of change who is an attractive figure. Similar concepts formulated by Linton (1936, pp. 343–44) and by Osgood and Tannenbaum (1955, pp. 42–55) have pointed out that acceptance is promoted by high esteem for the agents of change.

The conflicting values of the younger and older generations led to violent clashes in behavior. Indian children spied on their parents and reported idols found at home. Several children were beaten to death by their elders for destroying pagan idols. One Indian killed his own son for this reason. A group of pupils in Tlaxcala stoned an Aztec priest to death in the belief that he was a demon and bragged that they had been aided in their deed by God and St. Mary (Motolinía, 1950, pp. 243–50). The divided reaction of the two generations to the destruction of Aztec temples is described by Mendieta (1945, 2: 71): "Thus fell the walls of Jericho with shouts of praise and joy from the faithful children, while those who were not of that number stood by frightened, amazed and heart-broken, seeing their temples and gods fall to the earth."

375

The acceptance of Christianity had become an alternative as defined in Linton's theory of universals and alternatives (1936, pp. 282–83). Linton postulates that a folk culture consists of a core of universal culture elements shared by all members of the society and a small zone of alternative culture elements that compete for acceptance as universals. When a culture is changing very rapidly the alternatives increase while the universals decrease, causing the culture to lose pattern and coherence. Without a wide community of ideas the members of the group will not react to particular stimuli as a unit. The divided reaction of the Aztec to the destruction of pagan temples and idols reflected a sharp decrease in universals, accompanied by loss of cultural coherence.

The older generation began to grant Christianity a minimum of overt compliance without accepting its values. The Aztec hid pagan idols behind Christian altars and in the pedestals of Christian crosses in a futile attempt to mollify the Catholic priests without further offending their own gods, even though they feared those gods might have forsaken them. Some villagers worshipped images of pagan gods placed side by side with Catholic images of the crucified Christ and the Virgin Mary. "It may have been that, having a hundred gods, they wanted a hundred and one," Motolinía shrewdly observed (1950, pp. 48–49).

The joint worship of Aztec and Spanish images was a first attempt at syncretism of Indian and Catholic forms. This type of syncretism by simple addition of new gods to old had ample precedent in Mexican culture, which traditionally adopted deities of the numerous tribes that invaded the Valley of Mexico in preconquest times. The friars actively opposed this kind of syncretism by confiscating the Catholic images and destroying the pagan ones wherever they were found together.

Many adults who had been attending church on Sundays and feast days accepted Catholic baptism at the urging of the Franciscans. Motolinía reports that the friars often frightened the Aztec into receiving baptism in order to escape torture by the devil in hell (1950, p. 52). At the end of one sermon on the devil, the Indians became "so alarmed and terrified that they trembled to hear what the friars were saying, and some poor wretches began to come to baptism and to seek the kingdom of God, seeking it with tears and sighs of importunity." Jiménez Moreno points out that grave sanctions were imposed on those who persisted in pagan worship without receiving baptism (1958, p. 82). "It has not been emphasized sufficiently that a considerable portion, if not the majority, of the Indians of the ancient Mexican empire were obliged in the first half of the sixteenth century to abandon their ancient religion by force," he states.

There is some indication that the older generation associated Catholic baptism with a similar pagan rite which endowed baptismal water with divine power to remove filth from a newborn baby's heart. As late as the 17th century, it was common for an infant baptized by a Catholic priest to receive a Spanish first name and an Aztec second name in honor of the Catholic saint and the pagan god on whose day he was born (Serna, 1892, p. 282).

In order to stimulate adult participation in celebrations of the Catholic ritual calendar, the Franciscans initiated their own forms of religious syncretism. Gante conceived the idea of giving pagan songs and dances a Christian motif so they could be used at Catholic ceremonials in the same way they had formerly been used to honor Aztec gods. His conscious intention of fusing pagan and Catholic forms is clearly stated in the following letter (n.d., pp. 42–47):

In all their (Aztec) adoration of their gods they sang and danced before the gods. When they had to sacrifice some victims for some purpose such as obtaining victory over their

376

FIG. 4—INDIANS PRAYING BEFORE CHURCH, SAN MIGUEL ACATAN, GUATEMALA. (Photographed by Douglas Byers, 1927. Middle American Research Institute, Tulane University.)

enemies or for temporal necessities, before they killed the victim they had to sing and dance before the idol.

Since I had seen this and that all their songs were dedicated to the gods I composed a very solemn song about the law of God and the faith and how God made man to save the human race and how he was born of the Virgin Mary leaving her pure and entire.

I also gave them patterns to paint on their mantles so they could dance with them because this was the way the patterns had been used by the Indians . . . Then we invited all the people within ten leagues of Mexico City to come to the fiesta of the Nativity of Christ our Redeemer and so many came that they could not get into the patio.

In this way they first came to show obedience to the church and the patios were full of people.

Gante's innovation spread far and wide in Mexico and attracted hundreds of Indians to church ceremonies. However, adult participation in Catholic ceremonies was not accompanied by any profound value change. The real turning point in the conversion came with the miraculous appearance of the Indian Virgin of Guadalupe in 1531. This event brought about the emotional acceptance of a new faith, which has been aptly called Guadalupinist Catholicism (Jiménez Moreno, 1958, p. 92).

The dark-skinned Virgin appeared to an Aztec man on the hill of Tepeyac, where the Aztec goddess Tonantzin was accustomed to appear in former times. Tonantzin (also called Coatlicue) was one of three earth goddesses who apparently were three aspects of the same deity. Aztec legend identifies Tonantzin as the mother of the gods, including Huitzilopochtli who was created by divine conception. On December 9, 1531, Juan Diego saw a beautiful Indian lady dressed in shining garments on the top of the hill. She spoke to him in Nahuatl and identified herself as the Mother of God. Later she told the Indian that she was "one of his kind."

The Virgin requested that a church be

377

built on top of the hill "so that in it I may show and make known and give all my love, my mercy, and my help and my protection—I am in truth your merciful mother—to you and to all the other people dear to me" (Lazo de la Vega, 1956, pp. 41–53).

Juan Diego's vision fired religious fervor all over central Mexico. "From that historic moment total evangelization was an accomplished thing," Pope Pius XII proclaimed at a commemorative ceremony in 1945. Indians came from great distances, bringing offerings to the Catholic Virgin whom they called Tonantzin, and they erected a church on the spot where the vision occurred. It was very natural for the Aztec to associate Guadalupe with the pagan Tonantzin since both were virgin mothers of gods and both appeared at the same place. These pagan associations were denounced as "inventions of the devil" by Sahagún, who opposed the growth of the Guadalupan cult.

Despite Sahagún's misgivings, the Virgin of Guadalupe was not a mere Christian front for the worship of a pagan goddess. The adoration of Guadalupe represented a profound change of Aztec religious belief. The extent of this change can be seen by comparing Indian concepts of the Catholic Virgin and her pagan predecessor. The pagan Tonantzin was a dual-natured earth goddess who fed her Mexican children and devoured their corpses. She wore a necklace of human hands and hearts with a human skull hanging over her flaccid breasts, which nursed both gods and men. Her idol depicts her as a monster with two streams of blood shaped like serpents flowing from her neck. Like other major deities in the Aztec pantheon, Tonantzin was both a creator and destroyer. The nature and functions of the Virgin of Guadalupe are entirely different from those of the pagan earth goddess. The Christian ideals of beauty, love, and mercy associated with the Virgin of Guadalupe were never attributed to the pagan deity. The functions of the

Catholic Virgin are much broader and more beneficial to man than those of the Aztec nature goddess. Guadalupe protects her children (the Mexicans) from harm, cures their sicknesses, and aids them in all manner of daily undertakings. She is not a nature goddess. Her children repay her for her aid, not with human sacrifices, but with vows to make pilgrimages to her shrine and give her offerings of flowers, candles, and ex-votos. Only when a sacred vow is broken or some other grave religious error is committed does Guadalupe punish her errant child with sickness, misfortune, or death as Aztec deities used to do. Of the many "santos" and "Cristos" worshiped in Mexico, the Virgin of Guadalupe is the most benevolent and the most representative of Christian ethical values.

In the 16th century the Virgin of Guadalupe came to be a symbol of the new Indian Catholicism as distinguished from the foreign Catholicism of the conquerors. The Aztec adapted Catholicism to their own religious concepts by a process of fusional syncretism that eventually eliminated almost all visible vestiges of paganism. Guadalupinist Catholicism spread rapidly in central Mexico and became the focal value of Aztec culture. By 1537 some nine million Indians had been baptized in this area, according to Motolinía (1950, p. 133).

Pilgrimage centers where pagan gods had been worshiped before the conquest became centers of Catholic pilgrimages honoring the Señor de Chalma, the Virgen de los Remedios, and other famous saints. Before the conquest each Indian village had a patron deity whose idol was adorned with robes and jewels and presented with offerings. After the conversion each town adopted a Catholic patron saint whose image was likewise dressed in fine clothing and presented with offerings. Catholic confession was accepted in terms of its pagan counterpart. Pagan gods forgave confessed mistakes but once, so the Aztec resorted

378

Fig. 5—INDIANS ON STEPS OF CHURCH, CHICHICASTENANGO, EL QUICHE, GUATEMALA. (Photo by Frans Blom. Middle American Research Institute, Tulane University.)

to confession only in time of crisis or old age in order to secure recovery from illness or misfortune sent by an angry deity or in order to escape civil punishment for a crime. Aztec criminals, invalids, and old people confessed to Catholic priests in the belief that confession would restore their health and ensure judicial pardon of their crimes (Sahagún, 1938, 2: 32–33).

Village religion was supervised by the friars, who organized the Indians of their parishes into cofradías responsible for the celebration of Catholic feast days. Honor and prestige in the village were achieved by holding office in the cofradía, which put on a successful performance for the saints. Village fiestas included dance-dramas such as the one known as Moors and Christians which re-enacts the Spanish conquest of the Moors in Granada in 1492. The Indians reinterpreted this Spanish drama as a portrayal of the conquest of Mexico and added Hernan Cortés to its cast of characters. The friars permitted some Indian villages to retain pagan dance-dramas such as "Los Voladores," the flying-pole dance performed in conjunction with the feast of Corpus Christi (Madsen and Madsen, 1948, p. 24).

By 1555, barely a quarter of a century after the conquest, the conversion of the Aztec had been accomplished (Jiménez Moreno, 1958, p. 89). About that time there began a turbulent period of readjustment in which the Aztec lost the leadership of their beloved Franciscans. The Indians were caught in the middle of a feud between the friars and the secular clergy, who had started arriving in large numbers. Canonical law specified that the secular clergy were the proper parish administrators, but the friars had obtained special papal dispensation to carry out the early parish work since they were the only priests in central Mexico when the evangelization began. The broad powers of the Franciscan, Dominican, and Augustinian orders were bitterly disputed by the newly arrived secular clergy. In 1555 the First Provincial

379

Council of Mexico imposed strict limitations on the powers of the friars. The Franciscans were finally turned out of their jobs in 1640 when numerous parishes were transferred to the authority of the secular clergy. Throughout the controversy, the Aztec sided with the Franciscans and violently resisted the secular clergy, who tried to take over their churches and convents.

Interpersonal relations between the secular clergy and the Aztec were bad from the beginning. Obviously, Aztec hostility toward the secular clergy was patterned in part after that of the Franciscans. But there were other reasons. Many members of the secular branch never mastered the Nahuatl language and had to turn to the Franciscans for aid with confessions. Furthermore, the secular priests who came to Mexico in midcentury were accused of avarice, evil character, ostentation, unwillingness to put up with discomfort, and despising the Indians (Braden, 1930, pp. 215, 220–21).

The loss of Franciscan leadership produced a marked effect on Aztec Catholicism. Mendieta, writing in the latter part of the 16th century, contrasts the Aztec's irregular attendance at Mass in this period with his former faithful attendance. It became painfully obvious to the Catholic clergy that internalization of Christian moral values and metaphysical concepts had not taken place among the Aztec. The archbishop of Mexico charged that the Indians did not believe the articles of faith and the mysteries which the church celebrates. He further asserted that the Indians did not practice Christian ethics and were inclined to drunkenness, stealing, lying, and ursury (Braden, 1930, p. 248).

Some of the difficulties of implanting Christian values might have been averted if the Spaniards had trained a native priesthood, but Indians were not allowed to receive sacramental ordination as secular priests or enter the Orders during the colonial era. Mestizos also were barred from

the priesthood until 1588. From the 17th century on, Spanish priests had little to do with the development of Indian religion in many Mexican villages. This lack of clerical supervision gave free rein to the Aztec genius for religious syncretism.

Seventeenth-century worship of Catholic saints by the Mexicans was denounced as a form of idolatry by Jacinto de la Serna, who observed that some Indians thought the saints were gods (1892, p. 281). He reported that the Mexicans offered animal sacrifices and pulque to Xiuhtecuhtli, the Aztec fire god, and the Catholic saints, who were jointly worshipped at ceremonies held in private homes. Serna was surprised to discover that the Mexicans believed sickness was sent by vengeful saints.

Except for Serna's fragmentary report, there is little documentation on the process of integration whereby the Aztec made adjustments in both Catholic and pagan beliefs in order to fit them together in the Indian configuration of culture. However, the patterns of colonial syncretism and integration can still be discerned in the contemporary religion of a Nahuatl Indian village in the Valley of Mexico (Madsen, 1957).

Supernaturalism is the focus of modern Aztec culture and it penetrates all aspects of life in the village of San Francisco Tecospa. Religion today functions as an explanation of the ordering of the universe, the means of obtaining temporal necessities, the road to prestige, and an outlet for aesthetic expression. The forms of Indian religion are almost entirely Catholic as manifested in the veneration of Catholic saints, the celebration of Catholic feast days, and the use of Catholic sacraments. Religious beliefs represent a fusion of Aztec and Spanish traditions elaborated with local innovations.

The most important divinity in the village pantheon is the Virgin of Guadalupe, who is also called Tonantzin. She was born before the creation of mankind. Guadalupe is the mother of God and all the Mexicans. Like the Aztec earth goddess, Guadalupe fed both god and man with her milk. She is even more powerful than God because she can stop Him from destroying mankind. Indian cosmogony integrates Catholic divinities and biblical stories into the Aztec concept of multiple creations and destructions of the universe and mankind. The Christian God of love is transformed into a hostile Destroyer although He is also recognized as the Creator. He has lost his Christian omnipotence because his plans can be thwarted by the Virgin of Guadalupe. God and Guadalupe now figure prominently in the Aztec concept that the universe is ordered by a balance of opposites such as life and death, heat and cold, male and female. The universe of Tecospa is regulated by the opposition of male and female divinities as evidenced in the struggle between God and Guadalupe over the destruction of the world.

God and the Devil have replaced pagan deities as arbiters of human destiny in modern Tecospan fatalism. A man's fate is decided at birth by a battle between God and the Devil which takes place in the flames of the Aztec birth fire. If God wins the fight for the baby's soul, the child receives a good shadow but if the Devil wins the child receives a heavy shadow. A person with a good shadow is successful in life and his soul goes to heaven, but an individual with a heavy shadow is doomed to bad luck, poor health, poverty, lack of friends, commitment of sins, and hell.

Conflicting Christian and pagan concepts of the afterworld have been reconciled in a philosophy whose logical inconsistencies do not bother the Indians. Like the ancient Aztec, Tecospans believe that men who die in battle and women who die in childbirth go directly to the sky world regardless of their sins, while souls of drowned persons go to an earthly paradise inhabited by rain dwarfs. Heaven is divided into three parts: a garden of flowers

for children, a place for adults, and a place for God and the saints. In the adult part life goes on much the same as it did in Tecospa—people live in the same houses, wear the same clothes, and work in the same fields. Hell has three names: hell, purgatory, or Mitla, the name of the Aztec underworld. Devils called "pingos" burn firewood under condemned souls and jab them with pitchforks. Only witches and cold-blooded murderers are doomed to stay in hell forever. Sinners who die on the Day of the Dead are lucky because the gates of hell are open and they can go right through hell to heaven without being punished. Souls in heaven and hell come to earth to visit their families on November 2.

Catholic saints have lost their saintly character and become human-natured divinities who lie, lose their tempers, wreak revenge, and indulge in love affairs as the Aztec gods used to do. Unlike the pagan deity, the saint does not function as a specialized nature god in charge of the sun, the rain, or the earth. San Francisco, the village patron saint, performs a wide variety of functions such as bringing rain in time of drought, punishing theft of church property, curing illness, and generally protecting the village. With the consent of God and the help of Aztec rain dwarfs, San Francisco miraculously produces rain in Tecospa even when the saints of other villages have failed in this task. The images of the saints are clothed and worshipped and treated like divine personages even though Tecospans also speak of the saints as being up in heaven. San Francisco is the most popular saint in heaven. The most prominent Christs in the local pantheon are said to be brothers and they are classified as "santos."

Aztec ethics have been reoriented so that today man's primary obligations are to Catholic saints rather than to pagan gods. As in ancient times, the neglect of ritual obligations subjects the individual or the whole community to the vengeance of supernatural beings who punish Tecospans

381

with sickness, crop failure, and other misfortunes.

Virtues and vices are Aztecan. Bravery, the supreme virtue in Aztec religion, is highly valued in Tecospa where a man gains respect by fighting enemies who have wronged him. Beating up a witch who has threatened a man's family is considered a heroic deed. Other major virtues include the fulfillment of ritual obligations to the santos and industriousness in providing for one's family. Chronic drunkenness is disparaged because it interferes with a man's work. Personal ambition and avarice are despised. Adultery is a vice when it involves desertion of a spouse, but wives consider their husbands' extramarital relations as normal male behavior.

The Christian ethic of individual character perfection is lacking in Tecospa. The Indians do not love the Christian God nor do they think he loves them. They feel no obligation to love their neighbors or their enemies. Meekness, righteousness, and purity of heart are not virtues. The Tecospan concept of sin is mainly limited to those vices condemned both by Aztec and Catholic ethics, namely: witchcraft, premeditated murder, manifest disrespect for supernaturals, and failure to provide for one's family. The only major sin of Christian origin is bargaining with devils.

The Tecospa pattern of fusional syncretism extends to the other Nahuatl Indian pueblos in the delegación of Milpa Alta. Variations of the same general pattern are found in Indian and Mestizo communities in the delegación of Xochimilco and in the Nahuatl village of Tepoztlan across the mountains from Tecospa. Even in Mexico City and its suburbs, many Aztec beliefs are integrated into the supernaturalism of the lower classes, which is a far cry from the orthodox Catholicism of the educated urban dwellers. It is difficult to say how far the general pattern of religious syncretism found in Tecospa extends outside of the Valley of Mexico because the problem has not been adequately investigated. The cult of the saints in the Nahuatl Indian village of Tequila, Veracruz, seems to resemble saint worship in Tecospa (G. Soustelle, 1958, pp. 181–202). Carrasco's excellent study of economic, social, and religious interactions in modern Tarascan culture indicates that both the form and the ideology of Tarascan religion are largely Spanish in origin (1952b, pp. 23–56). However, he does mention a few native concepts such as belief in multiple creations and destructions of the universe and the polytheistic nature of worship.

The comparative analysis of religious syncretism in Aztec and Maya religions is a hazardous task largely because historical information for the Maya is less complete than for the Aztec. Spanish chronicles document the process of pagan resistance to Christianity but fail to show when, why, and how Catholic elements were accepted and modified by the Maya. Hence, it is impossible to delineate periods of postconquest change in Maya religion comparable to those observed in the history of Aztec religion after the conquest. My discussion of Maya religious syncretism is mainly limited to the Yucatan Peninsula since sources on that area provide a broader historical perspective than is available for other parts of the Maya region.

The religion and values of Maya culture survived the conquest intact to become the backbone of resistance to Christianity. By the time the Spaniards began the conquest of Yucatan in 1527, Maya ceremonial centers were in decline and many of the famous temples had been abandoned (Brainerd and Morley, 1956, p. 79). Hence the Maya had no centralized theocracy comparable to that of the Aztec which the Spaniards wiped out with one bold stroke. The grass-roots religion of the Maya was centered in widely scattered hamlets that were generally more isolated and more resistant to change than the towns of the Mexican plateau.

FIG. 6—INTERIOR OF CHURCH, SAN FRANCISCO EL ALTO, TOTONICAPAN, GUATEMALA. (Photographed by Dan Leyrer, 1937. Middle American Research Institute, Tulane University.)

As Maya culture was based on agriculture, so Maya religion was focused on the worship of rain, wind, and sky gods whose help was needed for growing crops. Prominent among these gods were the chaacs (rain gods), the pauahtuns (wind gods) and the bacabs (sky bearers). Each of these categories consisted of four individual deities who dwelled at the four cardinal points marked by four sacred trees which were represented by crosses. The Maya prayed to the cross as a god of rain. Roys believes that the pre-Columbian cross may have been personified as the cross is in Yucatan today (1943, p. 75; Tozzer, 1941, p. 207).

The Maya had adopted the Aztec practice of human sacrifice, but it never became the focus of Maya religion. When the Maya prayed for rain, crops, or health they customarily sacrificed small animals and made offerings of their own blood drawn from various parts of the body, in addition to offerings of food and copal incense. Only in case of community disaster such as a famine were human beings sacrificed to the gods. In time of drought the Maya threw live victims into sacred wells in order to obtain rain (Tozzer, 1941, p. 180; Roys, 1943, p. 81). I find no Maya equivalent of the Aztec concept that the strength and functioning of the gods depended on their regular consumption of blood and hearts obtained through human sacrifice.

Maya cosmological concepts and religious rites were generally similar to those of the Aztec. One distinctive form of Maya worship was the cult of the talking idol. Pilgrims came from great distances to the shrine of Ix Chel at Cozumel, where a large pottery idol of the pagan goddess answered the questions of her worshippers. From an adjoining room, a priest allegedly crept into the idol and impersonated the goddess.

The persistence of Maya religion accompanied by the rejection of Christianity was causally related to: (1) the long duration of the Spanish attempt to conquer the Maya; (2) the isolation and decentralization of the Maya; (3) the hostile nature of interpersonal relations between the Maya and the Spaniards during and after the conquest; and (4) the survival of the Maya value system.

The conquest of Yucatan lasted for twenty years (1527–46) and the conquest of Peten was not completed until 1696. During the period of Spanish military campaigns, there was a strong feeling among the Maya that their gods would help them kill the ruthless foreigners. After the conquest, Maya hatred of the Spaniards and their religion was strengthened by the cruel and inept methods of the Catholic missionaries.

The famous Fray Diego de Landa came to Yucatan in 1549. Although Landa and a few other Franciscans mastered the Maya language, more than half the friars never became proficient in the native tongue. Consequently the daily teaching of Christianity in Maya villages was left up to native schoolmasters who had received little instruction in Christian doctrine. Only occasionally did the friars visit the villages (Tozzer, 1941, pp. 69–70).

The Franciscans attempted to improve the teaching of Christianity by forcing the Maya to leave their own pueblos and move to convent towns where doctrine schools were established. Maya pueblos were burned when their inhabitants refused to move. The disastrous consequences of this forced relocation are reported in the Relación de Valladolid (ibid., p. 74):

There was in these provinces at the time they were conquered a large number of Indians and at the present time there is not the twentieth part (of this number). Principally, the diminution which has occurred and exists at present has been caused by the friars of the Order of St. Francis moving them from their old sites and native climate and waters . . . burning their pueblos and ordering them to be burned, settling them where they wished in places not so healthful nor suitable as those where they lived; the said friars making them work on the very sumptuous monasteries which they have built . . . and they never stop building, not having the consideration to order the work to cease at the time when the Indians need to attend to their own cultivating, on account of which the Indians have always complained because it has caused them to be lacking in supplies to sustain their lives. And for this reason, as well as on account of the moving and joining of the pueblos, and punishments under pretext of religious teaching the friars imposed, and other kinds of compulsion, and stocks which they have and use, they (the Indians) have come to the diminution referred to; and they are so afraid of them (the friars) that not only have they fled to the forests without reappearing, but some have died from pure grief and sorrow.

Franciscan attempts to gather Maya children in monastery schools were thwarted by the Spanish encomenderos, who engaged in a bitter feud with the friars. The encomenderos opposed the relocation of the Maya because it reduced the amount of forced labor and tribute they received from the Indians. Nevertheless, a considerable number of children attended monastery schools where they received Catholic baptism and learned to destroy idols including those of their own parents. This period of juvenile compliance was short lived.

In 1558 Landa "discovered" idolatry among those Maya who had been baptized in the Catholic faith. "This people . . . were perverted by the priests whom they had at the time of their idolatry," he wrote. "And they returned to the worship of their idols and to offer them sacrifices not only of incense but also of human blood."

The Inquisition that followed Landa's discovery was carried out on a scale never approximated among the Aztec. In 1562, Landa sent friars to gather information in the province of Mani where they found out that the common people, chiefs, elders, and schoolteachers were all guilty of idolatry. Testimony was extracted by imprisoning and torturing the natives. The types of torture included: the water torture in which

FIG. 7—SMALL CROSSES IN LOG IN FRONT OF SOUTHERN PIMA HOUSE, MEXICO. (From Lumholtz, 1902, 1: 128.)

the mouth was fastened open with a stick and water was poured in until the abdomen swelled up, after which the investigator stood on top of the victim until water mixed with blood came out of the mouth, nose, and ears; suspension by the hands and wrists with or without stones attached to the feet; scorching with wax tapers; scalding; tying the arms and thighs with cords which were twisted and tightened with sticks. Some 4,549 men and women were tortured by these techniques; an estimated 6,330 persons were whipped and shorn. A whipping on the bare flesh included as many as 200 lashes. It was reported that 157 Maya died in 1562 as a result of torture. Landa denied that the Indians had died "on account of said Indians having been hung up by said friars." If any Maya died during the period of the investigation, they must have hanged themselves in the bushes in order to avoid giving up their idols and evil ways, Landa insisted (ibid., pp. 76–79).

Yucatan Indians found guilty of idolatry were punished at public ceremonies. On July 12, 1562, Landa held his notorious auto de fe at Mani where convicted idolators were whipped with 100–200 lashes, shorn, and sentenced to wear the "sambenito," an apron-like garment bearing a likeness of the devil worn as a sign of infamy. Other punishments included: slavery sentences, loss of civil office and other honors held by Maya leaders, imprisonment, exile from the pueblo, the wearing of a rope

385

around the neck, and fines. Sometimes the Indian was required to attend Mass every two weeks and confess once a year.

Landa's attitude toward the Maya and the conversion is reflected in his comments on the *auto de fe:* "They (the friars) placed many (Maya) upon the scaffold wearing a paper coronet, and scourged and shorn, while others wore clothes with the sambenito for a time. And some, deceived by the devil, hanged themselves for grief, and in general they all showed deep repentance and a willingness to become good Christians."

The deep resentment harbored by the Maya against the Franciscans was expressed in a letter written to the King of Spain in 1567 by a group of native chiefs who complained that Landa and his companions had "tortured, killed, and put us to scandal" *(ibid.,* pp. 79–83).

Landa further antagonized the natives by burning Maya codices recording their knowledge of the calendar, plants, animals, and ancient customs. "They contained nothing in which there were not to be seen superstition and lies of the devil," Landa wrote. The burning "caused them much affliction" and "they regretted it to an amazing degree," he observed.

It is not surprising that the earliest forms of Christo-pagan syncretism among the Maya were associated with the cross, which was a symbol of major significance in both Maya and Christian religions. The Crucifixion seems to have been interpreted by the Maya as a new kind of human sacrifice. There are numerous reports of Maya human sacrifice after the conquest which may have been regarded as the type of collective disaster which required the supreme sacrifice. Christian teaching stimulated the native innovation of crucifying the victim who was nailed or tied to a cross. The body was sometimes removed from the cross before the heart was torn out. In other cases the cross with the body still on it was thrown into the local cenote. Roys believes

that postconquest crucifixion was associated with the worship of the rain gods and the cenote cult of human sacrifice in Yucatan *(ibid.,* p. 116).

Most of the native priests who performed human sacrifices after the conquest had Christian names, indicating that they had been baptized as Catholics. Toral reports that the lords and caciques who participated in human sacrifices had been baptized and "very well instructed in the matters of our Holy Catholic Faith" *(ibid.,* pp. 117, 119).

The instruction in matters of the Holy Catholic Faith produced an attitude of skepticism among the Maya as indicated in the words of a native priest who presided at the crucifixion of two little girls in the church at Sotuta about 1557 *(ibid.,* p. 116): "Let these girls die crucified as did Jesus Christ, who they say was Our Lord but we do not know if this is so."

After the girls were taken down from the crosses, their hearts were offered to pagan idols. In the town of Tecoh two boys were nailed to a cemetery cross surrounded by idols which received offerings of hearts.

Following Landa's death in 1579, there began in Yucatan a period of outward compliance with Catholic requirements such as baptism, ritual calendar observances, veneration of saints, and cessation of public idolatry in towns ruled by the Spaniards. When Fray Alonso Ponce visited the Yucatan Peninsula in 1588 he observed that the Maya of Yucatan were a "pious people" whereas those of Quintana Roo were "idolaters, apostates, and renegades" (Villa Rojas, 1945, p. 15; Jiménez Moreno, 1958, p. 77).

Quintana Roo had been divided among the conquerors in accordance with the encomienda system which encompassed the teaching of Christianity to the natives. By the end of the 16th century Quintana Roo had been almost deserted by the Spaniards owing to the poverty of the isolated forest region and the frequent Indian revolts against the encomenderos. In 1639 the few Indians living in encomienda villages burned churches, desecrated Catholic images and returned to the jungle, where they practiced their own religion which by that time probably included elements of Catholicism.

It was in the pagan environment of Quintana Roo that the cult of the talking cross began at the town of Chan Santa Cruz in 1850, three years after the beginning of the War of the Castes started by the Maya to win autonomy and rid the peninsula of whites. The Indian cause had seemed hopeless until the miraculous appearance of a small talking cross carved on a tree trunk. It claimed to be the Trinity sent to earth by God the Father to help the Maya in their rebellion against the whites. The talking cross was the invention of a Mestizo aided by an Indian ventriloquist who answered questions addressed to the cross. When a Mexican government expedition destroyed the cross and killed the ventriloquist, three new talking crosses came to replace the old one. The new crosses were identified as daughters of the original and were dressed in Indian costumes. Juan de la Cruz Puc, one of the early priests of the three crosses, spoke of himself as the Son of God. The names Jesus Christ and Juan de la Cruz came to be synonyms in Quintana Roo. Talking crosses appeared in other villages but their prestige was not as great as that of Santa Cruz, which became a pilgrimage center (Villa Rojas, 1945, p. 22).

Talking idols began to appear in Chiapas in 1867 just before the Tzotzil revolt. One of the inventors of the pottery idols told the Indians that they need not adore images representing non-Indians. Instead he proposed to crucify an Indian boy so the natives would have a Lord of their own to worship. The crucifixion was carried out in 1868 (D. E. Thompson, 1954, pp. 18–20).

The most distinctive aspects of contemporary folk religion in the Yucatan Peninsula are: the emphasis on worship of cross-

FIG. 8—ANCIENT STONE ALTAR WITH MODERN WOODEN CROSS SET IN IT, RANCHO UBALA, TONINA, CHIAPAS. (Photographed about 1925. Middle American Research Institute, Tulane University.)

es, which are usually personified; the persistence of pagan gods and rites; and the insignificance of the Guadalupinist cult.

The durability of pagan gods and rites is most evident in Quintana Roo, where Catholic forms are also an integral part of local religion. Native religion is focused on the cult of the cross and the cult of pagan agricultural deities, particularly the rain gods called chaacs. There are very few images of saints in Quintana Roo communities where the "santos" are crosses. "The saints are not intimately connected with the lives of the people," Villa Rojas writes (1945, p. 101),

387

"but the pagan deities and the crosses enter into their acts and beliefs at almost every point."

The patron cross of the village is regarded as the protector of the whole community and usually has performed many miracles. The whole village participates in the fiesta for the patron cross, which is honored with offerings of candles and food. When a village calamity, such as an epidemic, occurs the people appeal to the patron cross for aid. In theory all crosses act as intermediaries of God and Christ but a cross may acquire so much power that it comes to act in its own right. When community ritual obligations have been neglected, the patron cross may inflict punishment on the entire village by sending a drought or plague. In short, the patron cross fulfills the same functions performed by the village patron saint in other parts of Mexico. Sometimes the patron cross has an even closer relationship to the villagers since it may communicate with them. The talking cross of Chan Santa Cruz has lost its power of speech but now writes letters to make known its wishes or give counsel to those who seek it. In Quintana Roo the cross is housed in the church and worshipped primarily in a Christian context.

Cross worship is widely established throughout the Maya area in connection with both Christian and pagan rites. In northwest Guatemala crosses are divinities who see, think, hear, and communicate through a shaman-priest. The most important cross in the village of Jacaltenango is the huge one standing outside the church. Within the church the cross appears very little. Small crosses are found on hills, caves, ridges, town boundaries, and at the four corners of the village. In Santa Eulalia ancestral crosses kept on home altars pass from father to son through many generations. Images or pictures of saints may also be kept on the home altar but they are entirely secondary and subordinate to the family cross (LaFarge and Byers, 1931,

388

pp. 185–90; LaFarge, 1947, p. 114). Among the Chorti of eastern Guatemala the cross is sometimes thought of as a deity which is venerated and adorned but nothing is ever asked of it (Wisdom, 1940, p. 423).

The Chorti and the Mam-speaking Indians of Santiago Chimaltenango in northwestern Guatemala value saint worship more than cross worship (Wagley, 1949, pp. 390–431). But even in these Maya religions the saints seem less important than in the Valley of Mexico. In Maya folk religion the Catholic saints must share their honors with pagan deities. There is no Maya saint who fuses Christianity and paganism like the Aztec Virgin of Guadalupe. The Mother of all Mexicans is a foreigner to the Maya.

The worship of pagan agricultural deities still constitutes the core of Maya folk religion in rural areas. Of these pagan deities, the most important are the ancient rain gods called chaacs and the wind gods called pauahtuns. The most significant pattern of Christo-pagan syncretism in Yucatan folk religion is the compartmentalization of Christian and pagan cults. Pagan rites dedicated to Maya agricultural deities are performed by a shaman-priest called an h-men, whose prayers are said in the native tongue. Catholic rites are performed by a native chanter who recites prayers from the Catholic liturgy addressed to God, Christ, and various saints. The offerings made to Christian divinities are different from those made to pagan deities, and the rites of the two cults are usually performed in different places. Both pagan and Christian cults function to secure supernatural aid in obtaining rain, growing crops, and restoring health. They are complementary ways of dealing with the supernatural (Redfield, 1941, pp. 104–08).

The functioning of the two interrelated cults is illustrated in the rain ceremonies of Chan Kom and X-Cacal (Redfield and Villa, 1934, p. 139; Redfield, 1941, p. 107). During a drought in Chan Kom the people first held a novena before the patron saint to ask for rain. The nine evenings of prayer were led by a chanter with laymen participating. Special foods were placed on the altar of the saint. Some rain fell but not enough. Next prayers were addressed to the cross and God, but the drought persisted. Then the men of Chan Kom secured the services of an h-men to lead a ceremony dedicated to the chaacs. Some Yucatan villages still hold this cha'chaac ceremony at the local cenote where pieces of sacrificed turkey are thrown into the water where the rain gods dwell.

Pagan and Christian rain ceremonies in X-Cacal are performed simultaneously at separate altars in the same church. The h-men, beside his altar, addresses the pagan deities while the civil leader, called Nohoch Tata, kneels beside the other altar reciting Catholic prayers. There is no conflict between the two cults which are followed by the same congregation.

Whether or not the Maya themselves recognize a distinction between the two cults is a matter of debate. I would be inclined to agree with Villa Rojas' opinion that the natives do make a distinction but not in terms of historical origins. The very fact that both Christian and pagan rites are performed for the same purpose indicates that the Maya recognize two sets of deities who should be separately propitiated in different ways.

The compartmentalization of the two cults does not entail a rigid separation of all Christian and pagan elements in Maya folk religion. Through a process of incremental syncretism Catholic saints have been added to the Maya pantheon of nature gods. The chaacs are arranged in a hierarchy headed by St. Michael Archangel. This saint gives orders for rain to the captain of the chaacs who leads the pagan rain gods stationed at the four cardinal points of the sky. When the rain gods ride through the sky pouring rain from their calabashes they are sometimes accompa-

nied by the Virgin Mary, who has become a guardian of the maize and is often invoked by the h-men in his prayers to the chaacs. The Chorti of Guatemala attribute the production of rain to similar pagan deities known as "chicchans" who occupy the four world directions and bear the individual names of Christian saints (Wisdom, 1940, pp. 392-95). The pauahtuns, Yucatan wind gods associated with the four directions, are called St. Dominic, St. Gabriel, St. James, and Mary Magdalene (D. E. Thompson, 1954, p. 28).

Maya ethics are pagan. Man's primary obligations are making milpa and propitiating nature gods who run the universe and grant the temporal necessities of life. Gods who do not receive the proper offerings send sickness, drought, or other misfortunes to punish the negligent individual or community. The cessation of human sacrifice has not interfered with the orderly running of the universe by Maya agricultural deities, who are now content with animal sacrifices.

My analysis of the reasons for the contrasting processes and patterns of syncretism traced in this article may be summarized as follows:

The conquest decapitated the Aztec value system focused on war and human sacrifice, producing a strain for new religious orientations. This strain culminated in the fusion of Spanish and Indian traditions embodied in Guadalupinist Catholicism. The successful integration of the old and new religions was greatly facilitated by the paternalistic guidance of capable Franciscans who taught Christianity in the Nahuatl tongue, established warm personal relations with the Aztec, and encouraged certain types of religious syncretism. But the most important stimulus for fusion was the appearance of the dark-skinned Virgin of Guadalupe which enabled the Aztec to Indianize the white man's religion and make it their own.

The Maya value system focused on agriculture and worship of agricultural deities survived the conquest virtually intact to become a backbone of resistance to radical religious change. This resistance was strengthened by hatred of the Spaniards, whose missionary effort was marred by inability to communicate with the natives, cruel punishment of idolators, and burning of Maya pueblos. Indoctrination of the Maya was often left up to baptized natives who returned to paganism in scattered and isolated villages seldom visited by Catholic priests. Since the Maya of Yucatan felt no need for a new religion, they clung to their own, adding only those elements of Catholicism which could be accepted without impairing native religious belief.

Although the Maya and the Aztec adopted Christianity by different processes of syncretism, the contemporary folk religions of the two groups share many similarities based on their common heritages from paganism and Catholicism. The most obvious of these similarities are the Catholic ritual observances found not only in Middle America but throughout Latin America. Both Nahuatl and Maya folk religions adapted the Catholic saints and Christ to their ancient pattern of polytheism. Both folk religions worship images which are believed to possess supernatural powers and are treated like persons. Both retain a belief in dual-natured deities who grant men benefits and take them away at will. Both preserve an essentially pagan concept of ethics. In both Nahuatl and Maya folk cultures religion functions as an explanation of the ordering of the universe, a channel for dealing with the supernatural forces of nature, a focus of community activities, a means of aesthetic expression, and a road to prestige.

A study of religious syncretism in Middle America should include an appraisal of the influence of Protestantism and Spiritism, but little research has been carried out on these trends of change. The total number of Protestants in Mexico is very small but it is increasing. The 1950 census counted 330,-111 Protestants, but Protestant officials estimated that Mexico had nearly two million Protestants at that time. There are approximately 22 different Protestant sects in Mexico (Lewis, 1958, pp. 251–52). It is worthy of note that the most successful efforts of Protestant missionaries have been among Maya groups whose folk religion is relatively unaffected by the anti-Protestant influence of the Catholic Church.

The little information available on Protestantism in Mexico suggests that it may be accepted by a process of incremental syncretism without the complete abandonment of Catholicism. The town of San Pedro Martir in the Valley of Mexico is reputed to have a large number of Protestants who return to the Catholic church for baptisms, marriages, and annual fiestas for the village patron saint. A similar situation is reported by Redfield for Chan Kom, where six or seven families were converted to Protestantism in 1931. In response to the teaching of the Protestant missionaries, the converts at first renounced saint worship, drinking, and smoking, and established a rival cult of prayer meetings where Bible reading and hymn singing took place. The new cult created a schism in the community, but cultural homogeneity was later restored when the Protestants began to return to Catholic novenas and fiestas for the saints. A Protestant storekeeper who gave up selling liquor, cigarettes, and wax candles at the time of his conversion later started selling them again. The change to Protestantism in Dzitas made little or no difference in the participation in pagan rituals since Protestant missionaries direct their proselytism against Catholicism rather than against paganism (Redfield, 1941, pp. 144–46, 235).

Nash found that Protestantism appeals mainly to the marginal man who is not at ease in his social and cultural environment in the Indian community of Cantel located in the western highlands of Guatemala. The principal change accompanying the acceptance of Protestantism was a reformation of personal behavior including the elimination of drinking, smoking, and wife beating. The daily conduct of the convert was continuously supervised by his brethren to see that he conformed with Protestant rules of abstinence (M. Nash, 1958a, pp. 61, 66). If the Cantel and Chan Kom patterns are characteristic of Protestant missionizing in other parts of Mexico, it seems safe to predict that Protestantism does not pose any real threat to Catholicism in Middle America.

Spiritism and Spiritualism represent a major trend of change in the supernaturalism of Middle America as well as other parts of Latin America. Mexico City alone has some 25 Spiritualist "temples" and more than twice as many Spiritist temples, which are actually private houses as a rule. The Mexican Spiritist movement began in the middle of the 19th century and is based on the pseudoscientific philosophy of the Frenchman whose pen name was Allan Kardec. Spiritualism is a more recent development coinciding with the 20th-century missionary activity of United States Protestants in Mexico. The metaphysical distinctions between the rival cults of Spiritism and Spiritualism are rather insignificant and not generally recognized by the Mexicans, who commonly refer to members of both cults as "espiritualistas" (Spiritualists). Although the tenets of both cults are specifically anti-Catholic and have been officially denounced by the Catholic church, many Mexicans believe that the "espiritualistas" are Catholics. In the Valley of Mexico, Spiritist curing has been widely accepted by Catholic Mestizos as an addition to folk medicine without causing much change of religious affiliation (C. Madsen, 1966).

REFERENCES

Albert, 1956
Barnett, 1953
Beals, 1952
Braden, 1930
Brainerd and Morley, 1956
Bruner, 1956
Carrasco, 1952b
Caso, 1958c
Cortés, 1908
Demarest and Taylor, 1956
Festinger, 1957
Foster, 1960a
Gante, P. de, n.d.
Gillin, 1952
Jiménez Moreno, 1958
Kelman, 1958
LaFarge, 1947
—— and Byers, 1931
Lazo de la Vega, 1956
Lewis, 1958
Linton, 1936
Lumholtz, 1902
Madsen, C., 1966

Madsen, W., 1957
—— and Madsen, 1948
Mendieta, 1945
Merton, 1957
Motolinía, 1950
Nash, 1958a
Osgood and Tannenbaum, 1955
Paso y Troncoso, 1953
Redfield, 1930, 1941
—— and Villa, 1934
Roys, 1943
Sahagún, 1938
Serna, 1892
Simpson, 1959
Soustelle, G., 1958
Tax, 1952a
Thompson, D. E., 1954
Tozzer, 1941
Villa R., 1945
Vogt, 1951
Wagley, 1949
Wisdom, 1940
Wolf, 1959

20. Ritual and Mythology

E. MICHAEL MENDELSON

WITHOUT ADOPTING as radical a view as that held by Leach (1954, pp. 10–14) whereby myth, a statement in words, says the same thing as ritual, a statement in action, expressing "the individual's status as a social person in the structural system in which he finds himself for the time being," we can perhaps agree on the social anthropologist's viewpoint being directed to social relations rather than to the cultural contents of religion. In this sense, the present article, while considering various formulations about ritual and mythology in the area, will concern itself at times with variations in the position of ritual personnel. Leach's refusal to limit ritual activity to "sacred" activities agrees with the Middle American situation in so far as religious and political organization here have always been closely associated, and with the ritualization of nonreligious activities noted since Redfield's study of Tepoztlan (1930, pp. 147, 166).

Nor can one comment on this area without taking into account the conquest of the Indians by Spain in the 16th century and the various ways in which the Spaniards drove a wedge into the united politico-religious authority systems of the Indians. Indeed, the basis of a variational study must evaluate the state of evolution of these systems in different parts of the area, the kind of Spanish pressure exerted in different parts as well as the difference in the timing and orientation of a multitude of reports, in order to understand how Spain modified Indian notions concerning the proper locus of authority. The number of studies made on Middle America, the relatively short conquest period, and the cultural conservatism of Spain—recognized by Foster (1960a, p. 20) as considerably facilitating comparative studies—all make Middle America a fertile field for acculturation research in the broadest sense, but the writer attempting to summarize it is bewildered by the gaps in many reports according to the orientation of the reporters. It is difficult for him not to see the area from the vantage point of that part of it which he himself knows best.

I am best acquainted with the midwestern highlands of Guatemala and have concentrated my attention there on ritual and mythology. For the purposes of this discussion I have divided Mesoamerica into four subareas: the Atlantic lowlands, covering Yucatan, Quintana Roo, and British Honduras, but also extending into highland Chiapas and eastern Guatemala; the northern Guatemalan highlands; the midwestern or southern Guatemalan highlands; and central Mexico, with occasional references to outlying parts. Although the nature of ritual and myth is broadly similar over the whole area, the distribution of ritual personnel is of most significance as far as variational studies are concerned. This article will thus proceed from consideration of the latter to a more general study of the forms of ritual and the contents of myth envisaged as statements in words of the realities expressed in action by ritual.

The chief value of Redfield's seminal folk-urban continuum notion, and the studies clustering around it, appears to be here the underlining of the fact that, in the whole area, some Indian groups were less evolved than others at the time of the conquest and remained so afterwards; and that, in any subarea, certain groups have remained in folklike dependence on a more or less urban center. This viewpoint seems to have inspired one summary of the area: Cámara's division of groups into centripetal and centrifugal types (1952c, pp. 142–73) which covers both Indian and Ladino phenomena. Centripetal features—retention of pre-Columbian elements, importance of the community over the individual, hierarchy of ascribed status in the politico-religious organization—as compared to centrifugal features—secularization of life, the importance of the individual, achieved status, Catholic as opposed to pagan religious activity—lead one to identify the centripetal with the folk and the centrifugal with the urban situations. We shall meet these distinctions again in more detail below.

We must bear in mind a type of folk organization retained by many groups in outlying areas and often retreated into by more evolved groups when conquest deprived them of their upper social classes. Since the Spaniards naturally enough tended to concentrate on the more highly developed Indian communities, this type of organization has retained its nature in the geographic sense as well as in the historical sense, where it is represented by the kind of *República de Indios* described by Wolf (1959, pp. 212–32). Because of the scope of this article and because recent history has made political organization into the most elusive of our variables, we shall lay less stress on political authority than on religious, although the combined effect of Spanish political, military, and religious action on evolved communities appears, on the surface, to have caused more changes in the nature of religious authority than elsewhere, and this in a secularizing, politically oriented direction.[1]

[1] In the historical field I have consulted Borhegyi (1956b), LaFarge (1940), Gibson (1955), and major syntheses of Vaillant, Morley, Thompson, and Wolf. Detailed contributions came from Zavala (1945), Aguirre Beltrán (1953) and Goubaud (1952). In the sociological field, Doll (1952) and B. W. Starr (1949) have attempted surveys of the stewardship of the saint and politico-religious organizations, respectively. Cámara has treated the latter subject (1952, ch. 7), and the "Retention Index" from this source has also been used.

Detailed studies of particular communities include Redfield and Villa on Yucatan and Chiapas; Gann and Thompson on Yucatan, British Honduras, and Verapaz; Redfield on Tepoztlan; Foster on Tzintzuntzan; Parsons on Mitla; Bunzel on Chichicastenango; Tax on Panajachel; LaFarge on Santa Eulalia; Lincoln on the Ixil; Wagley on Chimaltenango; Adams on Milpas Altas; Wisdom on the Chorti; B. Paul and J. de Dios Rosales on San Pedro; Oakes on Todos Santos; M. Nash on Cantel.

An important dimension to these studies has been added by Foster's Spanish ethnography, especially by his article on cofradía and compadrazgo (1953a). He points out that, whereas the *cofradía-gremio* won out in Spain against the compadrazgo, the latter triumphed in America with the purely religious cofradías as a sideline. Of interest to us here are two points: (1) that the areas with high degrees of native retention seem not to need either, and (2) that the compadrazgo seems to have been more successful in central Mexico than in Guatemala. This may be related to the survival, in the latter, of other, often impersonal, mechanisms offering mutual aid: a village courthouse for disputes; a cofradía system which

In the marginal lands—this applies to subarea 1 and also, it would seem, to northern Mexico—we find a communal ritual activity, based on the fertility of maize, in which native priests, who are also shamans with long and sometimes hereditary tenure, play a leading role. (We distinguish here the priest, an intermediary between man and god(s), from the shaman, a possessor of supernatural powers in the realm of divination and medicine.) Catholic cult, more or less fossilized in its neo-medieval form, exists side by side with the native cult, almost a branch or aspect of it, and is not linked to the political organization. The individual's link with the supernatural is directed or mediated only by the priest-shaman and is situated for the most part in the fields or other natural spots. There are survivals here and there of the authority of lineage heads, to whom quarrels are taken instead of being referred to the political organization; the whole community pyramids upward directly and without intermediate hierarchization to one group of familial, political, and religious leaders.

___

defines social status, controls religious behavior, and buries the dead; and the systems of *posada* lodging and *recomendado* goods during travel.

Doll (1952) has noticed the similarity between marriage and stewardship in certain instances. In Mitla obligations incurred at one can be repaid at the other. In Atitlan we found that the manner of calling a cofrade much resembled the manner of calling a wife: many visits are necessary before acceptance is secured.

2 Wolf deals with the calendar in the whole area (1959, pp. 86–89); the most authoritative and detailed study for subareas 1–3 has been done by J. E. S. Thompson (1950). The calendar of subareas 2 and 3 has been dealt with by Miles (1952, pp. 273–84) and M. Nash (1957b). Nash suggests a direct correlation between the position of the shaman within the politico-religious system of subarea 2 and the retention of chronological elements, on the one hand, and the position of the shaman outside in subarea 3 and loss of these elements, on the other.

We feel that, on the whole, in the areas of maximum retention of calendric lore, the native deities are chosen and worshipped from among calendric powers, and have survived in that aspect rather than as direct representations of weather and agricultural deities.

In the northern Guatemalan highlands, in Verapaz, and the Chorti country, we find various forms of organization led by a group of prayer-makers with temporal and spiritual powers of a quasipermanent nature. These are native priests rather than shamans. There are shamans, some of whom play an important part in the divinatory aspects of community cult. The *principales*, native priests who have performed a number of community services, retain an exalted position until death, chose the new prayer-makers, maintain Catholic cult in the absence of a Catholic priest, and help in the selection of political officers. We thus have a group of leaders which is more homogeneous, less impersonal, more responsible for native cults of a communal nature whose influence on the municipality is strongly felt, than among otherwise similar groups in the southern highlands. The survival of calendric lore in the northern highlands raises problems as to the survival of noble castes here, possibly connected with lineage leadership, a factor which has largely disappeared in the area next under consideration.[2]

The northerners resisted·Spanish centralization, but the people of the southern highlands appear to have been strongly urbanized at the time of the conquest and thus to have borne the full brunt of it. The principales in the south are not priests of the native cult, but rather those who have passed through two interweaving hierarchies: that of the Catholic cult of the *cofradias* and that of the political organization of the municipality. We no longer have the direct, nature-oriented ritual of the marginal lands; rather, ritual is led by small, hierarchically organized groups representing the whole population, strongly linked to the Spanish-inspired municipal system and interested in the Catholic cult of the saints rather than in native deities. Here, passage through the ranks does not depend so much on personal inclination or charisma; the office is the man rather than the man the of-

Fig. 1—TE-AKATA, HUICHOL SACRED LOCALITY. (From Lumholtz, 1902, 2: 166.)

fice, and there are no significant offices of a permanent nature. With Bunzel's remarks in mind regarding the Catholic cult as an ecclesiastical arm of the secular state (1952, pp. 162–64), we can say that there has been a shift here in the nature of authority from one vested in native culture to one vested in the conquest culture. An economic factor may be noted in passing: the northerners do not seem to have been rich enough to entertain cofradías as fully as the southerners.

Subarea 4, central Mexico, appears to resemble subarea 3 more than any of the others, perhaps consonant with apparent pre-Columbian links of trade, cultural influence, and conquest between these two areas, as opposed to other links between the northern Guatemalan highlands and the Atlantic lowlands. There is less interrelationship between the political organization and the Catholic santo stewardships—though this is found, for instance, in Mitla—than in the southern Guatemalan highlands, possibly because central Mexico did not benefit so much from the retreat of the Spaniards in the "Century of Depression," which gave the southerners an opportunity to revert more closely to the native unified politico-religious basic system. Although stewardships promote an individual's prestige in Mexico as in Guatemala, the hierarchical and automatic passing through the ranks is less stressed here; the cofradía also seems less highly organized in its frequent division between those responsible for the image of the saint and those responsible for its fiesta. Much depends, as elsewhere, on local variations: Tzintzuntzan, in its stewardship system, shows signs of a vast Cath-

Fig. 2—CORA MOUNTAIN SHRINE, REGION OF EL MESA DE NAYAR, NAYARIT, MEXICO. (Photographed by Donald Cordry, 1938.)

olic program, with hospitals, convents, and chapels now decayed, while Tepoztlan exhibits interesting survivals of *barrio*—possibly ex-kinship—worship, a factor not found in the southern Guatemalan highlands.

An interesting shift in the position of the native ritualist is seen in subareas 1–4: the degree of his affiliation with the formal religious organization decreases. Correspondingly, there is a decrease in the native ritualist's hold over communal ritual to the benefit of the Catholic ritualist's and an increase in the native ritualist's relegation to individual and family ritual. The native ritualist is less involved in kinship matters, in effective control over political affairs, and in the hierarchization of social statuses, whereas the latter itself becomes less a matter of personal prestige attached to kinship, position, age and religious knowledge and more an impersonal matter of routine moving up the politico-religious ladder (Red-

field, 1941, pp. 366–68). As we move from subarea 1 to subarea 4, the shaman becomes increasingly an independent agent. He becomes divested of responsibility for good community ritual, he can become a focus for individual ritual involving either good or bad, white or black magic. Impersonal government structures lead to legalistic methods of handling quarrels in the community, leaving the shaman free to deal with less tangible individual matters. In addition, the Ladino element prevailing in the more developed areas forces all native ritual onto the shoulders of the outsider shaman and defines it more and more as bad, or black, magic.

A parallel shift concerns the nature of witchcraft. As one moves from societies in which power is vested only in one group towards those in which it is vested in different members of a hierarchical organization, witchcraft and sorcery accusations can be shifted from a point outside the society to one inside it: first the lower officials of the hierarchy, then the shaman, are open to such accusations,

Although the one body of leaders in the marginal groups can be tainted with suspicion, it is dangerous to accuse them. Thus witchcraft accusations can be shifted to outsiders or to a host of spirits responsible for sickness or disease far more numerous than in the more evolved areas. There is nothing that is specifically good or bad about these spirits; they are ambiguous or frankly amoral. Marginal-area witchcraft emerges against their background: the witch directs them into the bodies of his enemies and anti-witchcraft merges readily with all forms of the healing arts. Thus a fertile field for suspicion and accusation is provided which is lacking in the social setting, though, when it does erupt there, it may well be more violent than in more evolved areas. In subareas 2–4 uncertainty is much reduced in that both calendrical powers and santos are less ambiguous in their good and bad roles than native spirits. This trend towards personalization is also seen in the fact that spirits of subareas 3 and 4 are more anthropomorphized than those of subareas 1 and 2: we tend to deal more with humans and ex-humans than with winds and semimythical animals. The transitional nature of subarea 2 is marked by the mysterious time-watchers of the northern highlands—a kind of personalization of the powers inherent in the notions of "looking" and "seeing" as good or bad actions by powerful individuals on surrounding objects. As for the impersonal nature of office-holding in the more evolved areas, this may be reflected in the noninvolvement of the shaman in his work; he considers himself merely as a medium through which his client's accusations pass and apologizes to his client's enemies as soon as the ritual is over.

This argument would not be complete without reference to nagualism. Whether or not there has been confusion of a pre-Columbian notion of the spirit-animal protector with a belief in transforming witches of animal origin, the present system appears to have achieved balance in the notion that, although all or some people have animal companions, only bad people send them to harm others and do so as transforming witches. But there are variations in our subareas. In the marginal areas the companions come from nature, possibly in the form of a snake who swallows the apprentice shaman during his initiation. In these areas the companion would seem to be limited to priest-shamans or heads of lineages—another example of the concentration of power into the hands of one group. In the Guatemalan highlands, one finds that everyone has a companion but only witches know what theirs are and make use of them. This may be historically related to the survival of the calendar here, whereas it has disappeared in the lowlands. Further, beliefs about companions are sinking, in the more developed areas, into folklore. For this two factors are probably responsible. First, Christian notions of free

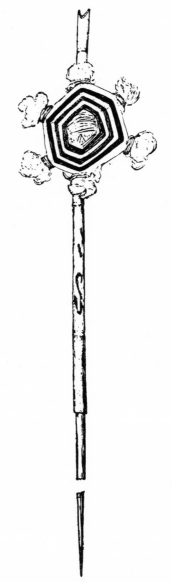

Fig. 3—CORA GOD'S EYE. Made as a prayer for health and life. (From Lumholtz, 1902, 1: 501.)

will interfere with the fatalistic Indian view of people as bound to a good or bad fate at birth; second, increased political activity brings into the open recognition of conflict as inherent in normal living and accepted as such by those who indulge in it. Thus the uncertainty as to who is a witch, recognized by M. Nash (1960) as part and parcel of witchcraft belief systems, is mitigated by direct recognition of the individual with whom one is in conflict. Redfield's conclusions in comparing Yucatec villages and towns (1941, p. 334) show that, in the villages, there are still enough beliefs linking sickness with spirits of nature and still enough family cohesion to obviate the need for personalized interpretations of illness and conflict in terms of witchcraft; whereas, in the cities, interpersonal conflict looms larger as confusion about native deities prevails and scientific knowledge infiltrates the world view. Lack of social and family cohesion in the city brings the outsider, as it were, into the gates.

We can therefore put forward as a significant variation in our subareas the fact that the more native ritual and native beliefs are relegated outside the formal politico-religious organization, the more witchcraft accusations tend to find a place within the group rather than outside it. At the same time, the influence of secularization tends to weaken belief in witchcraft until conflict, though perhaps not disease, is interpreted in nonreligious terms.

The foregoing summary enables us to divide the ritual of Mesoamerindian communities into three broad categories: the purely Catholic, the Christo-pagan (to use Madsen's term), and the purely pagan. It need hardly be said that the last category applies, with reservations, to apparently proved survivals of pre-Columbian ritual, none of which in all probability remain in their pure state. To some extent, we are dealing in all three cases with ideal types. We can use these categories, however, for a preliminary description of certain broad lines of ritual, reserving more detailed comment on certain problems for discussion below.

In the purely Catholic category, we can place ritual undertaken by a resident priest, Ladino or Indian, his appointed helpers from among the Ladinos and Indians, and the mass of the community in so far as they

attend these Catholic functions, together with Catholic ritual, usually based on missals and prayer books, by nonecclesiastical persons in communities without a priest. These activities cover normal Catholic procedure: Masses, processions of saints and some of the sacraments, especially baptism. Many observers have noted that Indians are more likely to accept baptism than marriage or funeral sacraments, and here we would probably accept Bunzel's reasons quoted above. In communities with groups of priest-trained *catequistas,* a certain number of (mostly younger) people will accept the other sacraments and attempt to get the rest of the population to do so too. They may, in the process, be reduced to attacking native deities or shamans who practice their cult and thus be brought into conflict with the traditional leaders of the community. As a result, in areas where this is possible, they may seek political power as opposed to religious and will thus underline secularizing trends within the whole system. Such a tendency is also to be found among Protestant converts who often give up the whole pattern of politico-religious concern when entering the new religion.

The priest may appoint a variety of officers: sacristans, bell ringers, missal reciters, acolytes—these offices can be used to avoid traditional offices by catequistas and other such rebels—or these officers may be chosen by literate people from among their own ranks in communities without a resident priest. In such cases, a priest is brought in on payment from the outside on the occasion of important fiestas.

In the Christo-pagan ritual, which serves as the main avenue of social prestige in subareas 3 and 4, as to some extent in 2, one finds the main concern focused on the care of community or community-section santos (Catholic saints adapted to Indian belief and ritual needs). Here, a member of the community will take upon himself, usually for a year, the responsibility for the annual fiesta of the saint. The responsibility is financial: he must pay for the ritual paraphernalia of the fiesta, the specialists (musicians, dancers, fireworks experts) employed, and the food which is distributed on a variety of festal occasions throughout the year. He must also make his presence felt at these ceremonies and direct their course, alone or with helpers. A variety of means is employed to ensure help in this financial burden. In cofradía systems, such as the Guatemalan, where the fiesta is paid for by a cofradía which also guards the santo's image in the house of its head, regular contributions are made by the subordinate cofrades and donations are brought by individual pilgrims. Elsewhere, a variety of public help is expected. In Mitla, a system of festal pledges is used; a kind of investment in other peoples' fiestas whereby a *cargador* insures himself against the time when he himself will be mainly responsible. In Tepoztlan, community lands ensure produce which will be used against the fiesta time.

The relative importance of fiestas differs in the area as a whole and, usually, some difference is found between involvement of the whole community and smaller groups, as well as between more ritualistic fiestas and more secularized fiestas associated with Independence Day or similar political or economic manifestations. In the latter cases the fiesta is accompanied by a fair or large market. Holy Week would seem to be general except for the Totonac (Tax, 1952a, p. 140); other church fiestas such as Corpus Christi, Day of the Kings, Day of the Cross, and All Souls' usually evoke wide response. Christmas is usually recognized as less important; New Year often has political overtones connected with the change-over of municipal officials. The patron saint's day is the occasion for community-wide fiestas in many, if not all, places except when another image has taken the patron's place as leader of the local supernatural powers. Throughout the area a fiesta is successful *(alegre)* if it is attended by many people,

FIG. 4—HUICHOL SHAMAN SINGING AND BEATING DRUM. (From Lumholtz, 1902, 2: 32.)

unsuccessful *(triste)* if not. A better opportunity of studying acculturation in fiestas is now provided by Foster's (1960a) very thorough chapters on Spanish ritual.

The actual ritual is centered mainly on processions of a religious nature, bearing the santos from the cofradía or mayordomía to the church for Mass and bringing them back again. In this respect, the ritual seems to parallel pre-Columbian rites involving the transport of subsidiary chapel figures to a central temple and back again. This means that there is usually a relation between the church and the sodality chapel: the cofradía may have an altar in the church corresponding to its santo for whose care and cleaning and adornment it will be responsible. My feeling (Mendelson, 1956, p. 1085) is that, on occasions when the church had to retreat from Indian villages for lack of priests, the church altars were

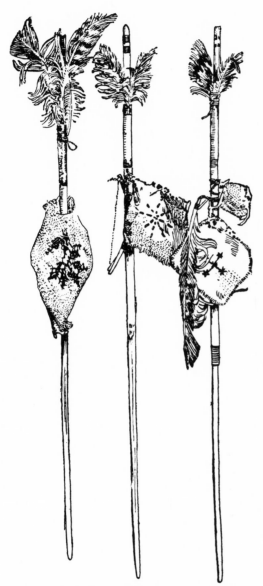

FIG. 5—HUICHOL BACK-SHIELDS. Hung on arrows, these express women's prayers for luck in embroidery. (From Lumholtz, 1902, 2: 209.)

divested of some of their contents, which passed into the cofradías and thus favored the church-chapel link. There would also seem to be some relation, in certain regions, between the original native performers of *barrio guachibales*, possibly still related to pre-Columbian kin-group cults, and the growth of cofradías, even though these

have now lost barrio associations in Guatemala. Curiously enough, Bunzel (1952, p. 171) refers to certain cofradías which are of ritual rather than political importance and whose santos are privately owned, have no cofradías, and are transmitted in family lines. These Chichicastenango cofradías seem to correspond fairly closely to those in Atitlan in which I have found the presence of native deities. Since Fuentes y Guzmán refers to a dichotomy between cofradías and privately owned, hereditary guachibales (1933, 6: 349), the cofradías of the southern highlands may have different origins for the politico-Catholic and the ritualistic-native, respectively.

Although detailed studies of stewardship behavior have rarely been made, various observers have commented on the extreme ritualization of the most intimate details of this behavior. Divisions between cases in which individuals take stewardships as the result of a vow or of social compulsion and those in which individuals volunteer or, on the other hand, show strong reluctance to accept a stewardship are not of great importance and are usually related to economic situations as well, probably, as to less tangible definitions of what constitutes appropriately modest behavior. The main point is that if a man can take office leading to social prestige, he will do so. The ritualization of behavior is linked by some observers with pre-Columbian patterns. Sovereign is the notion of the stewardship as a burden (*cargo*) as well as an advancement. The notion here is not only economical but seems to involve a concept analogous to that of the day and year bearers in the pre-Columbian calendars: man is in the world to carry it on through the medium of its pattern of offices; these are left behind when a man dies; the world is permanent. Doll (1952, p. 35) stresses the sacred-pledge aspect of this burden. In the marginal Yucatec areas, a man will die if he goes back on his pledge, a belief which even survives in secularized areas like Mitla. The son is often expected to fulfill the pledge for the father if he dies. In the old days, it is said, imprisonment followed refusal in Panajachel and Chichicastenango. In return for this burden advantages are conceived of as coming directly from the deity in marginal areas, from social recognition in more evolved parts. In this sense, too, rotation is stressed and nowhere is behavior more ritualized than in the transfer ceremonies after the annual fiesta.

In Atiteco cofradías, pleasure and relaxation are invested with a moral content: drinking, eating, smoking, dancing, praying, censing, are all part of the *servicio*. Thus food and drink cannot be refused, for they are gifts to the saint through human intermediaries; even a sleeping man must be wakened to take his share. Elaborate salutations and thanks to each person accompany these functions, and a man must even shake hands with each cofrade to be excused if he goes outside. Incense is a "present" from the chapel and is presented to each person who enters. The receiver passes it under his armpits and his headgear. All bits of paper and other rubbish deposited in the cofradía throughout the year are collected in a bag and used to fertilize the cofradía leader's field, together with bits of broken old censers. Rank determines how cofrades sit along benches, go in procession, and talk. Conversation is ritualized and speeches, especially at transfer ceremonies, are highly formal, the speakers standing obliquely to each other and shouting out their speeches simultaneously. This kind of elaborate politeness has been noted by Foster in Tzintzuntzan (1948a, p. 219) and is probably characteristic of Mesoamerica.[3]

Thus it is a blended type of religion,

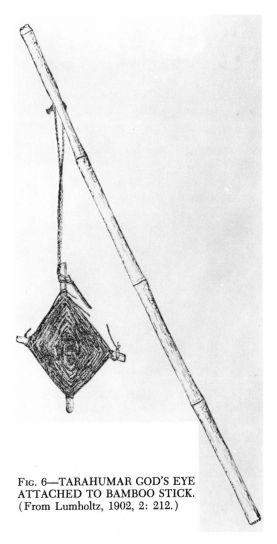

FIG. 6—TARAHUMAR GOD'S EYE ATTACHED TO BAMBOO STICK. (From Lumholtz, 1902, 2: 212.)

studied specifically in recent years by D. E. Thompson (1954), Madsen (1957), and Wolf (1959), that most aptly characterizes the whole of Mesoamerica. Foster (1960a) has shown that the culture of Spain was stripped down in the process of transfer to the New World; Wolf brings out the Reformation-like purge of Catholic ritual in its many accretions effected by the friars in America. The old gods, who were feared but not loved, failed the people (Wolf is here talking principally about the Aztec) and longing for peace was fruitful for the propagation of the Christian message. The peasants had not been interested in the

---

[3] Carrasco (1952b, p. 25) refers to "dramatizations and dances somehow related to the festival which is being celebrated" as "the most important folk additions to the Catholic liturgy." Kurath (1952, pp. 233–42) has summarized data in this field, and Correa (1958b) has published work on Guatemalan dances.

positions of a religious hierarchy which remained flexible at the level of the peasant household and resembled the old priesthood in that both types of priest were marked off from the common crowd by long training, fasts, penances, sexual abstinence, special dress, residence, and comportment.

In addition, writes Wolf (p. 171), the transition was eased by "an astonishing similarity in ritual and symbol between the old and the new religion." Both religions had forms of baptism, confession, communion, fasting and penance, pilgrimages, Virgins and Great Mothers, the cross, passion plays, and dramatic representations of sacrifice, the use of incense and holy liquor. We know, in addition, that some Catholics were not averse to using native ritual in order to attract the Indian to Catholic beliefs (Madsen, 1957, p. 134).

Although pagan ritual, as we have seen, is still communal in subarea 1, it tends in more evolved areas to be relegated to the sphere of individual ritual, most often associated with the life cycle and crises in individual existence. Carrasco (1952b) associates folk religion with unorganized activities: technological or life cycle. Foster (1960a) has differentiated between formal and informal acculturation, the latter being associated with the folk pole of the continuum. In both these writers, the folk pole is associated with traits which, in the present context, could be called pagan.

From the communal as well as the individual point of view, the deities that matter —and that always have mattered in the basic folk-society model—are those associated with the fertility and health or well being of essential crops, animals, and human beings. In this sense, they are available, either directly or as substitute santos, for rituals involving the whole group (production of good weather or rain) and individuals (production of fertility, good health, psychological well being). A communal ritual typical of marginal areas is described by Redfield and Villa (1934, pp. 138–43). A

Fig. 7—TARAHUMAR SHAMAN EXAMINING MAN ACCUSED OF SORCERY. (From Lumholtz, 1902, 1: 324.)

high gods of the priests but rather in the subsidiary gods of the agricultural cycle, weather, and health; like the Spanish peasants, they had recourse to magic, folk medicine, omens, and believed in witches which could transform themselves into animals. Both the Indian and the Catholic priests were trained in the manipulation of complex symbols, and the Indian priests of the militaristic period had already had much experience in relating new gods to old pantheons. Both "churches" had a tradition of flexibility: esoteric unity and exoteric diversity of the gods could coexist within one system. "As long as the priests remained in command, as ultimate mediators between gods and men and ultimate interpreters of this relationship, men could adapt the manifold religious patterns to suit their personal and local concerns" (Wolf, 1959, p. 169). Thus Catholic priests manned the pivotal

Yucatec priest-shaman directs the prayers in which an altar, consecrated native foods —subsequently eaten by all participants— and a ritual drink are used.[4] The chief rain god is impersonated by a dancer who waves the lightning machete and sprinkles water symbolic of rain. Small boys impersonate frogs, the musicians of the rain gods. In some parts of Yucatan, sacrificed turkeys are still thrown into the water of the local cenote, thus recalling the cenote cults of Chichen Itza. Women and children are excluded from these rites; indeed, as a whole, the less developed the community, the less women seem to play a direct part in the rites, although conjugality as a basis for participation in ritual—the family rather than a single man being a unit—seems to be found in the area from the Lacandones (G. Soustelle, 1959) to the cofradía regions of Guatemala and Mexico. Christian traits are to be found in this ritual, but the pattern is so close to pagan as to justify our use of the term here. It should be pointed out that some form of communal rain ritual, involving a tour of cofradías by leading elders and shamans as well as ritual for rain in "native" cofradías can be found in Atitlan, in the heart of subarea 3, and probably elsewhere. A substitute pattern in Christopagan ritual is the parading of the santo over the dry fields to show him or her the need for rain. This, since it is practiced in wholly Catholic countries too, can also be ascribed to pure Catholic ritual.

Throughout the area, divination and curing are associated with the native priest or shaman. Ritual patterns here follow closely the communal forms of ritual, except that they do not involve the same expenditures, processions, and food exchanges (cf. D. E. Thompson, 1954, p. 9). The native performer will divine and cure in the house-

FIG. 8—TARAHUMAR SHAMAN'S RATTLES. Length of longest 31.5 cm. (From Lumholtz, 1902, 1: 313.)

hold or he will take the individual on a tour of natural sites, chapels, or cofradías where he will say prayers for him, light candles, burn incense, and, possibly, promise some gift to the deity in case of recovery. Theoretically, shamans will often claim not to receive pay; in practice some kind of fee is usually received. Redfield (1930, p. 166) has described these medical usages as "a stock of traditional curative acts, tending to be ritualistic." Foster (1953b), among others, has pointed out the importance of psychological illnesses such as fright (*susto* or *espanto*) and suggested that the Amerindian seems more anxious and less stable than the Spaniard. He also shows that culturally accepted illnesses allow individuals to take ways out of anxiety, the results of ill-temper and shame in the very egalitarian *República de Indios* (pp. 216–17). In our opinion, the borderline between drunkenness and sobriety in the ritual drinking of Indian ceremonies allows the same kind of liberty. While santos may be invoked to cure illnesses, it is significant that the soul-stealing which takes place in most cases of psychological illness is thought to be effected by powers which resemble more closely

---

[4] Doll (1952, p. 49) points out that communal feeding off food devoted to the gods is associated with the stewardship in marginal areas, whereas smaller group meals take place in more evolved areas.

403

FIG. 9—TARAHUMAR OFFERING TESVINO AFTER A YUMARI DANCE. Cross covered with colored handkerchief. (From Lumholtz, 1902, 1: 344.)

the pre-Columbian deities. Madsen's *enanitos* (1957, p. 145) and Redfield's *aires* (1930, p. 165) are very close to the *tlalocs,* or rain gods, who, as we shall see, still form the basic pantheon of Mesoamerica; R. N. Adams (1952, p. 32) shows Christianized versions of these.

Madsen (1955a), studying shamanism in Mexico and Guatemala, comes to the conclusion that the phenomenon proper, involving the granting of supernatural power directly from a supernatural being to an individual, is rare. He contrasts this with situations in which the "shaman" is taught his knowledge. Granted that reports are unequal in different areas, this does seem to

be based on a confusion. In actual fact, short of believing in shamanism ourselves, we must agree that all shamans in some way or another do learn from living teachers. My own feeling about the difference may be that in some places shamans will defend their supernatural protector better than in others. In Atitlan the shamans would pretend that they received direct orders in dreams from Máximon and on pain of disobeying them they would go mad or die; laymen said—especially educated ones (and here secularization, the decline of myth into *creencias,* plays its part)—that they learned their prayers from other shamans. In fact, formal teaching seemed rare here; beginners learned by hanging about in cofradías while shamans said their prayers and trying them out first in private homes and natural sites—the home of native deities in Atitlan being in certain cofradías, not as more generally in the highlands (at Chichicastenango for instance) in the surrounding hills.

However this may be, Madsen accepts shamanism proper for the Tarahumara, Yucatan, the Popoluca, the Pokomam, the Valley of Mexico, and possibly the Chorti and the Mam. Thus it would seem that variation occurs more in the position of the shaman in society than in actual shamanistic belief and practice. The shift of emphasis from communal to individual would not seem to be a result of secularization of belief alone—since the individual if secularized in his beliefs would abandon native deities in any form of religion—but rather to the previously mentioned shift of emphasis from native culture to conquest culture in the realm of attitudes to public authority. Where the Cross triumphed most, the native deities and their cult lost most in public, though not necessarily, as we shall show, in private prestige.

Before we proceed to mythology, some confusing factors in the conquest situation must be examined. First, ritual, like mythology, tends to have an arbitrary appearance. Each community seems to have a collection of jigsaw-puzzle pieces, but no collection ever amounts to a complete puzzle. The pieces suggest an archetypal puzzle now lost: in any collection pieces will be found in different places; sometimes pieces will be entirely lacking; sometimes there will be two seemingly identical pieces kept on together side by side. Generally speaking, mythology will set the number of pieces which in turn will influence the available ritual. Only a complete history of the pre-Columbian myths in each area and the influence on them of the Spanish soldiers, officials, friars, and priests in each case would reveal the why and wherefore of each collection. At the same time, this very fragmentation, this absence everywhere of a complete puzzle, encourages two seemingly distinct processes. In one process, confusion is worse confounded by attempts to rebuild coherent systems. This process can still be seized in its living actuality among shamans of subarea 3 blending the pre-Columbian calendar with Christian day values or, in Atitlan, building a system out of the remains of the rain god beliefs with figures derived from Catholicism: twelve apostles plus Christ make thirteen, incidentally facilitated by the thirteen days of the native calendar.[5]

The other process, we suggest, is one of decomposition aided by the fragmentary and unsatisfying nature of the puzzle. Secularization can more easily work on such fragmented systems and thus myth can pass from living belief down to another level of

FIG. 10—ZAPOTEC WITH MINIATURE RANCHO-FIESTA, MITLA, OAXACA, MEXICO. At the cross of the *pedimento*, New Year's eve. (Photographed by Donald Cordry, January 1, 1942.)

"belief," in the sense in which all children in the West "believe" in fairy stories. The process of doubting what comes to be called mere creencias, I would call decline into folklore; Leslie (1960a, p. 21) defined this in terms of imagination and fancy, according to Coleridge.[6] At the same time this is not the whole story for certain sections of the population. We now refer to the traditionalists, the older people interested in upholding their social status and the offices and cults which maintain this. Here decomposition can be fought by holding on to bits and pieces because these were handed down from the fathers. This, essentially, is the notion of *costumbre* as it is held in Indian communities: so that practicing a certain custom becomes itself costumbre for lack of anything better. This attitude often goes with a glorification of the past at the

[5] Siegel (1941) has also analyzed cases of this sort in northern Guatemala. Foster (1953b, p. 208) points out that Tuesday and Friday are good days for curing both in Spain and in America.

[6] Foster (1948a, p. 220) shows a case in which symbolism takes the place of true belief in Tzintzuntzan though the ritual remains the same. The dead are offered food and are believed to be angry without it, but they are no longer thought to eat the food.

405

F_{IG}. 11—POPOLUCAS BEATING DRUMS IN HONOR OF SAINT, OCOZOTEPEC, VERA-
CRUZ. Saint is in bower at their right. (Middle American Research Institute, Tulane University.)

expense of the present: the old people were better at magic than the new, and so forth. Perhaps there is enough in pre-Columbian myths of world destruction to warrant this feeling about a golden age, which would not cause it to clash with an essentially cyclical view of history; perhaps the conquest itself had conditioned responses to decadence. Wolf writes (1959, p. 214): "The trauma of Conquest remains an open wound upon the body of Middle American society to this day." However this may be, there is usually in a community a group of people who will fight against the younger ones, secularized, Catholicized, or Protestantized as the case may be, and we may not be far here from Leach's considerations (1954) on the manipulation of different versions of myths by different groups, as we noted at the beginning of this article.

For these reasons any discussion of mythology must, in some way, take account of two poles: one in which the old cyclical view of pre-Columbian times is maintained as a statement in words of the rotation-burden system in action; another in which this cyclical view is interfered with by the linear or progressive view of history, saying

in words what social change says in action: that offices do die out, that old authority can be subordinated and new posts created, that new trades and new occupations can become more important than the traditional cycle of maize agriculture and small village-to-village peddling. Also, for reasons connected with fragmentation, it is virtually impossible to take bits of myth as they are on pain of emerging with a catalogue of heterogeneous items of little use to the social anthropologist. For this reason, I expand my suggestion offered earlier (1958a) that the rain god cycle is the basic myth of the area, justifying the regular progression of religious ritual, whether in town or in the fields, and that this can be substantiated from one apparently complete myth in the Huastec area and from fragments of similar myths in evidence elsewhere.

Stresser-Péan (1952) clearly presents the Huastec myth of the *Mamlab* as a cyclical one. The Huastecs remain respectful to mountains, which they think of as hollow and which they consider to be the home of the lightning gods. The Mamlab are divinized ancestors; the great god of lightning, husband to the goddess of the earth, once

406

drowned them long ago and took them to the eastern sea where the sun rises. They have become his servants, his miniature replicas. They drive the clouds over the earth in the guise of little men holding the lightning machete or ax. The clouds are feminine, and the little gods are said to drag the skirts of the sea goddess across the sky. The rains, fertilized by the male gods, fall on the crops and stimulate their growth. When young, the little gods circulate in the sky, brandishing their lightning weapons and fighting among themselves, making great noise with their thunder voices. Neolithic or bronze tools found near trees struck by lightning are considered to be fallen weapons. Occasionally, as in the case of an Atiteco legend of today, the god him-self gets stuck in a tree (Mendelson, 1958b, p. 125).

The clouds seem to rush towards the mountains, explained by the sexual desire of the godlings who meet with their females in the mountain caves. The females are frog goddesses whose call summons the rain of the warm season. The caves are then thought of as the scenes of orgies and nightly parties with dances and music and alcohol. But the Huastecs envisage love as a kind of sin or, at any rate, a kind of passing excess which weakens the lover in his physical as well as magical strength. Thus the godlings come out with the waters from the mountain sources and float towards the eastern ocean. They are then thought of as Ocel: degenerate, old, decrepit gods who

Fig. 12—CHAMULA INDIAN KNEELING AT ALTAR AND CROSS, LAS CASAS, CHIAPAS, MEX-ICO. (Photographed by Frans Blom about 1924. Middle American Research Institute, Tulane University.)

407

walk with lowered heads on the surface of streams or through the dank jungle. They now symbolize vegetation and often rest on certain kinds of plants whose leaves retain rain water. They are also masters of jungle animals, especially the dangerous ones. They still love dancing and improvise the drum by tapping on the stomachs of drowned beasts floating on the waters. They no longer carry weapons but only will-o'-the-wisps; their voices have become thin and plaintive like the voices of children. They no longer bring fertilizing rains but a variety of diseases.

But their drunkenness carries within itself its own regeneration. When floating in the sea they will swoon in a deep sleep of drunkenness like a momentary death. From this they will find the strength to start again as young gods of lightning and thunder. Stresser-Péan goes on to point out that these myths are expressed in dances which re-enact the life cycle of the gods and adds that, in Yucatan, cenotes seem to replace mountain caves; whereas in Guatemala, with a highland geography, there are two kinds of Mam "whose differential aspects have not been sufficiently studied."[7] He also feels that the Huastec myth should shed light on the relations between the Aztec Tlaloques of lightning, the Tepictoton of mountains and the Centzon Totochtin, the 400 rabbits of vegetation and drunkenness.

In other publications I have suggested that myths found in modern Atitlan, together with ritual native deities, show striking correspondences with the Huastec cycle (Mendelson, 1958a, 1958b, 1959, 1965). In this case, the Martins of cofradía San Juan seem strikingly like the godlings of lightning, while the old Mam or Maximón of cofradía Santa Cruz seems in many ways to represent the same god when old.[8] We have also suggested that the death of the Mam of the pre-Columbian calendrical five last days of the year is probably to be interpreted in a cyclical way in that he is likely to be re-born at the beginning of the new year. This cycle, taken together with J. E. S. Thompson's data on the Kekchi Mam (1930), suggests that the role of Mam and the role of Judas in another crisis of the year, Christian this time, may have merged in a way that exhibits the passing of pagan myth and ritual into the Christo-pagan field. The similarity of Easter and the Aztec festival of Toxcal adds subarea 4 to our picture (Madsen, 1957, p. 131).

Evidence for this cyclical myth being the basic folk type of myth of the area is further found in other sources. The Chac dancers of the Yucatec ritual described above wield lightning machetes; frogs— male, it is true—are attached to the corners of the altar. Madsen's account of the enanitos in Tecospa, as well as Redfield's equation of the Tepozteco aires with the Tlalocs are also significant. The widespread myths concerning the *dueños de cerro* in the whole area leave me in little doubt that they are related to the orgies of the Huastec godlings (Correa, 1955, p. 59).[9]

[7] D. E. Thompson, following J. E. S. Thompson, states that the Chacs are replaced in the Guatemalan highlands by gods of mountains who have dominion over fertility, rain, and the earth (1954, p. 28). For general data on Mam see J. E. S. Thompson (1930, p. 57 et seq.). Among the Chenalho (Guiteras Holmes, 1961, pp. 290–91), who seem to retain much of the old mythology, the mountain-rain-animal complex, represented by the 'Anhel,' is firmly subordinated by her informant to the Earth. Nevertheless, several traits of the basic myth we postulate here are present in Chenalho culture.

[8] A similar case of doubling is cited by J. E. S. Thompson in his paper on the moon goddess and is quoted by G. Soustelle (1959, p. 180) in commenting on the apparent separation of the old and the young moon goddess among the Lacandon. Foster (1953b, p. 213) shows the importance of the day of San Juan in Spain for curing and love magic.

[9] Wolf (1959, p. 218) contrasts the linear view of time held by non-Indians with their own "endless round," in which everyday labor issues into the magic moment of religious ritual, only to have the ritual again dissolve into the everyday labor that began the cycle. Compare the importance of the Tlalocs (p. 84) and the "heart of the land" theme (pp. 72–73) with Mendelson (1958b, p. 125, note 7). On the calendar's adaptation to a cyclical view of time, see Wolf, 1959, p. 88.

FIG. 13—IDOL HOUSE, PETHA, CHIAPAS, MEXICO. (Photographed by Frans Blom, 1928. Middle American Research Institute, Tulane University.)

One important point concerns the divinization of ancestors. Madsen clearly shows that the shaman whose soul becomes subservient to the enanitos becomes himself an enanito, or rain dwarf, on dying. In Atitlan we found evidence that the magic-working officials of cofradía San Juan became associated with the Martins at their death, indeed became Martins (the name deriving from San Martin) and reappeared in Atiteco society in moments of crisis, mainly weather and crop crises but lately political crises as well, in cases where the traditionalists were fighting Catequistas for the survival of native deities. Using Malinowski's concept of "current mythology," we can say that a cluster of such myths tends to accumulate around the personality of leading Indians in their lifetime, especially those connected with communal magic as in the case of the otherwise individually connected shaman of San Juan, and that this aids their transfer into the divine lists when they leave the world. Nothing in all this seems to conflict with pre-Columbian notions concerning the passage of certain people at death into divine realms.

The ritual of shamans, mainly concerned with what survives of the pagan cult, features throughout the area the same kind of elaborate politeness and consideration that is found in the ritualistic behavior of all Indian officials. In this case, however, the consideration is directed towards nature and the powers which own it. Surviving notions of four directions, sometimes involving a center in addition, notions concerning volcanoes or mountains bearing up the skies, an acute sense of the correct position of things reflected in the naming of series of objects and their citing in the prayers (Atiteco prayers follow fairly rigorously a directional pattern in citing natural features of landscape as well as church doors, pillars, crosses) ensure that no power which might conceivably influence the health of men and crops remains unattended. Objects of nature are of no significance

409

Fig. 14—QUEMADEROS FOR RITUAL OF THE BROKEN POTS, MOMOSTENANGO, TOTONICAPAN, GUATEMALA. (Photographed about 1938. Middle American Research Institute, Tulane University.)

unless they emit signals *(señas);* these are warnings of ownership. The *dueños* or owners bear their burdens much as human officials do. There are notions concerning the proper dosage of speech so that the dueño be not "molested," and great importance is placed on intermediaries and witnesses and watchers, thus leading to the justification of the shaman, as in the old Popol Vuh, as one "without whom the world would be all in silence." There are notions as to correct movement between one position and another *(viaje),* which are used to describe the movement of a saint from chapel to church, say, or the whole chapel to another head's house, as well as movements in the prayers from hill to hill and stream to stream, or the movements of angels in the skies opening the way for traders. Certain ritual acts appear to symbolize "viajes" such as the tying and untying of certain ribbons on saints' clothes during transfer ceremonies. The stylistic

trick of certain shamans—citing a basic name and then repeating it a number of times with other names attached—makes both for systematization in certain cases and for confusion in others, especially when the shaman is drunk. Guiteras Holmes' Chenalho material (1961, p. 307) brings out clearly why it is necessary to keep the Earth and other powers informed through prayer and ritual: everything that is meaningful to man has a soul, which must cooperate if one is to manipulate something for a desired result.

The cardinal notion in human affairs, parallel to that of positional ownership of aspects of nature (dueño), is that of fate or destiny (suerte). Man is thought of as "receiving" a suerte, much in the same way as a cofrade "receives" drinks or food or smokes. Almost all secondary characteristics or primary characteristics which have been relegated to the realm of creencias by Catholicism, such as the nagual a

410

man is born with or his specialization, depend ultimately on this basic destiny. So does a man's death: all the dead
whether good or bad people, if dying in a
certain, usually violent, manner, become
bad spirits. Hence comes the great emphasis on a calling or a "feeling for the job"
(sentido) in shamanistic ritual: however
much or little a man has to learn from other
shamans, he must have an inner strength of
purpose in reciting his prayers, without
which all knowledge is valueless. Hence too
comes a good deal of the laissez-faire and
tolerance of Indian society: a man's suerte
is not really his fault; one cannot dislike
him too much for being different to oneself.
J. E. S. Thompson (1954, p. 131) has analyzed Indian attitudes in a similar manner;
LaFarge and Byers (1931, p. 92) have
pointed out that the habit of delegating responsibility to various specialists has itself
helped to maintain elements of native ritual
alongside Catholic cults. More broadly, it
would appear that these notions are also
reflected in the general socio-economic out-
look of the area whereby the customs or
certain produce are thought of as the property of certain communities and are not
held or grown by members of other municipalities.

Summarizing the cyclical view of life
held by the traditionally oriented person,
we might say that the World, the *Santo
Mundo*, Nature in short, is owned in its
various manifestations by a host of spirits
which are, as in pre-Columbian times, one
in many and many in one, capable of being
good or bad but susceptible to human prayers, male and female or hermaphrodite,
scarcely dependent on time in that their
very antiquity is a guarantee of their efficacy in the present. These spirits are thought
of alternatively, or even simultaneously, as
a totality: Dios or Santo Mundo on the one
hand, and as parts of the totality on the
other; at any rate some kind of hierarchy
intervenes in any set of items.[10] All other
dueños are the servants (here angels fill in

Christo-paganism the role of subsidiary deities) and there is continual reciprocal activity between dueños and men's servants,
the shamans, with señas or miracles on the
one hand and prayers and offerings on the
other. The system is satisfactory as long as
this commerce continues to operate peacefully, as long as everything is in its proper
position, receives its due, speaks or is spoken to correctly. Men enter the world, serve
the dueños, carry out their servicios as
señas of this service, leave children behind
them to carry on the services and go out of
the world leaving it behind to their children as God left it to the first men. Strength
of personality and permanence of custom
are necessary in order to get through one's
allotted time, to escape the spirits when
they are angry, and to play one's part in the
upkeep of the world. This is all the more
necessary since catastrophes have been
known to happen: the world has died in
the past and presumably could die again.
For this reason no absolute certainty is
available to mankind: all observers will
have noticed the claim to ignorance about
the deepest reasons of life which the Indian will ritually make on a great number
of occasions.[11]

Writers on Mesoamerican religion can
usually be divided into those who, impressed by the omnipresence of formal to-
kens of Christianity or their impressiveness

---

[10] For an alternative, but not essentially unsimi-
lar, summary from an eastern Guatemalan point of
view, see Wisdom (1952, ch. 6), who lays emphasis on the economic aspect of payment to the
dueños (p. 126). This economic tone of ritual,
possibly more stressed in highland than lowland
context, is beautifully illustrated by Leslie in a
Mitla episode (1960a, p. 75).

[11] Compare D. E. Thompson's notion (1954,
p. 27) of the gods grouped in fours, such as the
Balams, being a way of dividing power to assure
a complete circle of magical protection for the
town.
Madsen (1957, p. 144) stresses the principle of
opposition between certain gods and, in the most
thorough study of "hot" and "cold" systems yet
made (1955b), relates this system to the *contrario*
principle, which is "older than God" in Tecospa.

Fɪɢ. 15—COFRADÍA ALTAR, SAN JUAN SACATEPEQUEZ, GUATE-
MALA. (Photographed by Matilda Gray, 1935. Middle American
Research Institute, Tulane University.)

for Indians (Gibson, 1955, p. 585), raise high the triumph of this religion, and the romanticists, as Wolf has recently called them (1959, p. 166), who are overwhelmed by the evidence of pre-Columbian survivals and speak of Mesoamerican religion as remaining predominantly Indian.

D. E. Thompson (1954) would appear to take the romanticist's view. He stresses the loss of face among Maya priests, leading to retention of pagan cults and revivalism, well analyzed here as in the Yucatec historical work of Roys, Scholes, Adams, and Tozzer. An interesting series of confusion factors is listed: Spanish crosses placed on pagan shrines and the stone piles of village exits; the coincidence of May 3 as the Day of the Cross and the date of after-sowing rains; features in architectural decoration leading to confusion of Chacs with angels as suggested by Pal Kelemen, Maya colors, directions, and four-fold symbolism compared to the Book of Revelations; the Virgin Mary painted as standing on a crescent moon; the sacrificial aspect of Christ selected rather than the youthful-god aspect in some parts while the young maize god is confused with the young Christ in others. Nativism attempted to create new Indian

gods and new Indian priesthoods on Ladino models while benefiting from similar confusions; such as talking crosses and pre-Columbian talking idols, Christ and sacrificial victims both going to heaven, crucifixion bleeding and sacrificial bleeding.[12]

We have not stressed in this article the importance of crosses in ritual but this is clearly brought out by D. E. Thompson (1954, pp. 23, 24), a whole chapter is devoted to it in LaFarge (1947, ch. 10), and Oakes takes the cross for her title at Todos Santos. In our subareas 1 and 2 the cross would seem to be an intermediary deity between native deities proper and Catholic

[12] Our Atiteco data suggest recent nativistic activity on the part of the rain priests 50–70 years ago and Maximón's role, as Judas, calls to mind Brinton's remark (1894, p. 36) that sodalities were dedicated to Christ's enemies out of hatred of the Church. The chief complaint of Atiteco shamans today is that "Maximón doesn't talk any more." Among the Chenalho (Guiteras Holmes, 1961, pp. 309, 317–18), as late as the Caste War of 1868–69, something akin to Wolf's "trauma of conquest" was considered responsible for the disappearance of many old customs. We surmise that similar recent disturbances account for much of the "death of the world" mythology in Santiago Atitlan.

Perhaps the most extraordinary attempt at nativistic revival today is D. H. Lawrence's The Plumed Serpent.

412

santos, linked to household worship with kinship-group associations. Nor have we treated the problem of images which, throughout the area, are mostly of the wooden Catholic type. Nevertheless other types still prevail. The Lacandon (G. Soustelle, 1959, p. 160) censers are called k'ur, which this author relates to the Yucatec word k'u (god) and the Spanish chroniclers' cu (temple of Yucatan or Mexico). In various parts stone idols are still used, such as the famous *Pascual Abaj* of Chichicastenango and a variety of small crosses, occasionally dressed in miniature Indian clothes. I have studied two "bundle" images in Atitlan (1958b, 1959). Among the Huichol, as reported by Zingg (in Doll, 1952, p. 62), certain votive bowls are associated with native priests.[13]

D. E. Thompson concludes that the form of worship remains Maya with power vested in individual images whose possession ensures their services and a cargador system which is pre-Columbian in origin. Vengeance by the santo when ignored or poorly served is not dissimilar to vengeance taken by pagan earth and weather gods. Catholic ritual is associated with towns and social life; pre-Columbian ritual centers on the milpa where techniques do not rapidly change and Ladinos and priests venture infrequently.[14] Thus, the more religious activities are centered in the town, the more likely native deities die out or find a niche for themselves in Catholic ritual; the more trade gains over the milpa cultivation, the less milpa deities can be said to matter.

Most observers, whether they lean more to Catholic or pagan supremacy, usually agree that it is in the field of ethics that the two religions differ most and had the greatest difficulty in adapting to each other (Madsen, 1957, p. 130). Broadly speaking, notions such as that of suerte tend to maintain the view that people are born good or bad and die good or bad deaths without their having much say in the matter. Catholicism, on the other hand, stresses the

individual's role in determining the manner of his death and the place he will achieve thereafter in the divine scheme of things.[15]

From the point of view of ethics and eschatology, the impact of Catholicism's theory of direct and unique divine intervention into history on Mesoamerican Indians does not conflict with Spain's temporal gift of Western notions of progress through gradual change as upheld by the present Mestizo population. To become a

[13] The whole question of idols is fully debated in Tozzer, 1941, pp. 111, 139.

[14] For D. E. Thompson (1954, p. 29), hunting deities have degenerated in subarea 1, perhaps because hunting was a privilege of the nobility. In Atitlan hunting is associated with the native deities of cofradía San Juan. Hunting is still of importance among the north Mexican tribes.

For a suggestion on the survival of rain gods in Mexico connected with their lack of need for sacrificial victims see Madsen (1957, p. 133).

[15] While in Atitlan, we confronted recent converts to the catequista movement, or Protestantism, with questions about the drowned: How could a good man become a bad spirit if he had served the God of Love well throughout his life? Responses to this kind of query require considerable mental agility on the part of informants.

In the articles previously cited, we have wondered, in examining sexual beliefs associated with Máximon, whether the fundamental Atiteco crisis in the coming together of the two religions did not occur when a theory of sin, brought about by disordered sexual relations and expiated by the consequent fertilization of Nature, clashed with another theory of sin, similarly incurred, but expiable only through a divinely inspired moral law at odds with any pagan theory of salvation through fertility (Mendelson, 1958b, p. 125). Curiously enough, while on this point, we found that those who were taking the most personalized view of conflict also took the most personalized view of sexual matters, looking for particular qualities of sexual attraction in individuals rather than general qualities of good character and willingness to labor.

Guiteras Holmes sees no break in continuity between the pagan view of the Earth as resenting man's presence, including his procreative functions, and the reinforcement brought to this view by Catholic teaching concerning sin. Her informant saw the Earth as both good and evil; his stress on the Earth's dangerous aspects was greater, however, than that of Atiteco informants (Guiteras Holmes, 1961, p. 308). One wonders whether other Chenalho people, not having suffered so many tribulations as Manuel, would have stressed quite so much the fearful aspects of the world around them.

Ladino and to become a better Catholic seem to be very much the same kind of thing, even in very secularized areas such as Michoacan, where the power of the Sinarquista movement has been noted by all students of things Tarascan. Becoming a better Catholic may mean the relinquishing of that total, if limited, picture of the world which is held by the traditionalist, without, until recent times at any rate, any very great positive gains. It also entails the progressive relegation into folklore of that which, in the traditional view, can still be qualified as living myth. The world to these people is still owned by dueños, as patron santos, but all these are servants to *Jesucristo* whose law is above all laws, whose path is better than other paths *(ley y camino)* and whose suerte was better than other suertes. Those who believe this will reject the idea of impartial service rendered to other dueños and will draw away from the stewards and shamans who serve them. They will enter the ranks of militant Catholic or Protestant organizations or political parties and attempt to acquire a broader view of life, one stretching beyond the boundaries of their municipality. For lack of education, their cosmology, biology, and medicine are the same as those of the opposing party but they consider the data as doubtful, open to conjecture, tainted by being held in common with idolaters and sorcerers. They try to reason about these data, contrasting, for instance, Biblical history with native views, and, as far as possible, attempt to readapt them to their new beliefs. But large areas of their thinking remain in suspension, unaided by the fact that rural Ladinos are often little more educated than the Indians themselves. They are convinced that new knowledge is available and valuable and patiently await its coming in a passive fashion.

Thus turning away from the traditional ritual and mythical system has involved some of these youths in organizations designed to "win support away from the folk organizations," as in the case of Catequistas; others or the same individuals have been brought to a view of community service as legal and voluntary rather than customary and morally obligatory. Carrasco (1952b, p. 35) has studied these trends in the Tarascan area while M. Nash (1958b), whose statements I quote here, has shown, taking the whole of Guatemala as his canvas, how the old politico-religious hierarchy insulated the Indian community from the wider world of the Nation and the Catholic Church. In the course of recent political revolutions, the nation has attempted to bypass the insulating group and to contact the Indian directly, involving him in the political party life of the new Republic and changing his notions of allegiance to the old principales. As far as religion is concerned, this process would appear to isolate the stewardship element from the political life of the community, relegating it in a sense to a position of passivity in regard to the communal life not too different from that of the shaman. In the process of Ladinoization, the cofradías may well become like the very secularized, voluntary groupings at present characteristic of the non-Indian populations of these municipalities and the shift of the locus of authority from native to conquest culture be finally consummated.

Technological change, together with the expansion of social contacts, will inevitably change Indian religion, and it is hard to disagree with D. E. Thompson's conclusion (1954, pp. 31–32) that costumbre will eventually be no more than a tourist attraction. At every turn in this article, we have come across Indian centripetal tendencies in ritual and myth: we might yet cite the tendency to relate by kinship the collection of saints inherited, more or less arbitrarily, from the friars, which probably parallels similar links in the pre-Columbian pantheons. How far these tendencies can win against progress depends, as Nash has put it, on the nature of the political group in charge and the extent to which the Indian is offered means of transcultural communication which do not insult his traditional view of life. As Nash rightly states, Guatemala—we can say here Middle America—"in microcosm exemplifies the political problems of the underdeveloped countries, still most of the world."

REFERENCES

Adams, R. N., 1952
Aguirre Beltrán, 1953
Borhegyi, 1956b
Brinton, 1894
Bunzel, 1952
Carrasco, 1952b
Cámara B., 1952c
Correa, 1955, 1958b
Doll, 1952
Foster, 1948a, 1953a, 1953b, 1960a
Fuentes y Guzmán, 1932–33
Gibson, 1955
Goubaud, 1952
Guiteras Holmes, 1961
Kurath, 1952
LaFarge, 1940, 1947
—— and Byers, 1931
Leach, 1954
Leslie, 1960a

Lumholtz, 1902
Madsen, 1955a, 1955b, 1957
Mendelson, 1956, 1958a, 1958b, 1959, 1965
Miles, 1952
Nash, M., 1957b, 1958b, 1960
Redfield, 1930, 1941
—— and Villa R., 1934
Siegel, 1941
Soustelle, G., 1959
Starr, B. W., 1952a
Stresser-Péan, 1952
Tax, 1952a, 1952b
Thompson, D. E., 1954
Thompson, J. E. S., 1930, 1950, 1954
Tozzer, 1941
Wisdom, 1952
Wolf, 1959
Zavala, 1945

415

21. Psychological Orientations

BENJAMIN N. COLBY

WHEN GILLIN (1952) described the ethos and cultural aspects of personality in Mesoamerica over a decade ago, he mentioned the paucity of data and the inadequacies of both theory and method. Adequate material for proper comparative work in the psychology of Indian culture is still not abundant. Most modern studies lack statistical or linguistic control and abound in subjective statements about "shy," "unimaginative," or "compulsive" natives. Validity and chance factors have not been controlled for in projective tests (Lindzey, 1961). "Blind" interpretations of Rorschach tests (according to criteria which are still debated among psychologists) have been combined with the anthropologist's account in a manner that only compounds the biases of the investigators' cultural background.

There are exceptions to the conditions deplored by Gillin in descriptive accounts reporting the informants' own words (Sahagún, 1950–66; Bunzel, 1952), in autobiographies (Sol Tax, 1950; Pozas, 1959c), in full context studies of specific psychological topics (Gillin, 1948; Paul, 1953), and in detailed comparative studies (Viqueira and Palerm, 1954). More recently high standards for descriptive validity have been set for linguistic control by Metzger and Williams (1963a). Questionnaires in the native language have been used to study attitudes and values (Colby, 1961b) and ethnic relations (van den Berghe and Colby, 1961). Francesca Cancian's detailed studies (1963) of family interaction have utilized psychologically oriented small-group theory. Laughlin (1962b) has penetrated to a new depth of understanding by participant observation in Zinacantan. Using a team approach, Vogt (1961, 1964a, 1964b) has made a variety of investigations in Zinacantecan culture, with emphasis on the use of key native terms.

Further work in Mesoamerican psychology requires a quality of data that is forthcoming only with good rapport, participant observation, understanding of the native language, and detailed information from many individuals. Information of this quality is possible only after years of living in a single community. My own fieldwork, on which much of this article is based, was done during eleven months with Zinacantecans in Chiapas.[1] Much more fieldwork is needed. The analyses and often speculative generalizations given here are prolegomena to further study and tests of validation in the field.

The psychological elements Gillin wrote about in 1952 are more useful for present-day Indian-Mestizo contrasts than for comparing one Indian culture with another; and as is to be expected in a generalized account, if any single culture be taken as a test case, a number of Gillin's elements either will not apply or will evoke questions that turn on frequency, intensity, or terminology. Nevertheless, Gillin provides a helpful checklist of characteristics, which I have classified for the purposes of this article:

A. In natural and supernatural relationships, the individual
   1. Seeks peaceful adjustment to the universe.
   2. Is abjectively submissive to natural and supernatural forces.
   3. Looks on work as an important value.
   4. Is incurious toward the world beyond the local geographical area.
   5. Lives for the present moment rather than for the past or future, yet is past-oriented in the sense of maintaining traditional ways.
   6. Is concerned about the soul in this life rather than in the hereafter.
   7. Extends religious concern to all spheres of life.

B. In social relationships, the individual
   8. Participates in religious activities in groups.
   9. Does not give orders to his fellows.
   10. Joins in group consensus for decisions.
   11. Is not ranked or stratified into classes.
   12. Counts less than the group.

[1] I am indebted to Evon Z. Vogt and the National Institute of Mental Health for participation in Project M-2100.

13. Is considered equally by the opposite sex.
14. Bickers little with his spouse.
15. Trains children permissively.
16. Is adjustive and permissive in social relations which nevertheless are accompanied by anxiety.
17. Is emotionally restrained.
18. Fears witchcraft.
19. Respects age.

Most of these characteristics will be discussed below, but not all of them are supported. Because the published data on the psychology of Mesoamerican cultures are sparse, this article will be concerned mostly with modern Zinacantecan culture and with the 16th-century Maya and Aztec cultures observed by Landa and Sahagún.

Two of these three cultures, Zinacantan and 16th-century Aztec, will serve for sketching a general "areal" pattern of psychological orientations. The scattered evidence in the ethnographies of Mesoamerican cultures suggests that the pattern is widespread enough to be called an areal pattern, but the examples here are taken from the two cultures mentioned, whose features are either well documented or were observed in the field. Other cultures will be cited where they offer relevant data. At the center of the pattern is a pessimistic world view; related to it are (1) concern about the alternate inhibition and expression of assertive behavior and (2) concern with social distance and social power.

In addition to this areal pattern of psychological orientations are two secondary variations, one concerning the relations between the sexes and the other concerning orientations toward group and self. Relations between the sexes differ for Nahuatl and Maya groups. Separation of the sexes characterizes the Maya cultures, particularly in the lowlands and in the Tzotzil-Tzeltal region; a (relatively) more relaxed and equalitarian relationship exists in the Nahuatl groups. Orientations toward group and self distinguish early and late Meso-american cultures. Nahuatl and Maya group-supportive orientations of the 16th century focused on restraining inappropriate expressions of self-assertion that might have led to social discord. They stressed a harmonious social order. Self-protective cultures of the 20th century center on the protection of the psychological integrity of the individual; situations are sought where the behavior of others toward the self is predictable and least menacing. With greater acculturation and a symbiotic relationship between Indian and national societies the self-protective orientation has become dominant since the time of the conquest. The areal pattern linking cultures at both periods embraces both the self-protective and group-supportive orientations.

AREAL PATTERN

The basic Mesoamerican pattern of psychological orientations includes a concern with the handling of assertive behavior, a preoccupation with social power, a pessimistic world view, a focus on male sibling relations, and "looking behavior."

Assertive behavior was a characteristic of a good Aztec warrior. According to Sahagún (bk. 4, pp. 38–39), it was particularly favorable for a warrior to be born or baptized on the day Ten Eagle:

It was a time of manliness, valor, grandeur, and bravery. It was a day sign of strength and courage. [Such a warrior] urged people on; he was spirited toward others; he instilled courage and valor; he was fearless of death. He hurled himself against the foe; he joined in the fray; he shook others off scornfully, drove them into corners, broke into enemy ranks, took after those who fled, threw himself upon them, was most intent upon the foe, and aroused complete terror. No one would give him occasion to quarrel; no one would dare him nor contain him, nor surround him, nor ridicule him. He would then seize one, grip him firmly, and rise up against and burst forth upon him.

This was because so was the day sign of the valiant, courageous, great warrior.

The bold aggressiveness prescribed for the Aztec can be shown through an apparition called the night ax, a headless man with a deep incision in the chest and abdomen which opened and shut with the sound of an ax sinking into a log. If he who witnessed such an apparition were not strong in spirit and fled in terror, he could call down upon himself sickness, slavery, sin, or death. If he were brave and assertive, however, he would plunge his hand into the chest incision, seize the heart, and demand such rewards as happiness, contentment, and material goods like flowers, tobacco, capes, lip pendants, and headbands (Sahagún, bk. 5, p. 158).

In a society that is expanding by warfare assertive behavior has its utility, but it may be difficult to encourage such behavior at one moment when it is needed and prevent it at another when inappropriate. To judge from the frequent mention of discord, confusion, and agitation in the Aztec literature, the channeling of assertiveness to avoid these conditions requires continual vigilance. Maintaining the social order is thus a conscious effort. Social harmony is never to be taken for granted but constantly sought in the regulation of day-to-day assertiveness and socially disruptive behavior considered basic in human nature.

In modern Zinacantecan society where warfare does not exist, there are very few occasions where assertive behavior is sanctioned. The clearest one is when a suitor and his party force entry into the house of his chosen bride and ask permission to court her (Fishburne, 1962). Otherwise, assertive behavior is present, in the Zinacantecan view, more as a potentiality or threat than as an actuality.

In Aztec life assertive tendencies appear in a socially controlled form as competition for wealth and status. This struggle for social power is a leitmotiv of Aztec thought.

Sahagún makes repeated references to surpassing and overcoming others and, conversely, to a fear of losing stature, of being inferior, of having to become a servant or someone else's "digging stick and tumpline."

All persons wished that they be given recognition, fame, and distinction; that they might not, on the contrary, be shamed, receive blame, be embarrassed, confused, belittled, confounded, or excluded from others. Each and every one therefore made him resplendent and admirable, each one separately proceeding with exclusive and undivided attention to feasting. They exalted and raised themselves; they surpassed and much exceeded themselves. There was vying and competition [Sahagún, bk. 4, p. 22].

The same desire for social prestige and power is one of the motivations for entering the *cargo* system of religious offices in Mesoamerica today, although now the situation is more complex because of conflict between ideals of equality and motivations toward social power. This complex relationship will be discussed in the section "Self-protective Orientation."

Tendencies toward self-assertion do not necessarily imply aggression. When channeled into economic and social competition or controlled in other ways, one cannot properly refer to self-assertion as aggression or hostility. But when assertion occurs as overt aggression, the questions of context, frequency, and intensity relative to other societies should be noted in an ethnographic study. This kind of detail has been lacking in accounts so far. Certainly none of the contemporary Mesoamerican societies live in the state of sustained high tension suggested in some ethnographies. People in many of these societies exhibit a keen sense of humor in everyday situations and maintain pleasant, harmonious relationships with each other. Zinacantecans show relaxed behavior most of the time. They are a witty lot and are particularly adept at puns, often ribald. Without some kind of quantitative measurement of aggression in specified contexts comparative studies of aggressive behavior have little utility.

Actual aggressive behavior, however, is not part of the areal pattern being discussed here. It is rather the native *view* of such behavior that is important. There is no doubt that in both modern and ancient societies in Mesoamerica, the view of human nature is pessimistic. Human (and supernatural) nature is seen as being self-interested, assertive, potentially evil, and not always to be trusted. There are certainly periods in the lives of a significant number of Zinacantecans and other Indians when anxiety and tension arise from witchcraft fears, as well as from the unpredictability and lack of control in other social relations. In Zinacantecan folk tales, ". . . personal relations, whether between man and god, between stranger and Zinacanteco, among fellow townsmen or between family members are shaded with distrust" (Laughlin, 1962a, p. 26).

Distrust and general pessimism appear in variations on a theme of orality. While feasting and drinking occupy a central and pleasurable part of ceremony and ritual, the oral imagery in the folk tales and folk beliefs reveals something more sinister. Zinacantecans believe that to dream of eating fruits and other foods will lead to sickness or death. They have beliefs about people or their souls being "eaten." The same expressions occur among the Tzutuhil (Paul, 1950b, p. 206), Chorti (Wisdom, 1940, p. 406), and Tepoztlan Nahuatl (Lewis, 1951, p. 377). Laughlin (1962a) has found cannibalistic themes in the folk tales of the Kekchi, Mixe, Mixtec, Tzotzil, and Popoluca. Among the Popoluca, "all unknown beings and individuals presumably are dangerous because of anthropophagous tendencies" (Foster, 1944, p. 243). The widespread belief among preconquest cultures of a cannibalistic sun god having to eat the hearts and blood of human victims for his existence is another variation of the theme.

Distrust is undoubtedly one of the reasons for the extensive proliferation of complex etiquette in both early and modern Mesoamerican Indian cultures. Etiquette brings in a certain amount of social control in situations where trust must be established. Etiquette reduces anxiety in situations of social difficulty because it structures the behavior of all concerned in a predictable way. Procedures for special requests, formal salutations, religious activities, settlement of disputes, and marriages are prescribed; here uncertainty and (one would presume) anxiety are greatest. Elaborate etiquette is followed in many Mesoamerican societies. Salutational etiquette lasts half an hour or longer in Chichicastenango (Bunzel, 1952, p. 95) and similar practices obtain among the Mixe (W. S. Miller, 1956, p. 199), Ixil (Colby, 1963), and Lacandon (Tozzer, 1907) as well as in the Tzotzil and Tzeltal cultures.

Why is it that etiquette and relationships of trust are so important or, conversely, why is it that concern over the lack of trust seems to underlie so much of Mesoamerican thought and action? Perhaps such patterns of behavior have their roots in childhood and in the socialization process. The simultaneous existence of a strong preoccupation with eating, drinking, and the mouth on the one hand and a concern about trust on the other supports Erikson's theory (1950) that unresolved problems arising during the early period of infancy (when the child's chief sensory stimulation is through the mouth) carry through into adult life in the form of distrust. It may be no accident that the principal means of handling trust in situations of formal etiquette is oral, i.e., feasting and drinking. In Zinacantan, bottles of *poš*, the local cane alcohol, are used to authenticate an agreement and bind the parties to it.

Information on this early, oral period of infancy in Mesoamerica does not exist in sufficient detail to test Erikson's theory. Available data suggest that some characteristics, such as weaning time, are similar in a large number of cultures. Weaning seems to occur on the arrival of a younger sibling in practically all the Mesoamerican cultures. The average is about two years or slightly earlier for all but the only child or the last child, where weaning may be as late as from three to five years. We have information on weaning for the Chorti, Cora, Ixil, Kanhobal, Mam, Mixe, Mixtec, Ocuiltec, Tarascan, Tepoztlan Nahuatl, Totonac, Tzeltal, Tzotzil, Yucatec, and others, but except for a study of Mixtecan socialization (Romney and Romney, 1963) and a detailed impressionistic monograph on Tepoztlan (Lewis, 1951), very little has been reported about child-rearing practices in detail. For instance, we know little about the kind and amount of attention a child receives directly after weaning. The early literature offers some help, however, on socialization. In describing the Mendoza manuscript, Humboldt (1814, pp. 182–83) mentions the Aztec life cycle: "At five years of age the boy carries loads, and the girl attends her mother spinning. . . . At eight years of age the instruments of punishment are shown to disobedient and idle children, and they are threatened; but it is not till they have attained ten years of age that they are actually punished." Sahagún gives most data on early socialization for the 16th century.

Another characteristic, widespread in Mesoamerica, that relates to weaning practices is the importance given to the male sibling relationship. If weaning occurs at the birth of a younger sibling, one might expect a certain amount of sibling rivalry,[2] a subject mentioned in a number of studies. Young Tepoztecan children can suffer from *chipilez* or jealousy, a childhood illness

[2] The new child may not always completely replace the older child, however. Viqueira and Palerm (1954) report instances where an older child shares the breast with a recently born sibling.

which begins when the child's mother again becomes pregnant. According to Lewis (1951, p. 377), the word comes from the Nahuatl *tzipitl*, meaning the last or smallest child. The Nahuatl term may be the source of the Maya *ch'ip* with the same meaning. The Zinacantecan word is *pečal*. The most complete documentation of early sibling rivalry is for San Pedro la Laguna (Paul, 1950b). Bushnell (1958, p. 263) reports sibling rivalry among the Ocuiltec Otomi; Bunzel (1952, p. 105), among adult Quiches in land disputes. I have witnessed a formal attempt to end a quarrel between two Zinacantecan brothers, the younger having failed in his obligations to assist the older, who was making bride-payments. The use of a go-between and a highly formal etiquette was necessary (Colby, 1960). Laughlin (field notes) reports that one Zinacantecan bit off his brother's nose in a drunken fight, a rather gruesome form of oral aggression between siblings. In spite of the intensity of some Zinacantecan sibling rivalry, however, the relationship between most brothers is one of trust and mutual help that can be relied upon when one has the duties of a *cargo* position (Frank Cancian, 1965, p. 172) or is making bride-payments. It is rather the *potentiality* of male sibling conflict which seems to preoccupy Mesoamerican Indians.

The older-younger brother distinction in Zinacantan is extended to older and younger brother *cargo* offices and to older and younger brother curers. Even in religious beliefs a single Christ child is replaced by two—an older and a younger brother (Laughlin, 1962a). The kin term distinction of older and younger brothers is probably proto-Mayan. The psychological importance of the distinction goes back at least to the 16th century among the Quiche, as portrayed in the *Popol Vuh* epic, where the principal protagonists are two younger brothers who change their older brothers into monkeys, an example of close cooperation and trust between two younger

brothers who show intense rivalry and aggression towards their older brothers. A similar version was found in a Kanhobal town (LaFarge, 1947, p. 50).

The mistrust and ambivalence that accompany some social behavior underly the activities designed to maintain distance between people interacting with one another. One form of such social disengagement can be observed in different kinds of "looking behavior." The way in which one person looked at another in 16th-century Aztec society could carry paralinguistic messages. In some contexts it is permissible, even desirable, that a person look directly at another, but at other times this is considered disrespectful. Of an Aztec ruler it was said "none might look up at him; none might come face to face with him" (Sahagún, bk. 3, p. 29). In 16th-century Quiche culture looking directly at a respected person was to be avoided. Conversely, one can infer from the *Popol Vuh* that to look directly into a stranger's face and call him by name is to exert dominance over him. In the *Popol Vuh* the defeat of the underworld gods at the hands of Xbalanque and Hunahpu begins when the gods inadvertently make themselves known to their adversary: "they showed their faces."

León-Portilla (1956, p. 189) speaks of the Aztec expression, "to take a face," which refers to the process of maturation and education. The synonymity of gaining a face with gaining social status occurs throughout Aztec literature. When an Aztec youth took his first captive, his face was said to have been washed by the sun god and the youth took "another face" (Sahagún, bk. 8, p. 75).

This imagery has persisted in modern Mesoamerican cultures. In Zinacantan Tzotzil the face and eyes are subsumed under the single word *sat*. This and another word *-b'a*, meaning forehead or crown, also represent a kind of self-concept. In Zoque the words for face, eyes, and self are all related. The word *win* means face and self,

421

and can be possessed by pronouns to mean myself, etc. The word *wit∧m* means eye, which W. L. Wonderly (personal communication) analyzes as deriving from *win* plus *t∧m,* which means seed. Similar semantic extension may lie behind the contemporary Quiche expression in Chichicastenango that when a youth reaches maturity his "eyes have been opened" (Bunzel, 1952, p. 96). The same expression in Tepoztlan refers to mature knowledge of sexual matters (Lewis, 1951, p. 291).

In Zinacantan the direct look of another person can be an invasion of privacy or a sign of affection, depending on the context. When relative strangers come together in conversation they are sometimes careful not to look at each other while speaking. Direct exchange of looks is particularly avoided between an unrelated man and woman who would not normally speak to each other but where the circumstances require it. On the other hand, I have observed what might be called "face tilting" between young Zinacantecan men at fiestas where two inebriated men will hold hands and stand facing each other very closely with the head moving sideways, first in one direction, then in the other.

The way in which the face and eyes are connected metaphorically with the concept of self-identity has many ramifications in Mesoamerica and has probably been reinforced and altered substantially by the Spanish belief in *ojo.* The Chorti represent such a case where, Wisdom states (1940, p. 314), "Individuals who are said to have 'strong blood' can, when emotionally agitated, cause fright in others who are susceptible by looking at them or coming near them." In describing magical fright Gillin (1948) mentions the Spanish belief; La Farge (1947, pp. 150–51) refers to "intensified attention" among Kanhobal Indians dealing with hostile people who are thinking about them and looking at them.

But concern with looking has much deeper roots than do the beliefs brought over by the Spaniards. The process of looking is intimately tied up with patterns of confession, curing, and praying. Only gods, priests, curers, or other specialists have the power of "looking" into a person's soul and "seeing" his sin. LaFarge (1947, p. 157) mentions a Kanhobal belief in the *ilum k'inal,* "watcher of time," who had a highly developed power of looking. This power was for the benevolent purpose of caring for the community's welfare. The seeing powers of an *ilum k'inal* had a protective influence over the people during travel and wartime. A related belief exists among the nearby Jacaltec Maya. In Zinacantan the name for a curer, *h?ilol,* can be translated literally as a seer, whose functions include praying to the gods who sometimes must be pleased with what they see about a person before being favorably disposed towards him. The major curing ceremony in Zinacantan is called the *muk'ta?ilel* or "great seeing."

The intimate connection between a person's feeling of self-identity and his face and eyes undoubtedly influences interpersonal disengagement brought into play between two Zinacantecans who converse together but who are not close friends. They keep a good distance between them and avoid eye-to-eye encounter. Unless they are drinking together, Zinacantecans often lessen the intensity of conversation with distracting activities, such as weaving hats (materials for which the men always have with them during crowded political meetings and on other informal occasions) or pulling off bark from a tree, or picking mud from the side of a house. This provides a distraction and displaces nervous energy which might otherwise intensify face-to-face interaction to the point of discomfort (Colby, 1959; Susan Tax, 1964).

The disengagement procedures used by the Indians towards anthropologists may give the false impression that their reserve and inhibition is a pervading psychological trait. Lewis speaks of "facial control" as one indication of the Tepoztecans' restrained behavior. Similar ethnographic statements have been made for other peoples, but usually do not specify the context. Lumholtz (1907, p. 300) specifies that the Tarahumara did not consider it polite even to look at another man's house. Until the context and meaning of these interpersonal characteristics are mapped out, however, there is little value in blanket statements about undemonstrative or unemotional Indians. Nothing is more moving, in fact, than the outpouring of emotions and tears at a curing ceremony, to name only one of many occasions of emotional display in Zinacantan.

RELATIONS BETWEEN THE SEXES

Below the areal pattern just discussed lies a pair of subpatterns affecting the relation between the sexes that differs for Nahuatl and Maya regions. The two Maya cultures, 16th-century Yucatecan and 20th-century Zinacantecan, maintain more separation between the sexes than do 16th- and 20th-century Nahuatl cultures. Though Nahuatl women usually have lower status than men, they can sometimes achieve a dominating economic position (Zantwijk, 1960, p. 30) and in other ways be held in equal esteem with men (Sahagún, bk. 4, pp. 10, 79). This is less so in Zinacantan, where women must always walk behind men or sit on the floor instead of on chairs as men do. A similarly low position is reported by Landa (1941, p. 127) for the Yucatec Maya, where women were required to step aside and turn their backs to let men pass. The two Maya groups also keep the sexes separate at mealtimes, and seldom, if ever, is there mixed dancing (*ibid.*, pp. 94, 391).[3]

The greater separation between the sexes among the Yucatecans is probably related to the belief that women were ceremonially unclean and that their blood as sacrifice was not acceptable to the gods (*ibid.*, p. 128), in contrast to the Aztec belief that a woman's blood *was* acceptable (Sahagún, bk. 4, p. 25). Though virgins were somewhat less dangerous in connection with religious activities than other Yucatecan women and were the only females allowed to prepare food for the priest (Landa, 1941, p. 106), the presence of any women, even virgins, was enough to destroy the purity and utility of sacrificial water (*ibid.*, p. 596).

Fears about the consequences of sexual relations are reflected in sex taboos. The three-year office of war captain, or nacom, in Yucatan, required sexual continence during the entire period. Continence was common in both lowland and highland Maya cultures and still exists in some of the remote groups in Guatemala and British Honduras.

In a general account of the character structure of Guatemalan (Maya) Indians, Goubaud Carrera (1948) mentions a strict enforcement of the separation of boys and girls in household activities and games. Each sex is taught that the other is dangerous. Boys are taught that woman has great power over man. Laughlin (1962a, p. 98) speaks of an underlying current of sexual anxiety which reaches its peak during Zinacantecan marriage ceremonies. The familiar Mesoamerican tales of spouses who turn out to be witches or potentially malevolent beings imply fear of the female sex.[4] Evidence suggests that some kind of anxiety underlies the relations between the sexes, particularly in the Maya groups. Recent developments in the psychology of sex

[3] Quiche and Cakchiquel Indians in Guatemala appear to have greater equality of the sexes than do the lowland Maya or those in the Tzeltal-Tzotzil region.

[4] The emotions of sex, aggression, and fear may be interrelated in many complex ways, one of which is suggested in Tzotzil and Tzeltal folktales where display of the genitals has a magical subduing power over aggressive supernaturals.

identity show that new theories and methods could be brought to bear in analyzing relations between the sexes in Mesoamerica, but so far the necessary data on socialization have not been recorded.

Two Orientations

Another pair of subpatterns that may have theoretical value distinguishes conquest-period and present-day Mesoamerican cultures. The conquest cultures were more oriented toward group-supportive characteristics than are contemporary cultures where the emphasis is self-protective. Group-supportive cultures, placing priority on social order and harmony, are exemplified by both Maya and Aztec cultures of the 16th century and, in very attenuated form today, by the Tajin Totonac and a few groups in western Guatemala. Self-protective cultures minimize subordination of self-interests to those of the group and have special beliefs about multiple souls and soul vulnerability. These beliefs reflect uncertainty about the individual's integrity, his self-identity, and his ability to cope with the world. They are mitigated, however, by cultural "devices" that bolster and protect the individual's conception of himself. Contemporary self-protective cultures include Catemaco Nahuatl, Chinantec, Chontal (Tabasco), Chorti, Huave, Kanhobal, Mam, Mazatec, Mixe, Mixtec, Popoluca (Veracruz), Tarahumara, Tecospa, Eloxochitlan Totonac, Tepoztlan Nahuatl, Tojolabal, Tzeltal, Tzotzil, and Zapotec.

A distinguishing feature of group-supportive orientation is the placing of blame for sickness or other misfortune on oneself rather than on others. Where confession or penance is more often used to cure sickness than is counterwitchcraft, self-interests will be subordinated to those of the social order. In self-protective societies, on the other hand, witchcraft is more often held accountable for illness. Witchcraft beliefs signify a loss of psychological control; the victim views himself as having lost the initiative to the witch until countermeasures are taken. Controlling the behavior of others is therefore more emphasized than controlling one's own behavior.

Another contrast lies in the way talking is regarded by the two types of culture. In group-supportive cultures proper speech is conceived as maintaining social harmony and order whereas improper speech can bring social chaos. In self-protective societies correct conversation requires a suitable distance between individuals; persuasive talking can bend others to the will of the talker.

The ideal of equality in relation to deference towards respected individuals is another criterion for distinguishing the two orientations. Group-supportive cultures minimize equalitarianism. Etiquette operates in a framework of prestige or social class differences (either ascribed or achieved). The cohesion of the social order in group-supportive cultures depends on these differences. Today fewer elements of the etiquette systems are based on prestige or social class, though vestiges still remain among the Ixil, Kanhobal, and perhaps some of the other less acculturated societies.

Self-protective societies emphasize to a greater degree the maintenance of personal integrity and self-respect regardless of social position. Such respect for the individual implies a certain equalitarianism, at least in the explicitly stated ideals of the culture, even though actual behavior sometimes belies it. In cultures with equalitarian ideals, etiquette is more likely to be based on power-empty hierarchies (such as age-respect hierarchies), which do not reflect social prestige or social power beyond that which comes with age to all people. Age-respect patterns of this type exist among the Chinantec, Chol, Chontal (Tabasco), Huave, Mixe, Quiche, Tzeltal, Tzotzil, and probably many others.

In summary, group-supportive cultures are concerned with protecting the social order; self-protective cultures, with the

424

image of the self.[5] In the former the maintenance of status hierarchies predominates, and fears center around the threat of social discord. In the latter the ideal of equality prevails, and fears focus on soul-loss or soul-damage. Group-supportive cultures are inward-projecting, with emphasis on self-control and on subordinating certain interests of the self to those of the group; self-protective cultures are outward-projecting with a self-interested emphasis on maintaining control over others. These characteristics are analyzed below in detail for three cultures: 16th-century Aztec, 16th-century Yucatan, and 20th-century Zinacantan.

Group-supportive Orientation

At the time of the conquest social rank in most of the Mesoamerican cultures was recognized by a person's place in processions or his position at ceremonial feasts, as well as by deference and the acknowledgment of prestige differences in other behavior. Landa (1941, p. 97) describes the way rank was recognized in Yucatan:

The Indians in making visits always take with them a present to give, according to their rank; and the person visited gives another gift in return. During these visits third parties speak and listen with attention, according to the rank of the persons with whom they are speaking, notwithstanding that all call each other "thou";

[5] In a personal communication William Wonderly has raised the question of whether a correlation between group-supportive societies and cultural vitality might exist. This would be an interesting and rewarding line of investigation in spite of the great difficulties in specifying operational criteria for cultural vitality. To speculate further, there may be a link between prolonged absence of the father (and hence of a father image for young boys to model themselves after) and greater concern about the self-image. (See Burton and Whiting, 1961, and D'Andrade, 1962, for one type of identity conflict arising from father absence during childhood.) Father absence increased when Indians no longer tilled their own lands but had to work for Spaniards and Mestizos at a distance from home. This might be one of many possible factors influencing the shift in orientation.

for in the course of conversation, the more humble is wont to repeat with great care the title of office or of dignity of him of highest rank. . . . The women are brief in their conversations, and were not accustomed to do any business for themselves, especially if they were poor; and on account of this the nobles laughed at the friars because they gave ear to the poor and the rich without distinction.

Differences in prestige and rank ordering at table are also described by Sahagún's Aztecan informants (bk. 4, p. 118): "The wine server, the server, first began; so he went to the one of highest rank, the first in rank, the one in first place. So he went in order, going in line, and so were left those of lesser rank, of inferior station, in last place."

Harmony in social relations depended on recognition of prestige in the 16th-century group-supportive cultures, and in the folk psychology of the time talking etiquette was the principal means of maintaining such harmony. Improper talking was greatly feared because of possible discord or anger (*ibid.*, p. 20): "But if in something he offended someone, sometimes letting slip an evil word, so misstating what he repeated in haste without reflection, he himself made it good so that the humiliation was not noticed. So he corrected and made good his words. Thus there was no anger."

Improper talking was one of the worst sins of the evil man in Aztec folk ethics. Such an Aztec "sinner" demonstrates the close linkage between bad talking and social discord (*ibid.*, p. 30):

Only and exclusively immersed in and dedicated to evil was the one then born. He was given only to talking; he went wrapped in discussion. Words were his hair. He was hot-tempered. He twisted words. Great was his glee if somewhere there was a shout; there he ran and listened to what was said. If somewhere there was discussion and something was said, he went among the people sowing discord; he went causing disagreements and dissension; he confounded and disunited them.

425

In addition to proper talking, social harmony was maintained by directing aggressive tendencies inward on the self, particularly in the practice of penance. The pre-Hispanic group-supportive cultures believed that only through denial and suffering would the much-sought-for goals of tranquility and social authority become reality. The belief is explicit in the counsel given to Aztec youths:

Remember one thing: go knowing, devoted, and dedicated to suffering. Perhaps he by whom we live will give thee something as thy deserts and merit [*ibid.*, p. 63].

If thou wouldst gain honor by such as this, O my son, be not shameless; do not faint; be not womanish. Give thyself completely to the torment; enter into it; deliver thyself to it with all thy force, so preparing for it, etc. For verily thou seekest and travelest into such places as thy elders, the old men, served. For they thus hurled themselves at and delivered to torment, and exposed themselves to danger and adversity. For not without reason did the merchants take and find leadership and the wisdom of old age, become leaders, and receive their authority in exchange [*ibid.*, p. 62].

Bloodletting was the most frequent kind of "torment" for the Aztec (*ibid.*, pp. 5, 25, and *passim*), Yucatec, and probably most of the other Mesoamerican cultures. It is difficult to imagine a more masochistic set of practices than these described by Landa (1941, pp. 113–14) for the Yucatecs:

Bleeding and penitence were other characteristics. They offered sacrifices of their own blood, sometimes cutting themselves around in pieces and they left them in this way as a sign. Other times they pierced their cheeks, at others their lower lips. Sometimes they scarify certain parts of their bodies, at others they pierced their tongues in a slanting direction from side to side and passed bits of straw through the holes with horrible suffering; others slit the superfluous part of the virile member leaving it as they did their ears, on account of which the general historian of the Indies was deceived saying that they practiced circumcision. At other times they

performed an obscene and painful sacrifice, those who were to make it gathered in the temple whereafter they were placed in a row. Holes were made in the virile member of each one obliquely from side to side and through the holes which they had thus made, they passed the greatest quantity of thread that they could, and all of them being thus fastened and strung together, they anointed the idol with the blood which flowed from all these parts; and he who did this the most was considered as the bravest; and their sons from the earliest age began to practice it, and it is a horrible thing to see how inclined they were to this ceremony.

Abstinence and bloodletting were preventive actions. Their proper observance kept the good will of the gods so that illness would not be sent as punishment. However, after sickness occurred, one of its cures was public confession (Landa, 1941, p. 491):

The Yucatecans naturally knew the wrongs which they did, and since they believed that death, sickness and affliction came to them for their wrong-doing and their sin, they had a custom of confessing themselves, when they were already suffering from them. This was the way that they did it. When, on account of a sickness or something else, they were in danger of dying, they confessed their sin(s); and if they were neglectful, their nearest relations or their friends reminded them of it. And thus they publicly confessed their sins to the priest, if he were present, or otherwise to their fathers and mothers; wives to their husbands, and husbands to their wives. The sins of which they most commonly accused themselves were theft, homicide, the weaknesses of the flesh and false witness.

Like penance, confession is another means of accepting responsibility for illness and misfortune where the blame is directed inward. In confession self-interests are subordinated to those of social harmony.

Confession, therefore, is one of the criteria for the group-supportive orientation. It is still practiced in the less acculturated areas today, including groups of Ixil-,

Kanhobal-, Mam-, Quiche-, and Tzeltal-speakers, though none of these cultures have a primarily group-supportive emphasis, with the possible exception of the Ixil. What might be called a borderline case is suggested in beliefs about illness for the Mixtec of Juxtlahuaca. There the prevention of illness is related to the control of aggressive impulses (Romney and Romney, 1963, p. 615); the blame for illness is rarely directed toward other people as in witchcraft accusations (p. 611).

Self-protective Orientation

In order to cope adequately with the world the individual must know the potentialities and limitations of his own abilities. Such knowledge constitutes part of a general self-concept that provides an anchor point for all plans and activities. Another aspect of the self-concept consists of percepts regarding the individual's body and its periphery. These percepts make up a body-boundary image which is sometimes soft and permeable, sometimes hard and strong. In our own folk psychology the word "thick-skinned" describes strong body-boundary attributes.

The main feature of Mesoamerican self-concepts is a very weak body-boundary image. This is of two kinds: the belief that impulses emanating from within the body (e.g., inner rage or sexual passion) can be contained or controlled only with difficulty, and the belief that defense against threats coming toward or into the body from the outside (e.g., witchcraft or the magical intrusion of destructive objects) is inadequate. Twentieth-century self-protective cultures emphasize the second belief.

Lack of precise information hinders the exact study of Mesoamerican self-concepts, including body-boundary images, but much can be learned indirectly from beliefs about the soul. Insecurity and anxiety are evident from belief in multiple souls and from widespread fear about soul-loss or soul-damage. A Zinacantecan has two main types of

soul. The first (*č'ulel*) is composed of 13 parts. If some of these parts become separated from a person, he will grow weak, get sick, or die. The second kind of soul (*čanul*) has an animal form. A person's *čanul* is kept in a corral inside a nearby mountain. If the gods in charge of the *čanuls* (Tzotzil plural, *čanuletik*) should become displeased with the behavior of any Zinacantecan, they will release his *čanul* to wander in the surrounding countryside. Any hunter may shoot the *čanul*, which then causes the death of its owner unless he is fortunate enough to have one or two *čanuls* in reserve.

One animal soul can be more powerful than another, depending on the kind of animal it is. In Zinacantan a person is not always sure about the strength or sometimes even the identity of his animal soul; nor is he certain whether his *č'ulel* is intact. It is the apparent association of social power and prestige with the power of one's soul, together with the uncertainty, that makes this an area of concern, particularly in matters of witchcraft.

If he does know what kind of animal his *čanul* is, it is still difficult for an individual to find out where he stands in a power relationship with others. At best he can be certain that another person is not more powerful than he and the curer (or *hʔilol*) representing him only if he has access to the maximum soul-power possible (three jaguars, according to one Zinacantecan informant). Even so, the health and effectiveness of the animal souls, no matter of what species, depend on the will of the gods, which may change at any time.

Though it is an assumption requiring validation by complex psychological tests, my inference from the data so far available runs as follows: The implicit Zinacantecan belief is that a person's general effectiveness in coping with his social milieu is determined by the state and power of his soul. If a man has a temporarily weakened soul, he may consequently suffer from poor health. But, more significant, if his *čanul* is an inherently weak animal (a rabbit, for example), his lesser abilities earn him a lesser prestige position that carries through his entire life. Social prestige therefore indirectly indicates one's soul-power. In a curious kind of reverse logic, members of the society actively (though implicitly) seek prestige-enhancing roles as proof to themselves and others that they have a powerful animal soul.

Soul-power and social power are so closely interrelated that the voluntary relinquishing of social power to someone else in an act of obedience would indirectly acknowledge inferior soul-power. Therefore, in situations of potential power conflict, where one person does the bidding of another, various ways of disguising the power difference implied in such action are employed by the person in command.[6] In such situations there thus exists a fiction of persuasion. Though individual Y will obviously obey individual X's order, both X and Y behave as though Y must be persuaded by X to carry it out. If Y does the bidding of X, he shows himself as having less social power in this instance unless X tries to equalize the power relationship by kneeling, chanting special words of supplication or self-abasement, and offering a bottle of homemade cane liquor or *poš*.

As the importance of the command increases and as the act of obedience demonstrates a particularly large power difference between X and Y, the persuasive procedures are prolonged further. Stretching out the conversation, making it repetitious, and showing resistance that requires further persuasive efforts exist in many areas of Zinacantecan life as a form of courtesy. Decisions are not made quickly or abruptly if they are to be binding. The more important the decision to be made, the greater the length of time necessary to reach agreement. The more resistance and denial, the more persuasion, and more bottles of *poš* consumed, the more important and binding the decision.

Patterns of persuasion, prolongation, and resistance preserve an equalitarian ideal in Zinacantan. But the ideal often does not coincide with reality; differences in social status and social power permeate many activities in Zinacantan, especially the respected year-long offices of religious *cargo*.

Frank Cancian (1965, pp. 162–63) arrived at a prestige-ranking scale of Zinacantecan religious *cargo* roles and then asked informants about the specific roles a named individual "passed through." When the informant made a mistake, it was usually only one position down or up in the ranked hierarchy. People are apparently rated by other members of the culture according to some implicit status scale, of which the actual *cargo* held is an external index not always precisely remembered.

My interpretation of the Zinacantecan situation is that a conscious ranking of other people cannot be done without some recognition of the individual's own position in the hierarchy. Since this hierarchy is an indirect indication of soul-power, such a conscious ranking would prove to be anxiety-producing. Anxiety is avoided by keeping social power rankings at the unconscious level while explicitly espousing an ideal of equality.

The equalitarian etiquette in Zinacantan requires a set of precedence rules; but if such rules were to follow lines of social prestige, they would nullify the equalizing effect. The apparent dilemma is solved by making age serve as the basis for precedence. In formal situations a younger person always bows to an older person, who in turn "releases" him by touching the top of his head with the back of his fingers. Two men of equal age both bow and release each other by one clasping the hand of the other, though this is now being replaced by

---

[6] In situations of relaxed dependency and in other contexts, directing others is perfectly acceptable, even to the point of being a cynosure in some of the religious roles.

428

a simple touching of open palms. Younger men of higher prestige (as evidenced by their *cargo* positions, wealth, or political power) will bow to older men of lower prestige or lesser political power. So in Zinacantan there are actually two hierarchies at work: the hierarchy of relative age (which might be termed power-empty) and the hierarchy of social prestige or social power.[7] The first has considerable dampening effect on the second but rarely nullifies it.

The keystone of Zinacantecan etiquette is speech behavior. The procedure for talking in such group-supportive cultures as the 16th-century Aztec was intended to keep social harmony and avoid disruption of the social order, but in the self-protective society of Zinacantan value is placed on the ability to persuade and control, on the one hand, and to maintain respect for personal equality and integrity, on the other.

Zinacantecan statements that a good talker is admired primarily because he can persuade the supernaturals to do his bidding reveal the controlling function of talking. Zinacantecans fear that if they cannot talk well to the gods, they may be brought into slavery in the supernatural world. An effective talker can cure the most serious illnesses and can even achieve countersorcery if he is more persuasive than the originating sorcerer.

Persuasive talking, therefore, is highly valued in some contexts, but in others it is not appropriate. In situations of potential social disharmony one uses a different style of talking for something of an equalizing purpose. How this works is shown by Robert F. Bales (1958) in his small-group studies where a correlation was found between volume of conversation and leadership. Leaders do more talking than other members of the group, and those who give an opportunity to reply are less disliked than other leaders.

In Zinacantecan culture, where much anxiety can arise over the ill feelings of others and over differences in social power or leadership, there is an unusual degree of equality in contexts where the emergence of a conversational leader might be disturbing. The listener participates in the conversation even if only to repeat the speaker's last words. Sometimes it is difficult, without knowing Tzotzil, to understand who is giving the news and who is receiving it. The talk consists of short phrases or sentences answered by the listener with repetitions, questions, and exclamations of surprise. The teller responds with repetitions, exclamations of affirmation, and so on. The style of talking can thus be something of a barometer for the disruptive or psychologically disturbing potentialities of a social situation.

It will be recalled that talking in 16th-century group-supportive societies was used both for controlling or influencing the behavior of others and for protecting the social order. Although the first function is found also in 20th-century self-protective cultures such as Zinacantan, the second seems to be replaced by a desire to protect the self-images of the speakers.

The threat of conversational leadership to the self-image is only one of several threats in a Mesoamerican self-protective culture. Another is witchcraft. The practice of confession has been subordinated to counterwitchcraft as one means of curing illness. The evidence suggests that illness through sorcery, though not the most frequent sickness today, is nevertheless much more prevalent than at the time of the conquest.[8]

---

[7] Though respect for age is probably more emphasized now, it was important also in earlier times. Sahagún (bk. 8, p. 71) mentions respect being shown to people of high status such as militia officers and judges, but old people, even if poor, were bowed to as well. Respect for age is also described by Landa (1941, p. 124) for the Yucatecans.

[8] See Siverts (1960, p. 24) and Villa Rojas (1946) for a discussion of witchcraft in the Tzeltal area of Oxchuc, and M. Nash (1960) in Amatenango.

In comparing four Yucatecan communities ranging from folk to urban, Redfield (1941, p. 327) found that the frequency of imputed witchcraft increases from the small village to the large city. "The significant fact is that in the villages sickness does not easily lead to or become an expression of hatred or fear of human beings. In the villages one does not often carry on one's quarrels by doing black magic to one's enemy." Redfield (p. 334) considers black magic to be an "expression of the insecurity of the individual in the unstable social milieu of the city."

The explanation for Redfield's observation is more likely historical than ecological. Increase in witchcraft from rural to urban areas seems to come through acculturation from old Yucatecan culture to modern Hispano-Yucatecan culture. Sickness attributed to witchcraft in 16th-century Yucatan is not reported by Landa and receives only brief mention by Sahagún (bk. 10, p. 31), whose informants lived in a densely settled metropolis. When compared to all the other evils imputed to witchcraft, particularly adultery and theft which, to judge from the severity of the punishment, were the two greatest sins in Aztec and Yucatec society, witchcraft sickness has a very small importance. Zantwijk's finding (1960, p. 57) that witchcraft (*nanahualtin*) was stronger among the more acculturated Catholic Macehualtin of Milpa Alta than among the Teomixica supports the general observation that the preconquest pattern, in which witchcraft sickness played a relatively minor role, substantially changed during the next four centuries.

Summary

Mesoamerican psychological orientations have been characterized in terms of a broad areal pattern consisting of (1) concern about assertive behavior, (2) preoccupation with social power, (3) pessimistic world view, (4) "looking" behavior, and (5) emphasis on trust and the male sibling relationship. Secondary patterns showed two distinctions: (1) between Aztec and Maya cultures according to the relationship between the sexes, with the conjecture that this distinction would hold for most Nahuatl and Maya cultures, and (2) between Mesoamerican cultures in the conquest period (Aztec and Yucatec) and at present (Zinacantecan), according to group- and self-orientations, also with a general application to other Mesoamerican cultures.

Social power, etiquette, and talking receive attention both in the literature about early group-supportive cultures and in present-day self-protective cultures. The differences lie in their functional importance. Class distinctions and equalitarian ideals are two among several features characterizing group-supportive and self-protective orientations, respectively. Witchcraft, penance, confession, and belief in multiple souls are others. None of these features are exclusive to one period or another; it is rather their relative emphases that have brought about changes in patterns.

The literature on other cultures in Mesoamerica contains fragments supporting these generalizations, but I have presented the argument in terms of three cultures for which information is most complete, so that the basis for these speculations may be clearer to the reader.

Personality study and cultural psychology in Mesoamerica are still undeveloped, yet there are many phenomena which will be of both theoretical and historical interest when explained by analysis and field testing. Some of these phenomena relate to social organization and various aspects of behavior not usually considered part of a "psychological" account. Obviously no two individuals and no two cultures are exactly alike, but theoretical advance comes only with the discovery of similarities, however broadly conceived.

REFERENCES

Bales, 1958
Bunzel, 1952
Burton and Whiting, 1961
Bushnell, 1958
Cancian, Francesca, 1963
Cancian, Frank, 1965
Colby, 1959, 1960, 1961a, 1961b, 1963
D'Andrade, 1962
Erikson, 1950
Fishburne, 1962
Foster, 1944
Gillin, 1948, 1952
Goubaud Carrera, 1948
Humboldt, 1814
LaFarge, 1947
Landa, 1941
Laughlin, 1962a, 1962b
León-Portilla, 1956
Lewis, 1951
Lindzey, 1961

Lumholtz, 1907
Metzger and Williams, 1963a
Miller, W. S., 1956
Nash, M., 1960
Paul, 1950b, 1953
Pozas, 1959c
Redfield, 1941
Romney and Romney, 1963
Sahagún, 1950–66
Siverts, 1960
Tax, Sol, 1950
Tax, Susan, 1964
Tozzer, 1907
van den Berghe and Colby, 1961
Villa Rojas, 1946
Viqueira and Palerm, 1954
Vogt, 1961, 1964a, 1964b
Wisdom, 1940
Zantwijk, 1960

22. Ethnic Relationships

JULIO DE LA FUENTE

OUR KNOWLEDGE of ethnic relationships in Middle America is generally a byproduct of other objectives rather than of studies directed toward that end. The few exceptions (Guiteras Holmes, 1948a; Romano, 1952; Morales, 1952; and especially Tumin, 1952) have elucidated the role of race in ethnic relationships and the kinds of social structures in certain biethnic communities, but do not offer comparisons or generalizations. Our information about ethnic relationships is therefore confined to southeast Mexico and Guatemala, and is incomplete even there.

We are further limited by many differences: in the amount and kind of information recorded in the investigations, the area considered (locality, community, or region), the method employed (anthropological or sociological), the emphasis on one or two of the interacting groups and the degree of the observer's bias and the correction of this. The studies have been much restricted to relationships between Indians and Ladinos (or Mestizos or *castellanos* or *gente de razón* [people of reason], depending on how they are called) disregarding small or vanishing groups that en-

432

lighten by contrast the relations between the important groups. More attention to Negroes, Anglo-Saxons, and other minorities would be valuable. Future investigations should systematically formulate the problems and standardize the data.

We here follow Redfield's definition of an ethnic group as one whose members' sense of identity stems from the same characteristics of race, genealogy, or culture. When we denote the Indians as an ethnic group, we make a convenient abstraction, because it would be more correct to so designate each of the linguistic-cultural indigenous groups throughout Middle America. We make another abstraction when referring to Ladinos as another group, ignoring the great differences between urban and rural Ladinos, and those of upper class and lower class. I choose the term Ladino arbitrarily, since other names are equally inappropriate and are restricted to parts of Chiapas and Guatemala. I am aware of objections to classing non-Indians of the upper class as Ladinos.

It is generally agreed that ethnic groups in Middle America are based on cultural rather than racial grounds. The Indians, as a group, tend to be relatively homogeneous physically, despite diversity shown by Amerindians and indubitable signs of mixture with Negroes or Caucasoids. Ladinos (here the term Mestizo would be appropriate) are physically more heterogeneous, ranging from pure Caucasoids to pure Amerindians. The Ladinos of the Altos de Jalisco (P. S. Taylor, 1933b) represent the "white race," with more admixture than have the other groups. Negroes, on the other hand, are generally defined racially rather than culturally, covering the whole range from diluted traits to definite Negroid traits.

The term *race* is used, somewhat more by Ladinos and Aladinados than by Indians, to refer to the primary stocks and additions such as the Indian race, the Mestizo, the Mixteca, the Yaqui. Ladinos tend to classify themselves as "white" or Mestizo and to classify the Indians as Indian. Race in Middle America is a sociological construction, in which absence of correlation between native physical trait and assumed race does not prevent the ascription of the latter. The concepts of race and their implications are examined below.

Language, literacy, surname, type of housing, place of residence, and various customs are the traits commonly considered when distinguishing Indians from Ladinos. Efforts have been made to differentiate these groups by ethos and personality (Gillin, 1952), but these criteria are relative, according to varying acculturation in different areas. In language it is the Indian who is regarded as speaking an indigenous tongue, even when Spanish is a second tongue. Conversely, the Ladino is he who speaks Spanish as mother or only tongue; speaking an indigenous language as a second one does not change his identity. The criterion loses validity in rural communities of Atlixco, Mexico, where farmers who work part time in the textile factories speak only Spanish but consider themselves Indian because of their principal occupation and their way of life, which differs from that of

the factory workers. It also loses validity where there is individual acculturation. Local differences dispute the meaning of monolingualism and the distribution of Spanish. The tendency for Ladinos to speak only Spanish (e.g., in San Luis Jilotepeque, El Chorti, Jamiltepec) and the necessity for Indians to learn Spanish to understand the Ladinos is one of the aspects of the deferential conduct that usually obtains between Ladinos and Indians. High indigenous monolingualism accounts for some bilingualism in Ladinos, as in Agua Escondida and Altos de Chiapas. Deriving from the high monolingualism of the Indians is their illiteracy, because even though the indigenous languages have been provided with an alphabet, it is little used in formal education.

The indigenous surname *(apodo,* or a name taking the place of the surname) is still a valid criterion in Yucatan, Villa Alta, San Pedro La Laguna, Veracruz, but in Agua Escondida and in Yucatan, for example, many Ladinos have an indigenous surname. The present tendency is toward a change to a Spanish surname.

Dress *(de huipil* and *de caites* in contrast to *de vestido)* is somewhat distinctive in areas of slow cultural change, but even here it is qualified. In most of the communities cited here Indians, both men and women, wear distinctive clothes, but in Villa Alta, only the women do. On the other hand, in east and southeast Guatemala and in Atlixco and Tantoyuca, Mexico, men and women dress like the rural Ladino. Semiofficial pressure, interdependence between language and costume, and type of occupation (even if temporary, as with braceros) weaken adherence to native dress. Deviation from native dress is slight in Los Altos de Chiapas, where indigenous organization is strong and where the Indians, by physical aggression, witchcraft, or other means, obstruct change. It is more rapid in areas such as Bajo Papaloapan, Mexico, where the reshuffling of the Mazateca population

433

has caused complete change in eight years. Individual articles of apparel or perhaps the whole costume (whether or not accompanied by linguistic change) give place, in parts of Mexico, to the intermediate items like *arrazonado, medio azul,* or *revestido.*

In numerous cases (Jamiltepec, Yucatan, central Oaxaca) it can be asserted that whoever lives in a *jacal* (Indian hut) made of vegetal and/or cheap materials is Indian, and whoever lives in a house made of more solid or modern materials is Ladino. However, in Bajo Papaloapan, Indians and Ladinos often live in similar *jacales.* The distinction persists, however, because Indians build their houses by reciprocal work and the Ladinos with wage labor. The Indian's house usually has one room; the Ladino's has many, or at least has an adjoining kitchen. The metate, hearth, and bed at floor level generally, but not always, mark the Indian; their position above the floor characterizes the Ladino.

The patterns of residence have some diagnostic value. The communities show varied distribution and composition. The tendency in Mexico is for Ladinos to be urban or semiurban, for Indians to be rural. This also occurs in Guatemala with some notable exceptions, e.g., Santa Rosa and Sacatepequez (Adams, 1956c, p. 33). The Indians of San Luis Jilotepeque form an island within a great Ladino region; the Ladinos of San Cristobal de las Casas, Agua Escondida, and La Cabecera de Villa Alta form islands within numerous Indian communities. In the last region Ladinos in towns are hardly more than a handful—the schoolteacher, a few farmers, some merchants—and so give rise to little ethnic interaction. In biethnic towns and villages, such as El Chorti, San Luis, Jamiltepec, Los Altos de Chiapas, Oaxaca, communication is greater, although Indians and Ladinos live in special wards or sections: Ladinos in the centers, Indians on the periphery. The villages of Los Altos are dispersed and generally Indian. One may often tell, therefore, from

the place of origin or of residence, to which group the individual belongs.

The strong religiousness of the Indians, the incorporation in their religion of non-Catholic concepts and practices, their forms of politico-religious organization, and special ideas regarding the cause of diseases and modes of treating them, mark them from the Ladinos. These differences are recognized in phrases such as "this is done only by the Indians" or "this is a custom of the Ladinos." However, one frequently finds patterns which are shared by both groups, with varying differentiations in form or function.

Indians do not exhibit social classes, although there are ranks in status or prestige, derived from age, experience, or officeholding in local hierarchies (religious and/or civil). Some stratification is based on economic and cultural conditions. Intra-Indian stratification is found among the Chortis, the Indians of Los Altos de Chiapas, and those of Villa Alta. Among the first, hierarchical distinctions are made between the more acculturated Indians, who live closer to the towns, and those more backward, rustic, and remote. In Los Altos de Chiapas, the Zinacatecos (as well as the Tileños) are considered, both by the Ladinos and by themselves, superior to other Indians (Colby and van den Berghe, 1960). This is true also in Villa Alta, as well as in other areas of interaction of Zapotecos with other less acculturated Indians. Indians at the top of these hierarchies begin to be like a superior social class within the Indian society just when they begin to merge into the Ladino lower class. Ladinos, as a group, have social classes. There are rural Ladinos, such as those of San Luis Jilotepeque, who acknowledge a superior class formed by those of "the society" and another formed by those of "the populace," the latter being the majority. However, the absence of social classes among rural Ladinos is perhaps more common (e.g., Agua Escondida, Cabeceras de los Altos de Chiapas, Pueblo de

Jamiltepec, Villa Alta). Ladino social classes are found, obviously, in cities.

The degree to which people identify themselves according to race or culture varies widely. In Arandas, where there are no linguistically defined Indians, Ladinos distinguish themselves mostly by race, blood, and genealogy. They overvalue their "white" race and blood, to which they attribute certain "superior" cultural traits; they undervalue Indians, their dark color, and the mixture of races (P. S. Taylor, 1933b). In San Luis Jilotepeque, "the members of each group view the others as if they were at least in certain aspects biologically different; among such aspects one finds not only physical appearance, but modalities of thought, opinions concerning life and intellectual inclinations and capacities. . . . from the *ladino's* point of view, at least, such differences show a natural inferiority on the part of the Indian and from the Indian point of view, they rather tend to represent a series of differences which are natural and impossible to eradicate, based on the different biological heredity" (Tumin, 1952). Biological mixture is also undesirable, being regarded as "contamination." In Los Altos de Chiapas, racial differences have some importance for the Ladinos: ideas about inferiority of the Indians are tied to them, e.g., some hold that blood mixture improves the Indian race (Cámara, 1952a). The differences given greatest significance are apparently those of a cultural order. Reports from Agua Escondida and midwestern Guatemala find that differences between Indian and Ladino are not conceived in biological terms (Tax, 1941). In San Pedro La Laguna, however, there is a minor belief in the superiority of dark color, which is extended to Indians, Negroes, and Ladinos. A town in Yucatan ascribes superiority to Anglo-Saxons, partly because of color or race but more because of culture. This situation obtains also in Villa Alta. In general, culture preponderantly defines group differences, and this has led to a definition of "social races" (Wagley, 1958).

Ladinos, whose intimate knowledge of the Indians is small, undervalue them as a group. They ascribe to Indians inferior traits and scorn many of their customs and beliefs as backward, infantile or gross, befitting primitive or rude people. The degree of contempt varies somewhat according to the acculturation of the Indians; it is greater in San Luis and Los Altos de Chiapas, where ethnic differences are pronounced, than in Agua Escondida, where they are not. A similar situation prevails in Villa Alta. However, Ladinos show some esteem towards certain Indian groups not only because of their acculturation but because of their subordinate position (Colby and van den Berghe, 1960), which gives them certain benefits. In Los Altos de Chiapas some 30 derogatory expressions are used for Indians; out of those about eight are directed at the Chamulas, who, on the other hand, are referred to by five or six laudatory expressions (De la Fuente, 1958a).

With certain exceptions, Indians accept their ascribed inferiority, but with varied repercussions. In Guatemala, Indians are likely to view cultural differences as natural and not to adopt Ladino patterns. In Mexico a similar view is offset by a conviction that it is possible, even desirable, to change cultures. Ladino detraction of Indian language, dress, houses, and some customs and beliefs, plus exaltation of their own, move Indians to seek change, more in some areas (Villa Alta) than in others (Los Altos de Chiapas). Security for the Indian is implied either way: either in ceasing to be an Indian or in continuing to be one. Cultural change, on the other hand, means only one thing: going from Indian to non-Indian.

Inequality of status between the two groups is manifested in the ethnic terminology and in social expressions and rules of conduct by which, in the generalized pattern, the Ladino receives deference from the Indian but does not return it.

435

Strictness of the rules and the occasions when they are applied vary from region to region. The term *indio*, used more often by Ladinos than by Indians, is known everywhere and connotes inferiority or contempt; this does not escape the awareness of the Indians, who are resentful when the word is used as an epithet. The Ladino who does not want to offend Indians therefore calls them by the acceptable names *lengua jeros, paisanos*, or local tribe or place names. Some names that Indians call Ladinos connote superiority *(gente de razón)*; others express the negative feelings inspired by the Ladinos.

Ladino paternalistic attitudes toward Indians are manifest in terms like *indito* or *muchachos*, the use of the familiar *tu* or *vos*, the use of first names regardless of the Indian's age or class. (It is common in Mexico for a Ladino of the upper class to address one of the lower class by those forms.) A possible high status of an Indian does not merit his being addressed by a Ladino as *usted, señor*, or *Don* as a Ladino would address other Ladinos of similar social position, although there are exceptions in Oaxaca and Yucatan. Indians who do not know Spanish return the familiar *tu* or *vos*, whereas the acculturated maintain social distance by using the forms of address that the Ladino expects.

San Luis Jilotepec is a good illustration of strict agreement by both groups to patterns of deferential conduct and social distance during casual meetings and events. Indians defer to Ladinos in the street, road, shop, church, government office, park, or home; Ladinos reciprocate grudgingly or not at all. Neither Indian nor Ladino behaves in that way toward his own kind. The only signs of break in the etiquette toward egalitarianism are in the reluctance of some Indians to remove their hats and remain bareheaded when talking to a Ladino, which irritates the latter; or in the acknowledged ability and even superiority of the Indians when musicians of both groups play the *marimba* together.

Differences in language, tradition, interests, and social position set off the two groups in other situations. In San Luis, street congregations, recreation, school and public parties, social visits, commensals, wakes, weddings, baptisms, private Indian social reunions, and Indian religious observances are activities in which each group participates more or less alone, or are peculiar to only one group, or involve both groups but the Indians remain on the periphery. In Agua Escondida social barriers are less pronounced: Ladinos show no reluctance to eat or to associate with Indians, children of both groups play together, and etiquette is less strict.

A pattern similar to San Luis holds true in Los Altos de Chiapas. There breaks in the old social order are evident. Until a few years ago Indians commonly walked only in the street, Ladinos on the sidewalk; the former yielded the way to the latter. Twenty or thirty years ago, when an Indian talked with his employer he was expected to remove his headgear, fold his arms, and bow his head in a submissive attitude. Today Indians sit on the benches of the public square; Ladinos avoid sitting next to them but if they do, the Indians do not get up. Commensality does not occur except in an official context, and even then Ladinos frequently impose segregation. If an Indian and a Ladino walk together or speak to each other, it is a business transaction or an order from Ladino master to Indian servant; except officially, there is no equal social interaction between Indian and Ladino (Colby and van den Berghe, 1960). Rudeness toward Indians (see below) is shown even by Ladino children, who sometimes insult or mistreat Indians, who usually express no indignation. What is said about Santa Eulalia (LaFarge, 1947, pp. 116–17) applies, with a brief addition, to Los Altos de Chiapas: the "stupid, brainless

Indians" are thus stigmatized more as an index of social class and culture than of race; with increasing exceptions the Indians are treated rudely and given the indulgence one gives to children. Indians can be treated well, but as animals, not as a common humanity. In contrast, Yucatan, Villa Alta, and central Oaxaca are areas in which deferential conduct persists less strictly and less often; the "rebellious" Indian who is not servile or even courteous is quite common.

Although the indigenous economy is often self-sufficient, Indians and Ladinos find themselves inextricably bound together in economic affairs which require close joint participation. The Indian is basically oriented toward agriculture, small-scale commerce, and home crafts which, like agriculture, are backward and poorly remunerated. The orientation of the Ladino is ultimately to nonmanual labor, although necessity may force him into agriculture (if possible, indirectly), shopkeeping, and other specialized work. Indians incline toward Ladino occupations, but few Ladinos engage in Indian occupations. Indians, as a group, occupy the lower part of the economic scale; Ladinos, as a group, occupy the entire scale. Economic relations among the groups, although greatly favoring the Ladinos, sometimes show a degree of equality.

Division of labor along ethnic lines is complementary rather than competitive. Among Indians competition exists in landownership and is increasing in handcrafts and business. In Santa Eulalia, Indians are farmers (both as landowners and as laborers) and servants; Ladinos are farmers, shopkeepers, and laborers. (We omit the specialized Indian occupations such as traditional musician, witch, curer.) Ladinos and Indians are landowning farmers or farm laborers in Agua Escondida, and the former do not feel dishonored by working in the field. In San Luis, Indians are either landowning farmers or farm laborers, as well as servants and artisans; Ladinos are also, in the main, farm landlords and laborers, but also comprise about 40 semi-specialists and specialists, among them the shopkeepers. Basically, this structure repeats itself in El Chorti, where Indians in the villages have a substantial number of traditional skills; and some in the towns have shops, just as the Ladinos do.

In Los Altos de Chiapas (including the city) Indians are landowning farmers and farm laborers, who engage in few crafts but compete (illegally) with the Ladinos' great alcohol industry. Under governmental influence they have in recent years become shopkeepers, artisans who begin to compete with Ladinos, and specialists in semiskilled occupations. Ladinos are absentee farmers (for them agricultural work is dishonorable), artisans, shopkeepers, specialists of all sorts. Indians of Costa Chica and Tantoyuca are landowning farmers and farm laborers, and have few skills not duplicated by those of Ladinos. Among them are also servants and professionals. Ladinos of these regions are absentee farmers, cattlemen, shopkeepers, and artisans. In Villa Alta, Indians are landowning farmers and farm laborers, artisans, shopkeepers and professionals; Ladinos are absentee farmers, shopkeepers, and schoolteachers.

In all except Agua Escondida and Villa Alta, Ladinos, as a group, are richer than the Indians, but generally there are some rich Indians everywhere.

The limited number of modern skills among Indians, combined with their low standard of living and their customs, restrict the jobs in which Ladinos want to or need to hire their services or be hired by them. Thus in such relationships as agricultural landlord to laborer, foreman to day laborer, master artisan to peon, master to servant, owner of the load to loader, the former are Ladinos and the latter Indians. An exception is Agua Escondida, where around one-third of the Ladinos had worked for Indians as laborers; in some instances Ladinos in El Chorti, Tantoyuca, and Villa Alta had been hired laborers for Indians. In Oaxaca it is common for indigenous master-artisans to be helped by Ladino peons; it is also common there and in other regions of Mexico for ex-Indians to have Ladino servants or laborers, agricultural or otherwise.

Labor legislation, although designed for both groups, does not protect Indians sufficiently. In Guatemala the vagrancy laws hurt the economically underdeveloped Indians more than Ladinos. In San Luis, Indian laborers doing the same work as hired Ladinos received less pay and less courteous treatment from their Ladino employers. In Agua Escondida this discrimination did not exist, but Chiapas is an extreme example of the unequal treatment in labor transactions. The hiring of Indians for work in the coffee plantations was, until recently, accompanied by induced intoxication; deceit and frauds tie the Indians through debt to the plantation. No Ladino was hired in that way. "Baldillaje" or semifeudal servitude persists on a small scale, binding the Indian to the farm. For a piece of poor land given by a Ladino to an Indian to cultivate, the Indian must return excessive work on Ladino land and illegal personal services. In this and in many other regions in Mexico, it is common for the Indian to be defrauded in the construction of highways. Similarly, in the construction of private or semipublic works which will benefit both groups equally, or more the Ladino than the Indian, it is the Indian who does most of the actual work. The Ladino's contribution of a cash fee equivalent to the work done by the Indian, although it equalizes participation, is inequitable because of the Indian's poverty. Indian servants are poorly paid compared with Ladinos. A somewhat egalitarian relationship in Tantoyuca—and a very unequal one in Chiapas—is that of godmother-mistress and god-

daughter-servant. The nature of economic activities generally dictates that when the two groups participate in the same work, they both perform it side by side.

In Guatemala and Mexico Ladinos generally do not object to selling artisan or professional services to Indians. The quality of service received by the Indian, however, is often poorer because of his ignorance, status, or the amount paid. Indians in Las Casas do not go to just any barbershop but to "barbershops for Indians" (which are second class and are patronized by lower-class Ladinos), where they are given seating, service, and treatment inferior to that given to Ladinos, but for which they pay a smaller amount (Colby and van den Berghe, 1960). If they should go to a first-class barbershop, which only a few ever do because of the price, they are directed to second-rate barbershops. In central Oaxaca the Indian's acceptance in a first-class barbershop depends to a great extent on his appearance.

And so it is that in some instances price and innovation override ethnic differences, whereas in others ethnicity predominates over price to the disadvantage of the Indian. Indians carry Ladinos' goods on their backs, but not vice versa. However, it is the Ladino who usually moves the Indian's goods on his beasts of burden or on some modern means of transportation. The young Ladino shoeshine boys of Las Casas, who go barefoot rather than wear *caites* (a type of Indian sandal), shine the caites of Indians. The poverty of these Ladinos partly explains the service. Indians formerly did not attend the cinema, but today some do, although they are often abused by Ladinos of the lower class. In the city, Indians were until recently, spectators at the fairs, since they were not allowed to use the mechanical rides, but in small towns they were permitted. With change, carnivals in the cities have become more permissive. In Oaxaca, Indians have been accepted on merry-go-rounds for 25 years.

438

In Los Altos de Chiapas, Indians who are hired for work at the coffee plantations are transported in buses and trains like cattle, in spite of the fact that their ticket (second class) entitles them to travel with relative comfort; but the hired Ladinos ride apart from the Indians and in better conditions. Equal service for equal pay also does not apply to Indians in local and regional transportation, where they are made to give up their seats to Ladinos if there are not enough seats, or they are sent to the rear, leaving for the Ladinos the best seats in front. Indians accept the discrimination, while sneering in their own language. In Oaxaca this kind of segregation is less frequent.

In Guatemala, impersonality of business relationships seems to be, if not invariable, at least very common. In the part of Mexico considered here, the peculiarity of small enterprises includes the right to bargain (as also in Guatemala) and the personalization of the business relationship. This personalization has two aspects: to be considerate to a client, and to take advantage of the ignorant and the outsider. The Indian thus frequently finds himself in a position of inequality with respect to the Ladino, mainly due to his ignorance, even though his position as a client reduces that inequality.

Los Altos de Chiapas typifies the most extreme inequality in these transactions. At the market and at the shop, the Ladino buyer receives from the Ladino seller preference over the Indian customer, even if the latter has arrived first or is already being waited on. The Ladino seller or buyer talks to the Indian in a patronizing or rude cutting way. Very often the Ladino, as a seller, cheats the Indian in weight, dimension, quality of merchandise, or in change; as a buyer he offers a price much lower than he would offer a Ladino and he bargains with him interminably. At the urban market Ladinos shove aside or strike the Indians as they move through the market place. Only a few Indians who sell much wanted merchandise (maize) are able to obtain a permanent spot.

Robbing intoxicated Indians in bars and forcing Indians to sell cheaper at the outskirts of the city and town before they get to market are daily occurrences (Bonilla Domínguez, 1953). These methods, which the Ladinos do not use among themselves, are rarely curbed by the law or the police, but they are condemned by the educated and upper-class Ladinos.

It is common for Ladinos and Indians in this area to deal with each other as customers, but when lower-class Ladinos are involved, this is merely formal. These relations are different in other cases: Indians try to have steady customers, whose houses they visit to sell their wares and from whom they receive better treatment. However, if the Ladino is a customary innkeeper and habitually puts up Indians, it is common for him to sell liquor to them and to perpetuate frauds, which are restrained only by his economic interest in the goods Indians bring. Indians tolerate to a high degree these and other forms of subordination and humiliation and compensate by petty thefts in the market place, damage to the property of Ladino merchants when intoxicated, and restrictions on some Ladino merchants in Indian communities. In one case, these restrictions coincided with the recent opening of Indian shops, helped indirectly by governmental action in their favor.

In Oaxaca, where socio-cultural differences between the two groups are less than in Chiapas and where the Indians have great commercial astuteness, not only Ladinos but also Indians capitalize on the opportunity to take advantage of the foreigner and the ignorant, be he Ladino or Indian. Even rustic and not very sharp Indians are victims of other Indians or Ladinos who buy from them "by storm." The principal difference is that Indians are not so rudely treated here as in Chiapas, and there is equality in the treatment of buyers. The existence in this area of numer-

439

ous Indian shopkeepers is another sign of the relative leveling of the two groups.

The practice, if not the concepts, of Catholicism makes for assembly of the two groups. This not necessarily egalitarian concurrence is massive at the Catholic festivals. The religiosity of the Indians, as well as extraneous intrusions that Ladinos see in the nominal Catholicism of the Indians, causes the former to undervalue the latter, describing them as ignorant and superstitious. The religious and curative concepts and practices peculiar to the Indians (sometimes officially persecuted in Guatemala) are a factor in the segregation of the groups. The intrusion of Protestantism is, at the same time, a cause for ethnic separation as well as consolidation. The priest, a Ladino by definition, usually plays a limited role in the relations of the groups in his character of occasional visitor to the towns, although he is instrumental in the creation of highly personal relationships between members of the two groups.

Santa Eulalia is a community in which the organization of religion—nominally Catholic and frankly pagan—is in the hands of the Indians even though Ladinos have a great formal participation, performing special roles in some festivities, in conjunction with the Indians. The participation of the priest is limited to officiating at festivities. Foreign Protestants, who have had little success in converting Ladinos and Indians, constitute, along with their few converts, a separate group.

Indians and Ladinos in Agua Escondida have separate brotherhoods, but there is some interaction among them, somewhat egalitarian. In San Luis, on the other hand, only Indians have brotherhoods, which are seen by the Ladinos as extraneous aggregates, in spite of their knowing that they function in the capital. The Ladinos used to monopolize two major festivals and the benches in church. Protestants are few and have little importance.

Against a background of strong paganism and social distance Los Altos de Chiapas presents a complex picture of relationships in process of being broken. Normally, in city and town churches, Ladinos and Indians sit and kneel where they please (although Indians who go to churches in the cities are few). In many town churches, where some saints are dressed like the Indians of the municipality and others are dressed in conventional robes, both kinds of saints often receive simultaneous adoration from the devout, who make their devotions in two different forms and contexts. In two towns a rope in the church separates the groups during important religious functions, during which guards prevent trespass. In two towns the cemeteries are divided into sections for Ladinos and sections for Indians. Generally, each group organizes the festivities of their respective saints, but in some places Indians and Ladinos participate together in the processions and other rituals which take place in church, street, and home. The modern dance at the festivity tends to be performed by Ladinos, with Indians as spectators. Occasionally Ladinos participate in the Indians' *misas de milpa*. Indians' common drunkenness and prowling during festivities give Ladinos the excuse to reaffirm their stereotype of Indians as subhuman, despite the fact that Ladinos themselves often behave the same way during their own revels. Indians have been strengthened by receiving increasing attention from the government, Catholics, and North American Protestants. The success of the latter in converting thousands of Indians (and some Ladinos) has moved Catholics toward a greater attention to Indians, as shown by the formation of militant catechistic groups.

A great Ladino-Indian interaction exists in Tantoyuca, stimulated by the Indians, whose religiosity and Catholicism are also greater here than the Ladinos' and very much appreciated by the priests. In this area Ladinos and Indians are separately organized for the upkeep of the Church, which devolves on Indians.

The concepts of state and nation, always vague among the Indians, are represented to them by major and minor public officials, some of whom sometimes visit their towns, and by low-ranking employees, soldiers, and policemen. All of these are Ladinos, whose functions the Indians interpret in terms of their experiences with them, generally more negative than positive.

In Guatemala, before 1944, the president designated the political chief of the department, who would designate the municipal intendant, who would designate the members of a municipal council (*juzgado*) and an auxiliary one, formed by Ladinos and Indians. In theory, certain posts had to be filled by election, but appointment was the usual procedure. If an election was held, the voters were Ladinos and so elected other Ladinos. In appointing Ladino officials, the intendant had the option of consulting with local Ladinos; in appointing the Indian counterparts, he would consult the elders of the Indian community (*principales*). People from the villages would participate in the municipal council, Indians usually predominating.

Parallel to the juzgado were the nucleus of administrative employees (tax collectors, etc.) and military police appointed by officials high in the government hierarchy, and the core of native authority sometimes unsuspected by the Ladinos. A member of the juzgado was the officer assigned to deal with the Indians. The proportional distribution of posts to Ladinos and Indians was fixed by law, but when it did not suit the Ladinos, they would obtain dispensation to modify it. Often the most important posts of the juzgado, the less inconvenient ones, and/or those with pay were thus held by Ladinos; the inferior ones, those without pay or degrading or bothersome, by the Indians. One could find a situation in which a secretary of juzgado who, along with the principales, controlled the Indians in the

Indian towns, was a Ladino, as were the administrative employees and the major, whose soldiers, on the other hand, were Indians. Few Indians in the military or civil service were then in a position to give orders to a Ladino; if by chance an Indian should occupy a post usually reserved for Ladinos, he would be resented (Wisdom, 1940, p. 224) and denied any respect from Ladinos.

Government seemed to the Indians to exist only for exacting obedience to orders, inflicting gratuitous services and unpaid labor, and extorting fines and fees. Requirements in construction and repair of roads, repair of towns, and military service weighed heavier on the Indians than on the Ladinos. Criticism of the system was punished. The amenableness of the Indians to local government would depend on whether they lived in a village or in a town: villagers would resolve their difficulties in traditional form by appealing to witchcraft, violence, or their moral authorities, causing the juzgado to persuade or coerce them to use legal means; townfolk, whose social controls had weakened, would frequently present their problems to the juzgado.

The Revolution of 1944 drew up a democratic constitution, which gave Indians the right to vote and to be elected to high office in the local hierarchies, various facilities (in San Luis, for example, the right to establish businesses), freedom to perform curative ceremonies without being bothered, and freedom from forced labor. However, the one time that the Indians in San Luis were asked to fill political posts they refused, claiming lack of experience, probably an excuse for not leaving their social place (Tumin, 1952). Therefore here and in other communities, even though the Indians had greater scope for their political aspirations, the Ladinos retained the real power.

In Mexico the constitution does not make ethnic distinctions—the Indian is a citizen just as any other—and so makes no legal stipulations regarding proportions of La-

441

dinos and Indians in the municipal government (*ayuntamiento*). In Los Altos de Chiapas it was common for Ladinos to monopolize the principal offices in the ayuntamiento of Indian municipalities, with the support of the municipal president of San Cristobal, who exerted control over the Indians in that way and through the Ladino secretaries, whom he appointed. Since 1943, with the inauguration of a Department (at state level) of Indian Protection, the ayuntamientos in the predominantly Indian municipalities have been filled by Indians. The nominations are made by the Indians themselves, validated by the official political party (of which Indians are nominal members), the chief of Indian protection, and other members of the political hierarchy, all Ladinos. (An office is given to a Ladino.)

Elections are merely nominal. The secretaries of the town continue to be Ladinos, who still exert control over Indians. The Chief of the Department of Indian Protection names secretaries and the governor ratifies them.

Having lost much of the control which they used to exert in the mixed municipalities, the Ladinos persist, nevertheless, in maintaining their influence, endeavoring by persuasion or threat to keep the Indians docile. Failing this, especially when the municipal president is young and antagonistic to them, Ladinos intrigue, threaten, and cajole until a more "docile" president is substituted. In matters of justice, Ladinos refuse to be judged by an Indian authority despite the fact that Indian authority is often lenient to Ladinos. Ladinos appeal—sometimes in vain—to the justice of the Ladino secretary or mayor. As in El Chorti, Indians live with permanent friction over the jurisdiction of authority. Their frequent crimes make them the object of an unfavorable balance of justice. In conjunction with the Ladinos, Indians participate in politics, sometimes with understanding and interest and sometimes not; they work, sometimes

without pay, on public works, to benefit their own communities. Even though they are far from achieving status equal to that of Ladinos, the increasing number of "rebellious" Indians and those who seek to be educated are evidence of role and status reversion however incomplete.

Various biethnic communities in Tantoyuca, Jamiltepec, Yucatan, and other areas show instances of monopolization of local government by Ladinos as well as Indian dominance. This the Ladinos resent. In Villa Alta the local municipal governments are wholly in Indian hands. On various occasions they have tried to elect Indian deputies but without success.

In Santa Eulalia, El Chorti, the municipios of the Guatemalan midwestern highlands and Chiapas highlands, the politico-religious organization of the Indians is still strong. In San Luis and the Mexican communities mentioned, they have a decreasing role as the national political life expands to the Indians and as other organizations compete for attention. These organizations involve the joint and more or less egalitarian participation of both groups, or an increase in the communication of the Indians with supralocal Ladino agencies and persons. In both countries the increased political participation of Indians has followed from their respective revolutions. In the Chiapas highlands the new organizations are the *ejidos* (land grants) and political locals (the former being biethnic in some cases and the latter in all cases), education committees, and a labor union of Indian workers from the coffee plantations; in Villa Alta, education committees and political locals, as in Dzitas; in Jamiltepec, ejido organizations (predominantly Indian in some cases), educational committees, and political locals, as in Tantoyuca. The diminishing importance of the old chiefs and the increasing value of young leaders now characterize all of the Mexican sub-area.

Formal education of the Indian is official-

442

ly recognized as an important means to national integration. "Education" of the Indian signifies, to a great extent, the transmission to the Indian, and his adoption of, Ladino culture and values. Spanish is the language of this education. Indian culture and languages are thus generally undervalued; Ladino culture and Spanish language are overvalued. Many Indians have adopted the official point of view and values so that special Indian education using indigenous languages blocks their desire to acculturate, wholly or partly.

Indian education is less effective than that of the Ladinos, because of ignorance of Spanish, the Indians' practical orientation, poverty, the academic emphasis of the curricula, the role assigned to women, and other causes. The Indians' attitude towards school ranges from extremely negative (reported for the tribal Indians of Quintana Roo) to unconditional acceptance by those who see it as the means for progress and change. The Ladinos' attitude is also variable: in San Luis and Los Altos de Chiapas Ladinos talk of the benefits that education would bring to the Indians, but they do little to extend and improve it. Some Ladinos, including teachers, consider education useless for the Indian, given the natural incapacity they ascribe to him, reinforced by the difficulty of teaching children. Others have a genuine desire to "civilize" the Indian and make him a Ladino. And others, according to the Indians, obstruct their education to maintain an advantage by keeping Indians ignorant (Villa Alta and Los Altos de Chiapas). There are complaints of discrimination (San Luis).

Teachers are chiefly Ladinos, a few ex-Indians, and, rarely, Indians. A Ladino or ex-Indian teacher is assigned to any ethnic group, whereas Indian teachers are assigned exclusively to their own people, as in some "projects" in Guatemala and Mexico. In some Mexican communities, the ex-Indian teacher is looked askance at by Indians and Ladinos, since they feel he may be poorly trained and not knowledgeable.

Self-segregation of the students on an ethnic basis, during recess and at close of school, as well as Ladino scorn for the poor Indian clothes, is reported in San Luis; self-segregation in Jamiltepec appears to be passing. In some instances, Ladino teachers and students (some Ladinos and others partly Ladinoized) of some schools in Chiapas, belittled and mocked Indian students who tried to take up Ladino traits (Guiteras Holmes, 1946b). The absence of Indian participants and spectators from school festivities in San Luis is quite contrary in Mexico, where the school is a major contributor to change in apparel among Indian children and an impetus to migration to cities or other regions. From Indian groups have come numerous skilled specialists, who did not find opportunities in their own communities and so migrated to urban centers. This loss keeps the home communities from making much advancement.

Ritual kinship crosses ethnic frontiers, thus creating relationships in which certain cases increase intergroup asymmetry. This increased asymmetry correlates with the width differences in the ethnic status of the groups. Some of the modifications in the patterns of San Luis are: (1) Indians initiate the ritual godfather role, Ladinos never, so no Ladinos have Indian godfathers, except a few in Jamiltepec. (2) The ritual kin maintains the proper respect relations (rarely in San Luis, frequently in Bajo Papaloapan and Jamiltepec). Reciprocity does not necessarily imply complete equality, especially in San Luis. The Indian, as Indian and as beneficiary of a ritual service, is doubly indebted and hence would be more respectful to the Ladino, who can be thus even more condescending. (3) Cordiality and courtesy do come from the Ladino *compadre* but rarely in San Luis. (4) Everywhere the two ritual kin derive benefit from the relationship— the Indians get favors, protection, and/or prestige; the Ladinos, services and/or

443

prestige—but the kind, frequency, and comparative value of the benefits vary considerably. (5) Godfathers tend to give godchildren necessary aid and protection, from childhood until they become adults. This feature of the relationship appears most developed (or is better known) in San Luis. (6) In "urban" situations the ritual kin relationship becomes secularized, because the Ladinos have so many compadres and godchildren that they forget their names or ignore some of their duties, as in Jamiltepec and Villa Alta in the relationship of *evangelio*. (7) The ritual relationships create or reaffirm ties without subverting the social order, but in Jamiltepec goddaughters sometimes receive encouragement from the godmothers to acculturate. There are in San Luis some peculiar aspects of ritual kinship, such as the taking over of the baptism festivity by the Ladinos in place of the Indian father.

Personal ethnic relationships are limited more than are impersonal ones, because of obvious factors: language, culture, occupations, and interests. Biological ideas of difference and physical differences also operate to limit personal relations. In the relationships one observes a carry-over from colonial days: casual sex relations between, most often, a Ladino and an Indian female; free unions on this pattern; few marriages, although more if ex-Indians are counted. Stable relationships require more or less acculturation on the part of the Indian.

In Santa Eulalia, Ladinos commonly rape Indian females; the only type of free union was one formed by an Indian in the process of Ladinoization and a Ladino female. He was, furthermore, the richest person among all Ladinos and Indians of the town. In another community, one Indian expected that good dowries to his daughters would bring them Ladino husbands. In Agua Escondida only casual unions are formed. In El Chorti are similar relationships and, apparently, free unions between Indianized

Ladino and Indian female. In San Pedro La Laguna and vicinity rape of Ladino females by Indians has occurred, as well as mixed free unions of all types, the Ladino females being unsophisticated.

In San Luis commercial sexual relations of Indian females, married and unmarried, with Ladinos took place without putting the Indian females in the same category with four well-defined Ladino prostitutes. Apparently, some of these relationships became concubinages. In the villages were some free unions and, apparently, one mixed marriage. The one mixed union, very unstable, was between an Indian and a Ladino prostitute. Ladinos and Indians denounce mixed unions, the former mainly because of their concepts of fixed biological differences, the latter, because of the cultural and economic differences. The tightest situation is in Arandas, where maintenance of purity of blood is limited to unions only of "whites." Prestige and family pride repudiate the daughter who disobeys this social norm.

In the Chiapas highlands rape of Indian servant-girls by Ladinos is reputed to be frequent. Ladinos rationalize this as an act of improving Indian blood (or race). In city and towns are numberless free unions and concubinages but marriages seem few and are usually between Indians (male or female) somewhat Ladinoized and Ladinos (male or female) of the lower classes. The services of Ladino prostitutes are infrequently bought by Indians. The towns of Villa Alta present many cases of semicommercial sexual relations of Indian females and Ladinos and few cases of free unions and marriages, which are limited primarily by the small proportion of Ladinos. Dzitas, in Yucatan, and Jamiltepec show many instances of all these relationships; proportionately Jamiltepec has perhaps even more, about 50 unions being in the capital.

Chiapas is the dividing line between a northern area (Mexico), where the Indian-Ladino structure is based on caste, and a southern area (Guatemala), where it is based on class. The main direction of mobility is from below to above, from Indian caste or class to Ladino caste or class. The reverse crossing does not take place because it lacks advantages. Acculturation is probably the basic mechanism in crossing, although amalgamation plays an important role. Crossing is legitimate when it does not hide the person's original caste or class traits; illegitimate, when it conceals them. The dividing line, however, is frequently tenuous, for acculturation substitutes cultural traits. Crossing, finally, requires a psychological willingness of the individual to consider himself a member of a different group. Instances of rigidity or lack of it follow.

To Ladinos and Indians of Agua Escondida, an Indian would turn Ladino if he were reared as such, or he would be considered originally Indian but Ladino because of habit. Ladinos incline to contribute to the crossing of Indians, but we have no examples. In the midwest highlands of Guatemala, it is agreed that theoretically an Indian becomes Ladino if he acquires Ladino habits or ways of living, but in practice this rarely occurs, and a single trait might denominate an Indian regardless of his Ladinoization.

The Indian, in El Chorti, who seeks to pass for Ladino moves to the town, changes costume, speaks only Spanish, pretends ignorance of Indian custom, hides his ethnic identity, and if possible marries a Ladino woman. Eventually he is considered a lower-class Ladino; but his origin is not forgotten by others, and his pretensions of being a Ladino are denied by lower-class Ladinos, although his children are considered fully Ladino. The desire to cross in San Luis is small. The children from mixed unions have greater chance of being considered and treated as Ladinos than the offspring of two Indians, even if they are educated among and as Ladinos. In practice, Ladinos and Indians consider all of them

Indians; and regardless of amount of acculturation and education, an individual continues to be considered and treated as an Indian. Only one woman tried to pass before both groups, without success. Thus, there is no crossing over, and Ladino status is attained by an Indian only where his ethnic identity is unknown.

In the Chiapas highlands some Ladinos encourage crossing but Indians show little desire. For some urban Ladinos, an Indian may turn into a Ladino, but not conversely, and the offspring of mixed unions would be Mestizo (Colby and van den Berghe, 1960). For the Indians, "an Indian is always an Indian." In the city, a man with marked Indian traits, viewed by some as Indian and by others as Mestizo, possessing some education and wealth, and married to a strongly Caucasoid Ladino woman of the upper class, was socially accepted as Ladino, as were his children. A certain number of Indians, married or living with Ladino women of the lower class, have crossed over to the Ladino group (ibid.). On the other hand, a small number of Ladinoized girls, who attempted to cross by hiding their origin, were considered Indian (Bonilla Domínguez, 1953). In a town a revestido Indian (one who has changed costume), with some schooling and married to a local Ladino woman, was considered and treated as a Ladino. In other towns many revestido Indians, with some wealth, sometimes married to rustic Ladino women, in this way identified themselves with Ladinos, contributing to Ladino festivities and settling their legal affairs with the Ladino secretary or mayor (who was considered Ladino, as were his offspring, but probably was not completely accepted).

In Villa Alta and central Oaxaca many acculturated Indians appeared to be considered (and considered themselves) Indian in origin but Ladino in culture (that is, not real Ladinos). They were not rustic and backward but were treated as Ladinos, whom they had joined by way of modern

445

specializations. In Jamiltepec *revestimiento* (change of dress) and knowledge of Spanish apparently account for a very fluid situation, with much crossing taking place.

Indo-Ladino relationships in four communities of Guatemala show two contradictory aspects: (1) Peaceful relations were without conflict, threat, hostility, or suspicion in Agua Escondida, where Indians did not interfere with the settlement of Ladinos and where an obstruction did not cause resentment or change in the good relations. (2) Similar relations in San Luis Jilotepeque were accompanied by mutual fear, underlying hostility, and Ladino intention to interfere with the rising of the Indians, but did not generate open conflict. (3) Peaceful relations in San Pedro La Laguna were impaired by Ladinos' potential threat to the security of the town, which brought about the town's refusal to sell any more land to Ladinos. (4) Peaceful relations were impregnated with Indians' "great and burning hate" toward Ladinos (caused by great offenses against their religion and probably also by the rape of Indian girls) and toward the Protestants. These attitudes are based on Indian rebellions and massacres of Ladinos when Ladinos formerly occupied Indian territory. The Revolution of 1944 gave rise to changes in the social order such as those described above, but were localized. Even if the Agrarian Reform was a factor of conflict, it did not give San Luis sufficient incentive to revolt, for here the Indians were satisfied with modest reforms in the distribution of the land. The decrease in Indian deference to age and seniority, and the acquisition by Indian young men of urban values, are other aspects of potential conflict.

Mexico presents a range of Indo-Ladino relationship from the peaceful and friendly, as in Yucatan (Redfield, 1941), to permanent conflict, accompanied by fear, resentment, threats, hostility, and open violence. In peaceful communities conflict is confined to the disparity that conservative Ladinos

find in what Indian behavior should be according to tradition and what it actually is *(ibid.)*. In hostile communities the conflict is a consequence of land problems, economic and cultural competition, political dominance of one group over the other, religious differences, and offenses of various sorts to individuals or groups.

In Tantoyuca the distribution of farms through agrarian reform, seizure of Indians' land by Ladinos, lack of Ladino cooperation in public works, destruction of Indian property, threats to them and assassinations of Indian leaders, all created a climate of fear and resentment between the Indians, who do not sell land to Ladinos and do not want the latter to live near them. This picture is similar (especially in the agrarian aspect) to Jamiltepec and many other Indian regions (the Tarahumara, Yaqui, Papago), where demographic pressure among Ladinos and political impotence of Indians lead to seizure of land, forests, and water. Except for some government intervention, Indians in these cases are basically on the defensive against predatory Ladinos.

In Villa Alta relationships are peaceful. There is some Indian resentment because of traditional Ladino dominance in political and cultural affairs. In central Oaxaca, Indian aggression is directed against other Indian towns and arises essentially from problems of land and prestige.

The Chiapas highlands are regions of acute and permanent conflict between Ladinos and Indians. Its origin lies in the messianic rebellions of the Indians before 1860; in other rebellions during the last 50 years; and in the settlement of Ladinos in Indian territory, where land is poor and scarce, although the forests constitute some wealth. The similarity of the hostility of the Chiapas Indians to those of Cuchumatanes, who have had similar experiences, is worth remarking. The actual causes of friction are numerous: formation of some ejidos of the Indians from Ladinos' farms; recent seizure of Indian lands by Ladinos; attempts of authorities and a Ladino alcohol monopoly to suppress the determined and illegal production of alcohol by the Indians and the consequent fighting and violence in these repeated attempts; restrictions imposed by Indians on Ladinos in matters of commerce; continuation of the Ladino penetration into Indian territory and resistance of Indians to it. This sums up the economic sources of conflict. Noneconomic factors are the ascent to power of Indians, and the dangerousness or criminality of some aggressive Indians and Ladinos, the Protestant penetration which gives rise to violent encounters between the Indians, and makes them suspicious towards Ladinos. Life in the towns is especially hazardous at times of religious festival during which Indians or Ladinos become intoxicated and threaten to or do attack those of the opposite group, who flee from the towns. (Intragroup aggressions are also common among Indians as well as among Ladinos.) The carnivals of the Indians give rise, on the other hand, to false rumors of rebellions which reach the city and frighten its inhabitants. Other Indians who occasionally inspire similar fears in Ladinos are in remote places: the Maya of Quintana Roo and the Yaquis of Sonora.

Guatemala (until 1944) and Mexico (until 1910) were similar not only because of their formation by similar peoples with similar cultures and as (until last century) a political unit, but also because of the system of ethnic relationships. In the epoch immediately preceding this, these systems were uniform: two castes co-existed in apparently stable equilibrium. Premises of biological origin, of which remnants are still well delineated, maintained, to a greater degree than currently, the positions of the castes, as well as conditioning the future. Equilibrium, and the conceptions on which it was based, began to be threatened during the latter half of the last century, in the northern area by social and scientific speculations which run counter to current opinion regarding the Indian and by the con-

structive interest about him (Stabb, 1959). The threat turned into a break with the treatment given to Maya and Yaquis and the social and political movement of 1910. A similar movement, that of 1944, attempted to produce similar effects in the southern area. In both cases, the incomplete process produced incomplete results.

Each local ethnic system, as well as the factors on which it depends, shows many similarities with other local systems: generally superior economic position of the Ladino group over the Indian group; cultural duality, with generally admitted overvaluation by Ladinos of their culture and language, and undervaluation of Indian culture and language frequently accepted by the Indians; racial duality, whether real or imagined, which in some cases rationalizes the positions of the groups, favoring the Ladino and undervaluing the Indian; constant narrowing of the ethnic relationships between the groups through traditional contacts and, more frequently, new ones in spite of the instances of breaks of the relationships; and the crossing of Indian to Ladino through acculturation and amalgamation. Some of the differences in the local systems, partly set forth above, are more of degree than of quality.

The basic tendency of change in the caste structure, which with more or less rigidity appears especially in the southern part, through diminution and annulment of the differences between Ladinos and Indians which give basis to the caste. The process is one way, from Indian to Ladino. That the tendency is more evident in the northern area than in the southern is indicated by the greater desire of Indians toward acculturation and toward national culture, smaller Ladino resistance to amalgamation and acculturation and more permissiveness in giving Indians positions of power. Acculturation means not only to adopt cultural traits, but to change "race," as someone might change costume, when race is negatively important.

447

As Colby and van den Berghe record (1960), the processes of change are conditioned, to a great extent, by communication. To this should be added the particular ideology of "lifting up the Indian." Communication implies roads and a better knowledge and use of Spanish by the Indians, two mechanisms which have received greater development in the northern area. Communication is a factor of amalgamation, although places like Agua Escondida, where both groups are bilingual, do not resolve themselves in greater amalgamation. That communication or isolation do not operate equally in all cases is suggested by the evidence. The isolation of Chiapas, not broken until recently, "explains" to a certain extent the conservatism of that region and the small number of mixed unions. However, Jamiltepec was (and still is) as isolated as Chiapas, perhaps more so; amalgamation has taken place there at an apparently faster rate. The presence of a third group, the Negro, might contribute to its explanation.

That the change from caste to class is not a peaceful process in the area is evidenced in the results—some temporary and others lasting—of the two social movements referred to, especially the one which took place in the northern area. Without well-delineated racial antagonism in the majority of cases, the relationships are not, strictly speaking, of castes but of classes or quasi-classes in competition. In these relationships, the old and the new form a combination not very different from that presented by ethnic relationships in the modern colonial world.

REFERENCES

Adams, R. N., 1956c, 1957b
Bonilla D., 1953
Cámara B., 1952a
Colby and van den Berghe, 1960
De la Fuente, 1952, 1958a
Drucker, 1959
Gillin, 1952
Guiteras Holmes, 1946b, 1948a
LaFarge, 1947
Morales, 1952

Redfield, 1939, 1941, 1946a, 1946b
Roberts, 1948
Romano, 1952
Stabb, 1959
Tax, 1941
Taylor, P. S., 1933b
Tumin, 1952, 1956
Wagley, 1958
Wisdom, 1940

23. Acculturation

———

RALPH L. BEALS

IN MIDDLE AMERICA the processes of acculturation antedate contact with European culture. In preconquest times periods of widespread similarities can be identified, sometimes accompanied by migration, military operations, and extended political controls over considerable areas. Some evidence for these processes is to be found in the native documents; more can probably be adduced from the archaeological records. Thus far preconquest data, whether documentary or archaeological, have rarely been analyzed from the standpoint of acculturation theories. The acculturation approach may have possible utility in future ethnohistorical and archaeological research. A little-recognized example is Kirchhoff's (1956b) interpretive text to the Relación de Michoacan.

Most studies of acculturation in Middle America either are concerned with the impact of Spanish culture on native cultures at or near contact times or focus on the impact of urbanism, industrialism, and nationalism on contemporary Colonial-Indian communities. In recent years some studies also have investigated modern examples of directed culture change. The 17th, 18th,

and 19th centuries have received little notice. Studies of directed culture change have not extended into the past, although Spanish policy in colonial times represents one of the most intensive and prolonged efforts at directed change for which substantial documentation exists. Some historians and anthropologists also have recognized the influence of Indian cultures on colonial Spanish culture, but this reciprocal aspect of acculturation in Middle America has been given little systematic consideration. Material on the colonial period is found in the work of such historians as E. B. Adams, Woodrow B. Borah, François Chevalier, Howard V. Cline, Lewis Hanke, Charles Gibson, J. Miranda, Robert Ricard, Ralph L. Roys, France V. Scholes, Lesley B. Simpson, Silvio Zavala, and others. Some of the important works are listed at the end of this article. They afford ample evidence that a rich harvest awaits the ethnohistorian. This article deals primarily with Indian acculturation, but devotes some attention to the reciprocal adjustments of Spanish-Indian social systems in the early period.

As used here the term *acculturation* re-

449

fers to changes and processes occurring in special situations where culture contact is massive and prolonged. Two aspects are distinguished: (1) the adaptations and modifications of the social systems in contact, and (2) the changes in cultural content of the systems in contact. Unlike Drucker (1958), I do not confine the term to situations where a culture in a subordinate position has lost complete freedom of choice. In Middle America the dominant Spanish culture also underwent change and lost complete freedom of choice. In his complementary article on nationalization (Article 24), R. N. Adams treats acculturation as leading to assimilation. I find it useful to consider this one possible end result of acculturation, involving a complete disappearance of one culture. Alternatively, cultures in contact may reach new equilibria in their interrelationships as well as undergo internal modification. Finally, the processes of acculturation are seen as primarily social and cultural. Individuals may change membership from one society to the other or develop dual membership or otherwise occupy intermediate positions between two cultures. More commonly, persons in dual or intermediate positions actually are occupying new roles within one social system, roles concerned with interaction and communication with another system.

Oliver LaFarge (1940) suggested the first historical framework for Indian acculturation, characterizing different phases for the highland Maya. Subsequently I suggested (1949, 1951, 1952) that this scheme could be applied to all Middle America. In modified form the main periods of post-conquest acculturation are: (1) Contact (including conquest where relevant) and Consolidation—referred to briefly hereafter as the Contact period; (2) First Colonial Indian, a period of intensive and in part directed acceptance of Spanish culture and changing social systems; (3) Second Colonial Indian (LaFarge's First Transition), a period of protected isolation, synthesis and

integration of surviving Indian cultures; (4) First Republican Indian (beginning with Independence), continued integration in the face of renewed pressures; (5) Second Republican Indian, renewed penetration of modern national cultures; (6) Modern Indian, efforts at incorporation or directed culture change with rapid acculturation.[1]

In presenting this outline of periods adapted from LaFarge, I have given no dates. Although the stages are widely and perhaps universally applicable to individual Indian cultures within Middle America, the initial and closing dates for some of the periods may vary by as much as a century for different groups. Important variables in the acculturation process consequently may differ from region to region; for example, Spanish culture and society in Middle America were substantially different in 1600 from what they were in 1520. Despite such qualifications, the stages given offer a useful framework for the discussion of both general trends and the variations within specific cultures and areas.

Contact and Consolidation Period

This period covers the time from first contact of a culture with Europeans to the consolidation of Spanish authority and policy. Emphasis in most historical studies has been on the fact of conquest, a term to be avoided for many reasons. Often the transition from first contact to relatively stable consolidation of Spanish authority took place without military operations. Further, the emphasis of most historical discussions on the military operations against Tenoch-

[1] Spicer (1961) has suggested a four-period classification for the Yaqui of Sonora. A similar four-period classification might be developed for other groups in Mexico if the emphasis were to be placed, as by Spicer, purely on the Indian cultures. In the LaFarge-Beals scheme an attempt has been made at compromise between crucial events in the dominant society and the reactions of native societies to the changed situation. Even so, Spicer identifies five types of cultural change taking place in three of his four periods.

titlan and subsequent activities in regions of resistance has almost totally concealed the fact that the Spanish initially appeared to many Middle American peoples as liberators, as in central Mexico, or as decisive factors in wars between competing groups, as in parts of Yucatan and elsewhere. Moreover, many past discussions fail to distinguish between the West Indies and Middle America. What was deplorable in Santo Domingo or Cuba often is assumed to be applicable to all Middle America.

Many aspects of the Contact period are under restudy and are discussed elsewhere, so only the most general remarks relevant to acculturation will be made here. Past interpretations either have overemphasized the colorful aspects of the conquest of Tenochtitlan examined solely from a European point of view in the tradition established by Prescott (1843) or have concentrated on the history and social organization of the Azteca or Mexica to the exclusion of other groups. Furthermore, study of the Azteca has suffered from the early bias introduced by Bandelier (1880b), whose interpretations were made through Morgan-tinted spectacles. Important new interpretations of the native cultures and the contact period include such works as Carrasco for the Otomi (1950a), Monzón on the calpulli (1949), Acosta Saignes on the Pochteca or merchants (1945), Aguirre Beltrán on the Señorío de Cuauhtochco (1940), Jiménez Moreno and Mateos Higuera on the Codice de Yanhuitlan (1940), Kirchhoff on the Tarascans (1956b), Caso on Mixtec and Aztec (1959), Chamberlain on Yucatan and Honduras (1948, 1953), and Roys on Yucatan (1943). Important studies by Paul Kirchhoff, Wigberto Jiménez Moreno and other Mexican scholars are still unpublished.

Many newer studies suggest that the controversial calpulli or a similar unit was the basis of the political and social structure over much of Middle America. These units were relatively small landholding social groups with the population concentrated either in a single community or in a dominant community with smaller satellite communities. Within each of these units existed stratified lineages, probably exogamous. One lineage may have been regarded as a chiefly lineage; at least it normally provided the principal rulers. However, heads of other lineages also participated in government as members of a council or in other capacities. (Some, e.g., Caso and Kirchhoff, still insist on the calpulli as a kinship unit or endogamous "clan.") It seems likely that the boundaries of such units often still are reflected in the boundaries of many existing municipios.[2]

Frequently such units were linked together by conquest, in what is preferably called a *señorio* (the term *cacicazgo* is also employed). In such cases one calpulli provided the top ruling group for the señorio, and members of this calpulli as a whole may have occupied a higher status within the society. At a higher level of organization, a number of señorios were sometimes linked together to form a larger state, as in the case of Tlaxcala. In other instances, both such states and individual señorios or unassociated calpulli might be dominated by a large urban center or by a confederacy of such centers (e.g., Aztec confederacy). The large urban centers in the highlands apparently consisted of several calpulli joined in a common residential center (but retaining separate landholdings) and organized for common purposes.

At the time of the Spanish conquest, the Aztec confederacy was mainly a military domination of other states, señorios or cal-

[2] The system outlined, or something very like it, seems fairly clearly established for most of the Nahua-speaking peoples and most of their neighbors such as the Mixtec and the Zapotec. The situation among the Maya-speaking peoples is much less clear, although the degrees of social stratification implied were at least as complex. The Tarascan area unquestionably differed in important respects, for in this area landholding may have been based on the individual rather than on calpulli and lineage.

451

pulli-type organizations. The main purposes of the domination were to ensure open avenues of trade and to collect fixed tributes. In addition, a portion of the lands of the calpulli organizations were commonly set aside for the production of tribute, the support of military garrisons, the support of religious establishments, and sometimes for Aztec nobility. The cultivation of such lands was either by communal labor of the "free" members of the lineage, through establishment of a serflike class atta hed to particular lands, by slaves, or by a system of tenant farming. This land division was superimposed on that existing in the "independent" calpulli where, in addition to communal lands distributed among the commoners or *macehuals,* some lands were owned by *pilli* or permanent nobility, and others were set aside for the support of temporary officials and local religious purposes. (Cf. Aguirre Beltrán, 1940, 1953; Caso, 1959; Kirchhoff, 1955, 1956a,b; Monzón, 1949; Wolf, 1959. For Yucatan see Roys, 1943).

The purpose of reviewing these basic socio-political structures is to clarify both the nature of the "conquest" and the subsequent administrative arrangements. The success of the conquest depended in part on the early establishment of communication channels, at first controlled by the Spanish. The recovery of a survivor of a Spanish shipwreck in Yucatan established a linguistic channel with Yucatecan Maya. The famous bilingual (in Maya and Nahua) Marina established a second initial linguistic link which made it possible for Cortés to perceive and to capitalize on the fundamental weakness of the empire of the Aztec confederacy. (Díaz del Castillo, 1927, contains abundant data.)

It now seems clear that in areas dominated by or threatened by the Aztec confederacy the "conquest" was essentially a native insurrection against the Aztecs for which the Spanish provided leadership. It is true that the first active allies, the Tlax-

calans, had not been brought under the domination of the confederacy. However, the Tlaxcalan state had been encircled and was hard pressed through the cutting of its normal trade routes, particularly for such essentials as salt (Gibson, 1952; Muñoz Camargo, 1947). More than 20 other groups, from the Chinanteca in Oaxaca to peoples in Panuco, followed the lead of the Tlaxcalans even after the first disastrous Spanish defeat at Tenochtitlan. A major member of the confederacy itself, Texcoco, defected to the Spanish-led insurrection. Many other independent groups such as the Tarascans remained neutral, as did many of the Aztec-dominated groups such as the Mixtec and Zapotec (Cortés letters in Díaz, 1927). "It was the intense hatred evoked by the Aztecs among their vassal states which made possible the conquest of the empire by a mere handful of Spaniards" (Simpson, 1950, p. vii. See also Simpson, 1952, pp. 22–23; Jiménez Rueda, 1951, p. 4; Gonzales Obregón, 1952, pp. 57, 60, 100).

The importance of these details to the matter of acculturation is to emphasize that for many groups the first contact and the "conquest" was not a traumatic conflict of cultures in at least the physical sense. For many groups the processes of the conquest were a continuation of ancient power struggles characterized by violent conflict and shifting alliances. (Significantly, the first major problem of the Spanish forces after the final capitulation of Tenochtitlan was to prevent their Indian allies from massacring all the survivors.) For not a few groups, the conquest was a liberation. Aguirre Beltrán's thesis of "culture shock" (1946, pp. 247–48) based on the abolition of polygyny is unacceptable. As Monzón (1949, p. 25) points out, polygyny was beyond the economic possibilities of the macehual. Jiménez Moreno's (1956) position on culture conflict likewise is extreme, if applied to all Middle America.

A revealing case history is provided by the Mixtecan community of Yanhuitlan

(Jiménez Moreno and Mateos Higuera, 1940). Yanhuitlan was first taken by the Aztec in 1486. In the 34 years before the fall of Tenochtitlan, Yanhuitlan or its close-by neighbors were involved in seven uprisings. Over 20,000 prisoners from the region are recorded as being sacrificed in Mexico City, including a thousand from Yanhuitlan. On one occasion the town and its fields and orchards were laid waste and, except for those taken for sacrifice to Mexico City, all who did not escape were killed regardless of sex or age. This list does not include various local wars with Mixtec and Zapotec señorios. In contrast, in the first 30 years under Spanish rule Yanhuitlan underwent no military occupation or conflict and for many years had no permanent Spanish resident. There is no evidence that tributes at any time significantly exceeded those paid to the Aztec confederacy. When converted to cash payments in 1560 they amounted to about 1 peso a year per person. Spanish rule, in contrast with the preceding Aztec period, was a time of peace and prosperity.

If the initial contact was not always a violent military conquest, neither did it take place at the same time for all groups. The first attempt at the conquest of Yucatan began in 1527 and ended in failure. The second and successful attempt did not begin until 1541; as in central Mexico, its success in part lay in the ability of the Spanish to capitalize on native power struggles between rival groups (Villa R., 1945, pp. 10–14). Spanish penetration was slow in other regions where no economic advantage accrued. The Mixe were not effectively controlled until about 1600. The Sierra de Nayar and some Maya-speaking groups were not pacified until the 18th century.

Once the major "conquest" of central Mexico is seen in the perspective of a native insurrection, the Spanish military achievement seems less remarkable than does the Spanish success in consolidating their position as heads of a unified state.

The continued Spanish presence in Middle America depended on the mutual accommodation of the European and native social systems. This accommodation began before the fall of Tenochtitlan. For central Mexico the main patterns were worked out by the end of the Second Audiencia in 1535. Actual implementation of these patterns in detail mainly took place after this date, and the process of accommodation and consolidation in some measure continued to the end of the First Colonial Indian period. Moreover, the effectiveness of the basic patterns of accommodation varied with the time, with the distance from the major center of control, Mexico City, and to some extent with the kinds of social patterns existing in the native groups. It may be noted, for example, that the Spanish adaptations failed almost completely with the nomadic nonagricultural peoples of the north.

Furthermore, it must be recognized that before the implementation of a system of accommodation was effective, some populations were destroyed and the social systems of others hopelessly disrupted. The activities of Nuño de Guzmán in Panuco and the northwest can only be described as those of a sadistic butcher. The expedition of Alvarado to Guatemala, especially on the Soconusco coast, was little better. On the other hand, it must be observed that these expeditions had the willing and possibly even enthusiastic cooperation, not only of such early native allies as the Tlaxcalans, but apparently of many survivors of the original Aztec-dominated confederacy. A case could be made that the extension of Spanish control was viewed by some Indian participants as a reconquest and extension of the hegemony of the Nahua-speakers of the Central Plateau.

Before we summarize the adaptations, some conditions of the conquest should be reviewed. Virtually all early exploration and conquest in the New World was undertaken by private enterprise under license from the Crown. Only in rare instances did

453

the Crown or its representatives subsidize or become a direct partner in the enterprises. Although in the Cortés expedition the governor of Cuba, Velásquez, not only issued the license but was a shareholder in the expedition, he was but one member of a corporate enterprise. Most of the important members of the Cortés expedition were shareholders and, when the enterprise succeeded, felt themselves entitled to a share in the profits.

Cortés's famous "treason" toward Governor Velásquez may consequently be viewed as actions by the majority shareholders (a) to seek a royal charter in place of a gubernatorial charter, and (b) to follow time-honored Spanish practice and establish a town or *cabildo* for which, as was common, a royal charter or *fuero* should be sought. The "citizens" of the new town (who were also shareholders in the expedition) then elected Cortés their leader or *adelantado*. Cortés subsequently acted under the assumption that the requests to the Crown would be granted and operated both as the active manager of the corporation and, through the authority of the cabildo, as a representative of the Crown. In this and in many of his subsequent actions he modified Spanish socio-political institutions but he did not abandon them.

The clamor of the "stockholders" for returns on their investment forced Cortés to introduce the encomienda system into Middle America, a step he took, however, subject to confirmation by the Crown and with important modifications from its Spanish and Antillean prototype. A second important action as an officer of the Crown was to persuade as many Indian groups as possible to become Crown subjects. In some cases, of which the Tlaxcalans are the most notable, the agreements included exemptions from the encomienda and the payment of tributes. More importantly, the way was opened for the Crown, in protection of its subjects, slowly to establish direct authority in what has been called the reconquest of Mexico from the original conquistadors (Simpson, 1952, chs. 5, 6).

Crown policy in the initial periods faced several problems.

(1) To ensure continued loyalty of the Spanish in Middle America in the face of separatist ambitions on the part of some conquistadors and settlers and to maintain minimal armed forces. This required some system of rewards and the Crown reluctantly continued the encomienda system with increasing limitations and restrictions. The holders of encomiendas acquired no land rights but only the right to collect tributes. Personal labor service was curtailed and eventually prohibited; rights to Indian labor were separated from the encomienda itself. *Repartimientos* of Indians —separated from the *repartimiento de tierras* (the encomienda)—were regulated, providing minimum wages, working conditions, and curtailing the maximum distance Indians could be required to travel. In addition, the use of Indians as porters or in sugar plantations and underground mining operations was early forbidden. Indian slavery was restricted and soon abolished.

(2) To maintain an adequate labor force, both for the support of the Spanish colonists and to provide revenues for the support of the colonial administration and the Spanish government in the metropolis. The repartimiento was part of the solution, but it also was necessary to maintain the labor force by preventing the depopulation that had occurred in the Antilles.

(3) To meet obligations of the Crown to its new Indian subjects. Contemporary Spanish political and social thought were consonant with the maintenance of the bulk of the Indian population as an agricultural peasantry and labor force. Belief in a stratified society was strong, as was belief that the health of the state required a wealthy nobility able to support and defend its retainers and dependents. At the same time the peasantry must be inducted into Spanish culture, a task laid primarily upon the

Church, especially through the various missionary orders, with the direct support of the Crown or of the encomenderos.

The implementation of these contradictory goals took a long time, and Spanish policy and administration were often uneven and vacillating as opposing interests struggled for influence and position. Much has been made of the arguments over the qualities and capabilities of the American Indian, culminating in the great dispute between Las Casas and Sepúlveda in 1550 (Hanke, 1959). Yet the doctrine of Natural Rights became basic to Spanish policy in Middle America when Cortés offered and the Tlaxcalans accepted the sovereignty of the Spanish Crown, together with Spanish recognition of property rights and the hereditary titles of rulers. The form of this agreement also implied acceptance of a native stratified society of a type not incompatible with Spanish thought, and laid the groundwork for the system of indirect rule by which alone Spanish administration succeeded.

The importance of the acceptance of Spanish authority is evidenced in the fact that even before the fall of Tenochtitlan Cortés was being called upon to be the arbiter of native disputes concerning dynastic succession. The way was paved thereby for the Spanish to assume the top position within the native hierarchy of office and power. Even high-ranking members of the native nobility were assimilated into the system and some who went to Spain, including members of the family of Montezuma, received high honors from the Crown and became permanent residents of Spain. After the fall of Tenochtitlan, Cortés appointed surviving Aztec officials to "the important offices which they had formerly held" (translation from Cortés letters, Simpson, 1952, p. 26).

Recognition of surviving upper classes was supplemented by encouragement of intermarriage. The majority of the companions of Cortés took Indian wives. Both legitimate and natural sons of Spaniards and Indians could go freely to Spain. Martín Cortés, illegitimate son of Cortés and Doña Marina, received the habit of Santiago directly from the king, fought in Germany and Algiers, and died in 1569 fighting a *morisco* uprising in Granada. As late as 1697 a royal cédula decreed that principal descendants of native nobility should receive the same privileges and honors as *nobles hijosdalgos* of Castile (Martin, 1957, pp. 92–95, reviews the data succinctly).

The Second Audiencia established the principle of limited self-government for Indian communities, perpetuating on the one hand the position of the native rulers, and establishing on the other hand governments which incorporated many features of the government of Spanish "free" towns (a type already declining in Spain). This decision was further implemented under the first viceroy, Mendoza. The general pattern involved a mayor, a council, judge, police chief, and a superintendent of public works. (English terms are used here because the Spanish terms employed vary from place to place.) Although not explicit in the documents, a number of religious functions and officials were incorporated, and the offices formed a hierarchy through which theoretically all men passed or could pass. Aguirre Beltrán (1953), Carrasco (1961), and Vogt (1961) have discussed the extent to which this form was consonant with pre-Spanish institutions and officeholding.

Powers of the officials included maintenance of internal order, protection of town rights, conduct of public works, collection of tributes, and selection of persons to work in repartimientos. Before the end of the 16th century powers were extended to include the arrest of Spaniards for certain offenses and their conveyance to the nearest Spanish courts. Often the cacique remained in office, either as an additional official or as a continually re-elected mayor. Along with these powers, he held lands apart from the community lands and often received

455

special tributes and service from townsfolk. Some caciques survived until Independence (Simpson, 1952, ch. 9).

The towns also held a specified land area much as did the calpulli. Most attention has been paid to the relocated towns, but some town charters specify aboriginal boundaries and holdings. Schmieder (1930) gives several examples. In the main, communal lands and lands of the caciques were respected where adequate authority existed. As the successor to Aztec government, however, the Crown laid claim to the so-called lands of Montezuma, lands set aside to produce tributes, to support religious establishments, to support garrisons, or regarded as unoccupied. The macehual, however, was generally left in undisturbed possession of community lands and, with the continuance in office of the caciques and perpetuation of the preconquest tribute system, for some time the bulk of the population, the macehual, experienced minimal disturbance in his life-ways. To his lands in theory, and often for some time in practice, neither Spaniards nor Indians of other communities had access.

The system of town government, perpetuation of the cacique and his successful Hispanicization (Gibson, 1955, 1959), and the continuation of land and tribute systems "bears the stamp of genius" (Simpson, 1952, p. 43). Its success may be measured by the fact that by 1600 "there was no regular military establishment in New Spain south of the Chichimec frontier" (*ibid.*, p. 88). The institutional arrangements also had the unforeseen effect of creating almost ideal boundary-maintaining mechanisms and are intimately linked with the persistence of many Indian communities to the present (Hinton, 1961).

Essentially the system of town government envisioned two "republics," one Spanish and one Indian. Other important decisions made in the consolidation period included the policy of placing the indoctrination of the Indians primarily in the hands

of the regular clergy of the so-called predicatory or missionary orders, primarily the Franciscans, Dominicans, and Augustinians, followed later by the Jesuits. A related decision was to emphasize the use of native languages. To this may be attributed the great production of grammars, catechisms, and other documents in native languages produced by the members of the regular clergy in the 16th century. In not a few cases the entry of the missionaries into special regions was delayed until they had proper linguistic preparation (Ricard, 1933).

The accounts of mass baptisms in the early contact period obscure the fact that close Church contact with many groups was actually in the First Colonial period. Although caciques and sons of caciques might be brought to Mexico City for education (especially at the famous school in Tlatilolco), appearance of either secular or regular clergy was rare in many regions. For example, only two of the many Dominican monasteries in the state of Oaxaca can be dated before 1550 (Kubler, 1948; Bishop Bartolomé Zarate as cited in Bancroft, 1883, 10: 728).

Another decision of some importance was to simplify the calendar of saints and to elaborate the pageantry associated with special religious celebrations in order to offset the colorful aspects of native religious events. Although perhaps not a matter of formal policy, the introduction of the auto or religious drama associated with some modification of the cofradía or religious-cult group was widely observed. Native dances deemed not "immoral" were often encouraged, even in the church (Foster, 1960a, pp. 164–234; Ricard, 1933, pp. 217–47). By the time of Jesuit entry into the Cahita area in the late 16th century this practice evidently was common (Beals, 1943, p. 66; 1945a, p. 202).

The separation of Indian masses from Spanish was also connected with the land policies and the gradual restriction of the encomienda. The encomendero, at first envisioned as a civilizing agent, was later discouraged from living on his encomienda. Indeed, early in the First Colonial Indian period residence in Indian towns of any Spaniards other than religious was prohibited (Simpson, 1950; Zavala, 1941; Martin, 1957, pp. 100–06).

For central Mexico, then, the basic patterns of adjustment of the two social systems in contact had begun to emerge in the Contact and Consolidation period. They were to be added to, elaborated, and in some extent implemented in the early part of First Colonial Indian and they were to result in somewhat different experiences where the effective contact period was later than in central Mexico. That these policies were not initially successful in many areas is a problem dealt with in the discussion of the First Colonial Indian period.

What is of primary importance here is that the problem of New Spain early came to be viewed as a gigantic attempt at planned culture change with the ultimate view of assimilation of the Indian population into a new stratified society at levels comparable to their position in the aboriginal stratified society. An important aspect of the planning was recognition that the process was reciprocal and required the modification of many institutions in the Spanish system. The many changes in material aspects of Spanish colonial (and even of Spanish metropolitan) culture have been too extensively documented to need discussion here. What is less frequently recognized is the extent to which adjustment to the native social system modified Spanish Colonial Society.

FIRST COLONIAL INDIAN PERIOD

This period began in central Mexico with the first viceroy, Antonio de Mendoza (1535–51). During these years the main features of Spanish administration became firmly established although additional implementation continued into the next century. The consequences of this consolidation were felt at later dates in more remote areas such as Guatemala or in the northern frontiers and regions such as Yucatan where the effective conquest came later. Crown policies were in general protective of the Indian population, and the effectiveness of administration gradually increased through time. Its accomplishments varied, however, with local conditions, the degree of resistance from Spanish settlers, and the character of high officials. Nevertheless, at times, enforcement of regulations against Spaniards was thorough and even drastic (as in the final abolition of Indian slavery).

For a very large number of Indians the First Colonial period was one of rapid acculturation under varying degrees of direction. Full understanding of this period would require a much more detailed study of the policies and activities of the missionary orders than is presently available, for there are indications of deliberate experimentalism in the early part of the missionary period.

The Franciscans, first in the field, initially were dedicated to formal educational and paternalistic approaches. Their educational efforts were directed especially toward the Indian elite. Of efforts at planned reconstruction of Indian societies the most notable is that begun by Bishop Vasco de Quiroga to establish the *Utopia* of Sir Thomas More among the Tarascans, vestiges of which still may be found in Michoacan (Zavala, 1941). The view that the simple poverty-stricken and humble Indian provided an ideal field for the re-establishment of primitive Christianity in accordance with Franciscan ideals had a powerful hold on many. At the same time there was an "anti-Indian faction" which held the Indian to be incapable of achieving the higher levels of Christian belief or Spanish culture, a view that apparently grew over time along with a shift toward increasing orthodoxy in religious matters.

The Dominicans were less impressed by

457

native simplicity and more dedicated to formal orthodoxy. Maintenance of native private property and minimum interference with native political institutions were parts of Dominican practice. The *Caja de Comunidad* was a Dominican innovation, a town treasury supplied by collective cultivation of communal lands or from community-owned livestock. The Caja was subject to abuse by Indian officials but at its best it paid the community tribute, cared for the indigent, provided for community improvements, and supported the resident priest. Early accusations of Dominican exploitation of the Caja seem poorly founded; such a possibility was forestalled in later times by placing the Caja exclusively under Indian control.

The Augustinians emphasized administration and organization. They also were the most active in establishing centers for training the Indians in new crafts and in new farming techniques. Alone among the three early orders, they consistently defended the admission of Indians to full communion whereas the other orders tended in time to lose confidence in the Indians' ability fully to comprehend and accept Christian doctrine.

As later comers, the Jesuits seem to have used a blend of established practices. They were notable for their flexibility and their adaptation of native observances. In the main, however, their activities in New Spain were in the northern frontier beyond the margins of Middle America.

All orders seem to some extent to have encouraged the continuance of town specialization and the existing systems of regional markets, adapting the latter to conform to the Christian calendar. More study of the missionary orders should throw important light on differences between surviving Indian cultures. (The superficial comments above are mainly from Barth, 1950; Bannon, 1955; L. Christensen, n.d.; Phelan, 1956; Ricard, 1933; See, n.d.)

Finally, of extreme importance was the training of native assistants as lay readers. In most areas there were never enough missionaries to provide a permanent resident in every town. Even in the rare instances where the number of missionaries equaled the number of towns, this condition lasted only for a brief period. Of necessity, most towns were merely *visitas*. Analysis of the vicarage of Totontepec and its 21 visitas among the Mixe (Schmieder, 1930) suggests that the single priest normally in residence would have spent approximately 30 days traveling over poor trails in very rugged country in order to reach all the visitas. Burgoa notes that at least three missionaries in this area were killed in falls from the rocky and steep trails, and that ". . . the distance between places and the ruggedness of the trails occupied their days, while nights sleeping in wastes among rocks and wild beasts, without shelter from the rains nor clothing for the snows, necessitated prolonged exposure to these embarrassments" (translation from Beals, 1945b, p. 12). Although conditions in the Mixeria may have been extreme, evidence elsewhere suggests that the majority of Indian communities were visitas without permanent resident missionary priests. Even a town with a resident priest often was so large in population as to prevent effective ministry.

Under these circumstances the functions of the missionary priest in purveying Spanish culture as well as in evangelizing the population were supplemented by native assistants, who in most cases had far more intimate contact with the population than did the priest (Ricard, 1933, pp. 117–18). Usually lay assistants were literate enough to read prayers and services, as well as to catechize the young or the unconverted; in addition they often secretly kept records of native practices. This has been documented only for the Maya area (LaFarge, 1940, pp. 287–88) but literacy in native languages is known to have been widespread in the 16th century and among some groups persists to this day (e.g., among the Yaqui).

458

The evidence of planned selectivity in the transmission of Spanish culture and the role of the lay reader suggests an important lead for further research. Nevertheless, planning alone does not account for all the selective transmission. Only Foster (1960a) has grappled with this problem, pointing out many cases where not only Middle America but all the Spanish New World seems to have received only one of several alternatives. For example, only one type of several Spanish plows seems to have been adopted in the New World. Foster (1960a, pp. 227–34) suggests that the process of "crystallization" occurred, i.e., the adoption of one satisfactory form lessened the probability that an alternate but not clearly superior form would be adopted. Foster suggests that the first transmission of Spanish cultural items was through direct contact in the Contact period, whereas after the rural-urban segregation of Indian-Spanish populations took place, transmission tended to be indirect with the growing Mestizo population serving as intermediaries. This view overlooks the importance of the continuing influence of the missionary orders. In many areas the relatively educated Indian elite also acted as intermediaries as late as the early 17th century and often beyond (Carrasco, 1961); nor were the Indians at first so isolated from urban contacts. Hawkes mentions the willingness of Indians to travel as much as 20 leagues to an urban center to file complaints or engage in lawsuits, this as late as 1572 (cited in Chevalier, 1952, p. 266). Nevertheless, as many writers have observed, apparently there was an early period of high receptivity on the part of the Indian populations. Bernal Díaz gives a compact account of the extent of acculturation (1927, 2: 546–47). Contributing factors to this receptivity undoubtedly were both intermarriage in the early period and some degree of acculturation of the Spanish population.

The main characteristics of the First Colonial Indian culture and the relations between Spanish and Indian seem to have crystallized within 50 or 60 years after the Contact period. The time for this varied, of course; in Yucatan, Scholes (1937, p. 131) places the crystallization point at about 1600, a function of the later conquest of that area.

Throughout the First Colonial Indian period Indian-Spanish relationships underwent a gradual change. Missionary supervision contributed to continuing alienation of Indians from native culture. At the same time a number of factors contributed to an increasing resistance toward new Spanish influences. The great epidemics in the latter part of the 16th century reduced Indian populations drastically, in many areas making it difficult for communities to maintain use and occupancy of lands. The caciques were in large measure destroyed economically also and their lands were usually sold to Spaniards. The caciques had been made responsible for the collection and payment of tributes and, although Spanish officialdom made real efforts to reassess tributes in terms of actual remaining heads of families, the problem was recognized too late and the bureaucracy worked too slowly for most caciques to survive (Chevalier, 1952, p. 273).

The opening years of the 17th century saw a major effort to concentrate the Indians in *congregaciones*. The evil effects of this move have been greatly exaggerated for Mexico, except for the nomadic peoples of the north. Much of the criticism by historians is based on the uncritical assumption that the village-dwelling Indians in Mexico were affected by the congregaciones in the same way as the Indians of the Antilles. Actually the same single concrete case of ill-effects of the congregaciones is cited for Mexico by a number of historians of the colonial period and refers to the Mixe of Nejapa, a mountain ranchería-dwelling people. Samplings of the archives by Simpson (1934) and Torre Villar (1952) indicate that for most of Mexico the early 17th-century congregaciones were consolidations of smaller communities, heavily depopulated by the disastrous series of epidemics. Plans were made after detailed consultation with the Indians involved and, if they proved unsatisfactory, in many cases the congregaciones were dissolved, the Indians returning to their original villages or hamlets.

The receptivity of native populations to Spanish culture clearly was quite variable. In some instances acceptance was perhaps inversely proportioned to the degree of contact and perhaps also related to previous history. The community of Yanhuitlan, later the site of the greatest Dominican church and monastery in the Mixtec region, except for one year (1529), had no permanent resident Dominican priest until 1535 or 1536. Apparently another period without Dominican residents occurred between about 1541 and 1548. All this time Yanhuitlan was the only "permanent" mission establishment for most of the Mixteca Alta (Jiménez Moreno and Mateos Higuera, 1940, pp. 21–23). Despite this lack of continuing direct contact, Yanhuitlan was the center for the introduced silk industry which, until ruined by oriental competition, not only appears to have paid for all the tributes but provided a sizable surplus. The will left by the cacique D. Gabriel de Guzmán dated 1591 itemizes the household furnishings of a relatively prosperous Spanish gentleman, including a number of European paintings and books considered of sufficient value to be itemized (*ibid.*, pp. 34–36).

Thus far the discussion has dealt with those Indian groups who accommodated to the new superordinate social system and survived for a significant time as identifiable social entities, many to the present day. Not all Indian groups so adapted. Not a few individuals became assimilated at a quite early time. The term Ladino originally meant a Spanish-speaking Indian; in 16th-century Mexico it was usually applied to an Indian who not only spoke Spanish

but who had adopted Spanish dress and culture. Near most Spanish towns were Indian *barrios* to supply the local labor force. Once the early practice of trying to rear the offspring of Spanish fathers as Europeans (and including them in the count of "Europeans") was abandoned, these barrios were gradually mestizoized. With the appearance of wage labor in the late 16th century, many Indians voluntarily left their homes to enter the labor force (Chevalier, 1952, p. 385).

Many areas early became practically depopulated, mainly in the regions of violent resistance or early unbridled brutality and exploitation. The effects of the Nuño de Guzmán expedition to Nuevo Galicia and Alvarado on the Soconusco coast have been mentioned. A less abrupt but still dramatic destruction of Indian populations is documented by Aguirre Beltrán (1958) for the southern Guerrero coast in connection with placer mining and cattle raising. Wherever initial impacts were not destructive, assimilation occurred gradually as in Huatusca (Aguirre Beltrán, 1940).

In areas not suffering the early impact of mining and warfare, population nevertheless declined markedly in the 16th century. Traditionally this decline is attributed to the encomienda, to the exploitation of Indian labor, and to the loss of lands, but modern studies suggest other causes. Simpson (1950, pp. 159–70) demonstrates that the Indians on privately held encomiendas survived better than did those on Crown-held encomiendas, while on the Central Plateau the greatest relative decrease took place in Tlaxcala, subject neither to the encomienda, to forced labor of the repartimiento, nor to tribute.

Land loss also is not an adequate explanation of Indian decline or disappearance. Although Spanish interest centered at first primarily on mining and somewhat later on cattle, only the so-called lands of Montezuma and vacant lands were originally distributed by land grants (in contrast to the tribute-collecting encomienda). Most early grants were for cattle raising. Even though some Indian communities also received such grants, in the main cattle raising was quite destructive of Indian crops. Efforts were made to move the cattle industry to the open spaces of the north or to the more depopulated areas of the coasts. By 1550, for example, all cattle raising in the valley of Oaxaca had been prohibited (Chevalier, 1952, p. 257). When cattle multiplied in the Valley of Toluca from their first introduction in 1535 to 150,000 in 1550, cattle raisers were forced at considerable expense to build confining walls; in the valley of Tepeapulco the Indians forcibly ejected all cattle (Chevalier, 1952, p. 124; Wolf, 1959, pp. 182–84).

The introduction of new diseases for which native populations possessed little resistance clearly was a major cause of population decline. Smallpox epidemics are recorded for 1520, 1531, 1545, typhoid (or typhus?) in 1545 and 1576; measles (more fatal to the Indians than smallpox) in 1595 (Wolf, 1959, p. 196). The 1576 epidemic alone is estimated to have caused more than 2,000,000 deaths. Influenza, yellow fever, and, probably most important in the depopulation of the coastal areas, malaria were also introduced. Syphilis, although probably a New World disease, apparently acquired new virulence and often epidemic proportions (Wolf, 1959, p. 196; Priestley, 1923, pp. 64, 184).

It should be noted that some groups also resisted acculturation. Numerous types of nativistic or revitalization movements sprang up. Best documented in the early period is the Mixton war in the Jalisco-Nayarit area in 1538–41, perhaps an aftermath of the bloody and disastrous Nuño de Guzmán expedition a few years earlier. Usually described in military terms, the Mixton war nevertheless included aspects of a messianic movement. Similarly oriented uprisings are known for the Tarahumara between 1645 and 1697 (Dunne, 1948, pp.

54–80) and the Acaxee around 1603 (Archivo General de las Indias). Such movements continued in Yucatan, including the War of the Castes in 1847 and its aftermaths, the still surviving groups organized about the Cult of the Talking Cross in Campeche (Villa R., 1945, pp. 20–28). Most Yaqui wars of the past and present centuries were essentially rational nativistic movements (Beals, 1945a, pp. 4–5). Riley and Hobgood (1959) report a modern movement among southern Tepehuane.

The final recorded serious uprising in Mexico City and nearby towns in 1692 presents interesting features. The revolt failed in part because of poor organization and poor execution of the plans. Perhaps even more important was failure of leadership to agree on goals. One group clearly wished merely greater access to the institutional structure of Spanish colonial society. The second group had nativistic objectives, seeking expulsion of the Spanish and return to pre-Spanish life, a goal hardly likely to be shared by the Tlaxcalans or others who may have remembered the dubious advantages of Aztec domination (Carta de un religiosa, 1951). Casarrubias (1945) and Gonzales Obregón (1952) give summary data on these as well as uprisings in Oaxaca, Chiapas, Chihuahua, Yucatan, and Nuevo Leon, although their interpretations need re-examination.

Nevertheless, except for such groups as were moving toward assimilation—and increasingly the assimilation was to newly forming Mestizo patterns rather than into the urban Spanish colonial patterns—the rate of acculturation slowed in the latter part of the First Colonial Indian period. In part this was to be expected as the new patterns crystallized. But nativistic sentiments also increased as the gulf between Spaniard and Indian widened. The Indian under mission rule was encouraged not to associate with Spaniards, and such contacts as he had were likely to be as an exploited party. Decrease in intermarriage and the

461

growing interposition of a Mestizo class between Spaniard and Indian cultures no doubt contributed to the growth of sentiments favoring isolation. The rise of wage labor in the northern mines, the growth of haciendas, the increasing availability of a Mestizo and slave labor force all lessened Spanish dependence on the Indian labor force (Wolf, 1959, pp. 202–11; Borah, 1951).

SECOND COLONIAL INDIAN PERIOD

This period in most areas is associated with the abolition of the last encomiendas and the secularization of the missions. These two events were not simultaneous but a rough date of 1720 serves to mark the beginning of the period in the central area. The characteristics of this period, however, began to emerge long before this date or before the major changes in Spanish institutions. Throughout the 17th century there was a slow decline in the encomienda and repartimiento, and missionary zeal for the programs of planned culture change diminished. Most of the century was one of stabilized interrelations between the two societies, characterized by diminished culture change and increasing alienation of Indian societies.

The withdrawal of the missionary orders left a linguistic wall about most Indian groups in Middle America. Despite repeated objections by the Crown, the missionaries had successfully prevented most Indians from learning Spanish. The secular priesthood, inadequate in numbers, had neither the obligation nor the inclination to learn native languages. At best, after a brief try, most secular priests lived in Spanish or perhaps Mestizo communities and paid but occasional visits to Indian towns. Even if a priest remained a resident, he had little knowledge of and virtually no communication with his parishioners. In addition, the successful transformation of the aboriginal stratified community into a democratic community with a hierarchy of civil-religious offices designed to share responsibilities within a community with defined membership and territory (Carrasco, 1961) created an ideal boundary-maintaining mechanism. Essentially each Indian community was now relatively free to innovate and consolidate in its own way.

Almost certainly the rise of nativistic sentiments along with increasing isolation brought about more or less conscious efforts to return to a native past. Such movements have been well documented, however, only by LaFarge (1940) for part of the Maya. Here the lay assistants of the priesthood played an important role, as they probably did elsewhere. As recently as the latter part of the last century we find most of the difficulties of the Mexicans with the Yaqui laid to the door of the temastianes or sacristans who, in fact, appear to be subordinate to the maestros or lay readers (Beals, 1945a).

The course of events in the last part of the 18th and most of the 19th century is unknown in detail for almost all Indian groups. It is probable that documentation is extremely scanty for this period, especially with the growing isolation of the Indian community. Evidence from surviving communities, however, makes it clear that in most groups a synthesis of European and native culture took place and became crystallized. Persistence of Indian communities depended in part on adherence to "los costumbres," closely related as they were to the civil-religious hierarchy, and on the maintenance of isolation through excluding outsiders, usually even by marriage. The fate of those communities which permitted the entry of Mestizos was an ever-present reminder of realities. Although broad regional resemblances exist, only such isolating mechanisms can at present account for the rich and infinite variety of the contemporary Middle American Indian communities.

FIRST REPUBLICAN INDIAN PERIOD

This period saw surviving Indian communities forced even more on the defensive. Some evidence suggests that the efficacy of colonial protective laws and Indian courts declined in the closing years of the colonial period but at least they existed. The Republic abolished these laws; and if in theory the Indian gained equality of citizenship, in practice equality meant greater susceptibility to exploitation. Unable in most cases to resist by force, the intensification of the boundary-maintaining mechanisms mentioned in the previous paragraph and increased attempts at withdrawal provided the only defenses. Unsuccessful communities often survived, but through a process of Mestizoization, losing their Indian identity as in the case of Huatusco (Aguirre Beltrán, 1940).

The extent to which Indians participated in the Independence movement is not well documented. In many parts of Mexico apparently the Indian was neutral and passive. In at least one documented case, the Yaqui, where the Indian took an active part in military operations, the result was increased conflict. In this case Independence was interpreted by the Indian to mean freedom from outside interference; in fact, it clearly turned out to mean freedom only for the creole class to impose its will and exploit the Indian. As a result, the three centuries of colonial rule with but a single revolt were followed by repeated uprisings, some of them persisting for several years, in the period between 1820 and 1928 (Beals, 1945a, pp. 4–5).

Second Republican Indian Period

In Mexico new pressures resulted from the Reform Laws of 1857, and their subsequent application to the Indians in later years justifies the establishment of a Second Republican Indian period beginning from that date. In Central America, however, conditions of the First Colonial Indian period persisted into the present century, perhaps altering substantially in Guatemala only at the termination of the Ubico dictatorship

in 1945 (Tax, 1952a, pp. 251–53). To some extent this appears true of more isolated groups such as the Mixe (Beals, 1945b).

The Reform Laws of Mexico were directed primarily against the Church and particularly against its land monopolies through prohibition of types of corporate ownership under the "Ley Lerdo." Breakup of communal landholdings of the corporate Indian communities and the creation of a landholding peasantry were also sought. The extensive church landholdings (estimated at more than 50 per cent of arable lands in Mexico) quickly fell into the hands of large landowners and speculators. Once the liquidation of Church lands was accomplished, the Indian communities came under attack. There seems good reason to believe that Indian communities lost more land through the Reform Laws in the past century than during the entire period since the close of the 16th century. Simpson suggests (1952, p. 259) that by 1910 less than 10 per cent of Indian villages retained any land but this is purely a guess. Little detailed study of this process has been made, although extensive documentation almost certainly exists (see Gruening, 1928; McBride, 1923; Tannenbaum, 1950).

Remote Indian villages, especially with communal lands of little value, often escaped losing their lands. To some extent this is true of Indian communities whose lands were held individually rather than corporately. Here, however, community organization had to be sufficiently "tight" to enforce the unwritten rule that individuals could sell lands only to other members of the community. A primary factor in this tight control was the vitality of the civil-religious hierarchy persisting from early colonial times. In many cases, even where during the Second Republican Indian period some outsiders had obtained land rights, the Agrarian revolution of 1910–20 saw a restoration of the closed community ownership (Beals, 1946, p. 12, refers to this process among the Tarascans), although

463

processes have nowhere been adequately studied.

The motivation behind the pressure on Indian lands and on the corporate Mestizo villages as well was not entirely the acquisition of additional lands. The new owners of the large estates were faced with an inadequate labor supply for their operation. If the land base of the Indian village could be destroyed, the Indians could be driven into the labor force, either as tenant farmers or as peons. Even under these circumstances, it seems likely that villages able to maintain the civil-religious hierarchy and the tightly integrated colonial Indian culture managed to survive or re-establish themselves after the agrarian revolution.

In the Second Republican Indian period then, as in the two preceding colonial periods, withdrawal, adherence to the status quo, resistance to outside influence—in other words, resistance to acculturative influences—was typical. Yet evidence is not wanting that this resistance was selective. Economic innovations certainly occurred. One example was the widespread adoption of coffee as a cash crop in the latter part of the last century. Another example, apparently somewhat later, was extensive adoption of dry rice as a cash crop by the Mazatec of Oaxaca, Mexico. In part, the introduction of coffee may have been by forced or voluntary workers on coffee plantations. However, the process has not been studied, if indeed documentation exists. The examples suffice to show, however, that even the most strict conservatism was selective and suggests that innovation was confined to cultural items rather than to key parts of the social system. To what extent the cultivation of a strictly cash crop had repercussions on the social system has not been investigated; certainly the results are not obvious.

MODERN INDIAN PERIOD

A Modern Indian period began in Mexico with the Agrarian Revolution. In Guate-mala this period, perhaps bypassing the Second Republican Indian period, began with the fall of the Ubico dictatorship. Where Indian populations persist in other parts of Middle America it is perhaps questionable whether the modern period has yet begun.

Characteristics of the Modern Indian period included, in Mexico at least, the essential merging of the Creole and Mestizo social systems, with Mestizos forming a substantial part of the new elite. Accompanying this shift was acceptance of the Indian backgrounds of Mexico and its utilization as part of the new nationalistic ideologies. For one thing, this movement led to extensive government support for archaeology, often with the overt purpose of creating tourist attractions but also with the less obvious one of glorifying the Indian past. At the same time the revolutionary ideology included the incorporation of the Indian into modern economic and political life, in effect, the inauguration of a new period of directed social and cultural change.

The new interest in "incorporating" the Indian in Mexico was accompanied by the birth of modern community and ethnological studies. The first major community study (Gamio, 1922) in Teotihuacan was motivated by applied considerations, the need to reform rural education. It was followed by the work of Redfield in Tepoztlan (1930), Bennett and Zingg among the Tarahumara (1935), Parsons at Mitla (1936), Redfield and Villa in Yucatan (1934), and Beals among the Cahita (1943, 1945a) and Mixe (1945b). These field studies between 1922 and 1933 were undertaken originally with ethnographic interests; all, however, became involved to some extent with the problems of culture change. They were followed by a growing number of community studies in Middle America, the most noteworthy perhaps being those sponsored by the Carnegie Institution of Washington and by the University of Chicago under the direction of Redfield.

The major theoretical direction of these studies was Redfield's (1934, 1941) folk-urban continuum approach. Although this framework has been found increasingly unsatisfactory (e.g., Foster, 1953c), it stimulated a great deal of research. The urban problems have been actively pursued in recent years. Lewis (1952, 1959b) has studied relations between Tepoztlan and Mexico City and other aspects of urban life; Whiteford (1960) has published on changing aspects of social class in Queretero; the Youngs (1960a, 1960b) have studied the impact of a planned industrial city on the rural area, largely unpublished; and George Foster and his students are working in Jalisco and Michoacan on urban influences but have not published.

The programs of planned culture change have been directed by various Mexican government agencies and more recently by projects sponsored by international agencies. In considerable measure the nature of these undertakings has been influenced by the Indigenista movement following the Mexican revolution. This movement, however, developed contradictory ideologies. At one extreme were essentially romantic ideas of restoring the Indian past, a past essentially unreconstructible in all its details. Others directed their efforts toward economic rehabilitation and the restoration of Indian dignity and autonomy. Still others sought complete assimilation through education and direct intervention in the Indian community (see Caso, 1954; Aguirre Beltrán, 1957).

Indian reactions to government-directed change by the 1940's had produced widespread disillusion in the dominant Mestizo class. The Indian proved resistant to planned changes and not a few Mexicans were reverting to prerevolutionary views of the Indian as a hopeless incubus on Mexico's economic and political progress. Anthropologists, on the other hand, were often convinced that the Indian cultures were again in a phase of rapid acculturation.

In fact, the Indians were changing; disconcertingly, however, they were changing in ways not anticipated by Mexican officialdom. Most particularly they were clinging to their "Indianness." Basically, the differences of opinion rested on different evaluations of the significant areas of change. Many officials, with little or no social science training, perceived the problem essentially to be one of introducing the symbols of "modernism," "progress," and "Mexicanness," and official pressures tended to be on such symbols. These were often clothing, housing, and customs divergent from those accepted by urban Mestizo officialdom. To the Indian, on the other hand, these were the symbols of his identity, essential to the maintenance of the social system by which for three centuries he had kept his individuality and through which he held what security he possessed.

The drive toward national uniformity in culture was not confined to official agencies. Carrasco (1952b) has shown the same tendency associated with religion in the Tarascan area. Although the folk religion of the Tarascans is almost wholly derived from the colonial Catholicism of the 16th and 17th centuries, it no longer conforms to the practices of modern Mexican national Catholicism. If Church efforts to modernize Tarascan religion ultimately succeed, clearly the time of success is far distant. Moreover, Indian reaction may again be disconcerting. Special forms of anticlericalism in defense of the folk religion are already rife, not only among the Tarascans but for the Yaqui, many Mixe communities, and no doubt in many others. Destruction of the folk religion is very likely to result not in acceptance of modern Catholicism but rather in the rise of religious indifference.

One reason for the resistance of Indian communities to alterations in the folk religion is the close linkage with the civil-religious officeholding hierarchy and its functions. Evidence is accumulating that in this system lie the major mechanisms for

465

preservation of the Indian community as social system. Forced introduction of a party system and destruction of the traditional officeholding patterns brought disastrous and rapid destruction of many Indian communities in Guatemala, particularly under the Arbenz regime. On the other hand, Nash (1955, 1958a) has shown that a community (Cantel, Guatemala) can adapt even to industrialism. Beals (1945b, pp. 34–37) describes ways, among the Mixe, of manipulating the system toward cultural change without disorganization. Beals (1945a) and Spicer (1940, 1954) both demonstrate the tight hold of the Yaqui civil-religious system on its membership. Spicer in particular shows how the system probably will terminate not through adaptation or assimilation but through loss of members who must ultimately make choices between participating in the modern economy effectively or remaining in the highly restrictive civil-religious system. Hinton (1961) has indicated the importance of the system in maintaining Cora culture. Guatemalan materials are summarized by R. N. Adams (1957b).

If contemporary Indian communities tend to resist acculturation in most aspects of the social system and in those parts of culture having symbolic values, the situation appears to be quite otherwise in nonsymbolic aspects of their cultures. Changes in technology, especially agricultural technology, or in matters of household economy as power corn mills, sewing machines, or improved water supplies are often eagerly accepted.

In recent years the most important source of directed change has been through the Instituto Nacional Indigenista (Caso, 1954) and pilot or training projects by UNESCO and OAS.[3] The Instituto Indigenista program concentrates on improved and more realistic educational facilities, health programs, agriculture, and communications, but makes no direct effort to manipulate the social structure or symbolic and belief

systems. The largest and oldest undertaking of the Instituto is in Chiapas and is under intensive study by research programs centered in Harvard University and University of Chicago. Other Instituto programs in 1961 included centers in the Tarahumara area, Nayarit, Mixteca Alta and Baja, Yucatan, Lower Papaloapam, and Sierra Mazatec. New centers have been approved for the mountain Zapotec and Mixe areas of Oaxaca. The major continuing UNESCO effort is the CREFAL[4] training program centering in the Lake Patzcuaro (Tarascan) area. Various agencies have carried out projects among the Otomi of the Valle de Mezquital over many years. Fisher (1953) has studied a UNESCO project in Nayarit. Somewhat different projects have been undertaken by the Central American Institute of Nutrition in Guatemala.

Many other unrealized opportunities for the study of directed culture change as well as of the relative importance of directed and nondirected change exist. For example, the often quoted assertion that improved communications may be more important than formal educative or other officially directed efforts in producing change (Beals, 1952, p. 270) needs verification.

One final comment must be made. The broad patterns of stages or periods in Middle American Indian acculturation utilized in this essay I believe to have some validity, although perhaps they should be modified in detail. A similar stage framework has recently been developed for a group of North American tribes by the various authors in *Perspectives in American Indian Culture Change*, edited by Spicer (1961). There remains, in both cases, the problem that the end product has been very different for various tribes.

I have elsewhere (1949) suggested historical and situational reasons for this diversity by brief analysis of three cases, the

[3] OAS, Organization of American States.
[4] CREFAL, Centro de Educación para el Desarrollo de la Comunidad en America Latina.

Yaqui, the Tarascans, and the Mixe. For the Yaqui I pointed out the steps leading to a remarkable synthesis of aboriginal and European influences, a conclusion which Spicer (1961) also reaches and documents in considerable detail. The Tarascans, on the other hand, are an instance of almost complete substitution of native cultural items by 15th- and 16th-century European elements, reworked and reinterpreted into a quite distinct and uniquely Tarascan pattern. The Mixe, because of isolation and missionary policy, present a marked case of compartmentalization in many features of their recent culture.

The three cases illustrate syncretism, substitution, and compartmentalization as predominant acculturative processes or "styles." Although fitting within the major patterns of events, the reasons for diversity in process can be at least partially identified. Analyses of other groups should give more generalizable results and possibly may also identify the operation of still other processes. (For a similar analysis for Guatemala see Edmonson, 1960.)

REFERENCES

Note. The references are confined to works cited, for the. most part only secondary sources, most of which contain extensive bibliographical guides.

Acosta Saignes, 1945
Adams, R. N., 1957b
Aguirre Beltrán, 1940, 1946, 1953, 1957, 1958
Archivo General de las Indias
Bancroft, 1883
Bandelier, 1880b
Bannon, 1955
Barth, 1950
Beals, n.d., 1943, 1945a, 1945b, 1946, 1949, 1951a, 1952
Bennett and Zingg, 1935
Borah, 1951
Carrasco, 1950a, 1952b, 1961
Carta de un Religiosa, 1951
Casarrubias, 1945
Caso, 1954, 1959
Chamberlain, 1948, 1953
Chevalier, 1952
Christensen, L., n.d.
Cline, 1946
Cortés, 1908
Díaz del Castillo, 1927
Drucker, P., 1958
Dunne, 1948
Edmonson, 1960
Fisher, 1953
Foster, 1953c, 1960a
Gamio, 1922
Gibson, 1952, 1955, 1959
Gonzales Obregón, 1952

Gruening, 1928
Hanke, 1949, 1959
Hinton, 1961
Homenaje Caso, 1951
Jiménez Moreno, 1956
—— and Mateos Higuera, 1940
Jiménez Rueda, 1951
Kirchhoff, 1955, 1956a, 1956b
Kubler, 1948
LaFarge, 1940
Lewis, 1952, 1959b
McBride, 1923
Martin, 1957
Maya and their Neighbors, 1940
Miranda and Zavala, 1954
Monzón, 1949
Muñoz Camargo, 1947
Nash, M., 1955, 1958a
Parsons, 1936
Phelan, 1956
Prescott, 1843
Priestley, 1923
Redfield, 1930, 1934, 1941
—— and Villa, 1934
Ricard, 1933
Riley and Hobgood, 1959
Roys, 1943
Schmieder, 1930
Scholes, 1937
—— and Adams, 1955
See, n.d.
Simpson, 1929, 1934, 1950, 1952
Spicer, 1940, 1954, 1961
Tannenbaum, 1950

Tax, 1952a
Torre Villar, 1952
Villa R., 1945
Vogt, 1961

Whiteford, 1960
Wolf, 1959
Young and Young, 1960a, 1960b
Zavala, 1935, 1941, 1945, 1951

24. Nationalization

RICHARD N. ADAMS

IN THE present article[1] "nationalization" refers to the process whereby the states of Middle America undertook to become nations, to consolidate their sovereignty, and to find a common expression of culture. Our specific interest is with the incorporation of the indigenous population. The territory of the Middle American states, at the time of their separation from Spain in 1821, included a wide variety and number of native peoples. Colonial policy had succeeded in encapsulating many of the Indian communities, thereby preserving some highly distinctive cultures; many others had never been brought under any real measure of control. A limited view of nationalization would concern itself wholly with the process whereby these Indian populations were, and are being, brought under the network of common symbols and interaction that permits the countries to be recognized as nations.

This process is complex. To understand what happened to the Indian, we must not only look into his particular and immediate

relations but also examine the factors that led to changes in these relations. The nationalization of the Indian involved the incorporation of his community within power structure of the state. The process of nation-making requires the substitution of the direct exercise of power over all individuals for the indirect exercise of power through corporate segments of individuals. The national power center must be able to communicate directly with, and exercise control directly over, the population. To do this, it is necessary to contain local and provincial power nuclei that can compete for control. In Middle America these local and regional nuclei have most commonly taken the form of haciendas and Indian communities. In some instances the perpetuation of the local centers resulted merely from environmental isolation; in others, this was combined with or replaced by cultural isolation. Although haciendas were culturally within the sphere of the country as a whole, communication and contact were difficult and time-consuming because of bad roads and distance. Indian communities, on the other hand, were separated both by distance and by different languages and customs. Nationalization

---

[1] An earlier draft of this essay benefited from comments by Julio de la Fuente, Jorge Skinner-Klee, and Eric Wolf.

was, then, always contingent on improved physical contact. In Indian communities it further required what Wolf has called "internal acculturation," the breach or elimination of cultural barriers to communication within the emerging nation.[2]

If we ask why this process must occur at all, or why it occurs at a particular time, we must look beyond the internal to the external relationships of the state. The factors leading to the incorporation of haciendas, Indian communities, and other local nuclei are to be found in the competition between growing states. In order to maintain hegemony over a growing society in the face of other growing societies, it is essential to maintain internal control.

Nationalization means the establishment of wider social relations and acculturation. The specific process of the former may be analyzed into the extension of political control over, and development of economic participation of, the entities concerned.[3] The present article focuses on the extension of political control over the Indian populations through a review of the policy and practice (in so far as data are available) of the efforts of the Middle American states to incorporate their Indian populations into the emerging network of national relations. We consider this over the period from the declarations of independence in 1821 until 1960, and cover the contemporary nations of Mexico, Guatemala, Honduras, El Salvador, and Nicaragua.

It is a quirk of history that less is known about the Indian developments of the 19th century than much of the colonial period.

[2] Eric Wolf's essay (1953) on this process in Mexico describes the formation of the state rather than the nation as conceived here. The present usage is preferred because it draws attention to the problem of nationalization as it confronts most of the world's states today. I am here considering the emergence of the nation at the point where Wolf's essay stopped: with the independence of the state from Spain.

[3] Of these, important portions of the processes are described in Articles 23 and 26.

470

One aspect of the struggles for state hegemony and nationhood was a cultural lack of interest in the condition of the Indian. Even today, when the Indian is mentioned in the national context in most Western Hemisphere countries, it is as "the Indian problem." Political autonomy and cultural independence led even sympathetic 19th-century observers to regard the Indian as something to be eliminated or, at best, avoided. If the present review leaves much obscure of the Indian's view of the 19th century, it will perhaps indicate something behind the national policies concerned with the Indian, and why he was subject to power and acculturative pressures. It will also indicate broad areas where intensive research can profitably be done.

At the time of independence there were three general kinds of Indians in New Spain: the northern hunters or "barbarians," the settled agricultural Indians of Mesoamerica, and the "forest" Indians of the Central American Atlantic coast. Collectively, the Middle American states held different relations with each of these types, and their policies reflect these differences.

The northern hunters at the time of independence were rapidly becoming predatory bands. Under the westward expansion of the United States peoples the Comanches, Apaches, and other hunting groups were increasingly being pressed out of their traditional lands by whites and displaced Indians. By the time of the Mexican War these bands posed major border problems for Mexico and were regarded as barbarian tribes that could be dealt with only through subjugation. Subjugation, however, by a state too weak to consolidate itself was itself a major problem.

The Central American Atlantic coast groups, the so-called "Jicaques"—the Payas, Miskito, Sumu, Rama, Ulva, and possibly also the Matagalpa—were partly agricultural but in a considerable degree dependent also on hunting and collecting. Stew-

TABLE 1

REGION	TIME OF CONQUEST		1821–1825		1950	
	Total Pop.	Indian % of Total	Total Pop.	Indian % of Total	Total Pop.	Indian % of Total
Mexico	11,000,000[1]	100%	6,800,000[2]	54.4	19,653,522[11]	27.91[11]
Guatemala	...	...	660,580[3]	73.6[5]	2,788,122[6]	53.5[6]
El Salvador	130,000[4]	...	250,000[3]	42.8[4]	1,855,917[8]	20.0[8]
Honduras	...	...	137,000[3]	? [15]	1,368,605[7]	9.2[7]
Nicaragua	...	...	207,269[3]	40.01[14]	1,057,023[9]	4.7[10]
Br. Honduras	...	...	...	...	59,220[12]	18.0[12]
Central America (minus Costa Rica)	[16]	...	1,600,000[2]	55.0	7,128,887	...

[1] For 1519; Cook and Simpson, 1948, p. 38 (minus Yucatan, Tabasco, and Chiapas).

[2] For 1825; Rosenblat, 1954, vol. 1, Table 3 facing p. 36.

[3] For 1821; Baron Castro, 1942, p. 554.

[4] For 1524; Baron Castro, 1942, p. 273.

[5] For approximately 1829, estimated from figures in Orellana, 1950, for the censuses of 1778 and 1880. Reproduced in Adams, 1957a, p. 279.

[6] Dirección General de Estadística (Guatemala), 1953, p. 93.

[7] Adams, 1957a, p. 607.

[8] Adams, 1957a, p. 488.

[9] Adams, 1957a, p. 160.

[10] This is a guess, allowing 25,000 for Atlantic coast, and 30,000 for the highlands and Pacific belt. See Adams, 1957a, pp. 156, 221, and 232–45. Rosenblat (1954, 1: 152) cites the 1920 census as giving a figure of 4.59%.

[11] For 1940; Caso and Parra, 1950, p. 20.

[12] For 1946; Rosenblat, 1954, p. 151.

[13] Baron Castro, 1942, pp. 124, 273.

[14] Squier (1855, p. 52) quotes Miguel Sarabia as estimating the population of Nicaragua of 1823 to be 173,213, two-fifths of which were Indians. In 1837 Galindo estimated the proportion at nearer one-third (ibid.).

[15] Galindo (Squier, 1855, p. 52) estimates there were no Indians in Honduras in 1837, but that the major portion of the population is Ladino. However, modern figures clearly indicate Indians to be present. Wells (1857, p. 554) estimates the proportion at that date to be about 28.6%. The 1825 percentage is probably similar to that of Nicaragua.

[16] Rosenblat's figure of 800,000 (1954, p. 102) seems too slight in view of the Cook and Simpson estimate for central Mexico. If the Central American loss and regrowth were proportional to that which occurred in Mexico between 1520 and 1825, then the 1520 figure for Central America would be in the neighborhood of 2,600,000.

ard (1949, 5: 765–66) has seen them as essentially a deculturated series of peoples, broken down under conquest and colonization. There is little doubt that by the 19th century they were in some part rapidly diminishing refugee populations (Stone, 1958). Until fairly recently, the main interest they held for the developing nations reflected their possible allegiance to a competitive power—first the English, and later other Central American republics.

Most of the Middle American Indians were the survivors of the pre-Columbian Mesoamerican states and tribes. These peoples, vastly reduced within the first century after the conquest, had, by 1821, regained something of their former numbers. Culturally they formed a set of individualistic corporate entities, with varying degrees of dependence on and hostility towards their oppressors. The latter-day policy of Spain was to contain them through local autonomy, under the direct supervision of intendencias and priests (Zavala and Miranda, 1954), often keeping them dependent on working in neighborhood haciendas for income.

In very broad terms, the northern predators were ultimately dealt with through a policy that paralleled that of the United States: extermination and pacification. The forest groups were gradually incorporated through policies similar to those followed in the colonial period, and more recently have been subject to welfare and development work. The Mesoamerican sedentary populations have been the major concern of nationalization, and have been treated to three kinds of policy, in sequence: Conservative, protectionist, and exploitative; Liberal, neo-Darwinist, extinction through absorption; and economic development, welfare, and incorporation through cultural-relativistic, directed culture change.

Once the territory of the state is delineated, population, resources, and acculturation may be regarded as the central issues of Indian nationalization. Population data on this area, still hard to come by, are summarized in Table 1.

There is clear evidence that a tremendous population decline followed the conquest. Between 1520 and 1620 the central Mexican population fell from over 10,000,-000 to around 2,500,000 (Cook and Simpson, 1948, p. 46). The population of El Salvador is estimated to have dropped from 130,000 in 1524 to 60,000 in 1551 (Baron Castro, 1942, p. 273). Colonial accounts leave little doubt that these figures are not unreasonable. Bishop Pedraza wrote of Honduras in 1547: "The land is so ruined and depopulated of Indians because of the great destruction wrought by past governors, that in some districts one can pass for thirty leagues without seeing a pueblo . . ." (quoted in Chamberlain, 1953, p. 245; see also Rosenblat, 1954, 1: 305). There is little question that this catastrophe left the way open in some areas for the regrowth of a

Mestizo population. Why this occurred in some areas and not in others rests on local conditions of history, and in many instances on factors which have not yet been studied (Adams, 1957a, pp. 283–88). The over-all effect, however, has been for indigenous areas to regrow in a patchlike way. El Salvador, and probably Nicaragua and Honduras, were already predominantly Mestizo at the time of Independence. Guatemala, like some specific parts of Mexico (adjacent Chiapas, Yucatan) was predominantly Indian. When the new states began to face the problem of national development, they differed significantly in the degree to which their populations were Indian.

Another significant aspect of the colonial population changes is that by 1821 the population of 8.4 million people (Indians and non-Indians), with a density of 3.5 persons per sq. km., was thinly and unevenly spread out over Mexico and Central America. This population was divided among the politically dominant Europeans and Creoles, the growing body of Mestizos, and the culturally isolated Indians. Probably well under 10 per cent of the total felt any real commitment to most of the issues that faced the new states. Under latter-day colonial policy, Indians were increasingly protected from the dominant group, and were clearly a problem in the development of a nation. Production was low among Indian and Mestizo alike; the soil was worked with primitive tools, varying from digging stick to hoe and wooden plow. In all, the condition of the new states, specifically in Central America, was well described by Alejandro Marure, who held that collectively they simply did not produce enough income or have enough educated people to run more than one country (quoted in Herrarte, 1955, pp. 141–42). The Central American situation was considerably worse than that of Mexico, since the latter was the colonial headquarters and could turn to some fairly experienced bureaucrats. Although some writers (*ibid.*, p. 135) regard the joining of

472

Chiapas to Mexico as a significant loss of valuable territory to the Central American states, subsequent history suggests that the inclusion of this Maya highland region in Guatemala would not have materially affected national history in the 19th century.

Although this essay is specifically concerned with Indian matters, we may mention by way of context similar problems that faced the developing states. The hacienda, already well recognized, grew stronger in the course of the 19th century. This was another corporate entity that mediated between the state and its members, and it was, therefore, a competitive source of power. Regional interests were far from being balanced by centralist interests. Yucatan seriously considered secession in the 1830's (M. W. Williams, 1929); Leon and Granada in Nicaragua were fast approaching the fratricidal conflict that was to inhibit national growth in that country for much of the century. The opposition of two philosophies of nationhood, at first Federalists against Centralists, and later Liberals against Conservatives, served as constant rallying points for action against the incumbent government. In the first half of the 19th century Mexico leaned toward the Centralist position, providing a basis whereon the Liberals, when they finally emerged victorious in 1853, found themselves working with a relatively united country. Central America, on the contrary, started out under a Federalist organization, broke up in 1838 into the separate states, and never again maintained a larger entity. The desire, however, never died, and provided one pretext (among various) for the continued strife and governmental debacles that characterized the area through most of the century (Perry, 1922).

The internal contradictions of the situation were perhaps best illustrated by the place held by the Church. Centralists and Conservatives generally regarded the Church as an important ally, indeed, colleague. This was manifest in the Santa Ana

regime in Mexico and Carrera's return to the Church in Guatemala (Holleran, 1949, pp. 128–46). Federalists and Liberals, on the other hand, saw in the Church a serious competitor to the development of the unified state, a draining of resources and manpower by an alternative power center. Priests did little to destroy this image, as they tried to retain over the Indian communities a control similar to that which they exercised in the colonial period.

In brief, unlike the United States that had a fairly clear, open, west into which to expand as its economy and population grew, the Middle American states tried to establish themselves in a territory already peopled with existing states: a multitude of corporate Indian communities; hacienda communities that, while low in productivity, were high in control over their populations; regional entities separated by restrictive economic barriers, a minimum of economic interdependence, and reluctance to contribute to the strengthening of a national government; and finally the Church, always a state within a state, that threw its weight in favor of maintaining its competitive position with respect to the state government wherever the latter did not seek it out as a colleague.

With respect to the Indian, each country of Middle America has followed a somewhat different trajectory of policy and action. Immediately following the 1821 declarations of independence, however, the Middle American states were united for a brief period in the new Mexican monarchy. After the Mexican declaration of independence in 1810, Hidalgo and Morelos issued a series of dispositions which abolished slavery, "caste" differences, Indian community titles and funds, any kind of personal service on the part of Indians except that for public benefit, and required that lands be given individually to the Indians (Gamio *et al.*, 1958, pp. 23–29). Iturbide, in his *Plan de Iguala* of 1821, reiterated that "All the inhabitants of New Spain, without any

473

distinction of European, African, or Indian, are citizens . . ." (González, 1954, p. 115). These pronouncements, the precursors of 19th-century Liberal policy toward the Indian, had no immediate effect whatsoever on the status of the Indian.

MEXICO

With the fall of Iturbide in 1823, Mexico lost its Central American members, and its Indian policy began to diverge from that of the rest of the states.[4] Although the 1823 *Acta Constitutiva* set up a Federal government, this government then created its member states, rather than the reverse. Opposition to formal centralism continued even through the revolution a century later, but in fact the state was centralized in form continuously after 1823 (Mecham, 1938). The Centralist government that took over at this time and dominated Mexico until 1853 was ". . . strongly nationalist, economically and politically conservative, and culturally European Catholic" (Cline, 1953, p. 41). Although it has been claimed that there has been a "constant preoccupation" with Indian problems in Mexico (Gamio *et al.*, 1958, p. 17), this period of Centralist domination is singularly sterile in legislation concerning the Indian. The major legislative acts and decrees during this period were those passed in the separate states.

From 1824 to 1826 Veracruz sent out at least six decrees, mainly concerned with the division of Indian communal lands among private individuals (Gamio *et al.*, 1958, pp. 167–72). The state of Occidente (later broken into the two states of Sinaloa and Sonora) issued a series of laws that were essentially a continuation of an enlightened Spanish colonial policy. They were concerned with returning lands to the Indians; guaranteeing them rights as citizens; maintaining the lands devoted to the saints; excusing the Indians from many

taxes, tithes, personal services to the curates, and paying for land titles; organizing them as militia against the predatory tribes of the north; and handling Indian rebellions. This provincially sponsored policy was evidently dropped by the time of the Liberal rise to power in 1853 (Ezell, 1955).

By the end of the first 10 years of Centralist power, the opponents in almost every issue, the Liberals, found at least one point of agreement: Indian communities must be destroyed (Chávez Orozco, 1943, p. 376). The Conservative policy, as expressed in 1830, called for the dividing up of Indian community lands if the majority of the inhabitants resolved to do so; and that a person receiving land could not sell it without previous permission of the *ayuntamiento* (*ibid.*, pp. 371–74). The Liberal viewpoint was much more extreme; it saw the Indian communities as simply one form of corporate entity that was hobbling Mexico's development (Cline, 1953, p. 43), and resented the accumulation of potential capital stored up in the community *cajas* (treasuries) and institutions, like hospitals, set up specifically for Indians (Chávez Orozco, 1943, pp. 369–70).

The 1853 "Revolution of Ayala," carried out by Indian Juan Alvarez, served to bring into power the Liberals, led by Benito Juárez. The new era was marked by no new and special concern with Indian policy, however, but rather an emphasis on consolidating the Mexican state and developing nationalism through economic progress and the elimination of foreign controls. The first significant step concerning the Indians was the so-called *Ley Lerdo* that broke up church landholdings. The law was designed to destroy all communal holdings, however, and provided a way for individual entrepreneurs to take over Indian communal lands in the following period of liberal growth. This was further written into the reform constitution of 1857 (Gamio *et al.*, 1958, pp. 39–55). The measure was essentially the same as that set forth at the time of

[4] See Parra, 1954, for a bibliographic and historical treatment of the period following 1850.

474

independence, but under the Reform, the government was positively interested in breaking the power of the Church, and in so doing pressed its new policy with considerable vigor.

The Liberal movement suffered an interruption (1861–67) during the French intervention. Even in the few years of its operation, the Liberal policy had created great distrust among the Indians. The laws and policy of Maximilian and his supreme commander, Bazaine, were directed both by more humanitarian views and by the real need to have the support of the Indians. In the last they were generally successful, but their laws against abuses on the haciendas, debt peonage, child labor, and so on, went generally unobserved in the midst of the Empire's unsuccessful efforts to remain in power (Gamio *et al.*, 1958, pp. 69–78; Dabbs, 1958). The return of Juárez and the Liberals marked the virtual abandonment of the Indian in favor of economic development.

The corporate quality of the settled Indians was not the most outstanding Indian threat to Mexico in the course of the 19th century. Although these groups represented an ultimate problem to integration on a national scale, a more immediate danger was presented by the marauding, predatory tribes of the southwestern part of the United States. From 1849 until the turn of the century Mexico attempted to control these "barbarians" through a number of measures: the establishment of forts and military colonies along the borders; the colonization of peaceful Indians in the area; and the payment of bounty for Indians dead or alive.

Even though the declarations made at the time of Independence included the northern hunters as "Mexicans by birth," the state early found itself treating them as wild foreigners. By 1830 the State of Occidente was specifying that Indian militia was to serve against the barbarians (Ezell, 1955, p. 210). In 1843 Mexico made a treaty with the Comanches to protect them and get them as allies against the Lipans and Caddos. In 1850 a treaty was made with an Apache group. The Treaty of Guadalupe of 1848 eliminated the apparent contradiction of a nation making treaties with its own citizens by placing the major tribal areas within the confines of the United States. The United States was technically responsible for containing the tribes but failed to do so. Indeed, as the century wore on, Mexico increasingly became the refuge of these groups seeking to escape United States troops. As late as 1930 a surviving band is reported to have attacked a northern Mexican village (Wellman, 1947, pp. 455–56, note 7). Prior to the Reform of 1853, missionaries were encouraged to continue their work, but the state was very lax in providing them with support. Priests were becoming increasingly scarce. The situation became so pressing by 1831 that the state even encouraged priests still loyal to Spain to remain on the job.

The first "military colonies" were started in 1847 but were not pushed seriously until after the French intervention. In this period refugee Kikapoos, Seminoles, and some Negroes came into Mexico, and the state established them in communities in return for their fighting against the predatory bands. The Seminoles left in 1861 (K. W. Porter, 1951), but the Kikapoos continue today as a Mexican Indian group.

Elsewhere in the state, settled Indians rebelled from time to time. Many of these occasions seem to have been touched off by loss of Indian lands, but in some instances they took on the quality of a civil war. Among the outstanding cases were the continuing insurrections of the Yaquis and related tribes of Sonora that lasted from 1825 until 1901;[5] a War of the Castes that kept Yucatan unstable from 1840 to 1909 (Cline, 1945); and the War of the Castes in Chia-

[5] Spicer (1945, p. 275) says there were Yaqui disturbances as late as 1927, and that the Yaqui are still highly concerned about their status.

pas in 1868–69 (Pineda, 1888; Pozas, 1959a). The final campaigns in 1901 against the Yaquis and Yucatecans engaged 15 per cent of the government's armed forces. It was against the Yaquis and Yucatan Mayas that exile and exportation of individuals were practiced. Yucatan Indians were sold to Cuban planters, and Yaquis were sent to Yucatan (González, 1954, pp. 139–63).

The period of Porfirio Díaz saw Mexico expand economically, increase production, and begin the exploitation of natural resources made useful by the industrial revolution. It may be argued that this was a necessary step towards nationhood, but the position of the Indian under the Díaz economic policies became insufferable. Haciendas gradually occupied almost all the lands of Mexico. The far northern and far southern states (Chihuahua, Coahuila, Nuevo Leon, Tamaulipas, Campeche, Yucatan, and Chiapas) consistently refused to pay any attention to the constitutional prohibition of debt peonage, and Chiapas, in 1880, even passed a law that claimed to make it legal (*ibid.*, pp. 131–32). The policy of acculturation was to ignore Indian differences; this resulted in the Indian receiving little or no protection, and sometimes even finding non-Indian clothing being prescribed for him. Spanish was required, and during the period from 1887 to 1910, the government published only two books in Indian language text (pp. 135–38).

Irrespective of their inhumanity, the Díaz policies were somewhat effective in reducing the strength of Indian communities. Loss of corporate lands, forced labor, incorporation of Indians on haciendas, and education policies succeeded in reducing the Indian-speaking proportion of the population to 12.9 per cent by 1910 (Caso and Parra, 1950, p. 18). The general disinterest of the Díaz regime in the Indian is reflected in the fact that the collection of Indianist legislation compiled by Gamio and his colleagues cites no national legislation concerning the Indian during the entire period (Gamio *et al.*, 1958).

The general practice of the Díaz regime reflected a form of social Darwinism, assuming that Indians were inferior to whites and would be eliminated by Liberal policies through natural selection. There were at the time, however, prominent Mexican thinkers who voiced notions of the natural equality of races, and who may be said to be the progenitors of what has since become known as *indigenismo* (Stabb, 1959). While their writings preached the ability of the Indian, perhaps the first manifestation of this philosophy on an official basis was the attempt by the state of Chihuahua in 1906 to initiate a program to help the Tarahumaras. This was never carried out, but in 1910 the Mexican Indianist Society was formed, followed by a rash of similar associations elsewhere in the country. In the same year the same group held the First Mexican Indianist Congress. These efforts were quickly swallowed up by the revolution, but they marked the beginnings of what was to be the major turn in public Indian policy for the new century (Comas, 1953).

The Mexican Revolution was a profound experience, both in the history of that country and for the world. It was for the 20th century what the American Revolution was for the 19th century. No mere issue of statehood was involved, but rather a vast social upheaval, affecting the furthest reaches of the republic. The Indian was involved in it, both as leader and follower. Changes did not occur overnight, however. In the early 1920's a special office, the "Procuraduria de Pueblos," was created to aid communities in regaining their lost lands, and a Department of Education and Culture for the Indian Race was set up in the new Secretariat of Public Education (Dirección General de Asuntos Indígenas, 1958, pp. 13, 123–30). In 1927 the Casa del Estudiante Indígena enunciated its objectives to ". . . eliminate the evolutionary distance that separates the Indian from the present epoch, transforming their mentality, tendencies and customs . . . to incorporate them within the Mexican community . . ." (Secretaría de Educación Pública, "La casa del estudiante indígena" [Mexico, 1927], pp. 35–37; cited in correspondence by Julio de la Fuente).

The agrarian reform, with the reinstitution of ejido lands, gave a start towards the economic development of the land-poor rural communities. Between 1922 and 1933 three-quarters of a million persons were involved in ejido grants, and by 1950 over 1.7 million ejido members were recorded, or 35.2 per cent of the total population engaged in agriculture (International Labor Office, 1953, p. 325). This program was not directed specifically at the Indian, nor did it serve to reincorporate Indian communities. The issuing of lands was controlled at the local level, but it was not done by municipal authorities, nor did it necessarily include even the majority of farmers within any given community. The area that has over the years received the greatest ejido grants is one which is only partially occupied by Indians today: the east-west belt extending from Veracruz to Jalisco and Michoacan. The areas of most intensive Indian occupation, Oaxaca, Chiapas, and the Yucatan peninsula, together account for less than 20 per cent of the beneficiaries, and less than 10 per cent of the number of ejidos (op. cit., p. 326).

There is some variation in opinion as to the degree to which the first two decades of Indianist efforts were still governed by a strongly Liberal philosophy. Ruiz U. (1956) suggests that the goal of total incorporation of the Indian was not entirely in keeping with the view of Gamio, Saenz, and others, who demanded recognition of the Indian as a "positive cultural force." Perhaps the difference existed more in method than in goal. The Indianists, then as now, aim toward elimination of the Indian as a socially corporate entity within the body politic.

The method that became dominant under the regime of Cárdenas, however, was to treat with them as entities through special programs and offices under the point of view that this was a much more effective way, in the long run, to make them parts of the nation than the simple Liberal preference of elimination through economic destruction.

In 1936 the Autonomous Department of Indian Affairs was established, followed the next year by a Department of Indian Education. In 1938 these two were combined, and in 1940 Cárdenas internationally proclaimed his support of Indianist policy at the First Inter-American Indianist Congress at Patzcuaro (Dirección General de Asuntos Indígenas, 1958, pp. 129–30; Gamio et al., 1958, pp. 111–12, 123). In 1947 the Autonomous Department of Indian Affairs was brought under the Secretariat of Public Education, and in the following year the National Indian Institute (INI) was created. Under the direction of Alfonso Caso and a group of Mexican anthropologists, the new Institute developed a strong positive program for extending certain phases of Mexican national culture to the Indian. The INI established local centers in which the efforts of the various agencies of the national government were coordinated in accord with principles of applied anthropology. The central purpose was to nationalize the Indian; ". . . we consider it essential that the indigenous community gain an awareness of belonging to a vaster social organization, that of the Mexican nation" (Caso, 1958a, p. 28; 1958b; Instituto Nacional Indigenista, 1955).[6]

Mexico may be said to have reached national maturity under Cárdenas. The expropriation of oil resources by the government and the establishment of a practical, scientifically conceived, program for the incorporation of the Indian represent an external and internal balance of control providing

[6] See Article 25.

477

the state with the economic resources and the political strength necessary to nationhood.

CENTRAL AMERICA

Following the break-up of the Mexican Empire in 1823, the Central American states wavered and finally settled on a confederation. The uncertainty of the times is indicated by the fact that El Salvador first declared herself to be part of the United States, before finally joining the rest of the states. Chiapas voted to go with Mexico, thereby splitting the highland Maya Indian area between Mexico and Guatemala. Stanger (1932) has pointed out that the Central American states simply divided themselves up in terms of the colonial population centers and colonial provinces.

The Federated States immediately followed a different path than that of Mexico. Whereas the latter turned towards a generally conservative practice, the Central American states came under the rule of Liberals. The Indian policy of the time was the reverse of that of Mexico. In 1824 priests were ordered to "extinguish" the Indian languages; in 1829 town mayors were ordered to force Indians and other day laborers to work on haciendas, since it was needed for agriculture. This was repealed in 1837, foreshadowing the return of the Conservatives. The years 1825, 1829, and 1835 saw repetitions of the order to give private title for lands. Although the precise effects of these laws are far from clear (Skinner-Klee, 1954, pp. 17–22), there is some evidence that the Liberal Indian policies contributed to their own elimination. The abolition of tithes, establishing civil marriage, and the generally anticlerical policies led priests to incite the Indian communities against the government. The introduction of the Livingston Code in 1837, which included, among other things, trial by jury, brought about an armed uprising in San Juan Ostuncalco. Following this, a general scattering of insurrections began.

Squier reports that they began with a cholera epidemic wherein the priests set the rumor that the Liberals were poisoning the water in order to kill off the Indians and to make way for entrepreneurial foreigners. This last reflected the Liberals' desire to bring about the immigration of whites under the belief that they were more likely to develop the country than would the Indian. The Indians then killed or chased out the doctors who had gone out into the countryside (Squier, 1852, 2: 426–27). Perhaps the best-known uprising was that at Santa Catarina Ixtahuacan where, in October of 1839, the Indians rose against tax-collecting agents of the new Liberal state of Los Altos. Montúfar (1879, 3: 407), in reviewing documentation of this event, holds that it was wholly and hypocritically inspired by the Conservatives. The documentation, however, and other reporters of the time (Dunlop, 1847, p. 211) make it clear that real indignation was felt against the Livingston Code and the tribute being pressed by the Liberals. It was from the general conflict of which this was but a part that Rafael Carrera emerged as the Conservative leader who, in Squier's opinion, achieved control over Guatemala by waging a War of the Castes through using Indians against Mestizos and whites.

This was not the first Indian insurrection. Immediately preceding the declarations of independence, the Indians of Totonicapan in 1820 were led by an elderly *principal* to set up an independent kingdom and presidency with various creole trappings. Four years later the Indians of the same region mutinied against the Ladinos, and sent representatives to Chiapas to regain annexation to the Mexican republic (Contreras R., 1951, especially pp. 51–52). In 1832 a revolt of the Indians of the towns on the south side of the volcano of San Vicente, in El Salvador, led to the proclamation of an Indian republic and attacks were made on nearby towns, ". . . putting to death indiscriminately all foreigners, creoles, and mestizos. . . . Conceiving that the conspiracy involved the entire Indian population, the government first resolved upon their general extermination, but . . . it was not undertaken" (Squier, 1852, 2: 421). That actual extermination of the Indian population was considered reflects the strong Liberal point of view of the government.

In instances where the relations with Indian groups did not vastly affect the way of life of the states, another attitude was evident. Bancroft (1887, 3: 616) records that "the government of Guatemala tried in 1831 and 1837 to bring the Lacandones under its authority, but all its efforts had failed. . . ." Squier (1855, p. 49) reports evidently the same event as occurring in 1836, and that ". . . the government of Central America made a kind of treaty with the Manches, in which the Indians acknowledged the sovereignty of the republic, but were to be exempt from the operations of its laws for six years, and furthermore, were never to be called in question as to their religion, nor disturbed in their practice of polygamy. Wherever the governments assume to exercise jurisdiction, it is through Indian officials. . . ."

When the Federation finally collapsed in 1838, Guatemala rapidly came under the long conservative dominion of Rafael Carrera, whereas El Salvador and Honduras tended to remain strongholds of liberalism. Nicaragua, split between the strongly liberal city of Leon and the conservative city of Granada, was kept in a constant state of conflict.

In some respects, the Central American states continued to face essentially parallel problems. Those with an Atlantic seaboard experienced the possibility of external intervention. Tempered by the continued strain toward refederation, nationalist ambitions of each were manifested principally in rejecting possibilities of union. Under these circumstances, the Indian was a secondary problem, since his nationalization could hardly be seen as a major issue so long as the states themselves were being federated and defederated every few years. The other side of the coin, the presence of England's control over the "Mosquito King" in Nicaragua, the colonizing attempts in Olancho and the temporary claim on the Bay Islands of Honduras, kept large portions of the isthmian region out of the control of local states until the Clayton-Bulwer Treaty of 1850. Even after this, however, the British landed troops at Bluefields in 1893, and the United States left troops in Nicaragua from 1909 until 1932. Finally, the Guatemalan treaty with Great Britain by which the latter retained possession of British Honduras (Belice) continues to be a matter of Guatemalan external policy today.

In a very real sense the Central American republics are only now entering the period of nationhood, and doing so in part by virtue of nations clearly emerging elsewhere. Much of the intervention during the 19th century was solicited by Central Americans, as was the first appearance of the filibuster William Walker. (See Bemis, 1943; Salvatierra, 1946; J.A.T., 1946; Bancroft, 1887, vol. 3; Rose, 1904.) The activities of such men, however, provided an image of external intervention that contributed to the idea of nationhood. In examining the process of nationalization in the Central American countries, one must constantly be ready to cast it against the background of the potential Central American union. For even today the low income and limited skills available in the populations of these countries argue for the advantages of confederation (Herrarte, 1955; Arriola, 1957).

GUATEMALA

With the triumph of the Conservatives in 1838, the tone of Indian legislation immediately changes to one of protection and isolation of the Indian within the state administration. In an 1839 decree the Indians are recognized as forming the greater part of the state, and as a distinct class, calling for a special set of laws, or code, for Indians, and a special commission to promote the condition of the Indian. The sale of alcohol was forbidden in Indian communities in the same year, and further decrees were forthcoming concerning the detailed behavior expected of Indian governors of towns. The governor tended to have general jurisdiction over all events, such as funds, justice, clothing styles, in the villages. Perhaps the most revealing legislation occurred in late 1851. First it is noted that the Indians of the Verapaz are "abandoning their customs," and that this is due to the fact that ". . . since they established the system to rule them (the Indians) by the same laws as the rest of the classes, the towns are dispersing, and the countryside is peopled with no policing, and the society lives threatened by the dangers that are notorious . . ." (Skinner-Klee, 1954, p. 30). Following on this is a detailed instruction to the *corregidores* as to how they are to keep up the Indian communities. Perhaps of particular interest is that repeatedly in these papers Carrera used the Spanish Law of the Indies as his guide, and in an 1851 decree ordered his judges to do likewise (*ibid.*, p. 32).

The general product of the Carrera regime was a caste society in which the Indians were kept thoroughly separate from the ruling whites and Mestizos. Strong alliance was made with the Church, and civil administrators were instructed to support the clergy in their dealing with Indians (Skinner-Klee, 1954, pp. 22–32; see also Holleran, 1949, pp. 128–46).

The return of the Liberals to power in 1871 ushered in an era similar to that which took place under Díaz in Mexico, but was carried out on a more modest scale and confined primarily to agricultural development. In the same year it was enacted that Indians and Ladinos (non-Indians) should be administered as one. Under Barrios in 1876–77, the major laws of the new policy were set forth. His forced-labor law was issued in 1876, under the rationale that agriculture was the only way that the country

could become wealthy, and that the negligence of the Indian ". . . made him a poor worker." Further, that the ". . . only way to better the situation of the Indians, removing them from the state of misery and abjection in which they are found, is to create needs that they will acquire through continuing contact with the ladino class . . . at the same time this will habituate them to labor that they become useful and productive for agriculture, business, and industry of the country . . ." (Skinner-Klee, 1954, p. 34). In the following year Barrios abolished communal lands, and pushed the establishment of Ladino communities in the thoroughly Indian region of the Cuchumatanes (LaFarge, 1940, pp. 283–84). In this region the pressure of Liberal policies evidently was not entirely appreciated. In 1898 the Indians of San Juan Ixcoy slaughtered some 30 Ladinos, almost the entire Ladino population of the town (Recinos, 1954, pp. 363–64).

In the matter of administration, the Liberals gradually tried to institute municiple organizations that combined both Indians and Ladinos where there were very large Indian populations. In 1927 this was formalized (although never strictly followed) by requiring that all municipalities in which a majority of the population was Indian have one-half the municipal council drawn from each ethnic group (Skinner-Klee, 1954, pp. 46–47, 92, 94). Modest attempts were made to change Indian customs through education, usually by setting up Indian schools in provincial or national capitals (*ibid.*, pp. 42–43, 51–68, 93, 120).

In the course of the first half of the 20th century, some of the Liberal measures were relaxed. Farmers were required to see to the health of their laborers in 1928, and debt peonage was finally lifted in 1934. On the very same day it was replaced with a vagrancy law and law of *jornaleros*, which served the purpose of keeping labor available but without this control being exercised directly by the *hacendados*. The major revisions came with the revolution of 1944, the new constitution of 1945, and the labor, agrarian, and Indianist acts that followed. A National Indian Institute was established and an Institute for Social Security; considerable emphasis was placed on rural education (Goubaud C., 1952). The policy followed by the Guatemalan governments in some respects resembled the pattern of the 19th-century Liberals, but with periodic injections of Indianist and welfare philosophy. The Barrios program served to bring about the break-up of some indigenous communities early in the century (Amir, 1957). The Liberal method of controlled elections for local offices was replaced in 1936 by appointed officeholders. This further broke down Indian organization in other communities (Ewald, 1957a). The introduction of the elective system, but this time combined with competitive political parties, brought about drastic changes in many other communities (Adams, 1957b, p. 50; Silvert, 1956). The National Indian Institute, unlike its Mexican counterpart, has never been given a serious role to play, and as recently as 1945 the country witnessed a politically inspired, but serious, uprising of the Indians of Patzicia in which quite a number of Ladinos were killed. In the old pattern, this was met with equal, if not greater, slaughter on the part of the suppressors of the uprising.

Guatemala is faced with international pressure to treat its Indians after the philosophy of the Indianists, but at the same time is in the difficult position of having better than half its population living in Indian communities of varying degrees of corporateness (Adams, 1956a). Furthermore, while the Indian population is slowly declining relative to the Ladino population, both are growing at significant rates (Dirección General de Estadística, 1959, pp. 35–37). The lack of effective internal acculturation is reflected in the external situation: Guatemala is still making forceful claims on British Honduras (Belice) as na-

tional territory. For a country with a low national income and few resources, the problem of the nationalization of the Indian in Guatemala is a major one.

HONDURAS

Following the break-up of the Central American Federation, Honduras essentially followed a Liberal policy towards the Indian. As Alvarado García (1958, pp. 15–16) has noted: "There have been few juridical dispositions issued in favor of the Indians of Honduras, because the democratic idea has prevailed that Honduras ought to be considered as brothers and equals, without taking into account race or culture. In Honduras one may say that there is no racial discrimination, but it is certain that the Indians and country people in general have been exploited by more educated people ('hombres más preparados'), and that the aborigines have provided the major part of the human material that has succumbed in our fratricidal wars." Indeed, the same author, in trying to compile Indianist legislation, could find nothing that concerned the Indian between a single brief decree of 1829 and the first labor law of 1851.

Honduras, like Mexico, had distinctly different kinds of Indians to contend with. In 1857 Wells (1857, p. 555) described the distinction as follows: "The Indians . . . are distributed throughout the state, but divided into two distinct classes: those inhabiting the plateaus and tablelands of the interior who may be classed as peaceable, industrious people, such as the Texiguats[7] and others cultivating small patches of vegetables and fruits, which they carry patiently to the nearest towns; and the others, the coast Indians and those wandering over the wilds of Olancho, such as the Poyas, Woolwas, Guacos, and the Caribs, who are located from Cape Gracias á Dios to Guatemala. These are principally employed as

[7] By 1954 the Texiguat group was among the most acculturated survivors of this general population (see Stone in Adams, 1957a, pp. 621–22).

481

servants, mahogany cutters, carriers, and muleteers."

The first general population to which Wells referred, surviving today as the Lenca and related groups of the southwestern highlands, were treated with a general Liberal policy. This meant no special laws, no special treatment or rights. A significant exception to this was made in 1864 when it was decided that due to a continuing conflict between the Ladinos and Indians in Intibuca and Yamaranguila, there would be a separate *alcalde ordinario* for the Indian communities (Alvarado G., 1958, pp. 20–21). This policy was rejected by the Ladinos of neighboring Marcala (Adams, 1957a, p. 612), and the state refused similar requests from the Indians of Ocotepeque in 1875 and of San Andres in 1884. The policy led to some Indian revolts, and "Curarán, Gracias, and Intibuca acquired fame as centers of militarism and insurrection" (Stone, 1954, p. 193). The rebellion in Curaran resulted in a decree in 1872 creating a new department between Choluteca and La Paz to handle the Indians.

This policy of strict civil control of Indian populations in the southwest did not hold for the treatment of the tribes of the north and east. These groups, called "forest Indians" in the Honduran records, were much more isolated and in fact began to receive special treatment by 1861. It may well be that the Honduran governments too recognized that the strictly Liberal policy being followed with the communities of the southwest might press the northeastern groups into alliance with the English or other foreign filibusters, as had occurred in the Mosquitia. Whatever the reason, the great Honduran Indianist, Father Subirana, began his work in the department of Yoro and in the Mosquitia, in 1858, and wrangled a decree out of the government in 1861 for a civil and military governor of the latter area to be charged with special concern for the Indians. Here the problem was to establish towns, encourage catechi-

zation, set up schools and permanent houses, and in general teach the Indians a "love for work, agriculture, and other practical arts." This policy followed in many respects what would be regarded farther north as a Conservative policy. Cooperation with the clergy was explicit. In 1864 there followed a whole series of decrees providing land for Yoro Indians, and in 1868 the Mosquitia was created a department (Alvarado G., 1958, pp. 16–34).

From 1869 to 1877 there was a special administrative system under a *curador*. This quickly developed into a fairly exploitative practice since the curador was given the right to 8 per cent of the Indian production and a companion instructor (*celador*) was to take another 12 per cent. In addition to this, priests were to take 5 per cent while catechizing. In all, these state representatives were officially to take 25 per cent of the Indian production for their own support; and no one was to say how much more they might accumulate. This was recognized by 1877 to be the old *encomienda* in disguise, and was abolished (*ibid.*, pp. 35–37).

From 1879 through 1929 there followed a series of specific measures that provided special treatment for the Indians of these regions. Marriage was encouraged by eliminating civil fees (1879, 1886, 1894); Indians were to have free commercial transactions (1884), and Daniel Quiroz, a priest who followed in the tracks of Subirana, was allowed free entry of goods in order to set up towns (1885); a monthly grant was made to the Payas of Culmi for their school (1891) and right to ejido lands was granted the same group in 1898. In 1893 an extensive law freed all the northeastern Indians of the constitutional municipal system, and established special governments with special agents for their towns. Taxes were lifted, along with military service, but education was to be pressed, and nonexploitative contacts with non-Indians were to be encouraged. In 1929 the Indians of the Montana del Flor (southern Yoro) were granted a tract of land for their exclusive use (Alvarado G., 1958, pp. 41–61).

Although Honduras ratified the Interamerican agreement setting up the Interamerican Indian Institute in 1941, the act seems to have led to no change in Indian policy. The institution of a cultural mission to the Mosquitia in 1953 (*ibid.*, p. 61) followed the earlier policy of incorporation through settlement and education, but further reflected the interest manifested by Nicaragua for portions of what Honduras considered to be her national territory. In the southwest communal control of land survives, but it should be noted that retention of ejido lands in this instance has not been contrary to government policy, and that ejido holdings are common through Honduras. The difference is that in the Indian region about 50 per cent of the land is communal whereas in the rest of the country, only 20–30 per cent is held in this manner (Adams, 1957a, p. 543). The southwest groups, however, have with few exceptions been forced into the patterns of civil control.

NICARAGUA

Nicaragua, like Honduras, has been concerned with two quite different kinds of Indians and has followed a different policy with respect to each. For purposes of this general history, Nicaragua may be divided into two parts, the central and Pacific highlands and coast, and the Atlantic highlands and coast (Adams, 1957a, p. 159). The eastern section of the central highlands blends into the Atlantic area and there is no basis at present on which to give any significant dividing line. The earliest specific reference that I have found concerning Indian "policy" unfortunately concerns this hazy area. In 1828 the municipality of Acoyapa, Chontales, passed an act stating that the Indians of the neighboring region were too indolent and lazy and therefore 2000 caballerías of land they were occupying would be appropriated for national use, specifically by the town in question (Guerrero C., 1956, pp. 158–59). This measure probably concerned the semiagricultural and semicollecting Atlantic coast Indians and there is no evidence that it reflected a general policy of Nicaragua at the time.

On the whole, in the early period there seems to have been no special legislation concerning the Indians. This may reflect the policy of the liberal Federation, but it probably also reflects a condition of little interest on the part of the Nicaraguans in it. Prior to 1877, so far as I can tell, the Laws of the Indies continued to serve as the model for treatment of Indian communities and their communal lands, and this is not typical of pronounced Liberal policy.

In 1832 a decree stated that all towns of the state should have ejido or communal lands in accordance with the size of the population of each. In 1859 a law was issued saying that anyone holding such land for four years or more would thereby acquire individual rights to it; furthermore, however, lands could be claimed outright in shorter periods. Although this led to the destruction of what may have been corporate Indian holdings, it should be noted that at this date no distinction is made between Indian communal lands and those belonging to a civil municipality. It was the latter that was the owner, not the former. The law may have led to the weakening of municipalities in general, therefore, since rent previously received for use of municipal land was reduced through such claims. The situation of the Indian communities at this period is reflected in Squier's comments (1852, 1: 290–91) on his visit to Sutiaba in 1849: "The municipality of Subtiaba [sic], in common with the barrios of some of the towns, holds lands . . . in virtue of royal grants, in its corporate capacity. These lands are inalienable, and are leased to the inhabitants at low . . . rates. . . . In fact, many of the institutions of the Indians in this country were recognized, and have been perpetuated by the Spaniards." Squier also reported (p. 294) that Nicaragua was a country without peonage, that the Indians ". . . enjoy equal privileges with the whites, and may aspire to any position, however high, both in the Church and the State."

In May of 1877 the first major blow to the indigenous communities came through a legislative decree that ordered the dividing up of municipal ejidos and Indian communal lands. With respect to the latter, title was to be given to individuals and that left over was to be sold off. As was the case in almost all such subsequent acts, the funds gained from such sale were supposed to be destined for education of Indian youth (Instituto Indigenista Nacional, Nicaragua, 1947, pp. 3–4). The same ruling concerning lands was repeated in 1881, 1895, and 1906, suggesting that it had not received effective compliance. The 1895 decree added the destructive clause that any lands for which the Indians failed to show incontrovertible title would automatically be considered to be municipal land. The 1906 decree provided a definition of an Indian community, stating that ". . . there exists a *Comunidad Indígena* in the localities where the population of this *caste* possesses land that does not constitute an integral part of the municipal lands" *(ibid.,* p. 30; see also Pérez E., 1955, pp. 14–19). As Pérez has pointed out, the stipulations of these decrees were not such that the Indian would be likely to take advantage of private ownership.

Following 1877, there have been two major breaks in this position. From 1914 to 1918 the earlier decrees were set aside, and it was made illegal to alienate Indian communal lands. Again in 1935 a similar legislative decree was issued, and continued in effect at least until the publication of the laws in 1947 by the Instituto Indigenista Nacional. During this entire period (from 1877 to the present) there have been a series of decrees establishing statutes and local tax policies *(arbitrios)* for certain of the Indian communities. Specifically Muymuy,

Jinotega, Boaco, Masaya (Monimbo), various communities of Matagalpa, Sutiaba, Sebaco, San Isidro, and some of the communities of Rivas were affected by these measures. During the period from 1914 to 1918, however, the statutes included the statement that the community land was inalienable. Following the decree of 1918 various steps were taken towards the further destruction of the communities. In that year the Indian community of Jinotega was declared "extinct," and the lands not being held privately would be sold by the municipality. In 1919, 1000 hectares of Indian Community land of San Isidro were expropriated. In 1925 a decree stated that only a "pure" descendant of tributaries would have a right to a parcel of land. In two decrees of 1931 the term "Indian Community" is no longer used; it is replaced by terms such as "community of agriculturalists" and specifically refers to "all residents." In the same year, it is prohibited to the Indian community of Masaya (Monimbo) to use its funds for fiestas.

The change indicated in the 1935 return to community land rights is reflected in a decree of 1945 in which the "extinct" Jinotega Indian community is given local tax regulations (Instituto Indigenista Nacional, Nicaragua, 1947).

The result of the change of policy of 1877 may be seen in the Indian communities of Sutiaba and Monimbo today. In both, the population has no land to speak of aside from the neighborhood house plots. Monimbo Indians, both men and women, work almost entirely as day labor; those of Sutiaba combine this income source with fishing (Adams, 1957a, pp. 238–45). There is no special policy with respect to anything Indian.

The Indians of the Atlantic coastal plain and adjacent highlands have, as in Honduras, undergone a somewhat different history. Here the issue of foreign intervention has played an important role. In the course of the 17th century England made claims

484

on this region, and established some control through crowning a "King" of the Mosquitia. Control was exercised through buccaneers and colonial governors at Jamaica and later from British Honduras. The first "King" was crowned in 1678, and England kept up periodic control, punctuated with armed interludes, until she agreed to withdraw all claims, the United States doing likewise, in the Clayton-Bulwer treaty of 1850 (Bancroft, 1887, 2: 599–607, 3: 244–53). Although there was a degree of international recognition of Nicaragua's claims following this, it rested mainly on the competitive interests of two English-speaking nations.

The Mosquitia Reserve was set up by treaty in 1860. Where the Indians came into direct contact with the slowly growing Nicaraguan settlements, such as in Chontales, the state sent out orders to set aside land on which the Indians were to be "settled and civilized" ("la reducción y civilización de dichos indígenas") (Guerrero C., 1956, p. 88). On the Reserve itself a new crisis in 1893 led to a new English intervention and a revolt in Bluefields of "Chief Clarence," a local leader. The end of this affair was the withdrawal of the English, a new convention being set up between the Nicaraguan state and the Mosquitia inhabitants in which rights were granted the Indians to local self-government, use of their own taxes, and exemptions from military service, but requiring allegiance to Nicaragua. The Mosquitia Reserve was at this time converted into the Department of Zelaya (J.A.T., 1946).

Following the incorporation of the Reserve into the nation occasional measures were taken to provide for the Indian population and to encourage its nationalization. In part this was being done through the efforts of mining operations which drew Indians in as labor. But in 1903 the central government decreed 3000 hectares for the use of Indians near Bluefields, and in 1918 Indians of the department were granted

their house sites. Neither of these seem to be very strong measures, and their utility may be interpreted (for lack of further information) in various ways. In 1934, 40,000 hectares of national land were given to the "Creole Indian Community of Bluefields" to be repartitioned among its members. The term "Creole" had officially been added to that of "Indian Community" for the Bluefields population in 1933. In recent years the competition with Honduras for the Coco River area, together with the increased availability of trained personnel and funds from international sources, has led the government to initiate a program of fundamental education in this area. Initiated in 1955, the program has been directed towards public health, agriculture, and educational goals (Boletín Indigenista, 1955, pp. 365–67; 1959, pp. 241–45).

In one respect Nicaragua and Honduras have followed similar courses in their Indian policies. It is perhaps not so remarkable if one considers that the two countries are parallel in general topography, Indian distribution, size and composition of colonial population. Both have followed essentially similar courses of republican history. Today both are generally free of external threats to their territorial integrity, except from each other, and both are turning to modest development programs in the Atlantic coastal areas. Honduras, however, continues to have more significant Indian enclaves in the interior, whereas the post-1877 policies of Nicaragua have effectively reduced the strength of surviving populations in Nicaragua. The much greater degree of acculturation and nationalization of the Nicaraguan central and Pacific highland Indians, in comparison with those of southwest Honduras, may be laid in a considerable degree to the fact that Nicaragua eliminated communal lands, whereas Honduras continued to support them. It should perhaps be added that we have almost no systematic information on the present status, legally, culturally, or socially, of contemporary Indians of the Nicaraguan central and Pacific areas (Adams, 1957a, pp. 332–38; Stone, 1957). Where ejido lands survive in Nicaragua, they seem in no way to be related to Indian populations. Rather they were latter-day allotments to new Mestizo populations (Pérez E., 1955, pp. 14–19; Guerrero C., 1955, 1956; Adams, 1957a, p. 169). The ratification of the Interamerican Indian Institute by Nicaragua in 1943 did lead to a flutter of activity, and the appearance of fugitive publications, but it seems to have played no role in national policy (Boletín Indigenista, 1943, pp. 261–65, 295–97).

EL SALVADOR[8]

Although specific information is lacking, there seems to have been a much greater depopulation in El Salvador, Honduras, and Nicaragua immediately after the conquest than in Guatemala and Chiapas. The maximum figure that Baron Castro could arrive at for El Salvador for 1551 was 60,000, based on an actual count of some 10,000 less (1942, pp. 198–99). A leading Salvadoran historian has stated that the ". . . Spaniards exterminated the Indian men . . . and appropriated the Indian women . . ." (Lardé y Larín, 1953, p. 91). Whatever the case may have been in this respect the significant population that survived at the time of Squier's visit was restricted mainly to the southwest region. Half a century earlier the Indian population was strongly concentrated in the western section, and in San Miguel only 28 per cent of the population was Indian (Adams, 1957a, p. 487).

In the middle of the 19th century Squier referred to two major Indian segments in the country. One consisted of the large towns in the neighborhood of Sonsonate (Izalco, Nahuizalco) and on the southern side of the San Vicente volcano (the Nonaulcos), in which Spanish was the main language. In the other, ". . . the aborigines have always maintained an almost complete isolation, and they still retain their original language, and, to a great extent their ancient rites and customs. This district is known as the . . . Balsam Coast" (1855, p. 331). He goes on to say (p. 334) that the Indians of this area reject visits from any outsiders, and prize their autonomy. This was evidently maintained within the state of El Salvador due to two conditions. First, the exclusive extraction of the balsam for export lay with them, and from this they realized the enormous sum of £20,000 annually. Second, they were under a local Indian government, and "their votes for presidents, deputies, etc., are always given in consonance with indications which they receive from the seat of government, and which they regard in the light of orders."

This picture reflects an adjustment evidently having been made by the state in order to keep up the extraction of balsam. The Indians retained their corporate quality under this arrangement, and had evidently developed something of the cacique system of articulation with the state that characterized Izalco a century later (Adams, 1957a, pp. 493–94; 1959, p. 214).

The course of Salvadoran Indian legislation is not known to me, but it is clear that today the municipalities of El Salvador no longer have large extents of ejido lands. Evidently many used to have a good deal of such territory, but the parcels have been sold off. It was reported to me in Tejutla that the ejido lands of that municipality were repartitioned in 1912 and divided among the Indians. Individual holders rapidly began to sell their shares (Adams, 1957a, pp. 471–72).

The Salvadoran view of the Indian is perhaps indicated by the coverage of the 1930 census wherein less than 80,000 Indians are reported for the total republic, and

---

[8] Published information of state policy towards the Salvadoran Indian has been hard to come by. This brief account is provided on an even more tentative basis than the preceding reviews.

70 per cent of these lived in the southwest departments (*ibid.*, p. 488). The present Indian population of the country can also be calculated as high as 400,000, however, if specific cultural criteria are used.

A major event in the Indian's view of himself within the national context followed on the insurrection of 1932 (Schlesinger, 1946). This uprising, apparently involving efforts on the part of local Communist agitators, brought about a reprisal even more bloody than the uprising itself; the state slaughtered 25,000–30,000 people (Lardé y Larín, 1952, p. 35, cites the former figure, informants in El Salvador tended towards the latter). It is ironical that the resolution suggested for the 1832 Indian uprising, namely, extermination of the Indian population, was in fact almost the solution chosen for the uprising of 1932. Evidently the Salvadoreans identified the insurgents as being Indian, and it was reported that after these events, surviving Indians ceased to wear their Indian costume when traveling to other parts of the country (Adams, 1957a, p. 504).

Although El Salvador established a National Indian Institute in 1943, in tune with the times, I know of no action taken through this organization, and by 1957 it was reported not to exist (Boletín Indigenista, 1957, p. 325). Nationalization of the Indian in El Salvador today is basically handled as part of the general problem of rural development. There seem to be few if any surviving Indian lands, and almost all the surviving Indians are extremely acculturated. Literacy and public health programs are directed at rural communities irrespective of whether they are Indian or not (*ibid.*, 1959, p. 219). Occasionally special activities are carried on in Indian communities, but there is no indication that such efforts represent any special policy of the government (*ibid.*, p. 325). In some sense, the Indian policy of El Salvador has been similar to that applied by Nicaragua to the Indians of the central and Pacific highlands, which is almost to say that no policy was applied at all. The results seem to have been about the same in both areas.

THE INDIAN AND NATIONAL CULTURE

The process of nationalization involves the extension of new cultural forms and their concomitant relations among all the peoples of the state. From this emerges a thing which has been called a national culture. The elusive formal quality of national culture need not detain us here, but something of its quality in terms of the Indian warrants comment.

In the early adaptation of the Spaniards and other Europeans to the New World, certain basic characteristics of Indian cultures were borrowed. Fundamental among these were items of ecological adaptation, specifically food products. This included both staples, such as corn and beans, and auxiliary products such as squash, chili peppers, turkeys. Essentially, however, the development of the variant cultures of the New World has followed the formal patterning of the Old World wherever possible. Things peninsular were regularly of greater prestige than local forms. This continued in force, in spite of elements to the contrary, during the Díaz regime in Mexico, when things Mexican and Indian were frequently depreciated in favor of things European.

One aspect of the Mexican Revolution was the introduction of new values placed on Indian symbols. Aztec heroes became state heroes, and the people of Mexico's prehistory were identified as the proper Mexican heritage. As a part of the same shift (but not as a result of it) things Spanish, European, North American, and generally foreign were correspondingly depreciated. To a much lesser degree there has been some element of this in Guatemala, but the impression is that it is more a reflection of the Mexican Indianist interest than it is a parallel discovery by the Guatemalans of their own Indian past. In

487

Mexico and Guatemala, however, the National Indian Institutes have been charged with the preservation of a limited number of things Indian, particularly the popular arts. The Museum of Popular Arts in Mexico has been responsible for a strong development in this field, and the tourist business in Guatemala has similarly stimulated extra production of Indian textiles (Caso, 1958b, pp. 123–55; Skinner-Klee, 1954, pp. 127–28).

There is a real question, however, of what kind of contribution the Indian past has made to the emerging cultures of these nations. Faced squarely, the network of common meanings and forms that compose the countrywide culture of a nation must reflect the way of life of the contemporary peoples, and cannot seriously be anything but a pale imitation of past forms (Wolf, 1956). In a review of the history of the Indian in the nationalization of these states, he certainly cannot be regarded as a major contributor to national development. Indeed, the barbarians on the outside and the corporate communities on the inside were essentially competitors for autonomy. The nation is created only through some destruction of this autonomy. Whether this destruction is obtained through the harsh Liberal policies of the 19th century, or the welfare-oriented Indianist policies of the 20th, elimination of some cultural differences is inherent and central to the process of nationalization. The policy of the Indianist, however, which is now being effected

in Mexico, and may yet have some influence in Guatemala, is that the new national culture incorporate some Indian traits rather than lose them. In this, Honduras, Nicaragua, and El Salvador have little left to draw upon. The colorful traits of their Indian heritage have for the most part disappeared, and the remainder lie among low prestige items of a fairly poor laboring class.

The national cultures of Middle America are also developing as part of an even broader international culture. Nations grow up in communities of nations, and the common Spanish heritage, combined with facing common problems of development at approximately the same time in the world's history, has led these countries to share a great deal of their "national" cultures with each other. Indeed, it is easier to find traits of regional and international distribution than it is to identify traits that uniquely pertain and represent one nation alone (Adams, 1958). Nationalization of a state, then, including the incorporation of the Indian, brings about a new culture. It cannot be completely described with either single or collective sources because it develops as an adaptation to the conditions, both local and international, in which it finds itself. Indian nationalization is a sub-process within the whole whereby new cultures are formed through the elimination of Indian communities. It cannot be understood unless seen in terms of nations developing within communities of nations.

REFERENCES

Adams, R. N., 1956a, 1957a, 1957b, 1958, 1959
Alvarado García, 1958
Amir, 1957
Arriola, 1956, 1957
Bancroft, 1887
Baron Castro, 1942
Bemis, 1943
Boletín Indigenista, 1941—
Bosch-Gimpera, 1958
Caso, 1954, 1958a, 1958b
—— and Parra, 1950
Chamberlain, 1953
Chávez Orozco, 1943
Cline, 1945, 1953
Comas, 1953
Contreras R., 1951
Conzemius, 1932
Cook and Simpson, 1948
Cotner and Castaneda, 1958
Dabbs, 1958
Dirección General de Asuntos Indígenes, Mexico, 1958
Dirección General de Estadística, Guatemala, 1953, 1959
Dunlop, 1847
Estudios antropológicos, 1956
Ewald, 1957a
Ezell, 1955
Gamio *et al.*, 1958
González, 1954
Gouband C., 1952
Guerrero C., 1955, 1956
Herrarte, 1955
Holleran, 1949
Instituto Nacional Indigenista, Mexico, 1955
Instituto Nacional Indigenista, Nicaragua, 1947

International Labor Office, 1953
LaFarge, 1940
Lardé y Larín, 1952, 1953
Mecham, 1938
Montúfar, 1879
Orellana, 1950
Parra, 1954
—— and Jiménez Moreno, 1954
Pérez E., 1955
Perry, 1922
Pike, F. B., 1959
Pineda, 1888
Porter, K. W., 1951
Pozas, 1959a
Recinos, 1954
Rose, 1904
Rosenblat, 1954
Ruiz U., 1956
Salvatierra, 1946
Schlesinger, 1946
Silvert, 1954, 1956
Skinner-Klee, 1954
Spicer, 1945
Squier, 1852, 1855
Stabb, 1959
Stanger, 1932
Steward, 1949
Stone, 1954, 1957, 1958
T., J. A., 1946
Tax, 1952b
Villa R., 1945
Wellman, 1947
Wells, 1857
Williams, M. W., 1929
Wolf, 1953, 1956
Zavala and Miranda, 1954

25. Directed Change

ROBERT H. EWALD

THERE IS nothing new about directed change in Mesoamerica, if by this term we mean the active and purposeful intervention by one group in the culture of another (Linton, 1940, p. 502). Foster (1960a, p. 10) has pointed out that, ". . . the Spanish conquest was marked by a consistent and logical philosophy of purposeful guided change that extended over a period of three centuries." Planned change did not stop when the Mesoamerican nations obtained their independence in the last century.

We shall limit the present discussion, however, to certain programs of planned change that have been conceived and executed by national and international agencies in the past two decades, especially since the end of World War II. It was during this time that UNESCO developed its program of "fundamental education," and that the National Indian Institutes of Guatemala and Mexico were created.

The considerations which motivate programs of directed change in Mesoamerica are similar to those in all underdeveloped nations of the world. UNESCO (United Nations, 1949, p. 9) stated these in a general way: "The aim of all education is to help men and women to live fuller and happier lives; in adjustment to their changing environment, to develop the best elements in their own culture, and to achieve the social and economic progress which will enable them to take their place in the modern world and to live together in peace."

The conditions requiring programs of action in Mesoamerica are much the same as those found elsewhere. Foremost is the poverty of most of the rural population, caused by either lack of good land or its unequal distribution. Countless rural families own too little land, too poor land, or none at all. Technology is crude, outmoded, and low in productivity. Subsistence agriculture is widespread. Monoculture is common.

Poverty, in turn, is closely related to health, a universal problem in Mesoamerica. Poor standards of health and sanitation are reflected in high infant mortality rates, in nutritional deficiencies, and in the high prevalence of intestinal parasites and respiratory diseases, all these conditions the

490

result of inadequate diet and housing, general absence of medical care, and unsafe water supplies.

Attempts to improve diet and health are hampered by (1) the physical isolation inevitable from lack of good roads and of communications services; and (2) the widespread Indian monolingualism, and the high rate of illiteracy among those who do speak Spanish. According to a recent estimate (Ministerio de Educación Pública [hereinafter cited as MEP], 1960d), 74.5 per cent of all Guatemalans are illiterate; Fisher (1953, p. 78) has estimated that about 50 per cent of the Mexican population cannot read or write. Finally, ". . . from the viewpoint of the person seeking change, the villager lacks a basic knowledge which would help him make best use of resources at his disposal or cope with coming changes. Besides his ignorance of writing, he knows nothing of rights and legal procedures, marketing, simple science, and mechanics" (ibid., p. 79).

All this can be summed up as a problem in "social integration," a phrase much used in Guatemala and Mexico. In both countries the major task is to teach Indians and peasants skills enabling them to participate fully in a larger social system, the nation. Caso (1958a, p. 27) states this philosophy: "As a policy, indigenism consists of a governmental decision, expressed by means of international agreements, and legislative and administrative acts, which has as its objective the integration of indigenous communities into the economic, social, and political life of the nation." In Mexico, Caso goes on to say, indigenism is expressed in an action program, in planned acculturation on the part of the government, the principal agencies for which are discussed below.

Directed change is an aspect of acculturation, a subject which has loomed very large in the anthropological literature of recent years, since the early exploratory statement by Herskovits (1938). Much of the theory implicit in programs of directed change has been elaborated by anthropology. Further, such programs are directed toward the kinds of communities which anthropologists study. It is commonly accepted, therefore, that the anthropologist is the person best equipped by training and interest, to foresee the consequences of planned change and, hence, to make policy recommendations to agencies of change. Anthropologists are being drawn, in increasing numbers, into active participation in such programs.

The majority of anthropologists are likely to accept the fact that change is inevitable. The task of the anthropologist, where he fills the role of adviser, is to examine the community cultures in order to predict sources of resistance, and to make recommendations for guiding change so as to bring about a minimum of disorganization and demoralization. Where the anthropologist is also the administrator, as is the case in the National Indian Institute of Mexico, he can far more actively participate in the process of change, even while realizing that much of the process lies outside any possibility of his control. But, whatever the role of the anthropologist, he quite clearly must operate within a substantially broadened concept of acculturation in the complex situations of Mesoamerica. Since directed change means the intervention of one culture in the affairs of another, it is crucial to specify just what cultures, populations, and agents of change are in contact.

A starting point is to create some sort of typology of subcultures within the Mexican and Guatemalan nations. Various classifications have been drawn up for the cultures of Latin America in general (Service, 1955; Wagley and Harris, 1955; Wolf, 1955b), and Adams (1956b) has provided a scheme for Central America. More recently Edmonson (1953) has pointed out the range of subcultures that exist in Mexico. It is possible, from examining these various schemes, to identify which elements in the populations of Guatemala and Mexico are the primary targets of directed change. Social integration in those nations aims at incorporating into national life all relatively backward, economically deprived groups, whether they be classified as Indians, campesinos, poor Ladinos or rural Mestizos. Examination of these same schemes, however, provides no sure clue to which population components are at the initiating end of directed culture change. A recent paper by M. Nash (1957a) is illuminating for this purpose.

Nash points out the importance, in developing a theory of change for Mexico and Guatemala, of identifying the sociocultural segment of the nation wherein the impetus for change originates. He suggests that in Guatemala, for example, the impetus for economic development must come from Ladino society, and within this broad category the only possible one of four segments is that which he refers to as the *masa media*. This middle class is literate, politically active, socially mobile, and impoverished. Such a group, having low incomes and high aspirations, and having no commitment to the existing economic system, is a likely source for social and economic innovations. Mexico too has developed such a class, but there is a very great contrast in the relative ability of the masa media in these two countries to politically control economic means. In Mexico 30 years of revolution have resulted in the placing of political and economic power in the hands of this class. A necessary course in gaining and holding this power has been to adopt a policy which appeals to the lower classes and the Indian population. Thus, Mexico is substantially ahead of Guatemala in the development of a government-financed program for the betterment of the Indian population. This is reflected in the relative strength and influence of the Indian Institutes of these two countries.

Where it is believed that culture change must begin with education—whether for improved literacy, health practice, or farming techniques—then the community is commonly regarded as the proper starting point, and its relations with other communities or cities tend to be ignored. If it is held that economic change is fundamental—a proposition to which we subscribe—then no peasant community is seen as completely isolated or self-sufficient, but as part of a wider social system. In promoting economic change the promoting agency clearly must deal with some unit intermediate between the community and the nation at large. Mexican anthropologists have found a natural economic unit in the Mexican solar market system. A corresponding theory of regional integration guides much of the work of the Mexican Indian Institute.

PROGRAMS OF DIRECTED CHANGE
General Background and History

We limit ourselves here to a review of the programs of some public agencies whose basic goal is "social integration." The methods of attainment of this aim differ with each agency. Groups have been established to deal with different aspects of culture change—medicine, economic development, literacy.

For analysis we classify various programs according to scope of operations, and approach and methods. (1) Single community programs with limited objectives such as raising public health standards or promoting home gardening, or basic transformation of local culture. The Cultural Mission program is of this type. The Rural Schools also operate within single communities. In theory they extend their efforts to the entire community, to raise standards of living through schooling. (2) Specific programs on a national or regional level. We include here campaigns to improve community hygiene, stamp out endemic disease, or to raise the level of literacy. (3) The National Indian Institute of Mexico adopts a so-called integrated approach, which sees community development as part of a broader regional program.

These categories are not mutually exclusive, and we shall not deal equally with each type of program. We are concerned mainly with Mexico because of the relative paucity of published information on Guatemala, which offers a few points for comparison. A brief historical sketch is essential to explain the growth of national concern for social integration, and to make clear the complex interrelationships between the numerous agencies involved in social integration. An obvious omission will be the vast land reform, or *ejido* program, of the Mexican government, a complex subject that lies outside the scope of this article. Mexican modern national concern with social integration is commonly recognized as having its roots in the Revolution of 1910. Caso states that integration was the pre-eminent objective of that revolution (Caso, 1954, p. 266), and from it have stemmed programs of action designed to "raise the level of acculturation" of the Indian. The much discussed "integral approach" is seen as having its origins in the early years of the revolution, and Gamio is generally credited with having formulated it.

In 1915 Gamio called for a thorough study of the entire Indian community—biological, linguistic, cultural, relations with other communities—as a preliminary to a scientific program of development to achieve social integration of the Indian. This integration was seen by Gamio and others as a necessary part of the growth of the entire nation. He was instrumental in establishing, in 1917, a Dirección de Antropología, to be headed by himself, to carry out his plan. Preliminary work was limited for practical reasons, to the Valley of Teotihuacan (Gamio, 1922).

The principal activities of directed change were in the education and health fields.

EDUCATION. Caso has provided a concise summary of the history of educational movements in Mexico (Caso, 1954, pp. 247ff.). Following the revolution the Escuela Rural was developed. Using the integral approach, these schools aimed to educate the entire community, to combat misery, poor health, social disorganization, isolation, and ignorance. This was new and experimental, not based on tradition. The original school comprised three grades, each with a specific level of instruction. In addition there were numerous extracurricular activities, and the teacher was charged with adapting the programs to the needs of specific communities. Each school was given a parcel of land, the produce from which was to be used to buy school furniture and equipment, and to improve teachers' salaries. This system grew rapidly, increasing from 309 schools and 399 teachers in 1922, to 16,054 schools and 16,405 teachers by 1952.

The first Cultural Missions (discussed in detail below) were created to give better preparation to the rural teachers (Caso, 1954, p. 249). Mission teams were to visit rural schools in those areas most densely populated by Indians, establish model schools, and organize committees. The Cultural Missions extended their work into the community—teaching by example the better use of natural resources and how to improve the life of the community.

At first, the Rural Schools and the Cultural Missions served Indian populations only. Rural areas were Indian areas by definition. Rural problems, therefore, were Indian problems. Hence educational work was carried on in Indian and Mestizo communities. Neither Rural Schools nor Cultural Missions had much success in 100 per cent Indian communities, for several reasons: (1) the profound difference in cultural values between workers and Indians; (2) the inability of teachers to carry out programs of material and technical betterment, because of Indian resistance to changes in their traditional culture; (3) In-

493

dian monolingualism; and (4) the inadequacy of methods used to educate Indians. The teachers did not know the Indian language, and had a negative attitude toward customs which they regarded as backward or useless.

The work of the two organizations was complementary, but in general the Cultural Missions have had greater success. They are staffed by numerous specialized personnel and have been able to undertake more thorough studies of geographical, demographic, and cultural aspects of communities before attacking their problems. They have specialized in forms and methods of education for the entire community. The Rural Schools face major problems just maintaining themselves in the pueblos. Further, Caso charges, Rural School personnel have tended to confine their activities too much within school walls, to compete with farm work for children's time, and to be ill-adapted to dispersed settlement patterns.

The most serious obstacle to Rural School work was the monolingualism of the Indian. The first task therefore was to teach Spanish. Monolingualism was a problem of such magnitude, according to Caso, that at times the incorporation of the Indian into national life was expressed in the simple formula: Give to all of Mexico one language. But preparatory grade-school Spanish could not overcome home language. This made teaching slow and difficult. There were numerous pleas on the part of teaching authorities for improved methods of teaching Spanish.

Rural School failure contributed to serious doubt of the Indian's capacity to learn. This led to an elaborate experiment in which many Indian youths from 26 language groups were taken to Mexico City, to a Casa del Estudiante Indígena. They were exposed as fully as possible to modern culture. Ultimate conclusions were that the Indian had the same capacity to learn as the rest of the population; that he could rapidly assimilate western culture; and that once integrated into urban life, he preferred

it to life in the Indian community. Since the Cultural Missions had not fully solved the problem of providing trained teachers, it was thought that this Casa del Estudiante Indígena would train Indian teachers, who would then return to their homes. But, by and large, these students preferred to remain in the city, in any employment they could find.

In general it was felt by Mexican authorities that the Cultural Missions and the Rural Schools had failed in the task of educating and integrating the Indian, and in 1936 an Autonomous Department of Indian Affairs was created, to "promote, direct and stimulate all action attendant on protecting centers of Indian population, for their elevation and betterment, and their assimilation to the Mexican population" (Caso, 1954, p. 254).

In 1937 the Department of Indian Education was created, within the Secretariat of Public Education and incorporating a number of centers of Indian education. These were to operate in exclusively Indian regions, and the pupils, mostly adolescents, were to receive three or four years of training in a wide variety of subjects aimed at integrating them into national culture. Later these centers were reorganized so as to stress economic instruction over Spanish and liberal arts subjects. The new objective was to provide each student with agricultural and industrial techniques which would lead to success in his home community. This program succeeded mainly in producing discontented individuals, few of whom were willing to return to their pueblos.

A new stage in the work of social integration began in 1939 with attempts to apply anthropological science. Under the auspices of the Department of Indian Affairs and the National School of Anthropology, a First Assembly of Philologists was held, resulting in the formation of a Council of Indian Languages. This council elaborated a project for experimentation in new teach-

494

ing methods. The conviction spread among high education authorities that the literacy of the Indian population could be achieved only by teaching in their native languages, and that once they gained a basic knowledge of the alphabet, the teaching of literacy in Spanish could proceed more rapidly. An Institute of Literacy for Monolingual Indians was created to carry out this goal.

A technical difficulty in the way of this program lay in the necessity of analyzing the various native languages, determining their structures, preparing texts based on these languages, and then training teachers. In 1945 the Institute of Literacy convened five groups of bilingual teachers, coming from five different areas of native speech. Each was given intensive training in anthropology, in general linguistics, in the linguistics of his particular area, and in special teaching methods. Each teacher was to return to his area to serve as an instructor for 30 rural bilingual teachers. The latter would directly develop the literacy campaign among monolingual Indians. Under the direction of social anthropologists and linguists, texts were prepared for the five languages. These were designed to teach reading and writing in the mother tongue. Spanish was to be taught orally, in actual situations, prior to teaching literacy. There was considerable opposition among professional educators to such a program. They considered it wasteful to teach an alphabet soon to be forgotten, and it would retard the teaching of Spanish. Despite such objections the Institute continued the experiment among the five original groups. Excellent results were reported only for the Tarascan area.

The Instituto Nacional Indigenista (INI) has initiated its own educative programs in two Indian zones, the Tarahumara and the Tzotzil-Tzeltal. INI stressed an integral approach. This includes building roads, teaching concepts of hygiene, new methods of cultivation, betterment of industry, and in general raising the economic level.

Caso (1954, p. 256) concludes that acceptance of the Rural School serves as an indicator of the degree of integration of Indian communities into national life. The establishment of Rural Schools in Indian communities is a reflection of the economic growth of the nation, a growth whose impact is felt in local communities. In résumé, Caso finds, the Rural School functions only as an integral part of the complex of western culture; it is impossible for it to function normally with its methods in pure Indian communities.

MEDICINE AND HEALTH. Attempts to improve local health conditions also have a long and complex history (Caso, 1954, p. 242ff.). Following the Revolution of 1910 there emerged a new philosophy in public health. Public assistance in health matters came to be regarded as a social obligation, as a necessity for national progress. The new focus was to be on communities rather than on the treatment of individuals. Preventive medicine was to be stressed, because of the small cost compared with that of curative medicine; also, preventive medicine emphasized the community approach. Early campaigns were aimed at eradicating endemic and epidemic diseases and at reducing the mortality rate from malaria, smallpox, and yellow fever.

A major handicap in every case was the shortage of trained medical personnel. Thousands of communities, with 69 per cent of the total population, were without any medical aid. The First National Congress on Rural Hygiene in 1936 promoted a policy wherein all doctors, pharmacists, and dentists would practice two years in rural areas before setting up practices in cities. Such a policy, however, proved to be unconstitutional. Later, a conference between national and university medical authorities resulted in a program in which pre-graduates were sent, at the end of their studies, to various places to practice for a six-month period. During the six months they were to be supported by the government. They were expected to carry out programs of sanitation, which usually meant little more than immunizing local populations for smallpox, whooping cough, and diphtheria. They were to do research on sanitary conditions, and to obtain data on epidemiology, on physical medicine, and on the economy of the community. They were also permitted to privately practice curative medicine, charging according to local ability to pay. This measure, while provisional and insufficient, resulted in getting numerous medical personnel into the field though usually in areas where the economic level made such service attractive. The medical trainee was required to remain in the rural community only for a short period, thus his impact on the local way of life was little.

To resolve such difficulties there was founded, in 1937, the Higher School of Rural Medicine, attached to the National Polytechnic Institute, with a training program more elementary than that of the Medical School of the National University. Students leaving this school were obligated to work for three years in rural communities.

In recent years the Secretary of Health arranged with governments of states to establish agencies of health and assistance, called Sanitary Units and Centers of Hygiene. These units develop programs of preventive and curative medicine, do research on sanitary conditions in the areas served, and learn the nature of existent medical practices. They also try to provide midwives and curing specialists with rudimentary scientific knowledge. These efforts in the main are confined to cities.

Wider medical programs are the *ejidal* medical services, at first under the direction of the Bank of Ejidal Credit, but later under the Secretary of Health and Assistance. By contract, costs of services are shared by both parties, and adequate medical and sanitary services have been achieved, especially in the more prosperous ejidos. Such services go only to organized ejidos. It is precisely the underdeveloped Indian community that cannot count on these services. For them the old Department of Indian Affairs created a medical department especially charged with supplying medical assistance, but the usual lack of funds prevents widespread penetration.

Cultural Missions

Mexico is notable for the number of national programs of directed culture change. One of the most comprehensive of these has been that promoted by the Department of Cultural Missions, an organ of the Secretariat of Public Education.

The Cultural Missions program goes back at least to 1923 (Hughes, 1950). In the early years the program was heavily criticized and frequently reorganized. A major reorganization of 1942 revived the nearly defunct program. Mission programs include general improvements in economic life, diet and dress, housing, and sanitation conditions. Other objectives lie in social and recreational fields, popular general culture, and patriotism.

The Department of Cultural Missions consists of certain salaried administrative personnel in a central office in Mexico City, and a specialized field teaching staff. Of the several kinds of Cultural Missions only the so-called Rural Missions are discussed here. At the time of the Hughes survey in 1950 there were 48 Rural Missions. Each was staffed with eight to ten persons, including a chief, a nurse, a doctor or interne, an agronomist or practical farmer, a home economics leader, a music teacher, and teachers of plastic arts, of recreation and sports, of carpentry, and of building construction.

The Rural Missions emphasize local initiative to solve local problems, with Cultural Mission personnel acting as advisers. Ideally the local people set up a series of committees for each area of planned activity. Each committee should have a chairman, secretary, and treasurer, in addition to other members. The chairmen of the several committees comprise a general Committee

496

of Economic and Social Action (Hughes, 1950, p. 22). This general committee is expected to draft a plan of work and to take responsibility for its execution. The Cultural Mission personnel cooperate with this committee, provide technical advice, and attempt to enlist public support. Change, it is believed, should be gradual and progressive, as sudden or spectacular change might not be understood or accepted. The local committees ideally should be permanent, carrying on after the departure of Mission personnel.

An adequate survey of the results of the total program is not now available. There have been reports on the activities and accomplishments of specific Rural Cultural Missions, however, and these serve to illustrate the methods, the achievements, and the weaknesses of the total program. We draw primarily on the reports of Whetten, Fisher, and Hughes, whose studies provide the best material for an evaluation of the program.

San Pablo del Monte, in the state of Tlaxcala, was the location of one of the 37 Cultural Missions in operation in 1942 (Whetten, 1948, pp. 440–51). The *municipio* then had a population of 8563, about 85 per cent of whom lived in the *cabecera*, San Pablo. According to Whetten's figures, 89.2 per cent of the people spoke Nahuatl, 38 per cent were monolingual. The lack of knowledge of Spanish, and the high illiteracy rate, were major problems for the Cultural Mission. Fortunately, in this case, the chief of the mission spoke fluent Nahuatl.

The following facts about San Pablo were relevant to the Mission program (Whetten):

1.   An agricultural economy was based on corn growing, no water for irrigation, and only a few expensive deep wells were available for drinking water.

2.   Some 1500 local women made from 25 to 50 pounds of tortillas daily, by hand, and carried them to the city of Puebla for sale. There they bought corn for the following day's supply of tortillas. Each paid a small fee to the Puebla market. About half these women rode the bus between San Pablo and Puebla.

3.   Many San Pablo men made a daily trip into Puebla, on foot or by bus, to work as unskilled laborers, especially during slack seasons in agriculture.

4.   Local political, and to some extent, economic, life was dominated by a *cacique*, despite the legal autonomy of municipal authorities. The cacique was said virtually to appoint the municipal president (an illiterate man at the time of Whetten's visit), and to make all important decisions for him.

5.   A resident priest in San Pablo served surrounding villages. His attitude toward the Mission was apparently neutral.

6.   Civil authorities participated in church festivals, and the president appointed a *mayordomo* to take charge of the annual fiesta for the patron saint, and other mayordomos for other saints. Fiestas were expensive and the outlay could ruin a mayordomo, but this great honor could not be refused.

7.   Religious and political life were intertwined, and it was apparent that the priest was in a position to encourage projects which would raise the general standard of living. He was said, however, to lack any interest in the material welfare of his parishioners.

The arrival of the Missioners was greeted with coolness, even suspicion and hostility. Two months elapsed before prejudice could be broken down sufficiently to begin work at all. The music and recreation teachers were instrumental in making friends among the local populace. The Mission personnel, as one of their first projects, attempted to organize a number of cooperatives for production, distribution, and consumption of goods. Fair success was achieved with a number of smaller cooperatives, including four small consumers' cooperative stores, but the fate of a more ambitious cooperative venture is very instructive in illustrating the sources of resistance to directed change.

In an attempt to organize the tortilla makers into a single large cooperative, it was suggested that they jointly purchase one or more mills for grinding corn, machines for making tortillas, and a station wagon or two to transport tortillas to Puebla and corn back to San Pablo. Further, it was suggested that permanent stands be set up in Puebla, with full-time personnel to sell the tortillas, thus eliminating the necessity of 1500 women making the daily trek. In purely economic terms, such a proposal was eminently feasible. Vested interests made such a cooperative impossible. The cacique led a monopoly on the bus service between Puebla and San Pablo, charging a fee for each person and each basket. The purchase of station wagons would have seriously curtailed this traffic. The owners of corn grinders vigorously protested the cooperative purchase of such machines. Puebla officials objected to the potential loss of market fees. Consumers feared that machine-made tortillas would not taste as good. Finally, the director feared that the cacique would use his considerable influence in state affairs to have the whole Mission withdrawn from the village.

The Mission remained in San Pablo for about three years. In the director's own estimation, the Mission did little more than give the community some help in improving their level of living. Only a fraction of the population was effectively reached. Whetten visited San Pablo in 1944, after two years of Mission work, and reported that confidence and hope for the future have been instilled in the inhabitants (Whetten, 1948, p. 451).

Rural Cultural Mission number 17 began its work in Teteles de Avila Camacho, Puebla, in March 1949 (Hughes, 1950, pp. 33ff.). This village of 800 persons is located along a highway in a favorable environmental zone. Here too corn was the basic subsistence crop, but fruit growing was also important. Harvests of fruit were good, and the fruit was much needed elsewhere in Mexico, but in the absence of any effec-

tive means of distribution, much was left to rot.

During the first four months of its work the Mission organized the Committee of Economic and Social Action, and the various project committees. Following general Mission practice, economic development was given special emphasis in Teteles. The agronomist for this Mission (actually an "empirical" teacher) was regarded as being especially capable. He donated to the villagers 2000 eggs from pedigreed chickens for incubation. After a time he began trading the eggs of blooded stock for "criollo" eggs. He encouraged the villagers to incubate the former, and he sold the latter in the market to defray his own expenses. Hughes observed the presence of pure-bred chicks in the flocks of many homes.

Work in health and hygiene is said to have been outstanding. This is usually regarded as a weak point in the Cultural Mission, but in this case a capable doctor was present, and his nurses were well trained. A committee of hygiene and health operated effectively to obtain cooperation with the home economics teacher in improving sanitation practices in the home. Many householders accepted the practice of cleaning their patios several times weekly. A campaign to rid the community of lice, flies, and fleas was highly successful, after initial objections to the odor of DDT were overcome by perfuming the spray.

Fisher (1953, pp. 80–81) was able to devote six weeks in 1947 to observing Cultural Mission number 25 in San Nicolas de los Ranchos, a village near Cholula in Puebla. The population of about 1000 included both Indians and Mestizos. The economy was typical: raising corn, cutting firewood for sale, and making a specialty item, metates, for export. Water for any purpose was scarce, and crops were usually poor.

Fisher lists the Mission personnel, their duties and abilities. The chief, he felt, was unusually well chosen, an enthusiastic man who gained the confidence of the community. The agriculturalists too worked with great enthusiasm, often devoting long hours to the introduction of new techniques and new ideas through demonstration. The important duties of the nurse were carried out with considerably less interest. A skilled carpenter and a capable mason devoted most of their time to building facilities for the mission itself, instead of to teaching. The music teacher, says Fisher, was more an embarrassment than a help to the Mission, owing to his very limited musical ability.

Fisher feels that the chief of the Mission and the agriculturalists were the principal agents in introducing new patterns, and that despite its limitations the Mission did effect changes that would prove to be permanent. He emphasizes the important point that trained personnel are a constant problem to the Mission program. In other communities visited by him the personnel achieved no rapport with the people, and even aroused resistance.

The preceding paragraphs point up only the highlights of these three Cultural Mission programs. Some other Mission activities are briefly summarized here. The Missions in general emphasize agriculture, and home gardening in particular is thought to be valuable for improving the daily diet. The poor results in this respect reported from Teteles correspond with results elsewhere. Even where gardens are started and vegetables harvested in abundance, the peasants fail to incorporate them into their diets. In a few areas, however, the cultivation of soy beans, for the diet and for sale, was successful.

All missions are concerned with the water supply, for drinking and for irrigation, and they especially encourage the protection of streams and wells. In Teteles the Committee for Economic and Social Action supervised the building of a small reservoir for drinking water, fenced against stray animals. Such measures are especially important to control water-borne disease.

Medical work is a basic activity of all Cultural Missions. Each team tries to train workers to vaccinate, give injections, bandage, give first aid, nurse the sick, and prepare diets for babies. In San Pablo the nurse vaccinated extensively against smallpox and typhoid fever, and organized 18 midwives into weekly classes. As in Teteles, health personnel cooperated with the home economics teacher to promote sanitation in the home. Householders are encouraged to whitewash homes and to build floors. A standard campaign is to get householders to build raised *braseros* (brick stoves), a measure designed to relieve the woman of the tedium of cooking at floor level.

Cultural Missions cooperate with the schools, which are regarded as primary community centers. Their principal service is to encourage the building of new schools or the rehabilitation of old, and the construction of teachers' dwellings, school furniture, and other equipment and facilities. According to Hughes (1950, p. 50), from 1942 to 1949 over 400 primary schools were constructed under Cultural Mission guidance. Cultural Mission number 19, in the Santiago Ixcuintla zone in Nayarit, aided 10 or 11 towns in the zone to build new elementary schools during a three-year period. During one year the program maintained 125 rural literacy schools in communities which had no other schools.

Poor recreational facilities and excessive drunkenness create a social problem in rural Mexico (Whetten, 1948, p. 438). Each team has a teacher of sports and recreation, who tries to organize team sports, dancing classes, and theater groups. The work of the music teacher in organizing singing groups and orchestras is another part of this campaign.

A partial assessment of the effectiveness and lasting contributions of the Cultural Mission program can be taken up at this point, but general remarks are reserved for the conclusion of this article. Hughes' statements concerning the major problems and weaknesses of the program are relevant here. In his words (1950, p. 63), "Cultural Missions have contributed greatly to the overcoming of the physical and mental isolation in which the *campesinos* and the Indians live; they have also given rural communities a sense of interdependence and relationship with the rest of the population." This is, of course, a fundamental goal underlying nearly all programs of directed change in Mexico. Caso (1958a, p. 28) observed that, ". . . we consider it essential that the indigenous community gain an awareness of belonging to a vaster social organization, that of the Mexican nation." Further, Hughes feels that the campesinos have been made better producers and consumers through the introduction of new crops and better animals, improved techniques, and better diet. The tasks of the woman have been lightened—by power mills, sewing machines, and a more equitable distribution of chores within the family. Recreation and music are supplanting alcoholism in the fiestas.

The weaknesses and difficulties of the program are many, something to be expected, considering the vastness of the undertaking and the limitations on resources. Viewing the program in prospect rather than retrospect, it would seem that a primary requisite for the success of any Rural Cultural Mission would be a highly trained and dedicated staff—dedicated because the isolated and difficult working conditions require more than ordinary interest in one's employment. Adequate salaries might provide sufficient motivation if such dedication were lacking. Salaries were generally low in 1950 (Hughes, 1950), although the general level of salaries has been increased since that time (Fisher, 1953, p. 80). This state of affairs contributes to the general absence of well-trained personnel from Mission staffs. Hughes' figures for 1949

(1950, p. 64) bear on this point. The total teaching personnel for the entire Cultural Missions program was only 436. These were graded according to level of training into four categories, A through D. The last consisted of persons with empirical knowledge (for example, of farming or carpentry) but no normal-school education, and included 216 persons, or nearly half the total number. Apparently it is an unusual Rural Mission that is staffed with uniformly well-trained persons, and this certainly contributes to the highly uneven accomplishments from one zone to another.

Another limitation of the Mission program is the time available to work in any given community: usually from one to three years, but sometimes less. Yet the ultimate aims of the program are so broad that they will require generations, not years, to complete. There is in Mission philosophy a distrust of immediate, spectacular gains; they build up high hopes and are followed by disappointment. Ideally, change should be accomplished slowly over a period from seven to 10 years. But, in practice, a Mission may spend at least six months establishing rapport, and hence is just able to start work in earnest when it must leave. This situation is only partially ameliorated by the recent policy of moving the Mission a short distance away, so that personnel can return at intervals, or can be visited by members of the community.

It may be stated as a general principle that the more unlike two cultures in contact, the less they will understand one another, and the more difficult it will be to introduce sweeping change. Caso (1954, p. 250) has stated this to be a weakness of the Mission program, and the Missioners themselves consider the Indians to be a special problem. Hughes (1950, p. 67) cites the Popolocas of Veracruz as a special case of a people not culturally prepared to receive guidance. Illiteracy and monolingualism make communication difficult. Further, they tend to be suspicious, and cooperate only half-heartedly if at all. Existing medical beliefs and practices oppose the work of nurses. The status of women is an important factor. The men refuse medical aid for their pregnant wives. Further, women are not allowed to visit literacy schools where the teacher is a man, a serious problem because no female teachers are available.

Hughes presents statistics to indicate the scope of the Cultural Mission program during the period 1942–49, and its achievements (1950, pp. 72ff.). It is very difficult, however, to assess the actual extent of change accomplished by the Missions in a mere presentation of figures. The meaning of his figures, for permanent significant culture change, can be determined only by more intensive study at the village level. To state, for example, that an increased use of steel plows or concrete privies reflects a basic change in attitudes or values would be at best an inference. At present we can do no more than note that change is occurring as a result of the efforts of the Cultural Missions, but without being able to assess its true extent.

As a consequence of Mission successes and failures Caso (1954, p. 256) states these propositions as guidelines for further development: (1) A project achieved in a short time will not take root or have permanent results in an Indian community. (2) Benefits last longer when the pueblo acquires them by its own efforts; they should not be presented as gifts. (3) Culture change should be accomplished through informal education, because this is the traditional way of teaching and learning. (4) An official organization wishing to act in an Indian community must first arouse the desire for progress; the people themselves must be stimulated to feel the necessity for, and to desire, change.

Supervised Rural Credit

One of the more recently conceived programs for inducing change at the community level in Mexico has been a project for administering credit, on a limited and supervised basis, sponsored by the Centro de Educación para el Desarrollo de la Comunidad en América Latina (CREFAL). This organization was founded in 1951 by UNESCO, with the collaboration of the Mexican government, the Organization of American States, and other agencies, and is located in Patzcuaro in the state of Michoacan. Its primary goal is to train personnel to participate in programs of community development, and to prepare educational materials. Its zone of operation comprises some 21 hamlets surrounding Patzcuaro.

Buitrón (1961, pp. 141–50) describes the program beginning in 1956 on the small island of Pacanda, Lake Patzcuaro. This site was selected because the community seemed to be beyond help. Buitrón states that an ideal community development requires two essential conditions: (1) the program should be able to count on the participation, and some initiative, of the community itself; and (2) technical and other services should be provided from the outside, for example by the national government. CREFAL operates on the premise that no community is beyond all help. In Pacanda the people owned at most their own rude houses and small patches of rocky land, without any irrigation water; the principal occupation of the men was fishing, of the women housework. The people were illiterate, tired of waiting, and hopeless. It would be impossible, in such a community, to begin directly with a program of development. CREFAL began by bolstering people's self-confidence.

Specialists, after analyzing local conditions, decided the program offering best possibilities of success was one of supervised credit to promote the raising of poultry. First, building facilities would require neither extensive nor fertile land. Any family owning any land at all could participate. Second, breeding of poultry was not foreign to these people, although they would have

501

to learn scientific methods. Third, the care of poultry would be sufficiently easy that women and children could do it. Thus, the head of the family would be free to perform his traditional occupation, thereby lowering the risk of losing a source of income before there was absolute certainty that the new project would succeed. Finally, there was a good market for eggs all over Mexico.

To finance this project CREFAL was able to secure a bank loan of 100,000 pesos. In the first months of operation the CREFAL specialists spent their time selling the idea to the people, explaining fully their obligations and responsibilities, directing and supervising the construction of chicken coops, buying chicks and raising them to an age of six weeks, and distributing them 200 to each family. CREFAL personnel were charged with receiving and weighing the eggs, sending them to market, paying off the bank loan with the proceeds, and distributing profits to the growers. It was hoped that in a short time an association of campesinos would be able to operate the project independently of CREFAL.

Buitrón makes no claim that Pacanda is now a developed community. Direction is still needed to encourage building better houses and to improve the diet, sanitary conditions, clothing, and education. Nevertheless, it is felt that the very success of chicken raising will stimulate some of this development. Thus, when fish were the only resource, people of Pacanda saw no need to learn reading and writing. But now, when they see the number of eggs coming in, the money received, the payments to the bank, the number of bags of feed being bought each week, and so on, they are beginning to feel the need for literacy, and are seeing to it that their children go to school.

Nayarit Pilot Project

The primary focus of the programs discussed so far has been to work within the community, to provide the needed knowl-

edge for change, and to stimulate efforts at self-help. The Mexican Pilot Project in Basic Education, carried out in Nayarit in the years following September 1948 is somewhat more ambitious in scope. An anthropologist, Glen Fisher, had abundant opportunity to observe and participate in this project, first during 1949-50 and again in 1952. His study (1953) not only reports extensively on this project, but gives an excellent summary of directed change in Mexico up to that time.

The Nayarit Pilot Project was first proposed by the Mexican government to a General Conference of UNESCO (Second Plenary Session, held in Mexico City in 1947), and its aims and goals are consonant with the general statement of the UNESCO Fundamental Education Programme, cited above. The area selected for the project was one of some 2000 sq. km., comprising 28 ejidos along the Santiago River in Nayarit. This is an area of fertile soil but low agricultural productivity. The general objective was to stimulate and to train the people to solve their own socio-economic problems. A director for the project was named by the Ministry of Education, and was to cooperate with various other state and federal agencies. Active work began in 1949.

Project work centered in the Santiago Valley, along the coastal plain, and was organized to concentrate on five aspects of valley life: reading and writing, economic life, domestic life, health and sanitation, and recreation. It was recognized that progress in any one of these areas required concurrent action in the others.

To judge from Fisher's estimation of results (1953, pp. 129–30), the activities of the project did not end in either total failure or complete success. Certainly, different aspects of the total program met with varying response.

Education could not proceed until schools were built or repaired and the teaching staff increased. The program also involved revising the curriculum and extending the services of the schools to people of all ages. Of particular interest were a projected normal school and an agricultural school, which were to supply personnel who would keep up the work of the project after outside administrators and technicians had left. Response to educational measures was highly variable. No apparent objections were raised to the kindergarten, but although some parents were enthusiastic, others had to be coaxed to send their children. Night schools were very well attended in some cases, and villagers even asked for increased offerings in this program. Teachers' institutes were most successful of all. From the enthusiasm with which they were accepted, Fisher feels that teaching personnel acquired through them an increased pride in their role.

Improvement in the economic area meant in particular the development of agriculture, which in turn required a solution of the land question created by the inequalities existing in the ejido system. According to project plans, ejido lands were to be redistributed along the lines of existing legal specifications. The one serious case of resistance was encountered here. As would be expected, such resistance was offered by those who benefitted from the *status quo*. The crisis endangered the success of the whole Pilot Project, so that the director himself became influential in calling off the reorganization. Little was accomplished in the way of improving farming technology. Attempts to introduce hybrid corn, better livestock, and better care of animals were received with apathy. Road building was to be an important part of changing the valley economy through improved communications, but this lay outside the scope of the project.

Health and sanitation involved such measures as drainage, installation of privies, and sanitary water supplies, improvement in habits of personal cleanliness, and improvement of food habits. A DDT campaign was planned to combat malaria. Plans also called for the establishment of a cooperative health service, with a public dispensary and a permanent nurse. There was little measureable response to these programs, however, and a definite fear of medical science was revealed in a number of instances.

Village alignment and physical planning achieved the greatest success, measured in cooperation and village initiative. The recreational plan involved an extensive program of activities for persons of all ages and both sexes, but although well received, apparently did not take root. In one ejido teachers claim that their recreational program has forced one of the two *cantinas* out of business. Fisher quotes the results of a survey made before and after a year of project activities (1953, p. 130), which suggests that changes have occurred in the use of leisure activities. Thus, reading as a favorite pastime increased from 10 to 19 per cent, and sleeping decreased from 47 to 27 per cent. Fewer people listed visiting the cantinas as their favorite pastime. Fisher suggests some possible long-range consequences of the Pilot Project, in terms of changing personality patterns, goals, and value orientations. Such changes are crucial, of course, to any and all programs of directed change, but existing studies are almost devoid of information in precisely these areas.

National Indian Institutes

All programs of directed change, whatever their specific goals, have recognized the importance of economic factors, but we contend that basic economic problems cannot be solved solely by action within specific communities. The economic growth of any community is tied to that of surrounding communities and, ultimately, to the economic growth of the nation. Consequently, the teaching of agricultural methods, the encouragement of new crops, of production for a market, and so on, can have but limited success if more fundamental problems remain unsolved.

503

This belief has been a guiding principle in the work of the Mexican Instituto Nacional Indigenista (INI) since its inception, and personnel of that organization have elaborated, over a period of years, what is in our opinion the most adequate approach to directed change in Mesoamerica.

The INI was created by law in 1948, as one of several national institutes affiliated with the previously created Instituto Indigenista Interamericano. The latter had been established by international convention in 1940, at the First Congress on Indian Affairs, held in Patzcuaro, Michoacan. A brief history, summary of organization, and statement of aims are given in a small publication of the INI (1955). A similar organization was set up in Guatemala in 1945.

Basic research, carried out in certain areas of the country as a preliminary step to extensive developmental programs, has been a key activity of the INI. A number of major field investigations have followed the tradition established by Gamio.

The basic philosophy and guiding principles of the INI have been expressed in numerous publications by anthropologists of that organization. The policy of "indigenism" is an aspect of social integration, INI's main concern. In Caso's statement (1958a) the regional scope of change is stressed. The organ of this regional integration has been the Coordinating Center. Aguirre Beltrán (1955) has made explicit the acculturation theory that underlies the development of the Coordinating Center Program.

Beltrán describes this (1955, p. 31) as a social theory based on direct experience in applied fieldwork. Early attempts at social integration, he finds, were handicapped by the existing state of knowledge of the "cultural reality" of Mexico. Most anthropological community studies conceived the community as an isolated, self-sufficient, static entity. These studies were rich in detail but failed to define the position of such communities within the social structure of the nation. It followed that programs of social integration were atomized according to the multiplicity of existing communities in the country.

As theory grew, the urban and national factors as transmission media for modification of the culture of the Indian community became salient. Integral investigation studies showed that Indian communities should be seen as satellites in a constellation, the nucleus in each case being an urban Mestizo community. Indian communities were interdependent parts of systematic wholes, with the actions of the parts inevitably affecting other parts and the whole.

This new orientation led to the first regional project for integral action. The definition of Indian and what is Indian ceased to be important, as did the study of the folk-urban continuum. "What became important was the integral development of the system, that is, of the *cultural region* that included Indians, mestizos and ladinos, inasmuch as their mutual dependence connects them so inextricably that it is impossible to think of the improvement of one without being concerned with raising the level of the others. Nor was it of practical importance to discover or investigate the different levels of acculturation. What seemed more urgent was a knowledge of the mechanisms of *cross-cultural integration* of the communities and the urban nucleus, for a study of the greater or lesser degree of interdependence; the lower the interdependence the lower the level of acculturation" (*ibid.*, p. 34). The new emphasis is on analysis and change among communities comprising a system.

Thus, the most isolated, self-sufficient communities seemed to be the least dependent. Policy, therefore, would be directed toward strengthening ties between these and the larger system, in order to break down isolation. This would be achieved by promoting all means of com-

504

munication—highways and national language—to raise the level of acculturation. "The basic objective is to achieve, within a discernible future, the constitution of a homogeneously integrated *cultural region* with a profile and character of its own, functioning smoothly within the aggregate of cultural regions which comprise the larger national society" (*ibid.*, pp. 34–35). Beltrán holds the main job of the Coordinating Centers is to accelerate peaceful integration.

A concise description of the organization of the Coordinating Centers is given by De la Fuente (1958b, pp. 30–33). These Centros Coordinadores Indigenistas were created by the President, and much of the activity of the INI is channeled into regional projects through them. "The Centers coordinate, in each area, the economic and technical resources of the Institute with those of the federal agencies functioning in that area, and other agencies representing Indians and non-Indians in that area." Heading each center is a social anthropologist. Under him is a team including other anthropologists, and technicians in the fields with which the Center is concerned —doctors, public health trainees, agricultural engineers and nurses. A third level of technicians include the *promotores*—bilingual Indians, natives of the region, who have been trained for the purpose of introducing new ideas, techniques, and ways of organization into the community.

The anthropologist in the Coordinating Centers often makes policy decisions, an unusual role in the majority of cases where anthropologists are advisors or administrators. As Beltrán has said (1955, p. 42), "Because the goal pursued is the integration and development of a region, it is assumed that the specialist in the social sciences is the person best fitted to handle the problems of daily living which arise through the contact of human groups belonging to different cultures." Therefore, it is the administrator who is subordinate to the anthro-

pologist, because the central interests of the one and the other are so different, and because the goal is the development of a regional system.

The "cultural promoter" implements the belief in indirect culture change through individuals from the groups to be changed. Indian and Mestizo communities have interrelations which have required the existence of certain intermediaries having the specific role of smoothing the functioning interdependence.

There is a school to train cultural promoters for the various Centers. The schools teach technical skills as well as educational techniques. The Tzeltal-Tzotzil project, established in 1951, is the oldest and best described Coordinating Center (De la Fuente, 1958b, p. 30f.). It operates from the city of Las Casas in the Chiapas highlands, and serves some 115,000 persons, mostly Indians.

Another center is Papaloapan, centered in the Nuevo Paso Nacional, along the border between Veracruz and Oaxaca. This collaboration with the Papaloapan Comcenter relocated 12,000 Mazatec Indians, in mission. They were resettled because a vast hydraulic project flooded many villages.

The Mixtec project has two Coordinating Centers, the High Mixtec in Tlaxiaco, and the Low Mixtec at Villa de Jamiltepec. The aim of the first project is to construct a road to Low Mixtec, and the preparation of the population for resettlement in the lower region. The Low Mixtec project involves working on sanitation problems, to protect the health of the immigrants from the higher region. Poverty and overpopulation have necessitated this move.

The Tarahumara Coordinating Center operates from the town of Guachochi, and its program affects 40,000 individuals, mostly Tarahumara Indians. Immediate goals include controlled lumbering operations, and a fair distribution of profits, since in the past the exploitation of vast forest resources has failed to benefit these Indians.

505

This economic development is a necessary preliminary to further development.

The Cora-Huichol Center was established in July, 1960. This is an area of low population density, low living standards, and low-level economy. Primary goals are better communications, rural industries and crafts, and improved agriculture, health, and education.

The National Indian Institute of Guatemala (IING) is not as broad in scope or as large an organization as the INI of Mexico. Its activities have been limited to investigation. Trained investigators have compiled a series of brief cultural reports for many of the municipios of that country, and several of these have been published as short monographs *(Publicaciones Especiales del Instituto Indigenista de Guatemala)*. In addition to its investigative activities the IING uses its influence in many specific projects (Instituto Indigenista Interamericano, 1960). Following are some typical activities for the year 1959: obtained equipment to prevent the overflow of a river at San Cristobal, Totonicapan; obtained 20 cement latrines for use in San Antonio Aguas Calientes; aided in the introduction of drinking water into Momostenango, and negotiated with federal government people to supply the labor; promoted highway construction; and set up a Department of Rural Economy to study and analyze Indian industries and their economic importance to the nation.

Another activity was the formation of the Integral Betterment Plan of Tactic, department of Alta Verapaz. Under this plan, teachers have been supplied with materials and supplies, including bilingual primers (Spanish-Pokomchi). IING personnel have encouraged and promoted the building of new schools. A new clinic gives medical aid to all who seek it, and dispenses medicine sent by the federal government. Included in this plan is the distribution of seed of various kinds, and assistance in planting and the development of new agricultural techniques.

In Guatemala the greatest stress, by far, in social integration, is placed on education, and the principal agency is the Dirección General de Desarrollo Socio-Educativo Rural (SER). The organization, functions, and affiliations of this agency are described in a publication of the Ministry of Public Education (MEP, 1960a). The SER falls within the Ministry of Public Education and is affiliated with various international agencies: UNESCO, Organization of American States, World Health Organization, the Servicio Cooperativo Interamericano de Educación, and others. This agency is charged with the development of "integral rural education" for the entire country.

Education, as conceived by SER, is synonymous with social integration. The many problems of literacy, public health, infant mortality, nutrition, housing, and so on, already listed as basic to Mesoamerica, all fall within the purview of rural education. And the approach to these problems is fundamentally through education—training of teachers, of local leaders, of children in the schools, and of the adult population.

One of the major problems of SER is that of training so-called "empirical" teachers— rural teachers who are actually in service but have never received a normal-school training and lack the credential. It has been estimated that over 40 per cent of all rural primary teachers are *empiricos* (MEP, 1960b, p. 2). In a land where there is a general shortage of teachers these persons cannot be dispensed with, and therefore the Program of Professionalization for Rural Empirical Teachers in Service is an important activity of SER.

In addition to their schoolroom duties, such teachers are expected to participate fully in the life of the community. They should initiate or cooperate in programs designed to improve community health standards, housing, and agricultural practices, and should stimulate the growth of hand-crafts, and of cultural and recreational activities.

It can be seen that this program corresponds closely to that of the Rural School of Mexico, which was intended to extend its activities outside the classroom into the community. It is too early to predict whether or not the SER program will suffer from the same defects as the Rural School of Mexico—that is, whether the teachers will fulfill their obligations or whether they, like their Mexican counterparts, will tend to confine their activities to the classroom.

One further program, sponsored by SER in conjunction with UNICEF and the WHO, is referred to as the Pilot Project in Nutrition and Gardening. This project, begun in November 1958, has now been in operation for nearly three years (MEP, 1960c). In general, the purpose of this pilot project is to improve the dietary habits of rural people, especially children and pregnant or lactating mothers. This is to be achieved through improved methods of gardening and livestock care, and through training rural people to augment their diet with the resultant increased production. Included in the program is the distribution of milk and vitamins to preschool children.

It is too early to predict the long-range results of this program in terms of altering the basic diet of tortillas supplemented with relatively small quantities of beans and even smaller quantities of meat and milk. It is maintained by SER personnel involved in the project that nutrition is the basic problem in Guatemala today, somehow more fundamental than general economic development. Whether attacking the problem at this level places an exaggerated faith in education remains to be seen.

CONCLUSIONS

In the preceding pages we have outlined some of the major programs which have aimed at the integration of certain elements of the population into the larger socio-cultural system of the nation. We have considered only those specific programs operating directly on the culture of the community, or clusters of communities. We do not imply, of course, that such communities are not changed as well from other sources. On the contrary, the establishment of a commercial enterprise—a bus line, a factory—may profoundly affect the lives of many people (M. Nash, 1958a). In the final analysis, the intent of much national legislation is culture change—economic or social development, for example. Thus, a federal road-building program is likely to have a much broader intent than the transformation of life in a specific community. Marroquín (1955) and Lewis (1951) have demonstrated the great importance to Tepoztlan of the road to Cuernavaca, built in 1936; my study of San Antonio Sacatepequez in Guatemala has stressed the significance, for culture change, of that community's location along Guatemala's major east-west highway (Ewald, 1954, 1957b). Beals (1952, p. 232) has suggested (in a humorous vein) that as an acculturative force, one road is worth three schools and 50 administrators.

It is precisely the influence of forces on the community, originating ultimately at the national, or even international, level, that complicates any attempt to assess the effectiveness of programs described in this article. That is, an agency such as any of those discussed might operate for a period of months or even years in a community that is simultaneously being affected by developments in the nation. A comparison of community studies made before and after the program of directed change would reveal unmistakably that changes have indeed taken place, but the relative effectiveness of these two factors would be difficult to assess. Fisher, however, believes that in Nayarit the Pilot Project was less important in producing change than were nationwide

507

elements (1953, p. 158), and suggests that the network of roads built in this area achieved more than all the Pilot Project technicians put together. The interrelatedness of these two factors is, of course, a further aspect. To what extent are road building and general economic development of the nation prerequisites to the effectiveness of a more localized program of directed change? We will return to this question.

Vital changes have occurred in Mesoamerica in the present century, especially in Mexico. Goubaud (1952) summarizes events in recent years in Guatemala, where an entire volume has been published by the Seminario de Integración Social Guatemalteca (Arriola, 1956) on this topic. Lewis (1960, pp. 93–101) cites changes in Mexico just since 1940: great population increase, rapidity of urbanization, achievements in agriculture and industry, and general improvement in the standard of living brought about by an increase in national wealth. In this and in an earlier publication (1951) he details changes wrought specifically in Tepoztlan, where dress, diet, mode of travel, recreation, and the influence of United States culture all underwent modification. Edmonson (1953, p. 229) notes the technological advances made by Mexico in the present century. Nash comments on the relative speed of change in Mexico compared to that in Guatemala, particularly in social class structure. "Mexico of 1910 was much like Guatemala of 1940" (1957a, p. 830).

The progress of directed change must be weighed in terms of the broader national situation within which any such agency must operate. This evaluation is indicated for a number of reasons.

First, the success of any program of directed change depends at least in part on the resources at the command of the directing agency. A constant theme, in the literature on governmental agencies, is inadequacy of funds and therefore lack of trained personnel. In the Cultural Mission program a relatively small number of teams had to spread themselves over great areas, spending only a minimum of time in any given community. Not only were teams too few, but genuinely competent specialists were a rarity on any of them. The difficulty of inducing trained medical personnel to work in rural areas lay in weak financial incentives. The National Indian Institute of Mexico has been well financed and is vigorous, when compared with Guatemala, where nothing like the Coordinating Center program has been undertaken. In short, budgetary problems may be at least as important as those of theory in planning culture change.

Second, the very existence of agencies interested in problems of social integration is related to developments on a national level. The study of such programs is, of course, a study in culture contact—contact between the cultures of those promoting change and of the communities receiving it. At least two distinct population elements are involved in each case. The emergent middle class in both countries is the national subculture wherein the primary impetus for culture change originates. Edmonson (1953, p. 230) refers to the middle class as "the minority culture which sets the tone of modern Mexico."

Third, a program aimed at substantially transforming the culture of a community could scarcely gain headway if that community remained impoverished and isolated. New farming techniques are of little interest to a peasant population that lacks the capital to put them into practice. Knowledge of improvements in diet, sanitary practices, modern medicine, or housing is of little value to an Indian who cannot afford these things. An impoverished community cannot hope to raise itself by its own bootstraps. Economic development of any community is related to the economic condition of the nation. A developed national industry is a major source of government wealth.

Without financial stability a government is hampered in building roads and schools, in training teachers, or in promoting public health measures and community development programs.

A flourishing national economy is, then, a precondition to a successful program of social integration. National authorities state as an ideal of the indigenist program that social integration is essential to the prosperity and well-being of the entire nation. But clearly such integration must originate at the top, not at the level of the unintegrated community. Where there has been substantial economic advance, as in Mexico, change in community life seems to be proceeding even in the absence of specific programs of directed change. And where economic advance is retarded, there appears to be little chance of a flourishing program of directed change. This argument appears to find support in Nash's essay (1957a).

In light of the foregoing discussion, which types of programs of directed change would have the best chance of achieving significant results? A program which operates within a single community, treating it as an isolated entity, depends for its success on the general economic condition of the people. In poor communities, with marginal economies, the first task would be to raise the level of living. But how? Most programs have depended on education—teaching about new techniques, new crops, or new means of marketing. The accomplishments of the Rural School in Mexico were negligible along these lines. The Cultural Missions, even with a broader concept of education—working with the total community, attempting to stimulate local initiative—have, in general, also accomplished little. The reasons for these failures are not far to seek. Admittedly, economic development must ultimately involve some of the things these agencies are trying to do. Crops must be diversified, diet improved, cash incomes increased, and crafts and industries developed. But correcting these

conditions solely through local initiative, even with excellent technical advice, or with the continued encouragement of a trained cultural mission, amounts to a "bootstrap operation." The causes of poverty do not lie solely within the community. An Indian community cannot flourish in geographic isolation from other communities or from the nation at large; it cannot flourish surrounded by other impoverished communities, amid conditions of poor communications, underdeveloped marketing, or general regional and national poverty.

What are the possibilities of effective directed change in other aspects of community life, if general economic conditions remain low? What hope of success can there be in introducing new elements into the culture, or eradicating practices deemed undesirable? Problems universal in Mesoamerica are illiteracy; alcoholism; high infant mortality; unhealthful conditions around the home—smoky rooms, absence of latrines, impure drinking water; the tedious life of the woman in the home. We would maintain that any attempt to solve most of these problems without first solving the general economic ones would stand little chance of success. Granted, a federal government can finance and even build a system for transporting water into a community, or can build and maintain a free clinic. But neither of the federal governments discussed in this article can stand the financial burden of doing these things for their entire nations. And it is not certain that something given for nothing will significantly alter behavior patterns. A people whose basic subsistence wants are scarcely satisfied might be convinced of the desirability of expending time and money in the building of latrines, houses with floors and chimneys, elevated fireplaces, and so on, but this is striking at the symptoms, not the roots, of more basic problems.

What of the problem of illiteracy? Schools are provided by the governments of both Guatemala and Mexico, and teachers are trained and paid by federal agencies, but high illiteracy rates characterize hundreds of communities which have schools and full-time teachers. Two basic problems confront school officials throughout rural Mexico and Guatemala: children are expected to contribute to the family economy, and parents are unconvinced of the need to educate their daughters. These problems are not limited solely to remote, isolated communities. I observed these factors at work in San Antonio Sacatepequez in western Guatemala. This pueblo is on a major highway, between two larger cities, and has a school staffed with six teachers, all with normal-school training. Most Ladino children attended this school for the full six years available to them. School records showed, however, that Indian children, on the average, received less than one year of education. The drop-out after the first year was over 50 per cent, by the third year over 80 per cent. Further, daily attendance was irregular, varying with labor needs in the agricultural cycle. Despite a national law requiring attendance of all children, local Ladino officials were very lax in its enforcement with regards to Indian parents. This in itself is a difficult social problem not to be solved by literacy campaigns. San Antonio enjoys an unusually favorable geographic location. In more remote communities in western Guatemala, the problem is compounded by the fact that teachers speak only Spanish, whereas many Indian children enter school having learned only their native tongue in the home.

There is at least some evidence, on the other hand, to show that a desire for literacy follows when more basic economic needs are met. In the CREFAL program of supervised credit in the Mexican community of Pacanda financial successes in poultry raising stimulated parents to send their children to school to learn the now required skills of reading and writing.

The social structure in any given community is likely to be geared closely to a complex network of economic factors—land ownership, ownership of transportation facilities, paid political positions—and almost any change will threaten existing interests. Goldschmidt (1952) has discussed the effects of introduced change on the existing social structure. He shows that the status of the local elite rests on certain symbols and that change threatens these symbols. Leaders are likely, therefore, to reject changes which threaten their position. Any attempt to promote change by working directly on the social stucture would seem to be foredoomed to failure because of the powerful opposition it would arouse, especially if the fortunes of the local elite are tied in with those of powerful figures at higher levels of government.

We would agree with Foster (1953c) that the social structure of the Mesoamerican community is geared to a pre-industrial peasant economy, and the processes of commercialization and industrialization on a national level would have the ultimate consequences of transforming this traditional social structure. In Guatemala, for example, the castelike nature of social structure in Ladino-Indian communities rests in part on Ladino control of land and other economic resources. But as general economic growth takes place and new alternatives are offered both Indian and Ladino (for example as factory workers, auto mechanics, or bus drivers) this traditional structure will be undermined. We offer these suggestions in support of our argument that many of the problems confronted by programs of directed change cannot be solved directly under existing economic circumstances; and that once general economic growth has taken place, many problems will be well on the way toward solution without directed intervention.

It would seem, therefore, that a program of change which aims at solving fundamental economic problems over the broadest area possible, as a basis for raising the general standard of living, would have the

510

maximum prospects for achieving significant results. Such a program would recognize the primary importance of economic growth on a national level, and would attempt to speed up development on a more localized level. This is, as we have seen, the basic program of the INI, through its Coordinating Centers. Basic problems are dealt with as part of an integrated program of community development, a program which recognizes that little significant change is possible so long as the rural population remains impoverished, isolated, and ignorant. De la Fuente (1958b, p. 31) summarizes the Institute's program: many sided investigations into the problems of each region, carried out by various specialists; many-sided action, including improvement of communications, local economy, health and education; and shifting the community from a purely local to a national orientation. There is general concern for all people of a region under development, though with central interest focused on the Indian. Action in depth is said to be possible because of relatively ample funds.

The total program of the INI should be of exceptional interest to anthropologists concerned with all phases of culture change. Perhaps nowhere else in the world have anthropologists been placed in the dual role of administrators and theoreticians of culture change, with such a relative wealth of personnel and facilities as provided by the Mexican INI. Certainly the Indian institutes of other Latin American nations lag far behind Mexico in this respect, even in Guatemala, which is relatively far advanced. The Coordinating Centers, for all practical purposes, are laboratories for the study of acculturation. Under conditions as fully controlled as the anthropologist is ever likely to experience, acculturation theory can be put into practice and the results closely observed.

REFERENCES

Adams, R. N., 1952, 1955, 1956b
Aguirre Beltrán, 1952, 1955
Arriola, 1956
Beals, 1952
Buitrón, 1961
Casagrande, 1959
Caso, 1954, 1958a
De la Fuente, 1958b
Edmonson, 1953
Ewald, 1954, 1957b
Fisher, 1953
Foster, 1953c, 1960a
Gamio, 1922
Goldschmidt, 1952
Goubaud, 1952
Guatemala, Ministerio de Educación Pública, 1960a, 1960b, 1960c, 1960d
Herskovits, 1938
Hoselitz, 1952
Hughes, 1950
Instituto Indigenista Interamericano, 1960

Instituto Nacional Indigenista, Mexico, 1955
Lewis, 1951, 1955, 1960
Linton, 1940
Manners, 1956
Marroquín, 1955
Nash, M., 1957a, 1958a
Parra and Jiménez Moreno, 1954
Paul, 1955
Ray, 1959
Service, 1955
Social Science Research Council, 1954
Tax, 1952a, 1952b, 1958
Thompson, L., 1950
Tumin, 1958
United Nations, 1949
Villa R., 1955
Wagley and Harris, 1955
Wallace, 1961
Whetten, 1948
Wolf, 1955b

26. Urbanization and Industrialization

ARDEN R. KING

Consideration of the place of the Middle American Indian in cities and industry involves many problems. Because the clouded conceptual and theoretical picture of urbanization and industrialization, and the paucity of Middle American material preclude a traditional description and analysis, one must depend on inferences more than is desirable. Demographic data do not permit the easy identification of Indians in cities or in mechanized industry, where socio-cultural data are also deficient—an understandable situation when one remembers the difficulty of defining an Indian, and that those Indians who engage in truly industrialized activity, meaning high mechanization, have to a great extent redefined themselves socially and culturally. This recognition does not clarify much, however, for we immediately encounter, especially in predominantly agricultural Middle America, the problem of mechanized agriculture. Are those Indians who are engaged in mechanized agriculture, either through individual effort, cooperative action, or as employees, industrialized in their economic behavior? This is difficult to decide, for it is conditioned,

among other factors, by geographical area, closeness of ties with the national whole through transport, communication, political action, and nationally oriented religious movements.

Strict definitions of urbanization and industrialization do not reveal the true situation. Modern industrialization is not dependent on physical location in an urban setting, and modern urban patterning of culture is not necessarily confined to cities. In Mexico and Guatemala it is a question of national culture and the cultural connections beyond national boundaries as part of industrialization and urbanization in the modern world. We are then confronted with the problem of the Indians' relation to the developing national cultures of Middle America. Manning Nash (1957a) has discussed the concept of plural cultures in Middle American countries; in light of this, we have then to determine how much national culture the Middle American Indian has adopted. This, in turn, implies an interest in national economic, political, and religious movements, or, at least, those factors which imply them.

The increasing importance of national

culture, urbanism and urbanization, industrialism and industrialization, as well as new population configurations, has been accelerated by the degree to which the economy is industrialized, the development of true industrial populations which follow a way of life conditioned by the use of organized production with national and international implications, the rise of mechanized agriculture, and the increased mechanical exploitation of natural resources. Such factors demand an increase in the efficiency and expansion of transport systems; this implies not only economic development on a national scale, but the increased influence of the national government and its accompanying value in the industrializing areas of nationalism. These, in turn, imply an increasing currency of a national language and an increased efficiency of a nationally planned educational system. Increased activity of the national governments has brought about drives towards education and national language learning, as well as spread of public health and medical programs. In some areas the latter have contributed to overpopulation, for which the traditional Indian economy increasingly fails to provide. Increased contact with the developing national culture has been enhanced by the opening of the religious world of the Indian to groups with national and international orientation. The increasing success of Protestant missionary groups implies a national orientation for the Indian convert and, as well, demands a major change in cultural orientation. That this has assumed some importance in Middle America is seen by the intensified activity of the Roman Catholics in pursuing the revival of orthodoxy with its national and international affiliation.

Twentieth-century urbanization and industrialization imply the presence of conscious agents of change—planned, or unplanned but desired, change in which the Indian has been either the primary or the incidental object of socio-cultural forces

drawing him into the nation and national culture. Government activities in education, language training, transport, communication, electricity, water resources, public financing, agrarian reform and the ejido movement, and the national Indian institutes are all either directed toward bringing the Indian into national culture or eventually achieve that effect. The development of economy on a national scale both provides for employment, when land poverty and failure of the ejido system force the Indian into industrializing areas, and exploits natural resources in formerly isolated Indian areas.

URBANIZATION OF MIDDLE AMERICAN INDIANS

The urbanization of the Middle American Indian is analyzed on the basis of his actual residence in an urban settlement and his adoption of an urban way of life. Several difficulties impose themselves: definition of the Indian for demographic purposes, utilization of the *municipio* as a demographic unit (the Guatemalan census differentiates the *cabecera municipal* from the remainder of the *municipio*), general lack of distinction between Indian and non-Indian in rural and urban population data, use of 2500 (Mexico) or 2000 (Guatemala) as the lower limit of an urban settlement which offers little realistic basis of comparison with urbanization in other parts of the world, and lack of descriptive data for Indians in large urban settings.

Without attempting a detailed demographic analysis here, we should at least delineate the general trends of Indian population changes in Middle America.[1] The identification of Indian populations in earlier censuses appears to have been based on a combination of culture pattern and lan-

[1] Except where specifically cited, demographic data are taken from (for Mexico) Dávalos Hurtado and Marino Flores, 1956; Marino Flores and Castro de la Fuente, 1960; Mexico, 1960; Parra, 1950; (for Guatemala) Adams, 1956c; Guatemala, 1957; Whetten, 1961.

513

guage. Recent censuses not only have utilized cultural patterns but have compiled separate data on populations with knowledge of an Indian language and/or monolingualism.

Table 1 shows that the striking difference in size of Indian populations of Mexico and Guatemala points up the major difference between the role of the Indian in urbanization and industrialization in the two countries. There has been a steady, although not progressive, decline of Indian percentages in both countries; the total number of Indians has increased, but the proportion is smaller. Data are not available for Guatemala, but it seems certain that the absolute number of monolingual Indians has also declined in both countries. However, the proposals of Wolf (1960, p. 4) that during times of political instability and economic decline there appears to be a return to Indian culture patterns and, probably, to monolingualism should be considered. The Mexican decrease in monolingualism is especially noteworthy and is directly correlated with the increase in the spread of a Mexican national culture.

Although the majority of Indians in Middle America are rural rather than urban, Indians are not necessarily the majority of rural dwellers. Here we must distinguish the Indian urban dweller, but the 2500/2000 definition of an urban settlement offers little help. Consequently, the determination of changes in rural and urban populations is similarly crippled by lack of distinction between Indians and non-Indians in the census data, although it is clear that those Indians who become urban dwellers have changed their cultural identification to a great extent. The following sections will therefore compare monolingual Indian population with knowledge of an Indian language, rural population, population actively engaged in agriculture, illiteracy, proportion of the population in centers of more than 2500 inhabitants and more than 5000

inhabitants, and the degree of internal migration within the country. Inasmuch as only a detailed demographic analysis of municipio census tracts would allow us to determine the exact distributions of these categories, the major political units of Mexico and Guatemala will be utilized for the comparisons. The central and western highlands of Guatemala, the southern and central highlands of Mexico, and the Mexican states which border the southern Gulf of Mexico are the regions which possess the greatest number and percentage of monolingual Indians in Middle America. These were also the regions of densest pre-Columbian population. The 10 political divisions in each country with the highest percentage of monolingual Indian population will serve as the basis of comparison for the categories listed above. The primary comparisons will be based on inspection of the rankings. However, in order to gain some measure of each country as a whole, rank-order correlations[2] have been run for all comparisons utilizing all political divisions.

Indian Urbanization: Mexico

The 10 Mexican states with the largest percentage of monolingual Indian-speakers are, in descending order: Oaxaca, Chiapas, Yucatan, Puebla, Hidalgo, Guerrero, Quintana Roo, Campeche, Veracruz, and San Luis Potosi. This gives a distribution of four Gulf Coast states, four central highlands states, and two south Pacific states. An indication of the concentration of Indian languages is seen when one compares this group with the highest ranking states for knowledge of an Indian language. There is almost a complete coincidence except that the state of Mexico replaces San Luis Potosi in the tenth rank. The rank-order correlation of $+$ 0.96 verifies the conclusion that

[2] This measure of comparison, Spearman's rank-order correlation, is used not to impart a specious exactness to the study but merely to offer a general alternative to comparison by inspection.

TABLE 1—GENERAL TRENDS IN INDIAN DEMOGRAPHY

	Indian	Bilingual	Monolingual
Mexico:			
1900	1,794,293 (15.37)		
1910	1,685,864 (12.98)		
1921	1,868,892 (15.11)		
1930	2,251,086 (16.05)		
1940	2,490,909 (14.85)	1,253,891 (7.47)	1,237,018 (7.37)
1950	2,447,609 (11.30)	1,652,540 (7.60)	795,069 (3.70)
Guatemala:			
1778	311,797 (78.4)		
1880	844,744 (68.9)		
1893	882,733 (64.6)		
1921	1,299,927 (64.8)		
1940	(55.7)		
1950	1,497,261 (53.6)*		1,011,167 (40.4)†

* Including 331,814 Spanish-speakers.
† This figure represents those who speak an Indian language in the home; although many speak Spanish, the vast majority are monolingual.

TABLE 2—RANK ORDER OF MEXICAN STATES

Percentage Monolingual		Knowledge of Indian Language	Rural	Agricultural	Urban	Towns of 5000+	Illiteracy	Internal Migrants
1.	Oaxaca	2	1	5	32	28	4	29
2.	Chiapas	5	5	3	28	26	2	31
3.	Yucatan	1	26	20	7	8	21	32
4.	Puebla	7	15	15	18	20	7	19
5.	Hidalgo	6	2	8	31	25	5	26
6.	Guerrero	8	3	1	30	31	1	28
7.	Quintana Roo	3	9	19	24	16	20	4
8.	Campeche	4	28	23	5	6	18	14
9.	Veracruz	10	16	18	17	23	11	15
10.	San Luis Potosi	11	12	13	21	19	10	16
11.	Mexico	9	8	6	25	30	9	23
12.	Queretaro	15	6	10	27	18	3	21
13.	Chihuahua	18	21	24	12	11	26	12
14.	Michoacan	17	13	7	20	27	8	27
15.	Sonora	14	22	25	11	17	25	11
16.	Morelos	16	20	17	13	9	16	6
17.	Tabasco	13	4	4	29	29	13	30
18.	Tlaxcala	12	18	11	15	32	12	18
19.	Sinaloa	19	10	14	23	22	14	17
20.	Nayarit	20	17	12	16	15	19	10
21.	Jalisco	25	23	22	10	12	17	22
22.	Durango	22	11	9	22	21	23	13
23.	Guanajuato	21	19	16	14	13	6	25
24.	Coahuila	26	29	29	4	4	28	7
25.	Aguascalientes	29	25	28	8	3	24	8
26.	Baja California del Norte	24	31	30	2	14	31	1
27.	Colima	28	30	21	3	5	22	5
28.	Federal District	23	32	32	1	1	32	2
29.	Nuevo Leon	31	27	31	6	7	30	9
30.	Tamaulipas	27	24	26	9	10	27	3
31.	Zacatecas	32	7	2	26	24	15	20
32.	Baja California del Sur	30	14	27	19	2	29	24

TABLE 3—RANK-ORDER CORRELATION
OF MONOLINGUAL MEXICAN STATES

Knowledge of Indian language	+0.96
Rural population	+0.56
Agricultural population	+0.53
Urban population (2500+)	−0.52
Urban centers of 5000+	−0.45
Illiteracy	+0.69

most of the use of Indian languages in Mexico is closely confined to those states with large monolingual Indian populations.

A comparison of the high-ranked monolingual Indian states with rural residence patterns reveals that, following the category limit of 2500 set by the Mexican census, only Quintana Roo, Oaxaca, Chiapas, Hidalgo, and Guerrero fall in the first 10, indicating a strong tendency for the Gulf Coast states and the central highlands to have town-dwelling Indians. A rank-order correlation of +0.56 for the nation as a whole, however, clearly shows the rural orientation of the Indian. The parallel situation that arises in the comparison of Indian-language knowledge and rural residence verifies this conclusion. However, a comparison of the rankings for monolinguality and agricultural occupation again shows the lack of rank coincidence, with Yucatan, Quintana Roo, Campeche, and Veracruz from the Gulf Coast and San Luis Potosi and Puebla from the central highlands ranking lower than the first 10 in agricultural occupation. But the national rank-order correlation of these two categories indicates the agricultural orientation of the Indian as +0.53. From the two preceding categories, it might be concluded that there are more monolingual inhabitants of urban centers in these states. Of the first 10 ranked monolingual Indian states, however, only Yucatan and Campeche possess a large enough percentage of their populations in settlements of this size or greater to be significantly different. Moreover, that these two strongly monolingual Indian states should possess this rank for urban dwellers indi-

cates that there are special circumstances in the Yucatan Peninsula, for the national rank-order correlation between monolingual Indian states and urban dwellers is −0.52.

In an attempt to gain a clearer idea of true urban population centers than a consideration of municipios with more than 2500 population gives, a comparison was made with the incidence of cities of more than 5000 inhabitants. Of the 10 states with the largest monolingual Indian population, those with the greatest population in centers of this size are Veracruz, Puebla, and Yucatan, ranking second, fourth, and fifth in the nation. Because there is a strong tendency for Mestizos to concentrate in the cities, however, a comparison of the percentage of this population with monolingual rank reveals that Puebla is dropped from this anomalous position but that Campeche (6) and Yucatan (8) maintain their high rank. That this is unusual is seen by the rank-order correlation between both Indian monolinguality and knowledge of an Indian language and 5000+ cities of −0.45. This observation is enhanced by a rank-order correlation between knowledge of an Indian language and centers of more than 5000 population of −0.56. But the conclusion that the Gulf Coast states have a large portion of the population in urban centers would seem to hold. Although this may not be indicative of urban Indians in a precise sense, it is certainly indicative of greater availability of urban and national culture patterns for the Indian-speaking populations of these states, if there is not, in fact, a large number of Indians in centers of this size.

Something of this sort may be inferred from a comparison of monolingual Indian

TABLE 4—RANK-ORDER CORRELATIONS
OF MEXICAN STATES WITH KNOWLEDGE
OF INDIAN LANGUAGE

Urban population (2500+)	−0.45
Urban centers of 5000+	−0.56

states and illiteracy. The Gulf Coast states of Veracruz, Campeche, Quintana Roo, and Yucatan rank 11, 18, 20, and 21, respectively, for illiteracy. When it it seen that the national rank-order correlation between these two factors is +0.69, we can only conclude that in the Gulf Coast region a strong acquaintance with, if not adoption of, urban life as part of the Mexican national culture is associated with the Indian-speakers of this region, for literacy can only mean literacy in Spanish. Certainly, differentiation must be made between the various sections of these states such as Veracruz. But the fact remains, that of the first 10 monolingual Indian states the Gulf Coast shows the highest urban tendencies. Puebla seems to present a different picture with its overpowering large urban center, unless the relatively large development of textile-manufacturing centers in the smaller towns is reflected here. A similar situation seems to prevail in the relationship between the Federal District and the state of Mexico. This state is often regarded as an anomaly because of its high ranking for monolingualism (11), rural (8) and agricultural nature (6), and its high illiteracy (9) in such close proximity to the Federal District, thus demonstrating the high level of conservatism among the Mexican Indians. However, this is a distortion of the demographic position of Mexico City. Although it is a magnet for all Mexico, it draws as heavily from the state of Mexico. In fact, one suspects that the majority of the population left in this state is distinctly Indian. All those who have tendencies toward becoming Mexicans are more strongly influenced by the presence of Mexico City next door than anything else. Thus, the entire position of the state of Mexico would be changed with regard to the factors considered above, if Mexico City were included. We see that for all intents and purposes Mexico City has no monolingual Indians, that individuals who admit knowledge of an Indian language are less than half of 1 per cent of the popula-

TABLE 5—POPULATION IN MUNICIPIOS OF MORE THAN 2500*

Region	Percentage Urban
Central	49.9
North	42.3
North Pacific	39.1
Gulf of Mexico	36.6
South Pacific	22.9

* Duran Ochoa, 1955, p. 36.

tion. The effect of the Federal District on the state of Mexico is seen by the intensity with which the ejido program was applied here. The greatest number of ejidatarios in Mexico are found here as well as the densest population of all states. Most of the ejidos are Indian, and the amount of land suitable for such land division is insufficient. Fábila and Fábila (1951, 2: 326–28) point out some of the ways in which this economic and population pressure has been relieved. There has been a heavy migration of women to Mexico City; large numbers of men work in the Federal District during the week and return with their wages to improve their land and houses. Obviously, this would not be possible if the state of Mexico were not efficiently linked by transportation to the city. It would not be daring to predict that this practice will culminate in the settlement of these workers in the Federal District or in one of the newer industrial centers, especially if the land pressures continue. In other words, the state of Mexico, and for that matter the central region of Mexico, cannot be considered apart from the Federal District, which has the highest urban population ratio of the five demographic regions of Mexico. Even discounting the greater drive of non-Indians to concentrate in large population centers, mere propinquity is a major force in urbanizing the Indian-speaker both demographically and culturally. One cannot believe that the Indian-speaking population has gone unaffected by the shifting of populations from rural to urban location. We need only note the great changes in percentages

517

TABLE 6—RURAL-URBAN POPULATION
CHANGE*

Mexico	Percentage Rural	Percentage Urban
1940	64.91	35.09
1950	57.42	42.58
Decrease	7.49	
Growth	1.6	5.9

*Duran Ochoa, 1955, pp. 201–05.

of monolingual speakers of Indian languages indicated above. The changes noted in Table 6 are not dissociated from linguistic changes. Although much of this change has taken place in the northern tier of states, the heavily Indian central region showed an urban increase of 3.96 per cent; even more surprisingly, the south Pacific region showed an increase of 7.8 per cent.

For Mexico some inferences can be drawn from these data. The major population trend in Mexico is towards urbanization, not only in the 2500 municipio ranks, but also in settlements of more than 5000. It is also apparent that the country, although still rural, is moving rapidly towards a more urban and a less agricultural orientation. It is in the states of the central and south Pacific regions—those regions of present-day and pre-Columbian Indian concentration—where these effects are less striking. But even here the major trends of the country are easily seen to be important.

These trends are among the more striking features of Mexican demography. From 1940 to 1950 the growth of large population centers had been apparent in all of Mexico, but especially in those areas where industrialization and commerce have developed. Likewise, the increase in communications and roads has been an accelerating factor. Of course, Mexico City has been the main center of growth, drawing migrants from all sections of the country; but there are few data on the migrating and commuting workers from the Indian regions of the state of Mexico. The Federal District is 94.5 per cent urban and the growth of the city in the last half-century has been phenomenal, in-

creasing from 368,777 in 1900 to 2,143,644 in 1950 to 4,173,272 (estimated) in 1960 (Cacho, 1961, p. 125). This is an excellent example of parallel growth in the remainder of Mexico. As indicated by the Dotsons (1956, p. 42), urban growth has been greatest in larger communities. The number of cities with less than 10,000 inhabitants has increased 1.5 times from 1900 to 1950, whereas those with more than 10,000 inhabitants have increased 4.4 times. In number, over these 50 years cities of more than 10,000 have increased from 54 to 159, cities of more than 100,000 from 2 to 10. The percentage of the Mexican population in cities of more than 10,000 has grown from 12 per cent in 1900 to 29 per cent in 1950. The rank-order correlation between urban population (2500+) and percentage of population in centers of more than 5000 is +0.79. The purpose in citing these figures is to indicate that opportunities for the urbanization of the Mexican Indian have not been lacking, that these trends have been so widespread in Mexico that the Indian had to participate.

It is perhaps in the growth of the true industrial centers that the effect is most clearly seen. During the last 17 years this growth has taken place in Orizaba and Nogales in Veracruz; Puebla; in the Valley of Mexico in such locations as Tlalnepantla, San Bartolo, Cuautitlan, Texcoco; in the Irolo valley, Hidalgo; Ocotlan, Jalisco; and in Zacapu and Apatzingan, Michoacan (Moreno, 1958, p. 83). In one sense, one might have predicted demographically that these regions would have developed by viewing the monolingual and bilingual Indian populations of these areas in 1940. At that date, less than 1 per cent of the Indian population of these cities were monolingual; only three—Orizaba (1.32), Texcoco (9.89), and Zacapu (16.05)—had bilingual Indian populations of more than 1 per cent (Parra, 1950). By inference, these regions demand a surplus of workers and, for the acculturating Indian, they become locations where a more complete identification with Mexican national culture can be achieved.

Obviously, the mere recitation of the growth figures for industrial cities tells us little concretely about the Mexican Indian population's role. Some indication of this can be gained by looking at the trends in internal and external migration in Mexico (Whetten and Burnight, 1956, pp. 545–50). The northern tier of states and the Federal District have been the most greatly affected by internal migration in Mexico. In 1940, 10.7 per cent of the total population were living in states other than that of birth. By 1950 this had increased to 12.9 per cent. In addition, there had been an absolute increase of 58.8 per cent. In 1940 two-thirds of all internal migrants were living in urban municipios, by 1950 three-quarters were in urban municipios. The political divisions with the highest urban concentration were also those with the greatest number of internal migrants: Baja California del Norte 59.9, Federal District 45.4, Tamaulipas 30.9, Morelia 23.8, Coahuila 19.8, and Nuevo Leon 18.3 (Duran Ochoa, 1955, p. 204). Obviously, with the exceptions of the Federal District and Morelia these are far from regions of heavy Indian population. The importance of Mexico City in this regard is apparent in the following immigrant rate: 1950–55, 142,000 per year; 1955–60, 175,000 per year (Cacho, 1961, p. 125). However, it is precisely these areas which have the greatest demand for labor.

Examination of the percentage of the internal migrants (Dávalos Hurtado and Marino Flores, 1956, p. 202) in the total population bears out the trends mentioned above, the first 10 ranked states being: Baja California del Norte, Federal District, Tamaulipas, Quintana Roo, Colima, Morelos, Coahuila, Aguascalientes, Nuevo Leon, and Nayarit. Of these, only Quintana Roo ranks in the first 10 monolingual states, and a national rank-order correlation between these two categories of −0.48 indicates little relation between them, as is expected.

TABLE 7—RANK-ORDER CORRELATIONS OF INTERNAL MIGRATION OF MEXICAN STATES

Monolinguality	−0.48
Knowledge of Indian language	−0.47
Urban population (2500+)	+0.66
Urban centers of 5000+	+0.38

Monolingual Indian migrants do not remain monolingual for long. Likewise, none of the states ranking high in knowledge of Indian languages is found in the first 10 internal migrant states; the national rank-order correlation of −0.47 between internal migration and knowledge of Indian languages is indicative of the strong relationship between monolingualism and knowledge of an Indian language—so much so, that one suspects that these two categories are not mutually, or in any other way, exclusive. As we go down the list of categories considered previously it is seen that none of the high-ranked agricultural, rural, or nonliterate states are high in internal migrants, with the exception of Quintana Roo in the second category.

However, of the first 10 ranked internal migration states seven are to be found in the first 10 urban states (2500+; number indicates urban rank): Federal District (1), Baja California del Norte (2), Colima (3), Coahuila (4), Nuevo Leon (6), Aguascalientes (8), Tamaulipas (9). Campeche (5) ranks 14 for internal migration; Jalisco (10) and Yucatan (7) fill out the list. A rank-order correlation of +0.66 between urban population and internal migration makes clear the goal of the migrants. As stated above, however, a better measure of urbanization lies in the percentage of population in settlements of more than 5000 inhabitants. When we compare internal migrant ranking with that of the larger settlements it is seen that seven states are high in both categories: Federal District (2/1), Aguascalientes (8/3), Coahuila (7/4), Colima (5/5), Nuevo Leon (9/7), Morelos (6/9), and Tamaulipas (3/10). Again Cam-

519

peche (14/6) ranks high in this regard, displaying the urban characteristics mentioned previously. Baja California del Sur (2) and Yucatan (8) diverge, ranking high in urban population and low in internal migrants, 24 and 32 respectively, from the main trends possibly showing factors of isolation from the chief movements of population. A rank-order correlation of +0.38 is not as striking as that for the previous urban category, but it appears, nevertheless, to be indicative of the relationship between migrants and urban residence.

How many of these internal migrants are Indian is impossible to tell, but Indians from areas where there is land poverty are known to move long distances for economic reasons, as is seen from the bracero movement. This movement has received careful study, covering both the United States and Mexico, but with little evaluation for the Indian specifically. Lewis (1961b, p. 293) and Gamio (1930a, 1930b) have pointed out the great effect of the United States braceros on local agriculture and the improvement of economic standards of the communities to which the braceros return. Some investigations of braceros in specific areas of the United States have been made. Flores (1950, p. 76) demonstrates a heterogeneous origin of the braceros in Wisconsin during World War II, but indicates that the majority of them came from the Bajio and Mexico City, the latter being far more important in terms of numbers. The effect of the returning bracero on his native community appears to have been greater before 1950 (Cámara B., 1956, p. 308). This is mainly due to the patterns of return. Before 1950 approximately 50 per cent returned from the United States; between 1950 and 1955 the percentage of returnees became very small. Cámara believes that this has been due to a greater acculturation to United States values and to the lack of opportunity to fulfill them in Mexico. The following instances may be indicative of the general Indian situation. Although the Oto-

mi, to cite an extreme case, have been the object of much planned culture change, the results so far have been discouraging. Some braceros, however, returning from the United States, have set about developing modern Mexican physical aspects of settlement such as the planning and construction of a town with a plaza (Cornejo Cabrera, 1961, p. 83). Aguirre Beltrán (1952, pp. 135–37) notes a strong bracero movement among the Tarascans, both to the United States and for work in mechanized and industrialized agriculture in the tierra caliente of Mexico. He attributes great influence towards the development of individualization and secularization of Tarascan life to the bracero movement. Kaplan (1960, p. 59) also indicates the influence of returning braceros on the mechanization of local industry in Michoacan; Fisher (1953, pp. 76–77) considers braceros one of the major factors in the government-directed program of culture change in Nayarit. This brief recital of internal and external migration in Mexico reflects the scarcity of definite information but indicates sufficiently that major population movements have affected the Middle American Indians in Mexico. More evidence is available from the central region of Mexico than from the more heavily Indian states of Oaxaca, Chiapas, and Guerrero.

None of the foregoing facts lead to precise knowledge of the relationship between urbanization and the Mexican Indian. There are, however, enough inferences to hypothesize that the Indian is becoming urbanized with the effect least strong in the southern region of the country. Here in a contiguous cultural block with the highland Indians of western Guatemala decreased urbanization would be expected. Given the increasing national unity of Mexico and the planned programs for Indians directed towards this end, it is likely that Indians have become increasingly urbanized and, less certainly, participant in industrial activity.

Table 8—Rank Order of Guatemalan Departments

	Percentage Monolingual Indian	Rural Indian Population	Urban Indian: 2500+	Urban: 2500–4,999	Urban: 5000–9,999	Urban: 10,000+	Spanish-speaking Indian	Cultural Indian	Illiteracy	Percentage Indian Internal Migrants	Percentage Ladino Internal Migrants
1. Solola		18	5	6	2		22	2	6	21	6
2. Totonicapan		14	9	8	4		18	1	11	22	4
3. Alta Verapaz		5	18	17	7		20	3	2	17	9
4. El Quiche		9	14	10			21	4	1	16	16
5. Chimaltenango		19	4	13	1		14	5	12	11	12
6. Huehuetenango		4	19	15	10		17	6	3	18	22
7. Suchitepequez		10	13	14		4	8	8	8	5	3
8. Quezaltenango		13	10	12	9	2	7	9	19	8	8
9. Baja Verapaz		8	15	11			13	11	3	12	19
10. San Marcos		3	20	20	8	5	3	7	17	13	18
11. Sacatepequez		22	1	1			9	13	20	20	10
12. Retalhuleu		15	8	9	3		6	12	11	4	5
13. El Peten		1	22	22			16	15	7	2	11
14. Izabal		17	6	19		3	19	19	15	3	1
15. Chiquimula		6	17	18	5		1	10	4	19	20
16. Guatemala		21	2	4	14	1	15	18	18	6	7
17. Jalapa		12	11	7	12		2	14	13	15	15
18. Escuintla		16	7	3	11		12	20	10	1	2
19. Santa Rosa		20	3	2			11	21	14	7	14
20. El Progreso		11	12	5			10	22	9	10	13
21. Jutiapa		2	21	21	13		4	16	16	14	21
22. Zacapa		7	16	16	6		5	17	5	9	17

Indian Urbanization: Guatemala

Guatemala data show that the process of Indian urbanization here is far less significant than in Mexico. National culture is less developed and the Indians have been less affected by directed culture-change programs. To make a comparison with Mexico, monolingual Guatemalan Indians will be placed in the same data categories used for Mexico earlier. The 10 highest ranking departments in monolinguality are selected for comparisons by inspection, and the rank-order correlations are presented for the entire country.

Table 8 lists the 10 highest ranked Guatemalan departments by monolinguality. Inspection reveals no strong coincidence between departments with high monolinguality and either rural or urban residence. Only San Marcos and Huehuetenango show high ranks within both categories for the heavy Indian areas. The rank-order correlations are +0.23 and +0.02, for rural and urban residence, respectively. This reflects the town nature of the western highlands of Guatemala and is directly comparable to the Mexican states of Oaxaca and Chiapas, which present a similar residential pattern. Guatemala has large areas of non-Indian rural population, and also what are termed Spanish-speaking Indians. This bears directly on the Guatemalan census category of the cultural Indian,[3] for it is here that the cultural change leading to a national identification is occurring. When one compares the first 10 monolingual departments with those ranking high in Spanish-speaking Indian populations, there is rank coin-

[3] This term is derived from the Guatemalan census category *indígena*. That it is not to be confused with monolingual Indian is seen in the instructions given to census workers: "En las localidades pequeñas hay cierta conciencia local, que califica al individuo como indígena o ladino." This forms the basis for the designation Indian, in addition to language, clothes, footgear, and other items. Hence, the term "cultural Indian" can be justifiably contrasted to that of "monolingual Indian" (Guatemala, 1957, pp. xi-xii).

TABLE 9—RANK-ORDER CORRELATIONS OF MONOLINGUAL GUATEMALAN DEPARTMENTS

Rural Indian population	+0.23
Urban Indian population	+0.02
Spanish-speaking Indians	−0.60
Settlements 2500–4,999	−0.04
Settlements 5000–9,999	+0.23
Settlements 10,000+	+0.24
All settlements 2500+	+0.12
Illiteracy	+0.40

cidence of only Suchitepequez, Quezaltenango, and San Marcos, three departments which are affected by larger cities and the presence, or proximity, of commercial agricultural activities. Conversely, when the first 10 ranking departments of Spanish-speaking Indian populations are compared to their rank in Indian monolinguality, the same three departments are involved. The rank-order correlation is −0.60 for all Guatemala, denoting the overwhelming Spanish-speaking population of cultural Indians in the eastern regions of the country. Comparing cultural Indians with Spanish-speaking Indians yields a coincidence of four departments within the first 10. However, a rank-order correlation for all Guatemala is more revealing: −0.34. The inference is that many of the Indian populations in eastern and southern Guatemala are becoming Ladino, but that there is no indication they are becoming urbanized. However, in becoming rural Ladino, the first step to participation in national culture is made, and, thus, the first move towards urbanization is achieved. This in no way implies that the latter will occur, simply that the opportunity is made available.

Of the two large sections of rural population in Guatemala (the north-central region with 92.7 per cent and the west with 85.2 per cent), except for San Marcos the departments which make up these regions do not rank high in Spanish-speaking Indian populations; but there is a greater number of departments with high-rank coincidence for cultural Indian populations and monolingual Indian populations. Eastern Guatemala has a large rural population ranging between 90.1 and 83.5 per cent for departments constituting this region. There are no high (first 10) ranking monolingual or cultural Indian departments here, but four of the first 10 ranked Spanish-speaking departments (1, 4, 5, 10) are found in the east.

It is far more difficult to speak of urbanization in Guatemala than in Mexico, for there are far fewer concentrations of population here. Of the Guatemalan urban centers with more than 2000 population, only 31 of 71 are in the west and north-central regions, the most intensely monolingual areas. But because these regions are also the most Indian this is an indication of larger Indian municipios than elsewhere. Of the urban centers between 5000 and 10,000 only one of 19 is in the north-central region, whereas 10 of 19 are in the west. The north-central region is far more rural than the west with its economic specialization and lesser dependence on rural activities. Of the centers with more than 10,000 population only one of five, Quezaltenango, offers the Indian possibilities of urban cultural adjustment.

The rankings of the Spanish-speaking Indian departments appear to show no correlation with states ranking high in urban Indian. That is, there is no high coincidence of first 10 ranks. Similarly, the rank-order correlation of all departments is −0.21. Where coincidence of high ranking for these categories occurs—Retalhuleu, Quezaltenango, and Sacatepequez—the effects of greater urbanization and industrialization in the form of commercial agriculture are present. Thus, Retalhuleu has important coastal-slope cultivation of coffee which invites an invasion of migratory workers who settle there. Quezaltenango, the second city of Guatemala, fosters urbanized life in the surrounding communities despite the conservatism of some Indian towns. Sacatepequez reflects not only

TABLE 10—PERCENTAGE OF POPULATION IN CABECERAS

	2500+	Department Rankings
Central	45.45	1, 2
South	22.50	8, 10, 12
North	20.00	7, 17
East	19.69	3, 11, 13, 15, 18, 20
West	19.43	4, 5, 6, 9, 14, 19, 22
North-Central	18.18	16, 21

the development of commercial agriculture but the proximity of Guatemala City.

Another measure of the urbanization of the Guatemalan Indians is the comparison of departments with residence in cabeceras. The greatest percentage of monolingual Indians in cabeceras lies in the western and central regions of the country. In cabeceras with more than 2000 population the picture changes. Table 10 shows that the central region is the most heavily urbanized part of Guatemala, and reflects the effect of Guatemala City and other large population centers. Likewise, given the Ladino emphasis on urbanization here, one could only expect a carry-over to the Indian population as revealed by the ranking of cabecera Indians in Sacatepequez and Guatemala in the central region. The drop in the percentage of persons in this size of center in the other regions of Guatemala again reveals the major urbanizing locations. The south is a highly Ladinoized area, where the greatest amount of commercial agricultural exploitation has taken place, requiring a large labor supply which has largely been filled by highland Indians. This is an extremely good area for Ladinoization to occur, but the difference between the southern region and the rest of Guatemala is not so great as to indicate a comparatively higher degree of urbanization. Nevertheless, the commercial exploitation of agriculture here offers far more opportunity to acquire urban attitudes that lead to national identification rather than to Indian town identification. The north is affected in its percentage by the presence of Puerto Ba-

523

rrios and other settlements dependent on commerce in most heavily rural regions of the country because of the large numbers of Spanish-speaking Indians in the process of Ladinoizing. The west, even though the Indian population is strongly concentrated in cabeceras, is not strongly urban, for 75 per cent of its cabecera population is in settlements of less than 2500 inhabitants.

The Guatemalan census defines urban as a settlement of 2000 inhabitants. Consequently, a consideration of the relationships between centers of various sizes (2500–4,999, 5000–9,999, 10,000+) and monolinguality is in order. Rankings and rank-order correlations display the strong settlement of monolingual Indians in towns of western Guatemala. Although high-ranking monolingual Indian departments include three western highland departments with high rank in the 2500–4,999 range—Solola (6), Totonicapan (8), and El Quiche (10)—the general statistical indifference of the urban-nonurban locus of monolingual Indian settlement in Guatemala is again indicated by a rank-order correlation of −0.04. Further, the strength of the western highland town pattern is revealed in the concentration of monolingual Indians in centers of 5000–9,999, where four western highland departments rank in the first 10, and a rank-order correlation of +0.23, although not conclusive, is reflective of the nonrural proclivities of the western highland Indians, and the concentration of Indians in Coban, Alta Verapaz. The rank-order correlation of +0.24 for monolingual Indians compared with population centers of more than 10,000 is of a different order than the previous categories, for the two ranking monolingual Indian departments here are Quezaltenango and Suchitepequez, reflecting modern urbanism in the former and commercial agricultural activities in the latter. The overall rank-order correlation for all settlements of more than 2500 and monolingual Indians, +0.12, again reflects western highland

TABLE 11—RANK-ORDER CORRELATIONS OF SPANISH-SPEAKING INDIAN GUATEMALAN DEPARTMENTS

Cultural Indian	−0.34
Urban Indian	−0.21
Settlements 2500–4,999	−0.12
Settlements 5000–9,999	+0.31
Settlements 10,000+	+0.20
All settlements 2500+	−0.02
Illiteracy	−0.74

patterns rather than any form of modern urbanization.

To discover a possible relationship between monolingual Indians and Spanish-speaking Indians in these larger centers of population, comparisons between Spanish-speaking Indian departments of high rank and those of high ranking of monolingual urban dwellers were made. The rank-order correlations revealed little of significance except that Spanish-speaking Indians tend to settle in monolingual Indian centers of 5000–9,999 and 10,000+ more than in centers of monolinguals of less than 5000 population. Inspection of the rankings revealed that possibly monolingual Indians dwelling in larger centers would be disposed to learn Spanish, and hence would not only become better equipped to live in urban centers but would predispose themselves to urban life and the acquisition of national culture as well. These are suggestive coincidences in rank: San Marcos ranked eighth in residence of centers of 5000–9,999 for both monolingual and Spanish-speaking Indians; Quezaltenango reflects its departmental capital status by ranking second in both these categories for centers of more than 10,000, and by ranking seventh in both categories for percentage of settlement in all centers of more than 2500.

Although the greatest concentration of Spanish-speaking Indians is in eastern Guatemala and is predominantly rural, it is patent that before the Indian can be urbanized, he must acquire Spanish. A comparison of Spanish-speaking Indians and the sizes of population centers mentioned above should reveal the nature of Indian urbanization in Guatemala.

Inspection of the rankings reveals that of the first 10 ranking Spanish-speaking Indian departments compared with population in centers of 2500–4,999 the following coincidences arise. Jalapa (2/10) is in a Ladinoizing area, whereas Retalhuleu (6/8) again shows the effects of commercial agricultural development on the coastal plain. Sacatepequez (9/1) shows the effects of proximity to Guatemala City and of commercial agricultural development. Santa Rosa (11/4) and the Baja Verapaz (13/7), although centrally ranked with regard to the incidence of Spanish-speaking Indians, appear to display the effects of a Ladinoizing trend among the Indians of this region, the east. Escuintla (12/2), also ranked centrally for Spanish-speaking Indians, demonstrates the effects of Indian internal migration for employment in commercial agriculture. Chimaltenango (14/6), Totonicapan (18/5), El Quiche (21/9), and Solola (22/3) again highlight the town nature of the western highland settlement patterns of the Indian population and their notorious exclusion of Spanish-speaking and culturally intermediate Indians. The rank-order correlation of Spanish-speaking Indian departments with centers of this size is indifferent: −0.12.

Five of the first six ranked Spanish-speaking Indian departments are also ranked in the first 10 of population centers of 5000–9,999: Chiquimula (1/7), Jalapa (2/4), Jutiapa (4/10), Zacapa (5/3), and Retalhuleu (6/2). With the exception of the last, which shows the effects of commercial agricultural development, these are areas of ongoing Ladinoization. However, three low-ranked departments in the Spanish-speaking Indian category rank high in centers of this population size: Chimaltenango (14/1), Totonicapan (18/8), and Solola (22/5). Although the Alta Verapaz (20/9) can be

added, it reflects the large monolingual Indian population of Coban. The effect of migratory labor is again apparent in Escuintla (12/6), but probably a residual population from this source is to be found in larger centers. The strong concentration of Spanish-speaking Indians in the eastern part of Guatemala, plus the high rank of these departments for settlements of this size and Ladinoization, strongly suggest that urbanization of the Indian is correlative with Spanish-speaking Indian populations through which the route to urban life is opened. A rank-order correlation of +0.31 for the country as a whole, though not highly significant, tends to verify this, if the heavy monolingual Indian concentration in the western highlands is viewed as the effect of community economic specialization. The regional effect of the cities of Quezaltenango, Totonicapan, and Sacatepequez cannot be discounted, for although we have compared monolinguality with community size, with the expected negative results for urbanization, we have no data to measure the effect and strength of the bilingual Indian.

That there are only five centers of more than 10,000 inhabitants again highlights the small-town, rural nature of Guatemalan demography. These are the centers of Ladinoization, however, and data available to measure this phenomenon in cities are lacking for Guatemala as for Mexico. Nevertheless, some measure of urbanization as an important factor in Ladinoization is seen in the location of three of these five population centers in departments with large Spanish-speaking Indian populations: Sacatepequez, Quezaltenango, Suchitepequez. These figures, verified by Ladinoization studies in smaller communities, suggest that changing linguistic affiliation is a necessary part of becoming an urban dweller for the Guatemalan Indian. It appears that Guatemala, the highest-ranking department in this category of population size, has some

525

strong influence over neighboring Sacatepequez, whereas the urban center of Quezaltenango has a similar but lesser effect in the western highlands. Izabal and Suchitepequez again reflect the effects of commercial agricultural development. The rank-order correlation of +0.20 is distorted by the paucity of settlements of this size, but possibly indicates a potential country-wide relationship between dwelling in large urban centers and Spanish-speaking Indians.

If the total population in centers of more than 2500 is compared with the Spanish-speaking Indian population, it will be seen that, similar to the equivocal settlement of monolingual Indians in this regard, no consistent pattern emerges: rank-order correlation −0.02. The high-ranking departments of Spanish-speaking Indian population with corresponding high ranks in this settlement category—Zacapa (5/9), Quezaltenango (7/5), Sacatepequez (9/2), and Retalhuleu (6/6)—are in large part offset as bases for conclusions by the departments of monolingual Indian concentration in such centers—Chimaltenango (14/4), Totonicapan (18/10), Solola (22/8). The high ranking of Retalhuleu (6/6), Escuintla (12/7), and Izabal (19/3) again show the urbanizing effect of commercial agriculture and its attendant development of commerce. Guatemala (15/1) is, in effect, the apogee of both Ladino aspiration and Ladinoization. It is to be wondered why the department of Guatemala, and the city itself, has such a small Spanish-speaking Indian population if a correlation is thought to exist between this and urbanization. It is possible that once a Spanish-speaking Indian attains economic self-sufficiency in Guatemala City or one of the nearby suburbs or small towns, he will not be identifiable as a Spanish-speaking Indian for long, for he already has taken the most critical step towards urban Ladino status. A similar situation may hold for Puerto Barrios in Izabal, although the Black Carib population affects this conclusion. But none of these large

526

centers has been sufficiently investigated to clarify the nature of this shift. On the whole, the Spanish-speaking Indian remains a cultural Indian because he is rurally oriented. As with so many other aspects of acculturation and assimilation through Ladinoization in Guatemala, the acquisition of Spanish is an absolute prerequisite to urban dwelling.

If control of the Spanish language, either as a bilingual speaker or as a Spanish-speaking Indian, is necessary to becoming urbanized, then literacy in Spanish is a further step into the Ladino world and to the acquisition of Guatemalan national culture, both of which accompany urbanization. Thus, of persons over seven years of age, 90.1 per cent of the Indians are illiterate, whereas 50.5 per cent of the Ladinos are illiterate, in a country that shows 71.7 per cent of the population illiterate. High-ranking monolingual Indian areas are also high ranked with regard to illiteracy although some of those departments possessing high rank for Spanish-speaking Indians also rank within the first 10 in illiteracy. Comparisons of this sort are rather meaningless when one discovers that Indian illiteracy ranges from 97.3 per cent in El Quiche to 73.2 per cent in Sacatepequez. There is an inherent contradiction here because the foregoing figures refer to cultural Indians, and the Guatemalan census makes no distinction between cultural Indians and Spanish-speaking Indians with regard to literacy, although literacy demands Spanish-speaking individuals. The north-central, the east, and the west regions of Guatemala have the highest rate of illiteracy among the Indians. However, those departments in the west with high ranking for Indian illiteracy also have a higher literacy rate, indicating that some sort of selectivity for literacy and the use of the Spanish language by cultural Indians is at work here. Moreover, if one considers the country as a whole and makes rank-order correlations, it will be seen that high-ranked monolingual Indian departments lean strongly towards illiteracy (rank-order correlation + 0.40); those with high ranking for Spanish-speaking Indians show a definite trend towards literacy (−0.74).

Even when one considers both Spanish-speaking Indian populations and the rates of illiteracy, as well as the correlations with various settlement categories, the bulk of the Guatemalan Indians are not urbanized. This may indicate, in a manner different from that attempted before, the ways in which the monolingual Indian assumes Ladino status and thus acquires the opportunity to adopt an urban status; for the monolingual Indian, even in Guatemala, has little chance of remaining monolingual and becoming an urban dweller.

There is one measure of the degree of Indian urbanization in Guatemala in lieu of specific data: the amount and nature of Indian internal migration. The Guatemalan Indian does not usually migrate for permanent settlement away from his native locality. Only 5.41 per cent of the total Indian population are living in departments other than the one of birth. Rank-order correlation comparison of monolingual Indian departments and total internal migration, whether it be Indian or Ladino, demonstrates this: −0.36. Indian internal migration in terms of total number tends to be correlated with monolingual Indian departments (+0.29), but involves relatively short distances and is confined mainly to the western highlands. More interesting is the indication of a relatively high internal migration of Ladinos into the higher-ranked monolingual Indian departments. A higher percentage of the Ladino population tends to be internal migrant in these departments than elsewhere (+0.22).

TABLE 12—RANK-ORDER CORRELATIONS
OF MONOLINGUAL
GUATEMALAN DEPARTMENTS

Total internal migration	−0.36
Indian internal migration	+0.29
Ladino internal migration	+0.22

TABLE 13—RANK-ORDER CORRELATIONS
OF INDIAN INTERNAL MIGRANTS AS A
PERCENTAGE OF INDIAN POPULATION
IN GUATEMALAN DEPARTMENTS

Total internal migrants	+0.88
Percentage Ladino internal migrants of Ladino population	+0.40
Urban population	+0.30
Urban Indian population	+0.11
Rural population	−0.31
Rural Indian population	−0.25
Settlements 2500–4,999	−0.12
Settlements 5000–9,999	−0.18
Settlements 10,000+	+0.43
All settlements 2500+	+0.16

More significant is the comparison of the percentage of the Indian internal migrants in the total Indian population with factors possibly indicating urbanization tendencies. A comparison with the total internal migrant population gives a rank-order correlation of +0.88, showing that Indian internal migrants are in departments receiving the greatest internal migration of all kinds. When this category is compared with the rankings of departments for percentage of Ladino internal migrants as a percentage of the total Ladino population, similar factors are clearly stimulating both Indian and Ladino internal migrants. This rank-order correlation is +0.40. Less certain is the correlation of the Indian percentage of total Indian population with the categories of urban population and urban Indians, for all inhabitants of municipios of more than 2500 are considered urban in the Guatemalan census, and the heavy small-town settlement of the western highland Indian tends to distort the urban nature of the Indian. The rank-order correlations are for percentage of urban population (+0.30) and for percentage of urban Indian (+0.11). Conversely, the rank-order correlation of the percentage of Indian internal migrants with total rural population is −0.31, for rural Indian −0.25.

Even more revealing than the preceding set comparisons is one in which the internal migrant percentage of the total Indian pop-

527

TABLE 14—RANK-ORDER CORRELATIONS
OF SPANISH-SPEAKING INDIAN
GUATEMALAN DEPARTMENTS

Internal migration	+0.17
Percentage Indian internal migrants of Indian population	+0.20
Percentage Ladino internal migrants of Ladino population	−0.37

ulation is correlated with size of urban centers by department. A negative correlation exists between Indian internal migrants and centers of 2500–4,999 (−0.12) and those of 5000–9,999 (−0.18), but a surprisingly high correlation exists with centers of more than 10,000 population (+0.43). For total population in settlements of more than 2500, a rank-order correlation of +0.16 displays a slight tendency for internal migrants to go to departments ranked high in this category. The effect of strongly developed town nature of the western highland Indian is again indicated, for only Quezaltenango with its large city is included from this area.

Although not as clear-cut, the comparison of the high-ranked Spanish-speaking Indian departments with internal migration does suggest that a possible, or developing, correlation exists. Correlations of Spanish-speaking Indians with internal migration is +0.17, with Indian internal migrants as percentage of Indian population +0.20. More interesting is the negative correlation of this category with percentage of Ladino internal migrants of Ladino population (−0.37), suggesting that in the high-ranked Spanish-speaking Indian departments of the east, Ladino status may be more accessible to the Spanish-speaking Indian.

Both inspection and rank-order correlations show that Indian internal migrants move to less Indian (less monolingual) departments, where they become employed in commercial agricultural developments or in the larger cities; in the case of the latter, these Indians generally move to the larger population centers. One may conclude that

the Indian internal migrant tends to be associated with processes of urbanization and Ladinoization, wherein the assumption of national culture, although much less developed than in Mexico, is still a factor in his life. It is significant that the areas of internal migration are mostly those farthest removed geographically or culturally from regions retaining much of Middle American Indian culture or, at least, Indian cultural identification. Opportunities are presented, by either design or circumstance, for the Indians to enter more fully into a developing Guatemalan national culture with its attendant urbanizing and industrializing features.

INDUSTRIALIZATION AND URBANISM

A brief summary of the scanty data dealing with industrialization will give some idea of the nature of the possible relationship between the process of industrialization and the Indian of Middle America. Industrialization and urbanization as processes cannot be separated conceptually, or actually, from urbanism and industrialism which can more easily be defined as culture patterns.

The few studies of Mexican Indians in industrial pursuits do not distinguish between those industrial workers who are Indians and those who are Mestizo. This failure to discriminate is caused partly by less industrialization in Mexico, partly by the greater extent of Indian acculturation in Mexico than Guatemala, and partly by the stated official policy of not recognizing an Indian industrial worker as Indian or of immediate Indian derivation.

The best data available in Mexico relate to Atlixco, Puebla; Centro Industrial Fray Bernadino de Sahagún, Hidalgo; and Paracho, Michoacan. In the region of Atlixco, Moore (1950, 1951) attempted to determine the factors leading to Indians' employment in textile factories. Using as test cases San Baltasar Atlimeyaya and San Juan Huilco, both villages having a common language and a common dependence on agriculture, both being partially self-sufficient and equally accessible to Atlixco, Moore discovered a differential in the percentage of Indians working in Atlixco's textile factories. Of the two villages San Baltasar was the more "Indian." However, its inhabitants worked more outside their settlement and identified more with the factory than did those from San Juan. This difference is largely attributed to poverty arising from land scarcity in San Baltasar and, thus, the necessity to seek work outside. Although Moore implies that Indians leave their settlements only because of such necessity, there is similar land poverty in other sections of Mexico, witnessed by the general failure of the ejido program (Fábila and Fábila, et al., 1955, pp. 116, 128; Simpson, 1953). Pozas (1959b), following Moore's work in Atlixco, states that in approximately ten years the influence of the factories in the Atlixco zone has brought about great changes. Although there is no extinction of Indian culture, those settlements which are not clearly and conservatively Indian culturally are most affected; but the effects on those settlements are not made by the Indians in the face of over-identical, for many adjustments have been population and the urban life engendered by the factories.

One of the major industrial developments in Mexico is the Centro Industrial Fray Bernadino de Sahagún, or Ciudad Sahagún, in the Irolo Valley, Hidalgo (Hernández Moreno and Nahmad, 1961). Hidalgo ranked fifth in monolingual Indian population in 1950 (8.4 per cent) and sixth in population with knowledge of an Indian language in 1950 (25.2 per cent). The industrial development began in 1952 in a former center of pulque production. The ejido movement had been a failure here, and the communities involved sold land for industrial expansion which, during a 10-year period, saw the installation of four major industrial sites with the coordinate founding of a new town. These new industries and the new town with its service clubs, labor unions, and modern facilities have formed a focal point for regional integration. The indemnity for ejido lands has taken the form of water systems, electricity, and schools. Older communities and the new one collaborate in the construction and use of public buildings, schools, streets, roads, telephones, water, public health facilities, sewerage, and a regional hospital. In a region formerly occupied by a population of monolingual and bilingual Indians the industrialization and modern urbanization have accelerated incorporation of these populations into the modern world of industrial urbanism. Even though the Indian in this area had changed greatly before the advent of Ciudad Sahagún, this instance demonstrates that when such culture patterns are presented for learning and exploitation the Mexican peasant, Indian or otherwise, easily adapts to industrial situations.

The effect of this industrial advance on pre-existing communities in this region was measured by the Youngs (1960a,b), whose study of 24 communities reveals that changes were related to the ease of contact with the industrial center and to the size of the community involved. Modern contact, facilitated by new roads, doctors, telephones, radio, etc., made an identification with national culture more easily achieved in the larger communities. Further, participation of entire communities accelerated socio-cultural change and acceptance of industrial urbanism far more than individual contact through employment in the industries. Such conditions of adoption of national culture, however, were more likely to occur in poor communities. Younger communities, usually established by the ejido movement, were more likely to accept national culture, and all that it implies, in the context of industrial establishments. Thus, the greater the opportunity for participation in national culture, the greater the probability of socio-cultural change.

The foregoing instance represents one of the few documented areas of Indian population subjected to a massive influence of industrial urbanism. Kaplan (1960) has reported the effects of increased mechanization in Paracho, Michoacan, a community formerly dependent on handcrafts for its livelihood. The shift mainly involved concentration of production in larger shops, which by mechanization is forcing the smaller home-based handcrafts out of business. Thus evolved a dichotomy of craftsman (homeworker) and shopworker, with the former clearly at a disadvantage. Because the mechanization was local and because the worker made little change in work habits, there was little resistance to the mechanization. The socio-cultural effects have all been in the direction of pointing the Indian community towards the adoption of Mexican national culture. The increased desire for education, the striving for the upward social mobility of children, and great increase in the level of education can only result in creating Mexicans where there were Mexican Indians before, and of fostering adoption of the unfolding patterns of industrial urban culture. This may not be achieved in Paracho, but individuals and families will be motivated to seek fulfillment of these patterns elsewhere.

Further discussion of the Indian in a modern industrial and urban situation would require inference from data which do not identify the Indian in this socio-cultural environment, and would lead to consideration of the acculturative process. A few points, however, demand mention here because the acculturative process and the partially achieved assimilation of the Mexican Indian involve Mexican national culture rather than a generalized Mestizo or Ladino culture and, thus, a Mexican version of modern industrial urbanism with its lack of geographical limitation.

We have mentioned the effect of poverty, especially land shortages, as the chief motivating force impelling the Mexican Indian

towards some sort of participation in Mexican national culture. Ejidos were an attempt to solve the agrarian problem. It has become more and more apparent that this program is essentially a form of cultural conservatism and cultural conservation (Aguirre Beltrán and Pozas, 1954, p. 207). The successful ejidos were accompanied by intensive irrigation in sparsely populated areas. Between 1940 and 1950 there were attempts to avoid the inherent minifundio trends of ejido development in densely settled areas, but these have been given up as failures except in regions where adequately large areas can be exploited through irrigation and mechanization.

Mechanization of ejido lands has been successful only through use of central equipment stations, but in areas where the individual tenure is less than 5 hectares. Although a plot of 5 hectares can be mechanized, in reality over 50 hectares are needed to finance purchase of equipment through the agricultural production. Agricultural planning in Mexico foresees an increase from the 33.89 per cent of agricultural lands mechanized in 1950 to 71.44 per cent in 1974, with a planned displacement of 1,650,000 persons from the land (Yañez-Perez and Moyo Porras, 1957, p. 306). Such a proposal, if implemented, would obviously bring the Indians, whether on ejidos or private holdings, into full contact with industrial agricultural production.

In areas of dense population the trend has been away from ejido acreage and toward private holdings (Fábila and Fábila, et al., 1955, pp. 116, 128). Where successful, agrarian reform and ejido conditions have thrown the Indians directly into consideration of, and action in, Mexican national culture (Wolf, 1956, pp. 1072–73). Agrarian reform has also replaced the hacendado with the merchant as the economic prop of the Indian, a powerful element in the loss of cultural isolation for the Indian. Along with this is the increase in communication between Indian culture and national culture through the location of the store in positions accessible to roads. The increase in road communication has been the Indian's strongest impetus toward national culture. Knowledge of the national culture, need to communicate in Spanish, and increasing poverty stimulate the Indian to acquire and use national culture. The returning braceros bring their knowledge of the outside world, their new goals, and their skill in mechanized agriculture. The role of the national government in organizing rural labor unions in the densely populated Indian areas of the south, where Indians work on plantations, points up the general effect of the propagation of the national culture by directed culture-change programs (Pozas, 1952a).

It is perhaps in contact with such government programs that the effect of modern national culture in Mexico is most strongly felt by the monolingual Indian. These programs have been described by Caso et al. (1954), Wagley and Harris (1958, p. 63), and Aguirre Beltrán (1955). Programs have been planned to develop literacy of the Indian language and thus perhaps to increase the number of true bilinguals in the Indian population. It has always been apparent, however, that once literacy is achieved the Indian will be impelled toward exploration of non-Indian culture, suggested in the great decrease in percentage of not only monolingual Indians but also cultural Indians in Mexico. Introduction of roads, consumer associations, agricultural and livestock improvement, electricity, and relocation for economic reasons hasten the Indian's entrance into the modern world.

Among the several evaluations of the programs of directed culture change in Mexico the most succinct is that of De la Fuente (1959), who reports an increase in horizontal mobility and communication, in the division of labor and internal heterogeneity, rationalism, and identification with the larger Mexican society. Less apparent cultural changes are better economic base and a greater identification with the nation; the freeing of large numbers of Indians from servitude and, by accepting medical services, from anxieties, fears, and social limitations present in Indian culture; the creation of small elites, showing the Indians that, with education, they can rise to social positions formerly thought to be for Ladinos only.

These conditions apply to the Indian in southern Mexico, significant because here lie the most intensely monolingual areas. He sees, too, the extent of the adoption of modern national Mexican culture and the degree to which the Indians have been prepared for its adoption.

Partly as the accompaniment of planned culture-change programs and partly as the result of increased evangelism, Protestant missionaries and the Acción Católica have been active among the monolingual Indians of Mexico, especially in the south. Essentially these activities implicate the Indian in the modern and supralocal world. Protestants are not a large element of the Indian population but their effect is greater than numbers would indicate. Especially from Oaxaca and Chiapas come reports of more converts and more chapels constructed (Cassaretto, 1956, p. 34). Two reports (Siverts, 1960; Slocum, 1956) describe effects of Protestant conversion on the Oxchuc Tzeltal by the establishment of a new school and the increase in literacy, the development of community centers with economic and political functions, the eradication of alcohol, an increase in civil marriage and birth registration, and the attendant economic betterment of the community. Perhaps this is an instance in which the Indian acquired the Protestant ethic (Beekman, 1956), but whatever the long-term effect of such conversion, it is in the political changes here that increased participation in Mexican national culture is most clearly observed. Within a relatively short period, 1948–54, the traditional religio-political organization and its practice of reaching political decisions by consensus was replaced by a system of political parties with different ideologies. It is significant that the two parties were organized in terms of Presbyterianism, which had broken the old socio-religious hierarchy, and of a counteractive movement from the nationally organized Acción Católica. Wonderly (1960, p. 208) reports that Indians in urban settings adjust more easily to urban life if native Protestants are leading religious activities.

Investigation of Indian migrants in the large cities of Mexico has been greatly neglected. Lewis (1959a) has considered the Indian in Mexico City, but has not oriented his material so as to permit easy identification of the Indian. His analysis (1959b, 1961a) of what he terms the "culture of poverty" in Mexico City does not show the part the Indian plays in this "culture," although it is certainly an important role. Lewis (1959a) cites a migrant Indian family which because of easy access to the village from which they come, has maintained kinship ties and community affiliation. Compadrazgo, however, has been modified to suit the urban situation. The family has become matri-centered in contrast to Indian village life, the children have greater freedom, installment buying has raised the standard of living, and greater social and economic aspiration prevails. Much emphasis is laid on education. Lewis makes it quite clear that this family (and many others) is strongly motivated towards adopting modern Mexican urban culture. He concludes that the migrant Indian to Mexico City is an urban peasant with relatively little change in culture, but gives no explanation for migration or for the fact that the children are far removed from the roles which the parents have stressed in the past. Following Warner's three-class system, Lewis ranges such Indian migrants from the lower middle class through all aspects of the lower class. He

observes that migrants who were rural landowners are more socially aspiring.

Butterworth (1962) reports that Tilaltongo Mixtec migrants to Mexico City display most of the characteristics mentioned by Lewis for migrants from Tepoztlan. This he bases on the fact that certain behavioral features do not follow the classical picture of western urban migrants: closer family ties, intensified compadrazgo interaction, and maintenance of close relations with Tilaltongo point to the difference of the Mexican Indian migrant pattern. The migrants have far greater identification with Mexican national culture partly from experience in the army. The implication that close ties with the village stamp these migrants as Mixtecs is belied by the fact that migrants shift for economic reasons and desire for education for both children and adults. Further, there is a strong preference that children be listed as Mexicans on their birth registrations rather than Indians, as would be the case if they were born in Tilaltongo. In fact, children in Mexico City are forced to speak Spanish rather than Mixtec. Many changes in the behavior of the Mixtec migrant plainly show that identification with the Indian village is passing, for both Butterworth and Lewis described first-generation migrants.

It is characteristic of Mexico that the city tends to swallow the Indian and convert him into a Mexican. Whiteford's study of Queretaro revealed that no individuals here are recognizable as Indian either by cultural standards or by language, but it is significant that the upper lower class refers to the lower lower class as Indians (Whiteford, 1960, p. 94), probably a reflection of the place Indian migrants have always occupied in the cities.

It is generally clear throughout Middle America that the recent Indian urban migrant occupies a far lower social position in the city than in his own community. Both Lewis and Whiteford indicate the lower-class position of the Indian depends mainly on his length of time in the cities. Economically the Indian migrants occupy the lowest positions with, of course, the lowest pay; and, as Lewis has emphasized, poverty is an overriding factor in their life. Both writers report the loss of rural orientation; it is here that the cultural experience of the Indian and the Mestizo rural dweller converge, so that the Indian migrant to the city becomes indistinguishable from other migrants and other residents of lower-class status.

This convergence is illustrated by Solis Quiroga (1957, pp. 156–58) in a survey of delinquency in the newly industrialized towns of Chalco and Tlalnepantla in the state of Mexico. With increased industrialized activity and population growth came an increased delinquency and crime. During 1940–50 crime mounted both in kind and in quantity but declined somewhat after this period. Crimes against persons remained static or lessened, whereas those against property increased, especially fraud. These trends were more marked in Tlalnepantla than in Chalco, but industrialization must have greatly affected the Indians in both settlements.

The Indian migrant has habitually settled on the fringes of the city, but with the changing ecology of the larger Mexican cities, more and more characteristics of west European and North American cities appear. Lewis (1959a, p. 401) and the Dotsons (1957, pp. 57–63) report that the centers of cities are deteriorating and now house more of the lower class. Likewise, the ecology of Mexico City itself is in such a state of flux that many former fringe areas are developing middle-class housing projects.

Industrialization and the role of Indians in Guatemala has been investigated only by Manning Nash (1955, 1958a), although some work has been completed by Hoyt (1951, 1955) on commercial agricultural exploitation and the workers employed. The industrialization considered by Nash is not an adequate measure of its effect on the Indian, for the textile factory at Cantel, an Indian town near Quezaltenango, was culturally isolated from the urban situation. Here, until national governmental intervention, industrialization adapted to Indian culture instead of the reverse. Cantel is an extremely good example of how industrial exploitation can be carried on without overriding the Indian, but it is also an example of how culture can change when the opportunity for fulfillment presents itself. As reported by Nash, the factory worker was able to maintain and strengthen the classical religio-political hierarchy with its emphasis on age ranking. With the intervention of the national government through labor unions and political parties, however, a group of young Indians became ready and able to be officials. Now came clear separation of the religious and political life of the town. Thus, even in an isolated industrial situation the rising influence of the modern industrial urban pattern is sharply brought forth.

Hoyt's work (1951) in the plantations of Guatemala shows that the influence of the national culture was far less among these Indians, although organization of labor unions and political parties was extensive among the foreign commercial companies. Hoyt (1955) indicates that working in the commercial plantations does not predispose the Indian toward adopting Ladino and national Guatemalan culture, but that nearness to towns and cities produces a strong Ladinoizing effect. Wage earning leads to more buying in stores; housing is better and different than traditional Indian; medical care has discredited magical curing; diet has changed little. Dessaint (1962) reached similar conclusions in his summary of hacienda and plantation Indians and, further, sees the rise of a rural proletariat class in Guatemala.

Two additional factors lead towards an urban view for Guatemalan Indians. The processes resemble those in Mexico. The role of the national government in programs of directed culture change has had lesser but similar effects. Along with labor unions, political parties mean greater participation in the national political life (Adams, 1957b). In many of the western highland communities strong efforts were made to break the influence of the religio-political hierarchies by placing younger men in control of political offices with direct connections to the national government. In many places this was successful, but the result appears to have been the separation of younger, politically conscious Indian men from their Indian communities and their search for Ladino status. Accompanying these political activities were strong agrarian reform movements. The two most authoritative works (Newbold, 1957; Schneider, 1958) on agrarian problems reveal relatively little Communist influence. The Indian interest and participation in the Unión Campesina and other rural unions was for land rather than ideology.

The role of Protestant missionaries in the break-up of Indian religio-political organization has not been as great in Guatemala as in Mexico, but the work by the Nashes at Cantel gives an idea of what might happen where the Protestants gain converts (J. Nash, 1960a; M. Nash, 1955, pp. 27–28). In Cantel the greatest influence of the Protestants came with the intervention of the national government through the separation of religious and political functions. Further, the high cost of cofradía membership and participation has induced the Indian to shift to a religion which does not financially deplete him. This has especially appealed to younger Indians, for Protestantism provides an alternative to the cofradía system. In Cantel the cofradías lost their importance, although after the direct influence of the national government was withdrawn there was a partial return to the previous religio-political system. A similar situation existed in Chinautla (Reina, 1960,

pp. 92–93), an Indian community adjacent to Guatemala City which had managed to retain its Indian character despite long close contact with the city. However, the conjunctive influence of the Protestant missionaries and the Acción Católica on the one hand, and the national government through land reform and the like on the other, brought about an identification of religious sects and political parties and the subsequent decrease in the relative importance of the cofradía system. The decline of governmental interference saw a drop in the importance of the Protestants. It would appear that the influence of both Protestants and Roman Catholics is greatest when there is conjunctive action from the national political level. It would appear, also, that industrial urban patterns of behavior (extended by increased road systems) must have been available. A study of political influence on the national level in Guatemala therefore shows a correlation between its effectiveness and the degree to which younger men of the community have been exposed to new culture patterns (Adams, 1957b). It is significant, moreover, that the social locus at which this influence is most felt is in the most vulnerable section of the classical religio-political hierarchy: the point at which the young man desirous of social recognition finds seemingly endless obstacles to that goal, the beginning of the long climb up the status ladder of the cofradía. If the interference of national culture in the religious, political, and economic life offers this age group fulfillment of these aspirations, incidents like those cited above will surely occur.

The Guatemalan Indian's place in industrialization warrants two observations: first, compared to Mexico the Indian has had relatively little opportunity to engage in industrial work or to live in cities; second, more cultural isolation exists among Guatemalan Indians, demonstrated by Reina (1960) in Chinautla and by Colby and van den Berghe (1961, p. 787) in

Quezaltenango. Despite Chinautla's proximity to, and economic coordination with, Guatemala City, little urban settlement or behavior was apparent before government intervention in land reform and the political alliances of Protestant sects. Then, as in Cantel and other western highland Indian communities, possibly a sufficiently thorough-going cultural change occurred before intervention to stimulate adoption of cultural goals different from those commonly held by most people in Chinautla. An additional factor in the urbanization and industrialization of Guatemalan Indians is the socio-cultural castelike status hierarchy for Ladinos and Indians. Even in Quezaltenango, the second largest city in Guatemala, with a long history of urban Indians, this caste line separates them from Ladinos and touches off internal stratification among the urban Indians themselves. This social separatism has not prevented the Quezaltecan Indians from engaging in industrial pursuits nor has it precluded their participation in modern culture although the latter is more the prerogative of high-status Indians. Nevertheless we shall have no clear idea of the Guatemalan Indian in industry or in a large urban setting until more is known both here and, especially, concerning the Indian migrant in Guatemala City.

Conclusions

Despite lack of data for the role of the Middle American Indian in urbanization and industrialization, it is apparent that in the 20th century he has not escaped the effects of these processes. He is also increasingly adopting an industrial urbanism culture pattern through the developing national cultures in Mexico and Guatemala. From both standpoints the Indian population in Mexico has become Mexican far more than has the Guatemalan Indian become Guatemalan.

This difference arises from greater growth of a Mexican national culture, which in turn is closely tied to the modern world. The most apparent instigation of this movement came with the Mexican Revolution and the derivative programs of government intervention in the affairs of the Indian. This intervention has been direct through land reform programs, literacy campaigns, and agencies of directed culture change; but it is only part of a larger, more pervasive change affecting all Mexico through expansion of industry, communication, and transport so that perhaps the indirect effect of the modern world is more decisive than those activities easily observed. The results of an earlier industrialization in Merida, Yucatan (Hansen, 1934), are paralleled in a recent utilization of industrial urban culture in the rural setting of the Papaloapan Project (Winnie, 1958). Less intensively, similar factors have been at work in Guatemala. The parallel between these two countries, even though the results are different in degree, points to national governmental intervention in the culture of the Middle American Indian as a significant element in deep and rapid culture change. It is not industrialization or physical urbanization that is important, but the spread of the culture pattern which accompanies the modern world of which the growing national cultures of Mexico and Guatemala are a part. What is happening to the Middle American Indian is radical culture change, whose source lies in the behavioral patterns associated with modern cities and industrial activity.

Much has been made of the effect of the Indian's culture loss in an urban situation. We have questioned the view that the Indian urban migrant is a victim of poverty, the assumption that Indian village life is inherently superior to urban life, the assumption that life in cities is detrimental to Indian migrants, the conclusions drawn from the study of first-generation migrants. We have had a far too rigid view of modern Middle American Indian culture, assuming that inherently the Indian is hyperconserva-

535

tive. There is, however, much evidence to support Blumer (1960) that "tribal" and "folk" groups newly employed in industry suffer much less maladjustment and dismay than has been theorized, and that adaptations are made with ease, alacrity, and willingness. Of course, the economic opportunity must be present for such shifts in cultural allegiance to take place. This opportunity is far less in Guatemala than in Mexico.

The introduction of the culture pattern of modern industrial urbanism will undoubtedly destroy present Middle American Indian culture. The increased impor-

tance of a national culture will bring this about more rapidly in Mexico; in Guatemala the change will probably cause the growth of a large rural proletariat which has no cultural identity as Indian, somewhat paralleling Mexican history. However, Mexico has had means of assimilating, economically and culturally, the Mexicanized Indians whereas this appears less likely in Guatemala. One might predict therefore that the culturally identifiable Indian will disappear rather rapidly in Mexico, but in Guatemala will traverse a slower and perhaps different route.

REFERENCES

Adams, R. N., 1956c, 1957b, 1961
Aguirre Beltrán, 1952, 1955
—— and Pozas, 1954
Beekman, 1956
Blumer, 1960
Butterworth, 1962
Cacho, 1961
Cámara B., 1956
Caso and Aguirre Beltrán, 1960
Caso et al., 1954
Cassaretto, 1956
Colby and van den Berghe, 1961
Cornejo Cabrera, 1961
Council on Foreign Relations, 1961
Dávalos Hurtado and Marino Flores, 1956
De la Fuente, 1959
Dessaint, 1962
Dotson and Dotson, 1956, 1957
Duran Ochoa, 1955
Fábila and Fábila, 1951
——, ——, et al., 1955
Fisher, 1953
Flores, 1950
Gamio, 1930a, 1930b
Guatemala, 1957
Hansen, 1934
Hernández Moreno and Nahmad, 1961
Hoyt, 1951, 1955
Inst. Interamericano de Estadística, 1960
Kaplan, 1960

Leslie, 1961b
Lewis, 1949, 1959a, 1959b, 1961a, 1961b
Marino Flores and Castro de la Fuente, 1960
Mexico, 1960
Moore, 1950, 1951
Moreno, 1958
Nash, J., 1960a
Nash, M., 1955, 1957a, 1958a
Newbold, 1957
Parra, 1950
Pozas, 1952a, 1959b
Reina, 1960
Reuter, 1934
Schneider, 1958
Simpson, 1953
Siverts, 1960
Slocum, 1956
Solis Quiroga, 1957
Stone, 1959
Tax, 1952b
Wagley and Harris, 1958
Whetten, 1961
—— and Burnight, 1956
Whiteford, 1960
Willey, Vogt, and Palerm, 1960
Winnie, 1958
Wolf, 1956, 1960
Wonderly, 1960
Yañez-Perez and Moyo Porras, 1957
Young and Young, 1960a, 1960b

REFERENCES AND INDEX

REFERENCES

Acosta, J. de
1590 Historia natural y moral de las Indias. Seville. (Other eds. 1880, 1940.)

Acosta, J. R.
1960 La doceava temporada de exploraciones en Tula, Hidalgo. *An. Inst. Nac. Antr. Hist.*, 13: 29–58.

—— and H. Moedano Koer
1946 Los juegos de pelota. *In* México prehispánico, 1946, pp. 365–84.

Acosta Saignes, M.
1945 Los Pochteca. *Acta Anthr.*, vol. 1, no. 1.

Adams, R. M.
1961 Changing patterns of territorial organization in the central highlands of Chiapas, Mexico. *Amer. Antiquity*, 26: 341–60.

Adams, R. N.
1952 Un análisis de las creencias y prácticas médicas en un pueblo indígena de Guatemala. *Inst. Nac. Indig.*, Pub. Especiales, no. 17. Guatemala.

1955 A nutritional research program in Guatemala. *In* B. D. Paul, 1955, pp. 435–58.

1956a La Ladinoización en Guatemala. *In* Arriola, 1956, pp. 213–44.

1956b Cultural components of Central America. *Amer. Anthr.*, 58: 881–907.

1956c Encuesta sobre la cultura de los Ladinos en Guatemala. *Seminario de Integración Social Guatemalteca*, Pub. 2.

1957a Cultural surveys of Panama–Nicaragua–Guatemala–El Salvador–Honduras. *Pan Amer. Sanitary Bur.*, Sci. Pub. 33.

1957b [comp.] Political changes in Guatemalan Indian communities: a symposium. *Tulane Univ., Middle Amer. Research Inst.*, Pub. 24, pp. 1–54.

1958 The problem of national culture in Central America. *In* Bosch-Gimpera, 1958, pp. 341–59.

1959 Freedom and reform in rural Latin America. *In* F. B. Pike, 1959, pp. 203–30.

1961 Social change in Guatemala and U.S. policy. *In* Council on Foreign Relations, 1961, pp. 231–84.

Adán, E.
1922 Organización social actual de los Zapotecas. *An. Mus. Nac. Arqueol. Hist. Etnog.*, 1: 53–64.

Aguirre Beltrán, G.
1940 El señorío de Cuautochco. Mexico.

1946 La población negra de México: 1519–1810. Mexico.

1952 Problemas de la población indígena de la cuenca del Tepalcatepec. *Inst. Nac. Indig.*, Mem. 3. Mexico.

1953 Formas de gobierno indígena. *Cultura Mex.*, Pub. 5.

1954 *Introduction to* Tlaxiaco, una ciudad mercado, by A. Marroquín. *Inst. Nac. Indig.*, Ed. Mimeográficas, no. 4.

1955 A theory of regional integration: the coordinating centers. *Amer. Indig.*, 15: 29–42. Same in Spanish entitled Teoría de los centros coordinadores, *Ciencias Sociales*, 6 (32): 66–77. Washington.

1957 El proceso de aculturación. Univ. Nac. Autónoma Mex.

1958 Cuijla: esbozo etnográfico de un pueblo negro. Fondo de Cultura Económica. Mexico.

—— and R. Pozas
1954 Instituciones indígenas en el México actual. *In* Caso, 1954, pp. 171–272.

Alaniz Patiño, E.
1946 La población indígena en México. *In* M. O. Mendizabal, Obras completas, 1: 29–98.

Albert, E. M.
1956 The classification of values: a method and illustration. *Amer. Anthr.*, 58: 221–48.

Alcalá Dondé, R.
1954 Una vieja tradición campechana. *Yikal Maya Than*, 15 (175): 30, 40–42.

ALVA IXTLILXOCHITL, F. DE
1938 Cruautés horribles des conquérants du Mexique. Paris.

ALVARADO GARCÍA, E.
1958 Legislación indigenista de Honduras. *Inst. Indig. Interamer.*, Ed. Especiales, no. 35. Mexico.

ALVARADO TEZOZOMOC, H.
1944 Crónica mexicana. Mexico.

ALVAREZ, I.
1955 A Yaqui Easter sermon. *Univ. Arizona, Social Sci. Bull. 26.*

AMEZQUITA BORJA, F.
1943 Música y danza de la sierra norte de Puebla. Puebla, Mexico.

AMIR, R. G.
1957 Magdalena Milpas Altas: 1880–1952. *In* R. N. Adams, 1957b, pp. 9–14.

AMSDEN, C. A.
1936 A prehistoric rubber ball. *Masterkey*, 10 (1): 7–8.

ANDERSON, A.
1957 Two Chol texts. *Tlalocan*, 3 (4): 313–16.

ANDERSON, A. J. O., AND C. E. DIBBLE
1951 The Florentine codex. Book 2: The ceremonies. Univ. Utah and School Amer. Research.

ANDRADE, M. J.
1946a Materiales sobre las lenguas Mam, Jacalteca, Aguateca, Chuj, Bachahon, Palencano, y Lacandone. *Maca*, 10.
1946b Materiales sobre las lenguas Quiche, Cakchiquel y Tzutuhil. *Ibid.*, 11.
1946c Materiales sobre las lenguas Kekchi y Pokomam. *Ibid.*, 12.

ANGULO, J. DE
1925 Kinship terms in some languages of southern Mexico. *Amer. Anthr.*, 27: 103–07.
1932 The Chichimeco language (central Mexico). *Int. Jour. Amer. Ling.*, 7: 152–94.

ANONYMOUS
n.d.,a Chronicle of Oxkutzcab. MS. Peabody Mus., Harvard Univ.
n.d.,b Huichol and Aztec texts and dictionaries. *Univ. Chicago, Summer Inst. Ling.*, Microfilm 27.
n.d.,c Relation of the capital city of Atitlan. MS. Univ. Texas Library.
1863 Historia de Welinna, leyenda yucateca. Merida.
1875 Zaccicoxol ó baile de Cortés: Coban. *Univ. Pennsylvania, Univ. Mus., Berendt Coll.*, no. 56.

1932 Natabal nu-tinamit—The memory of my village. *Maya Soc. Quar.*, 1 (2): 71.
1939–48 Collected materials on Chol, Tojolabal, and Tzotzil. *Univ. Chicago, Summer Inst. Ling.*, Microfilm. 26.
1944 Pastorela de viejos. *Tlalocan*, 1 (3): 169–93.
1945 México: leyendas y costumbres, trajes y danzas. Mexico.
1946 Cuendú hanga: Mixteco. Summer Inst. Ling. Mexico.
1952 El caballo endemoniado (tradición maya). *Yikal Maya Than*, 13 (145–50): 17–19.
1958 Präkolumbische Kunst aus Mexiko und Mittelamerika. Haus der Kunst, München.

ARCHIVO GENERAL DE INDIAS, SEVILLA (AGI)
Transcript in Bancroft Library, Univ. California.

ARCINIEGA, R. P.
1944 Monografía de Chamula, Chiapas. *Univ. Chicago, Micro. Coll. MSS Middle Amer. Cult. Anthr.*, no. 15.

ARIAS LARRETA, A.
1951 Literaturas aborígenes. Los Angeles.

ARMILLAS, P.
1949 Un pueblo de artesanos en la Sierra Madre del Sur, estado de Guerrero, México. *Amer. Indig.*, 9: 237–44.
1951 Technology, socio-economic organization, and religion in Mesoamerica. *In* Tax, 1951, pp. 19–30. Tr. by A. J. Rubel.

ARRIOLA, J. L., ed.
1956 Integración social en Guatemala. *Seminario de Integración Social Guatemalteca*, Pub. 3.
1957 Integración económica de Centroamerica. Organización de Estados Centroamericanos. Guatemala.

ARROT, C. R.
1953 La cerámica moderna, hecha a mano en Santa Apolonia. *Antr. Hist. Guatemala*, 5: 3–10.

ASCHER, R.
1962 Ethnography for archeology: a case from the Seri Indians. *Ethnology*, 1: 360–69.

ASCHMANN, H. P.
1946 Totonaco phonemes. *Int. Jour. Amer. Ling.*, 12: 34–43.

ASTROV, M.
1946 The winged serpent, an anthology of

American Indian prose and poetry. New York.

ASTURIAS, M. A.
1948 Leyendas de Guatemala. Buenos Aires.

AULIE, E., AND W. AULIE
1953 Terminos de parentesco en Chol. 4th centenario de la Universidad de México. *Mem. Cong. Cien. Mex., 12th Cien. Sociales*, pp. 151–58.

AVELEYRA ARROYO DE ANDA, L.
1956 La Cueva de la Paila, cercana a Parras, Coahuila. *In* Cueva d Candelaria, vol. 1. *Mem. Inst. Nac. Antr. Hist.*, 5. Mexico.

BAER, P., AND M. BAER
1949 Notes on Lacandon marriage. *SW. Jour. Anthr.*, 5: 101–06.

BAEZ, V. D.
1909 Compendio de historia de Oaxaca. Oaxaca.

BAILEY, H. M.
1958 Santa Cruz of the Etla hills. Univ. Florida Press.

BALCASTRO, P.
1931 Vocabulario de la lengua Opata. MS in Bancroft Library. Reproduced in Radin, 1931.

BALES, R. F.
1958 Task roles and social roles in problem-solving groups. *In* Readings in social psychology, E. E. Maccoby, T. M. Newcomb, and E. L. Hartley, eds.

BANCROFT, H. H.
1883 History of Mexico, 1521–1600. *Works*, vol. 10.
1887 History of Central America. 3 vols.

BANDELIER, A. F.
1880a On the distribution and tenure of land, and the customs with respect to inheritance among the ancient Mexicans. *Peabody Mus., Harvard Univ.*, 12th ann. rept. (1876–79), 2: 385–448.
1880b On the social organization and mode of government of the ancient Mexicans. *Ibid.*, 2: 557–699.
1884 An excursion to Mitla. *Papers Archaeol. Inst. Amer., Amer. Ser.* Boston.

BANNON, J. F. (S.J.)
1955 The mission frontier in Sonora, 1620–1687. *U.S. Catholic Hist. Soc.*, Monogr. 26.

BARBO DE PIÑA CHAN, B.
1956 Tlapacoya: un sitio preclásico de transición. *Acta Anthr.*, ep. 2, vol. 1, no. 1.

BÁRCENA, J. M. R.
1862 Leyendas mexicanas. Mexico.

BARKER, G. C.
1957 Some aspects of penitential processions in Spain and the American Southwest. *Jour. Amer. Folklore*, 70: 137–42.

BARLOW, R. H.
1945 The Tlacotepec migration legend. *Tlalocan*, 2 (1): 70–73.
1949 The extent of the empire of the Culhua Mexica. *Ibero-Amer.*, no. 28.

BARNETT, H. G.
1953 Innovation: the basis of cultural change. New York.

BARON CASTRO, R.
1942 La población de El Salvador. Madrid.

BARRERA VÁSQUEZ, A.
1948 El libro de los libros de Chilam Balam. Fondo de Cultura Económica. Mexico.

BARRIOS E., M.
1949 Textos de Hueyapan, Morelos. *Tlalocan*, 3 (1): 53–64.

BARTH, P. J. (O.F.M.)
1950 Franciscan education and the social order in Spanish North America, 1502–1821. Chicago.

BASAURI, C.
1927 Creencias y prácticas de los Tarahumaras. *Mex. Folkways*, 3: 218–34.
1928 La situación social actual de la población indígena de México. *Pub. Sec. Educación Pública*, vol. 16, no. 8. Mexico.
1929 Monografía de los Tarahumaras. Talleres Gráficos de la Nación. Mexico.
1930 Apuntes etnográficos sobre los Indios Otomies del Valle del Mezquital.
1931 Tojolabales, Tzeltales y Mayas. Talleres Gráficos de la Nación. Mexico.

BATALLA, M. A.
1945 Textile plants suitable for basketry. *Esta Semana*, March 3, 10, 17. Mexico.

BAUER, T.
1915 Unter den Zapoteken und Mixes. *Baessler Archiv*, 5: 75–97.

BEALS, R. L.
n.d. The history of acculturation in Mexico. MS.

1932 The comparative ethnology of northern Mexico before 1750. *Ibero-Amer.*, no. 2.

1933 The Acaxee, a mountain tribe of Durango and Sinaloa. *Ibid.*, no. 6.

1935 Two mountain Zapotec tales from Oaxaca, Mexico. *Jour. Amer. Folklore*, 48: 189–90.

1936 Problems in the study of Mixe marriage customs. *In* Essays in anthropology, presented to A. L. Kroeber, pp. 7–13.

1943 The aboriginal culture of the Cáhita Indians. *Ibero-Amer.*, no. 19.

1944a Northern Mexico and the Southwest. *In* El Norte de Mexico, pp. 191–99.

1944b Relations between Meso America and the Southwest. *Ibid.*, pp. 245–52.

1945a The contemporary culture of the Cáhita Indians. *Smithsonian Inst., Bur. Amer. Ethnol.*, Bull. 142.

1945b The ethnology of the western Mixe. *Univ. California Pub. Amer. Archaeol. Ethnol.*, 42: 1–176.

1946 Cheran: a sierra Tarascan village. *Smithsonian Inst., Inst. Social Anthr.*, Pub. 2.

1949 Conferencia sobre los indígenas contemporaneas de México. *Univ. Central de Ecuador, Filosofía y Letras*, pp. 38–52.

1951a History of acculturation in Mexico. *In* Homenaje Caso, pp. 73–82.

1951b Urbanism, urbanization and acculturation. *Amer. Anthr.*, 53: 1–10.

1952 Notes on acculturation. *In* Tax, 1952a, pp. 225–32.

—— AND P. CARRASCO
1944 Games of the mountain Tarascans. *Amer. Anthr.*, 46: 516–22.

——, ——, AND T. MCCORKLE
1944 Houses and house use of the sierra Tarascans. *Smithsonian Inst., Inst. Social Anthr.*, Pub. 1.

——, R. REDFIELD, AND S. TAX
1943 Anthropological research problems with reference to the contemporary peoples of Mexico and Guatemala. *Amer. Anthr.*, 45: 1–21.

BEEKMAN, J.
1956 The effect of education in an Indian village. *In* Estudios antropológicos, pp. 261–64.

BEESLEY, C.
1943 The religion of the Maya. *El Palacio*, 50 (1): 8–21.

BELMAR, F.
1902 Lenguas indígenas del estado de Oaxaca: estudio del idioma Ayook. Oaxaca.

1905 Lenguas indígenas de México. Mexico.

BEMIS, S. F.
1943 The Latin American policy of the United States. New York.

BENNETT, J. W.
1944 Southeastern culture types and Middle American influence. *In* El Norte de Mexico, pp. 223–41.

BENNETT, W. C., AND R. M. ZINGG
1935 The Tarahumara: an Indian tribe of northern Mexico. Univ. Chicago Press.

BERCKENHAGEN, H.
1894 Grammar of the Miskito language. Bluefields, Nicaragua.

BERLIN, H.
1947 Historia Tolteca-Chichimeca. Anales de Quauhtinchan. Mexico.

1951 The calendar of the Tzotzil Indians. *In* Tax, 1951, pp. 155–64.

—— AND R. H. BARLOW
1948 Anales de Tlatelolco. Mexico.

BERNAL, I., AND E. DÁVALOS HURTADO, eds.
1953 *See* Huastecos, Totonacos y sus vecinos.

BEVAN, B.
1938 The Chinantec and their habitat. (The Chinantec: report on the central and southeastern Chinantec region, vol. 1). *Inst. Panamer. Geog. Hist.*, Pub. 24. Mexico.

BIART, L.
1900 The Aztecs. Chicago.

BIRD, J.
1953 Two Guatemala wedding huipils. *Needle and Bobbin Club Bull.*, 37: 26–36.

BLOM, F.
1923 Las Chanecas of Tecuanapa. *Jour. Amer. Folklore*, 36: 200–02.

1932 The Maya ball-game *pok-ta-pok*. *Tulane Univ., Middle Amer. Research Inst.*, Pub. 4, pp. 485–530.

—— AND G. DUBY
1949 Entre los indios Lacandones de México. *Amer. Indig.*, 9: 155–64.

—— AND O. LAFARGE
1926–27 Tribes and temples. 2 vols. *Tulane Univ., Middle Amer. Research Inst.*, Pub. 1.

REFERENCES

BLUMER, H.
1960 Early industrialization and the laboring class. *Sociol. Quar.*, 1: 5–14.

BOAS, F.
1912 Notes on Mexican folklore. *Jour. Amer. Folklore*, 25: 204–60.

—— AND J. M. ARREOLA
1920 Cuentos en mexicano de Milpa Alta. *Ibid.*, 33: 1–24.

—— AND H. K. HAEBERLIN
1924 Ten folktales in modern Nahuatl. *Ibid.*, 37: 345–70.

BODE, B. O.
1961 The dance of the conquest of Guatemala. *Tulane Univ., Middle Amer. Research Inst.*, Pub. 27, pp. 205–92.

BOGGS, R. S.
1939 Bibliografía del folklore mexicano. Mexico.
1945 Bibliografía completa, clasificada y comentada, de los artículos de "Mexican Folkways," con índice. *Bol. Bibliografía Antr. Amer.*, 3: 221–68.
1949 Mapa preliminar de las regiones folklóricas de México. *Folklore Amer.*, 9: 1–4.

BOLETÍN INDIGENISTA
1941– Published as a supplement to *America Indígena*, by Inst. Indig. Interamer. Mexico.

BOLTON, H. E.
1919 Kino's Historical memoir of Pimeria Alto. 2 vols.

BONILLA DOMÍNGUEZ, C.
1953 El proceso de cambio cultural en medicina. *Inst. Nac. Indig.* Mexico.

BONILLA Y SAN MARTÍN, A.
1923 Los mitos de la América precolombiana. Barcelona.

BORAH, W. W.
1943 Silk raising in colonial Mexico. *Ibero-Amer.*, no. 20.
1951 New Spain's century of depression. *Ibid.*, no. 35.

BORHEGYI, S. F.
1956a Settlement patterns in the Guatemalan highlands: past and present. *In* Willey, 1956a, pp. 101–06.
1956b The development of folk and complex cultures in the southern Maya area. *Amer. Antiquity*, 21: 343–56.

BORN, W.
1937 The use of purple among the Indians of Central America. *Ciba Rev.*, 4: 124–27.

BOSCH-GIMPERA, P.
1958 Miscellanea Paul Rivet, octogenario dicata XXXI. Int. Cong. Amer. Mexico.

BOURKE, J. G.
1893 Primitive distillation among the Tarascans. *Amer. Anthr.*, 6: 65–69.

BOWER, E.
1946 Notes on shamanism among the Tepehua Indians. *Ibid.*, 48: 680–83.

BRADEN, C.
1930 Religious aspects of the conquest of Mexico. Durham.

BRAINERD, G. W.
1946 Wheel-made pottery in America? *Masterkey*, 20: 191–92.
1949 Forming of the jarro yucateco. *Ibid.*, 23: 56–58.

BRAND, D. D.
1943a An historical sketch of anthropology and geography in the Tarascan region. Part I. *New Mexico Anthr.*, 6–7 (2): 37–108.
1943b Primitive and modern economy of the middle Rio Balsas, Guerrero and Michoacan. *Proc. 8th Amer. Sci. Cong.* (Washington, 1940), 9: 225–31.
1951 Quiroga, a Mexican municipio. *Smithsonian Inst., Inst. Social Anthr.*, Pub. 11.

BRASSEUR DE BOURBOURG, C. E.
1861 Popul Vuh: le livre sacré et les mythes de l'antiquité américaine, avec les livres héroiques et historiques des Quichés. Paris.
1862 Rabinal-Achi, ancien drame Quiché. *In* his Grammaire de la langue Quiché. Paris.
1871 Bibliothèque Mexicaine-Guatémalienne. Paris.

BRINTON, D. G.
1882a American hero-myths. Philadelphia.
1882b The Maya chronicles. *Library Aboriginal Amer. Lit.*, no. 1. Philadelphia.
1883a Aboriginal American authors and their productions. Philadelphia.
1883b The folk-lore of Yucatan. *Folk-lore Jour.*, 1: 244–56.
1883c The Güegüence: a comedy ballet in the Nahuatl-Spanish dialect of Nicaragua. Philadelphia.

1885a The Annals of the Cakchiquels. *Library Aboriginal Amer. Lit.*, no. 6.
1885b On the Xinca Indians of Guatemala. *Proc. Amer. Phil. Soc.*, 22: 89–97.
1886 Notes on the Mangue dialect. *Ibid.*, 23: 238–57.
1890 Essays of an Americanist. Philadelphia.
1894 Nagualism. Philadelphia.
1896 The myths of the New World. Philadelphia.

BRUNER, E. M.
1956 Cultural transmission and cultural change. *SW. Jour. Anthr.*, 12: 191–99.

BUELNA, E.
1890 Arte de la lengua Cáhita. Mexico.

BUITRÓN, A.
1961 El desarrollo de la comunidad en la teoría y en la práctica. *Amer. Indig.*, 21: 141–50.

BUNZEL, R.
1952 Chichicastenango: a Guatemalan village. *Amer. Ethnol. Soc.*, Pub. 22.

BURGESS, D. M., AND P. XEC
1955 Popul Wuj. Quezaltenango.

BURGOA, F. DE
1674 Geográfica descripción de la parte septentrional del polo ártico de la América y nueva iglesia de las Indias Occidentales, y sitio astronómico de esta provincia de predicadores de Antequera, Valle de Oaxaca . . . México. *Pub. Archivo General de la Nación*, vols. 25, 26. (2d ed. 1934, Mexico.)

BURKITT, R.
1920 The hills and the corn: a legend of the Kekchi Indians of Guatemala. *Univ. Pennsylvania, Univ. Mus. Anthr. Pub.*, 8: 183–227.

BURLAND, C. A.
1949 Mexican deluge legends. *Atlantean Research*, 2 (4): 62–64.

BURTON, R. V., AND J. W. M. WHITING
1961 The absent father and cross-sex identity. *Merrill-Palmer Quar. Behavior and Development*, vol. 7, no. 2.

BUSHNELL, J.
1958 La Virgen de Guadalupe as surrogate mother in San Juan Atzingo. *Amer. Anthr.*, 60: 261–65.

BUTTERWORTH, D. S.
1962 A study of the urbanization process among Mixtec migrants from Tilal-

tongo in Mexico City. *Amer. Indig.*, 22: 257–74.

CACHO A., R.
1961 La Ciudad de México. *Rev. Económica*, 24 (4): 23–33.

CALENDARIO DE LAS FIESTAS
1959 Calendario de las fiestas titulares de la Republica de Guatemala. Inst. Indig. Nac. Guatemala.

CALNEK, E. E.
1961 Report on Chiapas ethnohistory. Nat. Sci. Found., Seminar on Chiapas.
1962 Highland Chiapas before the Spanish conquest. Doctoral dissertation, Univ. Chicago.

CÁMARA BARBACHANO, F.
1946a Monografía sobre los Tzeltales de Tenejapa. *Univ. Chicago, Micro. Coll. MSS Middle Amer. Cult. Anthr.*, no. 5.
1946b Monografía de los Tzotziles de San Miguel Mitontik. *Ibid.*, no. 6.
1947 Culturas contemporáneas de México. *Amer. Indig.*, 7: 165–71.
1952a Instituciones religiosas y políticas indígenas. *In* Hechos y problemas del México rural. Seminario Mex. Sociol. Mexico.
1952b Organización religiosa y política de Tenejapa. *An. Inst. Nac. Antr. Hist.*, 4: 32.
1952c Religious and political organization. *In* Tax, 1952a, pp. 142–73.
1956 Factores causales respecto al bracero mexicano. *In* Estudios antropológicos, pp. 305–10.

CAMPOBELLO, N., AND G. CAMPOBELLO
1940 Ritmos indígenas de México. Mexico.

CAMPOS, R. M.
1929 El folklore literario de México. Mexico.
1936 La producción literaria de los Aztecas. Mus. Nac. Arqueol. Hist. Etnog. Mexico.
1937 Tradiciones y leyendas mexicanas. *An. Mus. Nac. Arqueol. Hist. Etnog.*, 2: 71–191.

CANCIAN, FRANCESCA
1963 Family interaction in Zinacantan. Doctoral dissertation, Harvard Univ.

CANCIAN, FRANK
1964 Some aspects of the social and religious organization of a Maya society. *Actas y Mem., 35th Int.*

544

REFERENCES

Cong. Amer., (Mexico, 1962), 1: 335–43.

1965 Economics and prestige in a Maya community: the religious cargo system in Zinacantan. Stanford Univ. Press.

CAPLOW, T.
1949 The social ecology of Guatemala City. Social Forces, 28: 113–33.
1952 The modern Latin American city. In Tax, 1952b, pp. 255–60.

CAPMANY, A.
1931 El baile y la danza. In F. Carreras y Candi, Folklore y costumbres de España, 2: 168–418. Barcelona.

CARR, M.
1952 The historical origin of the Middle American 'disease' concept [1937]. Univ. Chicago, Micro. Coll. MSS Middle Amer. Cult. Anthr., no. 31.

CARRASCO, P.
1946 Paricutín volcano in Tarascan folklore. El Palacio, 53: 299–306.
1950a Los Otomies: cultura e historia prehispánicas de los pueblos mesoamericanos de habla otomiana. Pub. Inst. Hist., 1st ser., no. 15.
1950b Middle American ethnography. Pan Amer. Union, Social Sci. Monogr., no. 10.
1952a El sol y la luna: versión mixe. Tlalocan, 3 (2): 168–69.
1952b Tarascan folk religion: an analysis of economic, social and religious interactions. Tulane Univ., Middle Amer. Research Inst., Pub. 17, pp. 1–64.
1961 The civil-religious hierarchy in Mesoamerican communities: pre-Spanish background and colonial development. Amer. Anthr., 63: 483–97.

CARRIEDO, J. B.
1852 Leyenda zapoteca. Ilustración Mex., 3: 336–45.

CARTA DE UN RELIGIOSA
1951 Carta de un religiosa sobre la rebelión de indios mexicanos en 1692. In Biblioteca de historiadores mexicanas. Mexico.

CASAGRANDE, J. B.
1959 Some observations on the study of intermediate societies. In Ray, 1959, pp. 1–10.

CASARRUBIAS, V.
1945 Rebeliones indígenas de la Nueva España. Sec. Educación Pública.

Mexico. (Extracts appear in supplement to González Obregón, 1952, 2d ed.)

CASO, A.
1924–27 Un antiguo juego mexicano, el patolli. El Mex. Antiguo, 2: 203–11.
1932 Notas sobre juegos antiguos. Mex. Folkways, 7: 56–60.
1936 La religión de los Aztecas. Mexico.
1942 Culturas mixtecas y zapotecas. Biblioteca del Maestro. Mexico.
1944 El calendario de los Tarascos. An. Mus. Michoacano, pp. 11–36.
1948 Definición del Indio y lo Indio. Amer. Indig., 8: 239–47.
1954 [ed.] Métodos y resultados de la política indigenista en México. Inst. Nac. Indig., Mem. 6. Mexico.
1958a Ideals of an action program. Human Organization, 17: 27–29.
1958b Indigenismo. Inst. Nac. Indig. Mexico.
1958c The Aztecs: people of the sun. Norman.
1959 La tenencia de la tierra entre los antiguos mexicanos. Mem. Colegio Nac., 4: 29–54. Mexico.

—— AND G. AGUIRRE BELTRÁN
1960 Applied anthropology in Mexico. In Willey, Vogt, and Palerm, 1960, pp. 54–61.

—— AND M. G. PARRA
1950 Densidad de la población de habla indígena en la Republica Mexicana. Inst. Nac. Indig., Mem. 1. Mexico.

CASSARETTO, M. A.
1956 El movimiento protestante en México, 1940–1955. Tesis profesional, Univ. Nac. Autónoma Mex.

CASTAÑEDA, C. E.
1932 The first American play. Catholic World, January.

CASTETTER, E. F., AND W. H. BELL
1942 Pima and Papago Indian agriculture. Univ. New Mexico, School Interamer. Affairs, Interamer. Ser., Studies I.

CASTILLO, C. DEL
n.d. Migración de los mexicanos al pais de Anahuac. Fin de su dominación y noticias de su calendario. Fragmentos históricos sacados de la obra escrita en lengua Nahuatl por Cristóbal del Castillo a fines del siglo 16. Bibliothèque National. Paris.

545

CASTILLO LEDÓN, L.
1917 Antigua literatura indígena mexicana. Mexico.

CERDA SILVA, R. DE LA
1943a Los Tepehuanes. *Rev. Mex. Sociol.,* 5: 541–67.
1943b Los Coras. *Ibid.,* 5: 89–117.

CERVANTES, N. C. DE
1732 Vocabulario en lengua castellana y cora. Reproduced in Radin, 1931.

CHACÓN PINEDA, N.
1936 Xtagabene. *Neza,* 2: 2–6. Mexico.

CHAMBERLAIN, R. S.
1948 The conquest and colonization of Yucatan, 1517–1550. *Carnegie Inst. Wash.,* Pub. 582.
1953 The conquest and colonization of Honduras, 1502–1550. *Ibid.,* Pub. 598.

CHAPMAN, A.
1947 Tzeltal stories. *In* A treasury of Mexican folkways, pp. 479–90.

CHÁVEZ OROZCO, L.
1943 Las instituciones democráticas de los indígenas mexicanos en la época colonial. *Amer. Indig.,* 3: 73–82, 161–71, 265–76, 365–82.

CHEVALIER, F.
1952 La formation des grands domaines au Mexique: terre et société aux 16th–17th siècles. *Inst. Ethnol., Travaux et Mem.,* no. 16. Paris.

CHICAGO, UNIVERSITY OF
1959 *See* McQuown, 1959.

CHINCHILLA AGUILAR, E.
1951 La danza del Tum-teleche o Loj-tum. *An. Soc. Antr. Hist. Guatemala,* 3 (2): 17–20.

CHRISTENSEN, B.
1937 The Acatlaxqui dance of Mexico. *Ethnos,* 4: 133–36.
1947 Otomi looms and quechquemitls from San Pablito, state of Puebla, and from Santa Ana Hueytlalpan, state of Hidalgo. *Carnegie Inst. Wash., Notes Middle Amer. Archeaeol. Ethnol.,* no. 78.
1953 Los Otomies del estado de Puebla. *In* Huastecos, Totonacos, pp. 259–68.

CHRISTENSEN, L.
n.d. The Dominican missions in Oaxaca, Mexico. MS. Univ. California, Dept. Anthropology and Sociology.

CLAVIGERO, F. S.
1807 The history of Mexico. Vol. 1. Tr. from Italian by C. Cullen. London.

CLINE, H. F.
1944 Lore and deities of the Lacandon Indians. *Jour. Amer. Folklore,* 57: 107–15.
1945 Remarks on a selected bibliography of the Caste War and allied topics. *In* Villa Rojas, 1945, pp. 165–78.
1946 The Terragueros of Guelatao, Oaxaca, Mexico: notes on the Sierra de Juarez and its 17th century Indian problems. *Acta Amer.,* vol. 4, no. 3.
1952 Mexican community studies. *Hisp. Amer. Hist. Rev.,* 32: 212–42.
1953 The United States and Mexico. Cambridge.
1962 Mexico, from revolution to evolution. Oxford Univ. Press.

COE, M. D.
1965 A model of ancient community structure in the Maya lowlands. *SW. Jour. Anthr.,* 21:97–114.

COE, W. R.
1965 Tikal, Guatemala, and emergent Maya civilization. *Science,* 147 (3664): 1401–19.

COESTER, A.
1941 The danza de los conquistadores at Chichicastenango. *Hispania,* 24: 95–100.

COLBY, B. N.
1959 A field sketch of some recurring themes and tendencies in Zinacantan culture. Harvard Chiapas Project. Dittoed.
1960 Ethnic relations in the highlands of Chiapas, Mexico. Doctoral dissertation, Harvard Univ.
1961a Outline for staff meeting discussion on values in Zinacantan. Harvard Chiapas Project. Dittoed.
1961b Indian attitudes towards education and inter-ethnic contact in Mexico. *Practical Anthr.,* 8: 77–85.
1963 Ethnographic notes and materials on the Ixil Indians of Nebaj, Guatemala. Unpublished material on file at Laboratory of Anthropology, Santa Fe.

—— AND P. L. VAN DEN BERGHE
1960 Ethnic relations in southeastern Mexico. Harvard Univ. Mimeographed. Published in part in their 1961.
1961 Ethnic relations in southeastern Mexico. *Amer. Anthr.,* 63: 772–92.

COLLIER, MRS. DONALD
    See Carr, M.

COLTON, H.
  1943 Life history and economic possibilities of the American lac insect, *Tachardiella larrea*. *Plateau*, 16 (2): 21–32.

COMAS, J.
  1942 El problema social de los Indios Triques en Oaxaca. *Amer. Indig.*, 2 (1): 51–57.
  1951 *See* Homenaje al Doctor Alfonso Caso.
  1953 Algunos datos para la historia del indigenismo en México. *In* Ensayos sobre indigenismo, pp. 63–108. *Inst. Indig. Interamer.*, Ed. Especiales, no. 13.
  1955 Un ensayo sobre raza y economía. *Amer. Indig.*, 15: 139–58.
  1961 ¿Otra vez el racismo científico? *Ibid.*, 21: 99–140.

CONGRESO INDIGENISTA INTERAMERICANO
  1949 Segundo congreso. Acta final. Inst. Indig. Interamer. Mexico.
  1954a Tercero congreso. Acta final. *Ibid.*
  1954b Tercero congreso. Número especial del *Bol. Indig.*, 14: 169–228.
  1959 Cuarto congreso. *Ibid.*, 19: 125–80.

CONTRERAS R., J. D.
  1951 Una rebelión indígena en el partido de Totonicapan en 1820: el Indio y la independencia. Guatemala.

CONZEMIUS, E.
  1923 The Jicaques of Honduras. *Int. Jour. Amer. Ling.*, 2: 163–70.
  1930 Une tribu inconnue du Costa-Rica: les Indiens rama du Rio Zapote. *L'Anthropologie*, 40: 93–108. Paris.
  1932 Ethnographical survey of the Miskito and Sumu Indians of Honduras and Nicaragua. *Smithsonian Inst., Bur. Amer. Ethnol.*, Bull. 106.

COOK, S. F., AND L. B. SIMPSON
  1948 The population of central Mexico in the sixteenth century. *Ibero-Amer.*, no. 31.

COOK DE LEONARD, C., ed.
  1959 *See* Esplendor del México antiguo.

COOLIDGE, D., AND M. R. COOLIDGE
  1939 The last of the Seris. New York.

COOPER, J. M.
  1949 Games and gambling. *In* Handbook of South American Indians, 5: 503–24.

CORBETT, J. H.
  1939 Ball courts and ball game of the ancient American Indians. Master's thesis, Univ. Southern California.

CÓRDOVA, J. DE
  1942 Vocabulario castellano-zapoteco. *Inst. Nac. Antr. Hist.* Mexico.

CORDRY, D. B.
  1941 Zoque maize legend. *Masterkey*, 15: 58–59.
  1947a Two Huichol tales from the sierra of Nayarit. *In* A treasury of Mexican folkways, pp. 499–501.
  1947b Two Zoque serpent tales. *Ibid.*, pp. 501–02.

—— AND D. M. CORDRY
  1940 Costumes and textiles of the Aztec Indians of the Cuetzalan region, Puebla, Mexico. *SW. Mus. Papers*, no. 14.
  1941 Costumes and weaving of the Zoque Indians of Chiapas, Mexico. *Ibid.*, no. 15.

CORNEJO CABRERA, E.
  1961 Los Otomies: historia del grupo y de la cultura y su situación actual. *Rev. Mex. Sociol.*, 23: 53–90.

CORNYN, J. H.
  1925 Fábulas mexicanas. *Mex. Folkways*, 1: 13–16.
  1932a Ixcit Cheel. *Maya Soc. Quar.*, 1: 47–55.
  1932b X'tabay. *Ibid.*, 1: 107–11.
  1935 Evil for good. *Real Mexico*, 2: 18–19.

—— AND B. MCAFEE
  1944 Tlacahuapehualiztli: educación de los hijos. *Tlalocan*, 1: 314–61.

CORONA NÚÑEZ, J.
  1946a La religion de los Tarascos. *An. Mus. Michoacano*.
  1946b Cuiteo: estudio antropogeográfico. *Acta Anthr.*, vol. 2, no. 1, pt. 2.
  1957 Mitología tarasca. Mexico.

CORREA, G.
  1955 El espíritu del mal en Guatemala. *Tulane Univ., Middle Amer. Research Inst.*, Pub. 19, pp. 37–104.
  1958a Texto de un baile de diablos. *Ibid.*, Pub. 27, pp. 97–104.
  1958b La loa en Guatemala. *Ibid.*, Pub. 27, pp. 1–96.

CORTÉS, H.
  1908 Letters of Cortés: the five letters of relation to the Emperor Charles V. Tr. and ed. by F. A. MacNutt. 2 vols. New York.

COTNER, T. E., AND C. CASTANEDA
1958 Essays in Mexican history. Austin.

COUNCIL ON FOREIGN RELATIONS
1961 Social change in Latin America today. New York.

COVARRUBIAS, M.
1947 Mexico south: the isthmus of Tehuantepec. New York.
1954 The eagle, the jaguar, and the serpent. New York.
1957 Indian arts of Mexico and Central America. New York.

COWAN, F. H.
1946 Notas etnográficas sobre los Mazatecos de Oaxaca. *Amer. Indig.*, 6: 27–39.
1947 Linguistic and ethnological aspects of Mazateco kinship. *SW. Jour. Anthr.*, 3: 247–56.

COWAN, G. M.
1947 Una visita a los indígenas Amuzgos de México. *An. Inst. Nac. Antr. Hist.*, 2: 293–302.
1952 El idioma silbado entre los Mazatecos de Oaxaca y los Tepehuas de Hidalgo. *Sobretiro de Tlatoani*, 1: 31–33.
1954 La importancia social y política de la faena mazateca. *Amer. Indig.*, 14: 67–92.

CRAWLEY, A. E.
1914 Pallone, pelota, and paume. *The Field*, vol. 123, suppl., p. xviii (April, 25). London.

CROFT, K.
1957 Nahuatl texts from Matlapa, San Luis Potosi. *Tlalocan*, 3: 317–33.

CRUZ, W. C.
1935 El tonalamatl zapoteco: el mito y la leyenda zapoteca. Oaxaca.
1946 Oaxaca recóndita: razas, idiomas, costumbres, leyendas y tradiciones del estado de Oaxaca. Mexico.

CULIN, S.
1907 Games. *In* Handbook of American Indians north of Mexico, 1: 483–86.

CURTIN, J.
1899 Creation myths in primitive America. London.

CURTIS, E. S.
1908 The North American Indian. Vol. 2.

DABBS, J. A.
1958 The Indian policy of the second empire. *In* Cotner and Castaneda, 1958, pp. 113–26.

DAHLGREN DE JORDAN, B.
1954 La Mixteca: su cultura e historia prehispánicas. *Col. Cultura Mex.*, no. 1. Mexico.

D'ANDRADE, R. G.
1962 Father absence and cross-sex identification. Doctoral dissertation, Harvard Univ.

DARÍO, R.
1954 Folklore de la América Central: representaciones y bailes populares en Nicaragua. *Nicaragua Indig.*, (2a ep.), 2: 5–9. Managua.

DÁVALOS HURTADO, E., AND A. MARINO FLORES
1956 Reflexiones acerca de la antropología mexicana. *An. Inst. Nac. Antr. Hist.*, 8: 163–209.

DAVIS, E. H.
1920 Papago ceremony of Vikita. *Mus. Amer. Indian, Heye Found.*, 3 (4): 153–77.

DEDRICK, J. M.
1946 How Jobeʔeso Roʔi got his name. *Tlalocan*, 2: 163–66.

DE LA FUENTE, J.
1941 Creencias indígenas sobre la onchocercosis, el paludismo y otras enfermedades. *Amer. Indig.*, 1 (1): 43–47.
1942 Las ceremonias de la lluvia entre los Zapotecos de hoy. *Actas, 27th Int. Cong. Amer.*, 5: 479–89.
1947a Definición, pase y desaparición del indio en México. *Amer. Indig.*, 7: 63–69.
1947b Discriminación y negación del indio. *Ibid.*, 7: 211–15.
1947c Los Zapotecos de Choapan, Oaxaca. *An. Inst. Nac. Antr. Hist.*, 2: 143–206.
1948 Cambios socio-culturales en México. *Acta Anthr.*, vol. 3, no. 4.
1949 Yalalag: una villa zapoteca serrana. *Mus. Nac. Antr., Ser. Cien.*, no. 1. Mexico.
1952 Ethnic and communal relations. *In* Tax, 1952a, pp. 76–96.
1958a Relaciones étnicas en Chiapas. Mimeographed.
1958b Results of an action program. *Human Organization*, 17: 30–33.
1959 Los programas de cambio dirigido, sus características y sus resultados. *In* Stone, 1959, 1: 380–85.

DELGADO, A. I.
1950 La danza "cadenitas," una expresión

folklórica. *Cuauhtémoc: Rev. Cultura y Actualidad*, 2: 48–49.

DEMAREST, D., AND C. TAYLOR
1956 The dark virgin: the book of our lady of Guadalupe. New York.

DESARROLLO CULTURAL DE LOS MAYAS
1964 Desarrollo cultural de los Mayas. E. Z. Vogt and A. Ruz Lhuillier, eds. Wenner-Gren symposium at Burg Wartestein on the cultural development of the Maya. Univ. Nac. Autónoma Mex.

DESHON, S. K.
1959 Women's position on a Yucatecan henequen hacienda. Doctoral dissertation, Yale Univ.

DESSAINT, A. Y.
1962 Effects of the hacienda and plantation systems on Guatemala's Indians. *Amer. Indig.*, 22: 323–54.

DEWAR, J.
1957 Blanket for tortillas, an Otomi textile. *Masterkey*, 31: 105–06.

DÍAZ DEL CASTILLO, B.
1927 The true history of the conquest of Mexico. 2 vols. 2d ed. New York.

DÍAZ DE SALAS, M.
1960–61 Field notes of San Bartolome de las Casas. MS, Chiapas Project files, Univ. Chicago, Dept. Anthropology.

DIESELDORFF, E. P.
1930 The Aztec calendar stone and its significance. *Proc. 23d Int. Cong. Amer.* (1928), pp. 211–22.

DIRECCIÓN GENERAL DE ASUNTOS INDÍGENAS, MEXICO
[1958] Seis años de labor.

DIRECCIÓN GENERAL DE ESTADÍSTICA, GUATEMALA
1953 Sexto censo de población. Guatemala.
1959 *Boletín estadístico*, nos. 1–2. Guatemala.

DOCUMENTOS RELATIVOS AL AXE O NI-IN
1884 *Naturaleza*, 6: 372–84. Mexico.

DOLL, E. E.
1952 The stewardship of the saint in Mexico and Guatemala [1943]. *Univ. Chicago, Micro. Coll. MSS Middle Amer. Cult. Anthr.*, no. 31, item B.

DOLORES, J.
1923 Papago noun stems. *Univ. California Pub. Amer. Archaeol. Ethnol.*, 20: 19–31.

DONDÉ IBARRA, J.
1884 El ni-in. *Naturaleza*, 6: 200–04. Mexico.

DOTSON, F., AND L. O. DOTSON
1956 Urban centralization and decentralization in Mexico. *Rural Sociol.*, 21: 41–49.
1957 La estructura ecológica de las ciudades mexicanas. *Rev. Mex. Sociol.*, 19: 39–66.

DRUCKER, P.
1941 Yuman-Piman. Univ. California Press.
1943 Ceramic stratigraphy at Cerro de las Mesas, Veracruz. *Smithsonian Inst., Bur. Amer. Ethnol.*, Bull. 141.
1958 The native brotherhoods. *Ibid.*, Bull. 168.

DRUCKER, S.
1959 Field notes on Jamiltepec, a Mixtec and Mestizo village of Oaxaca, Mexico. MS.

DUGÉS, A.
1891 La *Llaveia dorsalis, nobis. Naturaleza*, ser. 2, 1: 160–61.

DUNLOP, R. G.
1847 Travels in Central America. London.

DUNNE, P. M.
1948 Early Jesuit missions in Tarahumara. Berkeley.

DURÁN, D., ed.
1951 Historia de las Indias de Nueva España e islas de la tierra firme. 2 vols. Mexico.

DURÁN OCHOA, J.
1955 Población, México. Fondo de Cultura Económica. Mexico.

DUTTON, B. P.
1939a La fiesta de San Francisco de Assisi, Tecpan, Guatemala. *El Palacio*, 46: 73–78.
1939b All Saints' Day ceremonies in Todos Santos, Guatemala. *Ibid.*, 46: 169–82, 205–17.

DUVALIER, A.
1960 La laca de Chiapa de Corzo: síntesis. *Acta Politécnica Mex.*, vol. 1, no. 6.

DYK, A.
1959 Mixteco texts. *Summer Inst. Ling., Ling. Ser.*, no. 3. Norman.

ECKER, L.
1930 Los términos de parentesco en Otomi, Nahua, Tarasco y Maya. MS in Mus. Nac. Antr. Hist. Mexico.
1937 Los dos "metoros": un cuento Otomi. *Invest. Ling.*, 4: 254–61. Mexico.

1939   Relationship of Mixtec to Otomian languages. *El Mex. Antiguo*, 4 (7–8):229.

EDMONSON, C. N.
n.d.   Field notes on Barrio Libre, Tucson, Arizona. MS in the possession of E. H. Spicer, Univ. Arizona.

EDMONSON, M. S.
1957   [ed.] Synoptic studies of Mexican culture. *Tulane Univ., Middle Amer. Research Inst.*, Pub. 17.
1959   The Mexican truck driver. *Ibid.*, Pub. 25, pp. 73–88.
1960   Nativism, syncretism and anthropological science. *Ibid.*, Pub. 19, pp. 181–203.
1961   Field notes on western Guatemala, 1960–61. MS.

EGGAN, F.
1934   The Maya kinship system and cross-cousin marriage. *Amer. Anthr.*, 36: 188–202.

EKHOLM, G. F.
1940   Prehistoric "lacquer" from Sinaloa. *Rev. Mex. Estud. Antr.*, 4: 10–15.
1942   Excavations at Guasave, Sinaloa, Mexico. *Amer. Mus. Natural Hist., Anthr. Papers*, vol. 38, pt. 2.

ELSON, B.
1947   The Homshuk: a Sierra Popoluca text. *Tlalocan*, 2: 193–214.

ENCISO, J.
1933   Pintura sobre madera en Michoacán y en Guerrero. *Mex. Folkways*, 8: 4–34.

ENGLEKIRK, J. E.
1957   El teatro folklórico hispanoamericano. *Folklore Amer.*, 17: 1–36.

ERASMUS, C. J.
1950   Current theories on incest prohibition in the light of ceremonial kinship. *Papers Kroeber Anthr. Soc.*, 2: 42–50.

ERIKSON, E.
1950   Childhood and society. New York.

EROSA P., I. R.
1932   El Kan Cah. Merida.

ESPINOSA RAMOS, A.
1949   El folklore literario de México. *Orientación Musical*, no. 89, pp. 5–7. Mexico.

ESPLENDOR DEL MÉXICO ANTIGUO
1959   Esplendor del México antiguo. C. Cook de Leonard, ed. 2 vols. Centro. Invest. Antr. Mex.

ESTRADA, G.
1937   El arte mexicano en España. *In* Enciclopedia ilustrada mexicana, no. 5. Mexico.

ESTUDIOS ANTROPOLÓGICOS
1956   Estudios antropológicos publicados en homenaje al doctor Manuel Gamio. Univ. Nac. Autónoma Mex., Soc. Mex. Antr.

EWALD, R. H.
1954   San Antonio Sacatepéquez: culture change in a Guatemalan community. Doctoral dissertation, Univ. Michigan.
1957a   San Antonio Sacatepéquez: 1932–53. *In* R. N. Adams, 1957b, pp. 18–22.
1957b   San Antonio Sacatepéquez: culture change in a Guatemalan community. *Social Forces*, 36: 160–65.

EZELL, P. H.
1955   Indians under the law: Mexico, 1821–1847. *Amer. Indig.*, 15: 199–214.

FÁBILA, A.
1940   Las tribus yaquis de Sonora: su cultura y anhelada autodeterminación. Dept. Asunto Indígenas. Mexico.
1959   Los Huicholes de Jalisco. *Inst. Nac. Indig.*, Pub. 2. Mexico.

—— AND G. FÁBILA
1951   México: ensayo socioeconómico del estado. 2 vols. Mexico.

——, ——, M. MESA ANDRACA, AND O. SOBERÓN M.
1955   Tlaxcala: tenencia y aprovechamiento de la tierra. Centro Invest. Agrarias. Mexico.

FALCÓN, E.
1949   La venta del cochino, leyenda yucateca. *Yikal Maya Than*, 10 (116–17): 47–48.

FELIPE SEGUNDO
1573   Ordenanzas para descubrimientos, nuevas poblaciones y pacificaciones. MS.

FERNÁNDEZ, J., AND V. T. MENDOZA
1941   Danzas de los concheros de San Miguel de Allende, Mexico. Mexico.

FERNÁNDEZ, M. A.
1925   El juego de pelota de Chichen-Itza, Yucatan. *An. Mus. Nac. Arqueol. Hist. Etnog.*, 1: 363–72.

FERNÁNDEZ DE CÓRDOBA, J.
1944   Tres impresos en lengua tarasco del siglo XIX. Mexico.

FERRERA, J.
1920   Pequeña gramática y diccionario de

la lengua tarahumara. Reproduced in Radin, 1931.

FESTINGER, L.
1957 A theory of cognitive dissonance. Evanston.

FISHBURNE, J. H.
1962 Courtship and marriage in Zinacantan. Honors thesis, Radcliffe College.

FISHER, G.
1953 Directed culture change in Nayarit, Mexico. *Tulane Univ., Middle Amer. Research Inst.*, Pub. 17, pp. 65–176.

FLORES, E.
1950 Los braceros mexicanos en Wisconsin. *Trimestre Econ.*, 17: 23–80. Mexico.

FLORES RUIZ, E.
1954 El sumidero, la leyenda de los Chiapas (el marco, la leyenda, la historia). *Abside*, 18: 415–35. Mexico.

FORTÚN DE PONCE, J. E.
1957 La navidad en Bolivia. Ministerio de Educación, Depto. Folklore. La Paz.

FOSTER, G. M.
1940 Notes on the Popoluca of Vera Cruz. *Inst. Panamer. Geog. Hist.*, Pub. 51. Mexico.

1942 A primitive Mexican economy. *Monogr. Amer. Ethnol. Soc.*, 5: 1–115.

1943 The geographical, linguistic, and cultural position of the Popoluca of Vera Cruz. *Amer. Anthr.*, 45: 531–46.

1944 Nagualism in Mexico and Guatemala. *Acta Amer.*, 2: 85–103.

1945 Sierra Popoluca folklore and beliefs. *Univ. California Pub. Amer. Archaeol. Ethnol.*, 42: 177–250.

1948a Empire's children: the people of Tzintzuntzan. *Smithsonian Inst., Inst. Social Anthr.*, Pub. 6.

1948b Some implications of modern Mexican mold-made pottery. *SW. Jour. Anthr.*, 4: 356–70.

1948c The folk economy of rural Mexico with special reference to marketing. *Jour. Marketing*, 13: 153–62.

1949 Sierra Popoluca kinship terminology and its wider relationships. *SW. Jour. Anthr.*, 5: 330–34.

1950 Mexican and Central American Indian folklore. *In* Standard dictionary of folklore, mythology, and legend, M. Leach, ed., 2: 711–16.

1951 Some wider implications of soul-loss illness among the Sierra Popoluca. *In* Homenaje Caso, pp. 167–74.

1953a Cofradía and compadrazgo in Spain and Spanish America. *SW. Jour. Anthr.*, 9: 1–28.

1953b Relationships between Spanish and Spanish-American folk medicine. *Jour. Amer. Folklore*, 66: 201–17.

1953c What is folk culture? *Amer. Anthr.*, 55: 159–73.

1955 Contemporary pottery techniques in southern and central Mexico. *Tulane Univ., Middle Amer. Research Inst.*, Pub. 22, pp. 1–48.

1959a The Coyotepec *molde* and some associated problems of the potter's wheel. *SW. Jour. Anthr.*, 15: 53–63.

1959b The potter's wheel: an analysis of idea and artifact in invention. *Ibid.*, 15: 99–119.

1960a Culture and conquest: America's Spanish heritage. *Viking Fund Pub. Anthr.*, no. 27.

1960b Archaeological implications of the modern pottery of Acatlan, Puebla, Mexico. *Amer. Antiquity*, 26: 205–14.

1961a The dyadic contract: a model for the social structure of a Mexican peasant village. *Amer. Anthr.*, 63: 1173–92.

1961b Traditional cultures and the impact of technological change. New York.

FOSTER, M. L., AND G. M. FOSTER
1948 Sierra Popoluca speech. *Smithsonian Inst., Inst. Soc. Anthr.*, Pub. 8.

FRIAS, D. V.
1907 Foc-lor de los pueblos de San Bartolome Aguascalientes. Nicolas León.

FRIEDRICH, P. W.
1958 A Tarascan *cacicazgo*: structure and function. *Amer. Ethnol. Soc.*, Proc. annual spring meeting, pp. 23–29.

FUENTE, J. DE LA
See De la Fuente, J.

FUENTES Y GUZMÁN, F. A. DE
1932–33 Recordación florida. *Bibliotheca Goathemala*, vols. 6–8.

GAMIO, M.
1922 La población del Valle de Teotihuacán. 2 vols. Sec. Agricultura y Fomento, Dirección Antr. Mexico.

1930a The Mexican immigrant: his life story. Chicago.

1930b The Mexican immigrant in the United States: a study in human migration and adjustment. Chicago.

1937a Cultural patterns in modern Mexico. *Pan Amer. Inst. Geog. Hist., Proc. 2d General Assembly* (1935). Washington.

1937b La importancia del folklore yaqui. *Mex. Folkways,* July, pp. 45–51.

1939 El índice cultural y el biotipo. *Quar. Inter-Amer. Relations,* April.

1942a Consideraciones sobre el problema indígena de América. *Amer. Indig.,* 2 (2): 17–24.

1942b Las características culturales y los censos indígenas. *Ibid.,* 2 (3): 15–19.

1946 La identificación del indio. *Ibid.,* 6: 99–103.

———, F. González de Cossío, and others
1958 Legislación indígena de México. *Inst. Indig. Interamer.,* Ed. Especiales, no. 38.

Gámiz, E.
1948 Monografía de la nación tepehuana que habita en la región sur del estado de Durango. Mexico.

Gann, T. W. F.
1917 The chachac or rain ceremony as practiced by the Maya of southern Yucatan and northern British Honduras. *Proc. 19th Int. Cong. Amer.,* pp. 409–18.

1918 The Maya Indians of southern Yucatan and northern British Honduras. *Smithsonian Inst., Bur. Amer. Ethnol.,* Bull. 64.

——— and J. E. S. Thompson
1931 The history of the Maya from the earliest times to the present day. New York.

Gante, C. de
1921 Narraciones tlaxcaltecas. 2 vols. Puebla.

Gante, P. de
n.d. Cartas de Fr. Pedro de Gante, O.F.M., primer educador de América. Comp. by Fr. Fidel de Chauvet, O.F.M. Printed by Fr. Junipero Serra, Provincia del Santo Evangelio de México.

García A., J. L.
1942 Leyendas indígenas de Guatemala. Guatemala.

García de Palacio, D.
1860 Collection of rare and original documents and relations, concerning the discovery and conquest of America. No. 1. Ed. by E. G. Squier. Albany.

García Payón, J.
1942 Interpretación de la vida de los pueblos matlatzincas. *El Mex. Antiguo,* 6: 73–90.

García Pérez, A.
1863 Descripción de la ciudad de Uruapan .... *Bol. Soc. Mex. Geog. Estad.,* 1a ep., 10: 469–77.

Garibay K., A. M.
1953 Historia de la literatura náhuatl (primera parte). Etapa Autónoma, de c. 1430 a 1521. Mexico.

1957 Supervivencias de cultura intelectual precolombina entre los Otomies de Huizquilucan, estado de México. *Amer. Indig.,* 17: 319–33.

Gates, W. E.
1924 The William Gates collection. *Amer. Art Assoc.* New York.

Gay, J.
1881 Historia de Oaxaca. 2 vols. Mexico.

Gerhard, P.
1964 Emperor's dye of the Mixtecs. *Natural Hist.,* 73: 26–31.

Gessain, R.
1953 Les indiens tepehuas de Huehuetla. *In* Huastecos, Totonacos, pp. 187–212.

Gibson, C.
1952 Tlaxcala in the sixteenth century. *Yale Hist. Pub.,* Miscellany, no. 56.

1955 The transformation of the Indian community in New Spain, 1500–1810. *Jour. World Hist.,* 2: 581–601.

1959 The Aztec aristocracy in colonial Mexico. *Comparative Studies in Soc. and Hist.,* 2: 169–196.

Gillin, J.
1948 Magical fright. *Psychiatry,* 11: 387–400.

1951 The culture of security in San Carlos: a study of a Guatemalan community of Indians and Ladinos. *Tulane Univ., Middle Amer. Research Inst.,* Pub. 16.

1952 Ethos and cultural aspects of personality. *In* Tax, 1952a, pp. 193–224.

1958   San Luis Jilotepeque. Seminario de Integración Social Guatemalteca.

GIRARD, R.
1944   El baile de los gigantes. *An. Soc. Geog. Hist. Guatemala*, 19: 427–45.

GLADWIN, H. S., E. W. HAURY, E. B. SAYLES, AND N. GLADWIN
1937   Excavations at Snaketown: material culture. *Medallion Papers*, no. 25.

GOLDSCHMIDT, W. R.
1952   The interrelations between cultural factors and the acquisition of new technical skills. *In* Hoselitz, 1952, pp. 135–51.

GÓMEZ, E. A.
1944   El Popol Vuh. Mexico.

GÓMEZ-MAILLEFERT, E. M.
1923   Folk-lore de Oaxaca. *Jour. Amer. Folklore*, 36: 199–200.

GONZÁLEZ, M. N.
1954   Instituciones indígenas en México independiente. *In* Caso, 1954, pp. 113–69.

GONZÁLEZ CASANOVA, P.
1920   Cuento en mexicano de Milpa Alta, D. F. *Jour. Amer. Folklore*, 33: 25–27.
1928   El ciclo legendario del Tepoztecatl. *Mex. Folkways*, 4: 206–29.
1946   Cuentos indígenas. Univ. Nac. Autónoma Mex.

GONZÁLEZ OBREGÓN, L.
1952   Rebeliones indígenas y precursores de la independencia mexicana en los siglos 16, 17 y 18. 2d ed. Mexico.

GONZÁLEZ PEÑA, C.
1940   Historia de la literatura mexicana desde los orígenes hasta nuestros días. Mexico.

GONZÁLEZ ROSA, J. M.
1949   Morras o yucas. A la uñita. La mojiganga. Convite al aire. (Folklore.) *Rev. Archivo y Biblioteca Nac.*, 27: 357–64. Tegucigalpa.

GORDON, B. L.
1957   A domesticated, wax-producing scale insect kept by the Guaymí Indians of Panama. *Ethnos*, 22: 36–49.

GORDON, G. B.
1915   Guatemala myths. *Mus. Jour., Univ. Pennsylvania*, 6: 103–44.

GOUBAUD CARRERA, A.
1935   El "Guajxaquip báts"—ceremonia calendárica indígena. *An. Soc. Geog. Hist. Guatemala*, 12: 39–50.
1945   Discurso pronunciado en la inauguración del Instituto Indigenista Nacional de Guatemala. *Bol. Indig.*, 5: 372–86.
1948   Some aspects of the character structure of the Guatemala Indians. *Amer. Indig.*, 8: 95–105.
1949a   Notes on the Indians of the finca Nueva Granada. *Univ. Chicago, Micro. Coll. MSS Middle Amer. Cult. Anthr.*, no. 21.
1949b   Notes on the Indians of eastern Guatemala. *Ibid.*, no. 22.
1949c   Notes on San Juan Chamelco, Alta Verapaz. *Ibid.*, no. 23.
1952   Indian adjustments to modern national culture. *In* Tax, 1952b, pp. 244–48.

——, J. DE DÍOS ROSALES, AND S. TAX
1947   Reconnaissance of northern Guatemala, 1944. *Univ. Chicago, Micro. Coll. MSS Middle Amer. Cult. Anthr.*, no. 17.

GRASSERIE, R. DE LA
  see La Grasserie, R. de.

GRIFFIN, J. B.
1949   Meso-America and the southeast. *In* The Florida Indian and his neighbors, J. W. Griffin, ed., pp. 77–97.

GRIFFIN, W. B.
1959   Notes on Seri Indian culture, Sonora, Mexico, *Univ. Florida, School Inter-Amer. Studies, Latin Amer. Monogr.*, no. 10.

GRIMES, J. E.
1959   Huichol tone and intonation. *Int. Jour. Amer. Ling.*, 25: 221–32.
1961   Huichol economics. *Amer. Indig.*, 21: 280–306.

—— AND B. F. GRIMES
1962   Semantic distinctions in Huichol (Uto-Aztecan) kinship. *Amer. Anthr.*, 64: 104–14.

GROPP, A. E.
1934   Manuscripts in the Department of Middle American Research. *Tulane Univ., Middle Amer. Research Inst.*, Pub. 5.

GROSSMAN, F. E.
1871   The Pima Indians of Arizona. *Smithsonian Inst.*, ann. rept. Bound in *Anthr. Pamphlets*, 19: 407–19.

GRUENING, E.
1928   Mexico and its heritage. New York.

GUATEMALA, DIRECCIÓN GENERAL DE ESTADÍSTICA

1957 Sexto censo general de población, Abril 18 de 1950.

GUATEMALA, MINISTERIO DE EDUCACIÓN PÚBLICA

1960a Memoria de labores realizadas por la Dirección General de Desarrollo Socio-Educativo Rural durante en año de 1959.

1960b Prospecto de los cursos de profesionalización para maestros rurales empíricos en servicio.

1960c Extracto del proyecto piloto de nutrición y horticultura.

1960d Plan del trabajo de la Dirección General de Desarrollo Socio-Educativo Rural para el año de 1960.

GUDSCHINSKY, S. C.

1959 Proto-Popotecan. *Int. Jour. Amer. Ling.*, Mem. 15.

GUERRERO, R. G.

1944 El hombre y la mujer. *Tlalocan*, 1: 253–58.

GUERRERO C., J. N.

1955 Historia de los ejidos de Boaco. *Nicaragua Indig.*, 2 ep., no. 7, pp. 33–39.

1956 El pueblo extranjero. Monografía de Chontales. Managua.

GUITERAS HOLMES, C.

n.d.,*a* World view and belief system. *In* World view in San Pedro Chenalho.

n.d.,*b* Background of a changing kinship system among the Tzotzil Indians of Chiapas. MS.

1946a Informe de Cancuc. *Univ. Chicago, Micro. Coll. MSS Middle Amer. Cult. Anthr.*, no. 8.

1946b Informe de San Pedro Chenalhó. *Ibid.*, no. 14.

1947 Clanes y sistema de parentesco de Cancuc. *Acta Amer.*, 5: 1–17.

1948a Organización social de tzeltales y tzotziles, México. *Amer. Indig.*, 8: 45–62.

1948b Sistema de parentesco huasteco. *Acta Amer.*, 6: 152–72.

1951 El calpulli de San Pablo Chalchihuitan. *In* Homenaje Caso, pp. 199–206.

1952a Sayula. Soc. Mex. Geog. Estadística. Mexico.

1952b Social organization. *In* Tax, 1952a, pp. 97–118.

1960 La familia Tzotzil. *Tlatoani*, no. 13.

1961 Perils of the soul: the world view of a Tzotzil Indian. Univ. Chicago Press.

HALE, K.

1958 Internal diversity in Uto-Aztecan: I. *Int. Jour. Amer. Ling.*, 24: 101–07.

HAMP, E. P.

1963 *Discussion and criticism of* Aboriginal languages of Latin America, S. Tax, ed. *Current Anthr.*, 4: 317.

HANDBOOK OF AMERICAN INDIANS NORTH OF MEXICO

1907 Handbook of American Indians north of Mexico. F. W. Hodge, ed. 2 vols. *Smithsonian Inst., Bur. Amer. Ethnol.*, Bull. 30.

HANDBOOK OF SOUTH AMERICAN INDIANS

1946–59 Handbook of South American Indians. J. H. Steward, ed. 7 vols. *Ibid.*, Bull. 143.

HANKE, L.

1949 The Spanish struggle for justice in the conquest of America. Philadelphia.

1959 Aristotle and the American Indian. Chicago.

HANSEN, A. T.

1934 The ecology of a Latin American city. *In* Reuter, 1934, pp. 124–42.

HARO, J.

1944 Un poco de folklore del istmo. *Anuario Soc. Folklórica Mex.*, 5: 255–73.

HARRIS, M.

1946 An introduction to the Chontal of Tabasco, Mexico. *Amer. Indig.*, 6: 247–55.

1959 Caste, class, and minority. *Social Forces*, 37: 248–54.

HARRISON, W. R.

1952 The mason: a Zoque text. *Tlalocan*, 3: 193–204.

HARTMAN, C. V.

1907 Mythology of the Aztecs of Salvador. *Jour. Amer. Folklore*, 20: 143–50.

1910 Le calebassier de l'Amérique tropicale (*Crescentia*): étude d'ethnobotanique. *Jour. Soc. Amer. Paris*, n.s., 7: 131–43.

HASSLER, J.

n.d. Las formas de salutación en el Pipil del golfo. MS.

HAY, C. L., ed.

1940 *See* The Maya and their neighbors.

HENDRICHS PÉREZ, P. R.

1939 Un estudio preliminar sobre la lengua cuitlateca de San Miguel Totalapan, Gro. *El Mex. Antiguo*, 4: 329–62.

1945 Por tierras ignotas: viajes y observaciones en la región del Rio de las Balsas. Vol. 1. Mexico.

1946 *Idem*, vol. 2.

HENESTROSA, A.

1936a Vini-gunday-zaa. *Neza*, 2 (10): 1–6. Mexico.

1936b Niza-Rindani. *Ibid.*, 2 (14): 1–4.

HENNING, P.

1911 Los Otomies del distrito de Lerma. *An. Mus. Nac.*, 3 (3a): 58–85. Mexico.

HERMITTE, E.

1958–60 Field notes of Pinola. MS, Chiapas Project files, Univ. Chicago, Dept. Anthropology.

HERNÁNDEZ, F.

1959 Historia natural de Nueva España. *Obras completas*, vols. 2, 3. Univ. Nac. Mex.

HERNÁNDEZ, F. J.

1946 Holidays and festivals in Mexico. Pan Amer. Union, Travel Division. Washington.

HERNÁNDEZ, P. M.

1905 De los primeros habitantes de la venturosa yucateca. Merida.

HERNÁNDEZ MORENO, J., AND S. NAHMAD

1961 La política económica del estado como factor del desarrollo social regional. *Rev. Mex. Sociol.*, 23: 147–68.

HERRARTE, A.

1955 La unión de Centroamerica: tragedias y esperanza. Guatemala.

HERRERA, A.

1884 El aje. *Naturaleza*, 6: 198–200.

HERRERA Y GUTIÉRREZ, M.

1890 La dolomía del distrito de Uruapan. *Mem. Soc. Cien. Antonio Alzate*, vol. 3.

1891 *Idem. Naturaleza*, 2d ser., 1: 397–99.

HERSKOVITS, M.

1938 Acculturation: the study of cultural contact. New York.

HEWES, L.

1935 Huapec: an agricultural village of Sonora, Mexico. *Econ. Geog.*, 11: 284–92.

HILL, A. F.

1952 Economic botany. 2d ed. New York.

HILTON, K.

1948 Raramuri oseríame: cuentos de los Tarahumaras. Summer Inst. Ling. Mexico.

HINTON, T.

1961 The village hierarchy as a factor in Cora Indian acculturation. Doctoral dissertation, Univ. California.

HOLLAND, W. R.

1963a Medicina maya en los altos de Chiapas. *Inst. Nac. Indig., Col. Antr. Social*, no. 2.

1963b Psicoterapia maya en los altos de Chiapas. *Estud. Cultura Maya*, 3: 261–77.

HOLLERAN, M. P.

1949 Church and state in Guatemala. New York.

HOMENAJE CASO

1951 Homenaje al Doctor Alfonso Caso. Nuevo Mundo. Mexico.

HOOGSHAGEN, S. A., AND W. R. MERRIFIELD

1961 Coatlan Mixe kinship. *SW. Jour. Anthr.*, 17:219–25.

HOOVER, J. W.

1935 Generic descent of the Papago villages. *Amer. Anthr.*, 37: 445–64.

HORCASITAS PIMENTEL, F.

1949 Piezas teatrales en lengua Náhuatl: bibliografía descriptiva. *Bol. Bibliográfico Antr. Amer.*, 11: 154–64.

HOSELITZ, B., ed.

1952 The progress of underdeveloped areas. Chicago.

HOTCHKISS, J.

1959 A summary of Chanal, Teopisca and San Bartolome. Working paper. Chicago.

1960–61 Field notes of Teopisca. MS, Chiapas Project files. Univ. Chicago, Dept. Anthropology.

HOWENSTINE, W.

1963 Lecture. Chicago Teachers' College North. MS.

HOYT, E. E.

1951 Want development in undeveloped areas (Guatemala). *Jour. Polit. Econ.*, 59: 194–202.

1955 El trabajador indígena en las fincas cafeteleras de Guatemala. *Cien. Sociales*, 6 (35): 258–68.

HRDLIČKA, A.

1903 The region of the ancient Chichimecs, with notes on the Tepecanos and the ruin of La Quemada, Mexico. *Amer. Anthr.*, 5: 385–440.

HUASTECOS, TOTONACOS Y SUS VECINOS

1953 Huastecos, Totonacos y sus vecinos. I. Bernal and E. Dávalos Hurtado, eds. *Rev. Mex. Estud. Antr.*, vol. 13, nos. 2 and 3.

HUGHES, L. H.
1950 The Mexican cultural mission programme. *Monogr. Fundamental Education,* no. 3. UNESCO, Paris.

HUMBOLDT, A. VON
1814 Researches concerning the institutions and monuments of the ancient inhabitants of America. Tr. by H. M. Williams. London.

HUNT, M. E.
1962 The dynamics of the domestic group in two Tzeltal villages: a contrastive comparison. Doctoral dissertation, Univ. Chicago.
1963 The family and domestic group in the highlands of Chiapas. MS, Chiapas Project files. Univ. Chicago, Dept. Anthropology.

HUNTER, W. A.
1960 The Calderonian auto sacramental *El gran teatro del mundo:* an edition and translation of a Nahuatl version. *Tulane Univ., Middle Amer. Research Inst.,* Pub. 27, pp. 105–202.

IBARRA, A.
1941 Cuentos y leyendas. Mexico.
1942 Juegos y deportes en México. *Anuario Soc. Folklórica Mex.* (1938–40), 1: 41–49.

IMENDIA, C. A.
1951 Del folklore salvadoreño: la canoa blanca. *An. Mus. Nac. David J. Guzmán,* 2 (8): 89–91. San Salvador.

INSTITUTO INDIGENISTA INTERAMERICANO
1958 Recientes datos estadísticos sobre la población de América. *Bol. Indig.,* 18: 6–7. Mexico.
1960 Guatemala: informe del Instituto Indigenista Nacional, 1959. *Ibid.,* 20: 119–32.

INSTITUTO INDIGENISTA NACIONAL DE GUATEMALA
n.d. Monograph series: Chuarrancho, no. 2; San Juan Sacatepequez, no. 3; Parramos, no. 5; San Antonio Aguas Calientes, no. 6; Santa Catarina Barahona, no. 7; Santo Domingo Xenacoi, no. 8; San Bartolome Milpas Altas, no. 9.

INSTITUTO INTERAMERICANO DE ESTADÍSTICA, UNIÓN PANAMERICANA
1960 La estructura demográfica de las naciones americanas. *País de nacimiento, nacionalidad y lengua, características generales de la población,* 1: 3. Washington.

INSTITUTO NACIONAL INDIGENISTA (MEXICO)
n.d. Memoirs, no. 1.
1955 ¿Que es el I.N.I.?

INSTITUTO NACIONAL INDIGENISTA (NICARAGUA)
1947 *Nicaragua Indígena,* vol. 1, nos. 4–6. Managua.

INTEGRACIÓN SOCIAL
1956 Integración social en Guatemala. Seminario de Integración Social. Guatemala.

INTERNATIONAL LABOR OFFICE
1953 Indigenous peoples. Geneva.

JENKINS, J.
1946 San Gregorio, an Otomi village of the highlands of Hidalgo, Mexico. *Amer. Indig.,* 6: 345–49.

JENKINS, K. D.
1964 Aje or ni-in (the fat of a scale insect): painting medium and unguent. *Actas y Mem., 35th Int. Cong. Amer.,* 1: 625–36.

JIMÉNEZ MORENO, W.
1956 La conquista: choque y fusión de dos mundos. *Hist. Mex.,* 6: 1–8. Mexico.
1958 The Indians of America and Christianity. *Americas,* 14 (4): 75–95.

—— AND S. MATEOS HIGUERA
1940 Códice de Yanhuitlan. *Inst. Nac. Antr. Hist.* Mexico.

JIMÉNEZ RUEDA, J.
1950 Historia de la cultura en México: el virrienato. Ediciones cultura. Mexico.
1951 *Idem,* 2d ed.

JOHNSON, F.
1940 The linguistic map of Central America. *In* The Maya and their neighbors, pp. 88–114.

JOHNSON, I. W.
1936 A Chinantec calendar. *Amer. Anthr.,* 38: 197–201.
1953 El quechquemitl y el huipil. *In* Huastecos, Totonacos, pp. 241–57.
1957 Survival of feather ornamented huipiles in Chiapas, Mexico. *Jour. Soc. Amer. Paris,* n.s., 46: 189–96.
1958 Twine-plaiting in the New World. *Proc. 32d Int. Cong. Amer.,* pp. 198–213.

—— AND J. B. JOHNSON
1939 Un cuento mazateco popoloca. *Rev. Mex. Estud. Antr.,* 3: 217–26.

JOHNSON, J. B.
1939a Some notes on the Mazatec. *Ibid.,* 3: 142–56.

1939b The elements of Mazatec witchcraft. *Ethnol. Studies*, 9: 128–50. Goteborg.

1940 Three Mexican tar baby stories. *Jour. Amer. Folklore*, 53: 215–17.

1950 The Opata, an inland tribe of Sonora. *Univ. New Mexico Pub. Anthr.*, no. 6.

JONES, C. L.
1940 Guatemala, past and present. Univ. Minnesota Press.

JOSEPH, A., R. B. SPICER, AND J. CHESKY
1949 The desert people: a study of the Papago Indians. Univ. Chicago Press.

JOYCE, T. A.
1929 Report on the British Museum expedition to British Honduras. *Jour. Royal Anthr. Inst.*, 59: 439–59.

KAMAR AL-SHIMAS
1922 The Mexican southland. Fowler, Indiana.

KAPLAN, B. A.
1951 Changing functions of the Hunancha dance at the Corpus Christi festival in Paracho, Michoacan, Mexico. *Jour. Amer. Folklore*, 64: 383–92.

1953 Technological and social change: Paracho, a case in point. Doctoral dissertation, Univ. Chicago.

1960 Mechanization in Paracho, a craft community. *In* Leslie, 1960b, pp. 59–65.

KELLER, K., AND M. HARRIS
1946 Masculine crab and mosquitoes. *Tlalocan*, 2: 138–40.

KELLY, I. T.
1943 Notes on a west coast survival of the ancient Mexican ball game. *Carnegie Inst. Wash., Notes Middle Amer. Archaeol. Ethnol.*, no. 26.

1944 Worked gourds from Jalisco. *Ibid.*, no. 43.

1947 Excavations at Apatzingan, Michoacan. *Viking Fund. Pub. Anthr.*, no. 7.

1953 The modern Totonac. *In* Huastecos, Totonacos, pp. 175–86.

1965 Folk practices in north Mexico. *Inst. Latin Amer. Studies, Latin Amer. Monogr.*, no. 2.

——— AND A. PALERM
1952 The Tajin Totonac. Part 1: History, subsistence, shelter and technology. *Smithsonian Inst., Inst. Social Anthr.*, Pub. 13.

KELMAN, H.
1958 Compliance, identification and internalization: three processes of attitude change. *Jour. Conflict Resolution*, 2: 51–60.

KENT, K. P.
1957 The cultivation and weaving of cotton in the prehistoric southwestern United States. *Trans. Amer. Phil. Soc.*, n.s., 47: 457–732.

KIDDER, A. V., J. D. JENNINGS, AND E. M. SHOOK
1946 Excavations at Kaminaljuyu, Guatemala. With technological notes by A. O. Shepard. *Carnegie Inst. Wash.*, Pub. 561.

KIDDLE, L. B.
1944 The Spanish word *jícara*: a word history with an appendix on the manufacture of *jícaras* in Olinala, Guerrero. *Tulane Univ., Middle Amer. Research Inst., Philol. and Doc. Studies*, vol. 1, no. 4.

KINGSBOROUGH, E. K.
1831–48 Antiquities of Mexico. 9 vols. Mexico.

KIRCHHOFF, P.
1943 Mesoamérica: sus límites geográficos, composición étnica y caracteres culturales. *Acta Amer.*, 1: 92–107.

1944 Los recolectores-cazadores del norte de México. *In* El Norte de Mexico, pp. 133–44.

1955 The principles of clanship in human society. *Davidson Jour. Anthr.*, 1: 1–10.

1956a Land tenure in ancient Mexico: a preliminary sketch. *Rev. Mex. Estud. Antr.*, 14: 351–61.

1956b La relación de Michoacán como fuente para la historia de la sociedad y cultura Tarascas. *In* Relación de las ceremonias y ritos y población y gobierno de los Indios de la provincia de Michoacan (1541). Madrid.

KIRSTEIN, L.
1935 Dance: a short history of classical theatrical dancing. New York.

KLINEBERG, O.
1934 Notes on the Huichol. *Amer. Anthr.*, 36: 446–60.

1952 Raza y psicología: la cuestión racial ante la ciencia. UNESCO, Paris.

KLUCKHOHN, F. R., AND F. L. STRODTBECK
1961 Variations in value orientations. New York.

KRETZENBACHER, L.
1952 Folk songs in the folk plays of the Austrian alpine regions. *Jour. Int. Folk Music Council,* 4: 45–49. London.

KRICKEBERG, W.
1918 Die Totonaken: ein Beitrag zur historischen Ethnographie Mittelamerikas. *Baessler Archiv,* 7: 1–55.
1933 Los Totonaca. Tr. from the German by Porfirio Aguirre. *Pub. Mus. Nac.* Mexico.
1948 Das mittelamerikanische Ballspiel und seine religiöse Symbolik. *Paideuma, Mitteilungen zur Kultur-Kunde,* 3 (3–5): 118–90.
1956 Altmexikanische Kulturen. Berlin.

KROEBER, A. L.
1931 The Seri. *SW. Mus. Papers,* no. 6.
1934 Uto-Aztecan languages of Mexico. *Ibero-Amer.,* no. 8.
1940 Summary. *In* The Maya and their neighbors, pp. 460–87.
1952 The nature of culture. Univ. Chicago Press.
1958 Cultural and natural areas of native North America. Univ. California Press.

KUBLER, G.
1948 Mexican architecture of the sixteenth century. 2 vols. New Haven.

KUNST, J.
1915 Some animal fables of the Chuh Indians. *Jour. Amer. Folklore,* 28: 353–57.

KURATH, G. P.
1946 Los Concheros. *Ibid.,* 59: 387–99.
1947 Los arrieros of Acopilco, Mexico. *Western Folklore,* 6: 232–36.
1949 Mexican moriscas. *Jour. Amer. Folklore,* 62: 87–106.
1950 Penitentes. *In* Standard dictionary of folklore, mythology, and legend, M. Leach, ed., 2: 851–52.
1952 Dance acculturation. *In* Tax, 1952a, pp. 233–42.
1956 Dance relatives of mid-Europe and Middle America. *Jour. Amer. Folklore,* 69: 286–98.
1958 La transculturación en la danza hispano-americana. *Folklore Amer.,* 18 (2): 17–25. Coral Gables.
1960 The sena'asom rattle of the Yaqui Indian pascolas. *Ethnomusicology,* 4: 60–62.
1963 Stylistic blends in Afro-American dance cults of Catholic origin.

Papers Michigan Acad. Sci. Arts Letters, 18: 577–84.
—— AND S. MARTÍ
1964 Dances of Anahuac. *Viking Fund. Pub. Anthr.,* no. 38.

LAFARGE, O.
1928 The ceremonial year at Jacaltenango. *Proc. 23d Int. Cong. Amer.,* pp. 656–60.
1940 Maya ethnology: the sequence of cultures. *In* The Maya and their neighbors, pp. 281–91.
1947 Santa Eulalia: the religion of a Cuchumatan Indian town. Univ. Chicago Press.
—— AND D. BYERS
1931 The year bearer's people. *Tulane Univ., Middle Amer. Research Inst., Pub.* 3.

LA GRASSERIE, R. DE
1896 Langue tarasque. *Bibliothèque Linguistique Amer.,* vol. 19. Paris.
1898 Langue zoque et langue mixe. Paris.

LANDA, D. DE
1938 Relación de las cosas de Yucatan (1566). Ed. Pérez Martínez. Merida.
1941 Landa's Relación de las cosas de Yucatan. Tr. and ed. with notes by A. M. Tozzer. *Papers Peabody Mus., Harvard Univ.,* vol. 18.
1959 Relación de las cosas de Yucatan. Intro. por A. M. Garibay K., con un apéndice en el que se publican varios documentos importantes y cartas del autor. 8th ed., Porrúa. Mexico.

LANKS, H. C.
1938 Otomi Indians, Mezquital Valley, Hidalgo. *Econ. Geog.,* 14: 184–94.

LARDÉ Y LARÍN, J.
1952 Guía histórica de El Salvador. *Biblioteca de Pueblo,* no. 13. San Salvador.
1953 La población de El Salvador: su origen y su distribución geográfica. *An. Mus. Nac. David J. Guzmán,* vol. 4, no. 12. San Salvador.

LARSEN, H.
1937 The Mexican Indian flying pole dance. *Nat. Geog.,* 71: 387–400.

LARSON, R.
1953 Proclíticos pronominales del dialecto huasteco que se habla en el estado de San Luis Potosí. *In* Huastecos, Totonacos, pp. 117–18.

LAUGHLIN, R. M.
1962a Through the looking glass: reflections on Zinacantan courtship and marriage. Doctoral dissertation, Harvard Univ.
1962b El símbolo de la flor en la religión de Zinacantan. *Estud. Cultura Maya,* 2: 123–39.

LAW, H. W.
1957 Tamakasti: a gulf Nahuatl text: *Tlalocan,* 3: 344–60.

LAZO DE LA VEGA, L.
1956 The miraculous apparition of the beloved Virgin Mary, our lady of Guadalupe, at Tepeyacac, near Mexico City. *In* Demarest and Taylor, 1956, pp. 39–53.

LEACH, E.
1954 Political systems of highland Burma. London.

LECHE, S. M., H. N. GOULD, AND D. THORP
1944 Dermatoglyphics and functional lateral dominance in Mexican Indians. Part 5: The Zinacantecs, Huixtecs, Amatenangos and finca Tzeltals. *Tulane Univ., Middle Amer. Research Inst., Middle Amer. Research Records,* 1: 21–64.

LEGTERS, D. B.
1937 The story of a hunter. *Invest. Ling.,* 4: 302–05.

LEHMANN, W.
1906 Traditions des anciens Mexicains: texte inédit et original en langue Nahuatl avec traduction en Latin. *Jour. Soc. Amer. Paris,* 3: 239–97.
1928 Ergebnisse einer mit Unterstützung der Notgemeinschaft der Deutschen Wissenschaft in den Jahren 1925/ 1926 ausgeführten Forschungsreise nach Mexiko und Guatemala. *Anthropos,* 23: 747–91.

LEHMANN-NITSCHE, R.
1926 Mitología centroamericana. *An. Soc. Geog. Hist. Guatemala,* 2: 408–14.

LEKIS, L.
1958 Folk dances of Latin America. New York.

LEMLEY, H. V.
1949 Three Tlapaneco stories from Tlacoapa, Guerrero. *Tlalocan,* 3: 76–82.

LEÓN, F. DE P.
1939 Los esmaltes de Uruapan. Departmento Autónoma de Prensa y Publicidad. Mexico.

LEÓN, N.
1901 Lyobaa o Mictlan. Mexico.
1902 Carta lingüística de México. Mus. Nac. Mexico.
1903 Los Tarascos, notas históricas, étnicas y antropológicas. *An. Mus. Nac.,* 11: 392–502.
1905 Los Popolocas. *Ibid.,* 12: 103–20.
1921 Supervivencias precolombinas: la pintura al aje de Uruapan. *Amer. Española,* 1: 332–39, 412–18.
1934 Los indios tarascos del lago de Pátzcuaro. *An. Mus. Nac. Arqueol. Hist. Etnog.,* ep. 5, 1: 149–69.

LEÓN-PORTILLA, M.
1956 La filosofía nahuatl, estudiada en sus fuentes. *Inst. Indig. Interamer.* (2d ed. 1959.)

LESLIE, C. M.
1960a Now we are civilized: a study of the world view of the Zapotec Indians of Mitla, Oaxaca. Wayne State Univ. Press.
1960b [ed.] The social anthropology of Middle America. *Alpha Kappa Deltan,* vol. 30, no. 1 (special issue).

LESSER, A.
1928 Bibliography of American folklore, 1915–1928. *Jour. Amer. Folklore,* 41: 1–60.

LEWIS, O.
1947 Wealth differences in a Mexican village. *Sci. Monthly,* 65: 127–32.
1949 Husbands and wives in a Mexican village: a study of role conflict. *Amer. Anthr.,* 51: 602–10.
1951 Life in a Mexican village: Tepoztlan restudied. Univ. Illinois Press.
1952 Urbanization without breakdown: a case study. *Sci. Monthly,* 75: 31–41.
1955 Medicine and politics in a Mexican village. *In* B. D. Paul, 1955, pp. 403–34.
1957 Urbanización sin desorganización: las familias tepoztecas en la ciudad de México. *Amer. Indig.,* 17: 231–46.
1958 México desde 1940. *Invest. Econ.,* vol. 18, no. 70. Mexico.
1959a The culture of the vecindad in Mexico City: two case studies. *In* Stone, 1959, pp. 387–402.
1959b Five families: Mexican case studies in the culture of poverty. New York.

1960 Tepoztlan, village in Mexico. New York.

1961a The children of Sanchez: autobiography of a Mexican family. New York.

1961b Mexico since Cárdenas. *In* Council on Foreign Relations, 1961, pp. 283–345.

—— AND E. E. MAES

1945 Base para una nueva definición práctica del Indio. *Amer. Indig.*, 5: 107–18.

LI CH'IAO-P'ING

1948 The chemical arts of old China. Easton.

LIEBAN, R. W.

1960 Sorcery, illness, and social control in a Philippine municipality. *SW. Jour. Anthr.*, 16: 127–43.

LINCOLN, J. S.

1946 An ethnological study of the Ixil Indians of the Guatemala highlands. *Univ. Chicago, Micro. Coll. MSS Middle Amer. Cult. Anthr.*, no. 1.

LINDZEY, G.

1961 Projective techniques and cross-cultural research. New York.

LINTON, R.

1936 The study of man. New York.

1940 Acculturation in seven American Indian tribes. New York.

LIPSCHÜTZ, A.

1944 El indio-americanismo y el problema racial en las Américas. 2d ed. Santiago, Chile.

LLAVE, P. DE LA

1832 Sobre el Axin, especie nueva de Coccus, y sobre la grasa que de él se extrae. *Registro Trimestre*, 1: 147–52. Mexico.

LÓPEZ RUIZ, M., AND M. MARTÍNEZ GRACIDA

1906 Ita Andehui: leyenda mixteca. Oaxaca.

LOTHROP, S. K.

1927a A note on Indian ceremonies in Guatemala. *Mus. Amer. Indian, Heye Found., Indian Notes*, vol. 4, no. 1.

1927b The potters of Guatajiagua, Salvador. *Ibid.*, 4: 109–18.

1928 Santiago Atitlan, Guatemala. *Ibid.*, vol. 5, no. 4.

1929a Christian and pagan in Guatemala. *Nation*, vol. 128, no. 3315 (Jan. 16).

1929b Further notes on Indian ceremonies in Guatemala. *Mus. Amer. Indian, Heye Found., Indian Notes*, vol. 6, no. 1.

1930 A modern survival of the ancient Maya calendar. *Proc. 23d Int. Cong. Amer.*, pp. 652–55.

LOWIE, R. H.

1956 The culture area concept as applied to North and South America. *Proc. 32d Int. Cong. Amer.*, pp. 73–78.

LUDEWIG, H. E.

1858 The literature of American aboriginal languages. London.

LUMHOLTZ, C.

1898 The Huichol Indians of Mexico. *Bull. Amer. Mus. Natural Hist.*, 5 (10): 1–14.

1902 Unknown Mexico. 2 vols. New York.

1907 Among the Tarahumaras: the American cave dwellers. *Scribner's Mag.*, July.

McAFEE, B.

1952 Danza de la gran conquista. *Tlalocan*, 3: 246–73.

McARTHUR, H. S.

1961 La estructura político-religiosa de Aguacatán. *Guatemala Indig.*, 1: 41–56.

McBRIDE, G. M.

1923 The land systems of Mexico. *Amer. Geog. Soc., Research Ser.*, no. 12.

McBRYDE, F. W.

1934 Solola, a Guatemalan town and Cakchiquel market-center. *Tulane Univ., Middle Amer. Research Inst.*, Pub. 5, pp. 45–152.

1943 The black lacquer mystery of the Guatemala Maya. *Sci. Monthly*, 57: 113–18.

1947 Cultural and historical geography of southwest Guatemala. *Smithsonian Inst., Inst. Social Anthr.*, Pub. 4.

McCLENDON, J. J. C.

1961 An ethnographic sketch of Topiltepec and Pochahuixco. MS.

McDOUGALL, E.

1947 Easter ceremonies at San Antonio Palopo, Guatemala. *Carnegie Inst. Wash., Notes Middle Amer. Archaeol. Ethnol.*, no. 81.

1955 Easter ceremonies at Santiago Atitlan in 1930. *Ibid.*, no. 123.

MACE, C.

1957 Collection of dances from Rabinal (Baja Verapaz), Guatemala. MS. Tulane Univ., Middle Amer. Research Inst.

McGee, W. J.
1898 The Seri Indians. *Smithsonian Inst., Bur. Amer. Ethnol.*, ann. rept., no. 17.

McIntosh, J. B.
1949 Cosmogonía huichol. *Tlalocan*, 3: 14–21.

—— and J. Grimes
1954 Niqui 'iquisicayara: vocabulario huichol-castellano, castellano-huichol. Mexico.

MacIver, R. M., and C. H. Page
1949 Society: an introductory analysis. New York.

McQuown, N. A.
1942 La fonémica de un dialecto olmeco-mexicano de la sierra norte de Pueblo. *El Mex. Antiguo*, 6: 61–72.
1955 The indigenous languages of Latin America. *Amer. Anthr.*, 57: 501–70.
1956 The classification of the Mayan languages. *Int. Jour. Amer. Ling.*, 22: 191–95.
1959 [ed.] Report on the 'Man-in-Nature' project of the department of anthropology of the University of Chicago in the Tzeltal-Tzotzil speaking region of the state of Chiapas, Mexico. Hectographed.

Madsen, C.
1966 A study of change in Mexican folk medicine. *Tulane Univ., Middle Amer. Research Inst.*, Pub. 25, pp. 89–138.

Madsen, W.
1955a Shamanism in Mexico. *SW. Jour. Anthr.*, 11: 48–57.
1955b Hot and cold in the universe of San Francisco Tecospa, valley of Mexico. *Jour. Amer. Folklore*, 68: 123–40.
1957 Christo-paganism: a study of Mexican religious syncretism. *Tulane Univ., Middle Amer. Research Inst.*, Pub. 19, pp. 105–80.
1960 The Virgin's children: life in an Aztec village today. Univ. Texas Press.

—— and C. Madsen
1948 The human birds of Papantla. *Travel Mag.*, 91: 24–28.

Mak, C.
1959 Mixtec medical beliefs and practices. *Amer. Indig.*, 19: 125–51.

Makemson, M. W.
1951 The book of the jaguar priest: a translation of the book of Chilam Balam of Tizimin. New York.

Malinowski, B., and J. de la Fuente
1957 La economía de un sistema de mercados en México. *Acta Anthr.*, ser. 2, vol. 1, no. 2. Mexico.

Mann, C. E.
1958 Ethnography of the lowland Mixe. Master's thesis, Mexico City College.

Manners, R. A.
1956 Functionalism, realpolitik and anthropology in underdeveloped areas. *Amer. Indig.*, 16: 7–33.

Maqueo Castellanos, E.
1936 El espectro de Guiengola: leyenda zapoteca. *Neza*, 2 (13): 4–7.

Marino Flores, A.
1956 Indígenas de México: algunas consideraciones demográficas. *Amer. Indig.*, 16: 41–48.

—— and A. Castro de la Fuente
1960 La población agrícola y la educación en la República Mexicana. *Inst. Nac. Antr. Hist.*, Pub. 4. Mexico.

Marroquín, A. D.
1954 Tlaxiaco: una ciudad mercado. *Inst. Nac. Indig.*, Ed. Mimeográficas, no. 4. Mexico.
1955 Factor económico y cambio social. *Amer. Indig.*, 15: 215–26.
1956 Consideraciones sobre el problema económico de la región Tzeltal-Tzotzil. *Ibid.*, 16: 191–203.

Martí, S.
1955 Instrumentos musicales precortesianos. *Inst. Nac. Antr. Hist.* Mexico.

Martin, N. F.
1957 Los vagabundos en la Nueva España en el siglo 16. Mexico.

Martínez, M.
1959 Plantas utiles de la flora mexicana. Ed. Botas. Mexico.

Martínez Gracida, M.
1898 Mitología mixteca. *Mem. y Rev. Soc. Cien. Antonio Alzate*, 11: 421–34.
1910 Civilización chontal: historia antigua de la Chontalpa oaxaquena. *Ibid.*, 30: 29–104, 223–325.

Martínez Hernández, J.
1909a Las crónicas mayas. Revisión y traducción del texto de las crónicas de Chicxulub, de Maní, de Tizimín, de Chumayel. MS. Biblioteca Cepada. Merida.

1909b El Chilam Balam de Maní. Códice Pérez. Merida.

1926 Crónicas mayas. La crónica de Yaxkukul. Merida.

1929 Diccionario de Motul. Merida.

MASON, J. A.

1912a The Tepehuan Indians of Azqueltan. Proc. 18th Int. Cong. Amer., pp. 344–51.

1912b The fiesta of the pinhole at Azqueltan (Tepehuan). Mus. Jour., Univ. Pennsylvania, 3 (3): 44–50.

1917 Tepecano, a Piman language of western Mexico. Ann. New York Acad. Sci., 25: 309–416.

1920 The Papago harvest festival. Amer. Anthr., 22: 13–25.

1921 The Papago migration legend. Jour. Amer. Folklore, 34: 254–68.

1936 Classification of the Sonoran languages. In Essays in anthropology, presented to A. L. Kroeber, pp. 183–98.

1940 The native languages of Middle America. In The Maya and their neighbors, pp. 52–87.

1948 The Tepehuan and other aborigines of the Mexican Sierra Madre Oriental. Sobretino Amer. Indig., 8: 289–300.

1950 The language of the Papago of Arizona. Univ. Pennsylvania, Mus. Monogr.

1952 Notes and observations on the Tepehuan. Amer. Indig., 12: 33–50.

—— AND A. M. ESPINOSA

1914 Folktales of the Tepecanos. Jour. Amer. Folklore, 27: 148–210.

MASON, O. T.

1904 Aboriginal American basketry: studies in a textile art without machinery. Smithsonian Inst., ann. rept. for year ending 1902, pp. 171–548.

MATEOS HIGUERA, S.

1930 Breve monografía y reglas del "patolli." Mexico.

MAYA AND THEIR NEIGHBORS, THE

1940 The Maya and their neighbors. C. L. Hay and others, eds. New York.

MAYAS ANTIGUOS, LOS

1941 Los Mayas antiguos: monografías de arqueología, etnografía y lingüística mayas, publicadas con motivo del centenario de la exploración de Yucatán por John L. Stephens y Frederick Catherwood en los años

1841–42. C. Lizardi Ramos, ed. Colegio de Mex. Mexico.

MAYER, M.

1958 Poconchi texts. Summer Inst. Ling. Norman.

MEADE, J.

1942 La Huasteca. Pub. Históricas "Editorial Cossio."

MEAVE, J. A. DE

1791 Memoria sobre la pintura del pueblo de Olinalan de la jurisdicción de Tlalpam dispuesta por su cura propietario y juez eclesiástico D. Joaquín Alejo de Meave. Gaceta de Literatura, 2: 173–178. Mexico.

1831 Idem. Gacetas de Literatura de Mex., 2: 213–20.

MECHAM, J. L.

1938 The origin of federalism in Mexico. Hisp. Amer. Hist. Rev., 18: 164–82.

MECHLING, W. H.

1912 Stories from Tuxtepec, Oaxaca. Jour. Amer. Folklore, 25: 199–203.

1916 Stories and songs from the southern Atlantic coastal region of Mexico. Ibid., 29: 547–58.

MEDELLÍN ZENIL, A.

1960 Cerámicas del Totonacapan. Univ. Veracruzana. Jalapa.

MEDINA, A.

1961 Informe preliminar sobre un paraje de Tenejapa. MS, Chiapas Project files, Univ. Chicago, Dept. Anthropology.

1961–62 Notas de campo y reportes sobre Tenejapa. Ibid.

MÉDIONI, G.

1952 L'art tarasque du Méxique occidental. Mexico.

MÉDIZ BOLIO, A.

1941 Literatura indígena moderna. Mexico.

MEIGS, P.

1939 The Kiliwa Indians of Lower California. Ibero-Amer., no. 15.

MENA, R.

1930 Educación intelectual y física entre los náhuas y mayas precolombinos. Mexico.

MENDELSON, E. M.

1956 Les Maya des hautes terres. Critique, 115: 1076–87. Paris. [Also in Seminario de Integración Social Guatemalteca, Cuad. 6.]

1958a The king, the traitor and the cross: an interpretation of a highland Maya religious conflict. *Diogenes,* 21: 1–10. Chicago.

1958b A Guatemalan sacred bundle. *Man,* 58 (art. 170): 121–26.

1959 Maximón: an iconographical introduction. *Ibid.,* 59 (art. 87): 57–60.

1965 Los escándalos de Maximón. *Seminario de Integración Social Guatemalteca.*

MENDIETA, G. DE

1870 Historia eclesiástica indiana, obra escrita a fines del siglo XVI . . . . Ed. García Icazbalceta. Mexico.

1945 *Idem.* 4 vols. Mexico.

MENDIETA Y NÚÑEZ, L., ed.

n.d. Los Tarascos: monografía histórica, etnográfica y económica. Inst. Invest. Sociales. Mexico.

1949 Los Zapotecos. Univ. Nac. Autónoma Mex.

MENDIZABAL, M. O. DE

1928 Influencia de la sal en la distribución geográfica de los grupos indígenas de México. Mus. Nac. Arqueol. Hist. Etnog. Mexico.

MENDNER, S.

1956 Das Ballspiel im Leben der Völker. Münster.

MENDOZA, V. T.

1955 La danza durante la colonia de México. *Tradición, Rev. peruana cultura,* 19–20: 13–18. Cuzco.

1956 Panorama de la música tradicional de México. Mexico.

MÉRIDA, C.

1938 Pre-hispanic dance theater. *Theater Arts Monthly,* 22: 561–68.

1940 Carnavales de México. Mexico.

MERRIFIELD, W. R.

1959 Chinantec kinship in Palantla, Oaxaca, Mexico. *Amer. Anthr.,* 61: 875–81.

MERTON, R.

1957 Social theory and social structure. Glencoe.

METZGER, B.

1959 The social structure of three Tzeltal communities: Omaha systems in change. *In* McQuown, 1959, sec. 25.

METZGER, D.

n.d. An interpretation of drinking performances in Aguacatenango. MS.

1959a The social organization of Aguacatenango, Chiapas: a preliminary statement. MS.

1959b A preliminary evaluation of institutionalized social control and its contribution to cultural pluralism in the highlands of Chiapas. *In* McQuown, 1959, sec. 23.

—— AND R. RAVICZ

1966 Field notes on Tenejapa Tzeltal. MS.

—— AND G. WILLIAMS

1963a A formal ethnographic analysis of Tenejapa Ladino weddings. *Amer. Anthr.,* 65: 1076–1101.

1963b Tenejapa medicine. I: the curer. *SW. Jour. Anthr.,* 19: 216–34.

MÉXICO, DIRECCIÓN GENERAL DE ESTADÍSTICA

1943 Sexto censo de población. Resumen general.

1953 Séptimo censo . . . .

1960 Octavo censo . . . .

MÉXICO, MINISTERIO DE FOMENTO, COLONIZACIÓN E INDUSTRIA

1884 Trabajos de la Secretaría de Fomento de la República Mexicana sobre el Axe.

MÉXICO PREHISPÁNICO

1946 México prehispánico: culturas, deidades, monumentos. J. A. Vivó, ed. Mexico.

MEZA, O.

1934 Leyendas aztecas. Mexico.

MICHEL, C.

1951 Cantos indígenas de México. Inst. Nac. Indig. Mexico.

MILES, S. W.

1952 An analysis of modern Middle American calendars. *In* Tax, 1952b, pp. 273–84.

1957 The sixteenth-century Pokom-Maya: a documentary analysis of social structure and archeological setting. *Trans. Amer. Phil. Soc.,* 47: 731–81.

MILLÁN MALDONADO, A.

1942 Folklore. Univ. Nac. Autónoma. Mexico.

MILLER, F. C.

1959a Social structure and changing medical practices in a Mexican Indian community. *In* McQuown, 1959, sec. 3.

1959b Social structure and medical change in a Mexican Indian community. Doctoral dissertation, Harvard Univ.

MILLER, W. S.

1956 Cuentos mixes. *Inst. Nac. Indig., Biblioteca Folklore Indig.,* no. 2. Mexico.

MINTZ, S. W.

1953 The folk urban continuum and the

rural proletarian community. *Amer. Jour. Sociol.*, 59: 136–45.

—— AND E. R. WOLF
1950 An analysis of ritual co-parenthood (compadrazgo). *SW. Jour. Anthr.*, 6: 341–68.

MIRANDA, J., AND S. ZAVALA
1954 Instituciones indígenas en la colonia. *In* Caso, 1954, pp. 29–167.

MOLINA, A. DE
1880 Vocabulario de la lengua mexicana. Leipzig.

MOLINA ENRÍQUEZ, R.
1925 Las lacas de México. *Ethnos,* ep. 3, 1: 115–24. Mexico.
1928 Lacas de México: los baules de Olinalá. *Forma,* 1 (6): 15–22. Mexico.

MONTAGU, R.
1959 Preliminary report on the city of San Cristobal. MS, Chiapas Project files, Univ. Chicago, Dept. Anthropology.
1960–61 Field notes of the fincas of the region of Ocosingo. *Ibid.*

MONTERDE, F.
1955 Teatro indígena prehispánico: Raninal Achi. Mexico.

MONTÚFAR, L.
1879 Reseña histórica de Centro-América. 7 vols. (1878–87). Guatemala.

MONZÓN, A.
1945 Restos de clanes exogámicos entre los Cora de Nayarit. *Escuela Nac. Antr.*, Pub. 4. Mexico.
1947 Planteamiento de algunos problemas indígenas. *Amer. Indig.*, 7: 323–31.
1949 El calpulli en la organización social de los Tenochca. *Inst. Hist.*, 1st ser., Pub. 14. Mexico.

MOONEY, G. X.
1957 Mexican folk dances for American schools. Univ. Miami Press.

MOORE, W. E.
1950 Utilization of human resources through industrialization. *Millbank Mem. Fund Quar.*, 28: 52–67. New York.
1951 Industrialization and labor: social aspects of economic development. New York.

MORALES, S.
1952 Relaciones étnicas en Chiapas. Notas de campo. MS.

MORALES GÓMEZ, A.
1944 El tlilamatl o libro de los dioses. Mexico.

MORENO, D. A.
1958 Los factores demográficos en la planeación económica. Ed. de la camara nacional de la industria de la transformación. Mexico.

MORGADANES, D.
1940 Similarity between the Mixco (Guatemala) and the Yalalag (Oaxaca, Mexico) costumes. *Amer. Anthr.*, 42: 359–64.

MORLEY, S. G.
1946 The ancient Maya. Stanford Univ. Press.
1947 *Idem,* 2d ed.
1956 *Idem,* 3d ed., revised by G. W. Brainerd.

MORRISON, H.
1928 A classification of the higher groups and genera of the Coccid family Margarodidae. U.S. Dept. Agriculture, Technical Bull. 52.

MOTOLINÍA, T.
1950 The Indians of New Spain. Tr. and ed. by E. A. Foster. Berkeley.

MUÑOZ, M.
1963 Mixteca Nahua-Tlapaneca. *Inst. Nac. Indig.*, Mem. 9. Mexico.

MUÑOZ CAMARGO, D.
1892 Historia de Tlaxcala. Mexico.
1947 *Idem,* 2d ed.

MUNSCH, A.
1943 Some magico-religious observances of the present-day Maya Indians of British Honduras and Yucatan. *Primitive Man,* 16: 31–43. Catholic Anthr. Conference. Washington.

MURDOCK, G. P.
1949 Social structure. New York.
1957 World ethnographic sample. *Amer. Anthr.*, 59: 664–87.

MUSEO NACIONAL DE ARTES E INDUSTRIAS POPULARES
1951 Native dress of the Sierra de Puebla. No. 2. Mexico.
1953 Obras selectas del arte popular. No. 5. Mexico.
1954 Los Huicholes. No. 7. Mexico.

NADER, L.
1960 Social grouping and conflict in a Mexican village. MS.

NASH, J. C.
1959a Amatenango del Valle. *In* McQuown, 1959, sec. 10.
1959b Social structure and social organization in Oxchuc, Chiapas. *Ibid.*, sec. 24.
1960a Protestantism in an Indian village in

the western highlands of Guatemala. *In* Leslie, 1960b, pp. 49–58.

1960b Social relations in Amatenango del Valle: an activity analysis. Doctoral dissertation, Univ. Chicago.

NASH, M.

1953–54 Field notes, Cantel. MS.

1955 The reaction of a civil-religious hierarchy to a factory in Guatemala. *Human Organization*, 13: 26–28.

1957a The multiple society in economic development: Mexico and Guatemala. *Amer. Anthr.*, 59: 825–33.

1957b Cultural persistences and social structure: the Mesoamerican calendar survivals. *SW. Jour. Anthr.*, 13: 149–55.

1958a Machine age Maya: the industrialization of a Guatemalan community. *Amer. Anthr. Assoc.*, Mem. 87.

1958b Political relations in Guatemala. *Social and Econ. Studies*, 7: 65–75.

1960 Witchcraft as social process in a Tzeltal community. *Amer. Indig.*, 20: 121–26.

1961 The social context of economic choice in a small community. *Man*, 61: 186–91.

NATIONAL SCIENCE FOUNDATION

1959 Vegetation project, Univ. Chicago.

NATURALEZA, LA

1884 La Naturaleza: periódico científico de la Sociedad Mexicana de Historia Natural, vol. 6, 1882–83. Mexico.

NEWBOLD, S.

1957 Receptivity to communist fomented agitation in rural Guatemala. *Econ. Development and Cult. Change*, 5: 338–61.

NICARAGUA, DIRECCIÓN GENERAL DE ESTADÍSTICA Y CENSOS

1954 Censo general de población. Managua.

NICOLI, J. P.

1885 El estado de Sonora: Yaquis y Mayos; estudio histórico de León. Mexico.

NOGUERA, E.

1942 Cultura tarasca. Biblioteca del Maestro. Mexico.

NORDENSKIÖLD, E.

1927 The Choco Indians. *Discovery*, 8: 95.

NORMAN, J.

1959 In Mexico: where to look, how to buy Mexican popular arts and crafts. New York.

NORTE DE MÉXICO, EL

1944 El norte de México y el sur de Estados Unidos. Tercera reunión de mesa redonda sobre problemas antropológicos de México y Centro América. Soc. Mex. Antr. Mexico.

NÚÑEZ CHINCHILLA, J.

1959 Panorama indigenista actual de la República de Honduras. *Bol. Indig.*, 19: 230–32. Mexico.

NUTINI, H. G.

1961 Clan organization in a Nahuatl speaking village of the state of Tlaxcala, Mexico. *Amer. Anthr.*, 63: 62–78.

NUTTALL, Z.

1909 A curious survival in Mexico of the use of the *Purpura* shell-fish for dyeing. *Putnam Anniv. Vol.*, pp. 365–84.

OAKES, M.

1951 The two crosses of Todos Santos: survivals of Mayan religious ritual. *Bollingen Ser.*, no. 27.

OCHOA, J. C.

1945 The phantom lover. *Tlalocan*, 2: 34.

OLMSTED, D. L.

1958 Tequistlatec kinship terminology. *SW. Jour. Anthr.*, 14: 449–53.

OLSON, R. L.

1933 Clan and moiety in native America. *Univ. California Pub. Amer. Archaeol. Ethnol.*, 33: 351–432.

OLVERA, J.

1956 El arte de las lacas en Chiapas. *El Maestro Mex.*, ser. 3, 6: 38–40.

1959 *Idem. El Sol de Chiapas*, January 21, 22. Tuxtla Gutierrez.

O'NEALE, L. M.

1945 Textiles of highland Guatemala. *Carnegie Inst. Wash.*, Pub. 567.

ORELLANA G., R. A.

1950 Estudios sobre aspectos técnicos del censo de población. Univ. Autónoma de San Carlos de Guatemala.

OROPEZA CASTRO, M.

1947 El diluvio totonaco. *Tlalocan*, 2: 269–75.

OROZCO Y BERRA, M.

1864 Geografía de las lenguas y carta etnográfia de México. Mexico.

ORTIZ, S.

1940 Lingüística familia Choko. *Univ. Católica Bolivariana*, 6.

OSBORNE, L. DE J.

1935 Guatemala textiles. *Tulane Univ., Middle Amer. Research Inst.*, Pub. 6.

1956 Four keys to El Salvador. New York.

OSGOOD, C. E., AND P. TANNENBAUM
1955 The principle of congruity and the prediction of attitude change. *Psychol. Rev.*, 62: 42–55.

PACHECO CRUZ, S.
1947 Usos, costumbres, religión, y supersticiones de los Mayas. Merida.

PADILLA, V. M.
1953 La chorrera del Celaque (folklore). *Honduras Rotaria*, 9 (119–20): 11, 23. Tegucigalpa.

PALERM, A.
1953 Etnografía antigua totonaca en el oriente de México. *In* Huastecos, Totonacos, pp. 176–86.
1954 La distribución del regadío en el area central de Meso-América. *Cien. Sociales*, 5: 25–26.
1955 The agricultural bases of urban civilization in Meso-America. *In* Irrigation civilizations, a comparative study, pp. 28–42. *Pan Amer. Union, Social Sci. Monogr.*
1956 Comentario. *In* Arriola, 1956.

PAPELES DE NUEVA ESPAÑA (PNE)
1905 Relación del pueblo de Amatlan. Ser. 2, 4: 314–19. Madrid.
1946 Relación de Asuchitlan. Ser. 2, vol. 7 suppl., Relaciones geográficas de Michoacán, no. 6. Ed. Vargas Rea. Mexico.

PAREDES, P. I. DE
1759 Promptuario manual mexicano. Bibliotheca Mexicana. Mexico.

PARRA, M. G.
1950 Densidad de la población de habla indígena en la República Mexicana. *Inst. Nac. Indig.*, Mem. 1. Mexico.
1954 Las grandes tendencias de la evolución histórica de la política indigenista moderna en México. *In* Parra and Jiménez Moreno, 1954, pp. xvii-ci.

—— AND W. JIMÉNEZ MORENO
1954 Bibliografía indigenista de México y Centroamérica (1850–1950.) *Inst. Nac. Indig.*, Mem. 4. Mexico.

PARSONS, E. C.
1928 Notes on the Pima. *Amer. Anthr.*, 30: 445–64.
1930 Spanish elements in the kachina cult of the Pueblos. *Proc. 23d Int. Cong. Amer.* (1928), pp. 582–603.
1932a Folklore from Santa Ana Xalmimilulco, Puebla. *Jour. Amer. Folklore*, 45: 318–62.
1932b Zapoteca and Spanish tales of Mitla, Oaxaca. *Ibid.*, 45: 277–317.
1936 Mitla: town of the souls. Univ. Chicago Press.

PASO Y TRONCOSO, F. DEL
1890 Invención de la cruz por Santa Elena. Mexico.
1902 Comédies en náhuatl. *Proc. 12th Int. Cong. Amer.* (1901), pp. 309–16.
1903 Leyenda de los soles. Relación anónima escrita en lengua mexicana el año 1558. Rome.
1954 Tratado de las idolatrías, supersticiones, dioses, ritos, hechicerías y otras costumbres gentílicas de las razas aborígenes de México. 2 vols. Mexico.

PASSIN, H.
1942 Sorcery as a phase of Tarahumara economic relations. *Man*, 42: 11–15.
1943 The place of kinship in Tarahumara social organization. *Acta Amer.*, 1: 360–83, 471–95.

PATIÑO, L. R. AND H. CÁRDENAS
1955 Informes agroeconómicos de la Mixteca de la costa. *Inst. Nac. Indig., Mimeo. Ser.*, no. 8. Mexico.

PAUL, B. D.
1942 Ritual kinship: with special reference to godparenthood in Middle America. Doctoral dissertation, Univ. Chicago.
1950a Life in a Guatemalan Indian village. *In* Patterns for modern living, division 3: cultural patterns, pp. 468–515. Chicago.
1950b Symbolic sibling rivalry in a Guatemalan Indian village. *Amer. Anthr.*, 52: 205–18.
1953 Mental disorder and self-regulating processes in culture: a Guatemalan illustration. *In* Interrelations between the social environment and psychiatric disorders, pp. 51–67. Millbank Mem. Fund. New York.
1955 [ed.] Health, culture and community: case studies of public reaction to health programs. Russell Sage Found. New York.

—— AND L. PAUL
1952 The life cycle. *In* Tax, 1952a, pp. 174–92.

PAUL, L., AND B. D. PAUL
1963 Changing marriage patterns in a highland Guatemalan community. *SW. Jour. Anthr.*, 19: 131–48.

PÉREZ ARCEO, L.
1923 Iktili . . . a fable from the Maya. *El Agricultor*, 10 (18), November 15. Mexico.
1954 U tzicablil Xtabay (la leyenda de la Xtabay). *Yikal Maya Than*, 15 (176): 56–59.

PÉREZ ESTRADA, F.
1954 Teatro folklórico hispanoamericano. *Nicaragua Indig.*, 2a ep., 1: 34–39.
1955 Las comunidades indígenas en Nicaragua. *Ibid.*, 2a ep., 8: 5–19.

PÉREZ GARCÍA, R.
1956 La Sierra Juárez. 2 vols. Mexico.

PERRY, E.
1922 Central American union. *Hisp. Amer. Hist. Rev.*, 5: 30–51.

PETERSON, F. A.
1959a Ancient Mexico. New York.
1959b Las fiestas. *In* Esplendor del México antiguo, 2: 819–36.

PHELAN, J. L.
1956 The millennial kingdom of the Franciscans in the New World: a study of the writing of Geronimo de Mendieta (1525–1604). *Univ. California Pub. Hist.*, no. 52.

PIKE, E. V.
1948 Head-washing and other elements in the Mazateco marriage ceremony. *Amer. Indig.*, 8: 219–22.

PIKE, F. B., ed.
1959 Freedom and reform in Latin America. Notre Dame, Indiana.

PIKE, K. L.
1937 Una leyenda mixteca: cuenta chihi. *Invest. Ling.*, 4: 262–70.
1944 Analysis of a Mixteco text. *Int. Jour. Amer. Ling.*, 10: 113–38.
1945a Tone puns in Mixteco. *Ibid.*, 11: 129–39.
1945b Mock Spanish of a Mixteco Indian. *Ibid.*, 11: 219–24.
1946 Another Mixtec tone pun. *Ibid.*, 12: 22–24.
1948–49 Cuento mixteco de un conejo, un coyote y la luna. *Rev. Mex. Estud. Antr.*, 10: 133–34.

PIMENTEL, F.
1874–75 Cuadro descriptivo y comparativo de las lenguas indígenas de México. 3 vols. 2d ed. Mexico.
1903 Obras completas. Vol. 2. Mexico.

PINEDA, V.
1888 Historia de las sublevaciones indígenas habida en la estado de Chiapas. Mexico.

PINTO, R. G.
1941 Los indígenas y la República Mexicana.

PITTMAN, R. S.
1945 La historia de Pedro Sa-kinemilea. *Tlalocan*, 2: 10–17.

PITT-RIVERS, J. A.
1954 The people of the sierra. London.
1963 Political organization in Chiapas. MS, Chiapas Project files, Univ. Chicago, Dept. Anthropology.

PLANCARTE, F. N.
1954 El problema indígena tarahumara. *Inst. Nac. Indig.*, Mem. 5. Mexico.

PORTER, K. W.
1951 The Seminole in Mexico, 1850–1861. *Hisp. Amer. Hist. Rev.*, 31: 1–36.

POZAS A., R.
1952a El trabajo en las plantaciones de café y el cambio socio-cultural del Indio. *Rev. Mex. Estud. Antr.*, 13: 31–48.
1952b Juan Pérez Jolote: biografía de un Tzotzil. Fondo de Cultura Económica. Mexico. (3d ed. 1959.)
1959a Chamula: un pueblo indio de los altos de Chiapas, Mexico. *Inst. Nac. Indig.*, Mem. 8. Mexico.
1959b Los cambios sociales y la industrialización. *In* Stone, 1959, pp. 373–79.
1959c Juan Pérez Jolote: biografía de un Tzotzil. 3d ed. Fondo de Cultura Económica. Mexico.

PRESCOTT, W. H.
1843 The conquest of Mexico. 3 vols. New York.

PREUSS, K. T.
1912 Die Nayarit-Expedition, Textaufnahmen und Beobachtungen unter Mexikanischen Indianern. Band I: Die Religion der Cora Indianer. Leipzig.
1932a Au sujet du caractère des mythes et chants Huichols que j'ai recueillis. *Univ. Tucuman, Inst. Etnol.*, 2: 445–57. Tucuman, Argentina.
1932b Grammatik der Cora-Sprache. *Int. Jour. Amer. Ling.*, 7: 1–84.
1935 Wörterbuch Deutsch-Cora. *Ibid.*, 8: 79–102.

PRIESTLEY, H. I.
1923 The Mexican nation, a history. New York.

PROMPTUARIO MANUAL MEXICANO
    See Paredes, 1759.

RADIN, P.
1916 The relationship of Huave and Mixe. *Amer. Anthr.*, 18: 411–23.
1917 El folklore de Oaxaca. New York.
1920 The sources and authenticity of the history of the ancient Mexicans. *Univ. California Pub. Amer. Archaeol. Ethnol.*, 17: 1–150.
1925 Maya, Nahuatl, and Tarascan kinship terms. *Amer. Anthr.*, 27: 101–03.
1929 Huave texts. *Int. Jour. Amer. Ling.*, 5: 1–56.
1931 Mexican kinship terms. *Univ. California Pub. Amer. Archaeol. Ethnol.*, 31: 1–14.
1933 Mixe texts. *Jour. Soc. Amer. Paris*, 25: 41–64.
1935a A historical legend of the Zapotecs. *Ibero-Amer.*, no. 1.
1935b Tehuano vocabulary and Tehuano texts. MS, Library of Miguel Covarrubias, Tizapan.
1945 Cuentos de Mitla. *Tlalocan*, vol. 2, nos. 1, 2, 3.
1946 Zapotec texts: dialect of Juchitan Tehuano. *Int. Jour. Amer. Ling.*, 12: 152–72.

RAMOS B., J.
1945 The phantom lover. *Tlalocan*, 2: 30–33.

RAVICZ, R. S.
1958 A comparative study of selected aspects of Mixtec social organization. Doctoral dissertation, Harvard Univ.
1959 Field notes on Cuauhtenco, a Nahuatl-speaking village of Tlaxcala, Mexico. MS.
1960 Field notes on Xochistlahuaca, an Amuzgo-speaking village of Guerrero, Mexico. MS.
1961 Field notes on Trique and Mixtec speakers of Oaxaca and Nahuatl speakers of Guerrero, Mexico. MS.
1962–65 Field notes on Mixtec. MS.
1965 Organización social de los Mixtecos. *Inst. Nac. Indig., Col. Antr. Social*, no. 5. Mexico.
1966 The washing of the hands: a structural element in indigenous interpretation of Christian baptism. *In* Homenaje para Roberto J. Weitlaner. Mexico.

RAY, V. F., ed.
1959 Intermediate societies, social mobility, and communication. *Amer. Ethnol. Soc.*, Proc. annual spring meeting.

RECINOS, A.
1913 Monografía del departamento de Huehuetenango, República de Guatemala. Guatemala. (2d ed. 1954.)
1947 Popul Vuh: las antiguas historias del Quiche. Fondo de Cultura Económica. Mexico.
1950 Memorial de Sololá: anales de los Cakchiquels. Seguido de título de los señores de Totonicapan. *Ibid.*
1954 Monografía del departamento de Huehuetenango. 2d ed. Guatemala.
1957 Crónicas indígenas de Guatemala. Guatemala.

REDFIELD, M. P.
1935 Folk literature of a Yucatecan town. *Carnegie Inst. Wash.*, Pub. 456, Contrib. 14.

REDFIELD, R.
1928 The calpulli-barrio in a present day Mexican pueblo. *Amer. Anthr.*, 30: 282–94.
1930 Tepoztlan: a Mexican village. Univ. Chicago Press.
1934 Culture changes in Yucatan. *Amer. Anthr.*, 36: 57–69.
1939 Culture contact without conflict. *Ibid.*, 41: 514–17.
1940 The Indian in Mexico. *In* Mexico today, T. Sallin, ed. *Ann. Amer. Acad. Polit. Social Sci.*, 208: 132–43.
1941 The folk culture of Yucatan. Univ. Chicago Press.
1946a Ethnographic materials on Agua Escondida. *Univ. Chicago, Micro. Coll. MSS Middle Amer. Cult. Anthr.*, no. 3.
1946b Notes on San Antonio Palopo. *Ibid.*, no. 4.
1950 A village that chose progress: Chan Kom revisited. Univ. Chicago Press.
1960 The little community. Univ. Chicago Press.

—— AND M. P. REDFIELD
1940 Disease and its treatment in Dzitas, Yucatan. *Carnegie Inst. Wash.*, Pub. 523, Contrib. 32.

—— AND S. TAX
1952 General characteristics of present-day Mesoamerican Indian society. *In* Tax, 1952a, pp. 31–39.

—— AND A. VILLA ROJAS
1934 Chan Kom, a Maya village. *Carnegie Inst. Wash.*, Pub. 448.

1939 Notes on the ethnography of the Tzeltal communities of Chiapas. *Ibid.*, Pub. 509, Contrib. 28.

REINA, R. E.
1960 Chinautla, a Guatemalan Indian community. *Tulane Univ., Middle Amer. Research Inst.*, Pub. 24, pp. 55–130.
1961 Culture retention and culture change among Itzas of Peten and British Honduras. *Univ. Pennsylvania, Mus. Monogr.*

REJÓN GARCÍA, M.
1905 Supersticiones y leyendas mayas. Merida.
1926 Tix'iz: a Isidra. *Bol. Univ. Nac. Sureste*, pp. 125–27. Merida.

RELACIÓN DE MICHOACÁN
1869 Relación de las ceremonias y ritos y población y gobierno de los indios de la provincia de Michoacán (1541). *Col. Doc. Ined. para la Historia de España*, vol. 53. Madrid.
1956 *Idem.* Reproducción facsímil del MS c. IV 5 de El Escorial, con transcripción, prólogo, introducción y notas por José Tudela . . . . Madrid.

RENDÓN, S.
1941 La alimentación tarasca. *An. Inst. Nac. Antr. Hist.*, 2: 207–27.

REUTER, E. B., ed.
1934 Race and culture contacts. New York.

REYES, L. G.
1963 Nonohualco. *El Dia*, April 27. [Article in honor of Roberto J. Weitlaner.]

REYNOLDS, D.
1956 Danzas guatemaltecas. *Americas*, 8 (2): 31–35.

RIBAS, A. P. DE
1645 Historia de los triunfos de nuestra santa fe, en las misiones de la provincia de Nueva España. *In* Beals, 1943, pp. 66, 67.

RICARD, R.
1933 La "conquête spirituelle" du Mexique. *Inst. Ethol., Travaux et Mem.*, no. 20. Paris.

RILEY, C. L., AND J. HOBGOOD
1959 A recent nativistic movement among the southern Tepehuane Indians. *SW. Jour. Anthr.*, 15: 355–60.

ROBB, J. D.
1961 The matachines dance: a ritual folk dance. *Western Folklore*, 20: 87–101.

ROBELO, C. A.
1911 Diccionario de mitología nahuatl. Mexico.

ROBERTS, R. E. T.
1948 A comparison of ethnic relations in two Guatemalan communities. *Acta Amer.*, 6: 135–51.

RODOZ, J. DE
1723 Arte de la lengua Tzotzlen o Tzinacantan. (Paris Dictionary.)

ROJAS, M. J.
1933 Ecaliztli ihuicpan tepoztecatl (batalla contra el tepozteco). *In* D. Castañeda and V. T. Mendoza, Instrumental precortesiano. Mexico.

ROJAS G., F.
1943 La institución del compadrazgo entre los indios de México. *Rev. Mex. Sociol.*, 5: 201–13. Mexico.

ROJAS GARCIDUEÑAS, J. J.
1935 El teatro de Nueva España en el siglo XVI. Mexico.
1942 Fiestas en México en 1578. *An. Inst. Invest. Estéticas*, 9: 33–57.

ROMANO, A.
1952 Relaciones étnicas en Chiapas. Notas de campo. MS.

ROMERO DE TERREROS Y VINENT, M.
1918 Arte colonial. Mexico.
1923 Las artes industriales en la Nueva España. Mexico.
1951 El arte en México durante el virreinato: resumen histórico. Mexico.

ROMNEY, A. K.
1957 The genetic model and Uto-Aztecan time perspective. *Davidson Jour. Anthr.*, 3: 35–41.

—— AND R. ROMNEY
1963 The Mixtecans of Juxtlahuaca, Mexico. *In* Six cultures: studies of child rearing, B. B. Whiting, ed., pp. 541–692.

RORTY, J.
1960 ¿Hay discriminación en México? La experiencia indigenista de Chiapas. *Amer. Indig.*, 20: 217–28.

ROSALES, J. DE D.
1949a Notes on Aguacatan. *Univ. Chicago, Micro. Coll. MSS Middle Amer. Cult. Anthr.*, no. 24.
1949b Notes on San Pedro La Laguna. *Ibid.*, no. 25.
1950 Notes on Santiago Chimaltenango. *Ibid.*, no. 30.
1959 Indígenas de Guatemala. *Amer. Indig.*, 19: 115–24.

Rose, R. H.
1904   Utilla: past and present. Danville, N.Y.

Rosenblat, A.
1945   La población indígena de América desde 1492 hasta la actualidad. *Inst. Cultural Española.* Buenos Aires.
1954   La población indígena y el meslizaje en América. 2 vols. *Editorial Nova.* Buenos Aires.

Roys, R. L.
1929   Annotated transcription of the Chilam Balam of Kaua. MS. Tulane Univ., Middle Amer. Research Inst.
1933   The book of Chilam Balam of Chumayel. *Carnegie Inst. Wash.,* Pub. 438.
1943   The Indian background of colonial Yucatan. *Ibid.,* Pub. 548.
1957   The political geography of the Yucatan Maya. *Ibid.,* Pub. 613.

Rubel, A. J.
1950   Field notes on the Chinantec of Ojitlan. MS.
1955   Ritual relationships in Ojitlan, Mexico. *Amer. Anthr.,* 57: 1038–40.
1957   Notes on the Tzotzil-speakers of San Bartolome de los Llanos, Chiapas. MS.
1960   Concepts of disease in Mexican-American culture. *Amer. Anthr.,* 62: 795–814.
1964   The epidemiology of a folk illness: susto in Hispanic America. *Ethnology,* 3: 268–83.

Rubín de la Borbolla, D.
1963   Arte popular mexicano. *In* Arte popular de Mexico (special issue of Artes de Mexico).

Ruiz U., R. E.
1956   The struggle for a national culture in rural education. *In* Estudios antropológicos, pp. 473–90.

Russell, F.
1905   The Pima Indians. *Smithsonian Inst., Bur. Amer. Ethnol.,* 26th ann. rept., pp. 5–391.

Sachs, C.
1933   Eine Weltgeschichte des Tanzes. Berlin.

Sahagún, B. de
1938   Historia general de las cosas de Nueva España. 5 vols. Ed. Robredo. Mexico.
1950–66   Florentine codex: general history of the things of New Spain (1575–77). Original Nahuatl text and English tr. by A. J. O. Anderson and C. E. Dibble. Books 1–5, 7–12. Univ. Utah and School Amer. Research. Santa Fe.
1956   Historia general de las cosas de Nueva España. 4 vols. A. M. Garibay K., ed. Mexico.

Salas, C. de
1928   Relaciones de Tetiquipa, Rio Hondo, Tecuicuilco, Atepec, Coquipa y Xatlianguez. *Rev. Mex. Estud. Antr.,* 2: 113–20.

Salvatierra S.
1946   Compendio de historia de Centro América. 2d ed. Managua.

Salz, B. R.
1955   The human element in industrialization: a hypothetical case study of Ecuadorean Indians. *Amer. Anthr. Assoc.,* Mem. 85.

Samayoa Chinchilla, C.
1934   Madre milpa. Guatemala.
1936   Cuatro suertes: cuentos y leyendas. Guatemala.
1941   La casa de la muerte: cuentos y leyendas de Guatemala. Guatemala.
1959   The emerald lizard: tales and legends of Guatemala. Indian Hills, Colo.

Sánchez Castro, A.
1947   Los mixes: historia, leyendas, música. Mexico.

Sánchez García, J.
1956   Calendario folklórico de fiestas en la República Mexicana: fiesta de fecha fija. Notas recopiladas y ordenadas por V. T. Mendoza. Mexico.
1958   La virgen de San Juan de los lagos en Mexico. *Anuario Soc. Folklórica Mex.,* 8: 57–79.

Sanders, W. T.
1956   The central Mexican symbiotic region: a study in prehistoric settlement patterns. *In* Willey, 1956a, pp. 115–27.

Santos, J.
1716   Cronología hospitalaria . . . de San Juan de Dios. Madrid.

Sapir, E.
1913   Southern Paiute and Nahuatl I. *Jour. Soc. Amer. Paris,* 10: 379–524.
1915   Southern Paiute and Nahuatl II. *Amer. Anthr.,* 17: 98–120, 306–28.

Sauer, C.
1934   The distribution of aboriginal tribes and languages in northwestern Mexico. *Ibero-Amer.,* no. 5.

1935 Aboriginal population of northwestern Mexico. *Ibid.*, no. 10.

SCHLESINGER, J.
1946 Revolución comunista. Guatemala.

SCHMIEDER, O.
1930 The settlements of the Tzapotec and Mije Indians, state of Oaxaca, Mexico. *Univ. California Pub. Geog.*, vol. 4.

SCHNEIDER, R. M.
1958 Communism in Guatemala, 1944–1954. *Univ. Pennsylvania, Foreign Policy Research Inst. Ser.*, no. 7.

SCHOEMBS, J.
1949 Aztekische Schriftsprache. Heidelberg.

SCHOLES, F. V.
1937 The beginnings of Hispano-Indian society in Yucatan. *Carnegie Inst. Wash.*, Suppl. Pub. 30.

——— AND E. B. ADAMS
1955 Relación de las encomiendas de Indios hechas en Nueva España a los conquistadores. Mexico.
1957 [eds.] Información sobre los tributos que los indios pagaban a Moctezuma, año de 1554. *Doc. para la Historia del México colonial*, vol. 4. Mexico.

——— AND R. L. ROYS
1948 The Maya Indians of Acalan-Tixchel: a contribution to the history and ethnography of the Yucatan peninsula. *Carnegie Inst. Wash.*, Pub. 560.

SCHULLER, R.
1935 Das Popol Vuh und das Ballspiel der K'ice Indianer von Guatemala, Mittelamerika. *Int. Archiv für Ethnog.*, 33: 105–16.

SCHULTZE-JENA, L. S.
1933 Leben, Glaube und Sprache der Quiche von Guatemala. Indiana, vol. 1. Jena. (Tr. into Spanish in his 1945.)
1938 Bei den Azteken, Mixteken und Tlapaneken der Sierra Madre del Sur von Mexiko. Indiana III.
1945 Leben, Glauben und Sprache der Quiche von Guatemala. Tr. into Spanish by A. Goubaud C.

SEDILLO BREWSTER, M.
1935 Mexican and New Mexican folk dances. Univ. New Mexico Press.

SEE, R.
n.d. Missionary orders in Mexico: a preliminary investigation. MS, Univ. California, Dept. Anthropology and Sociology.

SÉJOURNÉ, L.
1957 Pensamiento y religión en el México antiguo. Mexico.

SELER, E.
1923 Mythus und Religion der alten Mexikaner. *Geschichte Abhandlungen*, 4: 3–156:

SERNA, J. DE LA
1892 Manual de ministros de Indios. *An. Mus. Nac.*, 6: 261–479. Mexico.

SERRANO PLAJA, A.
1944 España en la edad de oro. Buenos Aires.

SERVICE, E.
1955 Indian-European relations in colonial Latin America. *Amer. Anthr.*, 57: 411–25.

SHATTUCK, G. C.
1933 The peninsula of Yucatan: medical, biological, meteorological, and sociological studies. *Carnegie Inst. Wash.*, Pub. 431.

SHEPARD, A. O.
1956 Ceramics for the archaeologist. *Ibid.*, Pub. 609.

SHIMKIN, D. B.
1941 The Uto-Aztecan system of kinship terminology. *Amer. Anthr.*, 43: 223–45.

SIEGEL, M.
1941 Religion in western Guatemala: a product of acculturation. *Ibid.*, 43: 62–76.
1943 Creation myth and acculturation in Acatan, Guatemala. *Jour. Amer. Folklore*, 56: 120–26.

SIGNORET, M. V.
1875 Essai sur les cochenilles ou gallinsectes (Homopteres—Coccides), 15e, 16e, et 17e parties. *Ann. Soc. Entomol. France*, vol. 44.

SILVA Y ACEVES, M.
1925 La colección folklórica de la Biblioteca del Museo Nacional. *An. Mus. Nac. Arqueol. Hist. Etnog.*, 3: 269–320. Mexico.

SILVERT, K. H.
1954 A study in government: Guatemala. *Tulane Univ., Middle Amer. Research Inst.*, Pub. 21.
1956 El nacionalismo: medida de su crecimiento en Guatemala. *In* Arriola, 1956, pp. 393–414.

SIMEÓN, R.
1889 Chrestomathie nahuatl, publiée pour le cours de langue mexicaine. Paris.

SIMMONS, M. L.
1960 Pre-conquest narrative songs in Spanish America. *Jour. Amer. Folklore*, 73: 103–11.

SIMPSON, L. B.
1929 The encomienda in New Spain. *Univ. California Pub. Hist.*, vol. 19.
1934 Studies in the administration of the Indians in New Spain. 2: The civil congregation. *Ibero-Amer.*, 7: 29–129.
1950 The encomienda in New Spain: the beginning of Spanish Mexico. Berkeley.
1952 Many Mexicos. 3d ed. Berkeley.
1953 Unplanned effects of Mexico's planned economy. *Virginia Quar. Rev.*, 29: 514–32.
1959 Many Mexicos. Rev. 3d ed. Berkeley.

SIVERTS, H.
1960 Political organization in a Tzeltal community in Chiapas, Mexico. *In* Leslie, 1960b, pp. 14–28.
1964 On politics and leadership in highland Chiapas, Mexico. *In* Desarrollo cultural de los Mayas, pp. 363–80.

SKINNER-KLEE, J.
1954 Legislación indigenista de Guatemala. *Inst. Indig. Interamer.*, Ed. Especiales, no. 18. Mexico.

SLOCUM, M. C.
1956 Cultural changes among the Oxchuc Tzeltals. *In* Estudios antropológicos, pp. 491–95.

SMITH, R. E.
1949 Cerámica elaborada sin torno, Chinautla, Guatemala. *Antr. Hist. Guatemala*, 1: 58–61.

SOCIAL SCIENCE RESEARCH COUNCIL
1954 Acculturation: an exploratory formulation. *Amer. Anthr.*, 56: 973–1002. (Summer Seminar on Acculturation, 1953.)

SOLIEN, N. L.
1960 Changes in Black Carib kinship terminology. *SW. Jour. Anthr.*, 16: 144–59.

SOLÍS ACALÁ, E.
1949 Diccionario Español-Maya. Yikal Maya Than. Merida.

SOLÍS QUIROGA, H.
1957 Industrialización y delincuencia.

Jornadas Indust., 4a ep., no. 52, pp. 123–60. Mexico.

SOUSTELLE, G.
1958 Tequila: un village nahuatl du Mexique oriental. *Inst. Ethnol., Travaux et Mem.*, no. 62. Paris.
1959 Observations sur la religion des Lacandons du Mexique meridional. *Jour. Soc. Amer. Paris*, n.s., 48: 141–96.

SOUSTELLE, J.
1935a Deux contes otomis. *Ibid.*, 27: 1–12.
1935b Le culte des oratoires chez les otomis et les mazahuas de la region d'Ixtlahuaca. *El Mex. Antiguo*, 3 (5–8): 97–117.
1935c Les idées religieuses des Lacandons. *La Terre et La Vie*, 5: 170–78.
1937 La famille otomi-pame du Mexique centrale. *Inst. Ethnol., Travaux et Mem.*, no. 26. Paris.
1955 La vie quotidienne des aztèques á la veille de la conquête espagnole. Paris.

SPICER, E. H.
1940 Pascua, a Yaqui village in Arizona. Univ. Chicago Press.
1945 El problema Yaqui. *Amer. Indig.*, 5: 273–86.
1954 Potam, a Yaqui village in Sonora. *Amer. Anthr. Assoc.*, Mem. 77.
1961 [ed.] Perspectives in American Indian culture change. Chicago.

SPIER, L.
1925 The distribution of kinship systems in North America. *Univ. Washington Pub. Anthr.*, no. 1.

SPINDEN, H. J.
1928 Ancient civilizations of Mexico and Central America. 3d ed. *Amer. Mus. Natural Hist., Handbook Ser.*, no. 3.

SPRATLING, W.
1960 More human than divine. Univ. Nac. Autónoma Mex.

SQUIER, E. G.
1852 Nicaragua: its people, scenery, monuments .... 2 vols. New York.
1855 Notes on Central America, particularly on the states of Honduras and El Salvador .... New York.
1861 Monograph of authors who have written in the languages of Central America and collected vocabularies or composed works in the native dialects of that country. London.

STABB, M. S.
1959 Indigenism and racism in Mexican thought: 1857–1911. *Jour. Interamer. Studies,* 1: 405–23.

STADELMAN, R.
1940 Maize cultivation in northwestern Guatemala. *Carnegie Inst. Wash.,* Pub. 523, Contrib. 33.

STANDLEY, P. C., AND S. CALDERÓN
1925 Lista preliminar de las plantas de El Salvador. San Salvador.

STANGER, F. M.
1932 National origin in Central America. *Hisp. Amer. Hist. Rev.,* 12: 18–45.

STANSLAWSKI, D.
1950 The anatomy of eleven towns in Michoacan. *Univ. Texas, Inst. Latin Amer. Studies,* no. 10.

STARR, B. W.
1952a Ceremonial structures in the present day Maya. area. *Univ. Chicago, Micro. Coll. MSS Middle Amer. Cult. Anthr.,* no. 31.
1952b Field notes on San Andres, Tuxtla. *Ibid.,* no. 33.
1954 Levels of communal relations. *Amer. Jour. Sociol.,* 60: 125–35.
1957 Notes on Santiago Tuxtla, Veracruz. *Univ. Chicago, Micro. Coll. MSS Middle Amer. Cult. Anthr.,* no. 40.

STARR, F.
1899 Indians of southern Mexico: an ethnographic album. Chicago.
1900–02 Notes upon the ethnography of southern Mexico. 2 parts. *Proc. Davenport Acad. Natural Sci.,* vols. 8, 9.
1908 In Indian Mexico: a narrative of travel and labor. Chicago.

START, L. E.
1948 The McDougall collection of Indian textiles from Guatemala and Mexico. *Pitt Rivers Mus., Occasional Papers on Technology,* no. 2. Oxford.

STAUB, W.
1919 Some data about the pre-Hispanic and the living Huastec Indians. *El Mex. Antiguo,* 1: 49–65.
1940 Algunos datos acerca de los indios huastecas pre-hispánicos y de los contemporaneos. *Divulgación Hist.,* 1: 424.

STECK, F. B. (O.F.M.)
1951 Motolinía's history of the Indians of New Spain. *Pub. Acad. Amer. Franciscan Hist., Doc. Ser.,* no. 1. Washington.

STEGGERDA, M.
1941 The Maya Indians of Yucatan. *Carnegie Inst. Wash.,* Pub. 531.

STEININGER, G. R., AND P. VAN DE VELDE
1935 Three dollars a year, being the story of San Pablo Cuatro Venados, a typical Zapotecan village. New York.

STERN, T.
1950 The rubber ball games of the Americas. *Amer. Ethnol. Soc., Monogr.* 17.

STEWARD, J. H.
1946–59 *See* Handbook of South American Indians.
1949 South American cultures: an interpretative summary. *In* Handbook of South American Indians, 5: 669–772.
1950 Area research: theory and practice. *Social Sci. Research Council,* Bull. 63.
1951 Levels of sociocultural integration: an operational concept. *SW. Jour. Anthr.,* 7: 374–90.

STOLL, O.
1884 Zur Ethnographie der Republik Guatemala. Zurich.
1889 Ethnologie der Indianerstamme von Guatemala. Leipzig.

STONE, D. Z.
1949 The Boruca of Costa Rica. *Papers Peabody Mus., Harvard Univ.,* vol. 26, no. 2.
1954 Estampas de Honduras. Mexico.
1957 Brief notes on the Matagalpa Indians of Nicaragua. *In* R. N. Adams, 1957a, pp. 256–60.
1958 A living pattern of non-Maya—non-Mexican Central American aborigines. *In* Bosch-Gimpera, 1958, pp. 669–79.
1959 [ed.] Actas, 23d Int. Cong. Amer., vol. 1. San Jose.

STORM, M.
1939 Hoofways into hot country. Mexico.
1945 Enjoying Uruapan. Mexico.

STRESSER-PÉAN, G.
1952 Montagnes calcaires et sources vauclusiennes dans la religion des Indiens Huastèques. *Rev. Hist. Religions,* 141: 84–90. Paris.
1953 Les indiens huastèques. *In* Huastecos, Totonacos, pp. 213–34.

SWADESH, M.
n.d. Kin terms common to Tarasco and Zuni. Inst. Hist., Univ. Nac. Autónoma Mex.

1959 Indian linguistic groups of Mexico. Escuela Nac. Antr. Hist. Mexico.

SWANTON, J. R.

1929 A point of resemblance between the ball game of the southeastern Indians and the ball games of Mexico and Central America. *Jour. Washington Acad. Sci.*, 19: 304–07.

T., J. A.

1946 Documentos en los cuales se refieren los sucesos ocurridos en Bluefields, República de Nicaragua en el año de 1894. *Rev. Acad. Geog. Hist. Nicaragua*, 8 (2): 49–68. Managua.

TANNENBAUM, F.

1950 Mexico: the struggle for peace and bread. New York.

TAX, SOL

1937 The municipios of the midwestern highlands of Guatemala. *Amer. Anthr.*, 39: 423–44.

1941 World view and social relations in Guatemala. *Ibid.*, 43: 27–42.

1944 Information about the municipio of Zinacantan, Chiapas. *Rev. Mex. Estud. Anthr.*, 6: 181–95.

1946 The towns of Lake Atitlan. *Univ. Chicago, Micro. Coll. MSS Middle Amer. Cult. Anthr.*, no. 13.

1947a Notes on Santo Tomas Chichicastenango. *Ibid.*, no. 16.

1947b Miscellaneous notes on Guatemala. *Ibid.*, no. 18.

1949 Folk tales in Chichicastenango: an unsolved puzzle. *Jour. Amer. Folklore*, 62: 125–35.

1950 Panajachel: field notes. *Univ. Chicago, Micro. Coll. MSS Middle Amer. Cult. Anthr.*, no. 29. (Contains autobiography of Santiago Yach from Panajachel.)

1951 [ed.] The civilizations of ancient America. Selected papers of the 29th Int. Cong. Amer. Chicago.

1952a [ed.] Heritage of conquest: the ethnology of Middle America. Viking Fund seminar on Middle American ethnology. Glencoe.

1952b [ed.] Acculturation in the Americas. Selected papers of the 29th Inst. Cong. Amer. Chicago.

1952c Economy and technology. *In his* 1952a, pp. 43–75.

1953 Penny capitalism: a Guatemalan Indian economy. *Smithsonian Inst., Inst. Social Anthr.*, Pub. 16.

1957a Changing consumption in Indian Guatemala. *Econ. Development and Cult. Change*, 5: 147–58.

1957b The Indians in the economy of Guatemala. *Univ. College of the West Indies, Inst. Social and Econ. Research, Social and Econ. Studies*, pp. 413–23. Jamaica.

1958 The Fox project. *Human Organization*, 17: 17–19.

1960 [ed.] Aboriginal languages of Latin America. *Current Anthr.*, 1: 430–38.

TAX, SUSAN

1964 Displacement activity in Zinacantan. *Amer. Indig.*, 24: 111–21.

TAYLOR, D. M.

1951 The Black Carib of British Honduras. *Viking Fund Pub. Anthr.*, no. 17.

TAYLOR, H. M.

1933 Spur-of-the-rock: hero of the Mayo Indians. *Pub. Texas Folklore Soc.*, 11: 5–47.

TAYLOR, P. S.

1933a Making cántaros at San Jose Tateposco. *Amer. Anthr.*, 35: 745–51.

1933b A Spanish-Mexican peasant community: Arandas in Jalisco, Mexico. *Ibero-Amer.*, no. 4.

TELETOR, C. N.

1945 Bailes que representan los indígenas en Baja Verapaz. *An. Soc. Geog. Hist. Guatemala*, 20: 51–56.

1955 Apuntes para una monografía de Rabinal (Baja Verapaz) y algo de nuestro folklore. Guatemala.

TERMER, F.

1930a Los bailes de culebra entre los indios quichés en Guatemala. *Proc. 23d Int. Cong. Amer.*, pp. 661–67.

1930b Zur Ethnologie und Ethnographie des nordlichen Mittel-Amerika. *Ibero-Amer. Archiv*, vol. 4, no. 3.

1931–36 Der Palo de Volador in Guatemala. *El Mex. Antiguo*, 3: 13–23.

1957 Etnología y etnografía de Guatemala. Seminario de Integración Social Guatemalteca. Guatemala.

THOMAS, C., AND J. R. SWANTON

1911 Indian languages of Mexico and Central America and their geographical distribution. *Smithsonian Inst., Bur. Amer. Ethnol.*, Bull. 44.

THOMPSON, D. E.

1954 Maya paganism and Christianity: a history of the fusion of two religions. *Tulane Univ., Middle Amer. Research Inst.*, Pub. 19, pp. 1–36.

THOMPSON, J. E. S.
1927 The civilization of the Mayas. *Field Mus. Natural Hist., Anthr. Leafl.*, no. 25.
1930 Ethnology of the Mayas of southern and central British Honduras. *Ibid., Anthr. Ser.*, 17: 23–214.
1933 Mexico before Cortez. New York.
1938 Sixteenth and seventeenth century reports on the Chol Mayas. *Amer. Anthr.*, 40: 584–604.
1941a Apuntes sobre las supersticiones de los Mayas de Socotz, Honduras Britanica. *In* Los Mayas antiguos, pp. 101–10.
1941b Yokes or ball game belts? *Amer. Antiquity*, 6: 320–26.
1943 A figurine whistle representing a ball-game player. *Carnegie Inst. Wash., Notes Middle Amer. Archaeol. Ethnol.*, no. 25.
1950 Maya hieroglyphic writing: introduction. *Carnegie Inst. Wash.*, Pub. 589.
1954 The rise and fall of Maya civilization. Norman.

THOMPSON, L.
1950 Culture in crisis: a study of the Hopi Indians. New York.

THOMPSON, R. H.
1958 Modern Yucatecan Maya pottery making. *Soc. Amer. Archaeol.*, Mem. 15.

TIBÓN, G.
1960 Olinalá. Mexico.

TOOR, F.
1926 I am cured of fright. *Mex. Folkways*, vol. 7.
1939 Mexican popular arts. Mexico.
1947 [ed.] A treasury of Mexican folkways. New York.

TORO, A.
n.d. Una creencia totemica de los zapotecas. *El Mex. Antiguo*, 2: 123–28.

TORRE VILLAR, E. DE LA
1952 Las reducciones de los pueblos de Indios en la Nueva España. Mexico.

TOSCANO, S.
1945 Informe sobre la existencia de jugadores de pelota mayas en la cerámica escultórica de Jaina. *Carnegie Inst. Wash., Notes Middle Amer. Archaeol. Ethnol.*, no. 54.
1947 Mitos y leyendas del antiguo México. *Biblioteca Enciclopédica Popular*, no. 182. Mexico.

TOZZER, A. M.
1907 A comparative study of the Mayas and the Lacandones. New York.
1941 [ed.] Landa's Relación de las cosas de Yucatan. Tr. and ed. with notes. *Papers Peabody Mus., Harvard Univ.*, vol. 18.

TREASURY OF MEXICAN FOLKWAYS, A
1947 *See* Toor, 1947.

TUMIN, M. M.
1946 San Luis Jilotepeque: a Guatemalan pueblo. *Univ. Chicago, Micro. Coll. MSS Middle Amer. Cult. Anthr.*, no. 2.
1952 Caste in a peasant society. Princeton Univ. Press.
1956 Cultura, casta y clase en Guatemala: una nueva evaluación. Seminario de Integración Social Guatemalteca. Guatemala.
1958 [ed.] Values in action: a symposium. *Human Organization*, 17: 2–26.

UGARTE, S.
1954 Catálogo de obras escritas en lengua indígena de México o que tratan de ella. Mexico.

UNDERHILL, R. M.
1937 Social organization of the Papago Indians. Columbia Univ. Press.
1938 A Papago calendar record. Univ. New Mexico Press.
1940 The Papago Indians of Arizona and their relatives, the Pima. Haskell Inst. Lawrence, Kansas.
1946 Papago Indian religion. Columbia Univ. Press.

UNITED NATIONS
1949 Fundamental education: a description and programme. *Educational, Scientific, and Cultural Organization, Monogr. Fundamental Education*, no. 1.
1954 The population of Central America (including Mexico), 1950–1980. *Dept. Economic and Social Affairs, Population Studies*, no. 16.
1956 Methods for population projections by age and sex. *Ibid.*, no. 18.

UNITED STATES, DEPT. AGRICULTURE
1869 The ni-in of Yucatan. *In* Rept. to 40th Cong., 3d Sess. (1868–1869), pp. 268–71.

VAILLANT, G. C.
1940 A sacred almanac of the Aztecs (tonalamatl of the Codex Borbonicus). Amer. Mus. Natural Hist.
1941 The Aztecs of Mexico. New York.

VALENTINI, P. J. J.
1899 Trique theogony: an alleged specimen of ancient Mexican folklore. *Jour. Amer. Folklore*, 12: 38–42.

VALLADARES, L. A.
1957 El hombre y el maíz: etnografía e etnopsicología de Colotenango. Guatemala.

VAN DEN BERGHE, P. L., AND B. N. COLBY
1961 Ladino-Indian relations in the highlands of Chiapas, Mexico. *Social Forces*, 40: 63–71.

VAN DE VELDE, P., AND H. M. VAN DE VELDE
1939 The black pottery of Coyotepec, Oaxaca, Mexico. *SW. Mus. Papers*, no. 13.

VÁZQUEZ SANTANA, H.
1931 Calendario de fiestas típicas. Mexico.
1940 Fiestas y costumbres mexicanas. Mexico.

—— AND J. I. DÁVILA GARIBI
1931 El carnaval. Mexico.

VELASCO, A.
1929 Semblanza de la villa de Zaachila. *Bol. Soc. Mex. Geog. Estad.*, 41: 131–71.

VELÁSQUEZ, P. F.
1945 Anales de Cuauhtitlan y leyenda de los Soles. *Inst. Hist.*, Pub. 1. Mexico.

VERA, L.
1925 La leyenda de Tzuatzinco. *Mex. Folkways*, 1: 11–13.

VERRILL, A. H.
1929 Old civilizations of the New World. Indianapolis.

VILLA ROJAS, A.
1939 Notas sobre la etnografía de los Mayas de Quintana Roo. *Rev. Mex. Estud. Antr.*, 3: 227–41.
1941 Dioses y espíritus paganos de los Mayas de Quintana Roo. *In* Los Mayas antiguos, pp. 113–24.
1945 The Maya of east central Quintana Roo. *Carnegie Inst. Wash.*, Pub. 559.
1946 Notas sobre la etnografía de los indios tzeltales de Oxchuc. *Univ. Chicago, Micro. Coll. MSS Middle Amer. Cult. Anthr.*, no. 7.
1947 Kinship and nagualism in a Tzeltal community, southeastern Mexico. *Amer. Anthr.*, 49: 578–87.
1955 Los Mazatecos y el problema indígena de la cuenca del Papaloapan. *Inst. Nac. Indig.*, Mem. 7. Mexico.

1961 Notas sobre la tenencia de la tierra entre los Mayas de la antigüedad. *Estud. Cultura Maya*, 1: 21–46.

VILLACORTA C., J. A.
1936 Memorial de Tecpan-Atitlan (Anales de los Cakchiqueles). Guatemala.

—— AND C. A. VILLACORTA
1933 Codices mayas: Dresdensis, Peresianus, Tro-Cortesianus. Guatemala.

VILLACORTA VIDAURRE, L.
1953 Los cerros y el maíz. *Yikal Maya Than*, 14 (169): 175–76.

VIQUEIRA, C., AND A. PALERM
1954 Alcoholismo, brujería y homicidio en dos comunidades rurales de México. *Amer. Indig.*, 14: 7–36.

VIVÓ, J. A.
1941 Razas y lenguas indígenas de México, su distribución geográfica. *Panamer. Inst. Geog. Hist.*, Pub. 52. Mexico.
1943 Rasgos tribales y nacionales del problema indígena. *Cuad. Amer.*, 9: 155–63.
1946 *See* México prehispánico.

VOGT, E. Z.
1951 Navaho veterans: a study of changing values. *Papers Peabody Mus., Harvard Univ.*, vol. 41, no. 1.
1955 Some aspects of Cora-Huichol acculturation. *Amer. Indig.*, 15: 249–63.
1957 Acculturation of American Indians. *Ann. Amer. Acad. Polit. Social Sci.*, 311: 137–46.
1960 On the concepts of structure and process in cultural anthropology. *Amer. Anthr.*, 62: 18–33.
1961 Some aspects of Zinacantan settlement patterns and ceremonial organization. *Estud. Cultura Maya*, 1: 131–45.

—— AND A. RUZ LHUILLIER, eds.
1964 Desarrollo cultural de los Mayas. Univ. Nac. Autónoma Mex.
1964a Cosmología maya antigua y tzotzil contemporanea: comentario sobre algunos problemas metodológicos. *Amer. Indig.*, 24: 211–19.
1964b Some implications of Zinacantan social structure for the study of the ancient Maya. *Actas y Mem.*, 35th Int. Cong. Amer., 1:307–19.
1964c The genetic model and Maya cultural development. *In* Desarrollo cultural de los Mayas, pp. 9–48.

VOORHEES, T. E.
1959 The formal analysis and comparison of Yuman kinship systems. Master's thesis, Stanford Univ.

W., P. A.
1951 Algunas observaciones acerca de la religión de los Mixtecas guerrerenses. *Rev. Mex. Estud. Antr.*, 12: 147–64.

WAGLEY, C.
1941 Economics of a Guatemalan village. *Amer. Anthr. Assoc.*, Mem. 58.

1949 The social and religious life of a Guatemalan village. *Ibid.*, Mem. 71.

1957 Santiago Chimaltenango: estudio antropológico-social de una comunidad indígena de Huehuetenango. Seminario de Integración Social Guatemalteca. Guatemala.

1958 On the concept of social race in the Americas. Mimeographed.

—— AND M. HARRIS
1955 A typology of Latin American subcultures. *Amer. Anthr.*, 57: 428–51.

1958 Minorities in the New World: six case studies. New York.

WALLACE, A. F. C.
1961 Culture and personality. New York.

WARKENTIN, M., AND J. OLIVARES
1947 The holy bells and other Huave legends. *Tlalocan*, 2: 223–34.

WATERMAN, T. T.
1917 Bandelier's contribution to the study of ancient Mexican social organization. *Univ. California Pub. Amer. Archaeol. Ethnol.*, 7: 249–82.

WEATHERS, K.
1946 La agricultura de los Tzotzil de Nabenchuac, Chiapas. *Amer. Indig.*, 6: 315–20.

WEIANT, C. W.
1940 Los Tarascos. *Monogr. Hist. Etnog. Econ.* Mexico.

1955 Notes on the ethnology of San Lorenzo, a Tarascan village of the sierra. *El Mex. Antiguo*, 8: 365–74.

WEITLANER, I.
1936 *See* Johnson, I. W.

WEITLANER, R. J.
1940 Notes on Chinantec ethnography. *El Mex. Antiguo*, 5: 161–67.

1941 Chilacachapa y Tetelcingo. *Ibid.*, 5: 255–300.

1951 Notes on the social organization of Ojitlan. *In* Homenaje Caso, pp. 441–55.

1952a Curaciones mazatecas. *An. Inst. Nac. Antr. Hist.*, 4: 279–85.

1952b El sol y la luna: versión chinanteca. *Tlalocan*, 3: 169–74.

—— AND R. H. BARLOW
1955 Todos santos y otras ceremonias en Chilacachapa. *El Mex. Antiguo*, 8: 295–321.

—— AND C. A. CASTRO G.
1954 Papeles de la Chinantla: Mayultianguis y Tlacoatzintepec. *Mus. Nac. Antr., Cien. Ser.*, no. 3. Mexico.

—— AND S. HOOGSHAGEN
1960 Grados de edad en Oaxaca. *Rev. Mex. Estud. Antr.*, 16: 183–209.

—— AND I. W. JOHNSON
1943 Acatlan y Hueycantenango, Guerrero. *El Mex. Antiguo*, 6: 140–204.

———, P. VELÁSQUEZ, AND P. CARRASCO
1947 Huitziltepec. *Rev. Mex. Estud. Antr.*, 9: 47–77.

—— AND E. VERBITSKY
1956 Field notes of the Cuicatec. Mus. Nac. Antr., Field Notes Files. Mexico.

WELLMAN, P.
1947 Death on horseback. New York.

WELLS, W. V.
1857 Explorations and adventures in Honduras. New York.

WEST, R. C.
1948 Cultural geography of the modern Tarascan area. *Smithsonian Inst., Inst. Social Anthr.*, Pub. 7.

—— AND P. ARMILLAS
1950 Las chinampas de México. *Cuad. Amer.*, 50: 165–82.

WHETTEN, N. L.
1948 Rural Mexico. Univ. Chicago Press.

1961 Guatemala: the land and the people. Yale Univ. Press.

—— AND R. G. BURNIGHT
1956 Internal migration in Mexico. *In* Estudios antropológicos, pp. 537–52.

WHITEFORD, A. A.
1960 Two cities of Latin America: a comparative description of social classes. *Logan Mus. Anthr.*, Bull. 9. Beloit.

WHITING, B. B.
1950 Paiute sorcery. *Viking Fund Pub. Anthr.*, no. 15.

WHITING, J. W. M.
1959 Sorcery, sin, and the superego. *In*

577

Nebraska symposium on motivation [not paged]. Univ. Nebraska Press.

WHORF, B. L.

1935 The comparative linguistics of Uto-Azteca. *Amer. Anthr.*, 37: 343–45.

1943 Loan words in ancient Mexico. *Tulane Univ., Middle Amer. Research Inst., Philol. and Doc. Studies*, 1: 1–17.

1946 The Milpa Alta dialect of Aztec. *In* Linguistic structures of native America. H. Hoijer, ed., pp. 367–97. *Viking Fund Pub. Anthr.*, no. 6.

WILLEY, G. R.

1956a Prehistoric settlement patterns in the New World. *Viking Fund Pub. Anthr.*, no. 23.

1956b Problems concerning prehistoric settlement patterns in the Maya lowlands. *In* his 1956a, pp. 107–14.

——, E. Z. VOGT, AND A. PALERM

1960 Middle American anthropology. Vol. 2. *Pan Amer. Union, Social Sci. Monogr.*, no. 10.

WILLIAMS, M. W.

1929 Secessionist diplomacy of Yucatan. *Hisp. Amer. Hist. Rev.*, 9: 132–43.

WILLIAMS GARCÍA, R.

1953a Etnografía prehispánica de la zona central de Vera Cruz. *Rev. Mex. Estud. Antr.*, 13: 157–61.

1953b Un mito y los mazatecas. *Bol. Indig.*, 13: 360–64.

1955 Ichcacuatitla: vida en una comunidad indígena de Chicontepec, Veracruz. MS.

WILSON, G., AND M. WILSON

1945 The analysis of social change: based on observations in central Africa. Cambridge Univ. Press.

WINNIE, W. W., JR.

1958 The Papaloapan project: an experiment in tropical development. *Econ. Geog.*, 34: 227–48.

WISDOM, C.

1940 The Chorti Indians of Guatemala. Univ. Chicago Press.

1950 Materials on the Chorti language. *Chicago Univ., Micro. Coll. MSS Middle Amer. Cult. Anthr.*, no. 28.

1952 The supernatural world and curing. *In* Tax, 1952a, pp. 119–41.

WOLF, E. R.

1953 La formación de la nación: un ensayo de formulación. *Cien. Sociales*, 4: 50–62, 98–111, 146–71.

1955a The Mexican Bajio in the 18th century: an analysis of cultural integration. *Tulane Univ., Middle Amer. Research Inst.*, Pub. 17, no. 3.

1955b Types of Latin American peasantry: a preliminary discussion. *Amer. Anthr.*, 57: 452–71.

1956 Aspects of group relations in a complex society: Mexico. *Ibid.*, 58: 1065–78.

1957 Closed corporate peasant communities in Mesoamerica and central Java. *SW. Jour. Anthr.*, 13: 1–18.

1958 The virgin of Guadalupe: a Mexican national symbol. *Jour. Amer. Folklore*, 71: 34–39.

1959 Sons of the shaking earth. Chicago.

1960 The Indian in Mexican society. *In* Leslie, 1960b, pp. 3–6.

1962 Sons of the shaking earth. Reprint of his 1959.

—— AND S. W. MINTZ

1957 Haciendas and plantations in Middle America and the Antilles. *Social and Econ. Studies*, 6: 380–412.

—— AND A. PALERM

1955 Irrigation in the old Acolhua domain, Mexico. *SW. Jour. Anthr.*, 11: 265–81.

WOLFRAM, R.

1951 Die Volkstänze in Österreich und verwandte Tänze in Europa. Salzburg.

WONDERLY, W. L.

1946a Phonemic acculturation in Zoque. *Int. Jour. Amer. Ling.*, 12: 92–95.

1946b Textos en Zoque sobre el concepto del nagual. *Tlalocan*, 2: 97–105.

1947 Textos folklóricos en zoque tradiciones acerca de los alrededores de Copainala, Chiapas. *Rev. Mex. Estud. Antr.*, 9: 135–63.

1960 Urbanization: the challenge of Latin America in transition. *Practical Anthr.*, 7: 205–09. Valhalla, N.Y.

WYLLYS, R. K.

1716 Padre Luis Velarde's Relación of Pimeria Alta.

XIU, J. A.

1954 El árbol que llora. *Yikal Maya Than*, 15 (176): 52–53, 60–62.

YÁÑEZ, A.

1942 Mitos indígenas. Biblioteca Estud. Univ. Mexico.

YÁÑEZ-PÉREZ, L., AND E. MOYO PORRAS

1957 Mecanización de la agricultura mexicana. Inst. Mex. Invest. Econ. Mexico.

REFERENCES

YOUNG, F. W., AND R. C. YOUNG
1960a Social integration and change in 24 Mexican villages. *Econ. Development and Cult. Change,* 8: 366–77.
1960b Two determinants of community reaction to industrialization in rural Mexico. *Ibid.,* 8: 257–64.

ZABALA CUBILLOS, M. T.
1961 Instituciones políticas y religiosas de Zinacantan. *Estud. Cultura Maya,* 1: 147–57.

ZANTWIJK, R. A. M. VAN
1960 Los indígenas de Milpa Alta. *Inst. Real Tropicos, Amsterdam no. 135, Sec. Antr. Cultural y Física,* no. 64.

ZAVALA, S. A.
1935 La encomienda indiana. Madrid.
1941 Ideario de Vasco de Quiroga. Fondo de Cultura Económica. Mexico.
1945 Contribución a la historia de las instituciones coloniales en Guatemala. Mexico.

1951 Los esclavos indios en Nueva España. *In* Homenaje Caso, pp. 427–40.

––––– AND J. MIRANDA
1954 Instituciones indígenas en la colonia. *In* Caso, 1954, pp. 31–94.

ZINGG, R. M.
1932 Tarahumara children's toys and games. *Mex. Folkways,* 7: 107–10.
1938a Christmasing with the Tarahumaras. *Pub. Texas Folklore Soc.,* 14: 207–24.
1938b The Huichols: primitive artists. *Univ. Denver, Contrib. Ethnog.,* no. 1.
1940 Report on archaeology of southern Chihuahua, III. *Univ. Denver, Center of Latin Amer. Studies,* I.

ZUNO, J. G.
1952 Las llamadas lacas michoacanas de Uruapan no proceden de las orientales. *Cuad. Amer.,* 63: 145–65.

hot-cold qualities: in sickness, 334, 335, 342–343, 350, 351. SEE ALSO Strength-weakness qualities

household. SEE Territorial units

housing, type of: as criterion of ethnic group, 433, 434

Huahuas: rituals of, 168

Huastec: fiestas of, 159, 168; games of, 200; kinship terminology of, 223 (fig. 29), 224 (fig. 30); love concept of, 407; mythology of, 406–407, 408; sacred objects and places of, 406

Huatusca: acculturation in, 460, 463; Mestizoization in, 463

Huautla: barrio system of, 262

Huave: age-respect patterns of, 424; fiestas of, 325; as fishermen, 325; kinship terminology of, 220, 230; as self-protective culture, 424; textiles of, 143 (fig. 5)

Huehuetenango: market system of, 93

Huehuetla: dances of, 174

Huejotzingo: schools in, Franciscan, 373

Huichol: acculturation of, 506; basketry of, 120; cattle of, 89; civil-religious hierarchy of, 289; clothing of, 149, 152; dances of, 165 (fig. 9), 166; the dead, fear of, 338; economic organization of, 88–90; fiestas of, 159, 161, 163 (fig. 7), 164 (fig. 8), 165 (fig. 9), 166, 181; kinship terminology of, 209, 211, 212 (fig. 9); musical instruments of, 188; sacred objects and places of, 395 (fig. 1), 400 (fig. 5), 413; shaman of, 399; sickness among, 334, 349; sports of, 195; textiles of, 138, 144, 148, 149

Huimanguillo: settlement pattern of, 69, 70; wealth accumulation in, 70

Huistec: clothing of, 149

Huitzilopochtli: as Aztec tribal patron, 370, 371, 377

Huitziltepec: kinship terminology of, 209, 211, 213 (fig. 10)

human nature: pessimistic view of, 419

humedad y riego. SEE Cultivation, systems of

humor: expressions of, 179–184, 191, 192 (fig. 1), 419; inaccessibility of data on, 191, 193; lacking in Indian literature, 191; obscenity as, 181, 194; verbal, 194–195, 204, 364, 419

hunters: northern bands of, 470

hunting: of "jicaques," 470–471; in mythology, 413 n.

Ihuatzio: fan-making in, 95

images: 413. SEE ALSO Religious beliefs, sacred objects and places

incense: 401–403. SEE ALSO Copal

incest: compadre-comadre, 240 n., 248 n.

Indian populations: biological definition of, 12–15; castes in, 13–14, 445, 447; census figures for, 20–24, 54, 60 (Table 3), 63 (Table 8), 67, 74–80 (Tables 15–18), 471 (Table 1), 472, 515 (Table 1); cultural definition of, 15–17, 435, 522 n.; descriptions of, general, 4–7; economic and social needs of, 17–18; etiquette toward Ladinos, 436; as ethnic group, 432–448; legal definition of, 14–15; linguistic definition of, 15–20 (Table 1), 21–24 (Tables 2–6), 433; pigmentocracy of, 14; racial discrimination against, 13–15, 17, 18,

435–448; racial mixture of, 12–15, 433, 435; relationships with conquerors, 13–15; slavery of, 13, 473; social stratification of, 13–15, 18, 434–435; somantic criterion of, no longer valid, 14–15

Indian Protection, Department of: creation of, 442

indigenist studies: history of, 15–20

industrialization. SEE Socio-cultural trends

infancy and childhood: baptism during, 239, 242, 243, 245, 247, 271–272, 312, 385, 444; education during, in Franciscan schools, 373–374, 375, 385; padrinos' role during, 238–251; sickness in, 334, 335, 337, 343, 345, 351, 354, 490; socialization during, 217, 239–241, 255, 420–421

inheritance: of barrio membership, 263, 264, 265; bilateral, 99, 265; as affects economy, 99, 265. SEE ALSO Descent

insect fat. SEE Aje

integration. SEE Socio-cultural trends

Interamerican Indigenist Congress: First, 16, 477; Second, resolutions of, 19; Third, final act of, 19–20; Fourth, final agreements of, 20

International Demographic Congress: First, resolutions of, 17

interpersonal relations: etiquette, 420, 421, 424, 430, 436; between Indians and Ladinos, 432–448; ingroup antagonisms, 304–306, 308–310, 312–314, 365, 398, 447; "looking behavior," 421, 430; respeto, 239, 240–241, 250; in sickness, 334–355; social statuses, 239, 284–296, 306, 396, 405, 417–430, 434–448; sodalities, cofradía, 266, 275, 279, 280, 286, 294, 301, 310, 312, 315, 319, 321, 324, 325, 367, 379, 393 n., 394, 395, 399–401, 403, 404, 409, 412 (fig. 15), 414, 456, 534. SEE ALSO Kin relationships, artificial

intoxication: ceremonial, 166, 403; mock, of dolls, 203; postconquest, 266, 371, 380, 421, 422, 438, 439, 440, 441, 499, 500; renouncing of, 390–391; of shaman, 410. SEE ALSO Alcoholic beverages; Pulque

irrigation: for agricultural purposes, 27–28, 36–41, 45, 49, 51, 55–56, 61; areas where needed, 28; by canals, 37, 269; communal labor for, 51; implements used for, 49; by wells, 37, 269—in Guatemala, 320; in the Mesa Central, 55, 59; in Teotihuacan valley, 56, 60–61

Ixil: etiquette of, 420, 424

jacal structures: as criterion of ethnic group, 434

Jacaltec: kinship terminology of, 227 (fig. 36)

Jacaltenango: fiesta in, 318 (fig. 1); labor in, communal, 300 (fig. 1)

Jalisco: fiestas in, 159, 160, 161, 181; pottery in, 113, 115

Jamiltepec: housing in, 434; Ladinos in, 433–448; mobility (class) in, 446; padrinos in, 244; residence in, patterns of, 434

Janitzio: fan-making in, 95

Jaracuaro: hat specialization in, 95

jaspé. SEE Textiles

jealousy: in children, 420–421

jokes. SEE Play, verbal

juggling. SEE Play

109 (fig. 4), 110 (fig. 5), 112, 115, 116–117; settlement patterns of, 65 (fig. 6), 66 (fig. 7), 67 (fig. 8), 82; textiles in, 146

migration. SEE Demography

military service: of Indians, 441

milpa. SEE Agriculture

Milpa Alta: fiesta in, 327 (fig. 7); witchcraft in, 430

mining: Indians used in, 460

Miskito: games of, 198; nationalization of, 470–471; sports of, 196

missionaries: Augustinians, 458; as affected civil-religious hierarchy, 294; Dominicans, 457, 460; drama used by, 364, 456; Franciscans, 372–373, 374–380, 384–386, 389, 457; Jesuits, 458; lay assistants to, 458; literature influenced by, 362, 363, 367

Mitla: conflicts in, settlement of, 304; festal pledges in, 399; marriage in, 303; padrinos in, 243, 245, 246, 247 n.; religion in, folk, 307; ritual, economic aspect of, 411 n.; sickness in, 345; stewardship in, 400–401; textiles in, 138, 140, 146; witchcraft in, 340

Mixe: acculturation of, 453, 458, 463, 465, 466, 467; age-respect patterns of, 424; agriculture of, 325; boss rule among, 305; cannibalism, in folklore of, 419; etiquette among, 420; fiestas of, 159; kinship terminology of, 217, 219, 220 (fig. 24), 221 (fig. 25); missionaries among, 458; pottery of, 106; as self-protective culture, 424; settlement patterns of, 269; sickness among, 334, 349; specialization of, service, 302; territorial units of, 256, 257, 262, 265, 269, 274; textiles of, 140 (fig. 2)

Mixtec: acculturation of, 505; barrios of, 262, 264, 265; cannibalism, in folklore of, 419; chronicles of, 363; compadre greeting of, 241 (fig. 1); fear of the dead, 338; fiestas of, 159, 164–165, 168, 177, 181; games of, 199; kinship terminology of, 213, 214 (fig. 12), 215; as migrants, 532; padrinos of, 244; as self-protective culture, 424; sickness among, 334, 339, 427; soul-loss among, 346

Mixteca Alta: textiles in, 156 (fig. 17)

mobility, class: Indian to Ladino, 445

moisture and irrigation. SEE Cultivation, systems of, humedad y riego

Montezuma: literature about, 364

moon: folklore about, 362

Morelos: fiestas in, 160, 161, 181

municipio. SEE Settlement patterns

mushrooms: hallucinogenic, 193, 250

music: formal and informal use of, 193; songs, 188–189. SEE ALSO Musical instruments

musical instruments: bells, 188; bow on gourd, 165; brass band, 179, 180, 188; conchas, 177; coronet, 180; drum, 167, 174, 182 (fig. 28), 183 (fig. 29), 185 (fig. 31), 188, 399 (fig. 4), 406 (fig. 11); fiddle, 170, 177, 180, 182, 188; flute, 167, 169, 182 (fig. 28), 185 (fig. 31), 186 (fig. 32), 188; gourd rattle, 166, 182, 188; guitar, 174, 180, 183; harp, 170, 180, 182, 187 (fig. 33); marimba, 168, 180, 181, 188, 271, 436;

notched sticks, 181 (fig. 27), 182; tabor, 169; trumpet, 188; violin, 174, 187 (fig. 33), 188, 271

nagual. SEE Soul

Nahuatl: fiestas of, 326; games of, 195–199, 200, 202; literature of, 363; puns among, 194; as self-protective culture, 424; sexes, relations between, 417; sickness among, 334–335; soul-loss of, 346; witchcraft of, 340

Nahuatl language: use of, 59, 69, 168, 177

narcotic drugs: use of, 192

National Indian Institute: of Guatemala, 481, 490, 506; of Mexico, 9, 477, 490, 491, 492, 495, 504–506, 511

nationalization. SEE Political behavior, political movements

nativistic movements. SEE Political behavior, political movements

Nayarit: braceros in, 520; fiestas in, 159, 161, 163 (fig. 7), 329; games in, 200, 201 (fig. 11); sacred places in, 396 (fig. 2)

Negroes: in Costa Rica, 24; in dances, 174; as ethnic group, 432–433

Nicaragua: demography of, 24 (Table 5), 471 (Table 1); literature in, 364; Mestizo population in, 472; nationalization of, 473, 479, 483–486

nopal: cultivation of, 39, 43, 58, 59

nucleated communities. SEE Settlement patterns

Nuevo Leon: nativistic uprisings in, 461

Oaxaca: age-grades in, 291; basketry in, 120, 121 (fig. 12), 123 (fig. 14); cattle raising in, 461; commercial relationships in, 301–302; compadre greeting in, 241 (fig. 1); crops cultivated in, 27, 464; demography of, 21, 514, 515 (Table 2); fiestas in, 159, 160, 162, 170, 174 (fig. 18), 179, 181, 184, 187; housing in, 434; Indian-Ladino relations in, 434, 437–448; integration in, 301–308; markets in, 87, 94–95, 301–302; nativistic uprisings in, 461; pottery in, 107 (fig. 3), 108, 109 (fig. 4), 111–113, 116; settlement patterns in, 59 (fig. 4); textiles in, 140, 144, 146 (fig. 8), 148

obscenity. SEE Humor

Ocosingo: sickness in, 272

Ocoyoacac: pottery in, 112

offenses, socio-ritual: as cause of sickness, 337, 342, 346, 348, 350, 355

offerings. SEE Religious practices

office-holding: impersonal nature of, 396–397

officials, local: alcalde, 286, 288–289, 295, 298; alguacil, 285, 288, 297; auxiliares, 259; cabildos, 257, 258; cacique, 455–456, 459, 497, 498; comandantes, 259; Comisario, 69; election of, 441, 442, 481, 486; jefes políticos, 295; juzgado, 441; mayordomo, 257–258, 285–286, 288, 297, 314, 315, 321, 322, 330, 497; of paraje, 257, 258; principal, 258, 264, 273, 276, 284, 285, 286–287, 298, 340, 349, 355, 394, 441; regidor, 286, 288–289, 295, 297; sacristán, 266, 285, 287, 298, 398, 462

Ojitlan: padrinos in, 244; sickness in, 349